Teaching
North American
Environmental
Literature

Modern Language Association of America
Options for Teaching

For a complete listing of titles,
see the last pages of this book.

Teaching North American Environmental Literature

Edited by
**Laird Christensen,
Mark C. Long,
and Fred Waage**

The Modern Language Association of America
New York   2008

MLA and the MODERN LANGUAGE ASSOCIATION are trademarks
owned by the Modern Language Association of America. For information
about obtaining permission to reprint material from MLA book publications,
send your request by mail (see address below), e-mail (permissions@mla.org),
or fax (646 458-0030).

Library of Congress Cataloging-in-Publication Data

Teaching North American environmental literature / edited by
Laird Christensen, Mark C. Long, and Fred Waage.
        p. cm. — (Option for teaching ; 22)
Includes bibliographical references and index.
ISBN: 978-087352-809-2 (alk. paper)
ISBN: 978-0-87352-810-8 (pbk.: alk. paper)
1. Environmental literature—Study and teaching (Higher) 2. American litera-
ture—Study and teaching (Higher) 3. Canadian literature—Study and teaching
(Higher) 4. Ecology in literature—Study and teaching (Higher) 5. Environmen-
tal protection in literature—Study and teaching (Higher) I. Christensen, Laird,
1960- II. Long, Mark C. III. Waage, Frederick O., 1943-
PS169.E25T43 2008
810.9'355—dc22   2008022971

Options for Teaching 22
ISSN 1079-2562

Cover illustration of the paperback edition: *Fall Maples over Doe River.*
Photo by Michael Joslin

Second printing 2010. Printed on recycled paper

Published by The Modern Language Association of America
26 Broadway, New York, New York 10004-1789
www.mla.org

Contents

Part III: Teaching North American
             Environmental Literature

Disciplinary Approaches

Interdisciplinary Approaches

Place-Based Approaches

John Tallmadge

Foreword: Out of the Woods

When I entered graduate school in 1969, no one had ever heard of environmental literature. People like John Muir, Aldo Leopold, and Rachel Carson were known as activists rather than as writers. Seminars dealt with poetry, drama, or novels rather than with what is now called creative nonfiction. Humanist discourse had soared into theoretical stratospheres on the wings of deconstruction and psychoanalysis. Meanwhile, the country was convulsed by movements calling for peace, civil rights, emancipation for women, and healing for the earth. It was hard to concentrate on the finer points of Renaissance poetry with a demonstration boiling in the street below. We squirmed in our chairs when Vice President Spiro Agnew lashed out at the "effete corps of impudent snobs who characterize themselves as intellectuals" ("Agnew").

With rain forests, rice paddies, and ghettos aflame, the humanities seemed irrelevant—small comfort to those of us who loved the wisdom and beauty of great books and aspired to a teacher's path. We wanted our scholarship to matter, but the academy, always a generation behind, had only critical theory, close reading, and a dusty canon to offer. So we struck out on our own. In my case, the army helped by snatching me from graduate school and packing me off to California, where, on weekend furlough,

1

I discovered the dramatic landscapes of Big Sur and the Sierra Nevada and, more important, the books and poetry they had inspired. Here were generous wild places that offered freedom and ecstasy after weeks of military routine; here were books that affirmed memory while they fed both imagination and desire. Literature and landscape combined to foster the most intense kind of personal transformation by engaging every faculty of mind, body, and sense. I wanted to study this process and practice it in my life. I wanted to pass its gifts on to my students.

But back in graduate school, the enterprise was a pretty hard sell. I had to come in by the backdoor of narrative theory and undergraduate seminars, where the students were glad to get away for a weekend in the Maine woods. I had trouble finding a dissertation adviser but eventually persuaded one professor with a penchant for the avant-garde. He had once come to a party bearing a concrete poem that broke in two when he dropped it on the floor; later, he wrote a recommendation that began, "Mr. Tallmadge came up with his dissertation topic all by himself." For the next decade I worked in English departments, teaching environmental literature around the edges of surveys and freshman composition and taking students to the wilderness at least once a year. It was a good, if somewhat marginal, life.

Meanwhile, the environmental movement was merging into the cultural mainstream. Organizations like the Sierra Club and the Wilderness Society had become dominant players in national politics. Activists found new inspiration in the classic works of Henry David Thoreau, John Muir, Robert Marshall, and Aldo Leopold even as a fresh generation of poets and writers were choosing natural history as a vehicle for exploring culture, society, and the conduct of life. By the mid-1980s, nature writing had become the most vital genre in contemporary American literature. Annie Dillard's *Pilgrim at Tinker Creek* won the Pulitzer Prize for its pyrotechnic style, religious ardor, and stunning insights into the dark side of nature. Barry Lopez's best-selling *Arctic Dreams* earned a National Book Award for its elegant celebrations of Native wisdom enacted in landscapes of sublime austerity and dignity. In her pathbreaking and tragic memoir, *Refuge*, Terry Tempest Williams showed that natural history was supple enough to handle the most pressing issues of the day, from nuclear testing, habitat destruction, and breast cancer to the intimate struggles of religious and family life.

This literary and political renaissance brought environmental issues more and more to the fore as we thought about how we could open up the canon and teach what we cared about the most. We got a boost from feminism, with its emphasis on the personal voice and witness, and from African American studies, which challenged dominant modes of discourse and social construction. Courses in environmental literature began to spring up on campuses all across the land. But it was not until the founding of the journal *ISLE: Interdisciplinary Studies in Literature and Environment* and the subsequent organization of the Association for the Study of Literature and Environment (ASLE) in 1994 that this far-flung network of scholars coalesced into a critical mass. Now ASLE supports the journal and hosts biennial conferences that provide a forum for the development and refinement of catalytic ideas. The study, teaching, and practice of environmental literature are recognized as worthy academic endeavors. You even see ads for ecocritics in the *Chronicle*.

It would be comforting to think that the field of environmental literature has finally arrived, but to me that image suggests slowing down, even a dead stop. I think of a train pulling into a station with a squeal of brakes and a gasp of steam. The pressure is off; the engine dies; the huge contraption lurches to a halt. But the fact is, environmental literature is still an emerging field. Witness the growth of ecocriticism, which now ranges far beyond its initial focus on nature writing. The environmental view has become a mode of omnibus critique, on a par, I would argue, with feminism, gender, race, culture, ethnicity, and even deconstruction in the challenge it mounts to dominant modes of thought, discourse, and social relations. Emergence seems like a richer and more accurate metaphor for the state of our field. I think of a butterfly breaking out of the chrysalis to spread its wings, of Dine ancestors climbing up through a great hollow reed into the light of this world, of the earliest humans walking out of the woods into African savannahs, of hikers emerging onto alpine meadows at tree line, where the view suddenly expands to exhilarating horizons.

We have, you might say, come a long way. It's now much clearer why and how environmental literature matters, not only to students, teachers, and writers but also to the academy and society as well. Everything starts with those first transformative encounters with nature, which, over time, develop into a sense of ecological identity, the personal stories that define who you are with respect to the natural world. Identity implies values, and values invite affirming experiences and actions. For some of us, these actions involve politics, for others teaching, for still others bearing witness through speaking or writing, but all these actions strive to affirm identity by making some sort of return for the gifts received from nature. If these acts encounter resistance, as they often do from an ignorant world, then one seeks affirmation through renewed encounter with nature, and the pattern repeats. Thus, for students, writers, and teachers, engagement with land and literature becomes a self-stoking cycle, a kind of life practice.

Environmental literature is also important for the humanities, and for two reasons in particular. First, it engages the humanities in pressing concerns of the day. We often blame environmental problems on industry, capitalism, bad science, or rampant consumption, and we think that technical fixes or clever new laws will solve them. But these address only the proximate causes. Environmental problems ultimately stem from our values, beliefs, and ideas about the proper relations between human beings and nature. We will never solve them without understanding those beliefs, subjecting them to critique, and transforming them with capable imagination. Such work has always belonged to the humanities, and this means that humanists now have a vital role to play as public intellectuals in a culture that is groping halfheartedly toward a sustainable future.

Additionally, the study of environmental literature invites the humanities to consider new methods of inquiry that range beyond its historic emphasis on text-mediated interpretation. As Lawrence Buell reminds us, the environmental imagination forces us to take account of the real world outside the text (*Environmental Imagination* 3–5). Nature matters as much as discourse about it; therefore, we should ground interpretation in multiple intelligences and modes of experience that range beyond reading. This approach, which I call a natural history of reading, offers one avenue of escape from the claustrophobia of New Criticism, deconstruction, and other methods that privilege textuality and the written sign above all.

The field has important implications for teaching and for education in general. As David Orr says, all education is environmental education (90). Because teaching is always a personal transaction, the best learning occurs when the teacher conveys lived truth. If one teaches from ecological identity, the class is a gift, and the work is transformative for all. The transaction is made even richer when students are taken into the field, where they can learn through all their senses, their heartbeat and their skin, as well as through reading and discussion. In a time of ecological stress, there can be few forms of social activism as vital or as far-reaching. For we are still a long way from a truly sustainable world.

The essays gathered here reflect the maturation of environmental literature as a field of study, a subject matter for teaching, and a body of imaginative writing that is broadly engaged with issues of contemporary political relevance as well as universal concerns of the human spirit. Eco-criticism has expanded well beyond its initial focus on nature writing to embrace a wide array of genres, themes, modes of discourse, interpre-tive methods, and cultural perspectives. Pioneer scholars rejoice to see the torch passed to an energetic new generation.

But there is a danger on the horizon, a tiny cloud no bigger than my hand. When fields succeed, they tend to become institutionalized, attract-ing resources, attention, and ambition. The academy, which rewards success, also breeds its own sorts of corruption: careerism, envy, rivalry, hermetic discourse, self-promotion that masquerades as objective critique. We have seen the same thing in religion, politics, and science, where fun-damentalist zeal, fascism, and reductionism result from what Barry Lopez calls "failures of imagination" (*Winter Count* 71). We can avoid this trap, I believe, by staying focused on the larger issues: the need to heal our relationship to the earth, our duty to nurture new generations of wise and committed citizens—everything that Gary Snyder has called "the real work" (*Turtle Island* 32).

Part I

Backgrounds

Fred Waage

Introduction: Teaching Environmental Literature— A Trek through the Field

The current volume is in effect a radically revised edition of the original *Teaching Environmental Literature: Materials, Methods, Resources*, published by the Modern Language Association in 1985. That the current volume covers only North American environmental literature and is longer and features more diverse contents than its predecessor is evidence of how explosively the field has grown. Similarly, the MLA's tentative plan for this volume to be the first in a series covering other continents' literatures is based on the internationalization of environmental literature study and teaching, which was scarcely touched on in the previous volume.

Teaching North American Environmental Literature owes its existence to the urgings of my coeditors, Laird Christensen and Mark C. Long, who contacted me about the possibility of a new edition. They persisted despite my feeling that, although the 1985 text was clearly inadequate in the twenty-first century, an expanded edition would merely replicate what was already being written in a rapidly expanding field. Clearly, they were right, and the assembling of this anthology has made clear the profound changes that have occurred in the teaching of environmental literature since 1985.

Before the 1980s, literary environmental criticism and pedagogy were, as Cheryll Glotfelty says in her introduction to *The Ecocriticism Reader*, "disunified," and "graduate students interested in environmental approaches to literature felt like misfits" (xvii). Although I can testify to the truth of this observation, I would, in the following pages, like to qualify it by tracing what I see as an interdisciplinary evolution toward the credibility in 1985 of teaching environmental literature. Subsequently, I will summarize the dramatic changes since 1985 that have made this new volume not just credible but important and necessary.

The 1970s: Toward Environmental Literature Pedagogy

One might find an era of origin in 1960s dissatisfaction with the rigid disciplinarity of most college curricula, concisely characterized in Students for a Democratic Society's *Port Huron Statement* as "an exaggerated compartmentalization of study and understanding" (J. Miller 335). C. P. Snow's *The Two Cultures and the Scientific Revolution* was having a strong impact in this area—for example, Snow's concerns initiated the novelist and nature poet Robert Morgan's lifelong quest to "elicit peace between two cultures in the language of his poetry" (Waage, "Mountains" 48). Into this time of disciplinary anxiety blazed the literary brilliance of Rachel Carson's epochal *Silent Spring*, and the innovative cultural criticism in Leo Marx's *The Machine in the Garden*.

Thus, introducing a 1966 issue of the *Saturday Review* (a "Science and Humanities" supplement, entitled "The Fragile Breath of Life"), the editor Norman Cousins, in the intense afterglow of Snow and Carson, and four years before Earth Day, envisages a "third culture":

> There is no doubt that the worlds of the systematic thinker and the creative artist have been productive and, in many respects, prosperous. But there is still a question of total relevance, a question concerning the uses to which brainpower and scholarship and artistry are put . . . a question involving the safety of the world environment. (42)

There is no doubt that Cousins's intuition that environmental concern could become the terrain for a productive alliance between the "systematic thinker" and the "creative artist" has become a reality in the last forty years. The voices of Earth Day itself, in and directly after what George Siehl calls the "environmental nova," expressed themselves in song and story as well as in expository ecological, economic, and political analysis. Marya Mannes delivered the ironic "Hymn of Thanksgiving" to the "Lords of Affluence and Avarice" at Earth Day ceremonies in New York City (248). John Stadler compiled a short story anthology he titled *Eco-Fiction*, defining its contents as neither science fiction nor "nature stories," but stories that seek "to make the reader think about his relationship with his natural environment" (ix). Robert Disch's *The Ecological Conscience: Values for Survival* began with a poem by Allen Ginsberg, written while overflying "[f]armland whirlpooled into mechanic Apocalypse"; it concluded with Snyder's essay "Poetry and the Primitive: Notes on Poetry as an Ecological Survival Technique": "poets don't sing about society, they sing about nature" (198). A 1970 bibliography tendentiously titled "*Where Have All the Flowers Gone?*," whose "purpose . . . is to encourage a greater awareness of the available information pertaining to ecology," intriguingly includes a number of "literary" texts, for example Edward Abbey's *Desert Solitaire*; Robinson Jeffers's *Not Man Apart*; Joseph Wood Krutch's *The Great Chain of Life*; and *Wellspring*, by Edward Hawkins, "an absorbing novel about the hypothetical crisis of the pollution of the drinking water of 40 million Americans" (35). However, nowhere in its entries is literature per se considered an operant term: the entry right above *Wellspring* is titled *Ecology of Waste Water Management*. (It is interesting to compare this bibliography with the extensive one of "Nature Writers after Thoreau" in Loren Owings's 1976 *Environmental Values, 1860–1972: A Guide to Information Sources*, which is quite extensive.)

In the 1970 "Oecology" issue of his journal *Io*, Richard Grossinger strongly argued for "a place in ecology for the poem as well as for the supernatural, spirits, plays, movies, as well as sanitary engineering, invention of the cotton gin." He continued:

> [T]here is nothing to join the Sciences and the Humanities, except perhaps the wish to be well-read. With ecology as the guiding principle they are joined of necessity and the poem, the play, etc., are taken out of the hands of those not concerned with its use, its meaning, its life. These people no longer isolate criteria of judgement, but must deal with the botanist, the geologist, even as these latter must deal with the phenomenological landscape.

Inspired by private, public, and governmental rhetoric and action, during the 1970s environmental education developed in public and private schools and universities, even in some cases becoming the curricular center of these institutions, as with the College of the Atlantic, whose opening was eagerly anticipated by Grossinger. Early on, the work of the creative artist was recognized in some of these programs as a particularly penetrating way into environmental understanding. In *Teaching For Survival: A Handbook for Environmental Education* (1971), Mark Terry suggested that new perceptions of "the oneness or of the interconnections in nature," inexpressible in "traditional prose exposition," lend themselves to the "agrammatical juxtaposition of words in a poetic form." The "creative writer" can lead us to "the very crux of the problem of environmental misunderstanding" (146).

So, increasingly, creative writing became enmeshed with environmental education. Anthologies of environmental writing were published for college literature and composition classes, beginning with Glen Love and Rhoda Love's *Ecological Crisis* (1970), which included writings by Joseph Wood Krutch and Peter Matthiesson and ballad-entwined prose by the folksinger Malvina Reynolds. Sheridan Blau and John von B. Rodenbeck's *The House We Live In: An Environment Reader* (1971) expressly contains writings that "represent nearly all the major academic disciplines and important areas of intellectual discourse," since "no single intellectual movement, academic discipline, political orthodoxy, or ethical stance" has either caused or will resolve "our present ecological crisis" (Introduction 2–3). As well as the likes of Stewart Udall and Lewis Mumford, *The House We Live In* includes writings by John Evelyn, Leopold, Thoreau, Albert Camus, Wendell Berry, and Susan Sontag.

Prefacing his 1972 college anthology *The Whole Earth: Essays in Appreciation, Anger, and Hope*, David McKain confesses, "I sometimes realize that I am losing touch with my environment precisely because of the terms I have used in trying to understand it"—namely the objectivity of "inert writing." More likely to motivate its readers is writing that is "personal, intimate," which conveys, for example, "arguments favoring the preservation of a salt marsh" not in terms of "energy cycles," or "production/respiration ratios," but in terms of odors, colors, "everyday experience" (x).

An interesting source for environmental literature's identity in the 1970s is Siehl's annual "Environmental Updates" in *Library Journal*. *Literature* here is used in the generic-scientific sense, that is, "writing about the environment," but as the decade progressed, the subjects and expository modes in this category increased and diversified. While most of the books in his 1971 article either analyze environmental problems or prescribe methods of combating them, the 1972 survey emphasizes the internationalization of environmental concern and begins with "overviews" in a "philosophical context," such as Rene Dubos's *A God Within* (3548–49). In mid-decade, literary nonfiction begins to invade Siehl's terrain, with texts by Abbey; John McPhee; and, on the ecotone of ecocriticism, Donald Worster's *Nature's Economy.* Of course, although in tune with third-culture rhetoric, the emergence of literary works on the environment has ironic overtones, since in the last decade the canon of environmental literature has expanded regressively and much cultural creation (maybe even *The Ecology of Waste Water Management*) that was previously considered nonliterary is now considered legitimately subject to interpretation from an ecocritical perspective.

In 1974, Carl Swanson made explicit a linkage between environmental studies as "third culture" and the centrality of literature in the field: "Environmental literacy in the future must include the human as well as the scientific, the artistic as well as the technological, the dreams and yearnings as well as the factual and quantitative" (13). "When I seek to do this," Swanson says, "to inject the human and the humane into the issues of environmental concern, I turn most naturally to the literary scene" since "the humanistic literature available for incorporation into environmental education courses is enormous and varied" (13–14, 16). In this context, he evokes writers as diverse as John Steinbeck, Harry Caudill, and Aldo Leopold.

I have not been able to trace *ab origine* the actual teaching of environmental literature (however defined) at the college level in North America. "Nature writing" is at least a minor part of some early environmental education texts and programs. Glen Love and Rhoda Love's teaching guide to *Ecological Crisis: Readings for Survival* suggests that students read Thoreau and keep their own Thoreauvian nature journal as an essay source. A proposed "interdisciplinary environmental field trip" for secondary students includes an English component: either composing a nature haiku or "an imaginative composition, telling how one of the living things around [a] pond might perceive the world in which he lives" (Osborn and Spofford 361). In 1973 Gerald Haslam wrote that "healing and preserving our wounded environment have become a tragically factionalized issue"; thus environmental literature should be central to these endeavors, since "literature reflects it all; the controversy, the pessimism, the hope" (42). He surveys the large amount of quality "affective writing dealing with man and nature" and suggests "a course on literature of the environment" aimed at "guaranteeing that there will be a future" ("Who" 47).

The contents of my own abortive, self-published, two-issue periodical, *Second Growth: Literature of Environmental Concern* (1975–76), show how many quality "affective writers" were willing to be defined as creators of such literature. Among those sending contributions in response to solicitation from a total unknown (myself) were Louis Ginsberg (Allen's father), Malvina Reynolds, William Stafford, Harvey Shapiro, David Ignatow, Peter Wild, and Richard Lillard (whose survey of recent environmental writing would later appear in my *Teaching Environmental Literature*). Another example of the willingness to engage environmental literature was the enthusiastic response to and participation in my special session (such sessions were new at the time) on environmental literature at the 1976 MLA convention, the first such session, to my knowledge, at that venue.

In the United States, particularly in the period 1978–80, when *Teaching Environmental Literature* was first conceived and initiated, there seems to have been a multiplication of interdisciplinary environmental courses and programs centered on literature. Many of the courses described in that volume, and the many others submitted that did not find their way into print, were initiated in the later 1970s. No doubt there was an environmental*ist* motivation for this development, considering the high profile of Love Canal, Three Mile Island, the Superfund, and Interior Secretary James Watt. The continuing problematic connection between environmental*ism* and environmental literature will be addressed toward the end of this introduction.

The Environment of *Teaching Environmental Literature*

Whatever the extramural origins, much was being done to introduce environmental literature into academic curricula during the early 1980s. In the light of then and now, it is amusing to look back on the readers' reports on the original *Teaching Environmental Literature* manuscript. One reader's first response was that it seemed to be an oddly "dated" collection of materials, since "man's relationship to his environment is no longer a 'sexy' political issue." Another, while "strongly recommending" the volume's publication, suggested it would encounter "a dubious audience unacquainted with the literature." To these views, John Tallmadge, a contributor to that volume and author of this volume's foreword, responded encouragingly, "Don't lose heart!" (Tallmadge). He was right; actual teaching practice in the early 1980s belied the readers' skepticism.

Many disciplines were reexamining their traditional paradigms with a view toward a new nonanthropocentric groundwork for discourse and found it in environmental studies. For example, Riley E. Dunlap, editing a special issue of *American Behavioral Scientist* devoted to this very development, states unequivocally that "[t]he social sciences have largely ignored the fact that human societies depend on the biophysical environment for their survival" (Dunlap 5) and proposes, for sociology, in place of a "Human Exemptionalism Paradigm," a "New Ecological Paradigm" (Catton and Dunlap 15). Around the same time, Kathleen S. Abrams asked rhetorically, "How can an English curriculum thrive without the inclusion of environmental studies?" (302).

Many of the course syllabi submitted to me, although they did not find their way into the volume, exemplified such a new paradigm in practice. In fact, in many cases it was their interdisciplinary inclusiveness grounded in ecology that made them seem too broad for environmental literature as I conceived it then. For example, three Dartmouth professors were team teaching a course entitled Nature, Science, Society, and the Humanist Tradition. Other courses being actively taught in the early 1980s were Bryan Norton's Humanities and the Environment, at the University of South Florida, and Robert Schultz's Technology, Freedom, and the Nature of Man, at the University of Denver, which, according to the syllabus, had a goal of questioning "the adequacy of traditional enlightenment political ideals in a world growing conscious of natural limits."

Geography and literature were linked early on, particularly geography characterized as landscape. Christopher Salter organized a Landscape and Literature session at the 1974 Association of American Geographers meeting, and a resulting resource paper suggests ways that literary works, particularly fiction, can be used in geography classes (Salter and Lloyd). It even quotes *The Monkey Wrench Gang*'s "rejection of man's purposeful alteration of the earth" (Salter and Lloyd 12). In 1979, Robert Riley could write, "The interaction between culture and environment is now being explored with a fervor that would have been unusual and unseemly a decade ago" (11). Thomas Matro could argue that environmental perception, manifested in poetry, "can be of practical use in landscape assessment and in the preservation of scenic beauty required by sound environmental planning" (16). The Smithsonian's 1984 bibliography *The Natural Environment: An Annotated Bibliography on Attitudes and Values* (an initial one was published in 1980) was inspired by "the recent efforts of others in education, philosophy, religion, the sciences, and the humanities to come to grips with and write about questions on ecological interdependence central to successful human civilizations" (Anglemyer and Seagraves 10). Under the category "Civilization" it annotates a category "Humanities (Art and Literature)"—which perhaps unfortunately suggests that art and literature are the only relevant humanities areas; it includes novels by Richard Adams and the poetry of Ted Hughes and Gary Snyder. Yet a glance at the same volume's "Education" bibliography will suggest how little "literature" (in the traditional sense, and despite the inroads chronicled above) figured in publications on interdisciplinary environmental-studies pedagogy.

A Tale of Two Texts

So we have the double image of *Teaching Environmental Literature* as innovative in 1985 and outdated in 2008—outdated precisely because the "ecological insurgency" (Buell) it participated in initiating was successful. The scope of that insurgency is a central justification for the current, more comprehensive, volume. If we temporarily beg the question of whether environmental literature must inherently be an agent for environmental advocacy or action, we see that a characterization of the main differences between the 1985 text and this one may show how important this new volume is.

The 1985 volume is characterized in part by my introduction, which posited "much turmoil and uncertainty in American higher education" (ix–x). It spent much of its time quoting Leon Botstein (writing in 1982; "Beyond"), the 1980 report *The Humanities in American Life*, and the 1983 National Commission on Excellence in Education report *A Nation at Risk*, all of which endorsed interdisciplinarity. The introduction's tone seems defensive today, as though it were summoning character witnesses for a text on trial. Admittedly, Botstein, in his 1997 study *Jefferson's Children*, as in 1982, bewails the lack of a moral and disciplinary "common ground" (211). He complains even while citing the late 1970s through early 1980s as a period of fundamental change in United States higher education, a change partially enabled through the women's movement and the age, class, and ethnicity diversification of students. But, in actuality, the academic role of environmental humanities has expanded and diversified so radically that the timorousness of 1985 is as unjustified as Botstein's aggravation in 1997. A survey conducted by the Brown University Center for Environmental Studies lists over 150 United States colleges with environmental studies departments or programs ("Environmental Studies Programs"). As of 2004, the Web site Enviroeducation.com, "the environmental education directory," boasted 2,361 listings. A glance at the Association for Literature and Environment collection of syllabi on its Web site (asle@umn.edu) suggests how many diverse academic departments are sites for environmental literature courses.

Another main characteristic distinguishing *Teaching Environmental Literature* is the first section; titled "Contexts," it includes an essay on the definition of environmental literature by Walter Clark, Jr. ("What"), and by three others, thus chronicling "American literary environmentalism" from the nineteenth century through 1985. Clark defines environmental literature as "literature that deals with physical surroundings, most especially biological surroundings, in such a way as to include, tacitly or explicitly, that which is surrounded" (6), that has aesthetic qualities, and that involves moral and political issues when possible. Bruce Piasecki's survey of pre-Darwin writing discusses many natural history and philosophy texts, but his earliest reference is to John Playfair in 1802. The most recent American environmental texts cited in Richard Lillard's survey—or in any of the other essays for that matter—date from 1983.

There are several indications of how this field and its bibliography have expanded in the last twenty years. First, the current volume acknowledges the worldwide creation of environmental literature, not just American (as a synonym for United States) creation. Second, the extreme diversification of written genres considered to manifest North American literary environmentalism shows that environmental literature is recognized in Native American orature and colonial texts from the earliest narratives of encounter. Third, generically diverse environmental works have been published in profusion since 1985, in a context where those works evince self-awareness about their generic identity, since environmental literature has become widely integrated into curricula from primary through postsecondary education.

In this regard, John Murray's comments in the preface to *Nature's New Voices* are telling. Important writers included in his anthology—Rick Bass, Gretel Ehrlich, John Daniel, Richard Nelson, Terry Tempest Williams—did not appear in my 1985 volume. Murray tells his readers that when he began college in 1971 "nature writing, as a literary genre, was not taught anywhere" (x), whereas, at the time he wrote in 1992, it was being "taught . . . in English or Environmental Studies departments, at nearly every university and college" (xi). In fact, says Murray, "so popular are courses in this subject . . . that [the MLA] published a[n] . . . instructional book to assist teachers with syllabi and pedagogy in the burgeoning new academic discipline" (xi). A fourth indication of the expansion of the field is that the "Contexts" section in my 1985 volume is now expanded from four essays into two sections and contains ten essays, including this one. In it, Patrick Murphy gives a panoramic view of the varieties of environmental literature in the United States, Canada, and Mexico. David Mazel and Ursula Heise discuss ecocriticism, the approach to criticism that evolved alongside the environmental literature canon (in fact, although the term was coined in 1985, it was not recognized as a term of art then). Catriona Mortimer-Sandilands covers ecofeminism, and Karla Armbruster animal studies, two vital areas of concern. Finally, under the section head "Mapping North American Environmental Literature" are essays by Jorge Marcone and Priscilla Solis Ybarra, Pamela Banting, Daniel J. Philippon, and Annie Merrill Ingram, surveying Mexican, Canadian, and pre- and post-twentieth-century United States writing.

Teaching Environmental Literature was divided into sections that defined and illustrated four modes of pedagogy: "traditional" classroom-centered courses focused on textual interpretation; "nature writing" courses; "field" courses using extramural sites beyond the classroom; and "regional studies"—courses that are multidisciplinary, team-taught, and defined in content by a particular geographic area. The editors of this current volume, on the other hand, have had to encompass more variety—in types of literature, tools of pedagogy, disciplinary approaches—which called for a more complex format. We decided to define environmental literature in more nuanced terms by dividing Part III, "Teaching North American Environmental Literature," into three sections: "disciplinary," "interdisciplinary," and "place-based" approaches. The essays contained in these categories embody different ways in which the pedagogy has radically changed. One change reveals critical approaches and areas of concern that did not exist or that were not seen as crucial to environmental literary creation and study in 1985 but that are vital components of teaching today. New to this volume are essays on teaching environmental literature and ecocomposition, electronic media, environmental justice, ecoethics, and black American literature. Essays in this volume also recognize the national, cultural, and ethnic diversity of environmental literature in a way that was not possible in 1985. Thus, they not only cover writing from Mexico and Canada but also address Native American, African American, Asian, and multicultural literary creation. Another development is that field study has greatly expanded and diversified since 1985. The current volume recognizes this diversity under the rubric "place-based," a usage of *place* lacking currency in 1985. There are essays on teaching the "literature of place," urban (Los Angeles) and rural (the Great Plains). Varied forms of bioregional teaching are discussed, including the University of Kentucky's Summer Environmental Writing Program, Franklin Pierce University's Monadnock Institute, and the Great Basin Institute at the University of Nevada, Reno.

The most significant impact on the environmental studies movement since 1985 has been the readily accessible personal computer, the Internet, and related modes of electronic communication: computer programs, VCR, DVD, and so forth. *Teaching Environmental Literature* was written right before the "new machine" became commonly used; its manuscript was inelegantly typed on a portable manual typewriter. This technological transformation is embodied both in this volume's pedagogical essays and in "Part IV: Resources for Teaching Environmental Literature: A Selective Guide" by Mark C. Long. Many courses described in this volume either involve or are centered on nonhardcopy materials, but they are all premised on students' ability to use a computer to create and access environmental literature or to obtain information related to it. The list of resources I included in 1985 seems fairly quaint now. I listed works available in sections titled "Environmental Bibliographies and Information Centers," "Periodicals," and "Organizations." These resources were not available on Web sites. In addition, where I referred the reader to organizations, all locations were identified by phone number and street address only. No pedagogical programs (such as the Monadnock Institute) were mentioned, since few existed. There were no Web sites that could be devoted to individual writers, literary genres, regions, and so forth, not to mention that no electronic directories and bibliographies existed. Finally, whereas syllabi of courses described in this volume are available at the Association for the Study of Literature and the Environment Web site, readers of *Teaching Environmental Literature* interested in obtaining the same were instructed to write to me, for transmission by what is now known as snail mail.

Flocks and Herds of New Developments

In an early 1970s collection of environmental-education essays, Peter Sandman says that "the media are clearly the best available tools of mass environmental education" (241). Little did he know, I presume, what "media" would come to include as the succeeding decade progressed. Every possible type of environmental information—scientific, humanistic, and anywhere in between—can be accessed or located online. But the "third culture" has expanded since 1985 in many nonelectronic ways as well.

Perhaps the single most important overall development after 1985 related to teaching environmental literature was the founding and subsequent expansion of the Association for the Study of Literature and Environment in 1992 and of its publications, programs, and conferences. One (but not the only) source of the organization was the *American Nature Writing Newsletter*, created in 1989 and edited by Alicia Nitecki. A major section of the newsletter was "Classroom Notes," descriptions by the instructors of environmental literature courses they had taught or were teaching. The "Classroom Notes" section continued when the newsletter was adopted and edited by the ASLE, starting in 1993.

Another example of how the field has expanded in traditional, nontechnological ways is the founding of publishers of and periodicals devoted to environmental literature: Island Press and Fulcrum Publishing in 1984 and Milkweed Editions, with its distinguished The World as Home series, shortly thereafter. *Orion Nature Quarterly* and the Orion Society were established in 1992; the organization's realm of activities has steadily expanded and includes conferences, a grassroots network, and *Orion-online*. Major publishers are increasing their lists of environment-related books by individual authors, and a new generation of teaching anthologies with environmental content is responding to proliferating college courses, especially in ecocomposition. A text that signals the trend to publish creative environmental nonfiction is Pantheon's publication of Terry Tempest Williams's first book—a best seller—*Refuge: An Unnatural History of Family and Place*. I have used in my own place-based ecocomposition courses—among the many anthologies available—Melissa Walker's *Reading the Environment* and Lorraine Anderson, Scott Slovic, and John P. O'Grady's *Literature and the Environment*. In the 1990s a number of university presses began to develop specializations in environmental literature, including scholarly texts and creative nonfiction. Notable are the University of Georgia Press; the University of Virginia Press, with its Under the

Sign of Nature series; Oregon State University Press, which took over publishing John Murray's annual Best American Nature Writing series in 1999; and the University of Nevada Press. Along with the *Orion Nature Quarterly*, post-1985 literary magazines publishing mainly environmental literature include *Isotope* (formerly *Petroglyph*), *Bear Deluxe*, *Gaia*, *Glimmer Train*, and *Heron Dance*. *Green Teacher* magazine was launched in the United Kingdom in 1986 and reinvented in Canada in 1991; it surveys interdisciplinary environmental courses and resources. The magazine launched a book series in 2004.

The field of environmental literature studies further expanded in the 1990s, when independent and university-sponsored interdisciplinary field programs involving literature and writing were initiated, many of which are described in this book. Examples of their remarkable variety include a program at the Women's Wilderness Institute in Boulder, Colorado, where one can attend the Writing in Nature workshop. The University of Montana's Wilderness Institute, affiliated with the university's College of Forestry and Conservation, began a Wilderness and Civilization minor in 1990. Among its many field courses, David Moore teaches Literature and the Environment. The Canyonlands Field Institute, founded in 1984 in Moab, Utah, holds an annual Desert Writers Workshop in the desert. At the John C. Campbell Folk School in Brasstown, North Carolina, Elderhostel students can participate in a five-day workshop entitled Exploring the Natural World—Walk, Watch, Retreat, and Write. Indoors, Brown College of Brown University created the annual Sally Brown Seminar on Environmental Literature, which was energized by its first Environmental Fellow, Dan Philippon—one of the contributors to this anthology.

A singular and vastly influential actor in the ecocritical insurgency has been the network of institutes developed at the University of Nevada, Reno, in the 1990s. Scott Slovic and others organized the Center for Environmental Arts and Humanities in 1995. The center collaborated with the preexisting Center for Environmental Sciences and Engineering on many symposia, conferences, and residencies. In 2004, the two centers were merged into the Academy for the Environment. The academy functions separately from the University of Nevada, Reno, English department's Literature and Environment Program, developed in 1996 by Slovic, Cheryll Glotfelty, and Michael Branch to offer master's and doctoral programs.

The study of environmental literature has, of course, also continued to develop not because of, but with the help of, technology. An example of the possibilities provided by Web-based programs is the *Our Land, Our Literature* Web site (bsu.edu/ourlandourlit) founded by Barbara Stedman of Ball State University, which features coverage of seventy Indiana writers whose work has a strong environmental content. Stedman was inspired to create the site in 1999 because "almost nothing had been written about the subject [Indiana's environmental literature] in literary, historical, or environmental scholarship" (Stedman). Ball State's collaborative faculty-student seminars gathered information for and designed the site. Interestingly, the Web site exists because the students' work was rejected for university-press publication, when reviewers claimed environmental literature scholarship had a "limited audience." Stedman suggests that "all states, all regions— not just the West—likely have their own heritage of such literature, equally deserving of investigation."

Rip Van Winkle Effect

Teaching North American Environmental Literature is invested in an ancestral, recurrent, and unresolved debate fundamental to the teaching of environmental literature: its relation to environmental science and to environmental*ism*.

Waking up in 2008 from a slumber of twenty years, one concerned for the environment and involved with its literature might, like Rip, cry out in bewilderment, "everything's changed!" But one might also resume old habits. For a person who shares Walter Clark's view that the environmental literature best for teaching does "raise moral or political issues" (Clark, "What" 6), the literature and teaching of the environment would seem changed, but the "old habits" of environmental destruction would seem the same—or, if anything, more encompassing and more dangerous, which environmental sciences have clearly established.

In fact, according to one school of thought, the rise of an entity definable as environmental literature, with all its encumbrances of criticism, institutionalization, and pedagogical correctness, has hindered efforts to change old habits because environmental literature has disengaged itself from interdisciplinarity. Susan Zakin ironically but interestingly dates nature writers' "abdication" of issues to 1988, when Barry Lopez wrote a letter to Edward Abbey regretting that he had not been more of an activist but renouncing that role (xiii–xiv). Zakin sees two schools of environmental writing: the current one, those who "take themselves rather too seriously," and the superseded one, those who are "passionate, funny, and unpretentious." "Saving the environment is as much an aesthetic issue as a moral one" (xiv). Michael Cohen in "Blues among the Green" quotes Slovic on the currency of belief that "the community of nature writers and eco-critics has become too chummy and self congratulatory—too self-satisfied and self-righteous" (21). Slovic speculates, "I wonder if books themselves are fence destroyers. I wonder what Abbey would think about my use of literature as a lens through which to view the natural world. Does the text come between me and the world, preventing a more direct and somehow *better* form of contact?" (*Seeking Awareness* 177).

To what extent then, does the enterprise of teaching environmental literature, whose success is represented in this volume, collaborate in the self-righteous abdication of an initiating rationale for its own existence? I think this and similar questions are crucial components of the enterprise itself and that a central purpose of this book is to represent the current state of a discipline fully established enough to be questioned about its credibility.

In closing this essay, though, I would like to suggest that criticism of the environmental literature movement's disengagement, institutionaliza-tion, and self-absorption are questions mainly operative within the com-munity of environmental literature writers and teachers rather than in the teacher-student transactional community. Rarely entering this discussion are the countless thousands of individual students whose feelings, ideas, and life courses have been profoundly affected by the educational expe-riences that this community has provided. Even under the premise that environmental literature must have an impact, through its readers and stu-dents, on "moral or political issues," its effect even on the one individual student constitutes such an impact. Everyone comes to the agora or the voting booth conscious of this effect, even if he or she has never chained himself or herself to a single tree. "Local knowledge is the grounding for global knowledge," says Scott Russell Sanders (*Staying* 114), which is true in the teaching of environmental literature, one receptive consciousness at a time. Slovic makes this point most eloquently:

> Perhaps the best we can hope for is, like Barry Lopez, to "create an environment in which thinking and reaction and wonder and awe and speculation can take place." . . . And we can hope, with no more guar-antee than the writers themselves ever get, that when our students' and readers' thoughts settle, their actions will follow suit, and the earth will be a little bit more secure. (171)

Patrick D. Murphy

The Varieties of Environmental Literature in North America

Literary analysis of representations of nature in North American literature have been appearing for at least 140 years, according to the research of David Mazel in *A Century of Early Ecocriticism*; writing about nature in North America predates the first entry in his book by at least another 300 years. We have, then, more than 450 years of written records of individuals setting down their feelings and thoughts about nature in both literary and nonliterary forms in a variety of languages. While storytelling and narrative art would move human aesthetic responses to the North American natural world back thousands of additional years, this volume is concerned with written and printed texts.

Fortunately, the term *literature* in the title of this essay allows for a further, although highly contested, narrowing of the field to survey. The label *fiction* is really of no help, since a considerable number of the texts studied in nature-writing and environmental literature courses are defined as nonfiction; in other words, when teaching a movements-in-literature graduate course in the summer of 2004 devoted to environmental writing, I included *Silent Spring* and other nonfiction alongside poetry and fiction. Some critics would like English teachers to ignore the concept of literature altogether and study nature-oriented texts including such texts as "science reports," from a purely rhetorical orientation. Doing so, however, would ignore the fundamental difference between any kind of nature-oriented text and most of the works those very same critics analyze and teach: the aesthetic dimension of writing that causes people to pick up and respond to a text as *literary* (see Philippon; Branch, "Saving").

So, while I organize my study of various nonfiction works under the heading of literature, I limit their inclusion to those works that have a significant aesthetic dimension. By that I mean that they have an emotive-affective quality to their writing, regardless of the rhetorical or narrative strategies applied. That constitutes the difference between the report that John Wesley Powell made to the House of Representatives in 1874 about his 1869 trip down the Colorado River and the edited and embellished version that he published for mass consumption in 1895. Such literary works move people precisely because they not only make appeals to reason and provide information, often highly scientific, but also elicit emotional responses. In essence, they are texts that provide both information and emotion rather than either one or the other.

A fear exists that if certain texts are defined as nonliterary they will never be taught. American studies, particularly those fields of study with a Puritan focus, developed out of this kind of fear—or recognition of neglect—and we now find sermons, usually those from the colonial period of North American settlement, in anthologies of literature. I would suggest that, instead of struggling to smuggle everything and anything into a course labeled literature, some texts important to our understanding of environmental issues and perceptions of nature ought to be taught in American studies, environmental studies, cultural studies, rhetoric, composition, history, and philosophy courses, with only a few of these courses housed in departments of English. For example, George Perkins Marsh's *Man and Nature* is a touchstone text for the history of environmental consciousness in North America, but it is hardly teachable as literature or even as a well-written work.

Additional qualifications are in order. First, for the readers of this volume, I do not quibble over the distinctions between such categories as nature writing, environmental writing, ecological literature, nature-oriented literature, and various terms that I and other critics have used in distinguishing how authors respond to the world. Rather, I consider all literature that engages nature extensively as environmental literature, so that the broadest scope can be provided and individual readers, teachers, and critics can make their own further distinctions. For my own taxonomy and remarks on other taxonomies that do differentiate along these lines, please see *Farther Afield in the Study of Nature-Oriented Literature* (see also J. Bryson; Elder, Introduction; Elder and Finch; Lyon, "Taxonomy"; Scigaj).

Second, I do not subscribe to the belief that works of environmental literature have to conform to anyone's particular theory of reality or of representations of that reality, such as "outer mimesis" (see Buell, *Environmental Imagination*, ch. 3), nor do I believe that works need to remain consistently fictional or nonfictional in content. For example, as ecocritics delve deeper and deeper into the history of the literary production of many canonical, revered texts of nature writing, they find frequently that repeatedly taught works of literary nonfiction contain substantial amounts of fictional writing. Although the natural facts may be accurate, the events, occurrences, direct experiences, and even documents are fictional, such as many of John van Dyke's alleged direct experiences in *The Desert* and other of his works of "nonficton" or the first several letters of Gilbert White's *The Natural History of Selborne* (see Wild; Allen). Another problem is aesthetic rearrangement: chronicles, journals, and diaries pretend to describe events in chronological order, when in fact they often rearrange events from different years according to artistic need. Two key examples are the nineteenth-century nonfiction books *Rural Hours* and *Walden*. Likewise, works of fantasy and science fiction can create worlds with descriptions that contain no verifiable natural facts or even that present events contrary to known facts. Such works still qualify as environmental literature because of the ethical lessons of the texts, as with Diane Duane's Young Wizard series of young-adult novels. More clearly controverting outer mimesis or an accepted empirical realism are those works by Native peoples that include events, characters, and actions in their textual realities that many readers would define as belonging to the spiritual realm, myth, or superstition, as in the novels of Linda Hogan, N. Scott Momaday, and Leslie Marmon Silko.

Third, as with struggles over the canon elsewhere in academia, conflicts exist in ecocriticism over the forms of literature that count; these conflicts mark an effort to distinguish serious or high literature from popular and formulaic works. Here, though, I am concerned not with how to limit what may be counted as environmental literature but with how to expand the conception of what may be included. Hence, popular genres, particularly of fiction, must also be taken into account and appreciated for expanding readers' understanding of nature and of environmental justice. Also, many works now considered serious today were written according to formulaic conventions and as popular literature in their own time. Important works of environmental literature, particularly works written in the latter half of the nineteenth century and the first half of the twentieth century, and especially those by women, continue to be dismissed from the American literature canon by being labeled local-color writing or children's literature. The realities of the reading market mean that one Gene Stratton-Porter book in its day or one Clive Cussler or Michael Crichton novel today that focuses on environmental issues or actions affects more readers in one year than does the assigning of *Walden* or *The Land of Little Rain* by all English teachers in a decade. That is not to say that we need to be teaching Stratton-Porter, Cussler, and Crichton but that we should not shy away from doing so if they fit into the pedagogical needs of a particular course, such as one on ethics in science or the contemporary adventure novel for nonmajors.

In the body of this essay, I focus initially on three major categories of environmental literature: nonfiction prose, prose fiction, and poetry, placing particular emphasis on environmental fiction and its variations, which have received scant attention compared with nonfiction and prose (lack of attention to Aristotle's foundational genre of Western poetics, drama, will be taken up toward the end). Then I will turn to ways to divide up these categories, as well as to recategorize them to construct different courses. These two approaches conform to the ways that literature courses are organized and structured in most English departments.

To encompass the earliest known written reflections on the nature of North America, one must begin with works alleged to be nonfictional. Also, critics should not use anachronistic criteria associated with the personal-essay form most favored by modern writers. Official and unofficial journals and diaries constitute the earliest representations. As a result of academic interest in autobiographies, captivity narratives, and personal diaries, a strong basis exists for literary analysis of these early works, even though few of them were intended for mass distribution. Scholars have noted that the writers of the Lewis and Clark expedition journals—a relatively late entry into this category of writing—attempted to capture accurately the significance, difference, magnitude, and beauty of the landscape they encountered, which were in contrast to the Old World or even to the heavily settled eastern coast of the North American continent. They were conscious of the limitations of their language and the need for creativity in describing not just the facts, as it were, but the *effects* of the natural world on them. And herein lies the literary merit and interest of many of these early texts.

Works such as J. Hector Saint-John de Crèvecoeur's *Letters* stand in marked contrast to the Puritan writing that preceded them, particularly the sermons. While Crèvecoeur and others saw the world before them as unique and as provoking new perceptions, and as they used fresh language to describe this world, Puritan authors bound by religious orthodoxy could not engage the natural world on its own terms and open up their ideologies and beliefs to ways of thinking compelled by the wilderness they confronted. Literary anthologies have made great progress in redressing the almost exclusive emphasis on the Puritan perception of the New World, but an insufficient number of colonial nature-writing texts have made it into their pages. As a result, historical surveys of environmental nonfiction, poetry, and fiction remain spotty for the years before the founding of the United States. As Michael Branch has cogently observed, the writing of the literary history of the early years of American environmental literature still awaits a significant upsurge in textual studies and textual editing ("Saving").

Alongside these early writings, there quickly sprang up what is loosely identified as the travel narrative, which was increasingly written with the intention of being sold to a reading public. The quality and accuracy of these narratives, of course, vary greatly. Frequently, allegedly first-person travel narratives were not at all based on actual direct experience but had their descriptive passages cribbed from other books or, when needed for effect, simply invented. A distinction ought to be made here between works circulated as genuine articles of travel experience, such as William Bartram's *Travels*, written in the 1770s and published in 1791, and works written as fiction, thereby signaling their own fabrications. It is useful to bear in mind that from very early on, settlement was not so much an act of military conquest or imperial expansion as it was a business intended to enrich stockholders in the Old World at the expense of commoners laboring under various forms of servitude. Hyperbolic stories of opportunities for becoming wealthy, for enjoying exotic but nonthreatening adventure, and for living in paradisial environments were encouraged by companies seeking to generate a sufficient workforce for their financial ambitions (see G. Sayre).

The rapid development of scientific thinking and investigation arising out of the European Renaissance and the multicentury amateur character of most scientific research helped the development of another nonfiction literary genre, the natural-history essay. While these often coincided with travel and exploration, some of the best writing in this form has come from individuals who remained close to home and studied the flora and fauna in which their daily lives were immersed. The literary dimensions of this form, and the travel narrative as well, were aided in the nineteenth century by the development of the Romantic movement and the strong interest in the sublime. The amateur character of the movement of scientific discovery behind this writing enabled active participation by women until, according to Nina Baym, it was taken over by professional male scientists and an academy hostile to female participation.

While women such as Jessie Benton Frémont and Mary Hallock Foote engaged in travel writing, especially after the Civil War, the extent of their participation was limited by the restrictions placed on their personal mobility. This opportunity is most clearly attested to by the first full-length work of nature writing by an American woman, *Rural Hours*, written by Susan Fenimore Cooper. Her younger contemporary, Henry David Thoreau, also showed how one can engage in such nature writing either by staying close to home, as in *Walden*, or by traveling farther afield, as in *Maine Woods*. Both authors recorded observations, experiences, and reflections in journals kept over many years and then rearranged them into a cycle of seasons. This technique continues to be a mainstay of much North American nature writing, such as David Mas Masumoto's *Epitaph for a Peach*. One attribute of this form, whether positive or negative for readers, is the tendency to focus on the experiences of an individual rather than on community or cooperation. Relatively few nature writers seem to include other people as a positive presence the way that John Burroughs does in some of his essays. Also, many of the authors, both men and women, make themselves, rather than nature, the hero of their stories and essays, as John Muir often does. Women writers, such as Mary Austin, more frequently prove the exception to this representation of heroic individualism than do male writers.

Biography and autobiography constitute both a specific form of nonfiction environmental literature and a dimension of almost all its other forms as well. Personal essays are, after all, autobiographical to some extent. At the same time, the development of the personal autobiography as a literary genre has its own history and is replete with works in which nature and environmental justice play major roles. The study and teaching of biographies and autobiographies from an ecocritical perspective considers how their authors focus on the individual hero while foregrounding the actions of the individual in relation to nature that makes that hero worthy of attention. Recent works that lend themselves to this kind of analysis include Dan O'Brien's *Buffalo for the Broken Heart* and Janisse

Ray's *Ecology of a Cracker Childhood*. And many of these works end up being both biography and autobiography, as with Teresa Jordan's *Riding the White Horse Home* and Don Schueler's *A Handmade Wilderness*.

What is perhaps most stunning when looking at the various forms of literary-nonfiction nature writing—and nature writing is what it is most commonly called—is how relatively consistent the form and structure of its various manifestations have remained for several hundred years. Although the epistolary form has faded for the time being, the travel narrative, the journal, the seasonal cycle, the natural-history essay all remain quite popular with writers and have regained popularity with readers in recent decades. Nature writing, and perhaps appropriately so given an overweening sense of the necessity and value of conservation, has undergone far less structural mutation than either poetry or fiction over the same period of time.

With poetry, there is probably much less to say about genre than in the case of either nonfiction or fiction, for several reasons. One, nature poetry, at least as pastoral, has been recognized as part of the Western and world canons for a very long time. There has not been a debate about whether such poems are literature, as has been debated with many of the works of nonfiction nature writing. Two, as a result of the influences of Chinese landscape poetry, haiku, georgic poetry, pastoral verse plays and narrative poems, and Romantic long poems, American nature poems are much more an integral part of a long international tradition than have been the personal essay and wilderness-experience journal. Three, while the names and the specific poems may change, nature poems have always composed part of any anthology of American or Canadian poetry, in English or French. Four, while there has been a general shift toward free verse and the rise of the modern poetic sequence, traditional forms, such as the sonnet and the villanelle, are still practiced by various writers, who also continue to produce elegies, odes, dithyrambs, dramatic monologues, and other historically established forms. Long narrative poems are still being written about nature, for instance, alongside sequences, lyrics, and elegies, and some of these are being written in fixed forms. Some of these long poems are historical in orientation, while at least a handful turn toward fantasy and science fiction.

The main discussion of the poetry genre has concerned distinctions among nature, environmental, or ecological poems, as well as what the term *ecological* means. As a result, the discussion has focused almost entirely on issues of content and ideology rather than on form and genre. A debate has also ensued about whether a nature poem, rather than an environmental one, can be written in an age of environmental crisis (see B. Bryson; Scigaj; Gifford, *Green Voices* and *Pastoral*).

But before moving on to fiction, I do want to emphasize that for an understanding of North American nature or environmental poetry it is absolutely crucial that teachers and students read beyond the anthologies. Anthologies invariably privilege shorter poems over longer ones and often skew the reception of a particular poet by emphasizing one phase, one tone, or one kind of poem over another. The historical significance of Joel Barlow's lengthy *The Vision of Columbus* (expanded, republished, and poorly received as *The Columbiad*) has largely been lost, while the attention given Robinson Jeffers's shorter poems provides the best example of this problem. Jeffers can easily be represented as a quiet, meditative nature poet or as a raging antihumanist political poet, even when just selecting anthology entries from his shorter poems. The same can be said of anthology selections for Wendell Berry and Gary Snyder, even though these three poets have markedly distinct bodies of work. Other examples include Robert Frost, Elizabeth Bishop, and Adrienne Rich. Anthologies also often make room for new works by decreasing the number of earlier works. As a result, the nature poetry of William Cullen Bryant, Henry Wadsworth Longfellow, and John Greenleaf Whittier is increasingly represented as less and less important, while difficult poets who may have a strong concern for nature, such as Charles Olson, may be bypassed along with highly influential although critically underappreciated poets, such as Kenneth Rexroth.

Although the genre of environmental fiction has received the least sustained attention and is discussed almost entirely by means of individual examples, it is the one that I believe contains the greatest variety of forms of nature-oriented and environmental-activist writing of any of the three genres. It is the only genre that encourages critics to consider whether to include commercial and generically formulaic works, such as those of the mystery and the detective forms of popular fiction. What can be said about novels applies as well to short stories, so I will focus on novels here. While today some would argue that Charles Brockden Brown truly deserves the label of first American novelist, in most readers' minds that honor still remains with James Fenimore Cooper. Despite, then, the emphases of modernist, New Critical, and much postmodernist approaches, the American novel tradition is firmly grounded in the natural world of this continent, and the same can be said for Canadian literature, where survival in nature has remained an abiding theme. Other major early American novelists, such as Nathaniel Hawthorne and Herman Melville, also gave serious attention both to representations of nature and, especially in the case of Hawthorne with his critiques of Puritanism, to popular perceptions of nature, while numerous lesser lights wrote novels that highlighted the nature of specific regions, for example William Gilmore Simms in *The Yemassee* and *The Cassique of Kiawah*. It is often forgotten by critics and unknown by students that these writers hoped to produce popular novels that would sell and often worked with the stylistic techniques and narrative devices of recognized genres, such as the romance and the fictional travel narrative.

The second half of the nineteenth century and the beginning of the twentieth century is marked by a proliferation of fiction set in the American West focusing on the life of its settlers and historical inhabitants; these lives are worked out in relation to the natural environments they encounter. Hamlin Garland, Helen Hunt Jackson, Mark Twain, Jack London, Mary Austin, to name a few, contributed to a literature that included, near the end of this period, Oscar Micheaux's novels about his own experiences as an African American homesteader in South Dakota, *The Conquest* and *The Homesteader* (which was made into a movie).

By the beginning of the twentieth century, with rapid industrialization and urbanization, we begin to see a distinction developing between nature-oriented novels and environmental justice novels, although neither label was in circulation at the time. It could be argued that this distinction carried over from the previous century when readers and writers increasingly differentiated the more traditional romance from the more modern novel. The romance lends itself to pastoral and nostalgic views of wilderness, rural life, and simplicity, while focusing on family ties and heterosexual love relationships; the novel has the capacity for muckraking, for evincing the new realism, and for representing the destruction of families from the strains and pressures of wage labor and urban life. The contrast can be seen by comparing Gene Stratton-Porter's *The Song of the Cardinal* (1903) and Harold Bell Wright's *The Shepherd of the Hills* (1907) with a novel published in between these two, Upton Sinclair's *The Jungle* (1906).

At the turn and early quarter of the century, the novel side of this equation could also be divided in two, between realism and naturalism. The major works of naturalism also turn toward nature, environment, and environmental justice and are distinguished by wilderness and agrarian locations, such as Frank Norris's *The Octopus* or any number of novels by

Jack London. While Sinclair took the realist, muckraking environmental justice novel to the city, Mary Austin took it to agriculture. While Willa Cather was working largely in the romance tradition in her depictions of farm life in the 1910s, with *O Pioneers!*, *The Song of the Lark*, and *My Antonia*, Mary Austin was publishing novels, such as *The Ford* (1917), that dealt with an environmental conflict that continues to define the American West: the battle over water. And, of course, major modernists often depicted nature and conflicts over land use in their fiction, whether Ernest Hemingway's psychological healing through fishing or William Faulkner's despairing over fields converted to golf courses. Again, writers in the mid–twentieth century were often diminished by critics if they could be labeled regionalists rather than universalists, as if only the urban environment delineated the fundamental features of the human species.

Just as World War II gave rise to a new kind of nature writing, such as Carson's *Silent Spring*, so too did its technological revolution give rise to new themes in fiction. Running across a variety of subgenres, the cautionary tale became a staple of serious and commercial novels. Dexter Masters's 1955 realist novel about the dawn of the atomic age, *The Accident*, stands out. This novel, written by a nuclear-development insider, may have been one of the most important of these cautionary tales to be suppressed by the State Department, which prevented David O. Selznick from making it into a movie (see Masters's foreword to the 1983 edition).

In many ways, science fiction matured into a literature worthy of ecocritical attention in the thirty years after the war with the publication of such environmental classics as George R. Stewart's *The Earth Abides* and a spate of novels that imagined the environmental havoc wreaked by nuclear war. Science fiction provided a vehicle also for critiques of colonialism and for the linkage between empire and environmental destruction, as in Ursula K. Le Guin's short novel, *The Word for World Is Forest*.

Environmental awareness has been promoted through what creative writing instructors at many universities have derisively labeled "genre fiction." This expansion, however, proves more of a challenge for literary analysis than the continued attention to nature and environmental issues by the authors of literature (nongenre fiction?). If critics and teachers are interested in reader response, reception theory, cultural studies, and the social impact of literary production, then environmental mysteries, ecological science fiction, detective novels focusing on environmental justice investigations, and alternate-world fantasies, as well as nature-oriented eutopian,

utopian, and dystopian fiction, are the works to be studying, teaching, and evaluating. I think this is particularly the case given the significantly large participation by women and minority writers in these genres.

Many contemporary Native American novels, for instance, are plotted as environmental mysteries, such as Louis Owens's *Wolfsong*, while Alaska seems to have spawned its own brand of regionalism in the form of environmental mysteries, such as *The Curious Eat Themselves* by John Straley. Karen Tei Yamashita takes on the North American Free Trade Agreement in the postmodern, multiply narrated *Tropic of Orange*, and Ana Castillo promotes local cooperatives and critiques the pollution of border industries in *So Far from God*. Genre fiction has taken on pressing issues of the day, from Michael Crichton's cautionary tale about nanotechnology, *Prey*, to Neal Stephenson's exposure of illegal dumping in Boston Harbor, *Zodiac*, to Clive Cussler's condemnation of the international trade in nuclear waste in *Sahara* to Barbara Neely's commentary on lead poisoning in African American communities in *Blanche Cleans Up* to John D. MacDonald's exposé of runaway development in Florida in *A Flash of Green*. And Nevada Barr has created, it would seem, a special subgenre of the travel narrative: the environmental–national parks mystery, as represented by *Blood Lure* and other novels in her Park Ranger Anna Pigeon series.

Despite the foregoing, however, organizing the study of environmental literature along the lines of foundational genres—fiction, poetry, and nonfiction prose—constitutes only one way, and probably the less common way, to approach the teaching of such literature. Although numerous genre courses include environmental literature or entirely emphasize environmental literature, such as the course I was teaching when writing this essay—Contemporary American Women's Fiction—many other courses are centered on topics or themes. And special-topics courses enable environmental literature to be considered from every conceivable angle. Let me here just outline a few of those angles.

Since numerous anthologies that include diverse genres are now available, one can teach environmental literature region by region, and occasionally even state by state. Many of these regions, such as the Southwest, Northwest, north woods, and Alaska, contain a significant body of writing by Native American and other groups frequently taught almost exclusively in ethnic-literature courses. These works need to become part of a new regionalism that does not focus exclusively on, or is not organized around, white settlement. Another approach that conforms to the curricular structure of departments of literature is to base courses on historical period. Of course, the periods of environmental literature may not square with the periods of literature recognized by a given department. Also, certain periods may be flush with one or another genre of environmental literature, but the diversity of works available ought to be kept in mind.

Numerous courses already in the catalogs may be taught as environmental literature, from courses on major American authors to those on ethnic literature to women's contemporary fiction to regional literature to modern American poetry, and on and on. Almost invariably professors use other criteria beyond coverage or representation to select their texts, and there is no reason that relationships between human beings and nature should claim any less validity than race, class, gender, identity, sexuality, war, or any other such topic. Although some ecocritics will no doubt find the concept abhorrent, even a course on postmodernism can be built entirely around works of environmental and environmental justice literature.

It should be pointed out also that using ecocriticism as a method for teaching a variety of North American literature courses will arouse student interest and may lead to pressure being placed on those who teach courses in literary analysis, cultural studies, and literary theory in the department to include ecocritical theory as an element of those courses. In like manner, courses that include American and Canadian literary works in transatlantic, transpacific, and hemispheric comparative literature study can also be built on an ecocritical foundation, regardless of genre. Finally, opportunities exist to teach courses that go beyond literary study but include literature. For instance, for several years I taught an interdisciplinary honors seminar titled Ecology, Gender, Culture: Other and Another and assigned a variety of American and Canadian fiction and nonfiction alongside nonliterary works.

The only area where little seems to be happening with ecocritical study and environmental literature is the genre of drama. Why? I do not believe this results primarily from neglect but more from an absence of highly suitable material for literary analysis. That is, drama has a strong potential for environmental and ecocritical analysis but not of the type generally applied to texts. The proscenium arch and the almost total verbal commitment to dialogue do not lend themselves to descriptions of nature or narratives about engagement with nature. Making a particular ecosystem, natural locale, or even an animal, plant, or tree a major character on a Broadway stage does indeed prove a daunting task. So, although I would be happy to be proved wrong here, it does not seem that the traditional stage lends itself to a flourishing of ecodrama.

Rather, street theater, installation art, and performance art seem to be the dramatic modes most often used to represent environmental themes. Since these usually presume the audience's participation in the action in a specific location, habitat, or environment, they cannot be adequately captured either on film or in script form for classroom study. Instructors who want to integrate such theatrical works into their literature courses need to resort to the field trip, just as they do with the integration of literature and field experience in environmental-studies classes. Rather than try to make such performances fit the typical literature classroom through some form of procrustean butchery, it seems much better to encourage theater and film departments to take up the labor of their presentation, production, and study. English departments are often accused of disciplinary imperialism, so let us refrain here from cause for such an accusation.

Grains of sand on the beach, stars in the sky, trees in the forest, fire ants in my yard—all serve as metonymic references to the subjects of environmental literature and as metaphoric allusions to the range of literary works, across genres and topics, that we can teach, with a little imagination, a little cunning, and the use of vague catalog descriptions. No doubt this survey has slighted or neglected a favorite subgenre, author, text, or course concept, but it is meant to be in no way definitive or limiting but rather suggestive and expanding. We are doing a great deal of teaching of environmental literature, and we can, and must, do even more. I hope this survey helps with that task.

David Mazel

Ecocriticism as Praxis

Ever since ecocriticism emerged in the late 1980s, leading ecocritics have tended to describe what they do in explicitly environmental-political terms. Henry Harrington and John Tallmadge, in a typical formulation, describe ecocriticism as "a mode of critique" whose "political roots in recent environmentalism are manifest" (ix). In the "Editor's Note" to a recent issue of ecocriticism's premiere journal, Scott Slovic sounds a similar note:

> Ecocritics and environmental writers, even those who delight in rarefied theory and idiosyncratic aesthetics, are normally engaged in an activist enterprise. At times the activism is rather oblique or subtle, but with a little inspection you can always discern the political implications of this branch of scholarship and literature. (v)

Lawrence Buell, in his influential *The Environmental Imagination*, defined ecocriticism as the "study of the relationship between literature and environment conducted in a spirit of commitment to environmentalist praxis" (430n20). And Michael Cohen declares flatly that ecocriticism "has an agenda" because it "was born out of the perceived disjunction between business as usual in the university and the environmental crisis" ("Blues" 10, 27).[1]

We are to believe, then, that ecocriticism is a kind of environmentalist politics. How, exactly, does it function as such? Cohen argues that ultimately the "role of the ecocritic . . . is to facilitate clearer thinking about human transactions with environments, and to facilitate better nature writing in the future"—and by "better nature writing" he means writing that moves beyond "personal narratives about nature produced from privileged positions of gender, class, and ethnicity" ("Blues" 29–30). Cheryll Glotfelty stresses the field's potential for inspiring curricular reform and student activism:

> An ecologically focused criticism is a worthy enterprise primarily because it directs our attention to matters about which we need to be thinking. Consciousness raising is its most important task. . . . A strong voice in the profession will enable ecocritics to be influential in mandating important changes in the canon, the curriculum, and university policy. We will see books like Aldo Leopold's *A Sand County Almanac* and Edward Abbey's *Desert Solitaire* become standard texts for courses in American literature. Students taking literature and composition courses will be encouraged to think seriously about the relationship of humans to nature, about the ethical and aesthetic dilemmas posed by the environmental crisis, and about how language and literature transmit values with profound ecological implications. (xxiv–xxv)

Slovic goes a bit further, suggesting that after students encounter environmental literature and attain greater awareness of the beauty and fragility of their natural environment, "their actions will follow suit, and the earth will be a little bit more secure" (*Seeking* 171).

Taken together, such statements suggest what might be termed a standard model of ecocritical praxis, a still largely implicit model in which a sophisticated and persuasive ecocriticism (a "strong voice in the profession") works as part of a larger program of environmental education to perform three key functions. First, in accordance with the manners and customs of the profession of English, it demonstrates the literary or cultural value of environmental texts and thereby legitimates their inclusion in freshman readers and upper-division course syllabi. These newly canonized texts then inform and inspire the students, who in turn, it is hoped, roll up their sleeves and join in the ground-level work of saving the planet. Second, by highlighting the ways in which environmental texts are structured by categories of race, class, gender, and sexuality, ecocriticism helps ensure that the planet is not saved at the expense of those whose voices have traditionally been excluded from the discourses of environmentalism.[2] Third, by thinking rigorously about the role of language in shaping our understanding of nature, ecocriticism clarifies what nature and environmentalism have meant in the past and what they might mean in the future, reminding student activists-to-be that as environmentalists they "are part of a discourse that itself has a history" (Cohen, "Blues" 21).

In this way ecocritical theory motivates and informs environmental activism and makes good on its "commitment to environmentalist praxis." In doing so, it necessarily finds itself implicated in many of the literary-theoretical debates of the past few decades—most notably, debates over feminism, multiculturalism, canon formation, and social constructionism.[3] The debate over social construction has proved particularly contentious, no doubt because ecocriticism desires to ally itself with an environmentalism that derives much of its moral urgency, political program, and cultural authority from the physical and biological sciences. Ecocriticism needs theory to gain academic legitimacy, but that same theory challenges key concepts—such as wilderness and nature—that lie at the heart of environmentalism and ecology. This conflict haunted ecocriticism from the beginning and simmered quietly until 1995, when William Cronon brought it to a boil with his essay "The Trouble with Wilderness; or, Getting Back to the Wrong Kind of Nature." It was this essay more than any other that highlighted the necessary, but inherently problematic, intersections between ecocriticism, environmentalism, and science—and dragged a number of practicing ecocritics into the so-called science wars.

Though the worst of the science-war hostilities appear to be behind us, the key issues that engendered them remain unresolved—as firmly rooted as ever in the murky borderland where the "human" merges with a "nature" that is at once the matrix out of which the human emerges and the other against which the human perpetually defines and redefines itself. Out of this conceptual mire emerge the kinds of questions that, in the discourses of environmentalism, pit the ecocentrist against the anthropocentrist. Are we part of nature, or above it? Are we to save nature for its own sake, or for ours? Does nature have intrinsic value and meaning, or only the value and meaning we assign it? Can we turn to nature to free ourselves from the "prison house of language," as Fredric Jameson terms it, or is our experience of nature inevitably shaped by discourse? In the physical and biological sciences, an analogous set of questions concerns the objectivity of the scientific method and locks scientists into battle with literary and cultural theorists. Can science transcend its social embeddedness and see nature as it "really is"? Do its claims move progressively closer to absolute and transcendent truths, or are they inevitably historically contingent and culturally relative?[4]

Much as some academics would like it to, ecocriticism cannot simply pick a side in these debates. For ecocriticism to do so would be either to jeopardize its alliances with environmentalism and the sciences or to alienate itself from a profession still largely committed to a social-constructionist theory suspicious of "nature." One way out of this dilemma might be simply to fold the human back into nature—not in the inflammatory "deconstructing nature" mode of the humanities but in the (no doubt equally inflammatory) mode of evolutionary psychology. Prompted in part by the growth of the cognitive sciences and in part by dissatisfaction with contemporary literary theory, a small group of literary critics has been developing an "evolutionary" or "adaptationist" literary criticism, which proposes to ground literary analysis in a biological understanding of human nature and thereby make ecocriticism consilient with the natural sciences. (At least one of these adaptationist critics, Glen Love, is also an ecocritic.) In the debate over this approach, one key question is the degree to which writers, readers, and critics—as products of evolution—are themselves shaped by the nature about which they write. Does evolution guarantee some form of bedrock "human nature," or is the only essence of being human the way we have transcended nature? Are cultural behaviors such as writing and reading literature explained in any significant way by reference to the brain's evolved physiological structures? Currently, at the beginning of what some claim to be a "cognitive revolution" that will revolutionize the human sciences and the humanities, these questions sharply set off the adaptationist critics against those—still the great majority—who remain committed to the primacy of discourse. Should this evolutionary program succeed, it could align literary studies seamlessly with biology and put an end to the science wars once and for all. Working against such an outcome are the deeply entrenched textualist biases of the humanities and, more important, the highly provisional nature of so many of evolutionary psychology's claims.[5] The current cease-fire may hold for a time, but it seems unlikely that ecocriticism will be mustered out of the science wars any time soon.

Fortunately, these difficulties need not be resolved for ecocriticism to perform its three main pedagogical functions. Just how well ecocriticism *has* performed them remains an open question. At this point, ecocriticism seems not to have had much of an impact on upper-division literature survey courses.[6] But if the growing number of environmentally themed freshman readers is any indication, it *is* making itself felt in the composition classroom—and the introductions to these readers suggest that what I earlier termed the standard model of ecocritical praxis is firing on all three cylinders. Typical is this excerpt from Peter Valenti's preface to his *Reading the Landscape, Writing the World*:

> The authors included . . . represent the widest diversity of gender and ethnic identities of any text focusing on the relations between people and their physical environment. Not only does it present traditional nature writers such as Rachel Carson, John Muir, Henry David Thoreau, Mary Austin, Aldo Leopold, Annie Dillard, and Barry Lopez, but it also includes such new voices as Clarissa Pinkola Estes, Terry Tempest Williams, David Quammen, Gretel Ehrlich, and Gary Nabhan. Other authors such as W. E. B. DuBois, Richard Wright, Mary Wilkins Freeman, Alice Walker, and Leslie Marmon Silko are not traditionally considered "nature writers," but they have produced some effective writing about the relationship between our human and our natural environments. And finally, writers such as Gloria Anzaldua, William Least Heat Moon, Luci Tapahonso, Marie DeSantis, Dayton Duncan, and Kathleen Stocking show how particular regions and cultures affect the way we see and write about our worlds. (v–vi)

In addition to accurately summarizing the core nature-writing canon of ecocriticism's formative years (Carson, Muir, Thoreau, Austin, Leopold, Dillard, Lopez) Valenti illustrates the two means by which that canon has been expanded: first, by the admitting of "new voices" from the genre of nature writing as it has been traditionally conceived and, second, by the expanding of the conception of environmental literature itself, so that authors already canonical in other contexts can now be viewed as green writers capable of contributing to a more inclusive environmentalism. This second step does not occur in a vacuum but with the aid of a social-constructionist ecocritical theory that, in this case, insists on attending to the way "particular regions and cultures affect the way we see and write about our worlds."

Ecocriticism's influence is even more clearly discernible in the preface to another freshman reader, *Constructing Nature: Readings from the American Experience*. The editors, Richard Jenseth and Edward E. Lotto, note that their diverse selection of texts was designed to help students "understand our complex and changing relations to nature" (v) and "place the various conceptions of nature historically" (vii). The editors do not argue that their readings will produce environmentalists per se—only that they can help students think more critically and perhaps become environmentalists who are better informed and more reflective:

> As individuals and as members of a culture, a social group, or a genera-
> tion, we experience and understand nature differently, and these differ-
> ences have implications for what we do and what we value. No matter
> what the particular issue—protecting spotted owls or banning the use
> of pesticides—we are always debating the broader, more fundamental
> beliefs about what (or who) nature is and how we relate to it.
>
> Such an approach to nature—seeing it as a socially constructed and
> politically contested idea, as well as a physical phenomenon—allows
> us to accomplish some important intellectual work. First of all, it allows
> us to think critically about some of the most important issues of our
> time. . . .With issues this important, it is easy to think in black-and-
> white terms. . . . The critical thinking fostered by considering different
> conceptions of nature allows us to move beyond the name calling. (v)

The aim here is comparatively modest. Jenseth and Lotto identify and
focus on just one problematic aspect of environmentalism that their ecocritically informed editorial efforts might help clarify. Forthrightly relating
theory to practice, they apply a sophisticated understanding of nature to a
set of street-level environmental problems, even as they sidestep the science
wars with the declaration that nature is at once "a socially constructed and
politically contested idea" and "a physical phenomenon." The result is a
freshman reader that uses the insights of ecocriticism to align the interests
of the academy (in teaching writing and critical-thinking skills) with those
of environmentalism—an example of the "standard model" in action.

Does that model ultimately work? Do students who read and write
about green texts turn into more thoughtful and effective environmentalists than they might have been otherwise? I have yet to see any empirical
research (or even anecdotal evidence) indicating that they do. Perhaps that
is why ecocriticism has thus far tended to measure its success in terms of its
acceptance by the academy and not of demonstrable political impact. Now
that ecocriticism has been accepted—now that it has indubitably arrived as
a form of literary studies—perhaps it is time for it to remember its commitment to environmentalist praxis and employ a more appropriate metric.

Notes

1. Not all ecocritics share these views. Among those skeptical of ecocritical
claims of political efficacy is Dana Phillips, who has accused Buell's ecocriticism of
laboring to "make its stance seem more militant than, in truth, it is" and claimed
more generally that "ecocriticism simply does not have the aura of radical chic its
promoters would like it to have" (160).

2. For an elaboration on this point, see, for example, Adamson, Evans, and Stein (*Reader*).

3. Even a casual perusal of the contents of ecocriticism's premier journal, *ISLE*, will reveal that ecocritics are working from a range of literary-theoretical approaches that might have surprised the field's pioneers back in the 1970s. For example, Sandilands employs queer theory to problematize our understanding of the work of a familiar green author, Sarah Orne Jewett ("Importance"). Jewett lived for a quarter of a century in a Boston marriage with Annie Fields, and Sandilands argues that Jewett's lesbianism led her "to resist the stifling Victorian gender and sexual conventions" closely bound up with the "deeply cherished (and conservative) nature ideals drawn from an older rural universe." Because her sexuality thus complicates the nature nostalgia underpinning so much of the emotional force of her work, we must "read Jewett *queerly* in order to understand her ecology" (60). Another example is Barbara Neely, the author of several detective novels and an activist interested in urban environmental issues. Her novels feature the character Blanche White, an African American housekeeper who repeatedly finds herself involuntarily cast in the role of amateur detective. *Blanche Cleans Up* explores issues of environmental racism while also contrasting life in wealthy areas of Boston with that in the impoverished and largely African American neighborhood of Roxbury. See Rachel Stein, "Activism."

4. To sample a variety of positions in these sometimes highly polemical debates over the ontological status of nature and the objectivity of science, see Haraway, *Primate Visions*; Cronon, *Uncommon Ground* (which includes Cronon's essay "The Trouble with Wilderness"); Ross, *Strange Weather* and *Chicago Gangster Theory*; Lewontin; Soule and Lease; and Gross and Levitt. For a recent exchange of views on the relations between science and ecocriticism specifically, see Love, "Science"; Levin, "Between Science"; and Clarke. For an argument from a respected scientist that the science wars were premised on a false dichotomy and generated more heat than light, see Stephen J. Gould, "Deconstructing."

5. The first prominent biologist to link an evolutionary understanding of human nature to environmentalism was Edward O. Wilson, who hypothesized that all humans share a trait he termed *biophilia*, "the innately emotional affiliation of human beings to other living organisms" (Kellert and Wilson 31; see also Kellert, *Kinship*). The most thoughtful advocate, theorist, and practitioner of an evolution-based literary criticism has been Carroll (see *Evolution*; "Organism"; and *Literary*). For an application of evolutionary literary theory specifically to ecocriticism, see Love, *Practical Ecocriticism*.

6. Despite their impressive degree of inclusiveness, neither the *Heath Anthology of American Literature*, fifth edition, nor the *Norton Anthology of American Literature*, sixth edition, contains any work by such ecocritical favorites as William Bartram, Susan Fenimore Cooper, John Muir, William Burroughs, Aldo Leopold, Rachel Carson, Annie Dillard, or Barry Lopez.

Ursula K. Heise

Teaching Ecocritical Theory

Between Darwinism and Poststructuralism

In the short time since its emergence—the Association for the Study of
Literature and the Environment (ASLE) was founded in 1993—ecocriticism
has turned into an astonishingly diverse theoretical field. This diversity
is the result partly of the intellectual and institutional context in which
ecocriticism crystallized and partly of its affiliation with the broad range
of political projects that are usually summarized under the label environmentalism. This spectrum of theoretical and political orientations makes
ecocriticism an exciting but also a challenging field to teach, an area that
raises quite different problems at the undergraduate than at the graduate
level of teaching. Put somewhat simplistically, undergraduates who are first
confronted with ecocritical theory usually need to be taught how specific
social, cultural, and historical contexts shape an understanding of nature
and of the threats it is subject to. Initially, they tend not to understand
that natural processes as well as phenomena such as resource scarcity or
environmental pollution are "real" not so much in the sense of objective,
incontestable facts as in the sense of facts perceived from within a specific
cultural framework. One goal of teaching ecocritical theory, therefore,

must be to give students an at least rudimentary understanding of what is usually (and perhaps somewhat unfortunately) called social constructivism in the humanities and social sciences. Graduate students in the humanities tend already to have some grasp of this theoretical perspective. In some cases, in fact, their undergraduate education has emphasized culturalist approaches so much that the graduate ecocritical instructor needs to counteract the tendency to relativize any claims about nature and biology in terms of their real or alleged ideological functions with a dose of sociological and scientific empiricism—with an emphasis on the fact that not all claims about nature are equally valid and on how one might go about judging their comparative adequacy. Teaching ecocritical theory to undergraduates and graduates, therefore, involves different challenges for the instructor.

These challenges are not, of course, unique to ecocriticism. Feminism, postcolonialism, and critical race theory have similarly struggled with the question of how to reconcile the aspiration to present better—that is, more factually accurate and logically consistent—histories and sociological accounts with the awareness that notions such as factuality and consistency are themselves culturally framed (Butler 28; Haraway, *Simians* 187; Harding 576; cf. Mazel, *American Literary Environmentalism* xiv–xv).[1] Yet the intellectual and institutional context in which ecocriticism faces this question differs from that of other theoretical projects. While most of the important social movements of the 1960s had made an impact on literary and cultural studies during the 1970s and 1980s, which led to several decades of political and academic coevolution, ecocriticism only emerged long after environmentalism had reshaped the political arena and given rise to other research fields in the humanities such as environmental history and philosophy. This delay is no doubt in large part a result of the skeptical stance that different strands of poststructuralism had taken toward claims about nature and biology between the 1960s and the 1990s; only when poststructuralism and new historicism had morphed into the theoretically far more diffuse project of cultural studies did the intellectual space open up to translate the political urgency of environmental concerns into the terms of literary and cultural analysis. With no single theoretical paradigm dominating literary studies any longer, ecocriticism confronted and gradually absorbed the full range of theoretical options from cognitive science and linguistics to Marxism and deconstruction.

A renewed interest in the biological and neurological foundations of the human mind and human culture during the 1990s, fueled by rapid innovation in genetic science and biotechnology, also helped make room for the ecocritical agenda. At the same time, however, the virulence of the so-called science wars, controversies over the nature and scope of scientific epistemology, peaked with Paul Gross and Norman Levitt's attack on humanistic and social-scientific critiques of science, the mathematician Alan Sokal's faux-poststructuralist reading of quantum theory in the pages of the journal *Social Text*, and the ripostes to both.[2] Environmental literary criticism took shape in this theoretical crucible of attacks and defenses of poststructuralist thought and scientific knowledge and had to negotiate its own mixed allegiances to scientific epistemology, literary analysis, and political engagement in this tumultuous context.

Yet the challenges for ecocriticism were not limited to fierce academic disagreements. By the early 1990s, what environmentally oriented "political engagement" meant was also far less unambiguous than it had been at the inception of the modern environmentalist movement in the 1960s. Several waves of political institutionalizations of environmentalism accompanied by countervailing attempts to reradicalize the movement led to the emergence of a wide spectrum of thought that ranges philosophically from deep ecology to social ecology and ecosocialism, and that politically encompasses projects that Timothy Luke has grouped under the labels restorational environmentality (e.g., radical groups such as Earth First!), preservational environmentality (e.g., The Nature Conservancy), conservational environmentality (sustainable development and green consumerism), and transformational environmentality (encompassing visions of structural change such as those articulated by Herbert Marcuse or Murray Bookchin [*Ecocritique* 197]).[3] While two recent surveys of ecocriticism, Greg Garrard's *Ecocriticism* and Lawrence Buell's *The Future of Environmental Criticism*, have diagnosed a shift from a deep-ecological to a more social-ecological emphasis in ecocritics' work over the last decade and a half, all the varieties of thought and praxis just mentioned persist in current environmental literature, art, and criticism.

It may not be possible to unfold the full spectrum of ecocritical philosophy and theory in classes dedicated primarily to the analysis of cultural artifacts. Yet any course with theoretical aspirations must include some consideration of the way in which the relation between nature and culture has been addressed in ecocriticism. Approaches to this relationship range from scholars who, basing themselves on evolutionary theory, see culture as the product of the human adapted mind all the way to poststructurally oriented critics who analyze different understandings of nature as they have arisen from specific historical and cultural contexts: in other words, from those who see nature as the foundation to understanding culture to those who see culture as the ground for understanding nature, with multiple shades of empiricism, essentialism, and constructivism in between. Presenting at least a survey of this spectrum allows graduate students to link ecocritical research meaningfully to other areas of literary and cultural theorization. For undergraduates, grasping this theoretical spectrum may seem like a tall order at first. Yet if the material is properly explained, the central pedagogical challenges tend to arise not from the grasp undergraduates have on such different theoretical approaches so much as from their realization that these perspectives cannot be easily reconciled, their difficulty in deciding which is most persuasive, and their recognition that the class may not offer clear-cut answers to these questions.

In what follows, I outline three central areas of theoretical inquiry that should be covered in both graduate and undergraduate courses: different ways of understanding the concept of nature and its translation into culture, environmentalist appropriations of ecological science and critiques of them, and the controversial role of realism and referentiality in ecocritical analysis.

Ozone Holes: Understanding "Nature"

One of the best avenues for approaching the ways in which environmentalist discourse in general and ecocriticism in particular negotiate the complex intersections of science and culture, realism and constructivism, is no doubt the British philosopher Kate Soper's magisterial book *What Is Nature?* Even undergraduates who at first need some guidance in understanding how Soper articulates her own viewpoint in her carefully nuanced discussion of different theories often end up finding it an indispensable tool in formulating their own perspectives. In a central passage of her argument, Soper analyzes in a rather Wittgensteinian manner the ways in which the concept of nature is habitually used, and she proposes a three-way distinction:

> Employed as a metaphysical concept, . . . "nature" is the concept through which humanity thinks its difference and specificity. It is the concept of the non-human, even if . . . the absoluteness of the humanity-nature demarcation has been disputed. . . . Employed as a

realist concept, "nature" refers to the structures, processes and causal powers that are constantly operative within the physical world, that provide the objects of study of the natural sciences, and condition the possible forms of human intervention in biology or interaction with the environment. It is the nature to whose laws we are always subject, even as we harness them to human purposes, and whose processes we can neither escape nor destroy. . . . Employed as a "lay" or "surface" concept, as it is in much everyday, literary and theoretical discourse, "nature" is used in reference to ordinarily observable features of the world: the "natural" as opposed to the urban or industrial environment ("landscape," "wilderness," "countryside," "rurality"), animals, domestic and wild, the physical body in space and raw materials. This is the nature of immediate experience and aesthetic appreciation; the nature we have destroyed and polluted and are asked to conserve and preserve. (155–56)

Soper explains carefully how environmentalist discourse, which manifests itself most obviously in the third usage, also draws, in sometimes contradictory manner, on the first two: it tends to foreground human beings' connectedness with their natural environment explicitly, but the fact that humans are called on to preserve this environment, whereas no one would think of encouraging beavers to stop building dams or of enjoining elephants to refrain from destroying vegetation, also implicitly marks human beings' exceptional status with regard to the natural world.

With these distinctions in the use of the nature concept in mind, Soper addresses the question of the social constructedness of nature to outline her own position of "critical realism," pointing out that

there is . . . a confusion in supposing that because we can only refer in discourse to an extra-discursive order of reality, discourse itself constructs that reality. What matters politically is not the positing of an independent order of nature, but the adequacy of its representations, and we can only dispute any given representation from a position which acknowledges that independence. ("Nature/'Nature'" 30)

If any claim about nature is culturally constructed, in other words, it becomes difficult to argue that environmentalist claims about it are more accurate or adequate than any others. Soper sums up this position pointedly by arguing that "it is not language that has a hole in its ozone layer" (151).

This qualified realism is cogent enough as a theoretical position and broadly resembles that of other cultural critics such as Terry Eagleton and, to a lesser extent, Katherine Hayles, who have emphasized the logically as well as politically debilitating effects of extreme constructivist arguments.[4] Yet Garrard, in a chapter from his recent book-length introduction to ecocriticism that might well be assigned along with Soper, has pointed out that the example of the ozone hole, so far from highlighting a natural phenomenon that is completely independent of cultural construction, in fact provides an instance of how nature is understood by means of cultural metaphor:

> The "hole in the ozone layer" is actually a good example of the scientific and cultural construction of global environmental problems, since the terms "hole" and "layer" are strictly metaphorical in this context. The latter is an area of increased concentration of ozone, which is actually present throughout the atmosphere. . . . [I]mages of the ozone hole are really simulated graphic maps. (167)

NASA satellite pictures that translate continuous gradations of ozone into a color-coded scale, he argues, convey a misleading impression of a discrete hole (167–68). Therefore, he concludes,

> [e]cocriticism demands attention to literal and irreducibly material problems such as ozone depletion, but it also depends upon the insight that scientific problems are never fully separable from cultural and political ones. The ozone problem is real, but it is mediated by a popularising metaphor, and framed within international political discourses that are not scientific, but ideological. (168)

Garrard does not intend his observation as a general critique of Soper's critical realism, with which he agrees in its fundamental outline. But his analysis provides a vivid example to students of how questions of language creep back in at just the moment when a reality outside language is being affirmed. In courses primarily concerned with theoretical issues, Garrard's discussion of Soper leads easily to the related problem of how environmentalists and ecocritics have interpreted ecological science, a question that I will address in the next section. But the exploration of the conceptual space in between strong realist and strong constructivist perspectives on nature can also serve as a framework for classes that aim above all at the interpretation of cultural practices and artifacts. Soper's distinction between different uses of the nature concept provides an interesting tool kit for students in analyzing how these uses manifest themselves in specific texts. In particular, variations in the way in which the surface concept of nature is structured at different historical periods and in different cultural communities open up a virtually unlimited field of exploration. Focusing just on nature's association with wilderness and its more ambivalent relations to "civilized" and urban spaces, for example, a class in American literature might trace the transition from the representation of nature as the "hideous and desolate wilderness" William Bradford claims the first pilgrims encountered in his *Of Plymouth Plantation: 1620–1647* to Henry David Thoreau's famous dictum that "in Wildness is the preservation of the World" ("Walking" 174). A comparatist course, meanwhile, might focus on the meanings that journeys to the forest and desert wildernesses of North America have for twentieth-century Canadian and United States writers compared with the significance that journeys into the jungle assume in Latin American texts by José Eustasio Rivera, Mário de Andrade, Rómulo Gallegos, Horacio Quiroga, Alejo Carpentier, or, more recently, Gabriel García Márquez, Mario Vargas Llosa, and Isabel Allende. In other words, the theoretical consideration of how concepts of nature are culturally framed can be translated into the more specific problem of how literary forms in different times and places shape ideas of the natural.

Harmonious Wholes: (Mis)Understanding Ecology

The attempt to connect the study of literature and culture to a scientifically informed understanding of the current state of global nature is one of the distinguishing marks of ecocriticism. Yet the relation between ecology (as well as other natural sciences) and environmentalist discourse has been complicated by environmentalists' ambivalent attitude toward science and technology, by their conception of ecology as a science that operates on the basis of assumptions and methods different from "normal" science, and by a perception of ecosystems as naturally self-regenerating that has been abandoned by ecology itself. As some recent critics of environmental history and ecocriticism have pointed out, this misattribution of a certain understanding of ecosystemic functioning to ecology resulted in the superimposition of a pastoral template on science, an imposition that is now being fundamentally reconsidered.

Since its emergence in the 1960s and 1970s, the modern environmental movement has relied on science as the basic foundation for its claims about the state of nature. From Rachel Carson's indictment of pesticide overuse in *Silent Spring* (1962) and Paul Ehrlich's analysis of demographic growth in *The Population Bomb* (1968) all the way to recent alerts about global warming, loss of biodiversity, and the potential hazards of new forms of biotechnology, environmental risks have been pointed out either by scientists themselves or by lay people who availed themselves of scientific insight. Many threats to nature and human health are difficult or impossible to detect without scientific research, and such research legitimates environmentalist claims for politicians and the general public. Yet even as modern environmentalism is unthinkable without this close association with scientific research, it is also true that environmentalists have often seen science and technology as as much a part of ecological problems as of their solution. This ambivalence is visible from Carson's scientific indictment of synthetic pesticides and herbicides that were themselves the products of technoscience to contemporary new-age approaches to human health that rely on scientific insight (or at any rate claim to do so) to question mainstream "Western" medicine (see A. Ross, *Strange Weather* 15–74). In the classroom, a sense of this ambivalence emerges easily through a study of excerpts from *Silent Spring*—an obligatory part of any class on eco-critical thought—in combination with, for example, an analysis of the self-presentation of the cosmetics company Origins on their Web site, which combines invocations of the "invigoration and inspiration, recreation and rejoicing, sanctuary and solace" to be found in nature and "ancient wisdoms" with quotations from the *American Journal of Preventive Medicine* (www.origins.com/about.tmpl).

But trumping science with better science is the least radical form that environmentalist critique has taken. More fundamentally, environmentalists have indicted the kind of empirical science that originated in Europe in the sixteenth and seventeenth centuries for opening up a divide between the subject and the object of knowledge that obscures human beings' connections with nature, for basing its methodology on an instrumental rationality that objectifies and fragments the nonhuman world, and for arrogating to human beings the right to intervene in and manipulate natural processes according to their own wishes. What is at stake in such critiques is something more serious than an indictment of excessive or misguided technoscientific practices: it is the very principles of scientific research that come to be seen as root causes of environmental crisis today, a diagnosis that makes it difficult to see how science could contribute solutions to ecological problems.

This argumentative tension was at least partially alleviated in environmentalist discourse by casting ecology, a discipline that had come into being in the late nineteenth century but only entered public awareness in the 1960s, as an "alternative" science. As opposed to the analytic fragmentation of normal science, it was thought, ecology offered a look at organic wholes and interdependencies that connected the planet as a whole. This idea of a holistic science led to, among other things, the enthusiastic reception of the atmospheric scientist James Lovelock's allegorization of planetary ecology as the superorganism Gaia. In its emphasis on homeostasis and balance, ecology "seemed to be a science that dealt with harmony, a harmony found in nature, offering a model for a more organic, cooperative human community" (Worster 363). While this view may have been partly based on public misunderstanding of a science that even then had diversified into a wide range of specialized subfields, it was also shared by some prominent ecologists of the day, the highly influential Eugene Odum among them (see Worster 362–69). More than a science, ecology seen from this perspective turned into a moral philosophy of sorts whose "goal . . . was to study nature as a model for society" (Worster 368), into a discipline whose holistic assumptions set it apart from the analytic, instrumental, and industrial science of the day.

Part of the reason why this view of ecology imposed itself among environmentalists as well as the public at large was that it was easy to assimilate to preexisting cultural templates. If Lovelock's portrayal of planet Earth as a cybernetic feedback system or superorganism could easily be interpreted as a contemporary version of age-old myths about Mother Nature, an understanding of ecosystems as naturally balanced, harmonious, and stable became just as easily associated with a pastoral vision of nature that has a long tradition in Western thought as a counterweight to the urban, military, political, industrial, and technological spheres. These connections can be effectively conveyed in the classroom through a combination of selective readings from Lovelock's *Gaia: A New Look at Life on Earth* and Odum's "The Emergence of Ecology as a New Integrative Discipline" with selections from the two classic studies of pastoral, Leo Marx's *The Machine in the Garden* and Raymond Williams's *The Country and the City*. It is hard to overstate the potency of this amalgamation of ecology with pastoral for environmentalist discourse, where it functioned not only as a source of inspiration for environmental literature, art, and cultural criticism but also as an underlying political ideal that catalyzed and shaped oppositional energies.

But during the 1990s, this view of nature came increasingly under fire as no longer in accord with the state of ecological science. The biologist Daniel Botkin's *Discordant Harmonies* outlined a view of ecosystems as constantly changing, dynamically adaptive, and often far from anything one would want to call equilibrium. Environmental historians such as Worster, Richard White, and William Cronon began to question the adequacy of an ideally balanced nature as a foundation for environmentalist thought and activism. Cronon's essay "The Trouble with Wilderness; or, Getting Back to the Wrong Nature," which was widely read among ecocritics, exposed the idea of wilderness as ideally balanced and harmonious in the absence of human interference as a construct of the American nineteenth-century cultural imagination. Dana Phillips's *The Truth of Ecology*, the first book-length critique of ecocriticism, accuses Worster of a lingering nostalgia for the old brand of holistic ecology whose demise Worster's own work diagnoses. At the same time, Phillips lambastes ecocritics for their "gross misunderstanding of ecology . . . and a correspondingly gross overestimation of the nearness of ecological thinking to poetic and other modes of essentially comparative thought" (76).[5] But it is Garrard who most eloquently articulates the challenge "of developing constructive relations between the green humanities and the environmental sciences. This is especially problematic in the light of developments in ecology that expose the rhetoric of balance and harmony as, in effect, versions of pastoral" (178). Garrard concludes:

> Postmodern ecology neither returns us to the ancient myth of the Earth Mother, whose loss some ecocritics lament, nor supplies us with evidence that "nature knows best." The irony is that a future Earth-orientated system of values and tropes will have to acknowledge contingency and indeterminacy at a fundamental level, but this only *increases* the scope and extent of our liability as the most powerful species on the planet. The poetics of authenticity assumes, against the evidence of ecology, that there is a fixed external standard we ought to try and meet. The poetics of responsibility recognises that every inflection of Earth is our inflection, every standard our standard, and we should not disguise political decisions about the kind of world we want in either the discredited objectivity of natural order [or] the subjective mystification of spiritual intuition. Ecocriticism is essentially about the demarcation between nature and culture, its construction and reconstruction. (178–79)

While Garrard shows persuasively that ecological science cannot provide ecocriticism with a definitive system of values, his call for new kinds of connections between scientific and literary analysis invites research projects that students can be encouraged to undertake, such as a consideration of scientific issues they may be familiar with in their cultural and aesthetic translations or an analysis of the engagement of specific texts, films, or other cultural artifacts with ecological realities.

Reference, Realism, and Mimesis

Such projects can then lead to class discussion of a third area of theoretical controversy: the role of realism and referentiality in ecocriticism. Phillips's *Truth of Ecology* takes ecocritics to task for naively casting literary texts as windows onto the natural world, without any detailed appreciation of the highly mediated nature of the "realities" one is apt to find in books. "[W]hy environmental literature should be deputized to make the presence and reality of the natural world available to us by proxy, when that world lies waiting to be explored by bookworms and bold adventurers alike, is a question insufficiently mooted . . . in ecocriticism" (7), he argues, and adds: "Ecocritics who want the world to be the text often describe environmental literature as a kind of writing, in the narrow sense of *inscription*, which bears little evidence of the freight associated with traditional genres and forms" (15). Rejecting such tendencies, Phillips urges instead that "ecocriticism should be *more* antirepresentational than other forms of criticism, not *less*" (18). Phillips's vigorous critique of ecocriticism in general and Lawrence Buell's seminal book *The Environmental Imagination* in particular need to be placed in context for students, who are not likely to be aware that one of ecocriticism's initial achievements was a reconsideration of the American nature-writing tradition, which, marginalized in the canon of literary studies beforehand, raises issues of realism and referentiality in different ways from narrative fiction. Indeed, it may make the best sense to assign Phillips in a series of readings, alongside those sections from *The Environmental Imagination* he criticizes and Buell's response to Phillips in his book *The Future of Environmental Criticism* (29–61).

In this book, in a chapter entitled "The World, the Text, and the Ecocritic"—which replicates verbatim the title of the first section of Phillips's book—Buell argues that

> even designedly "realistic" texts cannot avoid being heavily mediated refractions of the palpable world. . . . Yet it is equally clear that the subject of a text's representation of its environmental ground *matters*— matters aesthetically, conceptually, ideologically. Language never rep-

licates extratextual landscapes, but it can be bent toward or away from them. (33)

This rather bland formulation becomes far more interesting when Buell follows it up with no fewer than seven juxtaposed passages that portray trees, ranging all the way from the Koran, Thoreau, and Wordsworth to the Aboriginal poet Oodgeroo Noonuccal and the Japanese American novelist Karen Tei Yamashita. In his brief but penetrating discussion of these passages, Buell points to "a series of discrepant representational axes or continua—particular/general, factical/fictive, literal/figurative" and concludes that "mimetic particularity and referentialism don't tightly correlate" (37). While the divergent excerpts and Buell's general analysis of them may be hard to digest for students (especially undergraduates) in a first reading, this section of Buell's book could become the nucleus for a more detailed exploration of referentiality and mimesis that would include both more extended excerpts from the texts in question and a more in-depth study of different theories of realism, ranging from Erich Auerbach's seminal *Mimesis* and the writings of György Lukács to Roland Barthes's essay on "l'effet de réel."

Broadening the discussion from controversies in ecocriticism itself to theories that have informed literary and cultural studies at large over the last forty years will enable students to see how ecocriticism fits into and diverges from the practices of the discipline, both theoretically and critically. This section of the course could glance at another medium to bolster Buell's point about the disjunction between mimetic particularity and referentiality by concluding with a screening of the French filmmakers Claude Nuridsany and Marie Pérennou's documentary *Microcosmos*. The film provides an in-depth look at insects inhabiting an ordinary meadow in such close-up shots and from such unusual camera angles that they come to appear like aliens from another planet, an effect that is reinforced by the total absence of any spoken comment of the kind that usually accompanies nature documentaries. The concluding scene shows the emergence of a golden object from a watery surface that unfolds with all the slow-paced majesty of a mythological deity's birth, until the creature's high-pitched buzz and takeoff reveal that the spectator has in fact just witnessed the hatching of nothing more (or nothing less) than a mosquito. It is precisely the hyperrealism of the closeups that makes nature appear unreal in this film, pointing up the way in which our normal understanding of realism is tied to a particular scale of perception—as well as, by extension, to a host of other conventions that are conditioned by both our biomorphology and our highly variable cultural contexts.

The underlying principle of instruction in the kind of ecocritical theory I have outlined here—no matter whether the class is aimed primarily at theoretical issues or considers them a framework for the study of creative works and whether its main focus is British, Americanist, comparatist, or another national or regional literature—is to convey to students a sense of the specificity of theoretical problems that arise out of ecocriticism's engagement with the nonhuman world and with scientific research, as well as a grasp of how these problems might be approached in terms of theories and concepts that were developed in other areas of literary and cultural study. Ecocriticism has been successful in using a variety of theoretical paradigms from other areas for its own analytic purposes; but, in recent years, this success has led a number of environmental critics to worry that ecocriticism is increasingly becoming absorbed into the institutional matrix of literary study without yet having defined its own transforming contribution to cultural theory (see Levin, "Beyond" 186; Buell, *Future* 139; Mazel, this volume). Training our students to acquire theoretical fluency both inside and outside ecocriticism forms an important part of our work toward such a lasting contribution.

Notes

1. Harding and Haraway deny that they are relativists with regard to scientific fact, even as their theoretical stances are difficult to understand as anything other than relativism; I have discussed this problem in more detail in "Science, Technology and Postmodernism."

2. The text of Sokal's article as well as the responses to it are reproduced in *Lingua Franca* Editors, *The Sokal Hoax*.

3. David Pepper's *Modern Environmentalism* can be assigned or recommended in whole or in part as an easily accessible survey of the most important forms of contemporary environmentalist thought.

4. In his chapter "Culture and Nature" in *The Idea of Culture*, Eagleton asks, "[W]hy is everything reducible to culture . . . ? And how do we establish this momentous truth? By cultural means, one assumes; but is this not rather like claiming that everything boils down to religion, and that we know this because the law of God tells us so? . . . Is the belief that everything is culturally relative itself relative to a cultural framework? If it is, then there is no need to accept it as gospel truth; if it is not, then it undercuts its own claim" (92). Hayles negotiates the problem of constructivism by arguing that the real world imposes constraints on what sociocultural constructions are possible, in an approach she

labels "constrained constructivism." Eagleton and Hayles, neither of whom are themselves ecocritics, provide useful complementary views to the environmentalist perspective.

5. See Cohen's "Blues in the Green" for an account of the successive critiques that were leveled against ecocriticism in its original formulation.

Catriona Mortimer-Sandilands

"I Still Need the Revolution":
Cultivating Ecofeminist Readers

...I did not want to write poems
about stacking cords of wood, as if the world
is that simple, that quiet is not simple or content
but finally cornered and killed. I still need the revolution
bright as the blaze of the wood stove in the window
when I shut the light and mount the stairs to bed.

— Dionne Brand

Ecofeminist Criticism: Interpretation, Taxonomy, and Publicity

I have an almost phobic dislike of taxonomy. Although I suspect that a portion of that phobia resides in some deep vault of my unconscious, I have, more recently, absorbed from several sources a relatively rational distrust of modes of thinking that proceed mainly through separation, categorization, and static cross-sectional comparison. So when I was asked, some years ago now, what kind of ecofeminist I understood myself to be, my questioner seemed dismayed by the force of my response, which was that I did not actually identify with any of the then-current categories of ecofeminist thought: liberal, cultural, socialist, social. There are certainly significant differences (including, but not limited to, disciplinary ones) among, say, Karen Warren's emphasis on the role of hierarchical dualism in the degradation of women and nature in the Western philosophical canon, Maria Mies and Vandana Shiva's focus on how subsistence labor shapes women's resistant knowledge practices concerning natural resources and environments, and Patrick D. Murphy's Bakhtinian reading of ecofeminism as a movement aimed at recognizing women's dialogical relationships with the multiple others of the more-than-human world (*Literature, Nature*). But as much as I value scholarly debates about the relative conceptual, ethical, and political strengths and weaknesses of these positions, I have tried to engage in such debates without claiming a "brand" or berating other critics for not being of the same brand as I am.

What I am much more interested in is the sort of layered effect that occurs when one considers that all of these authors may be onto something. Call it bricolage, call it pastiche, call it postmodernism (I do not), but in my view the most interesting ecofeminist scholarship brings multiple theoretical perspectives to bear on particular issues of gender and nature, rather than the reverse. Lee Quinby indicated the promise of this kind of position over fifteen years ago in an essay in which she argues specifically against ecofeminist moves toward theoretical coherence and systematicity. Although demonstrably and admirably committed to theoretical rigor in her scholarship, Quinby understands clearly that taking up an ecofeminist perspective is rather like committing oneself to peeling an endless onion: for every layer of complexity revealed in the pulling of a particular theoretical line of question, another one is revealed below it. (To push that simile a bit: each layer of the onion is equally constitutive of the vegetable's particular quality of onionness, and thus no single layer need be afforded analytic primacy, but the more layers, the more flavor.) As indicated by recent collections edited by Greta Gaard and Patrick D. Murphy; Glynnis Carr; Thomas S. Edwards and Elizabeth A. De Wolfe; Virginia Scharff; Rachel Stein; and Melody Hessing, Rebecca Raglon, and Catriona Sandilands—not to mention monographs by, among others, Murphy (*Literature, Nature*); Louise H. Westling, Stein (*Shifting*), Krista Comer, Diana M. A. Relke, Stacy Alaimo (*Undomesticated Ground*), Elizabeth S. D.Engelhardt; and Sylvia Bowerbank—there is no shortage of writers who, inspired by ecofeminist questions, are willing to take on the literary responsibility for peeling away at the layers. (This list does not begin to include the many individual works of ecofeminist-inspired criticism that appear in *ISLE* and other journals and in important related anthologies such as Armbruster and Wallace and Adamson, Evans, and Stein.) Indeed, instead of indicating a move toward ecofeminist theoretical convergence, most of these works suggest a deepened commitment to questions of specificity and intersectionality in analyzing works of literature and the gender-nature relations of which they are part. In particular, I argue that careful attention to questions of place, race, class, sexuality, history, genre, embodiment, and culture has informed and enriched ecofeminist literary criticism through a process of proliferation in which theoretically varied interpretations of (and relationships to) texts build, from the particular, an engaged conversation rather than a theoretical systematicity.[1] In Gaard and Murphy's collection, for example, the result is a lovely constellation of voices that includes an environmental justice-framed analysis of magical (or, rather, "virtual" [Platt]) realism in Ana Castillo's *So Far From God*; a philosophically rich reading of Virginia Woolf, Clarice Lispector, and Hélène Cixous (among others) for their attentiveness to the alterity of the living environment (Donovan); a consideration of Jane Smiley's *A Thousand Acres* for its elucidation of an "ecofeminist standpoint" perspective that includes both land and body (Slicer); and an interpretation of Ursula K. Le Guin's "Buffalo Gals" that is focused on the work's challenge to simplistic theories of gender-nature hierarchy and dualism (Armbruster).[2] Each of these voices is theoretically informed, and there is certainly more than one direct challenge offered up among them, but in each case, the energy of the analysis derives from a desire to examine a text, passage, or relationship in a specific light, creating a combination of text and interrogation as a sort of revelatory offering to a greater ecofeminist critical public. (Or, "look what happens to the onion when I peel *this* layer.")

But how does one teach, indeed think of, this kind of proliferation without melting into a lame pluralism? How does one create (and imagine oneself as a part of) an engaged ecofeminist conversation rather than simply a shopping mall of unrelated critical possibilities? The temptation toward category is palpable: ecofeminism and environmental justice over here, ecofeminism and sexual diversity over here, ecofeminism and animal politics over here, ecofeminism and embodied attention to other beings over here, and so forth. But there is also a different direction. In my reading, ecofeminist literary criticism is, almost by definiton, deeply political, and this historical and ongoing commitment to politics forces polyvocal engagement rather than theoretical orthodoxy (on the one hand) or pluralist smorgasbord (on the other). By this statement, I mean two things. First, I argue that ecofeminist critics are aware that they are not reading and writing in a vacuum and that the texts with which they are working and the analyses they produce both influence and are influenced by the world, ecologically and politically. Politics and literature may not be identical, but neither can they be neatly separated, and there is thus a strong tendency in ecofeminist literary criticism to read literary texts *for* nature and *for* gender in ways that bring to light the specific power relations in which the texts intervene. Ecofeminist criticism is, then, a mode (or, rather, constellation of modes) of political reading: of reading with an awareness of power, gender, and nature built in, of reading to highlight the charged and urgent relationship between word and world, gender and nature, even if the nature of that relationship is only specified in the combination of theoretical perspective and text that forms a given ecofeminist interpretive moment. Second, I argue that ecofeminists have demonstrated (to bend Hannah Arendt's ideas more than a little), a practice of "reading in concert," in which an interpretation of a text should be understood as a creative act of revealing its ecofeminist possibility that is necessarily oriented to a public realm of deliberation and contest.[3] Cheryl Lousley, in an excellent paper delivered at the Northeast Modern Language Association Convention in 2002, has already drawn an articulate connection between Arendtian ideas of political judgment and ecological literary criticism in her argument that developing an ecocritical sensibility involves the cultivation of a practice of fine-grained aesthetic attention and judgment that is actually key to the development of political opinion (I would call it something like "reading the world closely").[4] She and I would agree, I think, that this work is necessarily done collectively, is oriented toward showing one's interpretive opinion in the light of the opinions of others. The desire, here, is not to unearth some essential truth of the text that precedes the interpretive relationship but to reveal a unique quality that is created in the act of interpretation between and among critics and texts. Here, a taxonomic representation actually gets in the way of this relationship; in Arendt's terms, a category may reveal "what" a text (or interpretation) is (ecocentric, anthropocentric, postcolonial, colonial), but only by holding the text up to the scrutiny of others—the "look what happens" orientation of the revelatory ecofeminist offering I mention above—does one see the individuality of an interpretation, the uniqueness of its judgment, the political and literary particularity of the relation between text and critic, and thus the ecological and feminist potential of the specific interpretive moment.

This is not pluralism; this is an interpretive public realm. As Arendt emphasizes, the public realm considers "the world itself, in so far as it is

common to us all and distinguished from our privately owned place in it"
(52). At the same time, however, that world appears to each of us differently; we discover the common world through the appearance of our
interpretations in the company of others—through speech and action "in
concert"—and thus find our interpretive plurality always and only in relation to commonality. My suggestion that ecofeminist criticism is an act of
reading in concert, then, indicates that interpretation is about the cultivation of judgment in the company of others. Beginning, perhaps, with a view
of the common world that would highlight relations between gender and
nature, ecofeminists read and write with a view to creating a common world
in which the particular interpretive creation—the carefully crafted reading
and revelation, the particular peeling of the onion—contributes to a common and plural, rather than systematic and univocal, political project.

Teaching Ecofeminist Reading:
Peeling Onions for the Revolution

If we are to understand ecofeminist literary criticism as a set of practices of
reading and writing that begins with a politicization of gender and nature
relations and proceeds toward a critical practice of reading in concert, then
it seems fair to suggest that the kind of layered, interrogative peeling of
onionlike layers of meaning mentioned above is a reasonable way to proceed toward plurality. Since gendered relations to (and in) nature are to
be illuminated in this kind of critical practice, I contend that the quality of
our reading is at least partly contingent on our ability to find the specificities of genders and natures as they are located in the particular social relations and textual strategies of the works we bring to the collective table.
So there are two elements of pedagogy here: the first lies in the idea of
teaching toward a common world (in which our ideas influence, converse
with, and are influenced by—but are never reducible to—others' ideas),
and the second lies in the idea of layering—of multiplicity, interconnection, and contingency—in students' own reading activities.

I understand teaching as a process of collectively cultivating ecological feminist reading and acting and the fragile public realm of the
ecofeminist classroom as not dissimilar, if also not identical, to the conference, anthology, or public meeting. Thus, as teachers and critics we can
begin this process with almost any text or relation at all. For example,
how does Henry David Thoreau's historically and philosophically specific

practice of masculinity influence the development of his ideas of nature, economy, labor, solitude, and virtue in *Walden*? Under what conditions is Thoreau able to renounce acquisition? Does gossip about his sexuality have an effect on our reading of *Walden*, perhaps on our perception of his preference for the (admittedly sensual) companionship of nature, in the chapter "Solitude"? What about the fact that Thoreau equates the "quiet desperation" of "the mass of men" ([1983] 50) with the then-extant slavery of the United States South? What about his frequent recourse to orientalism in his search for transcendent knowledges of the natural world? How do these racialized readings affect our views of Thoreau's nature philosophy—indeed, of his nature observation? And what about that beautiful passage in which he writes about the partridges that have built their nest in the woods behind his house (273–74)? There is an animation and immediacy to this episode—and, indeed, to several others scattered through the text—that seem to interrupt Thoreau's carefully composed reflections toward the transcendent. How, then, do these different layers of meaning—gender, class, sexuality, race, and species (as well as philosophy, of course)—suggest different dimensions of Thoreau's nature and our critical responses to it?[5] And perhaps most important: How do our different views of the embeddedness of nature in these relations (and vice versa) suggest, in their conversation and interchange, a more ecologically complex Thoreau? A more robust environmental ethic? A more plural and accountable movement?

Perhaps especially for a novice classroom, however, there are also texts and conversations that may be more obviously conducive to an ecofeminist reading. Here, I would point the reader toward Alanna Bondar's essay in this volume for an excellent range of Canadian texts of different ecological and feminist periods, orientations, and genres (and toward the anthologies I have listed above for a more continental range of ecofeminist reading materials). But by way of demonstrating the beginnings of an ecofeminist reading in concert, I would like to offer and juxtapose two texts as especially good onions: texts to peel, savor, and reflect on in layers.

In her 1997 book *Land to Light On*, from which the opening epigraph was taken, the poet Dionne Brand takes us into Ontario's "near north," to winter drives on long highways heading toward Haliburton, to a frozen place where she "can hear wood / breathe and stars crackle on the galvanized / steel" (11). Interwoven with this north of Brand's "out here" (1) are other places: the Caribbean of her memories and family and departure, "slow purple quietness of cocoa pods" (66); the painful Toronto streets, "subways tender as eggshells" (24), their immigrant familiarity and unfamiliarity; and the sites of violent events of global imperialism that appear not only in the "terrifying poetry of newspapers" (13) bought with hot coffee at northern gas stations but also in the everyday lives of her friends and family. And her own life: the second poem of the book recounts a white man jumping out of a truck to scream his sexism and racism, his "exact hatred" at her on a country road, "something about your cunt" (4). If the book begins with a powerful sense of Brand's uncomfortable being in the particular place of this northern landscape—"is not peace / is getting used to harm" (3)—then it ends with an equally uncomfortable understanding of "her own singular life," with an imperative to locate her discomfort in the world, in "the life of a child running with her to a refugee / camp on the Burundi border, caught / in the bulb of a television camera" (99).

As Bondar's essay indicates, Canadian women have written of (and in) complex relationships to the "awesome" natural landscapes of the northern wilderness. In my reading, Brand responds to these relationships, and to the landscape, by insisting on a different kind of awe: looking around her to the snow on the pine trees and up into the black and frigid air, she attempts to locate the words to name and understand the inexplicable racism that has just assaulted her on this winter road and cannot "find a language" (5). The quiet, like the act of stacking cords of wood, does not offer her solace or simplicity; it is not enough to allow her to be in this white place that does not welcome her, that does not recognize her possibility of belonging. To understand, to confront the racist and sexist relations by which this landscape is denied her, she has "to think again what it means that I am here" (9); this thinking traces the complex geography of Brand's discomfort and links urban Toronto with northern wilderness with a gecko climbing a dirt wall in Trinidad with global imperialism and massive human displacement. Against a dominant narrative of Canadian nationality in which immigrants find freedom and belonging in the act of building a home in the wilderness, Brand offers a story in which that very wilderness is part of multiple stories of home, dislocation, violence, disappointment, and loss. The particularity of the place, the pines and snow and the "[q]uiet, quiet, earfuls, brittle, brittle ribs of ice" (8), cannot be separated from the story of her coming to it and is fully inserted into relations of global capital, like "bananas floating in the creamy eyes of business / men" (100).

The responsibility of the poet, for Brand, is to find the language that can allow her to understand and challenge the relations of landscape in which she finds herself: "I still need the revolution" (7). Thus the text invites not only a complex but also a deeply political reading of nature and place (the writing of several poems in the second person—"*your* cunt" [4]—also implicates the reader in the politics). What happens if we look at the North as a landscape of ongoing violence, as a place that is not a refuge from but is, instead, profoundly part of a global web of ongoing violence connected through capital flows and individual stories of coming and going? Looking closely, we find a dense network of particularities, specific body-landscape relations that Brand offers to us in their sensual present: she describes the time of a Caribbean Sunday as "the violent / slowness of flour, the regular ruin of storms, seas, winds" (67); she offers an Ontario summer as "corn dangling bronze, flat / farm land growing flatter, eaten up in highways" (73). Yet the places are linked, and in complex ways; in the midst of overt references to imperialism in lists of nations and snapshots of atrocity, we find repeated mentions of sewing, "mouthsful of needles / and thread bristling and black cake packed for sisters / abroad" (59); of loss, "rooms across this city full / of my weeping"; and even of common rhythms of landscape, "this new / landfall when snows come and go and come again, / this landfall happened at your exact flooding" (69). For Brand, the particularity of place—tropical, urban, northern—is penetrated by the particularity of other places; every chapter of the world (to borrow the title of her final section) shows how particular relations to landscape form a plurality that speaks to and of a common world.

If one can thus speak (categorically) of *Land to Light On* as a sort of postcolonial, diasporic, and anti-imperialist poetic response to certain traditions of nature writing (not only Canadian ones), then the question remains: What does the political peeling of these different layers of meaning reveal about "nature"? How is the reading ecofeminist? To approach these questions I would return, perhaps, to the question of awe. For Brand, of course, dominant myths of an awesome and sublime northern nature are challenged when they are held up to the historical and ongoing fact of their constitutive racist and sexist violences and exclusions. But I think there is another layer. Brand writes "Maybe this wide country just stretches your life to a thinness / just trying to take it in" (43). It is not that Brand would like the chance to take a "Caribbean" gaze to this new place (whatever that might be), as if a "mother" language would, somehow, allow her the full potential for words and belonging denied her by anti-immigrant racism (and white-Anglo nature writing).[6] Rather, invoking a particular history of arrival that is sewn to the other places of her geography, she writes:

> It always takes long to come to what you have to say, you have to
> sweep this stretch of land up around your feet and point to the signs,
> pleat whole histories with pins in your mouth and guess at the fall
> of words. (43)

Having given up on "land to light on" (45, 47, 48), on the idea of a
safe home—impossible given a world that still so desperately needs the
revolution—Brand nonetheless commits to writing the place in which she
has found herself, a land that demands an awe and poetic attention that is
part of, and not beyond, the profanities of the everyday: "I'm trying to put
my tongue on dawns / now" (48), still guessing at the fall of words.

Jan Zita Grover's memoir *North Enough: AIDS and Other Clear-Cuts*
is an excellent text to read with Brand's for several reasons. Most obviously,
Grover's is also a challenge to, and a politicized redeployment of, a nature
writing that focuses on an individual process of coming to, and finding
meaning in, an impenetrable northern landscape of the Canadian Shield.
But the processes, and the meanings, are very different in the two texts. If,
as I have suggested, one ecofeminist pedagogical desire is toward a recognition and cultivation of plurality, then it strikes me as useful to show the
constitutive tensions between particularity of experience and commonality
of world through acts of juxtaposition. In other words, reading Brand
and Grover in concert might show how plurality may be cultivated in the
world of nature, as well as in the world of the classroom.

Grover, like Brand, enters the North from elsewhere:

> I did not move to Minnesota for the north woods. I had only the
> vaguest idea of what the term meant when I first saw them in early
> spring, the birch, aspen, and tamarack skinned of their needles and
> leaves. I thought they looked diseased. (3)

Grover goes on to write that she has moved to Minnesota to try to escape
"the plague that had consumed my life for the past six years," the AIDS
wars of San Francisco. A front-line care worker, Grover has burned out;
she seeks a geographic cure, "to find a place where I might be at peace
. . . where AIDS was still a background noise" (3). Of course, she can find
no such refuge; her problems, her rage, her guilt have moved with her into
the north woods, where she finds herself "still heavy with mourning, thick
with sorrow" (5) as she continues to watch old and new friends die, continues to wrestle with dimensions of loss that are deeply ingrained in her and
that simply cannot be escaped. No wonder everything looks diseased.

Grover does not detail her inner life on its own terms. What we see instead is her unfolding relation to the north woods landscape, interspersed with memories of the men who died as she was caring for them. In one story, Grover is piled into a real-estate dealer's jeep, looking for a rustic property in the woods, "that proverbial northwoods grail, The Cabin on the Lake" (12), and finding instead "the kind of logged-out, burned-over district that makes westward migration seem like a sensible idea. Miles of black oak and jack pine, much of it dead and down. Sand roads lined with scrub" (13). In the memories that follow and haunt her movement further into her Minnesota life, San Francisco looms large, and with it her work with persons with AIDS unnamed and, especially, named: Darryl, who is unable to eat the fried-chicken dinner that he has requested as a memory of his past sensual fullness; James, who has the terraced garden; Tom, with the orchids; Ed, Lou, Bobby, and Eric, who has himself memorialized with his parrot on a brick in the Golden Gate Bridge plaza. Grover describes one Castro memory in landscape terms: "the sidewalk is a slow-moving river, its central channel coursing with tanned, T-shirted men, tricked out in the playful colors that only gay men and conservative New Englanders seem to have the courage to wear" (38).

These dying and dead men, this ravaged community, this landscape of horrific epidemic do not just haunt Grover as she moves into the Minnesota north woods; they help propel a different kind of understanding of her new place in the world. Specifically, and despite her professed quest for a retreat, she begins to understand the north woods as a place that is beautiful not behind, but in the midst of, its wounds from clear-cuts and poverty and all-terrain vehicles. As she writes:

> The north woods did not provide me with a geographic cure. But they did something much finer. Instead of ready-made solutions, they offered me an unanticipated challenge, a spiritual discipline: to appreciate them, I needed to learn how to see their scars, defacement, and artificiality and then beyond those to their strengths—their historicity, the difficult beauty that underlay their deformity. (6)

This discipline of Grover's involves learning about, and coming to care for, the specific details of the landscape. In much the same way as her AIDS work had involved coming to know the peculiarities and personalities of the gay men for whom she cared, Grover learns about the historical idiosyncrasies, follies, and defilements of the north woods in addition to the specific ecology that supports and is affected by them. For example, she outlines the sad histories of logging and agriculture in the region, not-ing the extraordinary hubris and folly involved in attempts to "reclaim" the bogs for agriculture; rather than mourn the loss of the pristine forest landscape, however, she carefully cultivates an attitude of appreciation of what lies before her, beyond the aesthetic wilderness to the intricate details of human interactions with the species and landscapes of the region. In this manner, she comes to be able to find the beauty in, for example, landfills and clear-cuts; far from naïveté or technophilia, this ability is grounded in a commitment to recognizing the simultaneity of death and life in these landscapes, the glut of aspen-loving birds in the clear-cut, the swallows, turkey vultures, and bald eagles near the landfill. Writing against a bland relativism that would fail to distinguish at all among landscapes, however, she insists on a dialectics of loss that recognizes dying and of beginning that is born, unpredictably and fragilely, from death: "The charm lies in finding ways to live with such loss and pull from it what beauties remain" (81).[7]

One of the most beautiful passages in the book involves a particularly disturbing juxtaposition of Minnesota north woods with AIDS-ravaged bodies. On a dawn walk, Grover notes that a small meadow has appeared where last year there was water. "This," writes Grover, "is what I see: a former beaver pond, perfectly round and silted up, wind- and animal-seeded, moving slowly through the ordinations of succession. It is on its way to becoming a forest clearing, then a patch of forest" (22). Rather than mourn the loss of the pond, she greets the emergence of the meadow with a recognition of the in-process character of all that she sees. Then, on the next page, she describes changing the dressing on a sick friend's leg that has been macerated by Kaposi's sarcoma. Unwinding the reeking bandage, she wonders "how much of the world could I wind in something that was dying . . . returning to orderless matter?" Indeed, the leg is already quickly becoming something else: "It did not look like a leg. It looked like freshly turned soil, dark and ruptured." She is forced, in this juxtaposition, to ask of the leg the same question she asked of the meadow: Could she learn to see it "as creation as well as destruction" (23)?

Over the course of the memoir, Grover introduces us to the ironies and beauties of an underappreciated landscape—her sense of humor, com-bined with her skills in research and close observation, makes her an excel-lent guide—and in the process of doing so, which she also understands as part of her own healing, she helps us understand the possibility of an ethical relation to that landscape in the act of caring for it. One must note, here, that this is a carefully chosen caring, an echo of the resistant and nonbiological familial relations in which lesbians shouldered a huge burden of the work of taking care of gay men with AIDS during the 1980s and 1990s. For Grover, care is something we learn to do over time, and it involves making choices to observe and act in the world mindfully: to care for the world as it is, as we have contributed to making it, rather than as we would like it to be ideally. Thus, she writes, "We assume responsibility for a place when we are able to look both backward at the burden of its history and forward at our responsibility for those parts of its future that lie under human control" (164).

Clearly, Grover and Brand share more than the Canadian Shield. Their struggles to dwell in their particular landscapes are undertaken in the context of complex personal and political geographies; their movements into the landscape are shaped by currents of power that exceed their desires and are charged with the sensitivity of the outsider. Grover's north woods are thus colored with an ethics and aesthetics of AIDS and a chosen capacity to care, and Brand's near-northern Ontario is pierced by a racism and sexism that connects the place to multiple points of global violence. Both authors reveal a fragile and open-ended sense of connection to the landscape; both demand the location of landscape in historical and political context; both recognize the tensions involved in developing a relation to a nature that exceeds them temporally, spatially, and historically. But the differences are also instructive. Where Brand cannot find "land to light on," Grover delves into the particularities of place with the intent of staying around. Where Grover values the intimacy that "is the product of time committed to one place" (164), Brand rejects the possibility, in global relations of alienation and dislocation, of ever possessing a language to bring the land "home" no matter how familiar. On the one hand, perhaps, we have an ethical and political commitment to reading a particular landscape for its internal contradictions; on the other, we have a commitment—equally ethical and political—to reading a particular landscape for its location in larger, global contradictions. Both possibilities lead to an ecofeminist politics of interrogating the intertwined relations of gender, power, and nature; both offer nature as a site of keen reflection and significant action.

Of course, there are other stories to be told, other revelations of the particular that could, read in concert, illuminate another layer of relations, another contribution to an ecofeminist plurality (had I the space, for example, I might have offered Margaret Atwood's *Surfacing* into the mix, or perhaps even Aldo Leopold's *A Sand County Almanac*—and even those would be confining myself to the Canadian Shield, which is clearly not the only possibility). Pedagogically, however, the point, I hope, is clear: performed in relation to one another, the individual illumination of works takes on the character of a conversation about the world in which each voice achieves meaning in conversation with others. Following Quinby, if the tradition of ecofeminist literary criticism has taught us anything, it is that the voices of the particular must not be drowned out in a quest for systematicity. Instead, the active cultivation of a practice of ecofeminist reading demands a respect for the existence of the layers of the world, and for the political and ecological necessity of peeling and examining them both one at a time and in concert.

Notes

1. Other than this move toward proliferation, I might make two tentative generalizations about ecofeminist literary criticism. First, I would argue that eco-feminist critics have always gone "beyond nature writing," perhaps out of aware-ness of the historical and ongoing importance of other genres to the articulation of ecological feminist principles (which does not mean that there are no ecofem-inist readings of nature writing, or that ecofeminism doesn't challenge narrow definitions of what nature writing means in the first place: both of these themes are amply present in Edwards and De Wolfe's collection). Second, I would argue that ecofeminists have generally rejected New Critical modes of reading, likely because ecofeminists have insisted on the mutual sustenance of text and world as an ecological relation (if not on the necessary priority of the world) and also on the inextricable connection between literature and politics (which does not mean that ecofeminists have ignored the texts themselves, as works such as Alaimo's and Westling's demonstrate particularly well).

2. This collection also includes two essays on ecofeminist pedagogy (Tassoni, Gaard), both of which provide excellent perspectives on teaching that differ from mine.

3. Although the differences are more than this essay can address, I should point out that Arendt would probably not approve of this use of her work. For her own words on the subject, see *The Human Condition*. Arendt is a complex writer with whom to think ecologically, but she is well worth the effort.

4. I would make the following additional arguments about the specific prom-ise of literary criticism for this project. In the first place, criticism emerges precisely from a conviction that there is something to be learned from the particular (as opposed, say, to most social science, which privileges the aggregate); in the second place, it offers attention to the complex interplay between form and content, be-tween creativity and history, and between word and context, thus privileging not only particularity but contingency.

5. Of course, these layers are often much more theory-driven. For example, we could take Freud with us: What about Thoreau's mother, anyway?

6. Brand has no room for nostalgia, and she does "not long, long, slowly for the past" (68). The section entitled "Dialectics" shows a particularly interesting relation between the present of Brand's past in the Caribbean and the past of Brand's present in northern Ontario: "This pine was waiting, / this road already traveled" (69).

7. In much the same manner as Brand has no place for nostalgia, Grover has no place for sentimentality. On seeing a robin feeding from a puddle of human vomit, she notes, "Both deprived and blessed by no longer needing to mine other creatures' offcasts for our own sustenance, we have gone so far as to lose touch with what such substances as shit and vomit actually are" (116). For Grover, the sentimental separation of nature and human does neither any intrinsic good; the ethical art, for her, is to greet the complex interactions between and among them with intelligence (including ecological intelligence), wonder, and gratitude.

Karla Armbruster

Thinking with Animals: Teaching Animal Studies–Based Literature Courses

Over the years, I have talked with a number of fellow ecocritics about the varied paths in life that brought each of us to this field. For many, the catalyst was a deep connection to a particular place or a passion for the outdoors and wilderness in general. For others like me, though, the affinity for the natural world grew out of a love of animals. In "Why Look at Animals?" John Berger argues that until the nineteenth century, "[a]nimals interceded between man and his origin [in nature] because they were both like and unlike man" (4). It is precisely because of this liminality that they can remind us of our own connections to the natural world, and in this essay I will suggest several ways that teaching literature from an animal studies perspective can provide pathways into important ecocritical and environmental issues.

It is fairly obvious how literature can raise questions about issues directly related to animals, such as endangered species and the ethics of hunting and meat eating, and writers such as Aldo Leopold have used animals effectively to illustrate basic ecological principles (think of the wolf with the fierce green fire dying in her eyes in Leopold's "Thinking like a Mountain," a figure that functions to explain the importance of predators to ecological systems). Attention to representations of animals in literature and other cultural texts (such as the granting to human beings of "dominion" over animals in the book of Genesis) can also lead to critical discussions of anthropocentric, hierarchical thinking and its destructive impact on the natural world. From a pedagogical perspective, animals are an effective hook for students who may feel disconnected or alienated from "nature" in a larger sense. In a rapidly urbanizing and suburbanizing culture where people have to work to maintain a sense of how they are connected to local natural systems, animals are an aspect of nature that still intrudes, fascinates, and commands attention as significant other and not just background for human activities.

However, there is another, less obvious reason to think of animal studies as a way into larger ecocritical and environmental conversations in the classroom: as a great deal of recent theory and criticism in animal studies has demonstrated, animals—both literal and figurative—have much to teach us about the dynamics of power, the nature of otherness, and the construction of subjectivity as well as the ways that many of these dynamics transcend the human. In a profound way, they disrupt the nature-culture dualism that we ecocritics so often decry. In a discussion of Jacques Derrida's thinking on animals, Cary Wolfe expresses the idea that "the animal difference is . . . the most different difference, and therefore the most instructive" (*Animal Rites* 67), which speaks to the tremendous potential of animal studies to contribute to discussions of otherness and of the countless ways that human relations with nature are caught up in all kinds of other relations of difference based on categories such as gender, race, and class.

In this essay, I will explore the potential of animal studies to contribute to the study and teaching of larger environmental and ecocritical concerns, beginning with a discussion of some of the recent theoretical and critical developments in animal studies. Then I will provide an overview of some of the directions animal studies–based literature classes have been taking. I will end with a discussion of a sophomore-level literature class I developed called Humans and Other Animals, exploring how I managed to integrate some of the most interesting theoretical developments in the field in a way that was accessible to undergraduates.

Recent Theory and Criticism in Animal Studies

In his article "Academic Animals," Charles Bergman points out the tendencies among academics in the humanities either to treat animals as "little more than allegories of human fear and desire" or to give up on them as

"radically unknowable beneath human representation" (143). Instead, he
argues that we should take on the admittedly difficult task of representing
animals not in ways that make them contingent by denying them mind,
subjectivity, and agency but rather in ways that "responsibly place them
inside their own lives" (144). In his essay, "The Animal That Therefore
I Am (More to Follow)," Derrida makes a similar point when reflecting on
the dangers in writing about his cat (who disconcerts him by gazing at him
while he is naked): that the temptation is either to declare the cat unknowable or to appropriate the figure of the cat for his own uses. Anyone creating a class on animals and literature who takes this challenge seriously
will benefit from an outpouring of theory and criticism in philosophy and
cultural and literary studies in the past few decades.

Perhaps most surprising to those unfamiliar with animal studies is the
recent body of theory from philosophers and cultural critics that both
explores the ways the figure of the animal has been used to define the
human in Western culture and deconstructs the boundary between those
two categories. In the dualistic Western tradition, *human* has meant "*not* an
animal," and the distinction between these two categories has been based
on a myriad of qualities, including the possession of a soul, rationality,
the capacity for language, the ability to use tools, and self-consciousness.
However, this distinction has proved as unstable as it is important to humanistic notions of "the human," and the recent deconstructions of this dualism are significant not just because they open up possibilities for thinking
about animals differently but also because they provide insight into the ways
the category of "animal" has been used to exclude certain groups of human
beings from full moral consideration. As Wolfe explains in *Animal Rites:
American Culture, the Discourse of Species, and Posthuman Theory*, "[B]ecause
the discourse of speciesism . . . can be used to mark any social other, we need
to understand that the ethical and philosophical urgency of confronting the
institution of speciesism and crafting a posthumanist theory of the subject
has nothing to do with whether you like animals" (7). Ecofeminists have been
particularly vigorous about pointing out that many of the same dynamics
are at work in othering animals and in denying groups of people, such as
women, status as fully human (see Adams; Gaard, *Ecofeminism*).

No theorist has been more important in questioning Western philosophy's constructions of "the animal" and connecting them to the dynamics
of othering in general than Derrida.[1] As Wolfe points out, Derrida himself
claimed that he had long been interested in the question of animality,
considering it "the limit upon which all the great questions are formed

and determined, as well as all the concepts that attempt to delimit what is 'proper to man,' the essence and future of humanity, ethics, politics, law, 'human rights,' 'crimes against humanity,' 'genocide,' etc." (Derrida, "Violence" 63). Derrida's concern with animality is most clearly outlined in two interviews, "Eating Well" and "Violence against Animals," and in a series of lectures he gave at Cerisy-la-Salle in 1997, two of which are currently available in English translations: "The Animal That Therefore I Am (More to Follow)" and "And Say the Animal Responded?"[2]

In "Eating Well," as part of a discussion of Emmanuel Lévinas, Derrida critiques the way notions of human subjectivity rely on "carnophallogocentrism," a logic of domination dependent on carnivorous sacrifice that also evokes the violence that language does to the multiplicity of the living world, by turning "animals" into "the animal," for example (Wolfe, *Animal Rites* 66). In "The Animal That I Am," Derrida offers the "chimerical" word *animot* as an alternative to the violence of *animal*; his coinage includes a sense of the plurality of animals while also emphasizing the word's linguistic nature.

Significantly, Derrida also questions the idea that humans are the only beings who possess the capacity for language. In "Eating Well," he points out the circularity of using language to distinguish humans from animals while defining "language in such a way that it is reserved for what we call man" and states that many of the characteristics he has identified in language— the trace, iterability, *différance*—"*are themselves not only human*" (116). In Derrida's notion of *différance*, every word possesses meaning because of the ways it differs from other words, and it retains a trace of those differences within itself, an absent part of its presence. In addition to suggesting that the two halves of the dualism "human" and "animal" are interdependent in this way, Derrida's ideas reconceive "language itself in terms of the dynamics of *différance* that, because they are fundamentally inhuman in both their technicity and their extention to extrahuman processes of communication, institute the inhuman at the human's very origin" (Wolfe, *Animal Rites* 74). Derrida further explores this notion of communication as an ahuman process in his discussion of Jacques Lacan in "And Say the Animal Responded?" And what are the implications for animals? In "The Animal That Therefore I Am," he proposes not what one might expect—"'giving speech back' to animals"—but suggests the possibility of "acceding to a thinking, however fabulous and chimerical it might be, that thinks the absence of the name and of the word otherwise, as something other than a privation" (416). In other words, he revalues the ordinarily denigrated term in the opposition human/animal (as determined by the capacity for language).

While Derrida does not want to erase all differences between humans and other animals, he does return (in "The Animal That Therefore I Am") to the question of what we share with animals through Jeremy Bentham's famous question, "The question is not, Can they reason nor Can they talk but, Can they suffer?" (396; see Bentham 283n). Calling the ability to suffer "this non-power at the heart of power," Derrida points to the mortality that resides there "as the most radical means of thinking the finitude that we share with animals" (396). And he does not ignore "the reduction of the animal not only to production and overactive reproduction (hormones, genetic crossbreeding, cloning, and so on) of meat for consumption but also of all other sorts of end products, and of all that in the service of a certain being and the so-called human well-being of man" (394), noting the lengths we go to to hide the cruelty and violence of this system from ourselves and comparing it to genocide. "One should neither abuse the figure of genocide nor consider it explained away," he cautions, elaborating that

> it is occurring through the organization and exploitation of an artificial, infernal, virtually interminable survival, in conditions that previous generations would have judged monstrous, outside of every supposed norm of a life proper to animals that are thus exterminated by means of their continued existence or even their overpopulation. As if, for example, instead of throwing people into ovens or gas chambers (let's say Nazi) doctors and geneticists had decided to organize the overproduction and overgeneration of Jews, gypsies and homosexuals by means of artificial insemination, so that, being more numerous and better fed, they could be destined in always increasing numbers for the same hell, that of the imposition of genetic experimentation or extermination by gas or by fire. In the same abattoirs. (394–95)

Characteristically refusing the easy separation between humanity and its animal others, elsewhere he predicts that this violence "will not fail to have profound reverberations (conscious and unconscious) on the image humans have of themselves" ("Violence" 64).

Derrida's work on the problem of animality has occurred in the context of what he calls his performance of "deconstructive gestures . . . on philosophical texts" ("Violence" 63), and in particular Derrida takes on Martin Heidegger's notion that the animal is "poor in world" and Lévinas's assumption that the animal does not have a face (meaning it does not require the same ethical consideration as a human being). Overall, Derrida's work calls attention to the ways animals have been an ignored or repressed element in Western philosophy and, as Derrida puts it, questions "the self-interested misrecognition of what is called the Animal in general, and the way in which these texts interpret the border between Man and the Animal" ("Violence" 63).

Gilles Deleuze and Félix Guattari's work on "becoming-animal" has also been important to recent animal studies. Based on their exploration of Franz Kafka, the notion of becoming animal is another challenge to essentialized, unitary notions of human subjectivity. For Deleuze and Guattari, becoming animal has to do with opening up the territorial confines of human subjectivity to the multiplicity of life, the deterritorialized flux; they associate multiplicity with the animal tendency to run in packs: becoming animal "always involves a pack, a band, a population, a peopling, in short, a multiplicity" (*A Thousand Plateaus* 239). As Wolfe explains in *Animal Rites*, for Deleuze and Guattari, "the animal properly understood is a privileged figure for the problem of difference and subjectivity generally, because it foregrounds how the subject is always already multiple" (162). Becoming animal is a process (often) triggered by the multiple, unorganized, physical pleasures available from animals rather than a metamorphosis of human being into animal, and it is always temporary, because of the constant pressure of (oedipal) territorializing forces. However, Deleuze and Guattari see becoming animal as a positive way to escape the oppressive forces that organize and limit human subjectivity.

Equally exciting is the work of Donna Haraway, whose famous "Cyborg Manifesto" critiques the Western dualisms, including nature and culture, that "have all been systemic to the logic and practices of domination of women, people of colour, nature, workers, animals" ("Cyborg" 177). For Haraway, the figure of the cyborg, as represented in the second half of the twentieth century, disrupts the unity of human subjectivity, leaving the subject open to connections (which can be a vulnerability but also opens possibilities for useful alliances). The cyborg is associated with the idea that all perspectives are partial and situated (in contrast with the domineering, patriarchal, illusory gaze from nowhere): "Cyborg politics is the struggle for language and the struggle against perfect communication, against the one code that translates all meaning perfectly, the central dogma of phallogocentrism" ("Cyborg" 176). More recently, she has discussed the dog, a companion animal, as another figure that disrupts the nature-culture dualism, explaining that her examination of the amazing range of current genetic research and technologies focused on the dog leads to using nature-culture as "one word. Humans invented neither nature nor culture, therefore social constructionism as a strategy of analysis ends up being kind of anemic and nutritionally deficient" ("Birth"). As this statement suggests, much of Haraway's work moves away from anthropocentrism and into a sense of the pervasiveness of what she has described as nonhuman agency.

One of the most thorough and useful treatments of these "posthumanist" theories of animality is Wolfe's *Animal Rites*, in which Wolfe critiques various philosophical considerations of the animal, including those of Luc Ferry and animal-rights theorists such as Peter Singer and Tom Regan.[3] Relying on Derrida and the scientists Humberto Maturana and Francisco Varela, he focuses on the question of animals and language in order to develop a theory of cross-species, "inhuman" communication that can move beyond essentialist definitions of the human (and the animal). He then develops and uses this theory in readings of Jonathan Demme's film *The Silence of the Lambs*, works by Ernest Hemingway, and Michael Crichton's novel *Congo*. Wolfe has also edited a collection, *Zoontologies*, which contains not only a version of his most important theoretical chapter from *Animal Rites* and the English translation of Derrida's "And Say the Animal Responded" but also further explorations of what a posthumanist response to animals in literature, film, art, and social issues might be. Charlie LeDuff's "At a Slaughterhouse, Some Things Never Die" in particular illustrates the idea that the processes of othering at work in discourses and material practices involving animals are linked in important ways to the processes of othering human beings based on categories such as race and gender.

Another groundbreaking use of philosophical inquiry into the question of the animal is Akira Mizuta Lippit's *Electric Animal*, in which Lippit argues that the defining characteristic of modernity is the disappearance of wildlife and its reappearance in "humanity's reflections on itself: in philosophy, psychoanalysis, and technological media such as the telephone, film and radio" (3). In the process, he not only traces the idea that animals cannot be said to fully die (since they do not anticipate and dread death) through the work of various philosophers but also uses this idea to support the argument that animals linger, ghostlike, in the unconscious, literature, and film. He is particularly interested in examining the way literature maintains "a privileged relation to the nonliterary referent or nonlinguistic writing" and in using the figure of the animal to make contact "between literary and nonliterary worlds visible" (23), and he includes readings of works by Lewis Carroll, Kafka, and the Japanese writer Akutagawa Ryunosuke. Steve Baker's work on animals in visual culture, *The Postmodern Animal* and *Picturing the Beast*, also make sophisticated use of recent theory.[4]

One other work that connects directly to the challenge that Bergman and Derrida describe—that of writing about animals in a way that respects their lived realities, their otherness, and that does not simply appropriate them for human use—is *Representing Animals*, a collection edited by Nigel Rothfels. This collection grew out of a conference of the same name held by the Center for Twentieth Century Studies at the University of Wisconsin, Milwaukee, in 2000, and in fact it was this conference that in part inspired Bergman's critique of the humanities' approach to animals; as Richard Kahn describes in his review of *Representing Animals*, this conference embodied the basic tension in animal studies between those who see it as carrying the responsibility of advocacy for nonhuman animals and those who focus purely on the history, semantics, and aesthetics of representing animals. The essays in the collection explore representations of animals that span history, literature, film, art, and cultural practices such as cloning and foxhunting and, taken together, call attention not only to the cultural construction of those representations but also to the effects of those representations on actual animals.

There are several important monographs that extend recent developments in animal studies to literary texts in particular. Marian Scholtmeijer's 1993 *Animal Victims in Modern Fiction: From Sanctity to Sacrifice* explores the ways that Charles Darwin's theory of evolution is reflected in twentieth-century literary representations of animals, focusing on the sacrifice of animals to confirm the boundaries of the human and how this practice has changed over time. An earlier book, Margot Norris's *Beasts of the Modern Imagination: Darwin, Kafka, Nietzsche, Ernst, and Lawrence*, also traces the influence of Darwin on the representation of animals. In *Perceiving Animals: Humans and Beasts in Early Modern English Culture*, Erica Fudge explores the ways in which a variety of discourses, including the law, religion, education, science, and politics, worked to separate the human from the animal during the period 1558–1649; her treatment of Ben Jonson's *Volpone* is particularly relevant to literary scholarship and teaching. *Animal Rights and the Politics of Literary Representation*, by John Simons, takes on the challenge of developing an approach to literary criticism that treats animal rights seriously, and he discusses texts from antiquity to the present in thematic explorations of animal symbols, anthropomorphism, and animal-human metamorphoses.

Clearly situated within ecocritical discourse, Barbara Barney Nelson's *The Wild and the Domestic: Animal Representation, Ecocriticism, and Western American Literature* critiques the privileging of wild over domestic animals in nature and environmental writing of the American West. In *The Animalizing Imagination*, Alan Bleakley also addresses ecocriticism directly, arguing that attention to human-animal relations is crucial for the ecocritical project and for addressing the ecological crisis in general. To demonstrate, he applies an interdisciplinary approach to the role that animals (particularly textual and imagined animals) have played in human thought, religion, and art, including the work of Gustave Flaubert, D. H. Lawrence, and Ted Hughes. Randy Malamud's *Poetic Animals and Animal Souls* takes a stance of advocacy, arguing for the potential of poetry to reform human attitudes toward nonhuman animals; in the process, he provides both an ecocritically based framework for reading literary works about animals and detailed analyses of poetry by a number of twentieth-century American writers, including Marianne Moore and the Mexican poet José Emilio Pacheco.

Collections featuring literary and cultural criticism of animal representations include *Humans and Other Animals* and *Animal Acts: Configuring the Human in Western History*. The first, edited by Arien Mack and based on a special issue of *Social Research* (*In the Company of Animals*), grew out of a 1995 conference sponsored by the New School for Social Research. The second, edited by Jennifer Ham and Matthew Senior, includes discussions of authors ranging from Giovanni Boccaccio to the cartoonist Gary Larsen. Among the special issues of journals focusing on animals in literature are the fall 2002 issue of *Papers in Language and Literature*, *Living with Animals*; a 2005 issue of *Comparative Critical Studies*, *Literary Beasts* (Seago and Armbruster); and two issues of *Mosaic* titled *The Animal*.

Trends in Animal Studies Courses

Because literary and cultural studies tend to address animal studies in an interdisciplinary way, it is worth a brief overview of how animal studies courses are often approached in other disciplines. An invaluable resource in this area is the Web site for the Center for Respect of Life and Environment, an organization that (with the Humane Society) offers several annual awards for courses in animals and society. Descriptions of the award-winning courses, along with a collection of animal studies courses in various disciplines, are available at www.crle.org/prog_courses_main.asp. Another source for syllabi from humanities courses focusing on animals is the H-Animal Syllabus Exchange at www.h-net.org/~animal/syllabus.html.

Philosophy has one of the most well-developed traditions of offering courses that focus on animals. These courses include wide-ranging treatments of the ethics of various controversial human interactions with animals (agriculture, hunting, eating, experimentation, entertainment, captivity, genetic engineering, etc.), specific overviews of the various philosophical positions in the animal-rights movement, and broader treatments of animals in the philosophical tradition that stretches from Aristotle to Derrida. The ethics of human uses of animals are often addressed in biology, animal science, and veterinary medicine courses as well; some agriculture and veterinary schools require students to take a course on the ethical use of animals in research. In addition, a number of interdisciplinary courses have been constructed around the same kinds of controversial uses of animals we find in ethics-based courses, but these courses draw on not only philosophy and ethics but also artistic representations, spiritual traditions, sociology, history, economics, and public policy. A growing number of first-year seminars and composition classes take a similar approach. There are a few interdisciplinary courses on animals in society or animal studies that go beyond the obvious controversies to issues like the human-animal bond, the meanings of wildness and domesticity, and animal sentience and emotions. Anthropology courses in animal studies tend to focus on cross-cultural comparisons of human-animal relationships and on how cultural values, attitudes, and ideas influence human perception of, and behavior toward, animals. Such courses might explore topics like the domestication of animals, the use of animals for food, and the role of animals in religion. The varied and contradictory roles played by animals in contemporary North American society are a common topic for sociology courses, which also draw attention to the connections among speciesism, racism, and sexism. Religious studies courses often explore the symbolic and ritual function of animals or treat animals as part of larger examinations of science, religion, and the environment. Of course, there are environmental studies courses that either include or focus on animals as part of larger landscapes and ecosystems, emphasizing the importance of animals to human health and environmental sustainability.

Within literary studies, graduate courses would seem to be a wonderful opportunity to combine the study of animal representation with sustained discussion of some of the important theory in this area. I have had the opportunity to read the syllabi for two such courses—Cheryll Glotfelty's Representing the Other: Animals in Literature, offered at the University of Nevada, Reno, and Pamela Banting's The Question of the Animal, offered at the University of Calgary. Banting's course, which included Canadian literary texts from the nineteenth through the twenty-first century, explicitly privileged the purpose of expanding ideas of otherness to include animals, while the stated focus of Glotfelty's course was representations of animals in North American literature. Both courses began with discussions of animals in aboriginal–Native American traditions, stories, and poems, and both included examinations of the realistic wild-animal stories of the late-nineteenth and early-twentieth centuries and of the nature-faker controversy that sprang up in response to them (using Ralph Lutts's edited collection *The Wild Animal Story*). These courses included not just recent theory on the question of the animal but stretched beyond literature, traditionally defined, by taking on the work of naturalists and scientists such as Farley Mowat (*Never Cry Wolf*), Charlie Russell (*Grizzly Heart*), Dian Fossey (*Gorillas in the Mist*), and E. O. Wilson (*The Naturalist*). Both explicitly addressed controversial contemporary issues raised by various texts such as hunting, ranching, pet keeping, predation, and endangered species. Especially interesting is the discussion of "edibility" as a factor in human subjectivity in Banting's class, drawing on texts such as Val Plumwood's "Human Vulnerability and the Experience of Being Prey" and James Hatley's "The Uncanny Goodness of Being Edible to Bears."

There are numerous options for undergraduate courses as well. Courses focus on animals in the literature and culture of particular time periods (such as a course on medieval animals at Columbia University); they also consider specific species or other categories of animals (such as Barbara Barney Nelson's course on predators, featured in this volume). Some courses incorporate interdisciplinary perspectives in order to investigate issues of animal representation similar to those explored in the graduate courses (such as a course titled The Nature of the Beast offered at the University of Virginia).

Teresa Mangum's course Literature and Society: Capturing Animals (offered at the University of Iowa), which won the 2005 Animals and Society award for Innovation in the Study of Animals and Society, is noteworthy for incorporating service learning at the Iowa City–Coralville Animal Center. The course included literature such as J. M. Coetzee's *The Lives of*

Animals and *Disgrace*, Rudyard Kipling's *The Jungle Books*, Anna Sewall's *Black Beauty*, and H. G. Wells's *The Island of Doctor Moreau*, as well as appropriate theory and criticism and sociological work on animal shelters and companion animals. Service learning is a wonderful way to keep the situation of living animals as part of classroom conversations about animal representations, increasing the opportunities to explore the ways animals on the page (and screen) both affect and reflect animals in the world.

Humans and Other Animals: A Literature Course Drawing on Animal Studies

Most courses in my department are thematic, so it wasn't hard for me to find an opportunity to offer a literature course with a focus on animals, a course that I named Humans and Other Animals to foreground the boundary between those two categories (a boundary that I designed the course to question). However, I did face several more specific challenges. Our department is small, and each course needs to make a distinct contribution to our students' knowledge of literary texts and issues in the interpretation of literature. I was also concerned that some faculty members and students might perceive the course as less than rigorous because of the focus on animals. I addressed both of these concerns, in part, by including *Moby-Dick*, which is not taught elsewhere in our curriculum. Because it was a sophomore-level course open to majors and nonmajors, I felt I needed to incorporate theory sparingly—and in fact I integrated theoretical and critical texts as they came to seem helpful to class discussions and assignments instead of scheduling them into the syllabus ahead of time. Finally, as a course that fulfilled a general-education requirement for cultural understanding, my course needed to expose students to a variety of cultural perspectives on animals.

In the end, the most difficult thing about designing this course was choosing the texts, since there were so many possibilities, especially because I was not constrained by a particular time period or national boundary. So I selected five themes that I feel are particularly important to the study of animal representation and chose texts accordingly. (The current version of this course can be accessed on my Web site at www .pop.webster.edu/~armbruka/engl2110animals/engl2110animals.htm.) I began with the unit "Myths and Metamorphoses," which focused on stories of human-animal transformations from Native American and

European folk traditions, often as reinterpreted by contemporary writers. Our texts included Gary Snyder's "The Woman Who Married a Bear," Joy Harjo's "The Deer Dancer," Galway Kinnell's "The Bear"; two stories from Angela Carter's *The Bloody Chamber* (rewritings of the Little Red Riding Hood and Beauty and the Beast fairy tales from a feminist, postmodern perspective); and several stories from Ursula K. Le Guin's collection *Buffalo Gals and Other Animal Presences*. All these stories and poems introduced the idea of a culturally constructed boundary between humans and other animals by exposing students to the very different ways this boundary has been viewed in Native American and European cultures at different points in time: the Native belief systems evoked in the poems are much less dualistic than those of contemporary Western culture, and the European folktales rewritten in Carter's and Le Guin's work reveal a worldview in which the boundaries between the human and the bestial (both on a physical level, with the very real specter of the wolf at the door, and on a psychological level, with the idea of uncivilized passions lurking beneath a civilized exterior) appeared much more tenuous than they do to most of us today. With their insistence on maintaining these boundaries, the original folktales emphasize the ways our humanity has been defined in contrast with animals and animality, and the contemporary spin Carter and Le Guin bring to these tales suggests that breaching these boundaries might bring unexpected rewards in a hierarchical, patriarchal society.

Carter's and Le Guin's stories develop a significant subtheme in which women, especially young girls, possess a special vulnerability to "becoming-animal"; in other words, they are particularly able to open themselves up to that which exists outside human subjectivity. This theme allowed us to discuss ecofeminist ideas of how women have been perceived as closer to nature than men—a position that has been used to oppress them but that may also hold potential for empowerment. The overall focus on the categories "human" and "animal" and how their meanings and interpenetrability have varied in different cultures and time periods led to a discussion of how ideas about the relation between humans and other animals have changed over time in Western culture. At this point, I provided a primer on René Descartes and the ways his work solidified the boundary between human and animal by valorizing rationality and language as the characteristics that set human beings apart from—and above—other animals.[5]

In our second unit, "Natural Histories and the Real Animal," we examined texts that claim to teach us something about "real" animals, including John Muir's essay "The Water Ouzel," Jack London's story

"To Build a Fire," James Dickey's poem "The Heaven of Animals," and selections from Sue Hubbell's *A Country Year* and Douglas Adams and Mark Carwardine's *Last Chance to See*. This theme led easily into discussions of the ecocritically important issue of whether language can convey "reality." Without directly addressing structuralist and poststructuralist thought, we explored both the advantages and disadvantages of experiencing textual representations of animal behavior, animal thought processes, and even animal heaven (and by implication what animals most value). We discussed the extent to which language and culture always intercede between us and other animals in textual representations and, given that fact, whether such representations can ever bring us closer to "real" animals, as they often purport to do. Of course, the question of anthropomorphism came up in this context, and we found Randall Lockwood's "Anthropomorphism Is Not a Four-Letter Word" a very useful tool for analyzing different types of anthropomorphism in our texts and evaluating their drawbacks and benefits. The selections in this unit also raise the question of what makes a text "literary" and to what extent "literariness" can either stand in the way or advance the cause of conveying something "real" about animals or a particular animal.

Jack London's well-known story and the introduction and first chapter from *Last Chance to See* resonated most in this unit. Eventually, we brought in London's essay "The Other Animals," in which London argues that some animals possess certain forms of rationality, an important counterpoint to Descartes's ideas and a helpful window in to the "truths" of animal nature conveyed in London's story. Adams and Carwardine's book, based on their expeditions to find, learn about, and see endangered species including the aye-aye (a nocturnal lemur) of Madagascar and the Komodo dragon of Indonesia, is distinguished by a self-deprecating, witty style (Adams is the also the author of the Hitchhiker's Guide to the Galaxy series). The book, however, also raises important issues about what humans want from animals; why we seek out exotic and endangered animals; and how contrived experiences with these animals, such as those we have in tourist situations and zoos, do and do not teach us anything about these animals and their situations. We found John Berger's essay "Why Look at Animals?" particularly relevant to thinking through these issues.

Our third unit, dominated by Herman Melville's *Moby-Dick*, was called "Animals as Symbols." We primed the pump for the novel with some shorter readings, including Denise Levertov's poem, "Come into

Animal Presence," Robert Frost's poems "The Most of It" and "Two Look at Two," Elizabeth Bishop's "The Moose" and "The Fish," a number of poems by Mary Oliver, and Annie Dillard's essay "Living like Weasels." Our primary goal was to explore the implications of using animals as symbols: In what ways is this use different from or similar to other cultural uses of animals? What are the ethical implications of using animals as symbols? (Some of Scholtmeijer's ideas from *Animal Victims in Modern Fiction: From Sanctity to Sacrifice* were particularly helpful in discussing this question.) Can this practice ever bring us closer to animals, or must it always distance us from them? In what ways do literary texts critique their own tendency to objectify animals as representations of something else? How do writers find ways to refuse the temptation to turn animals into symbols, and how does such refusal affect the impact of their texts (we had a particularly good discussion of this issue after reading the Bishop poems). Many of our texts, we found, both use animals as symbols and comment on that use, finding a way to gesture toward the aspects of the animals and their lives that evade textual representation.

While our discussion of *Moby-Dick* was thorough and ranged far beyond the use of animals (and the whale Moby-Dick in particular) as a symbol, our thematic focus meant we paid special attention to certain aspects of the novel: the general impulse to see nature as sign and symbol at the heart of transcendentalism; the contrast between different characters' views of the great white whale (and thus of Melville's theme of the perspectival nature of knowledge); Melville's own commentary on symbolism (such as that found in the chapter "The Whiteness of the Whale"); the contrast between Ishmael's moments of empathy for the whales being hunted and his pragmatic justification for the human use of whale oil and blubber; the ways that Melville's commentary on hierarchies and power can be extended to apply to human attempts to dominate nature (such as Ahab's); the ideas raised about cannibalism and meat eating and what they imply for human relationships with nature; the basic contrast between realism and symbolism in the novel; and environmental readings of *Moby-Dick* such as Lawrence Buell's *Writing for an Endangered World: Literature, Culture, and Environment in the U.S. and Beyond* and Elizabeth Schultz's "Melville's Environmental Vision in *Moby Dick*." In the end, the ways the novel can be read as a critique of Ahab's insistence on turning Moby-Dick into a symbol not only vastly complicated our discussion of using animals as symbols but also proved a productive way into the novel for undergraduates.

The fourth and largest unit in the class took on a relatively amorphous topic and was titled "Human Relations to Animals." In this section we most directly discussed what would be considered environmental or animal-rights issues such as meat eating, hunting, euthanasia, and research on animals. In addressing these controversial issues, my goal was not to indoctrinate students but to present them with a complex range of positions on each topic. We began with a group of poems that express appreciation for some of the ways human beings benefit from other animals: William Cowper's "Epitaph on Hare," the passage beginning with "I think I could turn and live with animals" from Walt Whitman's *Song of Myself*, and Wendell Berry's "The Peace of Wild Things." Then we went on to literature that directly addresses humanity's ethical obligations to other animals: D. H. Lawrence's poem "Snake" and a chapter from Edward Abbey's *Desert Solitaire*, "The Serpents of Paradise," both of which focus on the much-maligned snake to explore and critique the ways human beings often fail in those obligations. David Quammen's essay "The Face of a Spider" and Robinson Jeffers's poem "Hurt Hawks" raise questions about other rationales for killing animals—namely, self-preservation and euthanasia. Joy Williams's "The Inhumanity of the Animal People" challenges readers with her scathing, witty indictment of those who dismiss animal-rights advocates and her defense of those advocates' basic principles. Alice Walker's essay "Am I Blue?" and Richard Nelson's essay "The Gifts" provide an especially helpful pairing in discussing the issue of killing animals for food, including the issues of hunting and vegetarianism.[6] Barry Lopez's essay "Renegotiating the Contracts" directly addresses the idea that people today are turning to animals for something missing in their lives, what that might be, and why people often seem not to find what they are looking for. Lopez's short, illustrated book *Apologia*, on road-killed animals, raises the question of what role ritual could and should play in our relationships with nonhuman animals.

The two works that generated the most discussion in this unit, though, were volumes of poetry: Chase Twitchell's *The Ghost of Eden* and Donald Finkel's *What Manner of Beast*. Twitchell's poems—beautiful, haunting, and often profoundly depressing—regularly take up contemporary relationships with animals as the symptom of a desacralized world, emptied of meaning by humanity's thoughtless, demeaning treatment of nature and animals. Two of Twitchell's poems almost guaranteed to change (at least temporarily) readers' views of the world are "The Devil I Don't Know," an elegy for animals and animal parts as packaged in a supermarket, and "Aisle of Dogs," which directly confronts pointless human cruelty to animals. Significantly, one of the few poems in this collection that offers any sense of hope or redemption, "The Smell of Snow," features a fantasy of the speaker being eaten by a fisher (a relative of the weasel and the mink) and thus reincorporated into the cycles of nature. Finkel's collection includes a number of poems about the famous language experiments with chimpanzees, movingly addressing not only the ways language can be used to control and manipulate others but also its potential to allow us to connect with those others, even others of another species (a potential that the scientists in the poems learn from their chimpanzee subjects). These poems confront their readers with the ways human language separates us from the natural world and the awesome burden of thrusting this separation on another species while addressing issues of experimentation on animals and removing wild animals from their habitats.

Our fifth unit, "Animal Voices," focused on texts that attempt to represent animal consciousness by making animals the narrators of stories or speakers of poems. I originally intended to include some of the Australian poet Les Murray's work from *Translations from the Natural World*: these fascinating poems, written from the points of view of animals, including eagles, pigs, and sea lions, experiment with language in a way that produces an estranging effect and emphasizes the nonhumanity of the speakers. However, because of lack of time, this unit was reduced to just one book, Barbara Gowdy's novel *The White Bone*, which captures the consciousnesses of several of its main characters—all African elephants—in a limited omniscient-third-person point of view. Gowdy's elephants are a fascinating blend of the seemingly realistic (there is a great focus on bodily fluids and various behaviors that are exhibited by real elephants) and the fantastic (the elephants have a complex language and cosmology, and some of them can communicate telepathically) that challenges readers to contemplate both human similarities to and differences from this species of charismatic megafauna. In our class, Gowdy's elephants also raised not only the issue of endangered species (there are several heartbreaking scenes of elephants being killed by poachers or dying of starvation because of drought) but also the important topic of "other minds," which allowed us to discuss Marian Scholtmeijer's claim in *Animal Victims* that "[t]he reality of other minds, other experiences, or simply other eyes watching us places the demand upon culture to comprehend the language of nature" (89).

I indulged myself in the last week of class with a final unit on a single species, the dog. In addition to being a dog lover, I find the dog particularly interesting in thinking about the human relationship with other animals— as the first domesticated species, it wobbles on the fence between nature and culture in a particularly telling way. The unit also gave us an opportunity to see how some of the issues we had discussed earlier in the class played out in an investigation of representations of a single species. We read John Muir's "Stickeen," which emphasizes the dog as a kind of window into all of nature, and ended with poems from Amy Hempel and Jim Shepard's collection *Unleashed: Poems by Writers' Dogs* (which could just have easily fit into the section on animal voices, since the speaker of each poem is the writer's dog). Although some of these poems were—like many literary works on dogs—remarkably heart-wrenching, others were light-hearted and thus gave us an upbeat way to end the semester.

In his 1963 work *Totemism*, the anthropologist Claude Lévi-Strauss wrote (famously, within animal studies) that nonhuman animals "are chosen [as totems] not because they are 'good to eat' but because they are 'good to think'" (89). As I have suggested, this is especially true for those interested in teaching ecocriticism and environmental literature, and I look forward to seeing more and more courses offered in this thriving area as time goes on.

Notes

1. Other thinkers who have engaged in the posthumanist project of questioning essentialist definitions of the human, according to Wolfe, are Julia Kristeva, Gilles Deleuze and Félix Guattari, Jacques Lacan, Slavoj Žižek, Stanley Cavell, Georges Bataille, René Girard, bell hooks, Michael Taussig, Étienne Balibar, Donna Haraway, Katherine Hayles, and Evelyn Fox Keller (*Zoontologies* ix–x).

2. The conference at Cerisy-la-Salle, titled L'Animal Autobiographique, was devoted to Derrida's work; his lectures from the conference were published in French in a volume with the same name.

3. Good sources for those interested in philosophical work relevant to animal studies are the collections *Animal Others: On Ethics, Ontology, and Animal Life* (Steeves) and *Animal Philosophy: Essential Readings in Continental Thought* (Calarco and Atterton).

4. It is worth mentioning that Reaktion Books, the publisher of *The Postmodern Animal*, has made a major commitment to the area of animal studies; for example, their series Animal features titles on individual species (such as the cockroach, the crow, the dog, and the whale), and their significance in human history and cultures. Fudge's *Animal*, an overview of human relations with nonhuman animals, is also published by Reaktion.

5. Although we did not use it, an essay by Le Guin entitled "Cheek by Jowl: Animals in Children's Literature" provides a useful overview and critique of Western thinking about animals and would be especially accessible to lower-level undergraduates.

·   6. H. Lewis Ulman's essay "Seeing, Believing, and Acting: Ethics and Self-Representation" offers an insightful analysis that puts these two works in conversation with each other.

Part II

Mapping North American Environmental Literature

Jorge Marcone and Priscilla Solis Ybarra

Mexican and Chicana/o Environmental Writing: Unearthing and Inhabiting

Both Mexican and Chicana/o literatures offer significant insights and challenges for environmental thought, especially for the ways that ecocriticism has understood environmental writing up until now. Each emerges from a distinct vantage point on either side of the United States–Mexico border, but they remain linked by common bioregions, immigration exchanges, and some shared narrative traditions. At this preliminary moment in the study of environmental themes in Mexican and Chicana/o literatures, any concise summary will fall far short of the abundant potential in both sets of writings. Even so, certain thematic elements emerge to make them both indispensable and easily applicable in any course concerned with environmental literature. This essay showcases the way both these literatures engage a social-justice agenda, the legacy of the Mexican Revolution, and the political ecology of dispossession. And yet each literature exists in, and pushes the limitations of, a particular critical context.

Mexican Environmental Literature: Nature, Political Ecology, and the Literary Imagination

Environmental literature is not an established term in studies of literature in Spanish. Consequently, there is no corpus in Mexican literature already recognized as environmental literature.[1] Plenty of environmental literature of course exists, if we follow Scott Slovic's definition, which he developed when facing the same problem in Tokyo more than a decade ago: "Do you have any traditional writing that deals with seasonal change, fishing, walking, farming, or hunting? Are animals ever mentioned in Japanese literature? Butterflies or stars? . . . You see, all of that is what we mean by environmental literature" ("Love" 17). For the purpose of this introductory essay, however, this definition is too broad. Lawrence Buell's definition of an "environmental text" as one characterized by the implication of human and natural histories, environmental ethics, and the environment as a process rather than as a constant (*Environmental Imagination* 7–8) helps us better narrow the selection of authors and titles concerned with the impact of environmental crises and influenced by environmental perspectives. We, however, tweak this definition in at least two important ways. We include some figures in the Mexican environmental imagination despite their limited affinity with current environmental ethics and visions of the human and the nonhuman. Additionally, we approach Mexican environmental literature as a process marked by three characteristics: its imbrications with nonenvironmental problems, its shaking of certain conceptions about the relation of literary creation and tradition to the world, and its renewal of the recurrent Mexican literary tradition of appropriating or engaging in dialogue with indigenous and pre-Columbian traditions.

The most significant environmental issues that have marked literary and artistic production in Mexico are soil erosion, deforestation, flooding, water pollution, destruction of biodiversity, demographic pressure, and the issues of political ecology in which all the above are involved. By *political ecology* we mean the question of how the access, use, and control of environmental resources are decided by and shared among different social actors. Accordingly, a central force in Mexican environmental literature responds to ideas of modernization and of development understood in particular as large-scale industrialization, urbanization, and centralization—a model that was consolidated in the period from 1940 to 1970. The overwhelming growth of Mexico City is particularly important for understanding the Mexican environmental imagination because it not only became the object of ecological concerns since the 1970s but also was the center of a media that since then has reported on environmental crises and contributed to environmental awareness (the term *ecocide* was coined in those years and in that context). Paradoxically, then, it was Mexico City that triggered several environmentalisms that attracted the attention and involvement of literary authors since the mid-1980s. An exception to this statement would be the region of Chiapas, in southern Mexico, where local awareness responded to the region's environmental degradation and loss of biodiversity and engaged with the idea of sustainable development, a political ecology developed on behalf of indigenous and peasant groups and aimed at the reappropriation of traditional knowledge and identity.

Pre-Columbian Mexican Literature

These texts are in fact not pre-Columbian but postconquest literature. Of the almost five hundred codices, or painted books, known to exist, only fourteen are considered pre-Hispanic. A few of the surviving pre-Hispanic texts were first collected in codices and studied during the sixteenth century by missionaries or by indigenous intellectuals themselves (O'Connell 9). Their cosmology has been invoked recurrently in modern Mexican literature, such as the dual nature of a supreme creator, the four or five successive ages of creation, and the important figure of Quetzalcoatl as both god and culture hero (O'Connell 13). Titles to keep in mind from the Mayas are the Popol Vuh (the text of which was set down by indigenous authors in the 1550s; see Tedlock); the Books of Chilam Balam, a group of seventeen books of which the best known is *The Book of Chilam Balam of Chumayel*; and the *Annals of the Cakchiquels*, also called "Memorial de Sololá." Regarding Nahuatl culture, in his *Literaturas de Mesoamérica*, the scholar Miguel León-Portilla recovers a number of *cuícatl* (song, hymn, poem) with themes such as the joy of spring and of being alive, songs of flowers and friendship, the speculation on death, and the transitory nature of life. Other sources, translated into English, are León-Portilla's *Pre-Columbian Literatures of Mexico*, John Bierhorst's *Cantares Mexicanos: Songs of the Aztecs*, Gordon Brotherston's *Image of the New World: The American Continent Portrayed in Native Texts*, J. H. Cornyn's *The Song of Quetzalcoatl*, and Edward Kissam and Michael Schmidt's *Power and Song: Poems of the Aztec People*.

The Colonial Period

The chronicles of the discovery and conquest of Mexico, or New Spain, written mainly by Spaniards, articulated debates analogous to current debates on modernization and development and in fact still inform these debates (Dowling 31–41). One of the first chronicles is the *Cartas de relación* (1519–26), by Hernán Cortés (1485–1547), which marks a curious beginning. These five letters, addressed to the emperor Charles I, manifest a utilitarian appreciation of nature that contrasts with the sense of wonder in the face of the New World that characterized earlier accounts, such as Christopher Columbus's. When America, a land radically different from what was known to the Europeans, was discovered, Cortés portrays it for the first time as a land similar to Europe and Spain. Challenging visions such as Cortés's, Gonzalo Fernández de Oviedo (1478–1557) devoted his *Historia general y natural de las Indias* ("General and Natural History of the Indies") to American geology, flora, fauna, and depiction of the Amerindian. Although only a part of this multivolume work deals specifically with Mexico, it is peculiar, among many other reasons, for bringing together human and natural history under two different visions: pessimism of history, optimism of nature (Gerbi 358–59).

Other important sources of Amerindian cultures were produced in this period (Dowling 38–39). Bernardino de Sahagún's (1499–1591) *Historia general de las cosas de Nueva España* (*General History of the Things of New Spain*) recorded explications of certain native codices, cultural practices, and religious beliefs and transcribed more or less verbatim what the Native "informants" actually said. Diego Durán (1537–88) emphasized analogies between Indian and European society and religion in his *Historia de las Indias de Nueva España y Islas de Tierra Firme* ("History of the Indians of New Spain and the Islands of Terra Firme"). The *Historia* is a series of three books available in English as *Book of the Gods and Rites and the Ancient Calendar* (the first two books), and *The Aztecs: The History of the Indies of New Spain* (third book).

Mexico City makes its first appearance with Bernardo de Balbuena's (1561?–1627) *Grandeza mexicana*, a poem on the origins and topography of the city, its buildings, arts, and festivities. Although it presents the city as an Arcadian paradise, it does so by erasing the Amerindian (Dowling 47–48). Almost two centuries later, Francisco Javier Clavijero's (1731–87) *Historia Antigua de México* ("Ancient History of Mexico") illustrates a significant moment in history when the pre-Columbian past; the mixing of races, or *mestizaje*; and the land, animals, and inhabitants of Mexico are becoming part of an identity that would soon become a catalyst for the process of political independence from Spain (Dowling 71).

The First Wave of Modernization: Realism and *Modernismo*

The literary movements of realism and naturalism in Mexico were framed by the dictatorship of Porfirio Díaz (1876–1909). Under Díaz, Mexico went through an intense process of modernization, including the industrialization of Mexican agriculture initiated when the doors to foreign investors and colonists were opened (Martín-Flores 113–14). At this time, seventy-five percent of all Mexicans lived in rural farming and ranching areas. The minority was composed of small landowners; the majority was made up of sharecroppers or contract laborers exploited by wealthy landowners who, by the closing years of the Díaz regime, controlled eighty percent of the national territory. José López Portillo y Rojas (1850–1923) describes the conflicts over the possession of land in his *La parcela* ("The Piece of Property"). However, the literature is usually focused on the feudal landowner who administers people's lives and honor. Despite this, criticism, racial prejudices; rejection of the city and praise of the countryside; and the erasing or masking of the specific traces of contemporary economic, political, and social events are common, as in Rafael Delgado's (1853–1914) *Angelina* and *Los parientes ricos* ("The Wealthy Relatives" [Martín-Flores 116–17, 120]).

Modernismo is a name and chronology for a style of writing, mainly poetic, that is generally agreed to have prevailed from the 1880s to the 1920s, which "purified romanticism and absorbed prevailing French influences" (B. Lewis 139). A group of lesser-known *modernista* poets revived a classical environment of greenery, quiet, and balance. The initial desire in *modernismo*, however, was to build an alternate reality through art in response to the dysfunctions that scientific positivism and capitalism fostered in society (B. Lewis 140–41, 144). Agustín Cuenca (1850–84), in poems found in *Las cien mejores poesías mexicanas modernas* (Castro Leal) and in *La lira mexicana* (1967), blended the human and the environmental in the *modernista* ethos: the detachment of the artist from society leads to the poet's yearning for an integration into nature's forgetfulness. In María Enriqueta Camarillo's (1872–1968) *El secreto* ("The Secret") and *Álbum sentimental*, the garden, the wood, the grove, and the path are retreats as much as passageways to a dark knowledge. Laura Méndez de Cuenca (1853–1928), in *Mariposas fugitivas* ("Fugitive Butterflies") and *Simplezas* ("Nonsense"), shares with other modernists a high regard for the landscape, "where the beloved is sought and the first steps toward cosmic transcendence are taken" (Lewis 156). Carlos Pellicer (1899–1977), who was not a *modernista* in a strict sense and who was under the influence of the avant-garde movements, deserves a special mention for his *Material poético* ("Poetic Material") and especially for his early poetry, since while rejecting the materialistic-technological age he resorts to its language for describing nature with sensuality and joy.

The Mexican Revolution and Its Aftermath

The novel of the Mexican Revolution can be reread from the point of view of postrevolutionary political ecology, or the process of land use and control that followed the revolution of 1910. The period was marked by a devastating process of soil erosion and deforestation, and the tension between large-scale and small-scale development of natural resources. The genre started with Mariano Azuela (1873–1952) and *Los de abajo* (*The Underdogs*). The larger frame of postrevolutionary corruption is well represented in the work of Gregorio López y Fuentes (1897–1966). In *Tierra* ("The Land") he helped fashion the image of Emiliano Zapata in postrevolutionary Mexico. *El indio* (*El Indio*) tells a story of dispossession as outsiders force the indigenous community to work as guides in the search for exploitable resources and move to possess the Indians' ancestral land. Agustín Yañez (1904–80) published another classic much later that also revealed renewed tensions with modernization, coming from Mexico City or the United States, in a small town in *Al filo del agua* (*The Edge of the Storm*). Juan Bustillo Oro (1904–89) offers us an unusual contribution from theater with his *San Miguel de las Espinas: Trilogía dramática de un pedazo de tierra mexicana* ("San Miguel of the Thorns: A Dramatic Trilogy about a Parcel of Mexican Land"). Set in the 1920s and 1930s, the drama is about a dam that is supposed to bring relief and prosperity to the peasants of San Miguel, a dry and hot desert ranch in northern Mexico. It brings, instead, violent death and bloodshed (Nigro 220–23). During the postrevolutionary years, the connection between nature, indigenous cultures, and national identity was elaborated by essayists such as Alfonso Reyes (1889–1959). His "Visión de Anáhuac" (1917) uses the valley of Anahuac, or Mexico, as the emblematic essence of a Mexican identity based on the synthesis of the peculiarities of Mexican geography and history (Stabb 319–20). He suggests not that there is a rigid geographic determinism in Mexican identity but that a link exists between the Mexican of today and the pre-Columbian

Indian because both peoples had contended with the same natural environment. In his "Discurso por Virgilio" ("Speech in Honor of Vergil"), Reyes surprisingly argues that the Western tradition, and the classics in particular, is not "foreign" to the American scene but is in fact a tool for revealing what is genuinely autochthonous (Stabb 320).

The genre of the novel of the Mexican Revolution continued even as development became entrenched in the country. Several fictions are set in the 1930s and 1940s, when efforts were made to implement the reforms of the revolution but landowners struggled to block and evade change. Juan Rulfo (1918–86) added to the corruption a serious dose of skepticism in the first decade of modern "development" with *El llano en llamas* ("*The Burning Plain*") and *Pedro Páramo*. The endemic soil erosion and flooding of the postrevolutionary period are well illustrated in both books. In *Los recuerdos del porvenir* ("Memories of the Future"), Elena Garro (1920–98) displays a lyric style for describing the natural world of Ixtepec, a small rural Mexican community, while at the same time tells the familiar story of dispossession. The confluence of political ecology and conflictive ethnicities and views of nature is at the center of the early literary career of Rosario Castellanos (1925–1974). *Balún-Canán* (*The Nine Guardians*) and *Oficio de tinieblas* (*The Book of Lamentations*) are the two novels of her Chiapas cycle. Carlos Fuentes (1928–) arguably closed the cycle of the novel of the Mexican Revolution with *La muerte de Artemio Cruz* (*The Death of Artemio Cruz*), which illustrates the accumulation of large holdings of land by using the laws, bureaucracy, and rhetoric of the revolution's land reform. The dramatic genre also has a presence with the work of Felipe Santander (1935–2001). In his *El extensionista* (*The Government Man*) a newly graduated agronomist is sent by the federal government to teach the *campesinos* of Tenochtlén how they really should be doing their farming. He witnessed and took a stance against the corruption and abuse of the local officials with the blessing of their counterparts in Mexico City (Nigro 223–24).

The Capitalization of Mexico City

Between 1950 and 1990, Mexico City went from two to twenty million inhabitants. Fuentes recorded that process in *La región más transparente* (*Where the Air Is Clear*). The nation stopped being imagined in terms of the rural environment and started to be mediated by Mexico City, which was receiving emigrants from every corner of the territory, including the

vast majority of the authors that will be included in this and the next sections, even as migration to the United States intensified. With a growth of
such magnitude and speed, the ideal of the urban collapsed. No longer the
privileged space of the domination of nature and social exchange, Mexico
City became the saddest possible symbol of the disaster hiding behind the
myth of unlimited growth. The concept of development itself went under
scrutiny (Stabb 328–29). The collapse of the urban also progressively represented the demise of the novel as the genre for representing the new
totality of the city. The shorter and less prestigious genre of the chronicle
would be the one to bring a solution to a city already perceived as frag-
mented, disseminated, and incomprehensible (Muñoz, ch. 1). Along with
ecological concerns, the chronicle focused on new lifestyles and subcultures.
The tragic events on the Plaza de las Tres Culturas, on 2 October 1968,
marked the end of any optimism about a developed and democratic Mexico
City. Elena Poniatowska (b. Paris; 1932–), in *La noche de Tlatelolco* (*Massacre in Mexico*), records the repression of tens of thousands of protesting
students, workers, and intellectuals by the army on that infamous night.
Poniatowska chronicles other crises of Mexico City in *Fuerte es el silencio*
("Silence Is Strong"), and *Nada, nadie. Las voces del temblor* ("Nothing,
Nobody: The Voices of the Earthquake"). The emblematic representation of the contemporary chronicle is Carlos Monsiváis (b. Mexico City;
1938–). In Monsiváis, the end of expectations of the city coincides with
the fantasy of technology, the consolidation of mass media as an institution of social mediation, and the surge of the "ecology of fear," or "*imagi-
nación del desastre*," the final and total ecological collapse of Mexico City.
Monsiváis's most important collections are *Días de guardar* ("Days of
Obligation"), *Amor perdido* ("Lost Love"), *Entrada libre; crónicas de una
sociedad que se organiza* ("Free Entrance: Chronicles of a Society Organizing Itself"), *Escenas de pudor y liviandad* ("Scenes of Decency and
Frivolity"), and *Los rituales del caos* ("Rituals of Chaos"). A collection of
his chronicles and essays translated into English is available in *Mexican
Postcards*. Other voices have followed Monsiváis's example, but they have
produced perspectives of their own regarding the impact of development
and globalization. Gabriel Zaid (b. Monterrey; 1934–), in fact, in his *El
progreso improductivo* ("Unproductive Progress") displays his perspective
on and portrays the humor of the worship of *desarrollismo* and proposes
unusual alternatives for the needs of a Third World country (Stabb 333–
34). In José Joaquín Blanco (b. Mexico City; 1951–), the city is the collapse of modernity, the indifference in face of colonialism by means of the

neoliberal free market, and the disintegration of the national in the hands of the transnational mass media. In *Función de medianoche* ("Midnight Show"), *Cuando todas las chamacas se pusieron medias de nylon* ("When All the Girls Wore Panty Hose"), and *Un chavo bien helado. Crónicas de los años '80* ("A Cool Kid: Chronicles of the 1980s") Blanco's approach to representing the city recalls the nineteenth-century flâneur that goes around the city discovering it sensually, against the logic of efficiency and velocity and without embracing a particular image of the totality. Finally, Juan Villoro (b. Mexico City; 1956–), who, in *Los once de la tribu* ("A Tribe of Eleven"), unmasks the complicity of nationalist discourses and the discourses for the integration of Mexico into the global world. "Fictions," rather than effective proposals for overcoming the conflict between tradition and modernity in Mexico, in fact reveal that this conflict will take a new form, or start a new chapter.

Ecocide and Unearthing

Octavio Paz (1914–98) published, by the time he became the 1990 Nobel Laureate, two books in which he evaluated the legacy of the twentieth century, the end of the cold war, and the implications of the world's ecological crises. Those titles are *Árbol adentro* (*A Tree Within*) and *La otra voz. Poesía y fin de siglo* (*The Other Voice: Essays on Modern Poetry*). At the dawn of a new era, or at the return to practicing forgotten or repressed traditions, Paz dares to propose the idea that poetry has a role in figuring out our times. "Almost 90 percent of his poetic production," concludes Adriana García, "reflects an obsessive need to re-create the cosmos; to find the Word, the expression that will capture the ever-changing yet permanent face of nature; to understand why the essence of the universe can only be achieved by translating the intangible that lies within the context of opposites" (199).

Paz summarizes some trends in Mexican poetry since the 1940s, including the pervasive impact of environmental crises and the contexts to which they belong for the relation between poetry and the world. It started as early as Efraín Huerta (b. Guanajuato; 1914–82), another influential figure in Mexican poetry. Since he wrote *Los hombres del alba* ("Men from Dawn") and *El Tajín*—evident also in his *Poesía completa* ("Complete Poetry")—Huerta has been concerned with the pollution of Mexico City and other elements contributing to its destruction: inequality in the distribution of wealth and the exploitation of the masses (García 194). Other topics in Huerta reappear in later poets, such as the preoccupation with universal destruction, represented by Hiroshima and Nagasaki, and with the coincidence between the fate of modern-day Mexico and the fate of destruction faced in the indigenous past. José Emilio Pacheco (b. Mexico City; 1939–) further addresses the connection between the ecological crisis and poetry raised by Paz. Progressively in Pacheco's work, his faith in the eternal cycles of nature and in the poetic tradition that speaks to it disappears (Binns, "Landscapes" [2002] 113). Key titles are *Los trabajos del mar* ("The Labors of the Sea"), *Tarde o temprano* ("Sooner or Later"), *Ciudad de la memoria. Poemas 1986–1989* (*City of Memory and Other Poems*), *Álbum de zoología*, and *El silencio de la luna* ("Silence of the Moon").

Homero Aridjis (b. Contepec, Michoacán; 1940–), like Pacheco, demonstrated in his works a shift in interest from the cosmic, and the awareness of a holistic interconnection between the human and the nonhuman world, to the dilemma of poetry after the loss of such connection caused by environmental crisis. Polluted rivers, sick trees, species in danger, apocalyptic warnings, and nightmare images of Mexico's future characterized his latest poetry: *Imágenes para el fin del milenio and Nueva Expulsión del Paraíso* ("Images for the End of the World and New Expulsion from Paradise"), *Tiempo de ángeles* ("Time of Angels"), *Ojos de otro mirar* ("Eyes Belonging to Another Gaze"), and *La montaña de las mariposas* ("The Mountain of the Butterflies"). Aridjis's novels *La leyenda de los soles* ("The Legend of the Suns") and *¿En quién piensas cuando haces el amor?* ("Who Do You Think of When You Make Love?") are set in Mexico City, in the year 2027, a year that coincides with the end of the Era of the Fifth Sun in the Aztec calendar. In both novels the city is on the verge of ecological disaster, and corruption, crime, drug trafficking, kidnapping, rape, and prostitution are rampant. And yet there is room for redemption in the forthcoming Era of the Sixth Sun (Binns, *Callejón* 144–48).

Dystopia and the crisis of the literary tradition are present too in other writers. In *La gota de agua* ("A Drop of Water"), by the novelist and playwright Vicente Leñero (b. Guadalajara; 1933–), water shortages and other changes in the urban ecology of Mexico City are juxtaposed with criticism of a host of other problems: an ineffectual bureaucratic system that seems to be set up not to function, inept technological solutions, and creative writing done completely removed from the surrounding reality. Fuentes's insistence on the persistent underlying pre-Columbian cosmologies in modern Mexico is made explicit with Mexico City's ecocide in his novel *Cristóbal nonato* (*Christopher Unborn*). The plot is set in 1992, after a fictional environmental disaster that would have taken place in 1990, although the establishment of corruption and political stagnation has managed to survive the catastrophe.

Carlos Montemayor (Parral, Chihuahua; 1947–) has journeyed from the countryside back to the indigenous peoples of Mexico through the experience of the city. *Abril y otras estaciones (1977–1989)* ("April and Other Seasons") collects three already published books of Montemayor's poetry and adds a new, previously unpublished collection, *El cuerpo que la tierra ha sido* ("The Body That the Land Has Been"), made up of poems that explore "land" as a way of being, a forgotten sensation in the body for those living in a state of alienation in the city. In recent years, he has been dedicated to the publication of indigenous literatures. A novelist, too, his novels tackle issues of political ecology in northern Mexico as well the relation between labor and nature. *Mal de piedra* (*Blood Relations*) and *Minas del retorno* (*Gambusino*) focus on the life and death of miners in northern Mexico.

The year of 2004 witnessed another environmental struggle in Huatulco, Oaxaca, where Leonardo da Jandra (b. Pichucalco, Chiapas; 1951–) and his wife, the painter Agar García, have lived since 1979. Both artists joined local communities in defending the land from a megaproject that would transform a natural reserve into a tourist resort. Jungle and literature have mingled too in Da Jandra's own fiction, which includes *Entrecruzamientos* ("Crisscrossings"), *Huatulqueños* ("People from Huatuko"), *Arousiada* ("The Saga at Arousa"), *Los caprichos de la piel* ("Whims of the Skin"), and *Samahua*. The connection among Chiapas, where Da Jandra was born; environmentalism; and the Zapatista uprising of 1994 is crucial in Efraín Bartolomé's work (b. Ocosingo, Chiapas; 1950–). An environmental activist, Bartolomé too was born in Chiapas and has written on the Zapatista uprising. *Ojos de jaguar* ("The Eyes of the Jaguar") includes poetry on reading the signs of the jungle, but mostly the poems are on the river; the humidity of the forest; and, above all, light. *Ciudad bajo el relámpago* ("City under Lightning") and *Cuadernos contra el angel* ("Logbooks against the Angel") articulate the encounter with the city after leaving Chiapas. His poetry up to 1997, always related to the nonhuman, is gathered in *Oficio: Arder* ("Profession: Burning").

Following the other migration, Alberto Blanco (b. Mexico City; 1951–) has taken residence in El Paso, Texas. Poet and author of short stories, and children's books, most of his poetry between 1973 and 1993 has been collected in *Amanecer de los sentidos* (*Dawn of the Senses*). Two basic themes in his poetry are the continuity of all living beings and of their survival and the notion that the senses are indispensable for reaching the awareness of the interconnectedness with the nonhuman, both abilities that urban life has atrophied (Forns-Broggi 216–17). Most recent titles include *También los insectos son perfectos* ("Insects Are Perfect Too"), *El corazón del instante* ("The Heart of the Moment"), and a few bilingual editions: *The Desert Mermaid / La sirena del desierto* and *El origen y la huella / The Origin and the Trace*.

Chicana/o Environmental Literature: Contestation and Inhabitance

Some Chicana/o writers affirm generations of ancestors in the United States, some even tracing their heritage back to sixteenth-century explorers and colonials, while others have roots in families who have only recently immigrated to the United States from Mexico. Marked by its relation to dual nations and a history of colonization and imperialism, Chicana/o environmental writing narrates an ongoing contestation of lands as well as a steadfast connection to place. Chicana/o writers often articulate this vision in lines rich with imagery of lands they long to fully inhabit, ranging from fertile river valleys and expansive ranch lands to urban barrios. However, very few Chicana/o or environmental scholars have taken note. Mexican American and Chicana/o writings present views from the population that inhabited the Southwest before the United States took over in 1848, as well as from their descendants and the countless immigrants arriving in different waves of migration throughout the twentieth century. Likewise, the writers represent a wide range of experience regarding the environment: from the perspective of a landed aristocrat to the bitter intimacy of a field-worker and the reluctant alienation of the urban barrio dweller. Some of this literature is familiar to many readers, though its environmental aspects have been underestimated until now. Still other selections are just now enjoying new readerships through recent efforts in recovery and republication of nineteenth- and early-twentieth-century works.[2]

This brief outline emphasizes four literary-historical eras, each concerned with a particularly dynamic period in Mexican American and Chicana/o literature written since 1848; the outline contextualizes one or two examples from each era.[3] These eras and genres include mid-nineteenth-century treatises and novels regarding land possession and dispossession, early-twentieth-century nature writing, mid- to late-twentieth-century civil rights treatises and poetry, and environmental justice writing up to the present day.

1848 and Its Aftermath

The first literary-historical era follows many important events on the North American continent: New Spain's violent colonization, Mexico's independence, and the United States' takeover of half of Mexico's territory. The middle of the nineteenth century brings the Texas Revolution (1836) and the United States–Mexican War ending with the 1848 Treaty of Guadalupe Hidalgo. Some of the Spanish and Mexican land grants protected under the Mexican government were challenged in the southwest territories by the new United States order.

The nineteenth-century writer and aristocrat María Amparo Ruiz de Burton (b. Baja California; 1832–95) depicts these events, which she experienced firsthand, in her novel *The Squatter and the Don*, providing apt examples of privileged California families valuing land as a resource, much to the detriment of its indigenous inhabitants, who never rise above servant status on the large ranchos. Yet she contrasts the Mexican (newly created "Mexican American") hacendados' land use to that of the new population: Anglo-American squatters. By depicting the debates between her protagonist Mariano Alamar and the squatters on his land Ruiz de Burton vividly portrays the extensive experience *Californios* shared with the land and how they took rainfall patterns into account, imposed grazing limitations on themselves, and even predicted the future success of wine vineyards. Ruiz de Burton offers a voice from an upper-class *Californiana* perspective, and her novels confront issues of land use and human impact on environment in very sophisticated, and sometimes enigmatic, terms.[4]

Ruiz de Burton is just one among many Mexican Americans of this era writing about the struggle to keep lands, though she appears to be the only one who channeled her protests into a novel.[5] Still, to understand the Mexican American relation to the environment, one must grasp this era's concern with land possession and dispossession, as well as the way these transitions in ownership severed the intimacy that local populations had long established with the environment. These insights can be, in part, gathered from Ruiz de Burton's novel and the countless letters and political statements written at the time. Good sources for these documents include David J. Weber's excellent collection *Foreigners in Their Native Land* and Nicolás Kanellos's recent volume *Herencia*.

A Revolution's Influence

Mexican Americans writing in the early twentieth century worked to make sense of the 1910 Mexican Revolution and its impact on both sides of the border. Their reflection on the revolution often emphasize land, which continued the nineteenth-century Mexican American writers' focus on possession and dispossession of territories. Yet twentieth-century writers add considerations of social justice and distributive access. Interestingly, this leads them to chronicle the relation between humans and nature, resulting in a distinctive style of nature writing. The era of Mexican American writing from the 1930s to the 1950s takes on a different aspect than conventionally expected in nature writing. In the context of Mexican American literature, the category nature writing undergoes a rigorous revision, uncovering complicity with colonial projects that threaten traditional environmental knowledge. Specific examples would include the work of two premier chroniclers of Mexican American "place": Jovita González (b. Roma, Texas; 1903–83) and Américo Paredes (b. Brownsville, Texas; 1915–99). Both these writers hail from the southern tip of Texas, a bioregion that challenges the idea of national boundaries even as its population remains starkly aware of the borderline marked by the river called the Rio Grande in the United States and el Río Bravo in Mexico. In distinctive style and method, these writers recount the human relation with the land in this fertile valley, recording the experiences of those closest to it: farmers and *peones* (ranch hands). And just as postrevolutionary Mexican environmental writings depict tensions between large- and small-scale development, so do the Mexican American writers.

Jovita González's research as an anthropology graduate student at the University of Texas during the 1920s involved gathering folklore from the Texas border region, which informed the thesis she wrote for her master's degree in 1930. Then she infused these stories into various short stories and two novels, *Dew on the Thorn* and *Caballero*. Her work makes clear that Mexican American oral narratives survived alongside centuries' worth of epistemological assault, in the process preserving a great deal of traditional environmental knowledge. Her writings exhibit a rich tradition of natural history and nature writing as it occurs in oral form in Mexican American culture of the time. Her novel *Dew on the Thorn* includes scenes in which conventional class divisions of the rancho are ignored as all persons living and working on the rancho gather around the traveling storyteller, as well as poignant moments when the local sheepherder passes his wisdom along to his young companion. Paredes also contributes to an alternative mapping of Chicano narrative with his landmark study *With His Pistol in His Hand: A Border Ballad and Its Hero*. Paredes earned his prominent place within Chicana/o cultural studies with his incisive scholarly studies, dense short stories, and compelling novels. However, his place-based writings, such as his short novel *The Shadow*, remain little explored for their environmental relevance. Paredes wrote *The Shadow* in the 1950s, but it did not reach publication until 1998. The novel portrays the embattled period that followed the idealistic 1910 revolution. The ideals of the revolution come through in the literature, and the novel form allows rich reflection on these ideals while communicating key environmental values and perspectives. Though the agricultural social order is idealized at this time, it is also shown to be in jeopardy because of an oncoming industrialization. *The Shadow* anticipates this transition and the nascent social- and environmental justice movements of the mid- to late-twentieth century.

Civil Rights Voices: Third Era

The middle to late years of the twentieth century see another major shift in Chicana/o literary history with the production of a civil rights movement and a new identity. The writings produced in this period, such as the poetry of Rodolfo "Corky" Gonzalez (b. Denver; 1929–2005), Lorna Dee Cervantes (b. San Francisco; 1954–), and Jimmy Santiago Baca (b. Santa Fe; 1952–) and the novel by Tomás Rivera (b. Crystal City, Texas; 1935–84) *Y no se lo tragó la tierra / And the Earth Did Not Devour Him*, begin to depict more explicit views of nature and environment in terms of justice, for Chicanas/os as well as for the land itself. Indeed, the Chicano nationalist movement makes political claims for the geographic territory of the United States Southwest. The landmark manifesto of the movement, "El Plan Espiritual de Aztlán," was drafted at the First Chicano National Conference in Denver in 1969 and boldly states that

> Aztlán belongs to those who plant the seeds, water the fields, and gather the crops and not to the foreign Europeans. . . . With our heart in our hands and our hands in the soil, we declare the independence of our mestizo nation. (Anaya and Lomelí 1)

Chicana/o youth from across the nation went to the convention in Denver, and they drafted "El Plan." The passionate language in "El Plan" betrays the Chicana/o frustrations of oppression, alienation, and dispossession and shows how the convention attendees desired enfranchisement in the form of reconnection to the environment—as property and as partner. They sought to regain control of geographic space, as a result not of firsthand experience as *hacendados* but of years of discrimination and economic injustices, to equitably distribute resources.

Baca is one of the most evocative poets from this era. His collections invite environmental readings in characteristically Chicano terms and context, invoking hybrid identity and a history of colonization as well as a dedicated pursuit of justice. In his poem titled "Invasions" from his *Black Mesa Poems*, Baca writes:

I am the end result
of Conquistadores,
Black Moors,
American Indians,
and Europeans,
bloods rainbowing
and scintillating
in me
like the trout's flurrying
flank scales
shimmering a fight
as I reel in.   (71)

These lines reveal a man reflecting on his hybrid ancestry during an unlikely moment: as he struggles with a rainbow trout in the Jemez River of northern New Mexico. His ethnic recitation succinctly lists a history of settlement and conquest in North America. Yet, instead of following up on these intricate narratives, the poet chooses to articulate his kinship with the trout. He shares with the trout "bloods rainbowing / and scintillating." They also share a courageous spirit, "shimmering a fight," when faced with death. The fisherman reels in, catching the fish and seemingly breaking his identification with it. Yet the trout continues with the poet. He carries it "dangling from scabbard stringer / tied to my belt" and it accompanies him as he surveys "the new invasion": "peer at vacation houses / built on rock shelves, / sun decks and travel trailers" (72). The poet and the trout start out as kin, then become foes on either side of a fishing hook, and finally end up together again, peering at the middle- and upper-class invasion of consumer values and land abuse. What might at first seem violence against nature—catching the fish—becomes an act of communion in comparison with the detachment of vacation homes and recreational vehicles. Both "El Plan" and Baca's poem, along with other writings during this period, make clear that Chicanas/os long to fully inhabit their particular places, all the while making clear the ways they have nurtured these connections over long periods of time.

Environmental Justice and Aesthetics

Chicana/o writing firmly plants environmental concerns in a colonial context, past and present. For Chicana/o literature, the colonial era began when the Spanish invaded the Aztec Empire, and the legacy of occupation endures to this day, appearing now in the form of environmental injustices. The writer Ray Gonzalez strikes this note in the opening lines of *Memory Fever*, locating his memoir of El Paso and the desert in

> the place where the earth accepted its fate at the hands of the pueblo people who fought to save their civilization, and of the Spanish explor-
> ers who came to cut open the earth for its riches and burn the pueblos down. (Gonzales 3)

This and other more recent Chicana/o cultural productions of the late 1980s and 1990s dialogue, directly as well as figuratively, with the environmental justice movement in works such as Ana Castillo's (b. Chicago, 1953–) *So Far from God*, Cherríe Moraga's (b. Whittier; 1952–) *The Last Generation*, Gloria Anzaldúa's (b. Jesus Maria of the Valley, Texas; 1942–2004) *Borderlands / La frontera*, and Helena María Viramontes's (b. Los Angeles; 1954–) *Under the Feet of Jesus*. Key to these recent writings, largely Chicana-feminist in nature, is a questioning of national borders and consideration of global economy's impact on individual women's lives. These are vital issues when considering environmental justice, and these writers tell these necessary stories with beautiful style that is not afraid to confront difficult issues. Castillo tells of a woman who becomes contaminated from factory work, develops cancer, and inspires a community response; Moraga considers the ways that oppression imposes violence on the Chicana/o relation to the land; Anzaldúa relates her personal experiences of reluctant alienation from her environment along the United States–Mexico border as well as her work to recover intimacy; and Viramontes tells the tragic story of a boy who suffers from pesticide contamination and of the girl who comes of age when she faces the barriers that keep her from helping him survive. These writings are plainly honest about the injustices happening every day, yet these authors refuse to give up struggling and attest to their hope with passionate and lyrical portrayals. In "There Must Be Something in the Rain," the singer-songwriter Tish Hinojosa tells the story of a little girl's death (the result of pesticide contamination) from the naive perspective of her young brother. His initial impression that the rain poisoned his sister shifts as the verses slowly reveal a different culprit. He finally realizes that he was mistaken to hold faith in the fact that "those airplanes cure the plants so things can grow." He ends with a pledge to "break the killing chains" even though "I'm afraid but I believe / That we can change these hurting fields." So too remains the commitment of Chicana/o writers.

Concluding Remarks: Just a Beginning

Alienation in the city, or on the United States-Mexico border; the embracing of or the resistance to living without national boundaries; the common need to address the local in the global; the claim of a hybrid ancestry and identity, accompanied by the painful game of memory and oblivion—all these themes speak to a shared but overlooked environmentalism in both traditions and a shared legacy of underlying currents for contemporary Mexican and Chicana/o literatures. They speak, too, of joint themes with other North American environmental writing, such as the overlooked resonance with Henry David Thoreau. He built his log-cabin retreat at Walden Pond when the United States was on the brink of waging war against Mexico, and his famous act of civil disobedience was, in part, to protest this war: "Witness the present Mexican war, the work of comparatively a few individuals using the standing government as their tool; for in the outset, the people would not have consented to this measure" (Walden [ed. Rossi] 226). Nevertheless, *Walden* appears to be a lost volume in the Latin American library of American literature. Jorge Luis Borges, in his accomplished capacity as a librarian, had very little to say about Thoreau. Other than quoting Emerson's remarks about Thoreau, Borges could only add:

> In 1845 he retired to a cabin on the shores of the solitary Walden Pond. His days were spent in reading the classics, in literary composi-

tion, and in the precise observation of nature. He was fond of solitude.
On one of his pages we read: "I never found the companion that was
so companionable as solitude." (27)

This is all Borges has to say, as if Thoreau's insistence, in the first chapter of *Walden*, "Economy," on the alienation of work and division of
labor in capitalist society, on the absurdity and cruelty of the economy of
growth, on colonialism and world commerce as worthy of condemnation,
and his scathing criticisms of the "lettered man" and of the educational
system were something alien to other literatures of the Americas. Opening up the literatures of the Americas for environmental study, each in
its respective context as well as together for its shared themes, not only
contributes vibrant voices from Latinas/os and Latin America but also
offers a dynamic new context for *Walden* and other landmarks of environmental writing. Fresh sounds of resonance, and dissonance, remain to
be heard from environmental writings across the Americas, past, present,
and future.

Notes

1. We are grateful to Brian Gollnick, from the University of Iowa; Danny
Anderson, from Kansas University; and Jeremy Larochelle, at Rutgers University,
for providing us with interesting suggestions included here.

2. The Recovering the United States Hispanic Literary Heritage project recovers, indexes, and publishes lost Latino writings from the colonial era through
1960. More information is available online at www.arte.uh.edu/recovery.

3. One may find in-depth analysis of select texts in the articles by Blend; Flys-
Junquera; Herrera-Sobek; Lynch; Platt; and Ybarra.

4. For further studies on Ruiz de Burton's rich and challenging texts, see
Aranda ("Contradictory"; *When*) Bost; and Montes and Goldman's recent collection of critical and pedagogical essays.

5. Ruiz de Burton's letters are also a rich source of information about land-
grant disputes. See Ruiz de Burton, *Conflicts*.

Pamela Banting

Abandoning the Fort: Cultural Difference and Biodiversity in Canadian Literature and Criticism

According to the back-cover blurb of the anthology *Canadian Culture: An Introductory Reader*, edited by Elspeth Cameron:

> The surest way to the hearts of a Canadian audience is to inform them that their souls are to be identified with rock, rapids, wilderness and virgin (but exploitable) forest. This critical statement no longer explains Canada's largely urban culture. Multiculturalism, feminism, postmodernism and regionalism—these and other vital movements jostle for expression in today's Canada. Wherever there's a centre, a new margin vies for attention. . . . But in the music, literature, painting, history and popular culture of this country, you can always find a soul.

The cover copy attempts to entice the prospective buyer by claiming that Cameron's book casts off the chains of an outmoded vision of Canada and Canadians—the vision of Canada as raw resources to be exploited and of Canadians as mere hewers of wood and drawers of water, or even of Canadians as lovers of the outdoors, and substitutes in its place the vision of an urban, officially multicultural, hip, world-class, globalist society with "soul." There are, however, several blind spots in the blurb. Most glaringly, the list of "rock, rapids, wilderness and virgin . . . forest" refers primarily to the Canadian Shield country most associated with the provinces of Ontario and Québec and completely ignores for the umpteenth time in Canadian history the provinces more associated with prairie, mountains, tundra, or ocean. In his review of Cameron's book, David Leahy remarks that "Cameron's 'Introduction' alludes to how multiculturalism, feminism, postmodernism and regionalism 'jostle for expression in today's Canada' but the vibrancy, and especially the stakes, of the recent and ongoing 'jostling' are not as evident as they should be in the body of the volume. . . . And why aren't there Newfoundland or Prairie voices, for instance, contesting or stretching the unity of Canada?" Cameron's view of Canada, even while purporting to toss out the old centrist vision of the nation, not only overlooks yet again the rest of the country in order to set Ontario up as representative of the whole but also insinuates that Canada's "largely urban culture" is somehow a new "margin," a logical sleight of hand.

The centrist vision of Canada—the idea that the nation per se consists of the provinces of Ontario and Québec and that the rest of the country's vast geography, complex history, rich culture, and engaging literature is merely a hinterland of "regions"—dates all the way back to the European settlement of Canada, which proceeded primarily in an east-to-west direction, but it persists even today. For example, the writers usually promoted as the best anglophone Canadian writers—Margaret Atwood, Alice Munro, Timothy Findley, Michael Ondaatje—all live (or lived) in Ontario.[1] The critic Allan Hepburn dismisses contemporary Canadian literature about rural places: "Canadian protagonists used to go to the local rink for a hockey game; now they go to Paris or Beijing. . . . They can identify Armani, but they can't quite place Massey-Ferguson. Historical expansiveness, international sophistication, and stylistic elegance have become signatures of the best new Canadian writing." In his opinion, such classic novels as W. O. Mitchell's *Who Has Seen the Wind?* (1947) and Ernest Buckler's *The Mountain and the Valley* (1952) "are defined by immobility and narrowness of experience." For him, the rural is the signifier of immobility, narrowness of experience, rusticity, ahistoricity, and unstylishness.[2]

While it is true that today the majority of Canadians live in cities, in an age of diversity and inclusiveness this fact does not seem to me sufficient or just cause for ignoring, relegating to the realm of the unfashionable, or otherwise disenfranchising Canadians who live in or are attached to smaller cities, towns, villages, rural areas, or wilder places. It is at best

ironic when advocates of race, class, gender, and ethnic diversity like Cameron dismiss the territory beyond the city limits, as if principles of equality
and dignity were applicable only to urban Canadians. This is merely "rep
by pop" ("representation by population") applied to literary and cultural
studies, yet another centrist ploy for continued monopoly over Canadian
culture. And for Hepburn to dismiss novels published six or seven decades
ago for their absence of portrayals of frequent international jet travel and
to denigrate the rural because it is not urban is simply illogical. The central Canadian project to encompass, represent, speak for, appropriate,
monopolize, and capitalize on the rest of Canada by perpetually flogging
the question of a singular Canadian identity is the subtext of much of this
urbocentrism.[3]

However, even though most Canadians now live in cities, many of
us do not feel it is necessary or desirable to choose between the natural
and the cultural worlds, nor, to put it another way, do we think that in
order to fully embrace cultural diversity we must necessarily shun biodiversity.[4] Given that so much intellectual energy over the past thirty years has
gone into assiduously and even ferociously deconstructing binary oppositions, it is ironic that so much of the rejection of rural and wilder places
is expressed in terms of binary oppositions: center versus margin, urban
versus rural, the Manolo Blahnik versus the cowboy boot, civilized versus
feral, city mouse versus country mouse.

These are just a few examples of recent attempts by some members of
the Canadian urban intelligentsia to vanquish narratives rooted in rural and
wilder places in order to get on with the important globalizing work of the
twenty-first century. But that agenda may not be so easy to accomplish,
given that so many works of Canadian literature bear on the environment.
Canadian environmental literature begins with the pictographs, orature,
and literature of the many aboriginal nations who have lived in this land
since time immemorial. These texts are stored not only in print but also
in collective memory, oral storytelling, ancient and contemporary cultural
practices, museums, and stone, and students of Canadian environmental
literature may wish to supplement their textbooks with field trips to the
museum, petroglyph and pictograph site, archives, reservation, or pow-
wow. Productive contrasts and comparisons may also be drawn between
these multifarious Native works and the published journals of early European
explorers and fur traders in which observations about the terrain, climate,
flora, and fauna of the New World dominate. Germaine Warkentin has
compiled a selection of such accounts in her anthology *Canadian Explo-*

ration Literature, and students may also read original trading-post journals and correspondence by visiting the *Hudson's Bay Company Archives*
site (www.gov.mb.ca/chc/archives/hbca/about/hbca.html).

Moreover, environmental, postcolonial, race, class, and gender criticism of Canadian literature can intermesh very productively. Not only do
the subjects of former colonies "write back" to the imperial center; the
land itself resists colonial inscriptions, as attested to in Native, explorer,
adventurer, and settler accounts.[5] In my fourth-year English course Studies in Canadian Literature: Nature and the Poetry of the Confederation
Period, for example, we examined both Native and white constructs of
nature at a time when treaties were being made between aboriginal and
settler peoples. In the treaty negotiations and other discourses of the era,
concepts of nature, land, earth, wilderness, plants, animals, landscape,
private property, corporate and government property, human rights, and
related topics were under discussion and in dispute.

The course began with a brief survey of the oratory, songs, ceremo-
nial performances, protests, letters, sermons, and other documents of
First Nations peoples before and after 1867, drawn from three sources:
An Anthology of Canadian Native Literature in English, edited by Terry
Goldie and Daniel David Moses; *Native Literature in Canada: From the
Oral Tradition to the Present* by Penny Petrone; and excerpts from treaty
documents of the period available from *Early Canadiana Online* (www
.canadiana.org/eco/index.html). After scrutinizing the discourse of some
of the government treaties, we read work by the Confederation poets,
poets born during the decade of the 1860s when Canada formally became
a nation: Charles G. D. Roberts, Archibald Lampman, Bliss Carman, Duncan
Campbell Scott, as well as Isabella Valancy Crawford and E. Pauline Johnson
(also known as Tekahionwake).[6] While treaty negotiations were going
on in the nineteenth century, the Confederation poets were trying, with
mixed success, to adapt their vocabularies, British poetic models, and pastoral associations to the Canadian landscape and climate.[7] In class, we considered whether, in certain respects, their poetry enacts a kind of aesthetic
land grab parallel to that of the treaty negotiations. That is, even as the
first generation of Euro-Canadian poets born and raised in Canada laid the
foundations of the postcolonial project by working toward a homegrown
poetic (asking where and what is here, and who we are as Canadians), their
poetry served the imperialist project by creating for literate, middle-class
Canadians an aestheticized image repertoire of Canada's geography, flora,
and fauna that helped assuage any guilt about building "our home on

native land."[8] *Floating Voice: Duncan Campbell Scott and the Literature of Treaty 9*, Stan Dragland's critique of Duncan Campbell Scott's poetry and his extremely problematic work as a bureaucrat with the Department of Indian Affairs, was pivotal in our examination of the poetry and politics of the contest for nature involved in imperialist nation building. At the origins of the much ballyhooed question of *the* Canadian identity, then, are the very answers to that question, in Native orature, pictographs, and literature—had European Canadians wished to listen to those songs and stories and read those texts instead of trying to erase, eradicate, and outlaw the languages and cultures in which they were composed. At this locus of the course, postcolonial and race, class and gender theories came together with ecocriticism and its potential to address questions of environmental racism and justice. As the Native writer Lee Maracle has observed in an important essay, the term *postcolonial* is an extremely problematic one for Native people in Canada, many of whom even today live in Third World conditions in a First World nation, and ought to be problematic for non-aboriginals as well. She states:

> We are the grandchildren of an abusive industrial British parent, and in fact are nowhere near a post-colonial literature. . . . Canadian writers still hover about the gates of old forts, peek through the cracks of their protective ideological walls and try to write their own yearnings for freedom from the safety of their intellectual incarceration. (14)

For Canadians to develop an authentically postcolonial literature, she argues, we must abandon the fort.

Abandoning the palisades and venturing into the territory beyond would also create a more conducive climate from coast to coast to coast, as the saying goes, for the reception of contemporary Canadian environmental literature. Unfortunately, instead of making progress toward a literary criticism that would include both city and country, metropolis and wilderness, in the literary landscape and break down the fort mentality, what we have is an increasingly strident attack on some of our most important contemporary writers about the natural world. It is as if some critics expect writers to march to the drum of critical passions and fashions and to select their subject matter accordingly rather than to write from their hearts, minds, and personal experience.[9]

Don McKay, for example, is widely regarded as Canada's finest contemporary nature poet writing in English.[10] However, his most recent collections, *Apparatus, Another Gravity, Camber*, and *Strike/Slip*, explore not nature in isolation but the intersections between the natural and the cultural. In an interview, McKay describes how his poems try to stitch together, not separate, the human and the more-than-human worlds and how he tries to take in the physical landscape, the cultural landscape, and the cultural history of the natural landscape (Babstock 53). For instance, his songs for the songs of various birds (such as his "Song for the Song of the Varied Thrush") are not imitations of birdsong but lyrical rejoinders to the melodies of selected avian species. In other poems he is intent on recovering the wildness in cultural artifacts—the hammer and saw, the knife and fork, the violin—and reminding readers of the wildness in each of us: "the muscle / in your mother's arm and back / and pelvis" and the "rotary cuff, the wrist, / having learnt the trick of witching wands and locks" (*Apparatus* 3). His prose poem "Camouflage" satirizes the idea that we can continue wantonly to pollute and deplete natural habitats because science and technology will save us in the end: the tongue-in-cheek prose poem gives us directions, postextinction, for fabricating a ruffed grouse in our own backyards using a clump of dead leaves the size of a football and an elderberry for an eye. But his attempt to mark out common ground between ourselves and other creatures has been scorned in the press by proponents of urbocentrism.[11] For instance, in his review of *Apparatus*, Kevin Connolly writes:

> If McKay has any obvious deficiency as a writer, it's that his poems often lack clout. *Apparatus* is punctuated with poems which are either direct tributes to particular birds and flowers, or turn on this kind of imagery. There's one entitled "Chickadee Encounter." Another, "Camouflage," is about the ruffed grouse, if you can believe it. . . . A reader has a right to expect more than *Masterpiece Theatre* meets *Hinterland Who's Who*.

Connolly, who particularly prides himself on being a lifelong urbanite, tars McKay's naturalist poems as lacking in "substance." However, it is clear from his review that Connolly simply does not care for poems about the natural world, a personal preference to which he is fully entitled but fallacious grounds for critique and dismissal.

When critics like Cameron, Hepburn, and Connolly draw such strict and reductive demarcations between center and region, east and west, diversity and what they see as the nondifferentiated, urban, and beyond the pale—or the jet set versus the Massey-Harris set, to adapt a John Prine lyric—what they fail to realize is that the recent Canadian literature of immigration, displacement, and official multiculturalism that they themselves seek to promote is the literature of entering a new country and a new landscape: it is the latest wave of settlement literature. In other words, it is the pioneer or sodbuster literature of the contemporary cosmopolitan milieu.[12]

It is extremely regrettable when critics believe that in order to advocate on behalf of the literature of Native, immigrant, diasporic, or other marginalized writers and groups, they must first clear the land of the literature of the rural—both the original wave of prairie sodbuster literature of approximately the 1920s to the 1950s plus any subsequent books that are agriculturally rooted—and clear-cut the literature of wilderness and wilder places. These sort of unsustainable critical assumptions and practices presuppose that if an immigrant to Canada chooses to reside in a city that person is not a settler, that only people who dwell in small towns or on farms are or were settlers, and that city dwellers and city life are diverse while country dwellers and rural places are all the same.

However, like our nation's geography, the field of Canadian literature is large and commodious and can contain multitudes, especially if one takes into account readers from outside the universities, those who are not confined to the limitations imposed by the thirteen- or twenty-six week syllabus and the politics of canonization. I would contend that there is room in Canadian literature not only for the literature of displacement but also for the literature of coming to terms with, accepting, even rejoicing in, and stewarding place, geography, landscape, nature, the regional, and the local, including urban nature. While the language of inclusiveness I am using here could be attacked as mere pluralism, to posit and then aggressively defend an economy of scarcity—that there is *not* enough room in the Canadian canon for such literature—and to castigate individual writers on such bases is at least as problematic.

Of course, convincing the imperial center to stop treating the rest of the country as if it were nothing but hinterland is an ongoing project. The only hope is to illustrate that central Canada too is a unique region with a distinctive, though not representative, literature and culture.[13] In their 1997 essay "Firing the Regional Can(n)on," Herb Wyile and Christopher Armstrong write that during the past few decades of critique along race, class, and gender lines, "The politics of spatial divisions and cultural differences within nations . . . has received less emphasis, even in a country as preoccupied with geography and space as Canada, but the situation is starting to change. . . . Literary critics in various parts of the country have joined such challenges in the field of history by addressing the regional imbalances that have existed historically in the canon as one of the major shortcomings of the way in which Canadian literature has been constituted" (1).[14] The general point of scholarly work in what is often referred to as "the politics of location" has been to foreground and analyze race, class, and gender differences that had previously been ignored, suppressed, or repressed. And the notion that people who live within a certain radius may have things in common was, in many respects, rightly suspect for its potential and actual investment in the hegemony of liberal humanism and colonialism or neo-colonialism. However, the time has come when place can and must play a renewed role in supplementing notions of agency and solidarity within, between, and among differences. It is time that "the politics of location" be opened up to include along with gender, sexuality, class, ethnicity, race, and physical ability the geographic coordinates of location.

Centrist bias, however, is not the only obstacle to a fuller appreciation of Canadian environmental literature. Another important problem is insufficient awareness of ecocriticism, as Susie O'Brien has argued and, to a large extent, I agree.[15] O'Brien notes, for example, that there is only one Canadian contributor (Neil Evernden) to *The Ecocriticism Reader* edited by Cheryl Glotfelty and Harold Fromm and that there is, to date, no parallel Canadian text. In her article "Nature's Nation, National Natures? Reading Ecocriticism in a Canadian Context," O'Brien points to a limitation in postcolonial criticism as it has been practiced thus far in English Canada:

> Though it has worked effectively to theorize the ways in which language and culture serve as vehicles for power in relationships between and within different human groups, postcolonial criticism has yet to address adequately the relationship between human and non-human worlds—a relationship which is of vital importance to many of the indigenous groups whose voices postcolonial critics claim to heed. (12)

While largely true, nevertheless this claim brushes past Canadian critical work of the 1970s and 1980s on regionalism and relationships between human beings (often referred to as "Man" in those decades) and landscape such as Laurie Ricou's *Vertical Man/Horizontal World: Man and Landscape in Canadian Prairie Fiction*; Dick Harrison's *Unnamed Country: The Struggle for a Canadian Prairie Fiction*; Robert Kroetsch's *The Lovely Treachery of Words*; Rudy Wiebe's essays, some of which are collected in *A Voice in the Land: Essays by and about Rudy Wiebe* (Keith) and in *Trace: Prairie Writers on Writing* (Sproxton), possibly because these texts are usually categorized under either thematic criticism or regionalism.[16] In other words, the relative lack of awareness of ecocriticism in Canada that O'Brien rightly laments is in part a question of naming. For instance, O'Brien herself mentions the thematic criticism of Northrop Frye and addresses Margaret Atwood's extension of Frye in her *Survival: A Thematic Guide to Canadian Literature*, but she does not categorize their work also as ecocriticism, which I think one could in the same manner that many of the articles in *The Ecocriticism Reader* are also hybrids and not "pure" ecocriticism.

As part of this triple project of deconstructing the politics of central versus marginal in Canadian literature, legitimating geography as a valid and significant component of the politics of location, and creating space for ecocritical approaches to Canadian literature about place and the environment, in another fourth-year course, The Literature of Southern Alberta,[17] the students and I attempted to conduct an archaeology of the texts[18] associated variously with the mountains, foothills, prairies, ranches, farms, parks, villages, towns, and cities between Calgary and the Alberta-Montana border, the geographic location where we all live, at least during the university term. First we reflected on how many literature courses are defined in terms of historical period or national boundaries and how the texts studied are canonical ones, and then we entertained the concepts and feasibility of distinctly regional and even bioregional literatures. Next we invoked the poststructuralist extension of the notion of "text" to other media beyond just the book. That is, the texts we studied encompassed a range of mediums and genres beginning with the petroglyphs at Writing-on-Stone Provincial Park in southeastern Alberta and excerpts from early reminiscences of Red Crow, a leader of the Blood tribe; William Gladstone, a former Hudson's Bay Company boat builder; the Pincher Creek storekeeper A. L. Freebairn; and both the memoirs of and a field guide by painter Annora Brown. We continued with creative nonfiction by the former guide and outfitter Andy Russell, *Trails of a Wilderness Wanderer*, and the former park warden Sid Marty, *Leaning on the Wind: Under the Spell of the Great Chinook*. We read novels set in the former mining communities of the Crowsnest Pass by Roberta Rees, *Beneath the Faceless Mountain*, and Peter Oliva, *Drowning in Darkness*. We read Fred Stenson's historical novel *The Trade*, about the Hudson's Bay Company's monopoly on the fur trade in western Canada after 1821;[19] W. O. Mitchell's novel about a professor who, while hunting, is attacked by a bear, *Since Daisy Creek*; short stories by the native Canadian writer Emma Lee Warrior; poems by

Shirley Bruised Head and Jon Whyte; essays by the park warden Kevin van Tighem and the environmentalist Stan Rowe; Patricia van Tighem's account of surviving a bear attack and its medical and psychological aftermath, *The Bear's Embrace: A True Story of Surviving a Grizzly Bear Attack*; a radio play about farm economics by the playwright Gordon Pengilly; and poetry by local cowboy poets. We also watched the television dramatization of Thomas King's novel *Medicine River* and Andy Russell's documentary *Grizzly Country* and listened to the music and lyrics of *Lost Herd*, a compact disk by the singer-songwriter Ian Tyson, who ranches near High River. Throughout the course we explored such topics as representations of nature, wilderness, animals, landscape, work, the rural, the town, and the city; the use of the vernacular; sense of place; local knowledge; mountain literature; and notions of community.

By examining a broad range of genres and forms created in southern Alberta by people of different gender, ethnicity, social class, language, history, traditions, politics, jobs, artistic disciplines, and semiotic systems, we had the opportunity to glimpse what the geography, history, and climate of the area had inspired; to extend the scope of postcolonial criticism beyond the aesthetic and sociopolitical realms to the natural world; and to demonstrate that nature and culture are not dichotomous but always already intermingled and interdependent.[20] As Fromm reminds us in his essay "From Transcendence to Obsolesence," "A thought may have no weight and take up no space, but it exists as part of a stream of consciousness that is made possible by food, air, and water" (38). Because little or nothing had yet been published about most of the texts on the course and because we wanted to celebrate the literature of the local area that is the source of some of our food and all of our air and water, we then collaborated in the creation of a class Web site, which is located at http://irena .blackmill.net/509/.

In an era when factory and motor-vehicle pollutants sully urban skies and agricultural and petroleum-industry chemicals concoct carcinogenic cocktails in the country air; when city parks can host the occasional black bear and coyotes can be easier to spot in the suburbs than in farm or ranch country; when it is estimated that in the city of Calgary, population one million, there are more gophers than people and raccoons nightly prowl the cities of Ontario,[21] the old-fashioned binaries of urban/rural, industrial/pastoral, center/region, and culture/nature are unsustainable. Producing an endless supply of books, critical articles, and newspaper commentary on how east is "hipper" than west, urban "cooler" than rural, does absolutely nothing to promote healthy natural *or* cultural diversity, neither of which we can do without. In fact, most ecocritics include books about wilderness and wilder places, rural *and* urban locales in their reading and teaching, as well as considerations of environmental racism, environmental justice, and grassroots activism in their practice. Rights, justice, and activism cannot be restricted to urban social-justice movements or even to Homo sapiens. As Christopher Manes writes, "a viable environmental ethics must challenge the humanistic backdrop that makes 'Man' possible, restoring us to the humbler status of *Homo sapiens*: one species among millions of other beautiful, terrible, fascinating—and signifying—forms" (26). What I have tried to do as a professor of Canadian environmental literature is, on the one hand, to examine our literature in terms of the multiplicity of dramas, both human and more than human, enacted in many different ecological zones and, on the other, to deep map one region or bioregion at a time.[22] This seems to me a more productive way to savor and interpret the literature of our country than obsessing over how to come up with a singular and yet somehow representative Canadian identity or exercising one's blind prejudices against country people. It is time to unbar the gates of the fort and walk outside.

Notes

A portion of this essay was previously published in "Birds, Bees and Grizzly Bears: Notes on Nature and Culture in Contemporary Canadian Literature," *Conspectus: A Journal of English Studies* 2 (2004): 6–22, and is being published in Polish under the title (in Polish) "The Culture of Nature: Notes on Contemporary Canadian Ecological Literature," *Canadian Literary and Cultural Discourses and the Concept of Nationhood: Constructing/Deconstructing Canadiannes,* edited by Miroslawa Buchholtz and Eugenia Sojka (Cracow: Universitas P, forthcoming). I wish to thank the editor of *Conspectus*, C. S. Biju, and the joint editors of the Polish anthology for their kind interest in my work, as well as Jim Frideres, University of Calgary, for inviting me to give a talk to a group of visiting scholars from India, out of which these papers later emerged.

1. Findley died in 2002.

2. Like Hepburn, the Toronto *Globe and Mail* lifestyle columnists Russell Smith and Leah McLaren tend to disparage anything to do with the country beyond the perimeter of downtown Toronto, even, in Smith's case, the so-called cottage country north of that city. Under the guise of getting in touch with her inner country girl, McLaren portrays the rural as simply an antifashion domain where one kicks off one's Manolo Blahnik stilettos and succumbs to flat-footed idleness, whiling away the preternaturally long days sipping mint juleps.

3. Class is the unacknowledged variable underpinning Hepburn's privileging of urban over rural.

4. In his book *Cultures of Habitat: On Nature, Culture, and Story*, the ethnobotanist Gary Paul Nabhan argues that ecological and cultural literacy are symbiotic: "In place of the formerly varied views of the natural world held by the myriad ethnic groups that have inhabited this continent, we are evolving a new, shared viewpoint—one not of experienced participants dynamically involved with their local environment but of observers, viewing the landscape from outside the frame. Because only a small percentage of humankind has any direct, daily engagement with other species of animals and plants in their habitats, we have arrived at a new era in which ecological illiteracy is becoming the norm" (164–65).

5. See my article "The Land Writes Back: Notes on Four Western Canadian Writers" and my anthology *Fresh Tracks: Writing the Western Landscape*, for elaboration on the notion of nature's own inscriptions.

6. Canada formally became a nation in 1867, though what are now the western provinces did not join until later dates.

7. As the critic W. H. New writes, "In many respects illustrative of late Romantic literary conventions outside the country—regular verse form, high ethical tone, pantheist sentiment, elevated diction—Confederation poetry also struggled with many Canadian dilemmas, especially those created by imperial conservatism, by the contrast between urban life and the values attached to rural poetic imagery, and by the disparities between literary landscape conventions and empirical landscapes" (*History* 115–16).

8. Canadian aboriginals often use this phrase, which parodies and ironizes the opening lines of our national anthem: "O Canada / Our home and native land."

9. I do not wish to imply the reverse either, that critics ought to serve writers, but it goes beyond the scope of critical practice when critics attempt to dictate what a writer's subject matter ought to be. Fortunately, Canadian writers continue to write about their relations with the natural world.

10. McKay has twice won the Governor-General's Award for Poetry, and his book *Vis-B-Vis: Field Notes on Poetry and Wilderness* was nominated in the nonfiction category. He has also been nominated for a poetry prize in Canada awarding the largest financial sum, the Griffin Poetry Prize.

11. For more on urbocentrism, see Wendell Berry's essay "The Prejudice against Country People."

12. Perhaps instead of sodbuster literature I should call it pavement-pounder literature to properly acknowledge its urban setting.

13. For example, the greater Toronto bioregion is bounded by Lake Ontario, the Niagara escarpment, and the Oak Ridges moraine and includes several watersheds that drain into Lake Ontario. The city is located in the temperate deciduous-forest belt at the most northeastern extension of the Carolinian forest (dominated by oaks and hickories) and the Huron-Ontario-Upper St. Lawrence mixed forests dominated by sugar maple and beech. Within the mixed forest belt, the Oak Ridges moraine is, as the name implies, an extensive, largely natural, and

farm-covered moraine just north of Toronto that has oak as well as maples and is important for feeding the streams flowing through the Toronto area into Lake Ontario. I would like to thank Greg Michalenko for generously supplying me with information about the greater Toronto bioregion.

What is Michael Ondaatje's depiction of Toronto in his much-acclaimed novel *In the Skin of a Lion* but a local narrative? The Canadian Caribbean writer Dionne Brand's novel *In Another Place, Not Here,* set in Toronto and on a Caribbean island, explores questions of place and displacement that would be susceptible to an ecocritical treatment. Critics' obsessive and colonial preoccupation with the fact that many of Alice Munro's short stories have been published in the *New Yorker* seems to have all but obscured the source of her stories' power: their accurate and beautifully crafted depictions of life in Ontario small towns and exurbia. If Toronto is indeed punctuated by the stilettos of the city's fashionistas, it is simultaneously marked by the tracks and traces of squirrels, raccoons, rabbits, skunks, snakes, toads, numerous species of birds, woodchucks, coyotes, and other fauna who make their living there.

14. In 1998 the journal *Studies in Canadian Literature* published a special issue, *Writing Canadian Space*; in 2000 *Essays on Canadian Writing* did a special issue titled *Where Is Here Now?*; and in 2001 an issue of *Canadian Literature* was devoted to nature writing and ecocriticism. Herb Wyile, Lisa Chalykoff, David M. Jordan, and Susie O'Brien are beginning to rethink regionalism. See W. H. New's *Land Sliding: Imagining Space, Presence, and Power in Canadian Writing* and Dallas Harrison's remarkable essay "Where Is (the) Horizon? Placing *As for Me and My House*," in which Harrison sets out to discover on which Saskatchewan town Ross may have based the fictional town of Horizon. Stephen Henighan's polemical *When Words Deny the World: The Reshaping of Canadian Writing* is a forceful critique of the Toronto-centric nature of Canadian literature and publishing.

15. A significant problem also is the vast extent of Canada's geography. Few Canadians are fortunate enough to have traveled to all our provinces and territories. Moreover, a great many books are published each year, making it virtually impossible to have read everything. I take issue not with any one critic's lack of comprehensive coverage of our nation's literature, something only New seems able to keep up with, but rather with those who mistake the literature of their own region as more significant, more worthy, or more representative than that of other provinces or areas.

16. While texts such as the aforementioned ones about prairie literature, which take the prairie geography and its literary representations as their subject matter, use the word *prairie* in their titles, this practice is not often followed in central Canada, where, for example, collections of essays or anthologies that contain contributions by writers—all or almost all of whom are from Ontario—will use the word *Canadian*, as if Ontario stood for all of Canada.

17. Both courses—Nature and the Poetry of the Confederation Period and The Literature of Southern Alberta—were offered under the general rubric of English 509, Studies in Canadian Literature.

18. I borrow this specific use of the term *archaeology* from Robert Kroetsch's seminal essays on Canadian literature.

19. *Lightning*, Stenson's subsequent novel, about the first cattle drive up from Montana to stock the Cochrane Ranche, was published after the course was over; it is set in Montana and the environs of Calgary and Pincher Creek, Alberta.

20. While we did not study postcolonial theory in this course, a significant number of the texts raise issues pertinent to that field. Students were able to observe from the primary texts how postcolonial and ecocritical concerns can overlap.

21. *Gopher* is the vernacular term for the small rodent otherwise known as Richardson's ground squirrel.

22. Other environmental literature courses I have taught include The Literature of Wilderness and Wilder Places, The Poetics of Space and Place, Writing the Rural, Nature Writing and Ecocriticism, Wild Semiosis: Reading Texts and Landscapes, Contemporary Women Nature Writers, and Local Motion: Movement as Ecological Practice.

Daniel J. Philippon

United States Environmental Literature before the Twentieth Century

Mapping United States environmental literature before the twentieth century is a daunting task, given that this writing spans more than five hundred years of nonnative travel and inhabitation across more than three million square miles of land and water. One merit of mapping such a vast literary landscape in such a small space, however, is that it allows one to forgo the "thickets of detail" that accompany longer surveys and instead to "top out [on] the high ridge and to take a look around," to borrow a metaphor from Aldo Leopold (qtd. in Meine, *Aldo* 126). What we discover from such a vantage point is the gradual emergence of a profound tension in environmental literature between the establishment and continuance of the United States as a political administrative state and the identities and geographies of the particular places that compose that state. As Barry Lopez has remarked, "The land itself, vast and differentiated, defies the notion of a national geography. . . . Yet Americans are daily presented with, and have become accustomed to talking about, a homogenized national geography, one that seems to operate independently of the land, a collection of objects rather than a continuous bolt of fabric" ("American Geographies" 60–62). If, post–September 11, the main priority of the United States government has become to protect the "homeland," we would do well to ask how pre-twentieth-century environmental writers both influenced and were influenced by this homeland—how they imagined and represented the land that is now the United States, how they helped create and contest its national geography, and how they helped transform and protect the particular places that define it.[1]

As I have argued elsewhere, metaphor is one of the most powerful figures of speech a writer can use (and be used by) when representing nature (Philippon). By comparing the unknown or unfamiliar with the known or familiar, metaphors do more than simply express the inexpressible; they also create frames of understanding through which a writer's worldview is made manifest. As such, metaphors not only function as windows into different ways of knowing shaped by personal, social, and cultural identities; they also imply different ethics, or preferred ways of acting in the world. At its most basic level, United States environmental literature before the twentieth century can be reduced to a clash of metaphors: is nature an object to be exploited or a subject to be appreciated? (Witness Lopez: is the land a collection of objects or a continuous bolt of fabric?) Environmental writing is rarely so straightforward, however, but rather is threaded through with a variety of competing metaphors that reflect the complexities of identity and ideology as well as the difficulty of "coming to terms" with the American landscape on a range of spatial and temporal scales.

Age of Exploration (1492–1620)

Few periods in United States environmental literature demonstrate these complexities and difficulties more than the age of exploration, during which European seafarers first came into contact with the North American landscape and its Native inhabitants. None of these explorers considered themselves Americans, of course, and even the colonists who followed them in the seventeenth century had not yet begun to imagine themselves as members of an independent nation. But in the written records of their encounters with this unfamiliar land and its people, these explorers revealed a conflicting set of responses that shaped the experience of subsequent residents and travelers in important ways. In particular, writing about North America from the late fifteenth through the early seventeenth century reflected the imperial hopes and dreams of its authors, the familiar European landscapes and creatures through which they saw this new world, and the fears and anxieties this new landscape engendered.

Although their imaginative geographies powerfully shaped European impressions of America, the narratives of early explorers are first and foremost descriptions of particular regional landscapes: the Southwest (claimed by Spain), the Southeast (parts of which were claimed by England, France, and Spain), and the Northeast (parts of which were claimed by England and France). Alvar Núñez Cabeza de Vaca's *La Relación* (1542), for example, contains the earliest known descriptions of the Gulf Coast and Southwest, including the first descriptions of the Mississippi River and the American bison, while Pedro de Castañeda de Nájera's *Narrative of the Expedition of Coronado* (c. 1562) describes the first European encounter with the Grand Canyon of the Colorado. In the Southeast, Jean Ribault's *Whole and True Discovery of Terra Florida* (1563) recounts Ribault's 1562 expedition to what are now the St. Johns River in Florida and Parris Island in South Carolina, and Thomas Hariot's *Brief and True Report of the Newfound Land of Virginia* (1588) describes Hariot's encounters with the flora, fauna, and Native people of what is now coastal South Carolina. In the Northeast, Samuel de Champlain explored the Atlantic coast as far south as Cape Cod, which he describes in several volumes, including *Voyages* (1613) and *Voyages et descouvertures* (1619).

Comparing the "environmental literature" of European explorers with that of the Native people of North America is a difficult undertaking because of large differences in literary form and cultural context. Most of the forms environmental literature takes today—including the personal essay, novel, short story, and drama—did not appear in America until the late eighteenth and early nineteenth centuries. Instead, Europeans described their explorations in the form of written journals, letters, and relations, while Native Americans expressed their "relationship" to the "land" (they would not have used such terms) in oral narratives, the meaning of which was dependent on changing performative contexts and thus was fundamentally altered when recorded by European observers. Despite these challenges, analysis of the metaphors used by both groups reveals large differences in their worldviews. In a story told to Europeans in 1610, for instance, an Indian of the Potomac River describes his tribe's chief creator-god as appearing "in the likewise of a mightie great Hare," and the four other gods as "the 4. wyndes," which vie for power in a landscape defined by its physical and spiritual presences (Strachey 101–02). Thomas Hariot, in contrast, describes a similar regional landscape in terms of both the challenges of its strangeness and the potential for its commodification. Acknowledging "the want of provision," "the want of English meanes, for the taking of beasts, fishe, and fowle," and "[s]ome want also wee had of clothes," Hariot nevertheless proclaims that "we found the soyle to bee fatter; the trees greater and to growe thinner; the grounde more firme and deeper mould [loose soil rich in organic matter]; more and larger champions [unbroken plains], finer grasse and as good as ever we saw any in England" (Hariot, conclusion).[2]

Colonial Period (1620–1776)

Commodity production was only one of many motives for the settlement of the North American colonies, and the frames through which these European settlers saw the landscapes they eventually came to call home were as varied as the nations from which they came. Due in part to this broad range of motives, United States environmental literature changes in several ways in the colonial period. For one thing, its authors show a much greater interest in and sensitivity to the nonhuman environment, both because their survival depended on it and because they hoped their detailed descriptions would encourage more Europeans to emigrate. In addition, because many settlers (particularly in New England) were driven by religious zeal, environmental literature expands in terms of the genres in which it is found, with sermons, hymns, and poems, as well as spiritual biographies, autobiographies, and diaries, beginning to make extended reference to the natural world and the human place in it. By the mid–eighteenth century, environmental literature also begins to reflect the impact of new scientific understandings of nature, as exemplified by Carl Linnaeus's *Systema Naturae* (1735), which systematized the classification of flora and fauna, and Comte de Buffon's thirty-six volume *Histoire Naturelle* (1749–88), which helped to lay the groundwork for Charles Darwin's theory of evolution.

Although many readers tend to imagine the southern colonies as a paradisial garden and the New England landscape as a threatening wilderness, writers from both regions in fact mixed these metaphors with regularity. As Leo Marx has written, "like all effective metaphors, each had a basis in fact. In a sense, America was *both* Eden and a howling desert; the actual conditions of life in the New World did lend plausibility to both images" (*Machine* 43). At the end of his *Generall Historie of Virginia* (1624), for instance, John Smith reminds his readers how far he has traveled "in this Wildernesse of Virginia" (333), while elsewhere he includes a description of the landscape as a fertile garden yielding twice as many bushels per acre as previously reported (267). Smith was hardly an accomplished naturalist, however, and it took until the early eighteenth century for writers with a better understanding of natural history to more fully assess the blend of agricultural productivity and mountainous wildness that together define the southern landscape. Robert Beverley's *History and Present State of Virginia* (1705), John Lawson's *New Voyage to Carolina* (1709), William Byrd's *History of the Dividing Line* (1728), and Eliza Lucas Pinckney's *Letterbook* (1739–62) each address distinct aspects of this blended landscape, combining an awareness of the utility of nature for colonial development with an appreciation of the landscape's beauty for its own sake.

In New England, where English Separatists and Puritans settled beginning in 1620, environmental literature took several forms, from the early catalogs of the Massachusetts landscape in Thomas Morton's *New English Canaan* (1632) and William Wood's *New England's Prospect* (1634) to the meditative poems of Anne Bradstreet (c. 1650–72) and Edward Taylor (c. 1668–1729) to the upstate New York *Observations* (1738) of Cadwallader Colden and the botanical manuscript (c. 1750–59) of his daughter Jane. Although Puritanism was the window through which most of the settlers saw their environment in the seventeenth century, the piety of late Puritans such as Cotton Mather and Jonathan Edwards was tempered somewhat by the rise of Enlightenment science. Edwards, for instance, cites Isaac Newton's theory of light in his essay "Beauty of the World" (1725) to argue for the ways in which natural beauties "shadow forth spiritual beauties" (305). Not every chronicler of New England nature was a Puritan, however, and much of John Josselyn's *New England's Rarities Discovered* (1672) and *Account of Two Voyages to New-England* (1674) reiterates Morton's and Wood's secular expressions of wonder about the unfamiliar (and often mythical) flora and fauna they encountered, while also noting the changes in the land the Puritans had wrought.

By the mid–eighteenth century, a wider horizon for colonial ambitions was also beginning to come into view, in part because of the work of several far-ranging pioneer naturalists and travelers. Louis Hennepin introduced the upper Mississippi and Great Lakes to readers in his *Description of Louisiana* (1683) and *New Discovery of a Vast Country in America* (1697), which included the first descriptions of both Niagara Falls and St. Anthony Falls (at the site of present-day Minneapolis). Although his travels did not take him as far west as Hennepin, Mark Catesby also helped shape perceptions of a continental geography in his *Natural History of Carolina, Florida, and the Bahama Islands* (1731–43), the first attempt at a comprehensive natural history of the southern colonies. And Peter

Kalm's three-volume *Travels into North America* (1753–61) combined Hennepin's enthusiasm for travel with Catesby's eye for natural phenomena (Kalm was a student of Linnaeus) to produce one of the most thoughtful descriptions of the American landscape and its inhabitants before the creation of the new nation.

Federalist Period (1776–1820)

Although the establishment of the United States as an independent nation is traditionally dated to the adoption of the Declaration of Independence in 1776, nation making is a process, not an event. Just as the consolidation of political power in the federal government continued through the end of the Revolutionary War in 1783 and the ratification of the Constitution in 1788, so did the nation's new identity emerge gradually over time.

A wide variety of residents and travelers commented on the landscapes of the eastern United States in journals and travel narratives during the Federalist period, but none more effectively fostered the idea of a national geography than J. Hector Saint-John de Crèvecoeur and Thomas Jefferson. Crèvecoeur, whose *Letters from an American Farmer* was first published in London, offered an idealized picture of the American landscape through the eyes of his fictional narrator, Farmer James. An environmentalist in the archaic sense, Crèvecoeur argued in his best-known essay ("What Is an American?") that "[m]en are like plants; the goodness and flavour of the fruit proceeds from the peculiar soil and exposition in which they grow" (Crèvecoeur, *Letters* [ed. Stone] 71). Generalizing from the five years he spent farming the "middle landscape" of Orange County, New York, before the revolution, Crèvecoeur portrayed the American landscape as a pastoral garden whose freshness and possibility purified men in their cultivation of it. Jefferson, a close friend, shared many of Crèvecoeur's Enlightenment beliefs about the perfectibility of man, and the writings of both men marked the eclipse of Calvinism by natural philosophy in America, a transition also reflected in and fostered by the establishment of the American Philosophical Society in 1743. *Notes on the State of Virginia* (1785), Jefferson's only book-length work, began as his attempt to answer a series of questions sent to him by the French diplomat François Marbois, but it grew into a document that not only applied the scientific method to the measurement of Virginia's resources but also employed a new aesthetic of "the sublime and beautiful" to defend the nation's character (see E. Burke). In a series of answers to Marbois's "queries," Jefferson refuted Buffon's theory that the animals of the New World were degenerate versions of European creatures; introduced his European readers to the uniquely American landscapes of Virginia's Natural Bridge and Harper's Ferry (the latter "worth a voyage across the Atlantic," according to Jefferson [(ed. Peden) 19]); and, like Crèvecoeur, celebrated the nation as the natural home of virtuous husbandmen: "Those who labour in the earth are the chosen people of God," Jefferson proclaimed (164–65).

The georgic vision of America espoused by Crèvecoeur and Jefferson was of course only one metaphoric conception of the environment at work in the late eighteenth century. From the Gothic landscapes of Charles Brockden Brown's major novels to the spectacular nature of Charles Willson Peale's natural history lectures, United States writers represented the new nation in a number of often contradictory ways. Likewise, many of the texts that appear so distinctively "American" today are perhaps better seen as literary maps of particular regional landscapes. The early American Romanticism of William Bartram's *Travels* (1791), for instance—which influenced Samuel Taylor Coleridge and William Wordsworth, among others—is partly attributable to the luxuriant vegetation and tropical climate of the southern colonies through which Bartram traveled in the 1770s. And while Lewis and Clark's Corps of Discovery served to extend the influence of the federal government across North America following the 1803 Louisiana Purchase, the "American epic" that their *Journals* (1804–06) are said to represent could also be seen as a record of their astonishing ignorance and arrogance as the explorers encountered the land and peoples of the high plains, northern Rockies, and Pacific Northwest for the first time. Less descriptive of any one place, Alexander Wilson's *American Ornithology* (1808–29) nevertheless also helped imaginatively knit together the various regional landscapes through which Wilson and other itinerant naturalists traveled, an accomplishment made all the more significant by the wider distribution of printed materials that technological innovations had made possible in the early nineteenth century—a development that also helped shape the growing Romantic movement.

Romantic Period (1820–65)

It would be difficult to overstate the significance of the Romantic period to the renaissance of United States environmental literature that began in the 1960s. All the values the Romantics held dear—the importance of emotion, imagination, and passion; the validation of individual experience as a means to knowledge; the assertion of the unity and beauty of the organic whole; and the preference for aesthetics over economics—remain powerful features of modern environmental writing. Yet what drove the Romantics' endorsement of these values, beyond a generational reaction against the excesses of the Enlightenment, was the technological innovation of their fellow Americans, who turned their backs on Jefferson's call to democratic pastoralism in droves. As developments in both industrial and agricultural technologies enabled the expansion of the nation's population, these same innovations also led to the destruction of much of the nation's environment, particularly the felling of its northern forests, the plowing of its prairies, and the extermination of its wildlife—including, most famously, the extinction of the passenger pigeon and the near extinction of the bison. As a result, Romantic authors began to see John Winthrop's sacred "Citty upon a Hill" as a polluted, degraded, and despoiled landscape, and they likewise began to see the wilderness not as the home of godless savages but as a place of purity, simplicity, and harmony (47). And with this reversal of early American views of the city and wilderness came a new source of national pride: a distinctively *American* wilderness (Nash [2001] 67–83).

A number of other significant changes during this period also helped shape the emergence of forms of environmental literature that are more recognizable as such today. Increases in literacy and leisure time created national audiences for such genres as the personal essay and the short story. The development of specialized fields of scientific study (including botany, zoology, ornithology, geology, astronomy, and anthropology) relegated natural history to an amateur pursuit—but consequently left natural history writers with a wide latitude in which to work. (The specialization of ecology was still a century off, but the German Darwinian Ernst Haeckel first used the term *oecologie* in 1866, and Darwin himself published *The Origin of Species* in 1859, opening the door to the ecological evolutionary worldview of many modern writers.) Furthermore, the writings of the Romantics also coincided with and helped spur the birth of what David Mazel has identified as forms of "early ecocriticism." As these changes were leading more and more writers to trumpet the virtues of "nature's nation" (P. Miller), they were also leading these same writers to embrace particular places with an intimacy never before seen in print. In the Northeast, an early version of this dual allegiance appears in the work of Washington Irving and James Fenimore Cooper, both of whom skillfully rendered the landscape of upstate New York from personal experience and used its history and folk-lore to invent a usable past for the nation. Another version can be seen in Cooper's concern about the costs of nation building, such as when Natty Bumppo, Cooper's quintessentially American "Leather-Stocking," mourns the "wasty ways" of his fellow pioneers, whose unrestrained hunting helped doom the passenger pigeon (J. Cooper 305). Using the local landscape as a symbol of the American wilderness was a dominant theme in much of the region's writing, including the novels of Nathaniel Hawthorne and Herman Melville and the poems of William Cullen Bryant and the schoolroom poets. And it can similarly be found, though much less explicitly, in the work of the southwestern humorists and in Edgar Allan Poe's Gothic tales. But it was in the nonfiction prose of Ralph Waldo Emerson and Henry David Thoreau—both residents of Concord, Massachusetts—that this tension between place and nation most thoroughly emerged.

"We have listened too long to the courtly muses of Europe," Emerson announced in "The American Scholar," and he more than Thoreau sought a truly national literature (70). Inspired by the landscape of Concord, Emerson nevertheless took philosophical flight from it, concerned more about "nature," generally speaking, than the particularities of place. In his first book, *Nature* (1836), Emerson spoke of "the woods" as if any American woods would do, claiming that in them "we return to reason and faith" (10). Laying out his vision of transcendental nationalism, Emerson stressed the need to transcend the material world and contemplate its spiritual aspect, arguing that Americans' "original relation to the universe" should come directly from nature, unmediated by history and tradition (7). Where Emerson was abstract, Thoreau was concrete, grounding his own metaphysical excursions in the biological realities of Concord's fields and forests. Thoreau also took the metaphor of "nature as spirit" and enriched it, adding a biting social criticism that nevertheless retained an element of Emersonian optimism. In *Walden* (1854), for instance, Thoreau offered a model of place-based spirituality (inspired in part by Susan Fenimore Cooper's *Rural Hours* [1850]) and wrapped his critique of nationalism and materialism in a thoroughgoing idealism about the promise of America. "[T]he only true America," Thoreau wrote,

> is that country where you are at liberty to pursue such a mode of life as may enable you to do without these [commodities], and where the state does not endeavor to compel you to sustain the slavery and war and other superfluous expenses which directly or indirectly result from the use of such things. ([1989] 205)

The tension between place and nation that lies at the heart of Romantic literature also played out in the hundreds of Western travel narratives that were published during this period, as well as in the many other works of environmental literature that both grew out of and helped foster the nation's manifest destiny, including John James Audubon's *Ornithological Biography* (1831–39), Thomas Cole's "Essay on American Scenery" (1836), Francis Parkman's *The Oregon Trail* (1849), George Perkins Marsh's *Man and Nature* (1864), and Frederick Law Olmsted's report "The Yosemite Valley and the Mariposa Big Trees" (1864).

Romanticism was ultimately wrecked, however, on the shoals of the Civil War, which solidified national identity at the cost of hundreds of thousands of lives and devastated much of the southern environment. Although many Romantic writers chose to ignore the war, turning instead to nature as a refuge from history, others—Emily Dickinson and Walt Whitman, in particular—managed to address its emotional and physical impacts without abandoning their long-standing investment in the natural world. African Americans, in contrast, found a more literal kind of refuge in wild landscapes, as many fugitive slave narratives attest, and as Harriet Beecher Stowe's *Uncle Tom's Cabin* (1852) vividly illustrates.

Age of Realism and Regionalism (1865–1900)

With the end of the Civil War and the beginning of Reconstruction, many of the nation's modern institutions began to grow in influence, and in three of these—the corporation, the museum, and the nonprofit organization— we can identify the major environmental worldviews of the age of realism and regionalism. In the corporation we can see the metaphor of "nature as resource," and with the completion of the transcontinental railroad in 1869 and the invention of both the telephone and the internal-combustion engine in 1876, corporations gained greater and faster access to both natural resources and information about those resources. In the museum, we can see the idea of "nature as object of study," a way of seeing also reflected in the rise of literary realism, which encouraged scientific accuracy in the representation of nature and eventually led to the "nature fakers" debate that questioned the truthfulness of Ernest Thompson Seton's *Wild Animals I Have Known* (1898) and other anthropomorphic wildlife stories (Lutts). And in the nonprofit organization, we can see "nature as endangered place," especially with the rise of such reform-minded conservation organizations as the Boone and Crockett Club (1887), the Sierra Club (1892), and the

Connecticut Audubon Society (1898), all of which were founded by American nature writers (Philippon).

If Romanticism arose in reaction to the Industrial Revolution, the environmental literature of the late nineteenth century was equally responsive to the increases in immigration and growth of the cities that accompanied industrialization. In particular, the rapid urbanization of the eastern United States spurred a "back to nature" movement that sent thousands of city dwellers outdoors to pursue nature study—particularly bird watching—as a relief from the stresses of urban life (Schmitt). The separation of "work" and "leisure" brought about by industrialization also led to the popularization of other, more strenuous activities, such as camping, hiking, and mountaineering, and together these varied recreational pursuits helped whet Americans' appetite for a wide range of environmental literature. Aided by new technologies for the mass production and distribution of books and magazines, and by the growing national market for literary work, writers responded in earnest, producing fictional and nonfictional texts about the environment almost as fast as publishers could sell them. Many of the era's attempts at producing a national fiction—such as the realist novels of William Dean Howells and Henry James—relegated the environment to the background, as a setting for human action, but much of the regional literature of the day, particularly that written by women, presented the environment as a character in its own right. Celia Thaxter's *Among the Isles of Shoals* (1873) and *An Island Garden* (1894), Sarah Orne Jewett's "A White Heron" (1886) and *The Country of the Pointed Firs* (1896), and Mabel Osgood Wright's *The Friendship of Nature* (1894), to name only a few such works from New England, all connected the experience of women in the domestic sphere to the health and well-being of the landscape that surrounded them. In the South and Midwest, regional literature took a slightly different tack, with "local color" often being provided principally by human characters; the major exception here is Mark Twain, whose *Life on the Mississippi* (1883) and *Adventures of Huckleberry Finn* (1884) became the foundational texts of an entire canon of Mississippi River literature.

Dominating the post-Thoreauvian nature writing of this period are "the two Johns"—John Burroughs ("John o' Birds") and John Muir ("John o' Mountains")—whose works are as distinct in subject matter and regional focus as they are in tone and approach. Burroughs, who was born and lived most of his life in the Catskill Mountains of New York, delighted in nearby nature, writing of the joys of rural life with a neighborly folksiness and a penchant for patient observation. Muir, a Scotsman raised in Wisconsin, was drawn to the rugged landscapes of California's Sierra Nevada, the preservation of which he helped to ensure through his energetic prose and outspoken political activism. Burroughs's *Riverby* and Muir's *The Mountains of California*, both published in 1894, illustrate these differences well. While Burroughs describes the birds and flowers he meets in his walks around the neighborhood, Muir climbs to the top of a hundred-foot-high Douglas spruce during a wind storm so he might "enjoy so noble an exhilaration of motion" (Muir 176). Despite their differences, these two men both shared a national stage that changed them immensely. Deeply influenced by Emerson's transcendental nationalism, they both published widely in the leading magazines of their day and eventually became friends with some of the nation's foremost industrialists, all of which contributed a complexity of meaning to their writings that remains to this day.

That Muir's reputation has continued to rise in popularity while Burroughs's has declined, however, reflects a shift in literary interest from east to west that also began to take effect during this period. Just as the Hudson River school of landscape painters was followed by the Rocky Mountain school, so did increasing numbers of environmental writers gradually turn their attention westward as the nation's knowledge of this unfamiliar landscape began to grow. Many of the West's explorers and surveyors were themselves the authors of classics of environmental writing, including Clarence King's *Mountaineering in the Sierra Nevada* (1872), John Wesley Powell's *Exploration of the Colorado River* (1875), and Clarence Dutton's *Tertiary History of the Grand Cañon District* (1882). Others approached the West through the lenses of realism—such as Theodore Roosevelt in *Hunting Trips of a Ranchman* (1885)—and through realism's literary offshoot, naturalism, such as Stephen Crane in "The Blue Hotel" (1897) and "The Bride Comes to Yellow Sky" (1898). In part because of the efforts of Muir, Roosevelt, and other environmental writers, the federal government began to protect portions of the West during this period, particularly through the creation of the national forests and the national parks, such as Yellowstone (established in 1872) and Yosemite (established in 1890). But as the reach of the federal government extended farther and farther into the West, American Indian writers (such as Charles Eastman and Zitkala-Sa) were also finding their voice, and the particular kind of regionalism they advocated would eventually evolve into much more militant forms of resistance.

The age of realism and regionalism culminated, in a way, in the World's Columbian Exposition of 1893, the "white city" that stood on the shores of Lake Michigan throughout the summer and fall of that year. To many at the time, nature appeared confined to the "wooded island" in the middle of the fairgrounds, a romantic remnant of the "continuous bolt of fabric" that once was America. But in fact the nature of realism and regionalism was all around them—a "collection of objects" that had been dominated, harnessed, and transformed—in the horticulture, agriculture, and fisheries buildings; in machinery hall, the mines and mining building, and the electricity building; and even in the railroad terminal that brought Americans by the millions to Chicago, "nature's metropolis" (Cronon). The challenge for environmental writers in the twentieth century became determining exactly what to do with such knowledge.

Notes

1. For an insightful meditation on the relation between environmental history and national history, see R. White ("Nationalization"). See Olwig for a detailed discussion of "the interlinked meanings of landscape and nature, and the ways they have variously been used to define the body politic" in Britain and America (xxiii). For a postmodern reconsideration of the idea of the United States as "nature's nation," see Mazel, *American Literary Environmentalism*.

2. Excerpts from this and several of the other primary texts I cite conveniently appear in Branch, *Reading*.

Annie Merrill Ingram

United States Environmental Literature of the Twentieth Century and Beyond

United States environmental literature of the twentieth century in many ways defines the field: other than *Walden*, the most frequently taught works in environmental literature courses are all twentieth-century texts: Mary Austin's *The Land of Little Rain*, Aldo Leopold's *A Sand County Almanac*, Rachel Carson's *Silent Spring*, Edward Abbey's *Desert Solitaire*, Annie Dillard's *Pilgrim at Tinker Creek*, Leslie Marmon Silko's *Ceremony*, and Terry Tempest Williams's *Refuge*.[1] While these texts represent one version of an emerging canon of environmental literature (a canon with a clearly presentist bias), they also share characteristics typical of United States environmental literature after the nineteenth century: a movement away from the generalities of a geographically defined region to the particularities of a human-identified place, along with a shift from "nature writing" to "environmental writing." The late-nineteenth-century debates over the role of nature in national politics opened up a new consciousness about people's responsibilities toward the natural world. The legacy of John Muir's fight for the preservation of Hetch Hetchy Valley in Yosemite is variously represented by writers who defend the beauty of underappreciated topographies (such as Austin and Abbey on the desert); those who educate readers about ecological destruction in lyrical, accessible prose

(Leopold and Carson); and those who make individuals' struggles indicative of larger sociocultural ills (Dillard's theodicy; Silko's and Williams's protests against nuclear testing). While the theme of solitary retreat to a remote spot of wilderness remains prevalent in some twentieth-century environmental texts, a growing awareness of the national and international significance of nature characterizes twentieth-century environmental literature's increasing engagement with the human-constructed world as well as with the natural world.

In the first decades of the twentieth century, United States environmental literature continued the nineteenth century's interest in regionalism and celebration of America's diverse geography with the addition of incisive cultural criticism. Nostalgia for the past and a critique of the present found voice in works that foregrounded livelihoods and places endangered by the country's increasing urbanization and industrialization. Liberty Hyde Bailey, a farm horticulturist and dean of the College of Agriculture at Cornell University, was an early proponent of the modern environmentalist ethic. He argues in *The Holy Earth* (1915) that the "dominion" of humans over the land "has been mostly destructive"; as an antidote to the destructive powers of greed and devastation, Bailey asserts that "the living creation is not exclusively man-centered: it is bio-centric" (247, 254). A resistance to anthropocentrism similarly characterizes Austin's *The Land of Little Rain*, in which the scavenging creatures and arid climate of the desert are as much protagonists of the narrative as the miners and indigenous peoples who dwell in the Owens Valley and Sierra Nevada foothills. Willa Cather's novels of prairie farm life *O Pioneers!* and *My Ántonia* chronicle the struggles of immigrants to work the land, a land whose immensity and stark beauty humble its inhabitants into awed appreciation. The more populated, longer-settled, and earlier-industrialized New England environments had their own champions in this period. Henry Beston's *The Outermost House*, a latter-day Thoreauvian narrative set on Cape Cod, hearkens back to *Walden*'s restorative solitude and critique of encroaching technology, while its biocentric approach to the animals and ecology of the Great Beach situates it squarely in a twentieth-century sensibility. The poetry of Robert Frost gave voice to the New England working class and highlighted the region's birches, pastures, stone walls, woods, apple trees, ponds, and fields. Like the work of Wendell Berry a generation later, Frost's poetry honors rural agrarian life without romanticizing it. Frost's contemporary, Robinson Jeffers, shared Frost's misanthropic cynicism as well as his appreciation for wild beauty in lyric and narrative poems about his home in Carmel, California, where the sounds of hawks, vultures, gulls, rocks, and crashing surf could almost drown out the sound of encroaching suburban civilization.

As the nation continued its rapid industrialization, writers of the middle decades of the century responded with works that showed how specific and beloved environments were suffering from the effects of human exploitation of natural resources. John Steinbeck's novel about Dust Bowl migrants, *The Grapes of Wrath*, particularized the experience of millions of displaced rural people during the Depression. William Faulkner's novels set in fictional Yoknapatawpha County, Mississippi, not only put Southern literature on the national literary map but also placed that tradition directly on the land, a terrain of swamps, cotton fields, and wisteria. The best-known and most influential work of this period, Leopold's *A Sand County Almanac* (published posthumously in 1949), outlined his conservationist theories and detailed his experiences at his farm on the Wisconsin River, where on the weekends he put into practice the principles of forestry and game management he taught during the week at the University of Wisconsin. In *A Sand County Almanac*, Leopold's articulation of a long-term biocentric perspective (in "Thinking Like a Mountain"), the significance of wilderness preservation, and his essays on "the land ethic" and a "conservation esthetic" won him recognition as one of the most important environmental writers of the twentieth century. Marjory Stoneman Douglas's *The Everglades: River of Grass* lovingly describes this endangered ecosystem and traces the history of its inhabitants from indigenous people to explorers to the modern-day conquerors whose impact seriously threatens the health of this fragile and complex environment. Joseph Wood Krutch's *The Voice of the Desert* stands between the work of Austin and Abbey as another testament to the remarkable life of desert regions, one that combines detailed natural history description with thoughtful reflection on animal consciousness. In passages that anticipate Dillard's fascination with intricacy and fecundity in *Pilgrim at Tinker Creek*, Krutch wonders at the lives of the Sonoran spadefoot toad, roadrunner, and tarantula.

The landmark work of twentieth-century environmental consciousness raising is Carson's *Silent Spring*, a work of carefully researched nonfiction that details the damaging effects of chemical pesticides on soil, water, air, flora, and fauna (including humans). Her articulation of rigorous scientific evidence in graceful prose won her a huge audience as well as the attention of the chemical industry (which mounted a vituperative campaign against her) and the United States government (which eventually banned the manufacture and use of DDT in the United States). Closely following the publication of *Silent Spring* was the passage of the Wilderness Act in 1964, whose purpose was "to establish a National Wilderness Preservation System for the permanent good of the whole people, and for other purposes" ("Wilderness Act" 120).[2] Other social developments of the 1960s and 1970s, including the civil rights and women's movements, combined with the creation of the Environmental Protection Agency and the first Earth Day in 1970, heralded a new era of environmental consciousness and a number of new developments in United States environmental literature.

Two of the leading figures in the post-Carson era of environmental literature are Gary Snyder and Wendell Berry. They began their writing careers in the late 1950s with the publication of poetry, Snyder with *Riprap* in 1959, and Berry with the poems that would later be collected in *The Broken Ground* (1964). Both also work in the genre of the essay, and Berry writes fiction as well, including a series of novels set in fictional Port William, Kentucky, a place as vivid and complex as Faulkner's Yoknapatawpha. Snyder's Pulitzer Prize–winning *Turtle Island* (1974) articulates his place-based philosophy in a collection of poetry (and a few essays) that starts by apostrophizing the ancient Anasazi people and ends "Everywhere, / At once."[3] Snyder and Berry continue to be activist writers today, most notably with Berry's impassioned responses to the events following September 11, 2001 (*In the Presence of Fear* [2001] and "Citizen's Response" [2003]), and Snyder's call for a politics of "reinhabitation." While they arrive at a common goal of critiquing contemporary consumerist culture, Snyder's primary influences are Eastern (Zen Buddhism, Chinese poetry), whereas Berry's are Western (Judeo-Christianity). Snyder's defense of wildness in *The Practice of the Wild* (1990) underscores his commitment to defining our home places not by political boundaries but by the natural zones of watersheds. Berry's work clearly derives from an American tradition of populist agrarianism, yet his support of the American family farm is not nostalgic. Rather, in works such as *The Unsettling of America* (1977), Berry links the decline of culture and agriculture to larger forces of mechanization and moral bankruptcy. A third writer whose politics significantly informed his literary work is Abbey. The nonfiction *Desert Solitaire* lambastes how industrial tourism disrupts the pristine beauty of Arches National Monument (near Moab, Utah). His novel *The Monkey-Wrench Gang* (1975), which chronicles the ecoterrorist activities of four idiosyncratic characters working together in the Utah-Arizona canyon country, inspired the formation of Earth First!, the radical environmental organization.

   Although women writers were active in producing environmental literature in the early decades of the twentieth century, the 1970s women's
movement brought a new focus on the gendered female experience in and
of nature. Works like Susan Griffin's *Woman and Nature: The Roaring
Inside Her* (1978) and Carolyn Merchant's *The Death of Nature: Women,
Ecology, and the Scientific Revolution* (1980) established ecofeminism as
an approach to the environment that explicitly associates the degradation
of the land with the degradation of women and argues for a new consciousness that foregrounds women's particular, embodied experience as
an important counteraction to androcentric, patriarchal environmental
abuse. Some of the work of this era explicitly rewrites the male experience from a female perspective—for example, Anne La Bastille's revision
of *Walden* in *Woodswoman*, which recounts her experience of a year of
solitary living on a lake in the Adirondacks. The work of Ann Zwinger
(*Beyond the Aspen Grove* [1970] and *Run, River, Run* [1975]) and Gretel
Ehrlich (*The Solace of Open Spaces* [1985]) places these women in their
home environments in the American West, where, with the keen observation of the naturalist, they advocate for the significance of wild lands.
Mary Oliver's poetry connects a love for nature to a love for self, in which
natural environments can inspire healing transformation. Dillard's Pulitzer
Prize–winning *Pilgrim at Tinker Creek* captures the wonder of manifold
creation while it contemplates the theological implications of a god who
created such a profligate, extravagant world.

   Even more overtly political are works such as Williams's *Refuge*, which
links climatological abnormality (the rising of the water level of the Great
Salt Lake) to biological abnormality (her mother's struggle with breast
cancer). *Refuge* is subtitled *An Unnatural History of Family and Place*,
clearly signaling both the tradition of natural history that informs it and
the departure from that norm necessitated by the horrors of above-ground
nuclear testing. Other women writers break from previous traditions of
nature writing by creating utopian science fiction: Ursula K. Le Guin's
The Left Hand of Darkness (1969) highlights the constructedness of gender roles through the presentation of an androgynous race of beings, and
The Dispossessed: An Ambiguous Utopia (1974) warns of the dangers of
colonialism and its inevitable cultural clashes. Le Guin's legacy of ecofeminist science fiction has influenced other women writers, including Marge
Piercy in *Woman on the Edge of Time* (1976), Octavia Butler in *Parable
of the Sower* (1993), and Starhawk in *The Fifth Sacred Thing* (1993), all
of whom envision alternative future societies that implicitly or explicitly

critique patriarchal gender politics and current practices of environmental destruction.

By the late twentieth century, new genres broadened the scope and audience of environmental literature and expanded definitions of what constitutes "environment." The literature of environmental justice includes fiction, poetry, drama, and creative nonfiction works that narrate the injustices of environmental racism and advocate the institutional transformations necessary to overcome these injustices—including the need to move environmental literature beyond its roots in a white, middle-class experience of nature. Cherríe Moraga's play *Heroes and Saints* (1994) and Helena Maria Viramontes's novel *Under the Feet of Jesus* (1995) address the consequences of migrant farmworkers' exposure to toxic agricultural chemicals. The environmental racism targeted at Native American communities is portrayed in Silko's novel *Ceremony*; in Linda Hogan's novel *Solar Storms* (1995); and in the poetry of Simon Ortiz, Ofelia Zepeda, Margo Tamez, and others. Winona LaDuke surveys environmental injustice throughout Native American lands in *All Our Relations: Native Struggles for Land and Life* (1999). Additional novels by Ana Castillo (*So Far from God* [1993]) and Barbara Neely (*Blanche Cleans Up* [1998]) relate the toxic effects of both corporate greed and social bigotry in the American Southwest and urban Boston, respectively.

Other new genres and current environmental issues suggest future trends of United States environmental literature in the twenty-first century. The growing genre of urban nature writing is especially relevant now, at a time when most American citizens live in urban or suburban areas. The very real threat of global environmental catastrophe has inspired a number of postapocalyptic, dystopian environmental works, including Jean Hegland's *Into the Forest* (1996) and T. C. Boyle's *A Friend of the Earth* (2000). As globalization threatens natural environments and traditional cultures worldwide, environmental writers increasingly turn their attention and powers to creating narratives that promote positive alternatives for cultural survival and ecological preservation. Transnational approaches to ecocriticism and environmental writing, along with border studies and multilingual works, will no doubt also influence future United States environmental literature. As environments continue to be politicized, so will environmental writing.

Notes

1. For evidence of the most-taught works of environmental literature, see Christensen and Blakemore's introduction to the syllabi collection on the Asso-

ciation for the Study of Literature and Environment Web site (www.asle.umn
.edu/pubs/collect/intro.html), the "Nature Writing Poll" (www.asle.umn.edu/
archive/biblios/poll.html), and Milkweed Editions' *World as Home* survey results
(www.asle.umn.edu/archive/biblios/topten.txt).

2. I quote from the preamble of Public Law 88-577, Senate bill 4, passed
by the 88th Congress on 3 September 1964; for a reprinting of the entire act, see
"Wilderness Act."

3. Final two lines of "As for Poets."

Part III

Teaching North American Environmental Literature

Laird Christensen

Introduction:
A Range of Approaches

In the two decades since the Modern Language Association published *Teaching Environmental Literature*, college courses that explore the intersection of literary and environmental studies have flourished in number and variety, in the classroom and beyond. No longer is it especially remarkable to spot an English professor leading a crew of students, journals in hand, to the fields or forests behind the campus. Those early attempts to design courses in environmental literature (which usually featured some blend of Henry David Thoreau and Annie Dillard, with a dash of Edward Abbey and a couple Gary Snyder poems thrown in) have given way to classes that turn a sophisticated ecocritical gaze on topics from Shakespeare to postcolonial literature. The significance of this interdisciplinary approach is confirmed by its growth in popularity and institutional support. Where once a few like-minded scholars gathered at regional conferences to argue that landscape might mean something more than setting, now more than a thousand belong to the Association for the Study of Literature and Environment (ASLE).

In the early years of ecocriticism, Fred Waage's *Teaching Environmental Literature* was one of very few places where instructors could turn to discover what their counterparts were doing at other institutions. That prescient collection of essays blended models of successful courses with visions of possibilities not yet attempted. Beyond its usefulness as a teaching resource, however, perhaps the greatest value of *Teaching Environmental Literature* was its announcement to those instructors scattered across the country, trailing their different drummer in apparent isolation, that they in fact belonged to a community.

Like *Teaching Environmental Literature*, the present collection of essays offers an album of snapshots, as it were, detailing the teaching methods of more than two dozen instructors. Just as we do not presume that nothing occurred between the pictures in a photo album, so we should not assume that the obvious gaps between these essays imply a lack of other approaches to teaching environmental literature. Indeed, for every essay included in this volume, we were forced to set aside many fine submissions. We were inspired and humbled to find ourselves sorting through evidence of so much innovative teaching. In the end, we chose to feature those essays that suggested the widest possible range of pedagogies. To avoid giving a skewed impression of how such courses are generally taught, however, we offer an overview of approaches to teaching environmental literature, made possible by the membership of ASLE.

The formation of ASLE in 1992 opened up new possibilities for dialogue and exchange between teachers of environmental literature, and it quickly solidified the community of scholars that Fred Waage had imagined back in 1985. I have often wondered how many foundering academic careers were rescued by ASLE. Certainly mine was. Disillusioned by the challenges of trying to study environmental literature at a large midwestern university, I was preparing to leave graduate school after completing my master's examinations. Although I was researching the work of George Perkins Marsh and Thoreau, my studies seemed always to lead me away from the wildness that inspired their words. Looking back, I recall with more amusement than frustration a professor's response to my study of Robinson Jeffers's poetry as deep ecology: "Spike trees on your own time," he advised. "You're here to study literature." It was a drier life than I preferred, less engaged than I could tolerate, and I was prepared to leave it behind when I received a flier announcing the formation of ASLE. Simply knowing that such a community existed gave me the faith to search out a doctoral program that valued a more interdisciplinary, experiential approach to literature.

My experience illustrates the primary function of ASLE, which is to sustain the community of scholars and teachers who share an interest in literature and environment. One step toward fulfilling this mission is to encourage dialogue about the courses we teach. Almost from the start ASLE has hosted an electronic discussion list, but the organization also tries to provide its members with more permanent resources.[1] One such resource is *The ASLE Collection of Syllabi in Literature and Environment*, which Peter Blakemore and I began compiling while serving as ASLE's graduate liaisons (Christensen and Blakemore).[2] By the time we finished editing the collection in November of 1998, it was clear that this sampling offered more than just a resource for other instructors. A careful examination of more than two hundred syllabi provides a glimpse of how curricular and teaching practices had evolved in the years since the appearance of Fred Waage's volume. Moreover, when considered alongside the increasingly diverse approaches included in the present volume, the collection reveals a community of teachers that is sufficiently self-aware to adjust and readjust its curricula, building on the innovations of others in the field.

Now, our sampling of syllabi is in no way scientific: Peter Blakemore and I simply solicited syllabi from the ASLE membership and received 208 submissions. Nor is our sampling comprehensive. I know of many relevant courses that were not submitted for inclusion in this collection. Nonetheless, I do believe that *The ASLE Collection of Syllabi in Literature and Environment* has much to tell us about how such courses have generally been taught. The following observations are meant to provide a basic context that might bring into relief the new approaches described in this volume.[3]

Trends in Teaching Environmental Literature

Most syllabi we received came from campuses across the United States, although sixteen of the courses were taught in Canada, Japan, Great Britain, Australia, and South Africa. They reveal that the teaching of literature and environment is not limited to one or another type of institution, nor to any particular region. Such courses are taught in liberal arts institutions, Ivy League schools, community colleges, and research universities. Of the 208 syllabi we received, 136 came from four-year public universities, led by the University of Nevada, Reno, and the University of Oregon (in part, because of their well-developed graduate programs in the field and the involvement of their faculty members in ASLE). The West is better represented than other parts of the United States, as one might expect of a field that first defined itself at gatherings of the Western Literature Association: seventy-seven of the syllabi came from west of the hundredth meridian, while forty-nine came from the Midwest, thirty-one from the Northeast, and twenty-three from the South. However, when one discounts the programs with specific curricular emphases in the field (the Universities of Nevada, Reno; Oregon; and California, Davis), the number of courses in the West falls to thirty-nine. It is worth noting that the concentration of such courses in Reno, Eugene, and Davis reflects an institutional commitment to environmental studies that could be duplicated in any region of the country. (While the abundance of undeveloped public lands in the West certainly encourages greater familiarity with wilderness, most ecocritics are well aware that "environment" is not a concept defined by the absence of human population.)[4]

Of the syllabi we received, one-third of them describe general surveys of environmental literature. This is not surprising for a new field of study: such courses function like a pioneer species, popping up in the open territory between disciplines. Once they have proved their worth, they create a suitable habitat for more specialized courses. Their primary survival technique—the way in which they fend off institutional skepticism—is to favor authors with solid literary reputations. Who would object to a literature course that features Thoreau, Herman Melville, or Willa Cather? (True, the appearance on a syllabus of someone like Abbey might send a few eyebrows arching, especially among administrators who know his work only by reputation, but instructors often distract the skeptic by flashing a few Pulitzer Prize winners, such as Dillard, Snyder, or Mary Oliver.)

The author listed most frequently in the syllabi we received—both in surveys and in more specialized classes—is Thoreau, whose work is assigned in eighty-two of the courses, followed by Abbey, in seventy courses. (In Thoreau's case, *Walden* is nearly always the required text; instructors who assign Abbey prefer *Desert Solitaire*, but only slightly, to *The Monkey-Wrench Gang*.) These authors are in a league of their own, based on number of appearances, followed at a distance by Aldo Leopold and Annie Dillard, each of whom appears in at least fifty syllabi. Other authors whose work appears in more than thirty syllabi are Terry Tempest Williams, John Muir, Barry Lopez, Gary Snyder, Leslie Marmon Silko, and Rachel Carson.

If we were to take these ten authors and create a syllabus around their major works, we would have a typical survey of environmental literature. I do not mean to sound dismissive: the first course I taught in this field, more than a dozen years ago, included most of those authors, and I continue to assign Thoreau, Leopold, Dillard, Snyder, and Silko in Images of Nature, a course required of all first-year students here at Green Mountain College. Indeed, it would be difficult to introduce students to North American environmental literature without some reference to these authors.

Of course, the risk of such consistency is that we create and reinforce a canon of environmental literature—which, like all canons, manages to exclude more than it includes. One of the most encouraging features of *Teaching North American Environmental Literature* is the picture it presents of how instructors resist this trend. As veterans of past skirmishes over canonization, most of us are eager to prevent our reading lists from ossifying, no matter how important those authors may be. Increasingly one finds in our syllabi ecocritical examinations of authors not usually associated with "nature writing," whether Don DeLillo or Toni Morrison. In addition, more and more writers of color are showing up in our syllabi, from Zora Neale Hurston to Ana Castillo. The move to diversify our reading lists should not be mistaken for token adherence to political correctness. It has simply become obvious to most instructors that a syllabus limited to European American voices fails to reflect the blend of cultures that have shaped and been shaped by North American environments. In addition to their fundamental inaccuracy, syllabi that assign only European American authors invite and justify charges of parochialism and irrelevance. Just as biological diversity can provide stability for ecological communities, so cultural diversity in a syllabus creates a steadier base from which to study the influence on human cultures of distinctive North American habitats.

While general surveys of environmental literature dominate ASLE syllabi, there is no shortage of more specialized approaches in the collection. The twenty interdisciplinary syllabi are generally from courses in other disciplines that use literary texts to illustrate a theme or reveal a historical process. The collection includes courses from architecture, journalism, geography, theater, and history, as well as a number of broadly conceived liberal arts courses that use literature to explore the interface between environment and culture. Another eighteen syllabi are from courses that teach composition through the use of environmental literature. David Sumner, who examined these syllabi in an article originally written for *The Ecocomposition Reader* and reprinted in Christian R. Weisser and Sidney I. Dolorin's *Ecocomposition*, observes that they fall into three categories: "environmental studies courses with a strong writing component, environmental literature courses with an emphasis on the skills necessary to write about literature, and composition courses with environmental readings that employ a 'mode' theory of composition" (265). The other types of courses most often included in the ASLE collection are those that explore a specific literary period, author, or theme and those that take bioregional or ecofeminist approaches to literature. Each of these categories is represented in *Teaching North American Environmental Literature*, and some were even included in Fred Waage's earlier volume. What is remarkable is the extent to which current approaches have been shaped by an interdisciplinary sophistication that would have been difficult to imagine in 1985.

One other trend worth observing in *The ASLE Collection of Syllabi in Literature and Environment* is the emphasis courses place on experiential learning. Nearly a quarter of the syllabi require students to keep journals— a percentage I suspect would be even higher today—not only to record responses to readings but also to reflect on their interactions with the local environment. Many of those courses require students to engage in environmental-perception projects, in which a series of journaling prompts asks students to become familiar with a specific observation post in ways that expand their normal frames of perception.[5] Field trips are another component of many of these syllabi. John Elder, who has long championed an embodied approach to teaching literature, recognizes the need to do more than simply lead students out of the classroom: "Many of us who teach nature writing delight in outings with our classes, in order to ground our discussions in observations like those the writers themselves made," he explains.[6] "We have arrived at a point, however, where we need to begin integrating this experiential dimension of teaching and scholarship in a more strategic way" ("Poetry" [1999] 650). One of the most exciting aspects of the present volume is the diversity of methods by which instructors follow Elder's advice in integrating textual and physical experiences.

There are three main patterns, then, present in the ASLE syllabi collection that reappear, in more sophisticated form, in *Teaching North American Environmental Literature*. First, an active resistance to canonization now seems firmly embedded in nearly every essay we considered for this volume. Even courses that retain an emphasis on the dominant tradition of environmental literature are careful to situate major authors in a context that includes previously excluded perspectives, as well as some consideration of the politics of inclusion and exclusion. Second, the growing presence on campuses of environmental literature surveys (those pioneer species) has created a "habitat" in which increasingly specialized courses can flourish. Other than those essays we solicited to provide some introductory context for this volume, we saw very few proposals that offered any sort of broad overview of the field. These specialized approaches to teaching environmental literature also demonstrate a more mature relationship with interdisciplinary scholarship and pedagogy: it no longer seems such a stretch for an English professor to discuss thermodynamics or forest succession in a literature course. And, finally, many of the essays included here demonstrate a growing facility at integrating intellectual knowledge and physical engagement in a local ecosystem. Those of us who have struggled in our classes to find the right balance between these two ways of knowing understand how productive those struggles can be, reshaping us as teachers. I trust that some of the methods modeled in this volume will lead us toward even more challenges, which always seem to offer unexpected lessons.

The diverse approaches to teaching environmental literature gathered in this volume present their own challenges in terms of categorization. After a long day of sorting through essay proposals, arranging and rearranging stacks on a long conference table, the editors finally chose to group the essays according to a sequence of perspectives defined by the crossing of two boundaries: the one that separates English literature from other disciplines, and the one that separates the classroom from the places where we live. At times the distinctions between our own categories will flicker and vanish, reminiscent of the biological overlap, or edge effect, that occurs in an ecotone. We accept that as a risk inherent in trying to impose precise distinctions on sets of dynamic, evolving processes.

So, if we imagine three concentric rings, each of which represents a different pedagogical context, the innermost ring represents English literature. Here, in "Disciplinary Approaches," a story or poem is examined primarily as a literary work within a dominant cultural tradition. The next concentric ring, "Interdisciplinary Approaches," represents how the study of literature complements, or is informed by, some other conventional academic discipline. Finally, the outermost ring moves beyond culture to the world itself, those life-sustaining biotic processes that form the fundamental context of any human activity. The essays in "Place-Based Approaches" describe courses that use literature to encourage a personal and physical engagement between students and their specific bioregions. Even as we begin with "Disciplinary Approaches," however, we find courses that refuse to be contained by conventional literary boundaries and expectations. When Anne Raine describes her classroom experience in "Teaching American Modernism as Environmental Writing," she confesses that she is drawn to this period precisely "because modernism's paradoxical

embrace of nature and modernity anticipates the ambivalence" of less environmentally inclined students. While Raine makes original use of a conventional period, Bernard Quetchenbach pokes holes in the boundary
between modernist and contemporary poetry in his essay, "Post–World
War II American Poetry as Environmental Literature." Of course, the transition between one and another literary period is usually much more gradual
than an undergraduate literature survey might suggest, but Quetchenbach
clearly demonstrates the continuity between various late-modernist spheres
of influence and contemporary environmental poetry.

In "'Ready to Come Home': Teaching African American Literature
as Environmental Literature," Jeffrey Myers opens a door that has long
been, at best, ajar. After considering reasons why African American writers
have often been left out of environmental literature courses, Myers makes
the case that many African Americans seem obvious choices for inclusion
in our syllabi—once we have redefined what counts as environmental literature. In a similar fashion, Joni Adamson expands our options for inviting
American Indian writers into our courses in "For the Sake of the Land and
All People: Teaching American Indian Literatures from an Environmental
Justice Perspective." Too often our courses rely on stories and poems that
model a grounded indigenous culture, she argues, while neglecting the
fact that American Indians continue to fight for their identity—and, in many
cases, their lives—against economic and environmental exploitation. As
essential as it is to include a diverse representation of American experiences in environmental literature courses, Scott Slovic's essay, "Teaching
United States Environmental Literature in a World Comparatist Context,"
demonstrates how we might gain additional insight into our own tradition
by comparing North American environmental writing with the literature
produced in Latin America, Australia, and the Pacific Rim.

Effective literature courses often function as conversations between
writers with different perspectives, but introducing students to those voices
is only the first step. Our methods for encouraging students to try on
new ideas are every bit as important, as SueEllen Campbell demonstrates in "Asking Ecocritical Questions." With remarkable thoroughness,
Campbell shares questions that can help students discover personal and
cultural relevance in any text. Katherine R. Chandler illustrates another
method of engaging students in "'The Machine in the Garden': Using
Electronic Portfolios to Teach Environmental Literature." Chandler's
decision to bring computers into her class Landscape and Literature convinced her that "the computer world can be as instructive as is the natural

world." Finally, while it has become common to use environmental literature in composition courses, Cheryl C. Smith models a new approach in
"Giving Voice to the Novice Authority: *Silent Spring* in the Composition
Classroom." By requiring students to discover independent research topics in Carson's groundbreaking book, Smith argues for the value of asking
students "to embrace their own initial lack of authority on a subject and to
let their knowledge develop as they write."

The following section, "Interdisciplinary Approaches," opens with
Glen A. Love's essay, "Teaching Environmental Literature on the Planet
Indivisible." Love, a pioneer of ecocriticism, has long argued the need to
root literary criticism in biology, honoring cultural distinctions while also
insisting that we must not overlook the traits that unite us as a species. In
this essay, Love describes his use of E. O. Wilson's *Biophilia* to enable a
comparatist approach to literature that moves freely between the sciences
and humanities. Barbara Barney Nelson also brings together biology and
literature in her essay, "Predators in Literature," based on a course of the
same name. Nelson encourages her students to develop advanced analytic
skills by assessing competing claims about predator behavior in literature,
history, and politics. Another model, "Reading the Landscape: Prairie
Education through American Literature," describes Mary Stark's collaboration with ecologist Stephen Johnson in a class that combined literary
accounts of a prairie ecosystem, long since plowed under in Iowa, with
slides and lectures that recover an absent natural history.

David Landis Barnhill, in "East Asian Influence on Recent North
American Nature Writing," describes the experience of exploring environmental texts in the interdisciplinary context of Asian studies, providing students an opportunity to wrestle with the important question of "whether,
how, and how much American writers can in fact adopt and adapt a 'foreign tradition.'" Other instructors are more interested in using literature to
help students reflect critically on the dominant values of our own culture.
Cheryl J. Fish, for example, in "Environmental Justice Issues in Literature
and Film: From the Toxic to the Sustainable," describes how the right
blend of poems, essays, and films can help students "see the complicated
nexus of resistance, compromise, 'progress,' and identity; although toxins
in our lands and cities impact us differently, they affect us all." William
Slaymaker, in "Ethnic Ecoethics: Multicultural Environmental Philosophy
and Literature," considers what we can learn about our own ethical constructs by exploring those of other cultures—particularly American Indian
nations of his own Great Lakes region. By choosing to teach environmental

philosophy through examples provided by contemporary Anishinaabe authors, Slaymaker demonstrates the postmodern possibilities of incorporating Western and non-Western philosophies into a workable ethic.

In "Teaching the Literature of Agriculture," Christopher Cobb explores environmental literature through the lens of agroecology, observing that farming is the practice by which our culture "is made out of nature." While encouraging familiarity with the Western tradition of agrarian writing, Cobb also models courses that focus on contemporary agricultural issues, such as the growing prevalence of genetically modified organisms or the loss of family farms. In "Ecofeminist Canadian Literature," Alanna F. Bondar confronts some of the challenges of creating a course in Canadian ecofeminist literature—beginning with the question of whether such a thing as Canadian ecofeminism even exists. Bondar proposes an agenda for developing such a course, including a system of classifications, questions of efficacy, and a roster of writers to teach.

I have long complained to friends, tongue in cheek, about the logo of ASLE, which features the silhouette of a person reading a book beneath a leafy hardwood. With each new mailing from ASLE, I tell them, I hope to find only the book beneath the tree, having inspired the reader to go out and explore the world beyond its pages. The essays included in the final section of part 3, "Place-Based Approaches," describe classes that use literature to encourage greater intimacy with the places where we live. We begin with an essay by Hal Crimmel, who provides a broad overview in "Place-Based Courses and Teaching Literature Outdoors." After explaining the educational value of regionally focused courses, Crimmel describes a variety of experiential approaches to environmental literature, proposing several models that are distinguished by the amount of time students spend out of the classroom.

This is not to suggest that less experiential classes cannot lead students to a greater familiarity with their local ecosystems, as Cheryll Goltfelty demonstrates in "Finding Home in Nevada? Teaching the Literature of Place, on Location." Based on her experiences with a class called Nevada in Literature, Glotfelty reveals the power of stories and writing assignments to forge an emotional connection between the reader and the local landscape. Following stories to a deeper experience of place is also essential to John R. Harris's class, Place, Community, and American Culture. In his essay, "Teaching Place and Community History to Undergraduates," Harris describes his attempts to push back the boundaries of what we define as *text* to include historical records, and even the landscape itself.[7]

Sometimes the instructor's greatest challenge is simply to help students recognize that their daily experiences are shaped by the place they call home—and *place*, in the context of human communities, usually means more than a host ecosystem. In "Children of the Asphalt: The Nature of Los Angeles Literature," J. Scott Bryson describes adapting his training in nature writing to a teaching position in the Southern California sprawl. By creating a first-year course around the theme of Los Angeles literature, Bryson helps students develop their skills in writing and analysis, understand the many layers of experience that define their city, and create a lasting sense of place by contributing to a public Web site on Los Angeles literature. In "The Trouble with Texts; or, Green Cultural Studies in Texas," Stacy Alaimo works through a similar challenge in "the North Texas metroplex, where no soaring mountains or raging oceans announce their presence, only a disregarded river and miles and miles of highways and suburban sprawl." By asking students to perform local field work that combines analyses of the relevant natural and cultural influences and by exploring the tensions inherent in a landscape that derives its meaning both from culture and nature, Alaimo opens the possibility of establishing a connection between her students and environmental writing.

The power of a personal experience, as expressed through writing, is also at the heart of Randall Roorda's "Living as Equipment for Literature: The Summer Environmental Writing Program." Like the groundbreaking New England Literature Program, which Walter Clark described in *Teaching Environmental Literature*, Roorda's program models a two-step approach to environmental education: after spending much of their time learning the local landscape with scientists and specialists, students are asked to integrate this knowledge into their own lives through personal-writing projects—"to make literature with the equipment of living," as Roorda explains. In "Experientially Teaching Canadian Travel Literature on the Trail and in the Classroom," Bob Henderson describes how literature informs an outdoor-education curriculum set in the north woods of Ontario. Henderson deftly links the literature to specific activities that the students engage in while traveling through a landscape that is "peppered" with stories. Heading south, Jerry Keir, in "'Come to Paradise—While It Lasts': Literary Ecology on Mexico's Costa Alegre," explains how literature adds another dimension to a remarkable interdisciplinary program on the coast of Mexico. From the poetry of José Emilio Pacheco to the fiction of Juan Rulfo, Keir uses literature to help students from the United States understand how cultural issues such as exploitation of *campesinos* and the effects of ecotourism play a role in shaping the biotic community they explore.

The remarkable diversity of approaches included in this section testifies to the health and vigor of our field and reveals just how innovative instructors have been in adapting earlier approaches to environmental literature. It also raises the bar in terms of what new hybrid courses we might expect to see in the future. The degree of innovation reflects the efficiency of our feedback mechanisms, which allow instructors to compare ideas for new courses and then share the results. Foremost among these mechanisms are those provided by ASLE: the electronic discussion list, which features sufficient diversity of voices that an instructor floating an idea for a course can be assured of having it vetted by multiple (and often unexpected) perspectives; *ISLE: Interdisciplinary Studies in Literature and Environment*, which publishes the best in ecocritical scholarship, pedagogy, and book reviews, compliments of Scott Slovic and his staff; and the biennial conferences and regional symposia that ASLE sponsors, at which panels and workshops on teaching are often among the best attended. In part IV, Mark C. Long has gathered an impressive array of additional resources for teachers of environmental literature. The wealth of such resources, those wonderful feedback mechanisms, seems to assure a continued flowering of approaches to teaching environmental literature.

Notes

1. To subscribe to ASLE's electronic discussion list, visit the organization's Web page at the following address: www.asle.umn.edu/discuss/welcome.html.

2. Soliciting, editing, and publishing this collection actually took several years, beginning with the initial suggestion by the then ASLE president Michael Branch in 1995.

3. Many of these observations drawn from the *ASLE Collection of Syllabi in Literature and Environment* were first described in a paper I delivered—"Trends in Teaching Literature and Environment: From Overview to Application"—at the 1999 conference of the Pacific Ancient and Modern Language Association, held at Portland State University.

4. See, e.g., Dixon.

5. Perhaps the best example from a general survey of literature and environment is Lawrence Buell's "Environmental Imagination Project," which he describes as a "practicum in environmental perception" (Christensen and Blakemore). He requires students in his American Literature and the American Environment class at Harvard University to select an outdoor observation post to which they will return each week and record their responses to a weekly set of questions. Beginning with an initial botanical, zoological, and geological inventory of their

spots, students move on through questions concerning how they construct their understanding of their places, how they use senses other than vision to perceive these places, how these spots have evolved through history, how the locations might look to a nonhuman inhabitant, how it feels to have another person with them in their places, and how some item in that place has changed over the preceding weeks. They are also asked to write about their spots in a way that imitates one of the authors they have been reading.

6. The best articulation of this approach is Elder's "The Poetry of Experience." See also Elder, "Voice."

7. Like most ecocritics interested in the practice of reading landscape, Harris follows the lead of Tom Wessels's *Reading the Forested Landscape: A Natural History of New England*.

Disciplinary Approaches

Anne Raine

Teaching American Modernism as Environmental Writing

Asked to describe their motivations for taking a literature course on modernism and nature, a striking number of students will begin with some variation on "I'm not a tree-hugger, but. . . ." Some identify themselves as environmentalists or describe transcendent experiences on mountaintops, but many are reluctant to confess an interest that might associate them with the stereotype of the naive, touchy-feely nature lover. Others view this stereotype as a standard to which they do not measure up, citing their own fondness for technological gadgets or lack of enthusiasm for backpacking trips as evidence that they lack the qualifications to be "really" interested in nature. Yet something draws them to the course, and most end up having thoughtful, interesting, even heartfelt things to say about the relationship between human beings and the nonhuman world. I have found that modernist texts offer particularly rich resources for twenty-first-century students and teachers, precisely because modernism's paradoxical embrace of both nature and modernity anticipates the ambivalence of students like these. Teaching modernist literature as environmental writing offers an opportunity to raise ecocritical questions with students who would be unlikely to sign up for a course on Henry David Thoreau, Annie Dillard, and Edward Abbey. Conversely, focusing on modernism challenges those already interested in ecocriticism to reexamine and refine received ideas about nature in the light of a body of literature that productively complicates our assumptions about what counts as nature writing, or indeed what counts as nature.

Modernist literature has not typically been read as concerned with environmental questions. Ecocritics, eager to promote the critically neglected genre of nature writing and to bring an ecological conscience to bear on literary studies, have tended to disregard modernism's formal experiments in favor of nature writing or the literature of wilderness, whose representations of and advocacy for nature are less equivocal and more easily interpreted.[1] Yet modernist texts offer rich resources for ecocritical inquiry. Many modernist writers shared a fascination with the nonhuman world and a lively curiosity about the popular and scientific discourses through which nature was being redefined, debated, and reimagined in the first decades of the twentieth century. Like their contemporaries in the booming fields of nature writing and nature education, these modernists used aesthetic practices to draw attention to the nonhuman world and to investigate human beings' place in nature. Unlike their "nature worker" contemporaries, however, modernist writers often sought to distance themselves from "Nature," a concept laden with nostalgic and sentimental associations, and to reconcile antianthropocentric reverence for nature's otherness with an optimistic faith in the power of human invention, scientific and aesthetic, to transform the material world and make nature new. This sometimes makes for dubious environmental politics, but it also produces a fascinating literature that anticipates current efforts to understand nature as a complex, dynamic totality that is partly produced by, yet irreducible to, human discourses and socioecological practices.

My course on modernism and nature, an advanced undergraduate seminar, is designed to address three challenges, each of which I discuss in more detail below. First, most of my students have had little or no exposure to ecocriticism, environmental theory, or environmental history; before our work can begin, I need to introduce them to some of the theoretical tools and historical information they need to read ecocritically. A second challenge lies in the formal demands of reading modernist literature; often, considerable time and effort must be spent grappling with each text before students feel confident enough to begin relating it to the historical and theoretical materials. Finally, there is a danger that getting students excited about modernism's rethinking of nature will result in an uncritical celebration of modernist innovation that devalues more accessible forms of nature writing and loses sight of the activist impulse that has been vital to ecocriticism from its inception. For that reason, I end the course with modernist texts that are centrally concerned with socio-ecological practice, and I include writing assignments that invite students to make connections between the literary texts and environmental issues they encounter in the world outside the classroom.

Reading Ecocritically: Theoretical and Historical Contexts

Lest students assume that their work for the course will consist of reiterating familiar commonplaces about nature,[2] I like to begin with a selection of theoretical readings designed to open up the question of what we mean when we talk about nature. An essential starting point is William Cronon's introduction to the anthology *Uncommon Ground*, which introduces students to the key premise that our understanding of the nonhuman world is shaped by culturally specific values and assumptions and that a key task for the critic is to identify and analyze the historical, cultural, and political factors that inform particular representations of nature.[3] I also assign the introduction to Lawrence Buell's *The Environmental Imagination*, another seminal text that helps identify the stakes of our project by considering how we might develop a less anthropocentric way of doing literary studies. However, the model of ecocritical practice that Buell advocates here tends to reinforce a straightforward distinction between nature on the one hand and human culture on the other. This distinction has been usefully complicated by accounts of the social production of nature coming out of Marxist theory and science studies. I assign Steven Vogel's "Marx and Alienation from Nature" to introduce the Marxist argument that the material world we live in is not natural but rather the product of embodied human activity and therefore capable of transformation. As Donna Haraway points out, however, the Marxist view of production disregards the agency of nonhuman nature; both Haraway's "The Promises of Monsters" and the introduction to Bruno Latour's *We Have Never Been Modern* (both of which I teach in short excerpts) offer challenging but useful efforts to rethink nature as an artifactual production resulting among particular beings and phenomena, both human and nonhuman.

Finally, I like to include Gary Snyder's well-known essay "The Etiquette of Freedom." The Marxist and science studies models speak to the modernist fascination with artifice and with the increasing hybridization of the organic and the technological; at the same time, these models of nature as produced rather than simply given challenge the counter tendency in modernism to idealize nature and the primitive as sites uncontaminated by human instrumentality. In contrast, Snyder's account of the persistence of "the wild" in human language and culture draws on insights from evolutionary biology to offer another way of complicating the binary opposition between nature and culture and an alternative perspective on modernism's interest in the materiality of language and the embodied nature of aesthetic experience. Like Haraway, Snyder seeks to reimagine "nature" as a heterogenous collective in which, as Haraway puts it, "the actors are not all 'us'" ("Promises" 297).

This is a lot of reading to pack into a small space on the syllabus, but I find it productive if approached in the following way. I assign four or five short but challenging selections to be read for the second class meeting. Each student is assigned one of the articles to focus on and writes an informal response paper identifying the main points of the article and discussing how its view of nature resembles and differs from the others. The students discuss their responses in small groups, and we then work as a class to build a conceptual map of the different theoretical perspectives. It is a rather grueling session, but allowing students time to share their ideas and confusions makes it less intimidating, and it has the advantage of plunging them into the kind of active reading and critical thinking the course will require. The result is an array of conceptual tools with which students can compare and analyze modernist investigations of nature; they will employ these tools in a midterm essay assignment that asks them to put one of the theorists in dialogue with one of the modernist texts.

Students also need some basic knowledge of the environmental-historical context to which modernist writers responded. Most students, even those who are involved in environmental activism, have had little or no exposure to environmental or conservation history. Accordingly, I assign selections from John Opie's *Nature's Nation: An Environmental History of The United States* to provide a useful overview of how industrialization, urbanization, and new scientific technologies were transforming the material environment, and a basic introduction to the different environmentalist discourses that emerged in response to these changes.[4] I supplement this overview with selected primary documents in conservation history: for example, writings by Gifford Pinchot and John Muir that show the conflict between utilitarian conservationism and aesthetic preservationism;[5] writings by female conservationists who interpret nature through sentimental discourse;[6] and excerpts from Mary Austin's *The Land of Little Rain*, which is often cited as an exemplary ecocentric and ecofeminist text. By analyzing the writings of early-twentieth-century conservationists and nature writers, students develop a second conceptual map in which to situate the more perplexing investigations of nature they will encounter in the modernist texts.

Practical Ecocriticism: Reading Modernism

Having explored these theoretical and historical contexts for our inquiry, students have a sense of what questions to ask as we turn to the modernist texts. Unfortunately, there is currently no overview of environmental questions in modernist literature that might be used to frame the course. Walter Kalaidjian's recent *Cambridge Companion to American Modernism* does not contain a chapter on modernism and environment. Hugh Kenner's 1975 study, *A Homemade World*, is probably still the best introduction to this approach to American modernism, and Douglas Mao's *Solid Objects* provides a suggestive reading of modernism as "foundationally ecological" (8), but neither is very accessible to undergraduates (though I do assign excerpts from Kenner during the units on Williams, Moore, and Stevens). Instead, I help define the field for students by grouping the authors in thematically related pairs and providing study questions and response-paper assignments that help students connect the modernist texts with theoretical and historical issues introduced in the other course materials. Where possible, I also provide images of specific landscapes that inspired each writer's environmental imagination. The various secondary materials "familiarize" modernism for students by helping them see how modernist texts respond to particular historical-material environments and public debates about nature conservation. At the same time, we foreground the ways in which modernist texts differ from nature writing and conservationist discourse; we explore how modernist writers use experimental literary forms to defamiliarize both conventional ideas about nature and the natural environment itself, and we consider what is gained and lost by writing about the natural world in such counterintuitive ways.

Our first unit, "Modernity and Alienation: Nature as Redemption?" introduces the theme of alienation from nature as explored in Willa Cather's *The Professor's House* and T. S. Eliot's *The Waste Land*. Cather's complex but accessible novel is an ideal introduction to modernism's reckoning with nature; by comparing her portrait of Tom Outland and the

Blue Mesa with preservationist texts by Muir and Austin, we explore how Cather at once shares and complicates the American ideal of nature as pristine wilderness through her emphasis on the acculturated nature of the mesa, the history of violent conflict over land use embodied in the figure of Mother Eve, and the way Professor St. Peter's romance with "Outland's country" seems to both enrich and impede his ability to come to terms with the realities of modernity and social life.

Cather's depiction of modernity as an emotionally sterile wasteland of empty consumerism gives students a concrete point of entry to Eliot's more oblique and challenging treatment of similar themes. After noting the similarities between the two writers' views of modernity, we discuss the difference between Cather's passion for the American landscape and Eliot's commitment to European cultural and literary tradition. Here, we ask to what extent Eliot's nature imagery and allusions to ancient fertility rituals suggest a literal faith in the redemptive power of nature, and to what extent he merely uses these images and allusions symbolically to talk about issues that are essentially cultural or psychological rather than environmental. We also consider how sexuality functions as one manifestation of "primitive nature" in the mechanized, alienated environment of Eliot's modern city.

Our second unit explores how William Carlos Williams's *Spring and All* and selected poems by Marianne Moore exemplify the modernist effort to "make nature new."[7] *Spring and All* is a direct challenge to Eliot's bleak vision, affirming that both natural and urban environments contain rich resources for a revitalized modern poetry. In contrast to Eliot's insistence that nature is meaningless without cultural traditions that give natural objects human meaning, Williams's eagerness to rescue the thing from the layers of cultural associations that obscure it suggests a more ecocentric orientation. But Williams also complicates what might look like a naive naturalism by defining the poem as "a machine made of words" (*Selected Essays* 256), exploring the vitality of urban spaces and technological objects as well as natural ones, and insisting that the only rose that is not "obsolete" is one produced through the technology of a cubist painting or a modernist poem (*Spring* 107).

William's conviction that technological and mediated sources of experience could be as "natural" as nature itself was shared by Marianne Moore, who similarly insisted that even the self-consciously mediated space of the modernist poem could yield "a place for the genuine" (*Complete Poems* 36). Moore's poems combine a passion for natural-historical accuracy and an explicit critique of human exploitation of nature with compositional methods that explore how nature is socially constructed. Her presentation of Mount Rainier in "An Octopus," for example, differs from Muir's and Cather's representations of national-park landscapes because its use of quotations foregrounds the position of a tourist whose experience is shaped by literary tradition, tourist guidebooks, and park regulations as well as by the park's natural features. Her portraits of animals ("The Jerboa," "The Plumet Basilisk," "The Pangolin," "He 'Digesteth Harde Yron'") similarly draw on museum experiences and explore the moral and epistemological complexities of making nature accessible to urban dwellers.[8] Unlike Cather and Eliot, Williams and Moore question the idea that modernity inevitably brings alienation from nature, and they invite us to consider how new technologies (films, museum exhibits, urban streetscapes, automobiles and other machines, experimental art) might provide new and intriguing kinds of access to nature or challenge us to define nature differently.

Our third unit, "Modernist Abstraction: Against Nature?" focuses on Wallace Stevens and Gertrude Stein, two writers who investigate problems of perception and representation in ways that emphasize the distance between the material world and the self-referential landscape of the text. Like Williams and Moore, Stevens insisted that poetry must "adhere to reality," yet poems like "Thirteen Ways of Looking at a Blackbird" and "Sea Surface Full of Clouds" foreground their own artificiality so self-consciously that they problematize any attempt to read them as simply "about" natural objects, rather than about *textual* blackbirds and clouds that function as elements in a poetic composition. Similarly, Stein insisted that compositions like *Lucy Church Amiably* and *Four Saints in Three Acts* were "about" particular natural landscapes (the pastoral countryside near Belley, France, and the arid plateau near Avila, Spain, respectively), yet these textual landscapes are even more radically abstract than Stevens's poems, mixing pictorial elements with counting games, grammatical exercises, and other forms of wordplay shaped less by fidelity to a natural scene than by relationships among words on the page.

Students often find this unit hard going. It helps to begin with poems like "Anecdote of the Jar" and "The Idea of Order at Key West" that raise the question of whether poetry is a sympathetic response to the natural world or the creation of an artificial world that is set against the natural one. These questions offer a way into the texts discussed above, which are more abstract and more exuberantly artificial. Another useful strategy is to construct two consecutive readings of each text, one in which we try to read the text as a representation of particular natural phenomena and a second one in which we focus on the moments in each text that are impossible to read naturalistically. Photographs of the French and Spanish landscapes can help students imagine how Stein's compositions might capture the feel of a place without representing it realistically. On the other hand, listening to a recording of *Four Saints* can help disgruntled students pick up on the opera's playful delight in the materiality of words; for some reason, they find it easier to entertain the idea of enjoying language as language when it's combined with music.

Of course, the question can and should be asked whether such radically self-referential texts are really about nature at all. For that reason, I like to end the course with William Faulkner's "The Bear" and Muriel Rukeyser's long poem "The Book of the Dead," two texts that use formal experimentation in the service of socioecological critique.[9] Although "The Bear" is often taught as part of the tradition of frontier literature, I emphasize how it resists that tradition by placing at the heart of the story not an idealized natural space (as in *The Professor's House*) but rather the commissary, symbolizing the complex landscape of the plantation system and, later, modern capitalism. While the story valorizes Ike's effort to repudiate his inheritance and embrace the wilderness ethic embodied by Sam Fathers, it also questions whether his idealization of wilderness and Native American culture will do anything to restore social justice or even to protect the wilderness he loves. Faulkner carries out this ambivalent critique in prose that enacts, rather than describes, the complexity of both nature and human society: in the wilderness sections, labyrinthine sentences force readers to relinquish their sense of direction in a textual wilderness as Ike does in a real one, and in the commissary, the intricate narration embeds us in the web of historical and economic relations in which everyone and everything is entangled (whites, blacks, Native Americans, animals, the land). By struggling through this confusing textual landscape, students can see how Faulkner uses formal difficulty to raise difficult questions of race, class, and socioecological responsibility that many more accessible texts gloss over.

Like "The Bear," Rukeyser's "The Book of the Dead" raises questions of action and accountability in a modern landscape that is at once ecological, economic, social, and political.[10] The poem documents a deadly outbreak of silicosis among miners at a hydroelectric project and silica mine in Gauley Bridge, West Virginia. Like Faulkner, Rukeyser uses experimental techniques to convey the complexity of the socioecological relationships that shape both human lives and the nonhuman environment, incorporating into the poem's mythic structure actual transcripts from testimony given at the congressional hearings, descriptions of silica-infected lungs seen through an X-ray machine, meditations on the physics of hydroelectric power, and landscape descriptions that critique the tourist guidebooks being produced by the Works Progress Administration. While she critiques both the tourist's idealized vision of rural nature and the capitalist's transformation of nature and human labor into profit, Rukeyser does not denounce the technological project of converting water power into electricity; instead, her investigation of the dam, the mine, and the miners' bodies emphasizes how human social life is irreducibly material, embedded in the natural environment in ways that are at once vital and sometimes deadly. Both a call to action and a multivocal, open-ended exploration of the relations between human and nonhuman nature, Rukeyser's poem is a fitting end to a course that aims both to complicate our ideas of nature and to connect philosophical and literary inquiry with public debate and socioecological practice.

Putting the "Critical" Back in Ecocriticism: Assessing Implications

I believe that modernist texts can enrich our environmental thinking by offering new and challenging ways to imagine the more-than-human world; I also think it's important to acknowledge the obvious limitations of modernist "difficulty" as a strategy for solving environmental problems and to point out how nature writing "proper" has been marginalized in a literary canon that valorizes modernism's emphasis on complexity, ambiguity, and formal virtuosity. My goal in raising ecocritical questions through modernism is not to duplicate American literary history's tendency, in Lawrence Buell's words, to "identify representation of the natural environment as a major theme while marginalizing the literature devoted most specifically to it" (*Environmental Imagination* 9). Rather, by showing students how modernist texts participate in ongoing cultural debates about nature, I hope to spark their interest not only in literary modernism but also in ecocriticism, nature writing, and environmental issues more generally.

For that reason, I sometimes include a "newswatch" assignment that asks students to keep track of and report on environmental issues in the news as a counterpoint to our literary investigations, and I like to end the course by discussing some of these contemporary issues and raising the question of how our study of modernism's rethinking of nature might affect (or not affect) our participation in other forms of environmental discourse and practice. I also encourage students to consider ways that they might include nonliterary or nonacademic materials in their term projects by putting literary-critical analysis in dialogue with, for example, their experiences volunteering for an environmental organization; their research into a particular environmental issue; or a journal project that explores the personal, ecological, and historical dimensions of a particular place. The results can be awkward and unwieldy, but they are also often the work that students feel most proud of and most personally invested in. Like the disjunctive moments in many modernist texts, the rough edges in these projects indicate a willingness to disrupt familiar forms, experiment with new ways of thinking, and investigate the complex relations between text and world. In my view, that's ecocriticism in action.

Notes

1. This is changing; in recent years a number of ecocritical anthologies have been published that expand the boundaries of nature writing to include a wider variety of genres and texts that have not previously been considered environmental. Coupe's recent *The Green Studies Reader* contains a section devoted specifically to modernism. In addition, in the field of modernist studies a number of critics have begun to explore modernist writers' complex engagement with nature and science.

2. For an important, if sometimes overly polemical, critique of ecocriticism's attraction to such commonplaces, see D. Phillips.

3. See also Soper, *What Is Nature?* and Raymond Williams's classic social history of nature in *Problems in Materialism and Culture*.

4. See also Schmitt (*Back*) and Tichi.

5. Selections from these and other conservationist texts, along with helpful historical introductions, can be found in Nash; Merchant (*Major Problems*); and Magoc.

6. See, for example, Adams-Williams; Anna Botsford Comstock, "A Little Nomad" (1903; rpt. in Anderson and Edwards); and Stratton-Porter (*Homing*). For useful discussions of women's nature writing and conservationism, see Norwood; Alaimo (*Undomesticated Ground*).

7. Although the poems from *Spring and All* are often anthologized and taught separately from the prose passages that surround them, I prefer to teach the poems and prose together; Williams's prose musings offer valuable points of entry into the poems and give students a sense of his complex and often contradictory take on the relations among modernity, nature, and the imagination.

8. Instructors should be aware that Moore's *Complete Poems*, the most widely available edition of her work, is not in fact complete; many of the poems are substantially revised, some do not appear at all, and the poems are not presented in

chronological order, obscuring the thematic connections between poems originally published together. *Becoming Marianne Moore: The Early Poems, 1907–1924*, brilliantly edited by Robin Schulze, is by far the most useful edition for scholarly purposes, but it is expensive and includes only the early poems. A fair compromise is the recent collection edited by Grace Schulman, *The Poems of Marianne Moore*, which presents all the poems in chronological order (though, confusingly, later versions are sometimes substituted for the poems as first published) and includes variant versions in the editor's notes.

9. Because of time constraints, I sometimes teach "The Bear" on its own rather than having students read all of *Go Down, Moses*. But I do prefer to teach the whole book if time permits, since the earlier stories provide information about the characters and plot that make "The Bear" somewhat less confusing, and "The Old People," "The Buck," and "Delta Autumn" especially extend Faulkner's meditations on the role of wilderness in modern life.

10. "The Book of the Dead" was originally published in Rukeyser's second collection of poetry, *U.S. 1* (1938), which is now out of print. It appears in the new *The Collected Poems of Muriel Rukeyser* and is also reprinted in full in Cary Nelson's *Anthology of Modern American Poetry*, which includes excellent notes, as well as a companion Web site containing historical information and critical perspectives (www.english.uiuc.edu/maps).

Bernard Quetchenbach

Teaching Post–World War II American Poetry as Environmental Literature

Poetry and Ecology

Poetry has played a traditional, nearly universal role in human attempts to apprehend and respond to nonhuman nature, so it is not surprising that American poets explore nature and ecology in this time of environmental crisis. Contemporary poets noted for environmental advocacy include Gary Snyder, W. S. Merwin, and Wendell Berry. Collections of nature and environmental poetry have been published by, among others, Maxine Kumin (*Nurture*), William Heyen (*Pterodactyl Rose*), and Denise Levertov (*The Life around Us*). *Learning to Live in the World*, an edition of William Stafford's nature poetry selected for adolescent readers, was published posthumously in 1994. A number of poetry anthologies, such as *News of the Universe* and *Poems for a Small Planet*, have been devoted to environmental themes. "Green" literary journals include *Albatross*, *Green Fuse*, and *Ecopoetics*, and poems have regularly been published in environmental magazines such as *Wild Earth*, *OnEarth*, and *Orion*. Poetry is covered in studies of environmental history and philosophy including Bill Devall's *Simple in Means, Rich in Ends* and Max Oelschlager's *The Idea of Wilderness*.

Poetry reveals and reconceptualizes connections, its elements forming a network of interacting parts analogous to a natural community. Because

173

poetry deals in provisional and fluid relationships, nature poets, despite being informed by science, tend to distrust scientific reductionism. In *Greening the Lyre*, David Gilcrest aligns poetry with ecology, which itself is opposed to "atomistic and mechanistic Newtonian science" (16). The deep-ecology philosopher Devall notes that Antler, whose poetry reflects his working-class experience, "writes from the inside of life" (75). Poetry's experiential quality makes it an apt vehicle for offering alternatives to "the house of concepts and abstractions and quantification taught in schools and demanded in environmental impact statements" (75).

Poetry's immediate, experiential character is emphasized in the work of post–World War II American poets, who sought to renew the genre's creative capacity by cultivating an impression of unpremeditated, internalized exploration. The contemporary poetry pioneer Theodore Roethke combines close observation of the natural world with a romantic sense of the relation between the individual and his or her surroundings. In "Night Crow," originally published in *"The Lost Son" and Other Poems* (1948), a crow rises from a snag to be met by a corresponding "shape in the mind" (47, line 3). In addition to Roethke, poets such as Snyder, Robert Bly, and Allen Ginsberg explore the inward-outward correspondence between the unconscious and nature, holding that the same technocratic or bureaucratic mind-set that disconnects people from the nonhuman also disconnects them from the "wild" or creative aspect of human life.

Nature poets, like nature writers in other genres, seek to balance intuitive and analytic approaches to their subjects. Contemporary poets whose work is clearly informed by the natural sciences include A. R. Ammons, Snyder, and Pattiann Rogers. These poets balance the scientific perspective with a strong emotional and spiritual attachment to the natural world, often, especially in the work of Snyder and Rogers, evoked through sensual or erotic imagery. For Rogers, nature, like the body of the green anole in "When You Watch Us Sleeping," is the source of "not merely truth, / but rapture" (320, lines 32–33); the sense of physical and spiritual immersion in natural processes both complements and counters the detachment associated with scientific observation.

Accustomed to the decidedly mediated relationship between human and nonhuman that characterizes modern life, contemporary students often find it difficult to approach the natural world directly. For humanities students especially, engaging the particulars of a nature poem may seem more the purview of science than literature. These students may find it helpful to move away from the classroom setting, a practice that might logically lead outdoors. Ammons's "Corson's Inlet," for example, can be read aloud by a class moving from place to place on the campus grounds, so that students more clearly experience the blending of sensuous and scientific perspectives that characterizes not only this poem but all genres of nature writing.

Nature Poetry, Ecopoetry, and Politics

Poetry critics such as Leonard Scigaj and J. Scott Bryson have found it useful to distinguish between traditional romantic and pastoral nature poetry and ecopoetry, which acknowledges and addresses the current systemic state of environmental crisis. In *Sustainable Poetry*, Scigaj asserts that ecopoets "present nature in their poems as a separate and equal other in dialogues meant to include the referential world and offer exemplary models of biocentric perception and behavior" (11). Bryson, in his introduction to *Ecopoetry*, an essay collection he edited, defines his subject as a newly developed "subset of nature poetry that, while adhering to certain conventions of romanticism, also advances beyond that tradition and takes on distinctly contemporary problems and issues" (5). In her foreword to *The Life around Us*, Levertov says that the contemporary nature poet, "although often impelled, as always, to write poems of pure celebration, is driven inevitably to lament, to anger, and to the expression of dread" (xi). Ecopoetry both updates and critiques Romanticism. For example, Merwin, according to the critic Jane Frazier, attempts to reestablish "contact with a lost, original world, free from the ontologically insular and physically threatening forces of industrialization and technology," while also addressing the "outright destruction" of nature characteristic of modern life (16).

Ecopoets have adopted a range of approaches to political issues. In contemplative poetry such as that of Stafford, the political force tends to be muted or implied. Stafford's "At the Bomb Testing Site," for example, embodies the earth's reaction to the impending human-generated chaos in the figure of a lizard sitting tensely, so that "[t]he hands gripped hard on the desert" (41, line 12). A more explicitly activist approach to the same subject can be found in Levertov's "Protesting at the Nuclear Test Site" (*Life* 21–22). That Levertov's political advocacy is informed by the environmental movement is established by her poem "*Silent Spring*," which offers in concise form the central argument of Rachel Carson's influential book about pesticide pollution (*Life* 37–38). The uneasy coexistence of traditional meditative and celebratory approaches to nature and the more politically active environmentalist perspective is as characteristic of contemporary nature poetry as it is of prose nature writing since Carson.

Some poets have expressed ambivalence concerning the significance of nature poetry in contemporary American life. In his essay "Rolling Up," for example, Louis Simpson criticizes contemporary poets who write as if "they looked with the eyes of the crow and listened with the ears of the beaver" (333). Simpson sees more relevance in acknowledging that, though he himself may not especially like to think so, "[t]here is as much poetry in a suburb as by a lake, if we have a mind to see it" (335). He does, however, differentiate between what he criticizes as his peers' tendency toward naive escapism and a Wordsworthian attempt to restore humanistic values through purposeful withdrawal into the countryside.

No contemporary American poet is more thoroughly immersed in rural literary traditions and lifeways than Berry. In addition to being a working farmer, Berry is notable for his oeuvre of mutually supporting writings in different forms and genres, including free-verse poetry, rhymed religious meditations, novels, short stories, and essays, most concerned in various ways with small-scale agrarian society and noncorporate literary and cultural endeavors. For Berry, the farmer and the farm are bound by ties of mutual dependence and affection that are in harmony with fundamental Western ethical and religious traditions but antithetical to industrial exploitation of the earth.

Though the pastoral or wilderness lyric remains its primary mode, contemporary ecopoetry is also set in urban and suburban environments, where the poet seeks to reveal as illusory the disconnection between modern life and the natural systems that support it. Taught as examples of urban ecopoetry, Ginsberg's "Sunflower Sutra" and Joy Harjo's "And If I Awaken in Los Angeles" may seem more immediately accessible to city students than pastoral poetry such as Berry's. Like many of Harjo's urban poems, the poems in Heyen's *Pterodactyl Rose* dispel the illusion that daily life in contemporary American communities is independent of both history and ecology. "Fast Food," for example, begins with the speaker in a McDonald's restaurant "eating my fragment of forest" (41, line 1) and ends with an ominous reminder that the current prosperity is temporary: "we flourish, at present, under the golden arches" (line 9).

The Poetry "Schools" of the 1950s and 1960s

The decades of "anthology wars" between "academic" and "open-form" poets that followed World War II featured a highly charged atmosphere of aesthetic debate and competing theories and manifestos. Poets working in open or organic forms set themselves in opposition to what they saw as the mechanistic, institutional verse of the mid-century. Partly on the basis of the poets' own friendships, publications, and statements and partly as a result of classification schemes later formulated by editors and literary scholars, prominent open-form poets whose work began appearing in the 1950s and 1960s have been grouped in loosely defined "schools." Figures associated with each of the schools write about nature, but natural imagery and environmental themes are particularly evident in the work of the deep-image poets, primarily Bly and James Wright; the Black Mountain poets, including Charles Olson and Robert Duncan; and the poets of the beat generation, among them Snyder, Michael McClure, and Ginsberg.

The term *deep image* was first applied to the work of a group of poets including Robert Kelly, Diane Wakoski, and Jerome Rothenberg, but it is most often used to refer to Bly, Wright, and others associated with Bly's journal *The Fifties* and its successors. *The Fifties* poets, at least in Bly's interpretation, view each individual human consciousness as linked to a shared awareness that pervades not only humanity but the universe itself. In his anthology *News of the Universe*, Bly's introductory essays reject the hierarchical idea that "[a] serious gap exists between us and the rest of nature" (8). To refute what he sees as Cartesian arrogance, Bly offers poetry that "grants consciousness" (84) to nonhuman life forms and natural phenomena.[1] Bly's position can fruitfully be contrasted with E. O. Wilson's attempt to relate aesthetics to Enlightenment-based empiricism in *Consilience*. In their own poems, Bly and Wright offer evocative, rural, frequently midwestern landscapes surrealistically filtered through the subjective consciousness of the speaker.

The Black Mountain, or projectivist, poets posit that, as Olson says in his seminal 1950 essay "Projective Verse," a poem "must, at all points, be a high energy-construct and, at all points, an energy-discharge" (16). The critic Jed Rasula connects the projectivist idea of "composition by field" to organicism, noting that "[t]he sensible adherence to physiological rather than metrical orders in composition was persuasive" during the 1960s (132). In his poem "Poetry: A Natural Thing," Duncan compares the creation of poetry to natural processes such as the growth of moose antlers (50, lines 22–27). Duncan's tone is ironic, but the principle established in his title is basic to projectivist theory. The Black Mountain poets have influenced the beat ecopoets McClure and Snyder, as well as Levertov, who attended Black Mountain College and is frequently identified with the projectivist group.

The Black Mountain poets have much in common with another major school, the beat generation, who generally share the projectivist belief that breath is a key to defining the poetic line. During the 1950s, beat writers saw the oppression of both nature and the human imagination as symptomatic of the paranoid mind-set of cold war America, and environmental concerns continued to characterize the work of several prominent beat figures as general awareness of environmental issues increased through the following decades. At the 1955 Six Gallery reading in San Francisco, most noteworthy for the first presentation of Ginsberg's *Howl*, Snyder read poems eventually included in *Myths and Texts* (1960), and McClure performed an early protest poem, "For the Death of One Hundred Whales" (Schumacher 215). McClure has characterized the beats as "the literary wing of the Environmental Movement" (R. Phillips). A central tenet of McClure's work is that acknowledgment of humanity's animal nature is essential to understanding human culture and actions. Ginsberg is noted for his antinuclear activism, reflected in poems like "Plutonium Ode." Snyder's contributions to ecopoetry and nonfiction prose place him among the foremost environmental writers of his time. Perhaps because their initial movement was so clearly youth-oriented, beat poets remain popular with students who are likely to find projectivist or deep-image poetry obscure or somewhat dated; for this reason, poems such as Ginsberg's "Sunflower Sutra" and Snyder's "Mother Earth: Her Whales" constitute an excellent introduction to postwar ecopoetry.

The Avant-Garde Experimentalists

During the late 1970s and the 1980s, a group of poets generally associated with the language school carved out a new direction in poetry, influenced by the experimental modernism of Gertrude Stein; by objectivism; by French literary criticism and language theory; and by the beat and, especially, the Black Mountain schools. Though he claims that their influence "obscured other possibilities," Rasula acknowledges the projectivists' role as important predecessors of experimental and avant-garde writers who have emerged in recent decades (132).

Perhaps because the antilyrical stance of most experimental poets distances them from the traditions of romantic and pastoral nature poetry, environmental concerns and natural imagery have not frequently been evident in avant-garde work, leaving the field of nature or ecopoetry mostly to lyric poets. Larry Eigner, however, is an example of a writer who can be seen as both a nature poet and an experimentalist. Jonathan Skinner's journal *Ecopoetics* publishes selections of "*Project*-ive (or 'applied') poetics" addressing environmental themes and subjects (6).

Recently, many poets, such as those whose work is represented in *The Iowa Anthology of New American Poetries* (2005), have been attempting to reintegrate the lyric and experimental modes; the editor, Reginald Shepherd, describes the anthology's "lyrical investigations" as poetry that "crosses, ignores, or transcends the variously demarcated lines between traditional lyric and avant-garde practice" (xiii).[2] The work of these poets features disjunctive syntax, uncertain point of view, and self-conscious imagery, demonstrating their acceptance of language's inability to transparently represent even the bedrock of individual experience. The resulting play between intellect, language, and perception recalls the work of Wallace Stevens; a poem such as Melinda Markham's "The Rock in the Garden Lets People In" can fruitfully be read alongside Stevens's "The Snow Man."

The work of emerging poets seeking to overcome the decades-long division between lyricists and experimentalists has the effect of restoring external reality to at least a tentative position in avant-garde poetry. For such poets, if the self and the external world do not reflect each other as relatively distinct, stable entities in the manner of romanticism, they are not completely separable either. Like Scigaj, the poet Leonard Schwartz turns to phenomenology in an attempt to reconceive the relation between poetic language and its subjects. In his essay "A Flicker at the Edge of Things: Some Thoughts on Lyric Poetry," Schwartz develops a concept of transcendence as the inevitable product of human imagination, concluding that "[t]ranscendental lyric is the poem written in the moment before the world of representations is created, before the trap of projection ensnares us, before the world we project upon gets its chance to fix us in place as bodies, objects, commodities" (112). The first strophe of Snyder's early poem "Piute Creek" concludes with "[w]ords and books / like a small creek off a high ledge / gone in the night air" (6, lines 16–18). Schwartz's position, though more skeptical, similarly acknowledges the limitations of being "in language" while recognizing that the poetic imagination can at least provisionally approach something like an objective reality beyond and before language.

Poetry of the Native American Renaissance and the Chicano Movement

American Indian cultures have had an enormous influence on American nature writing and ecopoetry. Poets including Mary Oliver, Richard Hugo, Heyen, and Stafford have written about figures and events in Native American history. Projectivist poets acknowledge a considerable debt to Native American oral tradition. Additionally, Snyder, Bly, and others have at times adopted the persona of the "poet-shaman" based on their understanding of Native American spirituality; Snyder, who studied anthropology in college, is especially influenced by tribal sources. Works such as Snyder's *Myths and Texts* and Galway Kinnell's "The Bear" incorporate unattributed materials from indigenous sources, leading to charges of cultural imperialism. Other criticism has focused on the failure of English translations to re-create the entire experience of oral-tradition literatures. "Total translation," conceived by translators such as Rothenberg, Dennis Tedlock, and David McAllester, attempts a more complete representation of indigenous voices in their own cultural context.

Despite the influence of Indian traditions on white writers, until the civil rights and black-arts movements had opened up opportunities for minority writers, publication of work by contemporary Native Americans was rare. Beginning in the late 1960s and continuing to the present, however, the work of a variety of American Indian writers has regularly been appearing in print. Observers such as Kenneth Lincoln dubbed the apparently sudden emergence of these writers a "Native American Renaissance." Native American Renaissance poets illustrate historical and mythic ties to traditional homelands, reservations, and urban enclaves. The setting of Simon Ortiz's "Canyon de Chelly," for example, links present and future generations, represented by the speaker and his son, to the ancient inhabitants of Anasazi sites in the canyon (*Woven Stone* 201–02). Harjo's *Secrets from the Center of the World* combines Stephen Strom's sweeping yet intimate landscapes of the Southwest with Harjo's loose narrative sequence of mythic prose poems. Since Harjo also performs selections based on the sequence with her band Poetic Justice, the poems, photographs, and music provide a multimedia experience of Native American Renaissance writing. Particularly adept in interview situations, Harjo is featured in a number of useful print and videotaped discussions. Harjo interviews can be found in the Lannan Foundation interview series (Harjo, "Joy Harjo"; "Power") and in Bill Moyers's *The Power of the Word*. Harjo maintains a Web site, including a Web log, which provides additional insight into her poetry and ideas (Harjo, *Joy Harjo*).

Although poems by American Indian writers have much in common with the work of other contemporary figures, poets of the Native American Renaissance clearly draw on their Indian heritage. In Harjo's "Eagle Poem" and "Song for the Deer and Myself to Return On" (*How* 85, 78), for example, animals appear as both physical and mythic beings and are responsive to ritual contact. In his introduction to the 1974 anthology *Come to Power*, Joseph Bruchac points to Leslie Marmon Silko's statement that her "writing is a gift to the Earth" as evidence that, he asserts, "the Indian vision is very different" from both Euro-American and African American concepts of literature (6).

Like the Native American Renaissance figures, poets of the 1960s Chicano movement base the legitimacy of their claims to intimacy with the American land on their indigenous status. Aztlan, an Aztec name denoting a place north of the Aztec empire in Mexico, represents a mythic home in the American Southwest. The "post-movement" Chicano poet Jimmy Santiago Baca establishes that defending the concept of homeland involves defending real places from, among other things, environmental degradation. In an interview with Gabriel Meléndez, Baca extols the heroism of the Chicano activist Rito Canales, killed by police acting as agents of a society that values development interests over the indigenous histories embedded, like Rito's blood, in the landscape itself (Baca, "Carrying" 72–73). In "Rebirth," sensitivity to pollution is a source of working-class solidarity: "Huntington Beach blackened with oil. / Rudy comes behind me and says / 'Fucking shame they do that to our shores.' / I suddenly realize how I love these workingmen" (*Healing Earthquakes* 333, lines 67–70).

It is important not to generalize or stereotype the diverse voices representing Native American, Chicano, and other minority literatures in the United States or to assume that indigenous people are inherently "close to nature." Chicano and Native American writers, however, have often recognized that the commercial and industrial forces that exploit nature endanger their communities as well. Additionally, writers such as Baca and Ortiz provide a critical look at environmentalism itself. Both reject the idea of a pure "natural world" separate from human culture and history. In "Black

Mesa," Baca's speaker climbs a "No Trespassing fence" to reach personally and culturally evocative sites (121, line 24). In the Meléndez interview, Baca rejects "the attitude that says, 'Leave this mountain alone because we want to come up here and hike and look at birds'" (Baca, "Carrying" 73). Ortiz's "A Designated National Park" juxtaposes the impersonal bureaucratic pronouncements of National Park Service signs with the observations of an Indian speaker who has "to buy a permit to get back home" (*Woven Stone* 235, line 15) but whose response to the environment at Montezuma Castle National Monument is informed by an intimate personal connection to the place and the people who lived there.

Regionalism and the Environmental Long Poem

From Walt Whitman's New York to Robinson Jeffers's California coast, the settings employed by American poets have provided context for the individual speaker. With the spread of both rootless modernity and environmental awareness, many poets have consciously become "place-makers," a term that the ecocritic Bryson adapts from the work of the anthropologist Keith Basso (*West Side* 9). Contemporary poets of place include Berry on his Kentucky farm, Baca in New Mexico, Richard Shelton in the Sonoran Desert, and John Haines in Alaska. Other poets, including Oliver, Kumin, Snyder, Stafford, Hugo, Bly, and Ted Kooser, exhibit sensibilities thoroughly grounded in regional landscapes and traditions.

Like prose writers inspired by Henry David Thoreau's *Walden*, American poets look to a nineteenth-century model, *Leaves of Grass*. Though Whitman's sweeping poems reflect his ambition to be a national bard, New York City and nearby Long Island provide a specific, textured environment in which many of the most memorable poems are set.[3] Twentieth-century examples of long, sometimes multivolume, works in which place plays an important role include such diverse texts as William Carlos Williams's *Paterson*, Hart Crane's *The Bridge*, and John Neihardt's *Cycle of the West*. Contemporary examples of environmentally significant long poems include Sharon Doubiago's *Hard Country*, Gary Holthaus's *Circling Back*, Baca's *Martin and Meditations on the South Valley*, Ammons's *Garbage*, and Snyder's *Mountains and Rivers without End*. Though different in approach, Merwin's *The Folding Cliffs: A Narrative* can also be considered an environmental long poem.

Typically, these works set autobiographical elements in a large-scale "environment" by adopting a regional focus, a journey format, or both.

Doubiago and Holthaus trace journeys that are personal as well as historical and geographic. The autobiographical content of Baca's *Martin and Meditations on the South Valley* is apparent when these "[n]ovels in verse" (Levertov, Introduction xiii) are compared with details revealed in the poet's autobiography, *A Place to Stand,* and elsewhere. Ammons links his own aging to the processes of decay occurring at a landfill he encounters along an interstate highway in Florida. Inspired by Japanese landscape-scroll painting, Snyder's *Mountains and Rivers without End* features an unusually expansive concept of bioregion, the Pacific Rim setting reflecting the habitat in which Snyder's life has been shaped. Based on events that took place on nineteenth-century Kauai, Merwin's *The Folding Cliffs* draws connections between the exploitation of Native Hawaiʻians and the environmental devastation wrought by colonial enterprises in Hawaiʻi and elsewhere. Merwin portrays the implication of Native leaders in the destruction of sandalwood forests as evidence of the disintegration of Hawaiian culture under colonial pressure and makes his criticism of manifest destiny explicit by references to the battle of the Little Bighorn and the Indian Wars on the North American continent. Though *The Folding Cliffs* is not autobiographical, it does constitute a declaration of loyalty to Merwin's adopted home.

Regional poetry can be incorporated into the classroom in various ways. Poetry related to the campus region can be included in period, topical, and genre courses. A book such as Baca's *Black Mesa Poems* can be especially useful in a class focusing on a particular region, since it incorporates local history and geography and addresses contemporary social and political issues in an accessible, dynamic style. Long narrative poems are also generally accessible and constitute a viable alternative to a work of nonfiction prose or a novel; Holthaus's *Circling Back* would be an appropriate text in a Western literature class, while Merwin's *The Folding Cliffs* might be included in a course focusing on representations of colonialism in literature. In a genre course, a regional voice serves to remind students that poetry need not be limited to distant times and places; students may be surprised to find that their own surroundings have been seen as a landscape for poetry. Library subscriptions to regionally focused literary magazines such as *Blueline, Potomac Review,* and *Black Canyon Quarterly* can also foster place awareness by introducing students not only to regional writing and writers but also to area publishers, book dealers, and events.

The contemplation of nature is a traditional subject of poetry. Moreover, a poem creates an "ecological" network of relationships. Environmentalists have long recognized poetry's potential for encouraging environmental awareness and demonstrating John Muir's maxim that "[w]hen we try to pick out anything by itself, we find it hitched to everything else in the Universe" (*First Summer* [ed. Cronon] 110). American poetry since World War II offers insight into shifting conceptions of the relation between the human and nonhuman and provides rich and diverse material for courses exploring the intersection of nature, ecology, and environmental literature.

Notes

1. Bly uses this phrase in his discussion of the Spanish poet Federico García Lorca, but it applies in general to the poems he collects. The anthology is subtitled *Poems of Two-Fold Consciousness.*

2. Shepherd notes that he derives the term "lyrical investigations" from Ludwig Wittgenstein (xiii).

3. Whitman's role as an urban poet has been frequently noted, and Long Island poets such as Heyen and Vince Clemente have discussed his connection to that area. For a recent examination of the role of the Long Island seashore as a sacred place in Whitman's work, see Killingsworth. See Fletcher for a discussion of the influence of Whitman's "environment-poems" on post–World War II poets such as John Ashbery.

Jeffrey Myers

"Ready to Come Home": Teaching African American Literature as Environmental Literature

A recurring issue in recent environmental literature scholarship and pedagogy has been the exclusion of works by and about people of color from
the American environmental literature canon—with a related effacement of
how race and racism intertwine with environmental issues. Confronting this
issue reveals much about what we consider "the environment" to be and
who "properly" speaks about environmental issues, with implications for
diversity in the classroom and environmental justice outside it. I would like
to discuss some of the reasons for the exclusion of African American literature in particular: a narrow conception of "nature-writing" as a nonfiction
form; a reluctance to think of urban space as "natural" space; a subordina-
tion of environmental justice issues to concerns over wildlife and wilderness
preservation; and the extremely vexed but nonetheless intimate history that
African Africans have had with the land with respect to slavery, Jim Crow–era
racial violence, and internal migration to northern cities. As I do so, I offer
a number of concrete examples of African American environmental writers
from Charles Chesnutt to Percival Everett and suggest ways of including
African American literature in the environmental literature classroom.

One reason for the early exclusion of African American writers from
environmental literature curricula was the lingering conception of nature

writing as a genre defined by the nonfiction essay collection. Thomas J. Lyon, in his valuable taxonomy of nature writing, discusses a number of categories and gives familiar examples: Rachel Carson's *The Sea Around Us*, for one, is a "Natural History Essay"; Edward Abbey's *Desert Solitaire* falls under "Solitude and Backcountry Living" (Lyon 22). None of Lyon's examples (not even in the revised, 2001 edition) are by writers of color, to which there are two somewhat paradoxical responses. First, the nonfiction nature-writing essay that has become the standard of the genre presupposes a degree of leisure, social status, and even safety that has been historically less available to African American writers in the United States, as well as a peculiarly Eurocentric stance toward the natural world. Expanding our conception of environmental literature to include other literary forms, from slave narrative to contemporary fiction, that foreground African American experience in the natural world opens up the possibilities immensely. That being said, there is, ironically, a significant body of nonfiction environmental literature by African American writers—essays and accounts that would fit perfectly into the Lyon taxonomy—that has been largely overlooked. The notion that African American writers have not contributed to the genre of environmental literature turns out, on closer inspection, to be something of a myth.

A Tradition of African American Environmental Fiction

The bias against thinking of fiction as environmental literature is doubtless one of the reasons that so few African American writers are included in anthologies. But even anthologists with a bias toward the nonfiction nature essay admit certain works of fiction into the nature-writing canon if they are sufficiently "environmental." Sarah Orne Jewett's "A White Heron" (1886), for this reason, has become a staple of environmental literature anthologies, demonstrating that the exclusion of fiction is somewhat selective. It is in the realm of fiction that African American writers make some of their strongest contributions to environmental literature, so for these writers it is doubly exclusionary to select against fiction in choosing pieces for curricula and anthologies. Vera Norwood, Rachel Stein, Karla Armbruster, and Kathleen R. Wallace have shown the possibilities for reading the novels of Toni Morrison, Alice Walker, and Zora Neale Hurston as environmental fiction. Beyond these, the number of contemporary African American fiction writers with an explicitly ecological consciousness is remarkable. Percival Everett's *Watershed* (1996)—about a black geologist who joins with a fictional Native American tribe to expose government contamination of the tribe's reservation's water supply—and his *God's Country* (1994), which is an Old West satire about a black tracker who leads a white homesteader on the trail of outlaws who destroy his home, criticize the dominant culture's racism and exploitation of the environment even as they explore the relationship of African Americans to the land. I teach *God's Country* in an American literature course that centers on themes of ethnicity and the environment, pairing it with either James Fenimore Cooper's *The Last of the Mohicans* (1826) or Mark Twain's *Adventures of Huckleberry Finn* (1885), to show how Everett deconstructs the way those novels tacitly endorse white appropriation of American landscape and racial hierarchy in the natural world. Many of the novels of the science fiction writer Octavia Butler display an ecological consciousness. In particular, her *Parable of the Sower* (1993), in which an African American adolescent girl founds a new religion called "Earthseed" in an environmentally degraded Los Angeles of the future, highlights issues of environmental racism and injustice.

The possibilities for African American place-based literature are practically limitless once urban space is configured as natural space. As Michael Bennett notes, there is an "anti-pastoral African American literary tradition" underlying the fact that "African Americans and their culture have . . . increasingly been involved in the process of urbanization" ("Anti-pastoralism" 195, 197). John Edgar Wideman's trilogy, *The Homewood Books* (1992), is dense with ruminations on the way place—the Pittsburgh neighborhood in which Wideman grew up, rendered fictively here and nonfictively in his memoir *Brothers and Keepers* (1984)—influences culture and personal identity in an urban setting (Buell, *Writing* 79–83). The title alone, combining the words *home* and *wood*, should make teachers of environmental literature take notice that something powerfully evocative of the environment is at work. The Pulitzer Prize winner Edward P. Jones's collection of short stories, *Lost in the City* (1992), explores his home terrain of Washington, DC, much as Wideman does Pittsburgh. I recently included Jones's story, "The Girl Who Loved Pigeons" (anthologized by Dixon in *City Wilds*), in a freshman writing course to model a writing assignment about students' own urban and suburban neighborhoods as environmental space.

Probably no contemporary African American writer of fiction expresses a stronger ecological consciousness than does Gloria Naylor in *Mama Day*.

Her 1989 novel follows a young, professional African American woman as she moves back and forth between her adopted home of New York City and her birthplace on an island, threatened with development in the novel, located off the Georgia coast that forms part of the Sea Islands. Not only does Naylor render both environments with equally fine attention to detail, she introduces the title character as a conjure woman who draws her power from a deep spiritual connection to the natural world. This novel pairs well in the classroom with a showing of *Daughters of the Dust*, the 1991 Julie Dash film about Gullah culture in the Sea Islands set at the turn of the twentieth century. *Mama Day* is also densely allusive to William Shakespeare's *The Tempest* and would pair well with that work, which is often taught as environmental literature.

This practice of spiritual magic is something of a motif in African American place-based literature, whether the anthropological *Mules and Men* (1935) of Hurston or the turn-of-the-century short-story collection, *The Conjure Woman* (1899) by Chesnutt. These well-known stories—in which "Uncle Julius" McAdoo spins tales of antebellum haunting and magic in an attempt to preserve his and his community's livelihoods—have been understood by a generation of critics, notably Houston Baker, Jr. (41–47), as deeply subversive of white supremacist ideology, but they also have a strongly environmental focus that until recently has not been pointed up (Myers 87–110). Another indispensable African American work from the latter end of the "Age of Thoreau, Muir, and Burroughs" (Lyon 67) is Jean Toomer's *Cane* (1923). With its dual settings in the rural South and urban North, *Cane* evokes both painful and beneficial connections to the land—a vital reminder, as bell hooks explains, "that black people were first and foremost a people of the land" ("Touching" 30). A contemporary of Chesnutt's, Pauline Hopkins, begins her magazine novel *Winona* (1902) by imagining an idealized interracial society set on an island in the Niagara River in the 1850s—the wilderness setting, in a space between the political borders of the United States and Canada, allowing Hopkins "to challenge contemporary racist ideologies" in the context of mainstream American culture's alienation from the natural world (Carby 128). That this society is broken up by the intrusion of Southern slave catchers, which moves the action to the "Bleeding Kansas" of John Brown, further underscores the way in which Hopkins explores these two themes. Hopkins's following novel, *Of One Blood* (1903), recenters her nature-based antiracism within an African diaspora literary tradition. Such a tradition, with a strongly environmental slant, similarly informs the work of contemporary writers such as Paule Marshall, in *Daughters* (1991), and Sandra Jackson-Opoku, in *The River Where Blood Is Born* (1998).

The Myth of African American Environmental Nonfiction

The well of place-based African American fiction is deep, but there is an abundance of nature-oriented nonfiction to match it. A good place to begin an exploration of this body of work is Evelyn C. White's essay "Black Women and the Wilderness" not only because her essay addresses in such a straightforward manner one African American writer's take on environmental-justice issues but also because the piece is itself an excellent environmental literature essay—a "Backcountry Living, Travel, and Adventure" essay in Lyon's taxonomy—that dispels the myth that there are no good examples of the genre by black writers. A brief comparison of White's essay with a passage from one of the most canonized works of contemporary environmental literature, Annie Dillard's *Pilgrim at Tinker Creek* (1974), illustrates some of the difficulties in conceiving an African American environmental literature and highlights White's success in doing so.

In the chapter "Stalking," Dillard describes her practice of sitting motionless on a footbridge, suspended over "one of the creek's nameless feeder streams," to observe muskrats (194). Her stillness and concentration allow the author to observe one of the animals so closely that she could have reached out and touched it. And yet, she says, "he never knew I was there" (198). She continues, "I never knew I was there, either. . . . My own self-awareness had disappeared. . . . I have often noticed that even a few minutes of this self-forgetfulness is tremendously invigorating" (198). For Dillard, such experiences are the crux of her visionary connection to the nonhuman world. It is an experience that, as Scott Slovic puts it, "frees the experiencer from the obstructive awareness of self" (*Seeking* 82). Such experiences—Edward Abbey describes how "the naked self merges with the non-human world, and yet somehow still survives intact, individual, separate" (*Desert* [1968] 6)—are a staple of contemporary environmental literature. Slovic identifies the conveying of such moments as part and parcel of one of environmental writers' most important projects: to "study the phenomenon of environmental consciousness and attempt to stimulate this heightened awareness among their readers" (*Seeking* 7). As such, this body of literature has had a vastly beneficial influence on the way people in the United States and elsewhere in Western culture have viewed the natural world.

But such "heightened awareness," however valid, proceeds unknowingly from a particular racial standpoint, as White's essay points out. White describes her initial discomfort—when she is teaching at a summer writing workshop in Oregon's Cascade Mountains—over the constant invitations to "trek to the lava beds, soak in the hotsprings, or hike into the mountains" (283). She cites the memory of two events that occurred during her childhood—the 1955 lynching in Mississippi of the fourteen-year-old African American Emmett Till and the 1963 church bombing that killed four African American girls in Birmingham, Alabama—as the reason for her "sense of vulnerability and exposure" (284). She describes a "fear I experience in the outdoors [that] is shared by many African American women and that limits the way we move in the world" (284). While she had enjoyed the sound of the river from inside her cabin or the view of the trees through the classroom window, White had felt "certain that if I ventured outside to admire a meadow or to feel the cool ripples in a stream, I'd be taunted, attacked, raped, maybe even murdered because of the color of my skin" (283). The forty minutes of stillness and concentration that Dillard needs to lose herself in the observation of the muskrat are an unattainable privilege for White. Unlike Dillard, White cannot "never know she was there." These contrasting views of the outdoors—the site of "self-forgetfulness" on the one hand, the site of "vulnerability and exposure" on the other—highlight the unconscious "race/power evasiveness" (Frankenberg 14–16) of much environmental literature in particular and of the mainstream environmental movement in general.

Even if White's essay ended here it would valuably address many reasons for the *apparent* lack of African American environmental writing. But White goes on to recover a connection to the outdoors familiar to any reader of environmental literature—and does so, moreover, from an African American cultural point of view. At the end of her essay, White recounts how she faces her fear of the outdoors by joining a rafting trip down the McKenzie River, and she describes her nearly palpable joy in finding that she can, as she says, "reconnect myself to the comfort my African ancestors felt in the rift valleys of Kenya and on the shores of Sierra Leone" (286). Her emphasis on the communal effort of paddling as well as her evocation of the positive nature-based experience of her African roots is a counterpoint to the solitary Euro-American "rambler" in nature that we trace back to Henry David Thoreau and John Muir. When she claims at the very end that "comforted by our tribal ancestors—herders, gatherers, fishers all—I am less fearful, ready to come home" (286), she is not only recovering an African American sense of place in North America. She is criticizing mainstream environmentalism's effortless appropriation—to the exclusion of African Americans, American Indians, and others—of North American nature as home (M. Evans 183). Teaching White's essay in a contemporary environmental literature course is a good way to spark discussion of topics ranging from differing cultures' attitudes toward nature to environmental racism.

White's essay, it turns out, is not an exception. Examples of African American environmental nonfiction are easily found, even within the traditional bounds of the nonfiction nature essay or book. A focus on "backcountry travel" might lead to Eddy L. Harris's *Mississippi Solo*, his 1988 account of canoeing the length of the Mississippi. It should be included in environmental literature courses organized around a number of themes: accounts of river expeditions; regional works on the Midwest, South, or the Mississippi; contemporary nature writing; or environmental justice. Along the same lines, Alice Walker's essay collection *Living by the Word* (1988), from which "Am I Blue?" is often excerpted, is replete with essays ("Everything Is A Human Being" and "Longing to Die of Old Age," to name just two) that deal directly with environmental issues or celebrate the natural world. The same is true of bell hooks, whose essays such as "Touching the Earth" and "Earthbound: On Solid Ground" are explicitly environmentalist in their call for "black folks" to "collectively renew our relationship to the earth" ("Earthbound" 70). In many cases, Walker and hooks mix environmental themes with themes of social justice in a way that seems atypical of Lyon's "taxonomy of nature writing." That is why a new taxonomy, such as can be found in T. V. Reed's call for an "environmental justice ecocriticism" is more apt (145). If we no longer insist on treating nature as separate from the human and define *environmental* to include issues other than wilderness preservation, then a book such as *Living by the Word* fits easily—in its entirety—into contemporary environmental literature courses that use essay collections such as Terry Tempest Williams's *An Unspoken Hunger* (1994) and Barry Lopez's *Crossing Open Ground* (1989).

A focus on urban space might include Harris's *Still Life in Harlem* (1996) or might just as easily include Wideman's *Brothers and Keepers*. Wideman's extraordinary memoir about his own and his brother's lives is a meditation on places and their influences on human lives, juxtaposing rural Laramie, Wyoming, where the author was teaching, against the urban neighborhood in Pittsburgh where he and his brother grew up—and juxtaposing both of these against the prison environment in which his brother is trapped. A focus on issues of environmental racism and environmental justice also would suggest the inclusion of Robert D. Bullard's *Dumping in Dixie* (1990), which focuses on the environmental degradation of poor African American communities in the South, or his *Confronting Environmental Racism* (1993), which includes essays about issues affecting not only African American but also Native American, Latino/a, and Asian American communities. If standards of environmental literature courses such as Williams's *Refuge* (1991) and Abbey's *Desert Solitaire* (1968) can take on political issues such as nuclear testing or the Glen Canyon Dam, there is no reason not to include books that address lead-paint poisoning, toxic-waste sites, and high asthma rates in poor urban neighborhoods. As part of a freshman writing course on environmental literature, I use the essays in *Confronting Environmental Racism* as models for a final research paper in which students explore a local environmental issue—such as a decision to situate a new power plant in a poor, densely populated Bronx neighborhood or the possibility of cancer clusters on Long Island. Along with these works by Walker, hooks, Harris, Wideman, and Bullard, I want to highlight two recent anthologies, both published in 2002, that do not focus exclusively on African American literature but that reconceptualize the environmental literature anthology in useful ways: *City Wilds*, edited by Terrell F. Dixon, which presents both fiction and nonfiction on the topic of urban nature, and *The Colors of Nature*, edited by Alison H. Deming and Laurent E. Savoy, which specifically addresses the need to represent the experience of the natural world by writers of color.

Going further back into literary history, Henry Bibb's *The Life and Adventures of Henry Bibb, an American Slave* (1849)—from which Carolyn Ross excerpts a passage in *Writing Nature*—recounts the author's escapes from slavery through "the wild forest," with "nothing to travel by but the sun by day and the moon and the stars by night" (Bibb 161). Even as an adolescent Bibb turned to the woods for temporary refuge from the torments of slavery (M. Dixon 3). Indeed, Bibb, throughout his account, continually contrasts the "beauties of nature . . . the green trees and wild flowers of the forest; the ripening harvest fields waving with the gentle breezes of Heaven" with the harsh fact of forced labor on that very land (Bibb 66). Similarly, he feels that his "chance was by far better among the howling wolves in the Red River Swamp"—into which he escapes with his wife and child—"than before Deacon Whitfield, on the cotton plantation" (131). I have recently taught Bibb's narrative in a course devoted to American environmental narratives and found that it holds up very well, in its entirety, to a complex ecocritical analysis: the work is no less "environmental" than William Bartram's *Travels* (1791) or Thoreau's *The Maine Woods* (1864), despite their difference in circumstances. Likewise, if writings about farm life have a place in environmental literature—Lyon reserves a whole category he calls "Farm Life" for writers from J. Hector Saint-John de Crèvecoeur to Wendell Berry—then surely chapters about black sharecropping such as "Of The Black Belt" from DuBois's *The Souls of Black Folk* (1903) have a place alongside them. And again, if memoirs of growing up in nature such as Janisse Ray's *Ecology of a Cracker Childhood* (1999) or Ivan Doig's *This House of Sky* (1978) are environmental literature, then Richard Wright's *Black Boy* (1945) is environmental literature.

As a white scholar and teacher of environmental literature, I found it all too easy, early in my teaching career, to ignore the implications of excluding African American writers—along with people of color in general—from the developing environmental literature canon. But as the environmental justice movement emerged as a major force in environmentalism, I became convinced that such a position served to reinforce the effacement, on the part of mainstream environmentalism, of the environmental concerns and experiences of people of color. I still teach—and greatly admire—the works of Thoreau, Muir, Leopold, Carson, Dillard, and their literary kin, but I no longer teach their culturally specific visions of the natural world to the exclusion of others. Indeed, in some ways most urban white students have more in common with the place-based experiences of some of the African American writers I have highlighted than they do with the likes of Thoreau and Muir. I have found that students—for somewhat differing reasons, both white students and students of color—come to value the understanding that a reading of African American responses to nature provides.

Joni Adamson

For the Sake of the Land and All People: Teaching American Indian Literatures from an Environmental Justice Perspective

In *Hunting for Hope*, Scott Russell Sanders recalls the joy in his seventeen-year-old son Jesse's face while the two were experiencing the risk and excitement of a whitewater-rafting expedition. In his recollection, he watches Jesse lean into the waves and catch his breath, happy and determined to meet the challenge of the water and waves. However, shortly before the two step into the raft, Sanders's son accuses his father of seeing clearly what ails the world environmentally but failing to live with joy and hope. Jesse pointedly asks his father why we should work for the environment, if all is already lost.

I was very moved when I first read Sanders's words about his son because I realized that, while raising my own three children, I also focused too often on the interlinked social and environmental issues we face in a world shaped by hundreds of years of racial oppression, gender and class discrimination, and multinational corporate and governmental irresponsibility. My daughter, Brittany, had once accused me of "always ruining everything." Brittany challenged me to give her not only the information and tools she needed to live a life in which she could contribute in meaningful ways to the building of a better world but also the hope that would carry her through that struggle.

I begin this essay with my own experience because many of my mostly non–Native American students come through the door on the first day of my senior-level course, Contemporary Native American Literature, bringing romanticized images of the "noble savage" and looking to me to teach them about the beautiful, ancient, oral traditions of America's indigenous peoples.[1] But, as they sometimes tell me, I "ruin everything," because we focus not only on ancient stories but on complex, interlinked social and environmental problems that are being faced by every tribe, band, and nation of American Indians today. Most Arizona students know something about the Hopi and the Diné (Navajo); however, high school lessons often leave indigenous peoples in a romanticized past. As a result, students know little or nothing of contemporary tribal cultures or their continuing battles for their people, communities, and environments.

When we read the contemporary works of post-1960s writers such as N. Scott Momaday (Kiowa), Ofelia Zepeda (Tohono O'odham), Simon Ortiz (Acoma), Leslie Marmon Silko (Laguna), Rigoberta Menchu (Quiche Maya), and Winona LaDuke (Anishinaabe [Chippewa/Ojibwe]), among others, we begin with discussions of the oral tradition, meaning the ancient creation stories, migration stories, customs, and ceremonies of the culturally diverse tribal peoples of the Americas. However, as Silko points out in *Yellow Woman and a Beauty of the Spirit*, among most tribal communities historical stories of colonial struggle and contemporary stories of how people have survived in the modern world and even of events that occur in local American Indian communities are considered just as sacred and as much a part of the oral traditions as the ancient stories.

In other words, contemporary American Indian people make no separation in their oral traditions between the ancient and the modern. For this reason, when students read contemporary American Indian poetry, prose, and novels, they read about Thought Woman's creation of the world as well as about uranium mining in the American Southwest. They read not only about the watery, mossy places associated with the creation of tribes but also about dubious contracts with multinational mining companies that are depleting sacred water sources. They learn about the Pueblo Revolt of 1680 and the American Indian movement of the 1960s and 1970s. As a result, I sometimes see that "you ruined everything" look in the students' faces. They want to know about beautiful ancient stories, but contemporary environmental problems are best avoided because they are too overwhelming. Students fear there is nothing they can do personally to stop the "machine in the garden." This sense of helplessness can lead to a loss of hope, as my daughter reminded me, that can disempower young people rather than give them the tools they need to address the challenges they face.

In this essay, then, I want to cover in very light strokes how I teach my upper-division course on American Indian oral and written literatures with the objective of giving students hope for the future while at the same time allowing them to confront contemporary environmental challenges. In broader strokes, I will focus on how I teach the work of one writer/ activist—Winona LaDuke. LaDuke's nonfiction and fiction often depicts community organizing that can be linked to the environmental justice movement. By examining the literature we cover from an environmental justice perspective, students take away from the course models for how they, too, can contribute meaningfully to the building of a better world, if that is something they choose to do.

Here let me make three points important to the teaching of this course. First, as I explain elsewhere (*American Indian Literature*), the origin of what has come to be known as the environmental justice movement is much older than usually acknowledged. It could be said that this movement began well over five hundred years ago, when indigenous peoples first began resisting exploitation and fighting for resources and lands that were being stolen by European colonizers. The Pueblo Revolt of 1680, for example, which is remembered in the oral traditions of the Pueblo peoples, brought together a loose coalition of oppressed, dispossessed, and poor Pueblo, Diné, Apache, detribalized Indians, and Hispanic people who "forcibly expelled the Spanish" (Adamson, *American Indian Literature* 53).

Over three hundred years later, in 1991, the First National People of Color Environmental Leadership Summit convened in Washington, DC. Over three hundred grassroots environmental leaders of Native, African, Latino, and Asian descent from all over the United States, Canada, Central and South America, Puerto Rico, and the Marshall Islands came together to discuss their experiences with "environmental racism" and to attempt to redress the "disproportionate incidence of environmental contamination in communities of the poor and/or communities of color" (Adamson, Evans, and Stein, Introduction 4).

Second, it is important to note that the movement for environmental justice brings together people of all races, classes, and genders, including people from diverse tribal groups, labor unionists, green business owners, mainstream environmentalists, Buddhist monks, and others. The "literature of environmental justice," as I define it in *American Indian Literature*, reflects this diversity. It includes oral traditions such as the stories told about the Pueblo Revolt of 1680, contemporary poetry, nonfiction prose, fiction, movement manifestos, Environmental Protection Agency documents, trade agreements, and the testimonies of people and groups who are challenging transnational corporate rhetoric about the benefits of "free" trade and globalization and who are working to gain a broader understanding of global politics, civil rights legislation, toxics issues, and multinational-trade-agreement law that is affecting the places they live, work, play, and worship.

American Indian poetry and fiction such as that found in Simon Ortiz's *Fight Back: For the Sake of the People, For the Sake of the Land* can be considered environmental justice literature because it depicts the same kinds of loose coalitions of peoples and groups we see in the environmental justice movement who are coming together to find a middle place where they can, by consensus, work toward common social and environmental justice goals. For example, in *Fight Back*, Ortiz depicts men of Pueblo American and Anglo-American backgrounds employed together in a mine. There, they discover their commonalities and some ways in which they might work together to address the injustices they face when their company refuses to maintain a safe workplace; depletes the resources in their surrounding community; and pollutes the air, water, and soil where they live.

Third, the inclusiveness of the environmental justice movement allows students of diverse backgrounds to imagine the ways in which they too, to use Ortiz's words, can work with others both like and unlike themselves to "fight back." As an Anglo-American professor, a woman, the daughter and granddaughter of railroad workers and union members, a mother, a consumer who makes choices, and a person who drinks water that likely contains contaminants, I talk to my students about the reasons why people like me, not just American Indians or grassroots environmental justice activists, should be concerned about what LaDuke describes as the "direct relationship between the loss of cultural diversity and the loss of biodiversity" (*All Our Relations* 1).

As an illustration of that relationship, LaDuke writes about Katsi Cook, who is "a Mohawk midwife turned environmental justice activist" (*All Our Relations* 11). Not only have the Mohawk survived the assault on their culture from broken treaties, boarding schools, and unemployment, they live in the Great Lakes region where an estimated twenty-five percent of all

North American industry is located. This puts Cook's people "downstream from some of the most lethal and extensive pollution on the continent" (15). Consequently, Mohawk mothers cannot nurse their own babies because their mothers' milk is saturated with polychlorinated biphenyls (PCBs). The question this raises for Cook is "How are we going to re-create a society where the women are going to be healthy? . . . The first environment is about a baby, a woman, and family" (qtd. in La Duke, *All Our Relations* 22). This question becomes the "middle place" from which I teach the course. I am not American Indian, and I am very careful not to position myself as an "expert" on all things Native. But I am a person concerned about the contamination of air, water, and land and about the ways in which this is affecting human health. I am also a person who has learned a great deal about these subjects from my American Indian students and from American Indian colleagues, friends, writers, and activists.

As students begin to understand Cook's concerns, they begin to understand their own connections to the interrelated loss of cultural diversity and biodiversity. To counter the loss of hope they sometimes experience when confronted with the extent of environmental degradation not only on Indian reservations but also in the urban areas where they live, I extend invitations to local, indigenous activists, elders, and writers and give students the opportunity to read activist biographies such as those found in LaDuke's *All Our Relations.* When they read about the experiences of these activists, they see how difficult the challenges are, but they also begin to see that it is possible for ordinary community members like themselves to take concrete, positive steps toward solving problems.

Also, the structure of the course itself, and the focus on American Indian literature and culture, helps students counter the sense that all the beauty has gone out of the world and there is nothing we can do to stop the destruction. The course begins with a unit that covers how and why American Indian oral traditions are kept alive in contemporary American Indian communities. Readings of N. Scott Momaday's *The Way to Rainy Mountain* and Silko's *Yellow Woman and a Beauty of the Spirit* teach students more about the creation stories, migration stories, customs, and ceremonies of the tribal peoples of the Americas. We discuss how the ancient stories inform contemporary experience and contribute to a developed sense of place and identity that builds hope and gives people the strength they need to engage in resistance to injustices.

We then study how the oral tradition teaches the sacredness and power of language and discuss how the ancient stories and more contemporary stories about local events are employed by elders, teachers, and family members to teach the values of the community to the young. We examine how variant versions of stories from the oral tradition strengthen a listener's powers of interpretation and ability to analyze both the old stories and current events. We ask questions about how and why contemporary writers attempt to transform oral traditions into written language and why they use new written forms of scholarship, nonfiction prose, poetry, and fiction to reach their own communities and expand their audience. To help answer these questions, we read my "Throwing Rocks at the Sun" and consider the Opata-Mayo activist Teresa Leal's argument that achieving a more sustainable, livable world will require reaching larger and larger audiences in accessible ways and different mediums and genres.

We then move to a unit on "Resistance, Transformation, and Regeneration" that covers the history of indigenous peoples in the Americas, examines contentious Indian-White relations from first contact through the massive loss of life due to pathogens; colonization; genocide; and, more recently, neocolonization by multinational corporations that extract the resources and exploit the labor of Indian nations while leaving behind toxic materials that pollute the air, water, and soil. We focus closely on the history of federal Indian policy in the United States and the importance of the issue of sovereignty among Indian nations in the fight to resist modern-day colonization by multinational corporations and to transform contemporary communities in ways that protect languages and cultures, ensure economic viability, and protect the environment.

We also briefly cover the history of Native literatures in the Americas by examining the Mayan almanacs, William Appess, John Rollins Ridge, Zitkala-Sa, and other pre-1960s writers. We ask questions about the role literature has played or is playing in ongoing battles to protect cultural diversity and biodiversity and discuss how both ancient and modern oral traditions—transformed into written forms such as scholarship, prose, poetry, and fiction—can be a kind of cultural critique that provides information and tools for the struggle.

The final two units of the course include readings of LaDuke's *All Our Relations* and *Last Standing Woman* and Silko's *Almanac of the Dead*. Since I have already written extensively in *American Indian Literature* about *Almanac of the Dead*, I will focus only on LaDuke's work. Over the course of these final units, we cover the emergence of ecocriticism as a field and discuss the problem with the interrelated, romanticized concepts of "wilderness" and Native peoples as "close to nature." I introduce

the environmental justice approach to literature-and-environment studies and Native American studies. We ask, What is environmental justice?
What is environmental justice literature? What would a just relationship
to community and place look like? We explore answers to these questions
as we read LaDuke's *All Our Relations* and examine the incredible acts of
resistance to interlinked cultural degradation and ecological destruction
mounted by each Native community organizer described by LaDuke.

LaDuke herself is not only a writer and scholar but an activist whose
perspectives and successful methods of community organizing are reflected
in her fiction. An enrolled member of the Mississippi Band Anishinaabeg,
she lives on the White Earth Reservation in Minnesota. As director of the
Honor the Earth Program (www.honorearth.com) and founding director
of the White Earth Land Recovery Project, she is systematically buying
back those parts of her reservation that have been questionably sold to
non-Anishinaabeg. In 1994, *Time* nominated LaDuke as one of the fifty
most-promising American leaders under the age of forty. She was well
known for her speeches and scholarly works even before she published
her first novel, *Last Standing Woman*, which traces seven generations of
Anishinaabe people.

In *Last Standing Woman*, LaDuke weaves most of the issues she
addresses in *All My Relations*, her nonfiction collection of biographies of
Native American grassroots environmental activists, into the context of
Anishinaabe oral traditions and seven generations of history. Interconnected stories are told in the voices of some powerful and some troubled
characters, who make clear connections between social injustices—racism,
sexism, domestic violence, unemployment—and environmental injustices,
such as stolen lands, corporate logging and milling, and contamination
seeping from a pulp plant. In an accessible genre likely to reach an even
larger audience than her scholarship or her nonfiction, LaDuke's characters reflect her own coalition building and writing activities at White
Earth.

In the novel, when the tribal council (which is profiting personally
from kickbacks from logging and milling corporations) attempts to sign
profitable leases, a determined group of people, mostly Anishinaabe, but
also some "progressive white people," form a coalition to resist giving
away reservation lands and resources (178). The tribal council refuses to
listen to them, so the Protect Our Land Coalition takes over the tribal
council's offices to make their point (147). One of the main characters,
Alanis Nordstrom, a half-Anishinaabe, half-Irish newspaper reporter who

has lived most of her life away from White Earth, returns home to tell the story to the world. She takes the following statement from Warren Wabun, a veteran of tribal political wars, numerous rallies, marches and takeovers:

> Ninety percent of this reservation is held by interests other than Native People. Our people have been forced into desperate poverty, and yet we watch our natural resources and wealth flow off this reservation, without any benefit to us. Now, the headwaters of the Mississippi River are threatened by contamination. This is our survival. We are not willing to surrender until there is some meaningful intention to negotiate. (180)

Later, Alanis hears Warren thanking the Great Spirit for the fax machine that will speed the story to the media and the world and bring pressure to bear on the tribal council. At that moment, Alanis is witness to the inseparability of ancient oral traditions and modern technology and written texts. Alanis's stories about tribal members committed to protecting their health and homes and the resulting negative media pressure force the tribal council to abandon its plans to sign leases with the corporations. The experience also convinces Alanis to move home and dedicate herself not only to writing but also to activism that will contribute to the building of a more livable, sustainable world.

Through the literature we read and the discussions in which we engage, my students and I explore activism as a function of being alive in the world and fully, joyfully engaged in the processes and forces that shape our world. I like to think that, like Sanders's son, Jesse, we are breathing and leaning into the waves and water. My students tell me that the course has changed the way they think about their world forever. They have examined the power and beauty of American Indian oral traditions and the possibilities for living in more sustainable ways; they know that unseen chemicals lurk in their water, and they wonder what will happen in the next seven generations if we do not attend to the issues and problems about which we have read. At the same time, they have examined the power of written texts and literary movements; they have pushed their discussions of environmental challenges beyond a focus on environmental racism and toxics and toward the positive and successful community activism we see in LaDuke's Honor the Earth Project and depicted in her fiction and nonfiction. Students have considered how LaDuke's savvy writings and organizing activities on behalf of her beloved White Earth increase her audience and raise the likelihood that many more will hear and understand—perhaps even act on—her message. This provides students with a powerful model for how their own actions, writings, and professional goals could result in a better, more just relation to people and place.

Note

1. The terms *Native American*, *Native*, and *Indian* are heavily laden with colonial history and political controversy. Joy Harjo and Gloria Bird note in *Reinventing the Enemy's Langauge* that "Native American" is a term invented in academe to replace the term "American Indian." They write that in "our communities we first name ourselves by tribe, but the general term commonly used is *Indian* in the United States" (20). Some American Indian authors, Ortiz for example, do use the term *Native American*. Throughout the introductory essay of *Woven Stone*, Ortiz uses the term Native American when referring to Indian people as an increasingly empowered political group and *Native American Literature* when referring to the growing body of poetry, fiction, and nonfiction by Indian writers. In this essay, I will use *Indian* or specific tribal names when referring to individual authors, *American Indian* when referring to groups that include more than one tribal group, and *Native American* when making references to the academic fields of Native American studies or Native American literature.

Scott Slovic

Teaching United States Environmental Literature in a World Comparatist Context

> *Our campuses are producing citizens, and this means that we must ask what a good citizen of the present day should be and should know. The present-day world is inescapably multicultural and multinational. Many of our most pressing problems require for their intelligent, cooperative solution a dialogue that brings together people from many national and cultural and religious backgrounds.*
>
> —Martha Nussbaum

The Ecology of Comparative Thinking

Those of us who routinely teach literature and writing from an environmental perspective will immediately find resonance in the philosopher Martha Nussbaum's linkage of education and citizenship. We tend to view our own work space—our offices and classrooms—not as rarefied retreats from society but as privileged vantage points from which to observe and reform society. We see our students not as pliable receptacles to fill with abstract knowledge but as collaborators—as fellow citizens—with whom to build a safer, cleaner, more just world. Of course, the obstacles to social justice and environmental protection are immense—and it is easy for idealists to lapse into despair. When daunted by the immensity of the world's problems and the steady loss of ground that seems to be the name of the game, it is helpful to think of the environmental educator Mitchell Thomashow's simple formulation: "you don't have to be optimistic to be hopeful" (*Bringing* 18). Despite the bleakness of the big picture, it is possible to live a "hopeful," constructive life, chipping away at the world's problems day after day.

As Nussbaum claims, the world is "inescapably multicultural and multinational" (8). All who study environmental topics, whether literary scholars, economists, or biologists, understand that phenomena such as climate, population, and pollution do not fit neatly in national—or even hemispheric—borders. Patterns of climate change, population impact, and ecological degradation may begin with local human behavior, but the effects of such behavior are far-reaching. Just as the outrageous actions of a single household can upset an entire neighborhood, the ill-considered tendencies of a single nation—or group of nations—can implicate the entire planet in a devastating trend. From an ecological perspective, it makes sense that we think both locally and globally. As John Muir famously exaggerated, "When we try to pick out anything by itself, we find it hitched to everything else in the universe" (*First Summer* [1911] 157). To study North American environmental literature without even a gesture toward literary, historical, and philosophical trends elsewhere on the planet is, some might argue, akin to studying the ecology of Jeffrey pines in a Sierra forest without noting the relation between Jeffreys and lodgepoles, junipers, piñons, aspens, seed-caching rodents, numerous bird species, fire, and the many other forces and creatures whose actions have an impact on the Jeffrey pines. To isolate a single species in an ecological system borders on nonsense—to read a single national literature in isolation, whatever the excuse, could be considered similarly shortsighted.

The United States, as has been widely recognized, is a leader in innovative thinking about nature and culture and the literary expression of these ideas, despite (or perhaps because of) the fact that American consumer behavior, business practices, and military actions are responsible for environmental degradation across the globe. Because of the richness and easy accessibility of American environmental writing in our own country, it is common for teachers of environmental writing and literature, from the high school level up through graduate seminars, to focus on home-grown authors, as if American culture somehow existed in a vacuum, isolated from and perhaps superior to the literary expression of environmental ideas in other parts of the world. This is an understandable perspective, but also a dangerous one. For one thing, the isolationist approach to teaching American environmental writing limits instructors' and students' access to powerful insights that come from other cultures. Another concern is that the supposed predominance of American environmental thought and literature creates a shady canopy that prevents other voices from thriving, resulting in an unhealthy intellectual monoculture. One of the best antidotes to isolationist ignorance and monocultural intellectual poverty is the effort to explore environmental literature in a multinational, comparatist context.

Nussbaum suggests that the three capacities "essential to the cultivation of humanity in today's world" (9) are "critical examination of oneself and one's traditions" (9); seeing oneself not only as a local citizen but also as a person "bound to all other human beings by ties of recognition and concern" and recognizing that "the world around us is inescapably international" (10); and using the "narrative imagination" to "think what it might be like to be in the shoes of a person different from oneself, to be an intelligent reader of that person's story, and to understand the emotions and wishes and desires that someone so placed might have" (10–11). Although she does not explicitly comment on the relevance of these intellectual capacities and education goals to environmental consciousness, the connection between these approaches and the teaching of United States environmental literature in a comparatist context seems clear.

American ecocritics have benefited from such publications as John Elder and Hertha Wong's *Family of Earth and Sky: Indigenous Tales of Nature from around the World* and Patrick D. Murphy's *Literature of Nature: An International Sourcebook*, which have made dramatic gestures toward revealing international traditions of environmental literature. But the idea of actually teaching international environmental literature remains daunting to many teachers in this country, most of whom are specialists in single national literatures or perhaps in anglophone literatures. However, there is a wealth of powerful international environmental writing that, if not originally written in English, is now available in translation. And, increasingly, there are ecocritics working throughout the world whose efforts make it possible for teachers in North America (and elsewhere) to use far-flung environmental texts in the classroom without fear of completely misrepresenting local cultural, aesthetic, and ecological issues.

Core Humanities and the Scrutiny of Fat Brother

One of the most common courses offered by American university instructors in the humanities is some sort of introduction to American literature and culture. For the better part of a decade, I have occasionally taught an introduction to American culture for large groups of undergraduates at the University of Nevada, Reno. This is the third part of a required humanities sequence for all undergraduates at the university—the first two segments emphasize classical and modern European culture. Often in this course, The American Experience, I have emphasized such themes as movement (migration/immigration) and sense of place in American culture. Inspired by many of the books and articles I had read by American and international authors in the wake of 9/11, I decided to refocus the course to consider the phenomenon of consumption in our society, with a particular emphasis on how America is viewed from outside its borders. It is perhaps a truism to state that one can appreciate criticism most deeply if that criticism is directed toward someone else. This is, for American university students, one of the virtues of Arundhati Roy's *Power Politics*. Her book indicts not only the American government's violent response to 9/11 (the absurdity of "bombing Afghanistan back to the stone age": "[s]omeone please break the news," she writes acidly, "that Afghanistan is already there" [113]) but also the Indian government's callous displacement of tens of millions of Indian peasants through cooperation with international energy speculators (many of them based in the United States) who are urging dam-building projects in the Third World, despite that most of the local people do not need—and will never benefit from—the energy produced by the eventual dams. The apparent indifference of the Indian government toward its own citizens and its harassment of writers and activists (including Roy herself) who speak up about the injustice they perceive is a useful story for American students as they turn to think about the role of the artist, today and throughout history, in our own cultural context.

Although this course does not concentrate on environmental literature per se, many of our readings are in fact examples of such literature. The course also provides an occasion to combine literary texts with historical and economic readings and with a broad range of cultural commentaries. We begin this course by discussing the American studies scholar James Farrell's "Shopping: The Moral Ecology of Consumption" as a way of signaling that even mundane daily activities, such as visiting shopping malls, can merit academic scrutiny. Farrell's concerned, evenhanded treatment of our society's habits of consumption helps set the tone for the entire class—our goal is not simple celebration or critique of America but rather analysis and explanation. We follow the Farrell article with a series of readings on the importance of dissent and freedom of imagination in a democratic society; in particular, we focus on Azar Nafisi's *Reading* Lolita *in Tehran: A Memoir in Books* and two essays, "Saying Grace" and "And Our Flag Was Still There," from Barbara Kingsolver's *Small Wonder*. In a way, Kingsolver's brief, accessible pieces serve as the centerpiece for the entire course because of her notions of the importance of outspokenness ("dissent") and the danger of arrogant selfishness ("hubris"). For me, her parable of Fat Brother and his family, presented in a single paragraph in the essay "Saying Grace," articulates the essence of why it is important to consider American culture—including American environmental literature—in a comparatist context. To do so is an immediate recipe for humility. "Imagine," she writes,

> that you come from a large family in which one brother ended up with a whole lot more than the rest of you. Sometimes it happens that way, the luck falling to one guy who didn't do that much to deserve it. Imagine his gorgeous house on a huge tract of forests, rolling hills, and fertile fields. . . . Your kids cry themselves to sleep on empty stomachs. Your brother must not be able to hear them from the veranda where he dines, because he throws away all the food he can't finish. He will do you this favor: He's made a TV program of himself eating. If you want, you can watch it from your house. But you can't have his food, his house, or the car he drives around in to view his unspoiled forests and majestic purple mountains. The rest of the family has noticed that all his driving is kicking up dust, wrecking not only the edges of his property but also their less pristine backyards and even yours, which was dust to begin with. . . . You're beginning to see that these problems are deep and deadly, that you'll be the first to starve, and the others will follow. The family takes a vote and agrees to do a handful of obvious things that will keep down the dust and clear the water—all except Fat Brother. He walks away from the table. He says God gave him good land and the right to be greedy. (24)

It does not take particular prescience to understand this harsh view of America's place in the international "family" of human beings (and other species). We proceed from Kingsolver to read Roy's *Power Politics*, noting Roy's analysis of the economic and social impacts of American corporations (especially, big energy) on her country on the other side of the ocean from North America. At the same time, we read and talk about T. Coraghessan Boyle's darkly comic novel, *The Tortilla Curtain*, which depicts the accidental relationship between a couple of undocumented Mexican workers and a yuppie nature writer who writes a column in homage to Annie Dillard called "Pilgrim at Topanga Creek" from his home in a Southern California gated community. The gap between haves and have-nots, between consumers and those whose land and lives are consumed by others, is engagingly and provocatively etched by writers from the Unites States and abroad. The epigraph of Boyle's novel comes from John Steinbeck's *The Grapes of Wrath*: "They ain't human. A human being wouldn't live like they do. A human being couldn't stand it to be so dirty and miserable." Whether comparing the lives of people within the borders of the United States or across borders, one of the crucial purposes of studying literature in any comparatist context is to cultivate the empathy needed to appreciate and validate other points of view.

Throughout the remainder of the semester, we trace consumptive tendencies in America—and resistance to these tendencies—back to the nineteenth century (industrialization) and before (colonization), reading *Walden* and Barry Lopez's *The Rediscovery of North America*, the autobiographies of Benjamin Franklin and Frederick Douglass, Morris Berman's *The Twilight of American Culture*, and Alan Brinkley's sharp and comprehensive history text *An Unfinished Nation*. Eventually, we turn to consider alternative possibilities for American culture—less hubristic and exploitative directions. We find articulations of some of these ideas in Paul Hawken's *The Ecology of Commerce* and Richard Nelson, Barry Lopez, and Terry Tempest Williams's *Patriotism and the American Land*.

While this course, called Consuming America, is not specifically an examination of environmental literature, it is in fact a broad introduction to American culture from an interdisciplinary, multicultural, and international viewpoint. Although the readings may stack up to appear like a rather bleak treatment of America, I try to put a positive spin on the powerful history of dissent, critique, and envisioning of cultural alternatives that defines our society. Openness to both the statements of international writers such as Nafisi and Roy and the outsider perspectives of Kingsolver, Lopez, and many other American writers is an essential part of the learning experience in this course. For the sake of briefly summarizing the material emphasized in this course, I have perhaps overstated the "messages" of the readings—in reality, the students themselves wrestle with the curious juxtaposition of Roy's analysis of modern India and Lopez's version of Spanish colonization. As I mention above, the criticism of the Indian government is, for some students, easier to swallow, at first, than the less-than-glowing version of our own history.

Comparative Geography: Red Centre and Brown Southwest

Although the title of this essay refers broadly to the teaching of United States literature in a world comparatist context, the reality is that it is often more manageable and bioregionally coherent to focus a course on specific groupings of cultures, texts, authors, and landscapes. My first foray in this direction was a course called Red Centre and Brown Southwest: An Introduction to Australian and American Desert Literature, which I offered at the University of Nevada, Reno, in the spring of 2003. The American Southwest has long been recognized as a region of spectacular natural beauty where complicated struggles among various groups have taken place. Perhaps as a result of these first two factors, the Southwest has produced some of the most exciting environmental literature, such as Edward Abbey's *Desert Solitaire*, Rudolfo Anaya's *Bless Me, Ultima*, Simon J. Ortiz's *Woven Stone*, and Terry Tempest Williams's *Refuge*. It seems a natural step to begin considering American desert writing in comparison with desert writing from other countries—and Australia is an obvious place to look for such writing, given that a vast portion of the Australian continent is extremely arid.

As mentioned in the discussion of core humanities above, it is much easier to analyze ourselves and our own culture by looking for similar traits in other people and other cultures and then allowing our reflections to boomerang back, so to speak, and illuminate ourselves and our own places. Sometimes it is simply hard to criticize what is too close to home. I had this in mind in creating the comparative United States–Australian desert literature course. One of my central goals was the consideration of how Native people have been treated and mistreated by so-called settler cultures in particular parts of the world, often represented as backward and unambitious despite their exquisite adaptation to rugged terrains and climates. So I began this course with poems by the contemporary aboriginal poet Jack Davis, especially his piece "From the Plane Window" in *Black Life* ("Some call it desert / But it is full of life / pulsating life / if one knows where to find it / in the land I love" [73]), and worked up to the recently published memoir *Rabbit-Proof Fence*, by Doris Pilkington, an eloquent narrative about the "stolen generation," the Australian government's practice of removing (basically, *stealing*) aboriginal children from their families and communities and absorbing them into white Australian society. We also read James Vance Marshall's well-known novel *Walkabout*, which brings together segregationist perspectives from the American South and aboriginal

Australian perspectives on nature and human relationships, concluding with a sort of fantasy of adaptation to place and worldview expansion. We balanced treatments of the politics and experience of aboriginal Australia with Native American readings from my anthology *Getting Over the Color Green: Contemporary Environmental Literature of the Southwest* and such books as Ofelia Zepeda's poetry collection *Ocean Power* and Gary Paul Nabhan's *Coming Home to Eat*. Nabhan's book implies that even non-Native people can, through careful efforts, learn to live relatively appropriately in desert places.

Other major themes in the course included the exploration of gender identity in frontierlike desert locales and the use of literature to record natural phenomena and tell stories of environmental appreciation. Reading Robyn Davidson's personal narrative *Tracks* and Susan Hawthorne's novel *The Falling Woman* helped raise issues of misogyny and power in the far-away and, for my students, neutral landscapes of central Australia—and I believe this made it easier for us to discuss the same issues in a close-to-home context when it came time to look at Williams's *Red: Passion and Patience in the Desert*. We also juxtaposed the politically probing chapters of Abbey's *Desert Solitaire* with the more meditative and scientifically factual essays of Craig Childs's *The Secret Knowledge of Water*, and then we traced some of the same themes of home, tourism, escape, and ecological awareness in Tim Winton's Western Australia novel *Dirt Music* and Mark O'Connor's poems from "The Centre" section of *The Olive Tree: Collected Poems*.

For me, it was a particular delight to introduce my American students to one small branch of the "gum tree of Australian literature" (perhaps more appropriate than our usual tip-of-the-iceberg metaphor) while guiding them to the beauty and social urgency of American desert literature. I found myself frequently drawing rough maps of Australia and America's desert Southwest on our classroom whiteboard—efforts to orient students and give them some stable geographic footing. Likewise, I took advantage of the insights and experiences of several students in the class who had spent time in Australia and were eager to use their personal perspectives as a way of making our readings more real, more relevant to our academic discussion here in the western United States.

Since most of my students had never ventured Down Under in person, I found it useful, too, to show the film versions of *Walkabout* and *Rabbit-Proof Fence*, mainly to give students an opportunity to view Australian desert landscapes. It turned out that most of the students had scarcely wandered beyond the downtown casinos since their arrival in Reno, so we also took a class field trip to Incandescent Rock, north of Reno, for a three-hour scramble through a landscape reminiscent of southern Utah's canyon lands and eerily comparable with parts of the Australian outback. Juxtaposing familiar and exotic texts, familiar and exotic landscapes, our purpose in this class was to open up desert places as intriguing and important and beautiful loci of contemplation.

In lieu of an actual field trip to Australia and as a means of benefiting from the external view of American culture that tends to occur when studying literature in a comparatist context, I collaborated two years later (during the Northern Hemisphere spring of 2005) with Ruth Blair from the University of Queensland on an experimental pair of overlapping courses. We matched up my Nevada course titled Toward an Ethic of Place: Literature of the American West with Ruth's Queensland course titled Literature and Environment, using three texts in common: Williams's *Refuge*, Silko's *Ceremony*, and Winton's *Dirt Music*. My students read a total of ten books (plus numerous shorter selections), while the Australian students worked with six book-length literary works and a course reader compiled for their class—so the actual overlapping of the classes constituted a rather modest portion of the curriculum. I included Winton's western Australian novel in my western *American* literature course because we can learn interesting things about the complexities of communities and places at home by considering the literary representation of comparable settings elsewhere in the world. Moreover, my students each gave class presentations on one of the shared books (*Refuge*, *Ceremony*, or *Dirt Music*), we made the two-page presentation write-ups available to the Queensland students by an e-mail discussion list, and we used the Nevada papers to prompt e-mail exchanges between the American and Australian students. The Nevada students soon came to recognize the similarities and differences between their own readings of Williams and Silko (and Australian author Winton) and those of the Australians. In particular, the American students noticed their own tendencies to accept uncritically the exotic narrative of Winton and the Australian students' idealization of both Silko's Native American narrative and Williams's bitter treatment of the medical implications of mid-twentieth-century nuclear testing in the Nevada desert. In Winton's novel, the character Luther Fox has lost his family in a car accident and ends up living on the margins of acceptable society, making a living by poaching fish. He finds a kind of personal salvation by striking up an affair with Georgie, the alienated wife of a prominent local fisherman, and also by "going bush" and thus forcing himself into an existential crisis through his experiences in the wild and remote setting of coastal, northwestern Australia. American students, who might have found some of the narrative elements in *Dirt Music* far-fetched if set in more familiar landscapes, were willing to suspend disbelief because the novel takes place in the strangeness of western Australia—and the sometimes cynical comments by Australian students ("this is not really how Australians behave") helped correct the illusions of readers in Nevada. Likewise, some of the e-mail commentaries the Nevada students sent to their counterparts in Queensland may have helped the Australian students realize that the struggles of cultural transition and disenfranchisement by the military-industrial establishment described by Silko and Williams are comparable, in certain ways, with the struggles of aboriginal communities and rural communities affected by nuclear testing and mining in Australia.

Ruth and I had initially hoped to arrange video conferencing between our students on opposite sides of the planet, but, for technological and time-zone reasons, we could not make that happen. It was also difficult, because of other goals for her class, for Ruth to assign her students formal presentations on the shared texts to match up with my own students' work. So we compromised by using the Nevada students' papers as discussion prompts and facilitating electronic correspondence between our two classes. I consider this a demonstration that even a course focused on a particular national literature (indeed, a *regional* literature, such as that of the American West) can benefit from a comparatist twist.

Environmental Literature South of the Border

My core humanities class described above, while including comparative components, tends to be focused primarily on American literature and culture—on what Nussbaum would call "oneself and one's traditions." The American and Australian desert-literature class extends the scope of awareness to a transnational level, guiding students to think about how desert dwellers in one part of the world might be "bound" to people on the other side of the planet through comparable landscapes and experiences. In recent years, I have also taught a graduate seminar on Latin American and Caribbean environmental literature that highlighted the otherness of cultural experiences and landscapes in a part of the world relatively proximate to the United States. From an ecological perspective, we in North America have much in common with the countries south of the United States–Mexico border, ranging from the birds that migrate north and south to the trading of goods and labor up and down our shared land and waterways. I have long been interested in the cultures and writings of Latin America and the Caribbean, but I felt painfully ignorant of the relevant literature—so I used several articles that had appeared in the journal *ISLE* and three relevant articles from Murphy's *Literature of Nature* collection as a foundation; began searching for translations of primary texts from French, Spanish, and Portuguese; and developed an exploratory graduate seminar. The primary goals of this course were to develop preliminary familiarity with a few of the major twentieth-century and contemporary writers of Latin America and the Caribbean and to determine whether the perspectives and methodologies of contemporary North American ecocriticism can be fruitfully applied to literary works that may not have been written from an ecological perspective similar to our own. For instance, Niall Binns writes, in "Landscapes of Hope and Destruction: Ecological Poetry in Spanish America," that "whereas [the British critic] Jonathan Bate sees in myth a way of curbing ecological mayhem, [the Mexican poet Octavio] Paz places his hopes in a poetry bound together analogically with itself and the universe" ([2003] 137).

Though admittedly a newcomer to the materials we studied in this class, I felt confident that I knew enough about the broad range of ecocritical techniques and viewpoints to suggest scholarly approaches that might be relevant to the readings we did together in this class. We actually started the seminar by reading the ethnobiologist Wade Davis's narrative *One River: Explorations and Discoveries in the Amazon Rain Forest*, in part to demonstrate the virtue of traipsing boldly and open-mindedly into untraveled territory—a virtue that is useful to keep in mind whenever beginning a comparatist pedagogical or scholarly project. Davis also makes it clear that there are deep ecological and commercial connections between the United States and its many neighbors to the south, thus reinforcing the importance of knowing something about cultures and environments elsewhere in the Western Hemisphere.

We had time to survey only one branch of the "rubber tree of Latin American and Caribbean literature" (apologies for reusing the tree metaphor), but this nonetheless enabled students to become acquainted with the writings of José María Arguedas (*Deep Rivers*), Homero Aridjis (*Eyes to See Otherwise / Ojos, de otro mirar: Selected Poems*), Miguel Ángel Asturias (*Men of Maize*), Alejo Carpentier (*The Lost Steps*), Jamaica Kincaid (*A Small Place*), V. S. Naipaul (*Miguel Street*), Pablo Neruda (*Extravagaria*), Octavio

Paz (*A Tree Within*), Derek Walcott (*Omeros*), Mario Vargas Llosa (*The Storyteller*), and Raúl Zurita (*Anteparadise*).

Several of the texts—including Davis's *One River*, Carpentier's *The Lost Steps*, and Kincaid's *A Small Place*—make clear that natural-resource exploitation and even something as apparently benign as tourism have dangerous implications for traditional cultures and local ecology. Other works—such as Arguedas's *Deep Rivers*, Asturias's *Men of Maize*, and Vargas Llosa's *The Storyteller*—emphasize the extraordinary indigenous narratives that explore the intersections between human beings, places, and animals in regions ranging from Peru to Guatemala. Naipaul's *Miguel Street* and Walcott's *Omeros*, like Vargas Llosa's *The Storyteller*, examine the phenomena of migration and cultural convergence throughout the Americas. And such authors as Paz and Aridjis, both from Mexico, con-template natural processes such as erosion and contemporary environmen-tal problems (for example, Mexico City's air quality and the endangerment of gray-whale birthing waters in the Gulf of California). A recently pub-lished scholarly collection called *Caribbean Literature and the Environ-ment: Between Nature and Culture*, edited by Elizabeth M. DeLoughrey, Renée K. Gosson, and George B. Handley, would greatly facilitate new versions of this course because it offers useful lists of authors and texts from throughout the region, historical background about relevant cul-tural and ecological issues, and theoretical contexts for the phenomena of hybridity and creolization.

It is exciting to list the texts for the above-mentioned courses and to sketch out the basic themes that emerge when such works are explored in the classroom, knowing that other regions in the world have produced similar riches of words and ideas, similar stories about how cultures belong to and violate the ecologies of their places. The study—and teaching—of United States environmental literature in comparison with literature from other places in the world enables us both to see ourselves reflected in distant mirrors and to use our "narrative imagination," as Nussbaum puts it, in order to appreciate the "emotions and wishes and desires" of other people in other places. Both of these intellectual practices—self-scrutiny and empathy—are crucial to the process of molding ourselves and our students into "good citizens" of the world.

SueEllen Campbell

Asking Ecocritical Questions

As an ecocritically minded teacher of literature, I begin with the premise that the environment matters. Then, borrowing tactics from many kinds of criticism, I ask all sorts of questions about the texts I read, and I teach my students to do the same.

Of course all questions are not equally productive: some dead-end quickly, some evaporate into the vast spaces of speculation; some are not really questions at all but are disguised as arguments, rants, or emotional reactions; some require information that is hard to come by in a classroom; some are too easy. So it matters how questions are constructed, how we ask them, how we teach students to develop their own. If questions are carefully handled, I have learned, even the simplest ones will open up into layered mazes of complications—and into unexpected illuminations.

What I offer here is a sample set of the questions I explore with my classes on the literature of nature and the environment. Some of these questions are what I see as necessary basics; others open into current ecocritical issues. Because all questions (and their key terms) can and should be qualified, modified, and elaborated for specific texts and contexts, and because when they are asked about particular texts they expand quickly, in this essay I have simplified them and made them generic, though I have occasionally gestured toward well-known and potentially productive examples. With a little coaching and thoughtful, talkative students at any college or graduate level, each paragraph below can easily fill a class period and provoke several term papers.

Beginning with the Text

In recent years I have found myself returning to the classic formalist questions about character, plot, point of view, imagery, theme, and so forth. These simple but potentially incisive questions can cut equally well through the smooth and nearly invisible surface of a book like Aldo Leo-pold's *Sand County Almanac*, the charismatic shield of a book like Edward Abbey's *Desert Solitaire*, and the challenging complexities of something like Henry David Thoreau's *Walden*. They are tools that help students grasp the basic structure and ideas of texts and also what the writer might have wanted to accomplish—two things I think it is important to consider from the start.

What kind of character is the person or narrator whose "voice" we are "hearing" as we read? What is this voice like? What kinds of sentence structures, words, images does the speaker use? What is his or her rhetorical stance? (Abbey's stance in *Desert Solitaire* is very different from Rachel Carson's in *Silent Spring*: but exactly how, and so what?) What is the primary grammatical point of view, and does it change? How is this technical choice connected to the conceptual (or perceptual) point of view? Anthropologists often act as participant observers, a concept that fits much environmental literature. Is the narrator an outsider-observer, an insider-participant, or both? In what proportions? (Compare Columbus with Lewis and Clark: where do they observe? where do they participate?) Does the narrator's conceptual point of view change through the text?

What other characters are important? Are some of them nonhuman, even inanimate? Is the setting a character, and, if so, how? Can a rock be a character? Can a blizzard? Can a farm? How about Walden Pond? the Missouri River, the Mississippi, the Colorado? How does each character add to the text? How does the narrator relate to these characters? How does the narrator filter what we learn about other characters?

How are animal characters perceived, described, and valued? As stimulus-response machines? As products of evolution, fighting to survive? As objects of our scientific inquiry? As servants to humans, or as imitation humans? Does the author personify or anthropomorphize animals? With what purposes and results? Does the text see animals as beings equal in value to humans, partly like us and partly different—partly mysterious? Consider Abbey's dancing snakes, John Muir's dog Stickeen, Barry Lopez's wolves or polar bear, Diane Ackerman's bats and penguins: how do these authors talk about these animals, why, and to what effects?

What is the basic structure of the text? Is it an almanac, journal, journey, rant, quest, physical or mental exploration, jeremiad, meditation, something else? Compare Leopold's almanac with the winter-to-winter time frame of Annie Dillard's *Pilgrim at Tinker Creek* or *Walden*'s summer through spring: their structures are similar but not the same, and their differences are interesting. What if we think about Meriwether Lewis's and William Clark's journals as a quest narrative? And what about a more complicated book like Terry Tempest Williams's *Red* or Dillard's *For the Time Being*?

How many plots are there? Can we distinguish, say, an event plot (what happens when), a telling plot (how the story unfolds), and a thematic plot (so what?)? Are there layers of plots? Is there a story behind the story? Do the climaxes of all the plots coincide? If not, why? If the text has chapters or subsections, how are they related to each other and to the plot? Does each part have its own plot, or are they, rather, installments in a book-long plot, or both? Is there an exterior plot and an interior plot, a physical one in the landscape, a second emotional or conceptual one in the narrator's mind? If so, does one direct the other? How else are they related?

Thinking about the Landscape

Environmental literature typically (or perhaps by definition) foregrounds the landscape, and ecocritics typically do the same thing in any text we read: that is, we assume at least as a hypothesis that places operate as more than just background settings and sources of imagery. When we consider the land itself as a critical factor, we most clearly distinguish ecocriticism from other current modes of literary study, but we also share with other current critical approaches an interest in human cultural, social, and political issues. These subjects are extremely difficult to separate, of course, and there are often excellent reasons not to try.

What kinds of nature and environment are of interest in this text? How does the author define these terms (explicitly or implicitly), and how useful are these definitions? What kinds of landscapes (wild, agricultural, toxic, restored, domestic, urban, suburban, feral, garden, etc.) are important, and how? (Contrast the desert wilderness of *Red* with the urban alleys of Robert Sullivan's *Rats*, the woodlot retreat of *Walden* with Leopold's farm.) What are the text's attitudes toward these landscapes? Do these attitudes challenge those held by the larger culture at the time the text was written? Now?

How intimately, how thoroughly, and in what ways does the author-narrator know these places? How many kinds of lenses are used to look at a place? How involved are the author-narrator's body, senses, imagination, heart, memory, curiosity, intellect, passion?

How aware is the author of the other living things in this place and how they relate to one another? How much does she or he think about what is not visible to a human observer, at this time? Is the human history of this place considered? Its environmental history? How it is (and has been) linked to other places through commerce, politics, ecology? Disturbing things about the place, such as pollutants and extinction? How the place has changed, recently and over deep time? What relations are visible in this text among the local, regional, and global? Are these categories understood in terms of bioregions, human cultures, political boundaries, watersheds, economics, ecosystems, worldwide forces (like climate change), something else?

What kinds of scientific information are present? How are facts framed and used? What scientific assumptions and models underlie them? What understanding of issues like evolution, environmental change, ecological relations, and so forth? How much faith in science is visible? How much is the information provided by science integrated with cultural information? What kinds of research has the author done? How much scientific literacy—or knowledge of the history of the natural sciences—do we need to be good readers of this text? What different things should we know to read William Bartram and David Quammen, and what is it like to read Bartram from the time of Quammen?

How might we describe the text's environmental politics? Is the author-narrator an environmental fundamentalist or a relativist? Is he nostalgic for something that has been lost? If so, is that nostalgia sentimental or robust? What is her attitude toward contemporary life—globalization, multinational corporations, sport-utility vehicles, virtual reality, shopping malls, agribusiness, consumer capitalism, other forces and issues of our time? If the text is older, what is its attitude toward the comparable issues of its own time? Is the text subversive or resistant to dominant forces and patterns? What alternatives does its response suggest?

When human desires (for jobs; mobility; prosperity; children; moving to richer, safer countries) conflict with other environmental values, how does the author-narrator choose? How concerned is the text with climate change, species extinction, habitat loss, toxic pollutants, resource depletion, population increase, warfare, desertification, disease, hunger, and so forth? What kinds of solutions does the text offer, if any? Are these solutions nostalgic? Misanthropic? Idealistic? What are their conceptual and practical implications? Is the author or the text activist? How? Compare Thoreau with Carson or with Rick Bass: what kinds of politics and activism does each enact?

What seem to be the author's religious, spiritual, moral, and ethical values, beliefs, and emotions? Does she or he regard the land (all or just parts?) as sacred, and, if so, how might we describe that vision of sacredness and its cultural contexts? Does the text use religious language or refer to specific religious beliefs or stories? (Dillard, Williams, and Gary Snyder speak overtly about religious ideas; how do their investigations compare with the ethical questions asked by Leopold or Kathleen Dean Moore?) How does the author understand the human position on the planet, our responsibilities to the rest of its occupants? What vision of happiness, fulfillment, or a good life does the text offer? (Think about the zest for life that is so evident in Thoreau's and Muir's books. What is its source?) What balance does the text offer between prohibitions (don't do this) and encouragements (do this)?

In what ways does the text deal with human cultural issues of identity, race, ethnicity, class, gender, sexuality, power, justice, and so on? Are race and ethnicity foregrounded, or not? Is this author conscious of the effects of his or her ethnic, racial, and class positions and their cultural histories? Does the author accept or resist these effects? Does the author's gender and sexual orientation affect the text? (How should we read Abbey's comments about women?) Does the text have anything to say about masculinity or femininity, about gender and sexual identity, perception, and behavior? (Compare Gretchen Legler's *All the Powerful Invisible Things* with Williams's *Red*.) What human power relations are evident, either present or past? Are some of them colonial or imperialistic? Are they economic, or class-based? What is the stance of the text toward these topics?

With these issues, does the text seem to be retrograde, old-fashioned, conventional, progressive, inventive, quirky? What connections does the text make or suggest between these human issues and the land, or between these issues and human relationships with the land? Is identity conceived of as partly, or significantly, ecological? Is place, or natural environment, seen as part of what creates identity? (Consider the work of Gary Paul Nabhan, Gary Snyder, Leslie Marmon Silko, or Keith Basso.) What is the author's or narrator's attitude toward other people on the land sharing the same place? What cultural issues beyond those directly connected to land are present in this text? Are they linked to land issues or seen as separate?

Carrying on the Conversation

Like other literary critics, ecocritics are interested in the cultural work done by texts and in the conversations that develop in communities of writers, books, and readers. The following questions address, in different ways, these conversations.

In what genres or subgenres is this text? What conventions does it make use of? Into what literary traditions does the author seem to be entering? (Think about what Robert Sullivan does with the model of *Walden* in his *Meadowlands* and *Rats*.) Does the text change, challenge, stretch, alter any significant conventions or traditions? Does it cross boundaries of genre, subgenre, literary tradition, or academic discipline? How, why, and so what? (What can we make of a highly unconventional book like Dillard's *For the Time Being*?) In what historical and current conversations—about what issues—is this text taking part? What are its contributions to these conversations? (What happens to the literary tradition of solitary encounters with wild nature when a writer like Kathleen Dean Moore has her children with her on river trips?) What elements of the author's life and historical circumstances seem important in shaping these contributions?

As readers, we're part of these conversations, too: what is the text's relationship to us? What does the author seem to want from us? What kind of reader does the text seem to want us to be, at least for a while? What if we are that kind of reader or can imagine ourselves to be? What if we aren't and can't or won't? What kinds of (ironic, skeptical, critical, historical) distances might we have as readers from the narrator's position? Can we try to read two ways at once, from our own assumptions and values and from those of the writer? What imaginative work does it take for us to see through the eyes of Christopher Columbus or Mary Rowlandson?

What are the main questions the author is exploring in this text? How overt or how subtle are these questions? (Some books foreground their questions—Rebecca Solnit's *Savage Dreams*, Dillard's *For the Time Being*,

Thoreau's *Walden*, and Moore's *Pine Island Paradox* are excellent examples. But all texts can be seen as asking them.) Are they common questions or startling ones? Concrete and specific or giant and cosmic? No single person, much less a single text, can ask all questions or consider all possible answers. To which questions is this text blind? Which questions does the author simply choose not to consider in this text? What does the text do with the questions it asks? Does it offer answers? Possibilities? Illuminations and insights? Does it simply embody, enact, or elaborate the questions? Does it see some questions as unanswerable?

What does this text help us understand about the world? about other people's perceptions of it, their ways of being in it? about all the other beings that share it with us? about our own perceptions, values, curiosities, passions? about actions we might wish to take? about our own possible places in the world? about the kinds of lives we wish to live?

Using These Questions in Classrooms

I use questions like these in two main ways. I ask them of myself as I read and prepare for class; they help me make sense of new texts and challenge me to think about familiar ones in fresh ways. I think about which are the most important, discussable, and incisive ones to ask about each text, and I revise and tailor them to focus on the issues I want to cover in class. Then I pose them to my students to start and continue class discussions. I also very often assign them as homework. That is to say, I ask students to write their own "good thinking questions"—clusters of focused, text-based and text-directed, open-ended, challenging questions, mixed (optionally) with bits of data, speculations, and thinking. (I typically ask upper-level undergraduates to bring to each class meeting two to four clusters of roughly 250 words each.) Then I'll have them use these questions to direct whole- and small-group conversations. This assignment takes a couple of weeks of intensive training at the beginning of the term and then runs itself.

In all the ensuing discussions, we mix big with small, giant generalizations with textual details; we zoom in and zoom out. We balance simplifications with complications. And we resist premature answers; if someone has a good answer, we try to build another question on that answer. I discourage questions like, will we ever learn to treat animals well? I ask instead that we think about what the author at hand might have to say about this "world question." I find that our discussions stay much more focused and that we do end up talking about the world issues anyway, just indirectly. I think often of an article I once read that suggested metaphors for kinds of class discussions. Some discussions, this article said, are like body-building or beauty contests, with each student parading his or her ideas before the rest of the class, whose job it is to admire and judge. Some are like wrestling matches, in which the best argument pins the weaker ones to the mat. And some are like barn raisings and quilting bees: everyone contributes a little something (a nail, a bit of stitching), and the product is truly communal. Classrooms full of questions, I believe, produce barns and quilts—or, to drop the metaphor, they produce students who can themselves recognize, create, and pursue good questions. I hope, in courses on environmental literatures, this may also mean that they produce good environmental citizens who will help create a healthy future.

Katherine R. Chandler

"The Machine in the Garden": Using Electronic Portfolios to Teach Environmental Literature

Whether we teach in an unremarkable setting, the most dramatic of mountain terrains, or a restless city, taking students into the out-of-doors is a natural extension of an environmental literature course. What could be more memorable than melding sensory experience with intellectual inquiry? Classes conducted beside a pond to read excerpts from Henry David Thoreau's *Walden* or on a creek bank to discuss Annie Dillard's *Pilgrim at Tinker Creek* create the kinds of crystallizing moments that teachers seek and that students remember. Thirty minutes consumed searching a square yard of garden or the edge of a bog can bring a student face-to-face with Sue Hubbell's bees or Barbara Hurd's rarely encountered sphagnum. Those types of learning moments I consider vital to my courses. What I had not attempted—in fact, never considered attempting—was hiking my environmental literature students into the "anti-natural" terrain of the computer world.[1]

Among deterring factors were the cement block walls of our windowless computer lab; walls and workstations are not surroundings I seek for teaching literature focused on nature. In this, I am not alone. Reviews of ecopedagogical articles and bibliographies confirm that others also move students into the natural rather than the technological world. A recent survey of members of the Association for the Study of Literature and the Environment, for instance, indicates that all "respondents include some outdoor activity in their curriculum" while "nearly all . . . are reluctant to use on-line instruction" (Erb 6, 5). Although Audrey Erb surveyed only a small percentage of the association's members, studies on teaching literature with an environmental focus substantiate that common practice is to encourage educators to take students out rather than remain in (Waage, Introduction [Part 4] 111–12; Thomashow, *Ecological Identity* 14–15). Indeed, ecoliterature faculty members have consciously steered away from technology toward experiential education (Kraft and Kielsmeier 154–55; Conrad and Hedin 382; Crimmel, Introduction; Cuthbertson et al.). "The teaching of environmental literature not only encourages but also demands that the boundaries of the traditional classroom be broadened or abandoned," Kandi Tayebi states, prefacing a journal issue focused on teaching environmental literature. "Students work in outdoor environments, study non-traditional genres, and connect their learning to life" (6). Service learning, social-justice projects, and other pedagogical methods that tend toward the immediacy of primary experience rather than the once-removed distancing of the electronic environment are typical of other participatory teaching strategies incorporated into American environmental literature courses (Dixon and Smith).

Studies of computer technology in environmentally related education specify skepticism or lack of computer training as additional reasons why English faculty members do not turn to the electronic environment (Bowers; Selfe and Selfe; Woodlief). Certainly my attitude toward computers and my lack of expertise with applications other than word processing factored into my personal reservations. Also, I thought that online environments fundamentally conflicted with my course goals—until I signed up for a workshop on electronic portfolios offered by our college's instructional technologists and writing center. With its title specifying "portfolios," the workshop appeared to be an opportunity to discover a way in which computers might aid my composition students. However, it was for my Landscape and Literature course that I became inspired.[2]

I discovered that electronic portfolios, or e-portfolios (as they are called), are more flexible as teaching tools than the title suggests. At St. Mary's College of Maryland, electronic portfolios are used not only in writing classes but for biology field studies, as student-teacher portfolios, and to organize and present senior capstone projects.[3] The author of *The Learning Portfolio*, John Zubbizarreta, points to versatility as one of the positive features of portfolios (15). Electronic portfolios are adaptable as learning tools and flexible enough to allow various kinds of uses and final products. With electronic portfolios, students also have documentation of their work that can be posted to the Internet, kept on a compact disc, or used as part of a résumé.

For Landscape and Literature I envisioned adapting the electronic portfolio to produce an art gallery, a virtual art gallery. My students could create Web sites that employed artworks to demonstrate course concepts. Since Landscape and Literature was designed for students in our cross-disciplinary environmental-studies program as well as for upper-level English majors, it invited an interdisciplinary approach. Incorporating a visual component in addition to advancing technological capability was a meaningful way of deepening and expanding a course whose title evokes the way we view with the eye.[4]

The gallery idea suited the objectives of the class and was a modification of the electronic portfolio that turned out to be quite successful. During summer planning sessions with one of our instructional technologists and the arts-and-letters reference librarian, I developed the art-gallery concept to include several exhibits illustrating the topics around which the course was organized. My plan was to have students working in groups to design pages for a gallery Web site. Each group would select a painting (from the Internet or a book) that enhanced its understanding of the literary works, then collaboratively write explanatory text to accompany the art.

The first concept I wanted students to grapple with was arcadia. I commissioned two groups to search for a painting portraying an idealized arcadia; two groups, a sentimentalized arcadia; and two, a complex arcadia. The groups averaged three students, but if the class were larger, groups could be set at a larger, manageable size. Each group was to choose the most illuminating image; download it into the exhibit; then add its explanatory text, which included lines from the literature we had read. Visitors accessing the finished site could view the six paintings composing the arcadia exhibit with their accompanying interpretive labels, then click on the next exhibit.

One group selected Albert Bierstadt's 1868 painting *Among the Sierra Nevada Mountains, California*, observing that it included everything an idealized arcadia could need: sublimely beautiful mountains, valleys, lakes, forests, waterfalls, and wildlife. Especially, though, it reflected "a perfect day when the storm gives way to a light that bursts through the clouds to illuminate lofty mountains, flowing waterfalls, and innocence suggested by grazing elk." In their accompanying text, this group refered to *A Journey from Patapsko to Annapolis, April 4, 1730*, in which Richard Lewis (to quote them), "describes scenery reminiscent of this painting saying, 'Far distant Mountains drest in blue appear, And all their woods are lost in empty air.' "[5]

One of the two groups exemplifying a sentimentalized arcadia chose Paul Gauguin's *The Swineherd, Brittany* (1888) because the viewer of the painting first notices the man as the central figure standing in the foreground. "Had he been back among the rocks and trees directly behind, in the town down the hill, or on the rolling hills in the distance," the students explain,

> we would see him blending with nature and would view the painting as an idealized Arcadia. However, with the man as the focal point and main actor in the piece, the viewer's thoughts are focused primarily on him. We wish to know his story. We want to know how he is feeling. It is these questions that capture the viewer and evoke the sentimental, as emotion and experience are aspects that drive this particular idea of Arcadia.[6]

Since the course was not structured chronologically but rather topically, students read and quoted works that ranged across four centuries of North American literature. A student discussing a sentimentalized arcadia in her preliminary electronic-portfolio writings quoted J. Hector Saint-John de Crèvecoeur's *Letters from an American Farmer* (1782), noting that Crèvecoeur is accomplishing something similar to what Gauguin was portraying by "painting through his words the American farmer as unsophisticated, simple, and artless," an individual who "rejoices in his work and the land around him."[7] Another student used James Wright's "Depressed by a Book of Bad Poetry, I Walk toward an Unused Pasture and Invite the Insects to Join Me" (1990) to explain a different kind of sentimentality, one that allows "Wright's speaker to retreat away from something (a book of bad poetry) to his arcadia," where he is "relieved and glad instead to be near 'ants, / who are walking up the fencepost' and to hear 'The old grasshoppers . . . a dark cricket . . . In the maple trees.' "[8]

The final type of arcadia represented was complex, and literary works as disparate as Maxine Kumin's "Territory," Wallace Stegner's "The Colt," Gary Snyder's "Marin-an," and Thoreau's *Walden* were used in the explanatory labels for the paintings. The artworks selected by the two complex arcadia groups could not have been more different: *Landscape with Carriage and Train in the Background* by Vincent van Gogh and *The Sheep* by Salvador Dali. Taking its lead from Thoreau's "Sounds" chapter, in which he describes the integral role that trains have taken in the lives of rural as well as urban people, the first group observes that in the Van Gogh painting

> we have a beautiful French countryside, but it may as well be New England. Thoreau's two-year stay at Walden Pond describes his own sort of Arcadia similarly. "And hark! Here comes the cattle-train bearing the cattle of a thousand hills. . . . The air is filled with the bleating of calves and sheep, and the hustling of oxen, as if a pastoral valley were going by." From this excerpt of *Walden*, we can see that Thoreau views the rumbling of a train not as an intrusion but rather as a welcome break in his day. The train in Van Gogh's painting has the same feel to it. The countryside seemingly embraces the train, which nearly disappears into the hillside. Even the smoke, generally a negative aspect of industry, fits perfectly into this natural scene. It floats from the engine and is quickly assimilated into the clouds.[9]

While this group focused on the introduction of technology into the edenic garden as the complicating factor, the Dali group concluded that, with its depiction of sheep as couches, armchairs, end tables, and other furniture in a modern living room, the uneasy portrayal of nature as culture demonstrated human beings' manipulation of the natural world. Dali's surrealistic representation, which merged the organic with the artificial, also suggested to them that a complex arcadia raised questions and challenged traditional understandings.[10]

The topics around which the course was organized and that were developed into gallery exhibits were

> Conceptions of arcadia
> American versus British notions of pastoral
> North American national parks' vision of pastoral
> Distinctions between pastoral, antipastoral, and postpastoral[11]

For the final exhibit, students were encouraged to use their own digital photographic images. In the future I will arrange for our class to join with a photography course during this project. Each class can expand the others' horizons: the literature students can introduce cultural concepts and verbal-aesthetic sensitivity, and the photography students can teach photographic skills and visual-aesthetic sensitivity.

Operating in the Electronic-Portfolio Environment

For ease of instruction at St. Mary's, faculty members usually employ a standard template designed by instructional technologists that defines the menu and folder structure of the electronic portfolio. Since the template specifies format rather than content, instructors and assisting technologists can easily adapt portfolios across genres and purposes.[12] For my Landscape and Literature course, I needed a template that allowed for flexible group work, an evolving syllabus, and creativity in student design even as it provided suitable guidelines for each assignment, the final structure, and copyright issues inherent in crafting a gallery of images. Since I also wanted the final product to display the class's progress to both students and public (Meyer, Schuman, and Angello), one of the primary challenges was inventing a structure that presented the gallery exhibits in an attractive and easily navigable way yet still tracked each student's learning process. *Dreamweaver* software allowed my students to populate the predesigned templates with information they were gathering, reflections on what they were discovering, and drafts written in preparation for their group's explanatory labels.

Included in individual electronic portfolios were exploratory writings that led students to what they finally composed for the Landscape and Literature Web site. The electronic portfolio, then, charted each student's discovery process. Although the students worked in groups, every student was given a separate electronic portfolio on a shared network drive. In this way, the portfolios were populated with each individual's definitional writings, responses to readings, reflections on the paintings, and drafts working toward their final exhibit pages. The page uploaded into the gallery Web site contained the chosen artwork accompanied by the collaboratively written label. Directions for the first exhibit on arcadia explain what each student incorporated into his or her electronic portfolio:

> Include a discussion of the selections from readings to date (you choose which selections) in relation to the three arcadias we are examining (at least two pages).
> Add your musings, ideas, drafts in preparation for defining your assigned version of arcadia (at least a page)

Develop your final definition—succinctly and eloquently written—no more than five lines.

Describe your individual responses to the painting that your group has selected. Contemplate how the painting exemplifies your particular kind of arcadia. Consider also how it amplifies the definition that you have articulated. Point out specific features in the painting that you wish viewers to observe. Your group will draw ideas from these reflections.

Incorporate your group's collaboratively written explanatory label that will accompany the painting. This will be the same in each group member's portfolio. Include some quoted lines from at least one of our readings in your explanation as a means of bringing together concepts revealed through the artwork with those revealed through the literature (this should consist of three thoughtfully developed, carefully polished paragraphs—this appears in public).

Create a "museum attic" (this is a storage location for images you have gathered, drafts of your group's labeling text, and thoughts you want to save).

Students thus came to collaborative meetings having already researched, written, and given thought to what they had, on their own, extracted from both readings and artworks.

As students posted their artworks with explanatory labels, I linked them to the main gallery located on the same network drive. The gallery was then uploaded to the Internet at the end of the semester, with drop-down menus allowing interested viewers to see individual students' work (posted with permission), including everything each student had written in preparation for the final product. By the end of the semester, we had an art-gallery Web site with multiple exhibits and, more important, students had learned additional skills and the material better than if they had only written papers.

At the inception of the course, however, I had to work out how the electronic portfolio would best fit into the semester schedule. This computerized gallery of images and texts, and especially the time that was needed to teach students how to use and populate it, had the potential to overwhelm other aspects of the class.

Unless it is immediately relevant, technology is often difficult to learn; therefore, I decided to spend a week near the beginning of the semester immersing the students in electronic portfolios. A week and a half of classes in the computer lab allowed students to learn basic *Dreamweaver* skills. Later in the semester, when students began individual projects to include in their final exhibit, I scheduled two additional lab dates. Our instructional technologist also met with each group separately and was available to meet with each person once he or she began their final, solo, project. Students, of course, did have to turn to computer-lab assistants for help throughout the term, particularly in the earliest projects, but, because the template remained the same for each exhibit, most developed a level of competence with the technological aspects of the course.

Assessing the Electronic Portfolio in the Classroom Landscape

True, we were not outdoors, yet I observed throughout the semester that students were learning in a deeper way than in previous semesters when we had remained in our classroom and not traveled to the computer lab. As the exhibits began to take shape, the value of turning to technology to help students understand both our cultural and individual relationships with the natural world became clear. When they could see an elegant, tree-lined lane leading to an eighteenth-century, gardened estate in Great Britain juxtaposed with the rutted mud trail through a nineteenth-century, open-field prairie farm in America, students better understood differences between American and British concepts of pastoral. They were able to visualize that, as one student observed, "British culture saw beauty in art rather than in nature untouched. . . . The American pastoral finds retreat in raw, unorganised nature, where beauty is seen in the untamed wilderness, which offers a sense of freedom."[13]

Accompanying their images in the *American versus British* exhibit were literary works such as Willa Cather's *O Pioneers!* contrasted with James Thomson's *The Seasons,* as well as Mark Twain's *Life on the Mississippi* contrasted with Andrew Marvell's "The Garden."[14] One student observed that colonists in the New World were often escaping controlling social constructs of the Old World.[15] If students had not also had images of *Harlestone House, North Hamptonshire* (artist unknown), depicted with fine lines and great detail in all of its manor-house formality, to contrast with Emil Armin's *Wild West,* with its broad-stroked waves of color suggesting the roughness of an adobe village, they would not have understood as well the differentiations. Oppositions in the two nations' pastoral literature such as ordered and chaotic, hospitable and inhospitable, constructed and discovered, enclosed and spacious came to students more clearly by creating the Web page art gallery.

"The cross-disciplinary aspect of this class is one of the most beneficial," one student noted in a course assessment, referring not only to the addition of art into the course but also to the addition of computer technology. Others specifically acknowledged learning benefits of the electronic portfolio: "Despite having to go to the lab to do them, I think the ePortfolios have been a great way to get us to focus our thinking and produce a product," and "I like how the ePortfolio gives me a place to work through and develop my thoughts." Several students commented specifically about how the electronic portfolio helped them make connections while it fostered out-of-class thought and discussion. If nothing else, promoting conversation outside class suggests the value of turning to the computer "terrain" in our environmental literature courses.

Electronic portfolios unquestionably enhanced my Landscape and Literature course. Yet this foray into the online environment was not free from trial. Surprising to me, most of my students were not nearly as computer conversant as I assumed they would be, which extended to their understanding of the Internet in general and the construction of Web sites in particular. Learning the fundamentals of the technology was time intensive and, for some, an emotional as well as a skill challenge. In fact, because the computer environment was not one with which many English majors felt comfortable, it turned out to be the most difficult aspect of the course.

During the first semester that I taught the course, one student remained committed to his antitechnology philosophy. There were other students who never developed a high level of comfort with the electronic portfolio, but only the one student resisted to the end, refusing, ultimately, to create his final exhibit Web page or submit his individual project in electronic form. "Talking about a text, fine, that's what we do," this student said; "designing a webpage—that's not literature. That's what computer science majors do."

This negative attitude turned into a positive when several students in the class came to me privately to say "that's just the way Robert is" and to assure me that he was not infecting the rest of the class with his uncooperative manner.[16] Indeed, I know that those who initially declared discomfort with the electronic environment worked hard to overcome those fears and to distance themselves from the attitude that Robert vocalized and exhibited. Several self-proclaimed technophobes subsequently employed this computer technology for papers, projects, and presentations in courses, and three others created electronic portfolios in which to showcase their senior-year projects.

In addition to the difficulty some students experienced while developing technological skills, we also encountered snags in locating artworks, a problem I had not foreseen while planning the course. We invited our reference librarian to one of our computer-lab classes, and she took the students through the steps of finding pictures. We learned that merely typing in "arcadia" was not the most effective (or, to students' surprise, time-saving) means of locating potentially appropriate images. Our librarian also assisted in clarifying the technological aspects of importing images into the electronic portfolio.

The most serious problem faced was related to the artworks, and it was one I had anticipated: copyright permissions. Since students were transferring artwork from the Internet into their exhibits throughout the semester, sources of images and acknowledgment of copyright had to be addressed. Issues relating to copyright and permissions for electronic publications are growing ever more complicated, so our reference librarian explained these matters and assisted students in requesting permissions and using the correct citation style. When I proofread before placing the project on my college Web site, I discovered that some students had not yet received (in some cases never would receive) permission, even though they had requested it. In some instances, students' queries had not been answered; in others, they had requested authorization from the wrong individual, institution, or organization. I later searched and requested permissions myself or tried to locate the image from another source that would grant consent to use it for an academic project. In the end, I had to remove several of the groups' or individual students' contributions because we could not obtain approval to use artwork. This time spent after the semester was not something I could afford or wished to repeat; having all permissions in hand will, in the future, be a requirement by the end of the semester.

On the positive side, I found that developing an electronic-portfolio art gallery promoted technological and presentational skills as well as enriched the content and sharpened the significance of our subject of study. Most important to me is that learning takes place. This semester-long project introduced students (and, I must confess, me) to the electronic environment in ways that I believe were meaningful and enduring. The project also maintains an easily available physical presence: since posting the project to our department Web site, I have had students report that prospective employers and academic institutions (for study-abroad programs or graduate school) have accessed the Web site for evidence of applicants' work.

This gallery concept of the electronic portfolio promoted other skills. Creating their portfolios allowed students to improve online research abilities and practice Web design. The gallery also had the advantage of being a more permanent public forum than in-class panels or talks, and it could be revisited by classmates in the process of understanding course concepts, and, because it was on the Web, by others outside class. All of us were able to witness ongoing revision during the semester before the final gallery was linked to the department's Web site. Also, the gallery's placement of the work of one group in relation to the work of others created opportunities for conclusions informed by comparison, adding a measure of dialogue to the process.

Cooperation as well as creativity also burgeoned. As Kathleen Blake Yancey observes, a successful portfolio, electronic or otherwise, is one that is "longitudinal in nature . . . diverse in content . . . and almost always collaborative in ownership and composition" (102). From the first, the collaborative assignments allowed students to turn to one another while developing comfort with the technology. Since Landscape and Literature is an upper-level course, student input was necessary to develop independent thinking, yet working in groups encouraged valuing others' reactions during the reasoning process. Collaborating also provided students with a means of venturing beyond comfortable and commonplace terrain and was one of the greatest benefits of this work. In terms of the course's environmental focus, a significant benefit in entering the virtual as opposed to the outdoor world is that students could draw on artists' impressions of nature in both comparative and evocative ways. Artworks accessible on the Internet invited us to "see" the world around us through the lenses of several perspectives. We witnessed in material form ideologies evolving (Old World to New World, for instance). We learned that each individual is a subject and has a perspective. The paintings and photographs helped students grasp abstract notions we encountered in the literature. The electronic portfolio is also valuable because it provides a way for students in a particular environment, such as an urban one, to experience—at least visually—a variety of settings beyond their own.

While the experiential aspect of the electronic portfolio is in the realm of technology rather than nature, the art-gallery approach in this landscape-focused environmental literature course aided students in developing a keener awareness of our cultural milieu as well as our relation with the natural world. By selecting artworks that amplified their literary texts then responding with how the two informed each other, students comprehended, in a memorable way, embedded cultural, aesthetic, and intellectual conceptions of nature. I would never advocate replacing outdoor experiences with computers, but, as we search for means by which we can improve the learning and the impact of our environmentally focused literature courses, I am now convinced that the computer world can be as instructive as is the natural world.

Notes

1. A previous article provided the foundation for this essay ("Exploring Environmental Literature Using Electronic Portfolios" *Academic Exchange Quarterly* 7.4 [2003]: 102–06). I thank the journal for permission to use that argument in constructing this one. I wrote the article with two colleagues from St. Mary's College of Maryland who assisted with my Landscape and Literature course: Sarah C. Magruder and Kerie L. Nickel. My deep gratitude goes to Sarah and Kerie for their permission to extend our original article and present it in this collection.

2. Unlike my other environmentally focused courses, which examine the nature-writing tradition, Landscape and Literature investigates canonized texts more commonly taught in English literature classrooms. In addition to Ralph Waldo Emerson and Henry David Thoreau, I wanted to include, for instance, Herman Melville and Zora Neale Hurston, Emily Dickinson and Sylvia Plath. Landscape and Literature is an upper-level undergraduate class examining canonized works in which nature is more than backdrop or setting. I used *Literature and Nature: Four Centuries of Nature Writing*, edited by Bridget Keegan and James C. McKusick, as our primary textbook because it provided us with "a range of literary genres: fables, ballads, odes, epic poetry, travelogues, short stories, portions of novels and dramas as well as the important nonfiction essay" (3). I used pastoral as a focus and a means of managing this wide historical and generic range of readings. Since "landscape" implies a culturally based view of the natural world, I wanted to emphasize ways in which Americans have related to and conceptualized their environment, particularly as derived from and in contrast to the British tradition. Focusing on pastoral provided us with a guiding yet evolving concept.

3. At 1,850 students, St. Mary's College of Maryland remains a small, public liberal arts college, and it is Maryland's public honors college.

4. For her ideas and insights during our brainstorming conversations, my gratitude to Lois Stover, associate provost for academic services at St. Mary's College of Maryland.

5. The students who designed this Web page were Margaret Stubbs, Karen Celedonia, and Rachel Smith. All quotations of student writing in this essay are used with permission.

6. Nicholas Ewenson, Joan Huston, and Karla Toper were the students in this group.

7. Daniel Lange made this observation.

8. This student was Claire Cambardella.

9. Kathryn Bogel and Brian Conlin were the pair who created this page.

10. The Salvador Dali–painting group was composed of Daniel Lange, Shaun Griffin, and James Bruland.

11. Two of the resources on pastoral that I used during the course were *The Machine in the Garden: Technology and the Pastoral Ideal in America*, by Leo Marx, and *Pastoral*, by Terry Gifford. For antipastoral and postpastoral, I employed Gifford's definitions.

12. The materials used in the St. Mary's College of Maryland electronic-portfolio workshop can be seen at www.smcm.edu/writingcenter/workshop/WWW_LocalRoot/index.htm.

13. The student making this observation was Meriah Burke-Raines.

14. Rachel Larsen and Rebecca Seward noted the contrasts between these North American and British works.

15. This comment was made by Dana Christianson.

16. To maintain anonymity, I have changed the name of the student.

Cheryl C. Smith

Giving Voice to the Novice Authority: *Silent Spring* in the Composition Classroom

What does it take to teach academic writing well—to mold new college students into solid expositors, prepared for the writing demands they will face as undergraduates? The answer that I explore here lies in engaging students in ethical debate; more specifically, it lies in using an interdisciplinary, multifaceted environmental text like Rachel Carson's *Silent Spring* as a focus for student research and writing. To use this landmark book is to successfully negotiate a tension in first-year writing courses: students need to be challenged to write with rigor in a way that prepares them for future coursework, but they do not benefit from being forced into a project that disengages them or, worse, totally bewilders them. This tension has, in part, produced what could be called one of the seminal debates in composition studies. Originating in the 1970s as the doors of the academy opened to previously disenfranchised groups of students, it is essentially a debate about how college assignments—indeed the very structure of higher education—privilege certain ways of knowing and continue to disenfranchise nontraditional students. As it has evolved, some primary issues of the debate have become the unequal access to the "discourse communities" of higher education and the dynamics of "contact zones" in the classroom, where learners from different backgrounds and skills sets come together hoping—or, some would argue, being wrongly required—to gain entry into privileged forms of knowing and communicating.[1] Can we strike some balance between honoring students' authentic interests and lives while still initiating them into the discourse communities of higher education? I believe so. In *Clueless in Academe*, Gerald Graff proposes one way to think about such a balance: "The point is not to turn students into clones of professors but to give them access to forms of intellectual capital that have a lot of power in the world" (9). In this essay, I propose a paradigm for resisting the urge to imagine entering freshmen as "professor clones" and, instead, for seeing them as both novices and authorities: as young adults whose intellects are already defined through their own experiences but are still lacking.[2] I advance a pedagogy that acknowledges what students bring to the classroom and their writing, including their personal worldviews and ethical inclinations, yet that pushes them to let go of old proficiencies and perspectives in order to try on new ones, if just temporarily. And I want first-year writing to initiate the mission of opening students to previously unexplored viewpoints and, ultimately, to the potential and promise that a higher education should afford.

Carson's work serves as an ideal vehicle for guiding students, as novice authorities, through an exciting research project that can be taken in multiple directions. This flexibility makes the book a perfect tool to teach the essential skills of academic-research writing while keeping class members interested in the challenging work because they get to shape their own topic. By providing a broad-based text as a springboard for their work, the instructor lays common ground for the class that prods students into new arenas, unfamiliar ways of thinking, and previously unasked questions. *Silent Spring* caused an immediate social polemic that still has not stopped; in this way, it is ideal for encouraging debate and playing devil's advocate about truly difficult ethical questions. In short, the book teaches critical thinking and careful analysis. But while the instructor can oblige students to think and question in rigorous ways, they retain the opportunity to carve out their own positions of investment.[3] Decades of divergent, emotional responses to the author's charges against the chemical industry easily accommodate a variety of interests, and writers can reflect on *Silent Spring* through many different lenses: economics, business and industry, women's studies, public policy, literary or historical studies, and science and technology.

And there is yet another reason for teaching the book: few current undergraduates study *Silent Spring*, even though it sparks emotional and intellectual responses, intrigues its readers, and has been enormously influential on many fronts. Of the hundreds of students I taught the book to at Tufts and Harvard in environmental studies, American studies, and finally first-year writing courses, only a handful had even heard of it; at my new school, Baruch College of the City University of New York, the situation is much the same. I would like to see Carson's work enjoy a revival in the academy, but, given that my primary concern is how best to give students the knowledge to write well and how to do this work through the intrinsically interdisciplinary framework of environmental ethics, the use of *Silent Spring* represents a flexible—or, in my experience, a model—choice: it is a text that works particularly well in the writing classroom. So I offer my experiences with it as a paradigm for generating student engagement with academic research and writing through the lens of environmental ethics. And I leave it to the knowledge and imagination of my readers to determine what other materials could function just as well as *Silent Spring* in managing to teach a broad range of students how to write proficiently and originally in and for the academic disciplines.

Background: Writing Pedagogy

In one of the most quoted phrases in composition studies, David Bartholomae names the problem college writers encounter every time they attempt to put pens to paper or fingers to keyboard: they face the prospect of having to "invent the university" (135). Our essay assignments ask students, explicitly or not, to gather and distill evidence in order to formulate a coherent argument that satisfies the demands of our discipline. But they have no solid grounding in academic disciplines; often, they do not even have the most basic experience in or exposure to disciplinary difference. As a result, our students' potential best works fall into the gap created when our (sometimes unspoken) expectations of them do not attempt to coincide with their actual knowledge and real potential for asserting authority.

By pointing out this gap, I do not mean to suggest that we should "dumb down" assignments or focus exclusively on giving students the opportunity to write about what they know. The privileging of what they know has led to advocating personal writing in composition courses as a means to facilitate students' voices of authority—their inner experts. To focus on personal writing, however, can limit the crucial first-year writing project to producing narratives instead of arguments or to using personal experience as evidence without discovering how to find and employ other types of evidence. In fact, environmental literature and nature writing have an established role in the academy as being able to stimulate precisely the kind of personal writing that I am *not* advocating here. Ann E. Berthoff offers a notable example of the confluence of personal and nature writing. She prescribes the dialectical or double-entry notebook for students to record notes on a topic and then later use the facing page to reconsider their original musings. And she specifically suggests using the dialectical notebook to have classes write about shells, seedpods, or "any natural object that can serve as "'text.'" Here, low-stakes, reflective writing encourages engagement with the natural world. Berthoff explains: "*reading the book of nature* is probably the oldest writing assignment in the world" (46). Indeed, free or informal writing on the human relationship to nature and the students' own sense of place tap into a vibrant and thought-provoking way of connecting with the environment. And mobilizing students' inner nature writers is effective in helping them understand the complex analogies that, for instance, Henry David Thoreau uses to explore the intricate ties between humankind and the natural world.[4]

But the project of academic writing does not stop there, and using environmental topics in first-year writing courses need not be limited to personal explorations. Our goal should be not only to make students better readers and more confident writers who can imagine for themselves a writerly authority but also to teach them how to approach complex theories and opinions that may, at first, be unfamiliar to them. To successfully approach such theories, students should be able to distill and mobilize evidence in order to advance an argument. All disciplines ask for something akin to an argument, position, or thesis, along with some kind of evidence thoughtfully and analytically marshaled in support of the thesis. Therefore, our composition curricula should endeavor to afford students the opportunity to write from a position of knowledge and confidence while teaching them how subject areas vary in demand and expectation, giving them skills that work across the academic disciplines.

And what works? In my first-year writing courses, I break it down to a set of four transferable skills that students can use in a variety of writing situations. I teach students to make sure their essays have a thesis, to use solid evidence, to structure an essay carefully and thoughtfully, and to try to write with a style that is at once their own and appropriate for their given audience. I repeat the significance of these four factors of good writing again and again, calling them TESS for thesis, evidence, structure, and style, and students come to remember the formula easily, especially since I reinforce the formula through the continuous writing that has become a hallmark of composition courses: informal prewriting, drafting, and revising. Finally, I stress that when given a choice, students should seek out writing topics that they feel passionate about or, at the very least, interested in. They do not have to know the topic intimately or be experts on it—in fact, they should be open to learning about their topic through the act of writing—but they should care about it.[5]

In trying to provide the content that gives a diverse set of individuals the opportunity to write from a position of investment, I have found that *Silent Spring* works well. Specifically, it works well with disparate audiences because it allows for a variety of perspectives and awakens ethical questions that touch everyone living in an industrialized society. For instance, a large segment of Tufts students are environmentally aware, perhaps drawn to the university because of its strong programs in urban and environmental policy. Certainly the self-selecting ones in my American studies and environmental studies introductory seminars came armed with knowledge and opinions on environmental issues. So while they had not, for the most part, read *Silent Spring*, they were not surprised by the government and industry abuses Carson decries; they could offer other examples of such abuses and quickly identify with Carson's message. Similarly, my students at Harvard were self-selecting, choosing my expository writing class on environmental ethics from a variety of offerings (at the time, it was the only expository-writing course on an environmental theme). All my Harvard freshmen had some strong, usually political and often geographic, relation to environmental concerns. A large number had grown up in unusual and rural landscapes (Alaska, Hawai'i, the countryside of Ireland) that had sparked a special interest in the natural world. In addition, most planned on concentrating in a physical science, a proclivity that may have given them an advantage with Carson's sometimes technical approach to the chemical crisis she defines.

When I came to Baruch and considered having students read selections from *Silent Spring* in my first-semester freshman writing course, I was concerned that what had made the text work so well in my prior experience would not be operative. Quite different from Tufts and Harvard, Baruch is a large, public institution and a commuter college. Eighty-five percent of Baruch's undergraduates pursue business degrees, which neither Tufts nor Harvard offer. In addition, Baruch students are urbanites. They all live in New York City; most grew up there. And perhaps most important, students would end up in my section of freshman writing by chance and through no special interest of their own in environmental questions. Could these students connect to Carson's text and manage to carve out personally invested approaches to an important ethical conundrum of twenty-first-century life?

I found that they certainly could. Many remembered, for example, when Rudy Guiliani supported extensive pesticide spraying in New York City neighborhoods and Central Park to control the spread of West Nile virus. They wondered if this was a safe and reasonable response. Several were especially intrigued by the individual testimonies in Carson's book and wanted to pursue questions of who suffers (and why those people in particular) as a result of decisions and mandates handed down from government or industry. From there, they could go on to consider, for example, acts of environmental racism, in which economically disadvantaged and largely nonwhite urban communities in their area were made dumping grounds for environmental toxins. Still others talked about the high rates of childhood asthma in urban neighborhoods, which has been linked to poor air quality. And not surprisingly, several were especially drawn to questions related to business ethics and environmental regulation. All of these represent issues that students may have encountered in the past, but Carson and her book provided a new context, new fuel they could use to generate informed arguments against the injustices and problems they identified. While my Baruch students' interests in the debates of *Silent Spring* have been markedly different from those of my past students, they have not been any less vigorous or invested.

In my experience, a text like *Silent Spring* that brings issues of environmental ethics to the fore can easily accommodate the needs and interests of diverse academic audiences. And the range of angles opened up by Carson's study has other significant benefits, as the following section shows. The book gives students the chance to pick their perspective and teachers the breadth of material to help foster distinct approaches so everyone in class can feel like enough of an expert—a novice with authority—to write with confidence. Instead of having to invent a position that does not really interest them, in relation to an audience foreign to them, students can critically consider their own ethical beliefs and use them to more legitimately enter the conversation that, at its best, is a defining dynamic of good scholarship.

The Assignment: Environmental Ethics and Research Writing

Environmental ethics and literature, much like the composition classroom itself, are ideal locations for inventing ways to write about something that matters. As Derek Owens notes in *Composition and Sustainability: Teaching for a Threatened Generation*:

> Not only do compositionists and their students inject material into courses that their colleagues and their students can't address, but they also orchestrate zones of inquiry that juxtapose eclectic webs of information, inspiration, and provocation, the likes of which can't easily be generated elsewhere in academe. (5–6)

Owens proposes mobilizing these eclectic webs into composition courses focused on sustainability, something that he argues is "absolutely crucial to [students'] intellectual, spiritual, economic, and physical survival" (7). I believe composition pedagogy can benefit from Owens's insights, even in courses not specifically about sustainability issues; his conviction can accommodate a more open-ended approach to the environment that engrosses students not already prone toward environmental activism, those whose instincts might be to eschew environmental issues as disheartening (a common complaint) or frankly uninteresting.

Silent Spring gives students an opportunity to study environmental hazards and to think about the ethics of unsustainable productivity but to write about these issues from highly flexible angles. The American chemical crisis of the 1960s resonates with a number of contemporary environmental concerns. These include the proliferation of genetic engineering in food production, the problem of disease control and particularly mosquito-borne diseases, the concern over estrogen mimics, the safety of food imports and the ethics of American pesticide exports, and the issue of where corporate responsibility fits in with the expansion of industry and technology. Students really enjoy debating what Carson refers to as the "giddy sense of power" that technological advancement can confer on some sectors ([1962] 68). As these angles suggest, research and writing projects inspired by environmental literature like *Silent Spring* can range from feminist studies on the reception and treatment of women in science and industry to political manifestos about the need to monitor government controls over issues of public health. Students have the opportunity to investigate and write about topics that genuinely concern them and often relate to their intended academic concentrations—science majors can focus on scientific angles, political science majors can write about issues of policy, business majors can look at industry responsibility—and the instructor has the pleasure of reading essays on a variety of subjects, all motivated by personal interest rather than coerced by a limiting assignment.

To foster a wide range of responses from the beginning, I present students with a statement about the book's impact before they begin reading. Here is an example of the kind of statement, along with some questions meant to stimulate discussion, that I put on the assignment:

> Immediately after the book's publication, the chemical industry painted Rachel Carson as a simplistic nature worshipper bent on subverting American progress, roundly dismissing her findings, but in his introduction to the 1994 edition of *Silent Spring*, Al Gore ranked it "among the rare books that have transformed our society" (xix). What a range of opinion on one book! The source packet I will provide and your own research will offer insight into the issues this pivotal text raised for its audience. You will read (or read about) specific responses to *Silent Spring* from the media, the chemical industry, scientists, and politicians. You will also read some of the first responses to the text as well as much later considerations of the text's relevance. These will help you to contextualize your analysis and consider questions such as: What kinds of readings—or misreadings—does the book tend to inspire? What have people gotten hung up on in the book? Why? How might Carson's work have reconceptualized (or failed to reconceptualize) how Americans think about the nature all around them? What changes in an ethical response to the environment has the book inspired? How can we understand the importance of Carson and the provocative nature of her text? It seems to either wildly enrage or spur her audience to action—few people feel neutral about it.

I use such a statement to lead into a collective brainstorming session on how students might narrow their approach to Carson's wide-reaching book. I want them to have some themes in mind before they start reading so they can annotate their text accordingly, and we generate a list of possible disciplinary angles: science and technology, politics and environmental legislation, the chemical (or other) industry and its ethics, feminist studies, social justice, economics and the environment, historical perspectives, and literary studies.

Once they read *Silent Spring*, of course, they will have to significantly narrow these broad angles. I select one, such as feminist studies, and spend a class session on it to model how students should move toward a honed thesis. We may read a brief article on the role women have historically

played in environmental activism in order to delve more deeply into issues
of women and public policy. Or, we may look at the misogyny in many of
the initial responses to Carson's 1962 publication and consider the friction
that may occur at the intersection of women, authority, and science in pre-
feminist America and now. Students can thus begin to see how the larger
context of their angles along with their particular interests works together to
define their arguments. To further foster the definition of their approaches
and get them going on their research, I distribute an intriguing cross section of sources. Often, it is too overwhelming for new students to be set
loose in their college library; they need a starting point, some materials to
get them grounded and to give them an idea of the many places—books,
periodicals, academic journals, government documents—that good evidence comes from. I try to compile an array of materials to distribute:
drawings, like Charles Shultz's cartoons depicting Lucy's idolization of
Carson; articles from the early 1960s, such as one in *Time* that responds
negatively to the social implications of *Silent Spring* and thus represents
the early stirrings of controversy ("Pesticides"); letters documenting her
struggles that Carson wrote to her close friend Dorothy Freeman as she
drafted the book (Freeman); chapters from books published on anniver-
saries of *Silent Spring*'s release, such as the American Chemical Society's
Silent Spring Revisited (Marco, Hollingworth, and Durham); more recent
examples of studies in environmental toxins, such as *Our Stolen Future*
(Colborn, Dumanoski, and Myers); testimonials from a 1992 congressional hearing on progress in monitoring environmental toxins (United
States); and articles from the *New York Times* (Cushman), the *New Yorker*
(Gladwell), and the *Wall Street Journal* (Begley) that reference *Silent
Spring* or its concerns. Each member of the class reads these materials, and
they all choose some articles or specific questions to investigate further
as they expand their individual projects. While I provide these sources to
help ground and inspire their continued research, I also use them as a basis
for discussing how academic writers use evidence. In seeing a range of
materials—some praising Carson as a courageous revolutionary, and others
condemning her for being an overzealous, one-sided, new-age nature
lover—students begin to grasp the many ways sources may be slanted
and biased. Further, I point out how some sources emphasize the book's
impact in a select, delimited field (say, the political arena), while others
(from articles in *Time* magazine to *Peanuts* cartoons) show how its message pervaded popular culture. Some reveal the immediate reactions the
text inspired; others demonstrate its continuing legacy. Such an array of

sources accommodates multiple treatments that I can use to encourage students to think about their stance in relation to their material. We talk about how they can mobilize their sources to work for them: to motivate their essays and highlight the tensions in their issue, to explore a counterargument, to enrich their argument conceptually, or to bolster their claims with historical facts or statistics.

Our many discussions on how to use sources, coupled with the enjoyment students find in crafting their personalized projects, help allay a growing anxiety for college professors: plagiarism. More and more higher education administrators and faculty members are noting that plagiarism is on the rise and that we need to address responsible source use at the freshman level.[6] In this new age of information technology, we are up against an Internet full of unreliable sources and, more ominously, paper-writing services. But perhaps even more formidably (since it is harder to calibrate), we are up against both students' uncertainty about how to write at the level we require and the pressure they experience in relation to school—feelings that can make them vulnerable to the "easy" solution of plagiarism. Carson's carefully researched book provides an ideal vehicle for discussing responsible integration of sources into an original academic argument. Students can see how Carson documented her claims and what gaps (or alleged gaps) her critics have denounced in her book, and the instructor can use these issues to open up considerations of responsible research, source use, and documentation. Her book promotes the broad, interdisciplinary understanding of a scholar's material that instructors of beginning academic writers can use to talk about boundaries and standards of quality scholarship. Further, many of Carson's indictments of government and industry officials condemn them for irresponsible communication of their findings to the public. They manipulated information, she contends, to call attention to or suppress certain details for their own purposes. In this way, the material in and around *Silent Spring* provides both a model and antimodel for conscientious reporting of researched findings, as well as ample opportunities for discussion.

Silent Spring helps the instructor strike the perfect balance between providing an already defined topic—one that promotes the rigorous relation to evidence that our students need to learn—and letting students find their own foci that interest and inspire them, drawing them into critical contemporary issues. Most undergraduates have not read Carson's book and are initially unaware of her importance in shaping the modern environmental movement; but, while they may not arrive at the topic already experts, they quickly appreciate her work because of its broad impact. The reality that Carson helped launch the Environmental Protection Agency and woke consumers up to the potential hazards of technological advances, an awareness that many young people take for granted, arouses readers' curiosity. All the related materials contribute to this curiosity to set students down a path of research, leading them through an original project and finally into a new knowledge and authority on a significant subject.

And in fact, when students are asked to embrace their own initial lack of authority on a subject and to let their knowledge develop as they write, they undertake tasks solidly in the tradition of the earlier American environmental discourse found in New England transcendentalism. These tasks are, therefore, challenges quite appropriate for a research assignment on environmental ethics or, I would argue, on *any* topic. Ralph Waldo Emerson reminds us that the magnitude of the natural world makes it "too bright almost for spotted man to enter without noviciate and probation" ("Nature" 543). Let us allow our first-year writing courses to be periods of apprenticeship like the one Emerson advocates for humanity just coming into a relation with nature. Composition courses can be holding patterns of probation, during which students are not expected to master and invent a disciplinary position too remote from their reality to matter but rather, as novices with authority, are encouraged to discover their ideas and stance in relation to material that is at once both specific and open-ended, fostering multiple arguments and approaches. Once discovered, the novice authority's voice and stance will lead more meaningfully into a rapport with academic disciplines. Through such a rapport, writers develop a rigor in relation to their material—and all students have a more equal opportunity to become successful, confident academic writers.

Notes

1. Joseph Harris's "Negotiating the Contact Zone" insightfully studies the attitudinal changes involving college access and writing, unpacking the terms I introduce here.

2. In their article "The Novice as Expert: Writing the Freshmen Year," Nancy Sommers and Laura Saltz summarize the findings of the Harvard Study of Undergraduate Writing, a longitudinal look at the writing experiences of 25% of the class of 2001. Sommers and Saltz give special attention to the writing first-year students do outside the required composition course, arguing, "We learn much from first-year students about their common struggles and abilities beyond our classrooms: that freshmen who see themselves as novices are most capable of learning new

skills; and students who see writing as something more than an assignment, who write about something that matters to them, are best able to sustain an interest in academic writing throughout their academic careers" (127). My approach to writing and learning owes much to how Sommers and Saltz, and the expository writing program at Harvard, think about the first-year writing project, the realities of our students, and the most effective methods for teaching them. I joined Harvard's writing program in 2001, the year the students in the Harvard study graduated, and, during my two years on the faculty, I took part in several discussions with my colleagues about the study and its findings. My teaching, as well as my Carson assignment, evolved greatly under the tutelage of the program's leaders.

3. Sommers and Saltz succinctly make the argument for the kind of approach to assignment construction that I am advocating: "The enthusiasm many freshmen feel is less for writing *per se* than for the way it helps locate them in the academic culture, giving them a sense of academic belonging. When faculty construct writing assignments that allow students to bring their interests into a course, they say to their students, *This is the disciplinary field, and you are part of it. What does it look like from your point on the map?*" (131).

4. I do not entirely dismiss the value of personal writing, but I do question a heavy reliance on it in first-year foundation writing courses. I believe personal writing can usefully have a small role not only in composition courses, as a vehicle for helping students explore voice and style, but also in literature courses, as a means to understand the genre of nature writing. I propose a project for using personal writing about nature as a means to explore Thoreau's *Walden*, to grasp the tenets of American transcendentalism, and to develop student voice in my article, "Writing like a Transcendentalist."

5. It is a general point of agreement for many teachers of writing and language that no one can learn to write well and meaningfully without having a central matter to engage, some integral focus on content. Peter Elbow communicates this common concern in his report on the 1987 English Coalition Conference, *What Is English?*: "participants kept trying to dismantle the dichotomy [between "solid content" and "empty skills"], stressing that you can't make meaning unless you are writing or reading about *something*; that practices are always practices *of* a content" (19). I am adding to this concern the challenge that, at least in first-year writing, students have the opportunity to write from a position of authentic investment.

6. At my school, Baruch College, City University of New York, plagiarism is a very active issue. The associate provost for faculty development oversees a task force on academic integrity that has published a student guide for distribution and discussion in first-year writing classes. The task force has also initiated several presentations and discussions in almost all departments, disseminating the alarming statistic that more than 50% of college students in the United States admit to recent acts of academic dishonesty such as cheating or plagiarism and letting faculty members know about procedures for reporting incidents (*Baruch College*).

Glen A. Love

Teaching Environmental Literature on the Planet Indivisible

Robinson Jeffers's startling poem "The Eye" depicts the Pacific Ocean as the great eye of earth, staring into space in infinite disregard of the human swarm whose aggressions occupy the other half of our globe-eyed planet. "[A]nd what it watches is not our wars," concludes the poem.

We have all seen the famous color photograph, taken from the *Apollo* spacecraft, of the beautiful cloud-laced ball that is planet Earth.. For the first time in human history, we saw, Gaia-like, our planet as it must appear to a dispassionate eye in the sky. The Earth-ball photo, now a poster often captioned "One Planet Indivisible," has become an emblem for ecological thinking, a tug on our reality chain, a reminder of Barry Commoner's first law of ecology that everything on Earth is connected to everything else (33).

This sense of a commonly shared biosphere—the region of the Earth's surface and atmosphere where life takes place—is now the context of all serious environmental thinking, just as it is increasingly becoming the realized context of all serious political, social, and economic thinking. For good or ill, like it or not, globalization is upon us.

This is not to say that the ecological microsystems of place and region and daily life will cease to be central in our human scale of things. What the *Apollo* photograph cannot show, because it reduces all the Earth's features to flatness and microscopic size, is the significance to our species of our everyday surroundings and existence. These will remain vital to us as the setting of our daily lives and as a corrective to an increasingly homogenized and intrusive mass culture. The enhancement of local and individual experience will continue to be the matter of literature and the arts. But from an ecocritical perspective, the local and the global are steadily transcending national boundaries in our thinking, however powerful these nation markers remain politically. What the eye in the sky watches is not just our wars, but more portentous and far-reaching global change.

What are the implications of planetary indivisibility for the growing new field of ecocriticism and the teaching and study of literature and environment? In what follows, I identify three important ecological-literary components of indivisibility—comparatism, human universality, and interdisciplinarity—and then recommend an introductory text that brings these facets of indivisibility into the English classroom and provides a coherent and distinguished introduction to the study of literature and environment.

First, the comparatist perspective. No outlines of national, cultural, or ethnic borders are drawn on the planet indivisible. Arbitrary human-drawn political boundaries of nations may dominate our past and present thinking, but they are nowhere to be found on Earth, as it might be seen by the impartial eye in the sky. Instead, great natural features seen in shades of blue, green, yellow, brown, white—oceans, forests, grasslands, deserts, mountains, the polar ice caps—draw our gaze. What we know to be urban megacenters are drably shaded spots in the latitudes between the middle of the Earth sphere and its ice-capped poles. From space, North America appears not as Alaska, Canada, the lower forty-eight states of the United States, Mexico, and Central America, but as merging landforms, islands, and vegetative zones punctuated by clusters of urban development.

Literary study in the past, my own included, has most often been placed within discrete national boundaries. But the emerging global awareness invites a comparatist perspective. "Comparative literature is to the humanities what ecology is to the natural sciences," wrote Joseph W. Meeker in his groundbreaking 1974 book, *The Comedy of Survival: Studies in Literary Ecology*. Meeker sees comparatists examining literature "as a characteristic activity of the human species which is unintelligible apart from its total context of historical and contemporary human life" (11). This sense of comparatist study as akin to the ecological understanding of underlying processes and relationships is basic to our developing sense of a globally sophisticated ecocriticism.[1]

A second powerful planet-indivisible consideration, drawn from the fields of biology, anthropology, and the related social sciences, is the existence of human universals. All modern biology, all the life sciences, are founded on Darwinian evolution, the understanding that humans are descended from early life forms and that evolution thus connects us to other animals and to all living things. Our own species, and all the rest of the earth's living creatures, followed long processes of development through natural selection. Our immense evolutionary journey as human beings is, in Loyal Rue's words, "everybody's story." Although we live in often deeply conflicted national, ethnic, religious, racial, and other cultural groupings, all of us as members of Homo sapiens have a common, species-specific, evolutionary heritage—with cultural variations, to be sure—and we share the great epic of our evolutionary antiquity, just as we share, in the only dot in the universe known to support life, our common home place. Thus there is a strong connection between biological thinking and ecocritical-environmental thinking.[2]

Convincing support for our shared evolutionary heritage is present in human universals, the startlingly large number of human behaviors and social practices found common to cultures around the earth. "Some anthropologists have returned to an ethnographic record that used to trumpet differences among cultures and have found an astonishingly detailed set of aptitudes and tastes that all cultures have in common," writes Steven Pinker. "This shared way of thinking, feeling, and living makes us look like a single tribe, which the anthropologist Donald Brown has called the Universal People, after Chomsky's Universal Grammar" (55).[3]

These human universals, potentially both harmful and helpful in their social effects, are present in our aesthetic creations, in the stories, music, dance, sculpture, drawings of human prehistory, as well as in written literature, which began only a few thousand years ago. The existence in literature of these human universals, reverberations of our species' shared human nature, account for the ability of people to read and relate strongly to literature from many cultures other than their own. While literary theory of the last two or three decades tends to emphasize the differences between the literature of nations, classes, races, genres, periods, and so forth, their commonalities are undeniable and, for those of us who see literature in an environmental context, increasingly important. Literary universals, as Patrick Colm Hogan observes, are hardly mentioned in recent literary criticism except to be dismissed politically as a means of oppression. What such dismissals are properly objecting to, though, as Kwame Anthony Appiah notes in his advocacy of literary universalism, "is Eurocentric hegemony *posing* as universalism" (qtd. in Hogan 225). Noting that literary universalism in no way excludes cultural and historical specificity, Hogan advocates convincingly the need to rethink this vital topic.

The third component of planetary awareness in ecocriticism is interdisciplinarity. As I argue in *Practical Ecocriticism: Literature, Biology, and the Environment*, ecocriticism demands that we cross disciplinary lines in our work. Nature is interdisciplinary, not neatly packageable into any single field of study.[4] Above all, I believe, ecocritics must become familiar with science, and the scientific fields that have most to offer us are the life sciences. Evolutionary biology, ecology, zoology, and the neurosciences and their intersections with psychology, anthropology, geography, geology, linguistics, and related fields are provocative and exciting territories for ecocritics to explore. Human interaction with the biosphere is widely seen as a defining issue of the twenty-first century, and biology promises to be the leading science. That prediction arises out of recent achievements in biological research and the growing integration of biological findings into related areas of the sciences and social sciences. The humanities, and especially our branch of it, cannot avoid the challenge of these new formulations, affecting, as they do, what it means to be human.

The term *eco* in ecocriticism must be more than a buzzword. The pioneering ecologist Eugene Odum, in a recent book *Ecology: A Bridge between Science and Society*, reminds us of ecology's function as the underlying and integrating science of today's world. He notes the rise of "interface" fields under the influence of ecological thinking (xiii). Though ecocriticism was an infant field in 1997 when Odum's book was published, it should now assume its place as part of the bridge between science and the humanities and contribute powerfully to the continuing study of literature and human values.

With these three concepts in mind—comparatism, human and literary universals, and literary-scientific interdisciplinarity—what would be an appropriate introductory text, a work of memorable literary substance and style, for use in a class on literature and environment? My first choice for such an introductory work for an environmental literature course is Edward O. Wilson's 1984 book, *Biophilia*. I choose this Wilson work because it is fairly short and very readable and because Wilson is perhaps the world's leading biologist and its foremost spokesperson for preserving species and biological diversity. Of equal importance, he is a writer of great talent, winner of two Pulitzer prizes (for *The Ants* and *On Human Nature*). He has been called America's most famous scientist and one of its greatest writers (Cooke 98).

The word *biophilia*, literally "love of life," suggests the book's thesis that as human beings we have a propensity for exploring and responding to life and lifelike processes. *Biophilia*, then, is a series of essays based on Wilson's global explorations as a naturalist, explorations that open up the fields of biology, conservation, and literature in surprising ways. With narrative-based essays like "The Superorganism" (on tropical leaf-cutter ants), Wilson not only describes the fascinating life of a species whose brain is its total society but also brings attention to the need for forest and species conservation in the tropics. With his essay "The Time Machine," Wilson retrieves the moment in history when Charles Darwin's revolutionary ideas reached leading American intellectuals in Cambridge, Massachusetts, like Louis Agassiz, Benjamin Peirce, and Asa Gray in May 1859. In this context, Wilson dramatizes the conflict between evolutionary and religious explanations of human origins and relates these to the continuing gulf between C. P. Snow's two cultures, the sciences and the humanities. In "The Right Place," Wilson looks at the habitat in which the human brain evolved, the savanna grasslands of Africa, and links this to the generalization from ecological science that "the crucial first step to survival in all organisms is habitat selection. If you get to the right place, everything else will be easier" (106). Such a perspective enriches our ecocritical study of place and region and expands our understanding of this vital literary territory.

In his essay "The Serpent," to my mind one of *Biophilia*'s most intriguing chapters, Wilson considers the snake from three perspectives: biology, the humanities, and culture. He traces the snake's image from conscious thought back to unconscious and evolutionary origins, from the zoological snake to Emily Dickinson's poem "A narrow Fellow in the Grass" to the venerated and feared serpent of mythology and religion. Wilson once again brilliantly expands the context of our traditional or Freudian reading of snakes in ways that reveal "the complexity of our relations to nature, and the fascination and beauty inherent in all forms of organisms. Even the deadliest and most repugnant of creatures bring an endorsement of magic to the human mind" (84). Toward the end of the book, Wilson's "The Conservation Ethic" is a powerful call for a new moral reasoning that looks to the biological roots of human motivation to understand how and why a "surface ethic" is not enough to halt the slide to myriad extinctions and despoliation in the natural world (138). "The more the mind is fathomed in its own right, as an organ for survival, the greater will be the reverence for life for purely rational reasons" (140). These snapshots of *Biophilia*'s chapters may give some sense of the value of Wilson's book.[5] As an introduction to evolution through natural selection, which is the foundation of all modern biology and ecology, *Biophilia* reveals to us in understandable terms the central principles of Darwin's great idea, perhaps the most important scientific discovery of all time. Our students are often seriously shortchanged by being denied, for any extraneous reason, exposure to evolution, the linchpin for all the life sciences.

As a distinguished nature writer himself, Wilson infuses his scientific knowledge with his narrative and reflective talents. *Biophilia* both models and encourages strong connections between the biological sciences and the humanities. Wilson's writing is rich in allusions—to literature, mythology, folklore, painting, and so forth—to the material of our professional lives. He explores the philosphical and ethical meanings of his scientific material with the sensitivity and insight that humanists welcome. Finally, in starting from stories about nature, about birds and ants and snakes and natural places, he invites our students to go with him, to draw on whatever experiences with nature they have had, for discussion and writing that can take them as far as they are willing to go. *Biophilia*, in short, is a worthy literary-biological analogue for our indivisible planet.

With *Biophilia* as the introductory text in a course in North American environmental literature, what works might follow? A rapidly expanding range of choices is revealed in the titles and contents of many recent anthologies and critical studies. The leading ecocritical scholar Lawrence Buell calls his recent book *Writing for an Endangered World: Literature, Culture, and Environment in the U.S. and Beyond*. Buell's title suggests the widening gyre, as do the titles of recent environmentally oriented collections like Scott Slovic and Terrell Dixon's *Being in the World*, Karla Armbruster and Kathleen Wallace's *Beyond Nature Writing: Expanding the Boundaries of Ecocriticism*, Patrick D. Murphy's *Farther Afield in the Study of Nature-Oriented Literature*, and Michael Bennett and David W. Teague's *The Nature of Cities*. Works like these underscore the view, held by many ecocritics, that environmental readings may expand our understanding of virtually any literary subject, and these readings assume many forms. For example, texts that cross North American national boundaries to bring together the literature and culture of an overarching ecosystem may encourage unique insights. Such a work is Laurie Ricou's *The*

Arbutus/Madrone Files, which explores the nature and culture of the Canadian and United States Pacific Northwest and offers innovative possibilities for a comparatist ecocriticism.

The portion of the Earth ball that is North America may be seen whole from space, reaching from the Arctic to Central America to the islands of the Caribbean. These landforms contain politically and culturally diverse countries and regions. A contemporary class in North American environmental literature is likely to recognize and represent many aspects of this diversity in its choice of texts. At the same time, this cultural diversity is underwritten, as is claimed here and as is represented in *Biophilia,* by a genetic evolutionary history that makes us all members of a species, a "universal people," in Donald Brown's words. The DNA in our bodies connects us intimately to all other people and, beyond that, to all life on earth.

For the writers we study and for us and our students as readers and intepreters, the bottom line is the complex and disquieting human animal, Homo sapiens. As the novelist Iris Murdoch writes, "We make, in many respects, though not in all, the same kinds of moral judgments as the Greeks did, and we recognize good or decent people in times and literatures remote from our own. . . . And this, when one reflects on it, is a remarkable testimony to the existence of a single durable human nature" (qtd. in Pinker 418–19). Literature is, from an ecological perspective, the record of people on a planet. It is many stories of human nature's capacity for hurt and help, for conflict and cooperation, on an indivisible sphere possessed of its own nonhuman imperatives. Our deeply grounded involvement with natural forces and a common evolutionary history, joined with the complexities of varied cultural and individual artistic experience, mark out the rich, troubling territory for ecocriticism and for the study of literature and environment.

Notes

1. See also Ursula K. Heise's trenchant argument for a comparatist perspective in ecocriticism, part of the *PMLA* "Forum on Literatures of the Environment" (1096–97).

2. The works of Joseph Carroll, particularly his *Evolution and Literary Theory* and *Literary Darwinism,* are central to the study of literature and evolutionary thinking. For specific ecocritical connections, and for fuller discussion of the ideas expressed in this article, see my *Practical Ecocriticism.*

3. See Donald Brown, *Human Universals,* and his recent essay, "Human Universals and Their Implications." Also see the work of Ellen Dissanayake, especially *Homo Aestheticus: Where Art Comes from and Why.*

4. For a recent overview of interdisciplinarity in ecocriticism, see Michael P. Cohen, "Blues in the Green: Ecocriticism under Critique" (17–19).

5. Further examination of the *biophilia* idea may be found in such works as Stephen R. Kellert and Edward O. Wilson's *The Biophilia Hypothesis*; David Sobel, *Children's Special Places*; Stephen R. Kellert, *Kinship to Mastery*; Peter H. Kahn, Jr., *The Human Relationship with Nature*; and Peter H. Kahn, Jr., and Stephen R. Kellert, *Children and Nature: Psychological, Sociocultural, and Evolutionary Investigations*.

Barbara Barney Nelson

Predators in Literature

Predators represent both one of the most controversial environmental issues and one of the most intriguing literary characters. From biblical lions' dens to mythological world-devouring wolves, predators began slinking across our psyches long before the first little girl took cookies to the first grandma. Predators in literature cross the boundaries of language, race, religion, class, and gender with ease. We call *ourselves* Black Panthers, Pink Panthers, and Grey Panthers, and we drive Cougars and Jaguars with a tiger in our tank, while wearing a leopard-print T-shirt. We call *them* gods, monarchs, changelings, tricksters, murderers, and thieves and have never answered, to our satisfaction, William Blake's burning question: "Did He who made the lamb make thee?" (489). Studying predators in literature provides an excellent forum from which to explore almost every aspect of environmental politics. Worldwide from persecution to protection, economics to religion, science to myth, predators paw at psychological and political pendulums that never seem to stop. Poetry, fiction, creative nonfiction, children's stories, and sometimes even science itself are filled with imaginary animals, heroes and villains, honesty and corruption, metaphor, big bucks, and insanity.

Good science is arguably the most important aspect of teaching environmental literature and the most difficult for a nonscientist to judge. Scientists have leveled much criticism at ecocritics, including the embarrassing closing session of the 1999 Association for the Study of Literature and Environment conference during which a woman stood up at the back of the room, identified herself as a scientist, and said that she had been hearing how this new ecocriticism would enlighten the sciences, but so far all she had heard was bad science. So, my goal was to ground my course in good science. My dissertation had been on animals in literature, and I developed my freshman composition courses around examples and research assignments connected to endangered species and world predators. Through the years those interests and courses began to develop my interdisciplinary research skills, as well as my familiarity with the political issues involved. In addition, I read extensively in predator research, attempted some interdisciplinary publishing, and subjected my work to corrections, comments, and rejections from experts in the field like Warren Ballard, the former editor of the *Wildlife Society Bulletin*; Dave Ankney, a University of Western Ontario emeritus professor of zoology and the former director of the Canadian Wildlife Federation; and Guy Connolly, the wildlife biologist at Animal and Plant Health Inspection Service Wildlife Research Center in Fort Collins, Colorado. I also consulted with people from my own university: the Distinguished Professor Emeritus of Biology Jim Scudday and current members of our science faculty.

Especially helpful were two of our alumni: Rocky McBride, the director of Faro Moro Eco Research, a new jaguar-conservation program in Paraguay's western Chaco, and his father, Roy, who is both a trained scientist with a master's degree in biology and the trapper who caught the last remaining wolves for the Mexican-wolf captive-breeding program. Roy and his trained hounds have been catching Florida panthers for that endangered species program since its inception in 1973. Both McBrides have traveled the world catching leopards, wolves, bears, snow leopards, pumas, hyenas, Cape hunting dogs, cheetahs, caracals, jackals, ocelots, jaguars, and a number of the smaller cats. They were especially valuable when providing guidance in finding contradictory and controversial scientific viewpoints and helping me understand the often subtle and obscure distinctions between them. Both appeared as guest lecturers, as did the retired United States Customs and Border Protection agent and tracker, Vince Lavallee.

I also attended several wildlife symposia listening to various predator experts, including the Department of the Interior senior wolf scientist, L. David Mech, author of *The Wolf: The Ecology and Behavior of an Endangered*

Species and *The Way of the Wolf*, and I invited Ed Bangs, the United States Fish and Wildlife wolf-recovery coordinator, to appear on my panel discussing representation of wolves in literature at the 2004 Western Literature Association conference. Over one Thanksgiving break, I journeyed to Coahuila, Mexico, as a guest of Diana Doan-Crider, a member of the International Union for Conservation of Nature and Natural Resources bear specialist group, to one of the ranches where she did her landmark black-bear study. Although I highly recommend mixing science and humanities, I caution that collaboration with scientists and wildlife professionals will significantly increase humility, at least for the "soft" scientist involved. So, although sometimes painful, without their expertise, I would surely have had a tiger by the tail.

These interests, contacts, and research excursions eventually evolved into a sophomore-level introduction-to-literature survey course. Called Predators in Literature, the course covers some of the basics of genre (poetry, fiction, natural history, essay, folklore) as well as period (Middle Ages, Renaissance, Enlightenment, Romanticism, transcendentalism, realism) and introduces several approaches from modern literary theory (feminism, Marxism, orientalism, and ecocriticism). The course lends itself to traditional literary discussions on death, religion, and human psychology, as well as contemporary discussions about power, dialogics, and deconstruction, although students are not always aware of their own theoretical insights. One student explained that if Eskimo or Indian knowledge of nature were accepted by the scientific community, science would be enhanced. Another thought possibly that the label given to the wolf's howl, the "call of the wild," made people feel that they were missing out on something.

I organized the course into four parts: the predator in gender and children's issues, the predator as evil, the predator as God, and the predator in history and science. Texts have included *Wolf Songs: The Classic Collection of Writing about Wolves*, edited by Robert Busch; Jack London's *The Call of the Wild*; Barry Lopez's *Of Wolves and Men*; Jean Craighead George's *Julie of the Wolves*; Jim Corbett's *The Temple Tiger*; and David Baron's *The Beast in the Garden*. My greatest challenge was incorporating a wide variety of readings without asking students to purchase thirty books. Instead of reading Farley Mowat's *Never Cry Wolf* or William Faulkner's "The Bear," we watched clips from movies. Instead of reading Cormac McCarthy's *The Crossing*, we listened to Brad Pitt read the wolf scenes on tape. Instead of reading Nicolas Evans's *The Loop*, we simply compared his imaginary description of the treble-hook loop (456–58) with a description of treble hooks rolled in fat and used instead of poison in rural Mexico (McBride, *Status* 64). Short selections ranged from beast fables to natural history to prize-winning fiction to peer-reviewed science, including brief excerpts from predator scientists who have become writers for the popular press, like Alan Rabinowitz and Mech. To stay within copyright fair use boundaries, sometimes I read a poem or "told" a story instead of distributing copies. Each section was literature-based and supplemented with an eclectic collection of charts and graphs, photographs, magazine ads, videos, tape recordings, trapping catalogs, technical bulletins, Defenders of Wildlife publications, and guest lectures.

Education theorists recommend a local or regional connection as a teaching tool to improve student interest and retention. Our university mascot is the wolf, or lobo, and we are located close to the Mexican border and surrounded by ranch country, so the predator is of significant local interest. In class we make fun of our bookstore's decals showing cat tracks as wolf tracks, and students bring in found items like pages torn from a Ducks Unlimited catalog selling items sporting Labrador tracks that are actually cat tracks. We retell a local ranchwoman's mountain-lion hunting story (Stillwell), peruse border-trading-post records on fur buying in our university archives, and read how wolves were treated here in 1908 (O. W. Williams). We often find surprises and mysteries. For example, the last wolf killed in Texas was our university mascot in 1974, the victim of a suspected poisoning (L. Owens 1).

Since my university is an open-admissions institution, serving the Mexico border area of west Texas, established for the purpose of educating future teachers, I try to model and incorporate innovative teaching methods into the course. As an example, even in testing I try to recognize the importance of "the I in nature" (McFadden) by asking students to produce an essay combining their own personal experience (childhood stories, gender, ethnicity) with their observations on Lopez's chapters on fable, fairy tale, and Indian storytelling as well as with short excerpts from around the world: a young Masai killing his first lion (Saitoti), a Korean woman taming a tiger with bowls of rice ("The Tiger's Whisker"). During deer hunting season, one student confessed that the class had caused him to think about these stories as he walked back to the truck from his deerblind. He said the class had been a great experience and had caused him to think about animals more than he had in the past.

Another example is a class drama that I wrote, which is based on the nature-faker controversy (Lutts). With their lines typed onto index cards and simple "costumes" like a cleric's collar for William J. Long and a bird's-nest-adorned hat for John Burroughs, the players pull their desks into a circle. The chorus (usually me) begins each "scene" by introducing the situation. In turn the players read their lines as we move around the circle of chairs, ending with comments from media and literary critics, including Julie Seton. In scene one, the characters each try to top one another as "wild" humans, showing photos of themselves in their "wilderness" garb (Roosevelt and Seton in buckskins, Long on snowshoes) or sharing descriptions of their primitive innovations (Muir's eagle-feather pen and Sequoia ink). In scene two, they top each other with their natural-history observations. In scene three, they each go a little "over the top" as Seton sees a fox ride on a sheep's back or Long watches a bird cast its own broken leg with mud and sticks. Even saintly Burroughs and John Muir speak incriminating nature-faking lines. In scene four, accusations are traded, become political, and cause tearful responses. And so it goes, round and round, until the last scene, when it all seems to boil down to promoting books. Joseph Knowles, who claimed to have walked off into the Maine woods naked (wearing his fig-leaf costume), is exposed with his snug cabin and food cache, but he proudly announces that his book, *Alone in the Wilderness*, has sold 300,000 copies. All lines read by the students are direct quotations with citations provided. During the hour in which students perform the play, they seem to develop a far better understanding and more retention of the nature-faking controversy, the characters involved, and its possible influence on contemporary writers than would be possible if I spent equal time on lecture. Student players are able to bring alive the role of nature writers and popular books in politics, advertising, and education. In an essay for the test on this section, one student observed that he and his fellow students were often at the mercy of the stories because most of them had never seen a wolf and probably never would. When unscrupulous authors combined science with exaggeration, only wolf scientists would be able to separate fact from fiction. Although the student felt sure most people would get beyond the idea that werewolves prowled the night looking for blood to suck, he worried that many false claims hidden in other tales were not so easily detected.

The class also spends considerable time analyzing the role of literature and animals in politics. One interesting rare book inspired an exploration into predators and poisons as political symbols. In 1929 *The Last Stand of the Pack* was authored by a popular fiction writer, Arthur H. Carhart, in collaboration with Stanley P. Young, the principal biologist of the United States

Biological Survey at the time—or, in other words, the government preda-
tor-hunters' boss. The book seems to have been intended, at least partly, to
combat the rising popularity of the Anti-Steel Trap League (later Defenders of Wildlife) by creating larger-than-life legendary government trappers
like Bill Caywood, demonizing nongovernment trappers, and swaying the
reader and rancher to support funding for government predator control
(Carhart and Young 36–39, 50). According to political scientists, "It is
characteristic of large numbers of people in our society that they cannot recognize or tolerate ambiguous or complex situations, and that they accordingly respond chiefly to symbols that oversimplify and distort" (Edelman
699). Politicians often manipulate apathetic voters by stirring up emotions
through successful symbols. Government agencies effectively use symbols
that evoke a threat to public safety to create support for funding. Politicians
can emphasize the threat and then reassure the voter with a promise for
protection. Public health issues like cancer or rabies are good examples, and
predator control enjoyed a doubling of its funding almost every ten years,
throughout the twentieth century (MacIntyre 333). The most useful political symbols are those that can be identified with certain voters and parties.
But, according to political scientists, those symbols are also the most dangerous: "Symbolism in politics is an inherently treacherous subject" because
"[t]he general public does not have the time, education or inclination to
check elite claims against the complex, remote and uncertain yardstick of
reality" (MacIntyre 680). However, Carhart and Young's book may have
backfired on the predator program. With field notes from the hunters obviously available to the authors, some of the wolf behavior is quite accurate,
but most is jazzed up and polluted by Carhart with anthropomorphic wolf
thoughts like: "Somehow the man on horseback . . . had touched a chord
in the heart of the lonely old wolf" (84). Consequently, the year it was
published, instead of dwelling on the heroics of the government trappers,
another popular author of the day, Mary Austin, noticed the predator's own
potential for a new kind of symbol in her review of the book. She "admits
a sympathy almost wholly engaged on behalf of the Pack, feeling that the
country could well have spared a last pack, and reimbursed the losers among
cattle men, for the sake of a pack to study, a pack to provide the last fillip of
wildness" ("Wolf Pack"). Eventually politicians noticed the same potential
for the wolf as symbol.

The drama behind the ban against poisoning predators is a classic
example of the political use of predators and poisons as symbols. According to political scientists, in the mid-sixties, the Republican president

Richard Nixon was looking for the "least expensive" way to grab head-lines through a symbol for a new cause established by his administration: environmental protection. One of his first executive decrees was to create the Environmental Protection Agency (MacIntyre 340). Two important books had skyrocketed to the best-seller list just before Nixon's search for a symbol: Rachel Carson's *Silent Spring* and Farley Mowat's *Never Cry Wolf.* Mowat presented the wolf pack as a model for modern human beings because wolves are outdoorsy, physically fit, and faithful to a mate; share child-raising duties; are both protective and gentle; and, in Mowat's char-acterization, acted as surrogate human parent figures who would nurture all human children. Carson demonized chemicals. So the class traces the use of chemicals by villains from Merlin to Faust to Romeo and Juliet to Snow White to modern industry in Carson as well as how chemicals them-selves, such as compound 1080, become villains. Obviously both wolves and chemicals hold deep symbolic meaning in the public psyche.

As Nixon's staff began to check into the possibilities of using either wolves or chemicals as a political symbol, the two came together dramati-cally in the predator-poisoning program. Sheep ranchers benefited most from the poisoning program, and they were extremely loyal to the Repub-lican party. Nixon's advisers thought they would take a direct hit and still vote Republican (MacIntyre 340). Sheep ranchers were also very symbolic to the liberal voter. Although the symbol of the lamb had once enjoyed much protection through its association in the Christian religion as a rep-resentative of the common man, those days—probably thanks to Muir (B. Nelson *Wild* 74–91)—seemed to be over, and demonization of preda-tors was easily dismissed as a holdover from fairy tales or as misdirected "scapegoating" by sheep raisers frustrated over their shrinking industry. Just one year before Nixon's reelection bid, sheep ranchers had also cap-tured negative media attention for illegally poisoning eagles (obviously another political symbol) with thallium sulfate.

Consequently, Nixon's advisers found predator poisoning a perfect political symbol. Stopping the poisoning program would grab headlines, would not upset other western Republicans too much, would not affect farmers at all, and would probably even benefit government predator con-trol, since the program had become not only a political liability but also a white elephant to the agency because the incredible success of compound 1080 threatened to make government trappers and their funding obsolete (MacIntyre 349). Identification with the persecuted wolf was also sublimi-nally likely for Republican businessmen. Forty years earlier, in her review of Carhart and Young's book, Mary Austin had noted the businessman's preference for identifying with the wolf pack rather than the monkey. She says that

> of all the hunting beasts, the wolf pack, as this book goes to show, most resembled the human economic pack in pattern, in the quality both of leadership and of submission to it, in foresight, in wariness, in evasion and attack, and in ruthlessness. . . . Altogether the book is a fable for economists, a document for psychologists.

The real sheep, the real predators, and the real poisons involved had nothing to do with Nixon's political move, and no amount of good science or common sense could have stopped the alpha male's Executive Order 11643. As predicted, banning the use of predacides on public land and by government agencies gained Nixon many votes and lost very few. Even sheep ranchers were somewhat naively confident that after the election, their Republican president would make amends (MacIntyre 383).

Ironically, although begun by the Republican Party, symbols of the EPA and protection for predators are now associated with the Democratic Party. During an election year, the class watches for developing predator symbols, and I bait discussion with questions like: Have Democratic environmental voters become so loyal to the party that they are now in the same position as sheep ranchers in the sixties? Can these environmental voters be counted on for loyalty if the party decides to grab some headlines and votes at the expense of predators? Which political party will exploit the predator symbol? Which books will have been or will be best sellers between now and the next election? During the 2004 presidential election, students brought in fascinating combinations: a George W. Bush ad comparing wolves to terrorists and an article warning that compound 1080 could be used by terrorists.

The written and oral research project for the course asks students to locate an intriguing passage in a literary text that we had not read in class (I provide selections but encourage students to find their own favorites), to briefly tell the story (which also helps expand exposure), and to find the science to support or refute its accuracy. It proves to be a demanding and sometimes surprising assignment, in which my greatest challenge is to wean students from doing their "research" on the Internet, where they find biased propaganda rather than good science—although even science can sometimes conflict and sound more biased than it should. Willa Cather's gruesome scene of wolves chasing Russian sleighs through a snowy night and eating the entire wedding party is a good example of literature conflicting with science. Students found peer-reviewed, reputable scientists claiming that wolves never harm people, and, on the other hand, published science articles listing hundreds of children and adults killed by wolves in rural India (Jhala and Sharma; Rajpurohit), as well as identifying a female scientist (Klinghammer) and others (McNay; Scott, Bentley, and Warren) killed by wolves in North America. Terry Tempest Williams's story "Lion Eyes" provided another source for conflicting science about cougar eye color.

The education theorist Robert J. Sternberg, writing on teaching for wisdom, says that science teaching should

> no longer be about facts presented as though they are the final word. . . . [It should teach] that the paradigms of today, and thus the theories and findings that emanate from them, will eventually be superseded . . . that, contrary to the way many textbooks are written, the classical "scientific method" is largely a fantasy rather than a reality, and that scientists are as susceptible to fads as are members of other groups. (171)

So we also discuss pseudoscientists or scientists as characters, as hero, advocate, legend, savior, movie star, lover, and despot. Many well-known predator scientists have appeared in these roles (e.g., Pringle).

To introduce the research project, I use material illustrating that the conflict between imaginary and real exists even in science (Sealander and Gipson; McBride et al.). When discussing the importance of physical sign, I include both David Abram's sophisticated thoughts on our lost ability to "read" stories on the land as well as Australian aboriginal art based on tracks. To practice for the research project, students compare Ernest Thompson Seton's "Lobo: King of the Carrumpaw" with Roy McBride's story of catching one of the last Mexican wolves: "Las Margaritas" (*Status* 55–62). Students then look for details in the literature where the author actually could have gleaned the details by interpreting physical sign as opposed to imagining or projecting behavior onto an animal. They quickly gain awareness and skills in separating imagination from reliable field observation. Their confidence increases when they discover that even scientists seem to have a difficult time separating the real from the imaginary, and thus students are then more inclined to question and look for alternatives.

The course also emphasizes the importance of the scientist as writer. McBride's material has been subjected to political editing for publication in government documents, and his science has been changed in the popular press and plagiarized by another author. So his material led to discussions about the importance of academic honesty, accuracy in the stories that shape our worldview, and the role of economics and ethics in publishing (B. Nelson, "Trap"). Comparing McBride's trapping techniques, his sympathetic feeding of a chained wolf, and his desire to break up a dog-against-wolf fight in Mexico (McBride, *Mexican Wolf* 33, 25, 19) with Cormac McCarthy's fictionalized versions (50, 113–22, 83) also helps me bring in connections to Mexico, an important consideration at a school serving students from along the Mexican border, and leads to discussions of racism, environmental justice, and the responsibility of the fiction writer to facts and sources (B. Nelson, "Crossing"). My borderland students usually feel that McCarthy's representations of Mexico and Mexican people are far from accurate and personally enjoy reading the McBride material. They often judge McBride's work as good literature and trust his accuracy because they know him by reputation and know he may have sat at one of the very same desks they now occupy.

Our analysis was further supplemented by Wallace Stegner's plagiarism in *Angle of Repose* of Mary Hallock Foote's letters and diaries (Hall). Farley Mowat's work, *Never Cry Wolf,* exploited Adolph Murie's wolf research in a similar manner. Although Mowat received negative reviews in scientific journals like *Journal of Wildlife Management* (Pimlott) and *Canadian Field Naturalist* (Banfield), was chastised by Mech (*Wolf* 339–40), and was exposed as a "nature faker" in the popular press (Goddard), none of this has kept his book from being heavily adopted by well-meaning teachers as a great nonfiction text accurately portraying wolves. Brief excerpts from Austin's 1934 short story "Speaking of Bears," Ralph Lutts's *Nature Fakers,* and a *Wildlife Society Bulletin* opinion piece on "the lynx affair" (Thomas and Pletscher) were also used to reinforce the idea that appropriating and misrepresenting predator science are widespread and ongoing problems.

The course also includes brief creative writing assignments: write a fable using good science, write an animal legend using good science, pick a favorite animal story from the readings and change the gender, or write a contemporary coyote story with a lesson for modern college students while trying to incorporate some good science. One student who moonlights as a bartender wrote "Coyote's Bad Bar Experience": "Every Thursday night the same Coyote came into the bar, always putting on a show. After a couple of drinks he would always make a scene." So the bartender and the patrons decide to play a trick on coyote by serving him drinks with hardly any alcohol to see if he will pretend to be drunk.

So Coyote orders another drink and the bartender makes it with almost no liquor at all. One after another the Coyote drinks. The bartender making each drink with less and less liquor. Finally, Coyote starts to get loud and make a fool of himself. Dancing around, talking to the patrons, Coyote begins to become so obnoxious.

Then the bartender says, "Coyote there was very little liquor, if any, in some of your drinks." And the story continues:

Coyote could feel the embarrassment on his face. The Bartender said, "Look, I don't care if you come in here, but we are tired of you trying to put on a show to make us think you are drunk. You are a fake and we are tired of it. Why don't you just be yourself? People will like you better for it." . . . [And he] never showed his face in the bar again.

Although the good science was only subtly included, the implication was that still to this day coyotes attempt to be themselves and no longer frequent bars or pretend to be drunk anymore (story used by permission of Kathy Lavallee Burkett).

In the section on gender, we trace the evolution of the Little Red Riding Hood story, and I incorporate photos of female hunters, little girls posing with dead animals, women wearing fur coats, and little girls who are adopted by wolves. Students often observe that in George's *Julie and the Wolves*, the alpha male is a noble savage who protects his family as well as Julie. Students realize that by humanizing these predators and making them appealing, readers forget that they can be dangerous and need to be reminded that the characters are romanticized. Excerpts from Terry Tempest Williams's "Undressing the Bear," Austin's "Bitterness of Women," and Ursula K. Le Guin's "The Wife's Story" provided perspectives ranging from female bears as victims to man-destroying mama grizzlies to a good wolf husband and father who turns into an abusive "were-human." In addition, we talk about the way predators have been objectified like women and Native American "noble savages" to serve as art, pets, entertainment, music makers, and tourist attractions, as well as about predators' roles in subliminal advertising.

Marxist criticism is especially enlightening in the section on the predator as thief and murderer. Modern scientists have investigated and discredited some of the legendary wolf stories by comparing the huge sizes of wolves in the tales to their real, much smaller skulls that had been sent to museums. Seton claimed the king of the Currumpaw died of a broken heart over his mate's death, but the scientists found the king's actual skull has a bullet hole between the eyes (Gipson, Ballard, and Nowak). Ironically, several reputable historians treated Seton's story as historical fact during the Leopold Forum: El Lobo (held in Las Cruces, New Mexico, in February 2003).

During the section on predator as god or benevolent animal, my class reads various coyote tales, discusses the hierarchies in Aldo Leopold's "Thinking like a Mountain," and analyzes McCarthy's wolf as Christ and Madonna figure (Robisch). We analyze the fictionalized characters created by modern writers that demonize trappers as alchemists (McCarthy 17), abusive men who raise nose-picking, dirty sons (Stegner, "Wolfer"), guilt-ridden loners who have no friends or family (N. Evans), and hallucinating ne'er-do-wells who visit prostitutes (Mattheisson, "Wolves"). My rural students, who often trap animals themselves, resist these descriptions: Nicholas Evans's *The Loop*, for example, portrays trappers as mean, dirty, and unethical. My students grant that a few trappers may exist who fit the description to some degree, but they feel it is more likely that the author simply used the trapper as a convenient villain and never actually knew any real trappers himself.

The course attracts students majoring in biology, natural-resource management, wildlife management, agriculture, criminal justice, and education. Students have expressed mixed reactions toward me in the course evaluations, some admiring my knowledge of predators and others finding my background weak. However, they all enjoyed the topic, the attempt to connect literature to science, and especially the McBride guest lectures. Even though almost all complained about the heavy reading load, they still said they would recommend the course to a friend. I was humorously shocked when one student said the course description was very misleading; this student was disappointed when the course was not about human predators. I try to keep my own biases hidden and present the material as fairly as I can, but I was quite surprised when one student commented that my class seemed like a PETA (People for the Ethical Treatment of Animals) meeting. Sometimes, though, students succinctly articulate almost my own belief that predators are neither morally good nor morally evil. They are what they are, with no romantic trappings. We all agree that the ideal situation is for literary authors to stop representing their romantic ideas about predators as science and for readers to recognize the difference.

My own criticism of the class is that thus far I have been unable to organize a field trip during which students can experience seeing or at least tracking a wild predator. I also wonder if our search for accurate science sometimes becomes more of a focus than the literature and the reasons we read literature. Only occasionally do students seem to find deep philosophical meaning in the science. Sometimes they also give a new slant to widely accepted observations, such as when one student wondered whether an alpha wolf becomes a dominant animal because of its ability to hold the pack together—to give it comfort, coordination, and community—rather than because of its aggressive nature or formidable bite. Because of my own enthusiasm for the topic, I do try to cover too much material and can provide only brief introductions to complicated concepts that most nonmajor undergraduates find daunting. The brief excerpts often do not do the authors or the topic justice. So I look forward to offering the interdisciplinary course at the graduate level some day.

In conclusion, I believe this course illuminates the deep psychological and literary basis of many vital environmental issues that future government employees, teachers, scientists, and politicians will deal with daily. Yet these issues are seldom addressed in our monocultural disciplines. To quote Ed Bangs, the United States Fish and Wildlife wolf-recovery coordinator, "Wolf management has nothing to do with reality." To be fair, I take his quote out of context. He goes on to say that it is all about human values. I would argue that it is all about the stories we read and tell, but maybe we are talking about the same thing.

Mary Stark and Stephen R. Johnson

Reading the Landscape: Prairie Education through American Literature

How can studying prairie ecology and natural history help with reading American literature based on a landscape that is no longer widely available? How can studying the literature help in prairie restoration? Many contemporary readers and some PhDs in literature lack the knowledge of the prairie ecosystems and their eradication for farmland that early American authors describe. Interdisciplinary collaboration can help readers understand the metaphors inspired by the lost landscape.

In Iowa and neighboring prairie states many efforts have been undertaken to form public awareness of what was lost and to create roadside and larger prairie restorations. Still mainstream Iowa and America in general have been slow to realize the importance of tallgrass prairie. As a teacher of environmental literature and an Iowan, I had never seen a prairie and had much to learn. I could not distinguish prairie dock from burdock. Mary was curious about the "vista" so many authors described. Further, as someone who wrote a dissertation on Walt Whitman's *Leaves of Grass*, Mary lacked understanding of its controlling metaphor and his image of the American nation. When Mary asked her classes at Central College in Pella, Iowa, to write about their knowledge of the state's natural history, most of the students indicated almost no knowledge of their home environment. The class needed a reader who knew the tallgrass prairie.

Stephen, whose PhD is in plant ecology from Kansas State University, agreed to help Mary and the class understand the landscape described in the literature.

In teaching a prairie unit in Mary's Nature Writing and Environmental Literature course, we first establish a context for the fragility of the prairie ecosystem that once dominated one-third of the United States. In Iowa, only one-tenth of one percent of prairie remains in a state that was once eighty to eighty-five percent tallgrass prairie, the most endangered ecosystem in America (Samson and Knopf xi; Joern and Keeler 13). Because so little prairie remains, it is no wonder that many twenty-first-century readers lack the knowledge of prairie natural history and the opportunity to see the vistas and understand the references in the literature. We found that slides from Stephen's Konza prairie research, videos of prairie landscapes, and service-learning field trips to prairie remnants and reconstructions animated the literature.[1]

For instance, so that we could visualize the Iowa landscape before the steel plow was invented in 1837–40 (Weaver 172), Stephen showed slides of the vast Konza prairie, near Manhattan, Kansas, which survived because its rocky soil inhibited even the steel plow. Stephen's photographs and research experience on Konza Prairie Research Natural Area (now Konza Prairie Biological Station) are particularly significant, since Konza is a long-term biological research area where the vista was saved. Konza prairie is 3,487 hectares of nearly virgin prairie—with only some parts significantly grazed (Knapp et al. 7). Diversity prevails in a healthy prairie: researchers have found 529 species of plants on Konza (80). It was on Konza that Stephen studied the effects of fire on prairie cordgrass (*Spartina pectinata*), diversity of spiders in wetlands, and the effects of fire and grazing on prairie orchids.

After some background on prairie natural history, we continue the prairie unit with a chronological approach, tracing the changes in the prairie landscape as reflected in the literature. The students write journals as they read the written descriptions of tallgrass prairie by Native Americans as well as early European and later colonizers to show how they responded to treeless vastness and prairie fires. For instance, John Bakeless's *America as Seen by Its First Explorers: The Eyes of Discovery* includes journal entries from members of the Coronado expedition. Here the explorers are presumably the first Westerners to see strange beasts such as the bison and a seemingly endless vista. For these "strangers . . . there was only a flat expanse of grass . . . stretching illimitably away until it met the sky in a huge ring that closed the white men in" (94).

The students next explore excerpts from the journals of Meriwether Lewis and William Clark; for example, on Saturday, 25 August 1804, Clark describes Spirit Mound in South Dakota (Bergon 35). Photographs from *Lewis and Clark's Green World: The Expedition and Its Plants* (Earle and Reveal) as well as *Lewis and Clark on the Great Plains* (Johnsgard) show visually what the journals depict in words. Then, in *Our Natural History: The Lessons of Lewis and Clark,* the biologist Daniel Botkin retraces the tracks of the expedition and the prairies of Spirit Mound. He also emphasizes America's need for prairie and an understanding of its natural history. He notes that because prairie "was diminished so early in the development of North America," many environmentalists focus on less-altered landscapes (257). Botkin delineates three reasons why the prairies are still significant: they have deep fertile soil, feature biological diversity, and provide "messages for us about how we can approach solutions to environmental issues today" (257). Stephen further explains other practical benefits of the tallgrass prairies as the "lungs of the continent" that filter the air we breathe and help with carbon sequestration and even climate change (Altman and Larrabee).

After discussing current environmental concerns, the students investigate more historical roots by reading journal entries from Zebulon Pike's expedition in 1806 as well as from Stephen Long's exploration in 1819. Both authors chronicle the diversity and vastness that they witness in the prairies.

As the unit unfolds, the students continue to record their observations about the literature and landscape, linking their reading to the context of prairie education. We move to the writings and artwork of George Catlin and highlight a section of Washington Irving's "Tour of the Prairies" with a focus on bison and bees, followed by a look at William Cullen Bryant's poem "The Prairies." These authors, publishing in the 1830s and 1840s, speculate about the changes in the prairie and guide us on the chronological tour of prairie literature. For instance, in *The Letters and Notes on the Manners, Customs, and Conditions of the North American Indians,* Catlin carefully describes bison and forecasts the demise of the species because of the "extravagancies" of both "red men and white" (256–57). Irving also describes the slaughter of bison in his "Tour of the Prairies" and notes changes to the landscape because of invasive species; the honey bee is "harbinger of the white man" (973). In his 1832–34 poem "The Prairies" Bryant refers to the exotic honey bee as a symbol of change: "The bee, / A more adventurous colonist than man, / With whom he came across the eastern deep, / Fills the savannas with his murmurings" (1044).

The speaker in the poem celebrates the diversity and the characteristic vista of these "Gardens of the desert": "I behold them for the first, / And my heart swells, while the dilated sight / Takes in the encircling vastness" (1042). But the speaker further notes rapid changes in the prairie landscape due to westward expansion: "In these plains / The bison feeds no more" (1044).

For Whitman in the 1870s, the diversity of the tallgrass prairie reflects his major image of democracy. To understand the metaphoric title of *Leaves of Grass*, it is important to describe the literal—what the grass looks like and the prairie's context. In "Walt Whitman's Prairie Paradise," Ed Folsom acknowledges the difficulty many contemporary readers have in understanding the title of *Leaves of Grass* because many only know the manicured lawn:

> Whitman's key image of grass often is interpreted as though he had been imagining a flawless Chemlawned expanse of bright green cut blades, thus evoking democracy as a plot of nearly identical individuals forming a uniformly colored oneness in which all the weeds and non-conforming grasses have been eradicated. (48)

As Robert Sayre states in the introduction to *Recovering the Prairie*, "To understand the metaphor, we need the fact"(6). To help students understand the metaphor Whitman uses, we provide an overview of the golf-course lawn, which, although a landscape we see all around us, is not exactly what Whitman had in mind with his focus on diversity and strong, deep roots clumped together as a metaphor for the states. In 1879, Whitman saw the Midwest prairie as endless and marveled at the tiny patches of farms as gardens in the sea of grasses (52). In contrast, we show current photographs of farmland and of lawn and urban sprawl that clearly invert Whitman's vision. Now the prairies are the tiny parcels against a sea of change.

Willa Cather, however, chronicles the most drastic changes in the landscape. Cather was born in Virginia and moved at age ten to the prairies of Nebraska; she integrates the beauty, diversity, and literal diminishing of prairie into *My Ántonia*. Ántonia thrills at the life teeming around her in the Nebraska landscape and protects a little grasshopper that hops from "the buffalo grass and tried to leap into a bunch of bluestem" (39). Coming from Virginia, Jim Burden, the narrator, is overwhelmed by the prairie: "Between the earth and that sky I felt erased, blotted out"(8). Yet Jim slowly grows to appreciate the prairie. To animate Cather's textual passages about movement ("there was so much motion in it; the whole country seemed, somehow, to be running" [15]), we juxtapose slides of the wind blowing gayfeather and Indian grass on the Konza landscape. Another photograph presents butterfly milkweed growing next to a barbed-wire fence to accompany Cather's description: "I saw a clump of flaming orange-coloured milkweed . . . I left the road and went around through a stretch of pasture" (232–23).

Cather also is the eye that views prairie destruction. She describes how quickly the prairie was ploughed: "The old pasture land was now being broken up into wheat fields and cornfields, the red grass was disappearing, the whole face of the country was changing" (306). Only tiny remnants of prairie remained just thirty-nine years after Whitman's observation of endless vista. Cather describes little prairie islands surrounded by graves:

> Years afterward, when the open-grazing days were over, and the red grass had been ploughed under and under until it had almost disappeared from the prairie; when all the fields were under fence, and the roads no longer ran about like wild things, but followed the surveyed section-lines, Mr. Shimerda's grave was still there, with a sagging wire fence around it . . . so that the grave, with its tall red grass that was never mowed was like a little island. (118–19)

Similarly, Whitman describes grass as "the beautiful uncut hair of graves" ("Song" 34, line 110). With the eradication of prairie vistas, these little cemetery remnants are now the small, enclosed areas described as "paradises" by Whitman. It also seems ironic that many of the prairie remnants survived around railroad tracks—since the railroad was not only the symbol of western expansion and of progress but also the conduit for pioneers as portrayed in *My Ántonia*.[2]

The continued destruction of the prairie advances the chronological and literary tour to Aldo Leopold's *A Sand County Almanac*, which shows the devastation following the elimination of the prairie. For instance, Leopold narrates an experience he had with a particular compass plant (*Silphium laciniatum*) in a tiny graveyard remnant established in the 1840s. He had watched this compass plant protected behind a fence until he noticed that the highway department had removed the fence and cut down the *Silphium*. He called the cutting "one little episode in the funeral of the native flora which in turn is one episode in the funeral of the floras of the world" (46).

The students sense that something "lost" marks the passage of the landscape in the literature. When we view *America's Lost Landscape: The Tallgrass Prairie*, they are often astounded by the rapidity of the dramatic transformation of the land. We then include Curt Meine's "Reimagining the Prairie: Aldo Leopold and the Origins of Prairie Restoration," which creates a synthesis of the class readings:

> Far from the landscape of democracy that Bryant and Whitman projected—the "very earthform of nondiscrimination," as Ed Folsom characterizes it—the prairie landscape that Leopold observed was one of deterioration. (145)

Meine, however, shows how following Leopold's new "land ethic" and "reimagining" the prairie landscape can help in restoring not only the land but also the readers who can reconnect with the lost landscape (157).

To culminate the unit, the class looks at 150 years of Iowa as a state; we clearly see the changes in landscape as captured in *Broken Ground*, a musical composition by Jon Chenette. To celebrate Iowa's sesquicentennial in 1996, Chenette arranged poems by Ray Young Bear, Dan Hunter, Ed Hirsch, Mary Swander, Paula Smith, and Michael Carey, which inspired Chenette's music. Hunter's "Only the Wind" features the cemetery where the wind "bends the grass on the graveyard's broken ground."

In addition to addressing regionalism and the local color associated with the prairie landscape, we mention the reading process and how background or a disciplinary lens shapes meaning. "Rhizomes" by Paula V. Smith from *Broken Ground* describes these horizontal roots as the "Anchor and balance for the waving sea / of grasses." For instance, Stephen's background in the study of soil and plants allows him to read the poem and explain and draw the vocabulary of "culms and rootlets" and "nodes" in context.

Similarly, Stephen reads Ed Hirsch's "Iowa Flora" first for factual details of which plants are "indigenous" and which "alien weeds"; he can explain the characteristics of invasive species with their biological agenda "that no state legislation could control." Once we establish the literal, we then extrapolate metaphorically with Hirsch's theme of human immigration and America as competition on many levels.

As David Orr reminds us, it is time that all Americans gain a fundamental understanding of the importance of ecology. Glen Love exhorts humanists to work together with colleagues from other disciplines to become "scientifically literate" ("Science" 79). This approach is ecology for the general public rather than for scientists. The 2001 and 2002 annual meetings of the Ecological Society of America (ESA), however, focused on communicating ecology to the public. Some scientists are asking for more collaboration with colleagues from other disciplines, as demonstrated in the 2007 ESA workshop "Communicating Science to the Public: The Where, Why, and How of Engaging the Public."

We enjoy collaborating; Mary is definitely including more natural history into the environmental literature and writing classes—a natural fit, it seems. Natural history as a discipline "is going extinct. And nowhere more quickly than where we need it the most—in our colleges and universities" according to Thomas Eisner and Mary Woodsen in "The Science of Wonder: Natural History in the Balance." Eisner and Woodsen advocate that natural history literacy is crucial: "How, except through a fundamental knowledge of natural history, can we imagine creating a recovery plan for a threatened or endangered species" as well as "conserving any part of nature?"

Perhaps if the general public understands the wonder, intricacy, and fragility of prairie, people might be inspired to "recover" or restore it. The Iowa Prairie Network espouses education as one of its main goals. Awareness is also of primary importance according to Pauline Drobney, a refuge biologist at Iowa's Prairie Learning Center at the Neal Smith National Wildlife Refuge (http://iowaprairienetwork.org).

Here in Pella we have a distinct connection to prairie. In fact, one section of Pella was first called Strawtown because of the rudimentary homes made from the thick prairie sod. Pella's historical village includes a sod-house replica, which we visit. Many students in the class are motivated to help with prairie service projects at Central College's field station and at the Neal Smith National Wildlife Refuge.

The literature can be a catalyst for approaching "environmental literacy" through the humanities (Orr 86). As John Elder writes, "Rather than assuming that science and the humanities must remain forever discrete, environmental education needs more boldly to inhabit the ecotone where they join and commingle, where something new may evolve" (*Stories* 8). Joining prairie education with the works of American authors can help in understanding the literature and can give readers glimpses of this greatly diminished ecosystem. Reciprocally, the literature can inspire readers to respect and perhaps even restore prairie to what Whitman calls the "Prairie States" (*Leaves* 402).

Notes

1. Stephen also created several visuals to help present information to third graders as well as college students. One overhead, for instance, depicted the difference in root systems between a tallgrass prairie and a tropical rainforest. This shows that carbon is stored in the soil of a prairie but is in the above-ground biomass of a rainforest. Another visual depicted fire as the metaphoric representation of what some indigenous people call the "red buffalo" (Altman and Larrabee.) A third indicated the importance of mycorrhizal association. Other illustrations suggested the effects of fire on plants; another showed plant competition.

2. Our focus on the railroad links us to the Cajun Prairie in southwestern Louisiana, which is composed of a group of linear remnants along railroad rights-of-way. According to Stephen and his colleague Larry Allain, "Less than 40 ha of the 1,000,000,000 ha of pre-settlement prairie in southwestern Louisiana remain, making Cajun Prairie one of the most imperiled ecosystems in North America" (qtd. in Vidrine et al.). Rice culture removed the vista of what was once eleven million acres of prairie. As in Iowa, less than one-tenth of one percent of the Cajun prairie remains in a natural condition—yet these areas still maintain a high diversity of prairie flora. In an area much smaller than Konza, the Cajun prairie may have 600 plant species ("Location").

David Landis Barnhill

East Asian Influence on Recent North American Nature Writing

In the late 1940s, Kenneth Rexroth published a beautiful nature poem with a title that no doubt puzzled most readers: "Hojoki." In the poem we read, "The waterfall is muffled, / And my ten foot square hut lies / In the absym of a sea / Of sibilant quiet" (*Complete Poems* 285). Later in the poem the narrator thinks "of Buddha's infinite / Laugh in the Lankavatara, / Lighting up all the universes," and then speaks of how "[t]he thin bladed laurel leaves / Look like Su Tung-p'o's bamboos" (286). To understand these references we would need to discuss Japanese Buddhist literature (*Hōjōki* ["An Account of My Ten Foot Square Hut"], the famous autobiographical essay by the Japanese Buddhist poet Kamo no Chōmei [1153–1216]); Chinese Buddhism (the Lankavatara Sutra); and Chinese painting and aesthetic theory (for example, the Neo-Confucian and Buddhist poet-painter Dongpo Su, 1037–1101).

Although there is no precise starting point for East Asian influence on nature-oriented literature in the West, we can take Rexroth's nature poetry in the 1940s as a sign that the influence had become significant.[1] That influence has continued to increase with the writings of Gary Snyder, Peter Matthiessen, Gretel Ehrlich, Ursula Le Guin, and many others. East Asian culture has become a major factor in American nature writing over the past half century. How, then, can we bring that into our courses on North American nature writing?

The Multiplicity of Influence

Obviously, teaching the role of East Asian culture in American nature writing poses difficult and distinctive challenges. One challenge is the complexity of that influence, which has included religion, poetry, travel diaries, drama, painting, and garden art. In terms of religion, Buddhism has been the most prominent religious tradition for American writers, but several distinct forms have been significant: Zen, Huayan, Tibetan, and the general Mahayana bodhisattva ideal. In addition, Daoism and even Confucianism have also been important.[2] The traditions of Chinese and Japanese nature poetry have been central, while the travel journals of the Japanese poet Bashō and the Japanese Noh drama have also had a strong impact.[3]

It would, of course, be impossible to expect students to gain a sophisticated understanding of all these different traditions in a course on North American nature writing. But we should avoid giving in to a common view that the influence is limited to, say, Buddhism and haiku. So I think it is important to point out at the beginning of any discussion of the significance of Asian culture that there has been this multiplicity of influence and then to give at least a brief summary of each tradition. One can then highlight references to Tibetan Buddhism or Daoism, Chinese aesthetics or the Noh drama as they appear in the readings (as all of these do, for instance, in Snyder's *Mountains and Rivers without End*). One can also provide an introductory bibliography to these traditions for those students who want to pursue them in a research paper or simply on their own.

Teachers, having offered an initial sense of the breadth of influence, can then place the focus on those traditions that are most germane to the particular writers studied: for Matthiessen's *The Snow Leopard*, Zen and Tibetan Buddhism; for Ehrlich's *Islands, the Universe, Home*, Daoism and Japanese culture; for Le Guin's *The Dispossessed*, Daoism; and so on.

The Foreignness of East Asian Culture

But when we do consider any of these traditions, we face another challenge: the foreignness of East Asia to the Western tradition and especially to most of our students. The challenge is not only understanding specific ideas and values but also the general problem of dealing with a foreign culture. Students find the material more understandable and interesting if we take the time to discuss with them some of the problems, approaches, and theories concerning cross-cultural understanding.

I have found it useful to first have the students themselves discuss how we should conceptualize these traditions and their relation to the West. Usually they offer a variety of answers and attitudes, and they end up illustrating in an initial way different concepts of religion or cultural tradition. They begin to consider whether, how, and how much American writers can in fact adopt and adapt a foreign tradition. This discussion helps them move away from simplistic approaches and creates a space to bring in theories about cross-cultural relations, such as those found in culture studies and feminism.

Eventually, such a discussion allows the instructor to point out the extremes of uncritical embrace and naive dismissal. Uncritical embrace denies the substantial cultural differences and the complexity of the ideas involved. It rejects any kind of otherness, making different cultures open for easy and superficial consumption. (Parallels between this attitude and colonialism are worth pointing out.) Actually this perspective can be disabused easily by getting students to grapple with an idea such as the Buddhist notion of nonself, in which the distinction between subject and object, consciousness and reality, is rejected. Individual passages from various writers illustrating this view of the self (e.g., Matthiessen in *The Snow Leopard*) can give the students an initial sense of cultural difference, generating a sense of "estrangement" that can open them to a new perspective on their own culture.[4] Naive dismissal, on the other hand, denies the real impact that East Asia has had on North American nature writing. It asserts that, because East Asian culture is foreign, we are inextricably alienated from it. As a result, the argument goes, attempts at adapting East Asian culture into nature writing are inauthentic, and East Asian culture is irrelevant to ecocriticism. In a slightly different context, one scholar of the religions of India, Gerald Larson, has argued that in current attempts to use foreign cultures as conceptual resources for environmental ethics, "[i]deas and concepts come to be construed as 'things' or 'entities' that can be disembedded from their appropriate frameworks and then processed and made to fit into our own frameworks" (270). (Again, parallels to colonialism are worth pointing out.) For Larson, concepts such as Dao or dharma cannot be utilized because they are embedded in the culture of their origin, a culture that is profoundly different from our own. Any attempt to import them as conceptual resources fails to be successful either philosophically or socially. Otherness has been absolutized.[5]

Consideration of such a view is an opportunity to bring cultural theory and history into the discussion. Arguments for dismissal are often based on an essentialist assumption that religions and cultures have a singular core, which makes them discrete, unchanging phenomena unavailable for intercultural exchange. There are, I think, at least two ways to present to students a middle path between uncritical embrace and a dismissal of cultural interchange. The first is the notion of "anotherness," first articulated by Mikhail Bakhtin and applied insightfully to nature writing by Patrick D. Murphy. One of the advantages of the idea of anotherness is that it is sophisticated but makes a simple point: another person, social group, or culture—or the nonhuman world of nature—has real distinctiveness, but at the same time qualified relatedness is real, and relative understanding is possible. As Murphy has said, "What if instead of alienation we posited *relation* as the primary mode of human-human and human-nature interaction without conflating difference, particularity and other specificities? What if we worked from a concept of relational difference and *anotherness* rather than Otherness?" (*Literature, Nature* 35).[6]

Another way to help students conceive of cultural difference is by what I call an ecosystem approach to culture.[7] Ecology has taught us to see nature not as a collection of separate discrete building blocks but rather as an interdependent system that consists of a single field of interrelated energy flows. The "things" of an ecosystem are (to borrow Snyder's phrase ["Introductory Note"]) formal turbulences in the energy flow: temporary forms that cannot be isolated from the rest of the field. In addition, ecosystems are distinguishable from one another but are not isolate and discrete; they overlap and blend together in ecotones. Furthermore, ecosystems are not permanent and unchanging but transform in many ways, from small shifts in population levels to the process of succession to large-scale catastrophic changes that permanently alter the biotic community.

Such an ecological view of culture affirms both distinctness as well as interrelationship, continuity, and change. It helps students see that we cannot simply *adopt* the concepts, values, myths, and so forth of other cultures but that we can *adapt* them. Similarly, individuals in one culture cannot claim to become members of another culture, but they can recognize a deep interconnectedness and learn from other cultures.

Such cultural theories are supported by history. The history of most religions is a history of transformation and cultural interchange, which can be illustrated to the students by considering Western culture. I like to point to the Hebrew Bible and the works of Aristotle, texts of two extremely different cultures, and then note that Thomas Aquinas brought them together with great persuasiveness. In spreading from India to China to Japan and now to the West, Buddhism has traveled through very diverse cultures, both influencing and being influenced by the new culture.[8] In the words of the historian of religion Thomas Tweed, "religion is hybrid" ("Night-stand Buddhists" 87n2), and the same can be said of the cultures that religions exist in.[9]

East Asian Themes in American Nature Writing

While it is worthwhile to have students wrestle with the issue of foreignness and cultural interchange, clearly the most pressing issue in teaching the significance of East Asian culture in North American nature writing is explicating the ideas and values that inform the writers. Here the pedagogical issue is less how to teach but what to teach. I have found it useful to focus on a few major ideas and values that appear frequently in various works of North American nature writers.

In terms of views of nature, one of the key themes is change, something emphasized by both Buddhism and Daoism as well as in Chinese and Japanese literature. Change is a complex theme, and it is important for students to attend to differences in the way the notion of change is developed in nature writers.

In some cases, change is portrayed as an ongoing process, which undercuts our common-sense notion of stability and endurance. For instance, as Matthiessen contemplates the natural world of the Himalayas, he states that "[a]ll phenomena are processes, connections, all is in flux" (*Snow Leopard* 65). Other times, stable cyclical change is presented, as in Rexroth's "Another Spring," with its strong Chinese flavor: "The seasons revolve and the years change / With no assistance or supervision. / The moon, without taking thought, / Moves in its cycle, full, crescent, and full" (*Complete Poems* 211).

There are darker sides to the East Asian notion of change. The Japanese aesthetic of *aware*, for instance, involves a bittersweet realization and sorrowful acceptance of the ephemerality of all that is beautiful. Such a sensitivity is evoked, for instance, when Rexroth exhorts his daughter to "[b]elieve in all the fugitive / Compounds of nature, all doomed / To waste away and go out" (*Complete Poems* 538).[10] Snyder emphasizes the traditional Buddhist notion of impermanence as the uncertainty of life, but turns it into an essentially celebratory view. "To be truly free one must take on the basic conditions as they are—painful, impermanent, open, imperfect—and then be grateful for impermanence and the freedom it grants us" (*Practice* 5).

The notion of interrelatedness is another central theme in East Asia and American nature writers influenced by it. This idea is both startling to students in its divergence from common sense and familiar to many of them in its similarity to ecology. Our culture tells us that nature is made of distinct and largely independent things, but Buddhism, Daoism, and Neo-Confucianism all insist that interconnectedness is radical and fundamental. But even for nature writers, it can be a struggle to really shift to such as view. Ehrlich, for instance, confesses, "I fight against the optical illusion of separateness" (*Islands* 165).

One way nature writers have evoked radical interrelatedness is with the Buddhist image of Indra's net. With this image, the universe is presented as a vast web of many-sided and highly polished jewels, each one acting as a multiple mirror. In one sense each jewel is a single entity. But when we look at a jewel, we see nothing but the reflections of other jewels, which themselves are reflections of other jewels, and so on in an endless system of mirroring. Thus in each jewel is the image of the entire net.[11] One of the first, though unidentified, uses of this image is found in Rexroth's poem "Doubled Mirrors," in which the narrator sees

> . . . tiny points of cold
> Blue light, like the sparkle of
> Iron snow. I suspect what it is,
> And kneel to see. Under each
> Pebble and oak leaf is a
> Spider, her eyes shining at
> Me with my reflected light
> Across immeasurable distance.
>   (*Complete Poems* 322)

This essential interrelatedness is Buddhist sunyata: "emptiness," "nothingness," or "void." These translations often throw students off track.

Sunyata designates not some absence of reality or the existence of some other reality underlying phenomena but rather reality characterized by interpenetration, empty of separate "thingness." This is also the Buddhist version of "oneness," not a monistic denial of distinctions but an affirmation of radical interrelatedness of all parts of the whole.[12] One important implication of such a view, found in both East Asian Buddhism and a number of American nature writers, is a rejection of a hierarchy of value in nature. As Snyder has put it, "Although ecosystems can be described as hierarchical in terms of energy flow, from the standpoint of the whole all of its members are equal" (*Place* 76). Here is one of the places where it is helpful to highlight the connection between an East Asian idea and contemporary environmental philosophy in the West, particularly deep ecology. A discussion of the ethical implications of such a nonhierarchical view can help students see the broad relevance of East Asian culture.

Interrelationship refers not simply to the natural world but to our place in it: we are fully embedded in the web of life. We see such a view presented in some of Le Guin's Daoist-inspired works. In *The Dispossessed*, the protagonist Shevek reflects on those who are able to realize this essential connection. "There are souls, he thought, whose umbilicus has never been cut. . . . It was strange to see Takver take a leaf into her hand, or even a rock. She became an extension of it, it of her" (185). Snyder, referring to Indra's net and Huayan Buddhism's Avatamsaka Sutra, presents the view common in deep ecology that because of interpenetration, our true self is nothing other than the whole of nature. "The Avatamsaka ('Flower Wreath') jewelled-net-interpenetration-ecological-systems-emptiness-consciousness tells us, no self-realization without the Whole Self, and the whole self is the whole thing" (*Place* 189). Again, we can help students overcome the strangeness of such ideas by noting the similarities to contemporary environmental philosophy.

Another common element in nature writing that has links to East Asia is animism. Nature is often portrayed as having a vitality and spiritual power, even in things we consider inanimate. Ehrlich, speaking of a visit to Japan, puts it in terms of Shinto kami, "deity" or spiritual presence and power: "Everything I saw seemed imbued with the kamisama" (*Islands* 110). In *The Snow Leopard*, Matthiessen frequently uses the term "ringing" to suggest the vitality of the mountains: "These rocks and mountains, all this matter, the snow itself, the air—the earth is ringing. All is moving, full of power, full of light" (180). Animism also runs throughout Snyder's poetic sequence *Mountains and Rivers without End*. Le Guin presents a view that combines a deep sense of the vitalism of nature and Buddhistic relational holism:

> It was the universe of power. It was the network, field, and lines of the energies of all the beings, stars and galaxies of stars, worlds, animals, minds, nerves, dust, the lace and foam of vibration that is being itself, all interconnected, every part part of another part and the whole part of each part, so comprehensible to itself only as a whole, boundless and unclosed. (*Always Coming Home* 308)[13]

Helping students comprehend such views of change, interrelatedness, and vitalism is, of course, a challenge. But one way is to point out the affinities such views have with the science of ecology. This field of study has helped us see that nature is not merely a collection of individuals we can stick into abstract categories of genus and family but a dynamic, inter-locking system of energy flow and nutrient exchange in a single field of being. The correlation between East Asian views of nature and ecological thought has been explored in a number of books.[14]

Other themes are more difficult to associate with Western science. A key idea in the Buddhist view of reality—one that also involves the Buddhist view of consciousness—is "suchness" or "thusness." Suchness refers to the world as it is, devoid of our dichotomizing abstractions and intellectualizing interpretations. For Buddhism, our conceptions, categories, dichotomies, and interpretations of reality distort its true nature. In particular, our view of things as discrete and ourselves as separate from a "world out there" keeps us from experiencing phenomena as nodes in a limitless field of being. It is possible, however, to apprehend reality "directly." Needless to say, such a possibility appeals to some nature writers, and I have found that students are quick to enter a discussion of whether such an ideal is possible or desirable.

Matthiessen speaks of this idea in *The Snow Leopard*, presenting the Buddhist ideal strikingly while noting his own failure to fully realize it. "The secret of the mountains is that the mountains simply exist, as I do myself: the mountains exist simply, which I do not. The mountains have no 'meaning,' they are meaning; the mountains are" (217–18). All categories cover up the radical simplicity of reality.

> For those who would see directly into essential nature, the idea of the sacred is a delusion and an obstruction: it diverts us from seeing what is before our eyes: plain thusness. . . . No wild and tame, no bound or free, no natural and artificial. Each totally its own frail self. (Snyder, *Practice* 103)

Such a view is clearly significant for nature writing, in terms of both metaphysics and epistemology or psychology. It is also significant aesthetically. To say that the study of literature is the study of literary meaning may seem like a truism to us, but in a very real sense it is false from a Buddhist point of view. The Buddhologist William R. LaFleur has analyzed the Buddhist "critique of symbols." Symbols are a problem for Buddhism because they point us away from direct experience of immediate reality, and this concern influenced East Asian literature, particularly nature poetry:

> This critique of symbols brought [Buddhism] into a very specific aesthetic mode. . . . It requires the return of a poet's perceptions and mind to the simple recognition of phenomena. This recognition is powerful because it represents a renewed simplicity rather than a naïve simplicity. This aesthetic mode lives off the way it redirects our focused attention to phenomena for their own sake. It does so with stunning effect by reversing the symbolizing habit of the mind. The poetry that results from and expresses this aesthetic mode invites us to see things in and for themselves; it deliberately rejects the attempt to discover "meanings," implications hidden or coded into a poem. (LaFleur, *Karma* 23–24)

Not surprisingly, it is difficult for students to grasp the meaning of what seems to be a declaration of meaninglessness, but their understanding can be aided by considering Western writers who discuss this type of experience. For instance, Rexroth's poem "Spring" begins with a startling statement: "There are no images here / In the solitude, only / The night and its start which are / Relationships rather than / Images." The narrator repeats the statement that there are no images, only "Shifting darkness, / Strains of feeling, lines of force, / Webs of thoughts . . ." Later in the poem Rexroth states that the night or a tree "doesn't mean / Anything. It isn't an image of / Something. It isn't a symbol of / Something else" (*Complete Poems* 610). The lack of meaning is not the despondent meaninglessness of nihilism. Just as Matthiessen states that the mountains are without meaning, Rexroth presents a Buddhist "critique of symbols," a rejection of a bifurcated sense of meaning, in which the meaning of something stands outside it. His statement is an affirmation that the night is what LaFleur has called a "plenum," wholly full of meaning in and as itself ("Japan" 239).[15]

The themes of change, relationship, and meaning are brought together in the conclusion of Rexroth's poem. After the statement that the night is not an image or symbol of something, we read, "It is just an / Almond tree, in the night, by / The house, in the woods, by / A vineyard, under the setting / Half moon, in Provence, in the / Beginning of another Spring" (611). The tree is actually a set of relationships in the limitless wholeness of the night. To use Le Guin's words cited above, the tree, night, house, woods, vineyard, moon, and Provence are "all interconnected, every part part of another part and the whole part of each part, so comprehensible to itself only as a whole, boundless and unclosed." And the night and tree are full of value and meaning in the Buddhist sense of suchness, while symbolic meaning is an abstraction from the wholeness of the moment in a world of constant transformation.

Implied in the Buddhist view of suchness is an ideal of consciousness that students often find both puzzling and appealing. The mind loses both its interpretive mode and its sense of being a subjective consciousness perceiving an objective world. In what we might call a "total absorption," mind and object merge. Ehrlich asks, "Where do I break off and where does water begin?" (*Islands* 196). Rexroth writes of a similar experience in viewing the night sky after putting down his telescope: "I can no longer / Tell where I begin and leave off. / The faint breeze in the dark pines, / And the invisible glass, / The tipping earth, the swarming stars / Have an eye that sees itself" (*Complete Poems* 536).

Such a spiritual and aesthetic perspective accentuates the present moment and the need for full, even absolute, attention. In Japanese this is called *nen*. As Matthiessen explains, "Nen is mindfulness, attention to the present with a quality of vibrant awareness, as if this present moment were one's last" (109–10). Meditation is aimed at achieving this state. "The purpose of meditation practice is not enlightenment; it is to pay attention even at unextraordinary times, to be of the present, nothing-but-the-present, to bear this mindfulness of *now* into each event of ordinary life" (257). Here it is useful to ask students to reflect on whether they have ever had such an experience. I have found that usually several students will recognize similar moments, particularly as they are involved in sports or the arts, and such a discussion helps other students consider this ideal more seriously.

With such views on nature, it is not surprising that East Asian culture and nature writers influenced by it see the natural world as having unqualified value. Of her visit to Japan Ehrlich wrote:

> I wanted to see how and where holiness revealed itself, to search for those "thin spots" on the ground where divinity rises as if religion were

a function of geology itself: the molten mantle of sacredness cutting through earth like an acetylene torch, erupting as temple sites, sacred mountains, plains, and seas, places where inward power is spawned. (*Islands* 90)

With splendid simplicity, Rexroth puts in this way: "He who lives without grasping / Lives always in experience / Of the immediate as the / Ultimate" (*Complete Poems* 671). Indeed, Rexroth spoke often of the sacramental character of nature, and Snyder has done the same in more ecological terms of a "sacramentalized ecosystem" (*Place* 67).

The East Asian influence on nature writing has not been limited to views and values concerning the natural world. There are ethical, social, and political dimensions as well, and a consideration of them forces students to go beyond the stereotype of the Chinese poet living in solitude on a mountain. The Mahayana Buddhist ideal of the bodhisattva is found in many of the writers, especially Rexroth and Snyder. Kannon (Avalokitesvara) is the most famous bodhisattva, known particularly for hearing all of the cries of every being who suffers. In Rexroth's masterpiece, *Heart's Garden, Garden's Heart*, written when he was living in Japan, Kannon is referred to on many occasions, as when we read, "He who hears / The crying of all the worlds." He also quotes the bodhisattva vow, "I will not enter Nirvana / Until all sentient creatures are saved" (*Complete Poems* 669). Compassion arises because we are radically interrelated to one another. At the very beginning of *Mountains and Rivers without End*, Snyder quotes the Indian Buddhist saint Milarepa: "The notion of Emptiness engenders Compassion" (ix). Snyder's poetic sequence could be interpreted as a multifaceted exploration of compassion.

One distinctive feature of American Buddhism and of nature writers associated with it has been the transformation of passive compassion for individuals into an active social commitment. Rather than focus on religious withdrawal from the pain-filled world, they have emphasized a sense of responsibility to it. Rexroth puts it this way, "I have tried to embody in verse the belief that the only valid conservation of value lies in the assumption of unlimited liability, the supernatural identification of the self with the tragic unity of creative process" (*Collected Longer Poems* iii). Le Guin has argued that much current science fiction has retreated from human needs, in part out of despair for the future:

Such hopelessness can arise, I think, only from an inability to face the present, to live in the present, to live as a responsible being among

other beings in this sacred world here and now, which is all we have,
and all we need, to found our hope upon. (*Dancing* 103)

Snyder states that Buddhism "values such old-fashioned terms as responsibility and commitment" (*Real Work* 153).

This sense of social responsibility has led to radical political critique.
Le Guin describes the current power structure in this way: "Civilized
Man says: I am Self, I am Master, all the rest is Other—outside, below,
underneath, subservient. . . . I am that I am, and the rest is women and
the wilderness, to be used as I see fit" (*Dancing* 161). Snyder personifies
environmental destruction in striking imagery: "A bulldozer grinding and
slobbering / Sideslipping and belching on top of / The skinned-up bodies of
still-live bushes / In the pay of a man / From town." Then he concludes with,
"Behind is a forest that goes to the Arctic / And a desert that still belongs to
the Piute / And here we must draw / Our line" (*Turtle Island* 18).[16]

Drawing on Buddhist and Daoist ideals, Rexroth, Snyder, and Le Guin
offer an alternative to the exploitive authoritarian state and the individu-
alized consumerism of modern culture: communitarian anarchism. The
notions of nonhierarchical interdependence, the spiritual value of every
being, and the sacrality of nature, as well as the rejection of materialistic
desires, lead to an ideal of small-scale, egalitarian societies. Like Rexroth,
Snyder presents a stark contrast between the nation-state and a communitarian society.[17] In "Buddhism and the Possibilities of Planetary Culture,"
Snyder argues that "[t]he State is greed made legal, with a monopoly on
violence; a natural society is familial and cautionary. A natural society is
one which 'follows the way,' imperfectly but authentically." Such a society
would be in close harmony with the local bioregion. "If we are lucky, we
may eventually arrive at a world of relatively mutually tolerant small societies attuned to their local natural region and united overall by a profound
respect and love for the mind and nature of the universe" ("Buddhism"
43). Le Guin explains the social vision she portrayed in *The Dispossessed*
and other books:

> Odonianism is anarchism. Not the bomb-in-the-pocket stuff, which is
> terrorism, whatever name it tries to dignify itself with; not the social-
> Darwinist economic "libertarianism" of the far right; but anarchism,
> as pre-figured in early Taoist thought, and expounded by Shelley and
> Kropotkin, Goldman and Goodman. Anarchism's principal target is the
> authoritarian State (capitalist or socialist); its principal moral-practical

theme is cooperation (solidarity, mutual aid). It is the most idealistic, and to me the most interesting, of all political theories. (*Wind's Twelve Quarters* 260)

Needless to say, these radical political views can make for vibrant discussions in which students end up relating East Asian ideas to their own political views.

Sympathizers and Parallels

So far I have been referring to writers who demonstrate explicit adherence to Buddhism or, in the case of Le Guin, Daoism.[18] But to help students understand the full presence of East Asian culture in American nature writing, we need to broaden our range. Tweed has argued that in studying American Buddhism, we need to include not only adherents but also those who have been influenced by it without becoming converts. He uses several terms to describe such people: sympathizers, night-stand Buddhists, shoppers, not just Buddhists, and dharma hoppers. These people, Tweed argues, may be more marginal to the study of American Buddhism than adherents, but they are still important to the full story. The same holds true of East Asian influence in American nature writing. Discussing examples with students not only helps them see the diversity and range of influence but also, I think, makes East Asia seem more relevant because one need not convert to a foreign religion in order to draw from East Asian culture. One example is Wendell Berry. Berry is a useful example in part because he is recognizably a Christian writer working in the American tradition of agrarianism. But Berry has gleaned from Confucianism as well, and East Asian poetry has affected his own. Once in the early 1970s, I went to a poetry reading of his, but instead of his own works, he read from Ezra Pound's translations of early Confucian writings. In *An Eastward Look,* Berry published nineteen original haiku poems and nine "Chinese painting poems," and he included several haiku in his collection *Given: New Poems. Standing by Words,* a collection of essays, takes its title from the Chinese word *xin* ("faithfulness"); the ideograph of *xin* is made of the symbol for a human being standing beside the symbol for words. (The Chinese character *xin* appears on the book jacket.) His essays are sprinkled with references to Confucianism, and the understanding of many of his themes can be enriched by placing them in the context of

Confucian thought. Like Neo-Confucianism, Berry emphasizes our relatedness to others, including the natural world, focusing on the individual, family, and local community as the root and context for moral responsibility. Berry also highlights the issue of propriety—what is proper for human beings given our relatedness and the limited resources of the world—as do Confucians. William Theodore de Bary has briefly analyzed Berry's works in the context of the contemporary relevance of Confucianism (29–33), and he calls Berry an "American Confucian/Christian" (29). Berry is not, however, a Confucian in the same way he is a Christian but rather seems to fit Tweed's category of a "night-stand" Confucian, drawn to and drawing from Confucianism without any adherence to it as a religious tradition.[19]

We can add another category to Tweed's analysis, although it is a category of a different kind. Tweed's categories all refer to people who have some explicit interest in and knowledge of a religion and who have been influenced by it in some way. There is also what we could call parallels. By that I mean writings that have significant similarities to, in this case, East Asian culture but lack direct influence. Some students are inclined (even eager) to recognize parallels, but they often have difficulty going beyond acknowledging superficial similarities. As a result, it is worthwhile to spend time considering how to deal with parallels.

One example is John Muir. Michael Cohen has noted some of the similarities between Muir's spiritual view of nature and classical Daoism, and he argues that there is support for George Sessions's notion that Muir is a "Taoist of the West" (Cohen, *Pathless Way* 120). Muir seems to have had no knowledge of Daoism, but the parallels (and contrasts) are intriguing. Henry David Thoreau is a more complex case. Especially when he was younger, Thoreau read and wrote about Asian religion and culture, particularly Hinduism. Beongcheon Yu analyzes the direct impact of the Asian texts he read, but then goes on to argue that there are significant parallels between Thoreau and Daoism, even though Thoreau knew virtually nothing of that tradition (Yu 40–54).[20] In this case we have a night-stand Hindu and a parallel with Daoism.

A contemporary example of this dual relation with East Asia is Scott Russell Sanders. Sanders draws on many spiritual traditions, from Buddhism to the Quakerism, even though he is a practicing Methodist. In particular, his notions of the ground of being and the inexhaustible source are closely related to the Daoist notion of nonbeing. He is, we could say, a night-stand eclectic, but there is more. I have argued elsewhere that in important ways his spiritual view of nature is closer to the Neo-Confucian tradition than the Daoist or Buddhist, even though, I believe, he is quite unfamiliar with Neo-Confucian thinkers. A consideration of the parallels between Sanders and that syncretic Chinese tradition is illuminating.[21] In fact, Sanders is a useful context to return students to the issue raised at the beginning: whether, how, and how much nature writers can draw from such a different culture.

The significance of East Asian culture to North American nature writing is continuing to grow, making it increasingly important to analyze the ideas and values that have been incorporated by nature writers. The issues involved are complex, and the pedagogical challenges are substantial, but we must include East Asia in our courses on nature writing to help our students recognize the intercultural richness found there.[22] Central to the success of teaching this dimension of the genre, I think, is maintaining an unresolved dialectic, affirming the strangeness of East Asian culture and yet helping students see that some of the ideas and values are not inextricably foreign. North American nature writers have demonstrated the "anotherness" of East Asia by adapting in various ways elements of that culture into their writings.

Notes

1. Buddhism and East Asian poetry first became a significant presence in Rexroth's poetry in *The Phoenix and the Tortoise,* a long poem of philosophical reverie published in 1944. Actually, Asian culture had influenced American nature writing early on, with Ralph Waldo Emerson and Henry David Thoreau. However, their access to texts and their understanding of Asian culture (primarily Indian) was severely limited, and the influence of Asia on nature writing largely died with their passing. Rexroth began a very different period of influence, with somewhat different pedagogical issues.

2. The romanization of Chinese was formerly based on the Wade-Giles system, in which this native Chinese religion was written Taoism. It is now written Daoism in the pinyin system, which has become the accepted system of romanization. Huayan Buddhism used to be transliterated as Hua-yen. Because so many books that used the Wade-Giles system are still useful, another challenge for students and teachers is to deal with two different ways of writing a single Chinese term.

3. For translations of Bashō's haiku and travel journals that emphasize their relevance to nature writing, see my *Bashō's Haiku* and *Bashō's Journey.* The Noh drama has been important in particular to Rexroth, especially his *Beyond the Mountains,* and Gary Snyder, in particular his *Mountains and Rivers without End.*

4. I have found Darko Suvin's discussion of the role of estrangement in science fiction to be helpful in analyzing the creative effect of cross-cultural divergences on students.

5. Calvin Martin has made a similar claim concerning Native American culture. He has argued that the American Indian is a "miscast ecologist" from which we cannot learn. "The Indian will not and cannot function as our spiritual leader in teaching us wise land use—a new land ethic—because his traditional interpretation of the world beyond him is profoundly different from our Western cosmology. . . . To suggest that we might adopt such an Indian world view is preposterous" because "[w]e are, after all, Industrial Man" (137–38, 145, 146).

6. Murphy uses the term "interanimation" to describe Bakhtin's view of the dialogical relation of mutual influence between people ("Anotherness" 23). I would argue that there is also cultural interanimation. For a discussion of Snyder's adaptation of Native American culture in terms of anotherness, see my "An Interwoven World."

7. I have discussed this theory in some detail in "An Interwoven World." John Elder briefly suggests the idea of cultural ecosystem in his book *Imagining the Earth* (38).

8. The Buddhologist Lewis Lancaster has spoken of "portable Buddhism" and argues that it was the first world religion, "the first to transcend boundaries of language, kinship patterns, political structure, cultural areas, geography" (4). There are numerous books on Western, especially American, Buddhism. See Coleman; Prebish; Prebish and Baumann; Prebish and Tanaka; Seager; Tweed, *American Encounter*; and Williams and Queen.

9. There are various studies of Asian influence on American literature in general. See Ellwood; Kern; Kodama; Miner; and Yu.

10. Ehrlich refers to *aware*, which she defines as "beauty tinged with sadness," in describing autumn in *The Solace of Open Spaces* (127).

11. For an explication of this image in Snyder's works, see my "Indra's Net as Food Chain: Gary Snyder's Ecological Vision." For but one of Snyder's many uses of this image, see his "Nets of Beads, Webs of Cells."

12. For an analysis of what I call "relational holism" in Buddhism and its relevance to deep ecology and ecofeminism, see my "Relational Holism."

13. Snyder makes a similar statement when talking about bioregionalism in *Practice of the Wild*: "The sum of a field's forces becomes what we call very loosely the 'spirit of the place.' To know the spirit of a place is to realize that you are part of a part and that the whole is made of parts, each of which is whole. You start with the part you are whole in" (38).

14. See, for instance, three books in the Religions of the World and Ecology series published by the Harvard University Center for the Study of World Religions: Girardot, Miller, and Xiogan; Tucker and Berthrong; and Tucker and Williams.

15. For another Buddhist denial of "meaning," see Snyder's "Piute Creek": "A clear, attentive mind / Has no meaning but that / Which sees is truly seen" (*Riprap* 6).

16. Matthiessen has voiced social criticism as well, but in his strictly Buddhist writings he has focused more on inner spiritual development and its relation to

the natural world. Although his Buddhist views underlie his social perspective, he tends not to put political criticism in Buddhist terms.

17. Rexroth wrote a history of communitarian societies: *Communalism: From Its Origins to the Twentieth Century.*

18. Le Guin has published a personal rendition of the most famous Daoist classic: *Tao Te Ching: A Book about the Way and the Power of the Way.* In her introduction she said of this text, "Of all the deep springs, this is the purest water. To me, it is also the deepest spring" (x).

19. The significance of East Asian culture in Berry's poetry and essays seems to be stronger in his earlier writings than in the more recent ones, but the Confucian dimension of Berry's writings and the correlation between his poetry and Chinese verse deserve more serious attention than they have yet received. Although Berry does not mention the early Confucian thinker Xunzi (third century BCE) or later Neo-Confucianism, many of his views seem to coincide with those thinkers.

20. Le Guin has referred to this parallel in her postapocalyptic novel *City of Illusions.* The book refers to the "Old Canon" (the *Daodejing*) and the "New Canon" (*Walden*), and several characters are "Thurro-dowists."

21. See in particular Sanders, "Ground Notes" and "Telling the Holy," in *Staying Put* (123–41 and 143–69). For an analysis of Sanders in terms of East Asian culture, see my "Through an Eastern Window."

22. This overview has been highly abbreviated; other important themes and genres were not even mentioned. Other themes include the journey, yin and yang, the limits of rational knowledge, and spontaneity. Genres include the Noh drama, travel journals, and *haibun* (haikulike prose, as found in Snyder's most recent collection of poems, *Danger on Peaks*).

Cheryl J. Fish

Environmental Justice Issues in Literature and Film: From the Toxic to the Sustainable

Environmental justice as we know it today in the United States emerged as a social movement in the second half of the twentieth century, in the wake of civil rights activism and the need to redirect ecology to address the uneven distribution of environmental impacts. During the 1980s and 1990s, scholars and teachers in the humanities began to work under the rubric of ecocriticism, environmental humanities, or green cultural studies, culminating in the founding of the Association for the Study of Literature and the Environment (ASLE) in 1992 (Winkler). They began to interrogate the assumptions that drive environmental-social policy, production, and consumerism in different communities and examine the relation these factors have to the arts and poetics. Since then, there has been a growing body of scholarship produced and courses offered in various disciplines. Those of us who teach and write about environmental justice complicate and challenge traditional versions of environmentalism, in order to more thoroughly interrogate the economic, historic, gendered, raced, and nationalistic components of environmental policies and to include more diverse voices. In addition, we study the implications of representing nature-culture and urban-rural binaries and attempt to raise awareness about the factors that put certain groups at higher risk of toxic exposures. Then, in our classrooms and beyond, we engage in processes that enable us to become part of meaningful and pragmatic solutions. Literature and film that address environmental justice and its overlap with social and economic justice; ecofeminism; and the links between production, consumption, and environmental hazards reach students in powerful and provocative ways and illustrate links between poetics, politics, and praxis.

On the first day of an interdisciplinary American studies seminar titled Environmental Justice in Literature and Film at a small New England liberal arts college, many students articulate their passion with vague notions of what such a course might entail; what soon emerges is a recognition of how this work will spur ethical problems in a way that seems overwhelming and personal while also revealing a complex set of local, national, and global issues. Questions quickly emerge: What counts as "environment," and what are the implications of this definition? If a "green building" employs nonunion workers, is that a contradiction? Why are the environmental perspectives of indigenous people and the poor ignored? To best grapple with these questions and others, the study of environmental justice ideally draws on interdisciplinary materials from the humanities, social sciences, popular culture, and science and technology studies and examines the convergence of rhetoric, grassroots activism, legal and governmental policies, and modes of representation. Through such an engaged inquiry, we see ourselves as potential agents of change—stretching what Robert Figueroa calls our "moral imagination" (325). In our classroom, we attempt to find hope amid the chaos and pain these issues raise and see ourselves as part of communities that have a stake in pressing for alternatives. A key tenet of the environmental justice movement is the demand for more public participation, as well as for a more open, communicative, and participatory political process (Schlosberg 13). In fact, as we study the ways in which writers and filmmakers bring environmental justice into the public eye and how their use of language, image, and technologies prove that toxicity is embedded in the body, body politic, and psyche, the class begins to consider how we can go beyond the walls of the classroom to our families, communities, and jobs in continuing the work. Thus this type of class lends itself to service learning or connection with an internship in which students could work on the most pressing community issues.[1]

We begin with a unit called "Roads to Environmental Justice" in order to understand how environmental justice became "one of the largest and most active social movements in the U.S. . . . addressing the concerns of urbanites and people of color that had been overlooked by mainstream environmental organizations" (Bennett, "Manufacturing" 169). As Dorceta E. Taylor explains, the movement is made up of thousands of grassroots environmental groups nationwide; before the emergence of the environmental-justice movement, mainstream environmental organizations were mostly made up of white and middle-class members (40).[2] It is useful to give students a handout that contextualizes landmarks of the United States environmental movement—such as the founding of the Sierra Club in 1892; the Clean Air Act in 1955; the publication of Rachel Carson's *Silent Spring* in 1962; the first United States Earth Day in 1970; and the toxic-waste case of Love Canal in 1978. Then, to emphasize how principles of environmental justice have been articulated, it is important to read and discuss the contents of a manifesto from the Multinational People of Color Environmental Leadership Summit (www.weact.org); this meeting brought together over three hundred community leaders from the United States, Canada, and Central and South America in Washington, D.C., in 1991. It includes such statements as:

> Environmental justice demands that public policy be based on mutual respect and justice for all peoples, free from any form of discrimination or bias.

> Environmental justice calls for universal protection from nuclear testing, extraction, production, and disposal of toxic-hazardous wastes and poisons and nuclear testing that threaten the fundamental right to clean air, land, water, and food.

> Environmental justice affirms the need for urban and rural ecological policies to clean up and rebuild our cities and rural areas in balance with nature, honoring the cultural integrity of all of our communities, and providing fair access for all to the full range of resources.

In early sessions of a course, I would recommend that students view a short video to more fully understand and visually intuit the struggles of particular communities. For instance, *And Justice for All* includes the landmark environmental justice case of the African American community's struggle in Warren County, North Carolina; the *Documentary Highlights of the First National People of Color Environmental Leadership Summit* will help situate students at the event where the manifesto was drafted (www.ejrc.cau.edu/videoarch.html). These short films and readings can illuminate the historical context in which we shall locate the study of literary texts, nonfiction prose, and fictional film.[3]

Dialogues in Literature and Film

The gist of my course examines how writers, artists, and filmmakers engage with questions raised by environmental injustices that we hear about in the news, some of which have been publicized by activists and nongovernmental organizations. Many of these writers and artists would consider themselves activists, or they come from an oppositional perspective; others draw on spiritual and cultural values in their work; we are anxious to know what types of sustainable alternatives they propose. A breakthrough anthology that uses the format of the roundtable for one of its first chapters, *The Environmental Justice Reader: Politics, Poetics, and Pedagogy*, edited by Joni Adamson, Mei Mei Evans, and Rachel Stein, includes activists, educators, and academics from different ethnic and geographic locations who lay out approaches to issues ranging from water rights to writing accessibly that hit home. "Introduction as Conversation," in Alison H. Deming and Laurent E. Savoy's *The Colors of Nature: Culture, Identity, and the Natural World*, provides an accessible frame for how American culture can be seen in the language of environmentalism as an ecosystem in itself and for how

> contemporary nature writing has moved beyond narratives of solitary encounter in the wild to explore how people and cultures have been shaped by and have shaped the land. It bears witness to the wounded relationship between people and the Creation and explores how literature might have political agency in reshaping the legacy. ("Introduction" 5–6)

In the same collection, the poet Yusef Komunyakaa writes in his essay "Dark Waters" of his upbringing in Bogalusa, Louisiana, a hotbed for racism in the 1950s; he claims racial and environmental toxicity tainted both social and natural landscapes. When he writes of the disparity in economics at the center of the racial and cultural divide, he notes "[s]uch things aren't accidental; everything is planned and perfected with the same attention as is given to any weapon." His focus on prescribed ideas about the distribution of environmental and social ills and the effect these have on health and psyche are key issues addressed throughout the semester. Nevertheless, he claims, "We need to trust each other" (107–08). Such contradictions, and the need to work collaboratively across difference despite a history of dispossession, emerge again and again. In fact, literary texts, such as poems by Simon Ortiz, can illustrate and mediate the struggle between place, justice, modernity, and consumerism in a neoliberal global economy.[4] Ortiz points to connections we desperately need to be making despite the ease with which we experience *disconnects* between ordinary life and global crisis:

> Merle Haggard and Willie Nelson sing on *Austin City Limits*. They look like old white men on TV. Because they are. . . . And the forests are burning. They're all burning. Indonesia is burning, down, Indira says. Soon the U.S. will send a $3.4 billion plutonium-powered Casini space craft to Saturn. . . . Does Saturn have forests to burn like the Amazon, like Indonesia, like Oregon and Idaho and Montana? Don't worry, it's safe. ("Meanwhile" 140)

We turn to Lawrence Buell's essay "Toxic Discourse," which illustrates just how deeply embedded in Western language and culture is the rhetoric of toxicity, as well as how this discourse challenges traditional understanding of what counts as environmental movement or ethos. Buell and other academics who contributed to the "Forum on Literatures of the Environment" (in the October 1999 issue of *PMLA*) call for greater cross-fertilization across disciplines and the need for transnational connections between ecocriticisms and cultural studies. But claiming that the awakening to the toxicity of everyday life leads merely to outrage, acquiescence, impotence, denial, and desperation does not take into account the responses of those who venture beyond despair—who count themselves among the participant witnesses and whistle-blowers and create what the artist and environmental educator Cinder Hypki calls "geographies of hope" (qtd. in Di Chiro 306). In the literature and film we examine, personal history, outrage, and humor intersect with the needs to document ethically and to represent empirically the evidence of the effects of toxins, whether in memoir or muckraking journalism or through the use of postmodern pastiche and parody.

In the light of my desire to turn to narrative that is highly provocative and entertaining, two examples bring postmodern techniques to bear on civic responsibility, environmental injustice, and personal agency. They are Ruth L. Ozeki's novel *My Year of Meats* and Judith Helfand and Daniel B. Gold's 2002 documentary film *Blue Vinyl*. These works document environmental injustices and toxic poisoning at the level of the manufacturing and consumption of our food and shelter. Both offer female protagonists who use "toxic humor" to get their activist messages across and who, in going up against powerful corporate entities, poke fun at themselves. This makes them likable "heroines" who enable viewers and readers to identify with their quest for knowledge and their transformative empowerment. Both protagonists show the intersection between class and race where environmental justice is concerned. Ozeki especially illustrates an ecofeminist linking of casual violence against women with the mistreatment of animals. Helfand and Gold's film puts at the center Helfand's middle-class Jewish American parents, who have the luxury of contemplating what, if any, materials would be an apt replacement for the blue vinyl siding and would not offend their suburban Long Island neighbors; an important counterpoint is offered by an African American family displaced by poisonous water from the polyvinyl chloride plant that manufacturers vinyl siding outside Lake Charles, Louisiana. They cannot sell their house, so they load the humble abode onto a truck to relocate it. Helfand presents herself as a muckraking raconteur with a single shingle of blue vinyl tucked under her arm, and she incorporates interviews, cartoons, and information from transnational corporations, activists, victims, and academic experts.[5] The film establishes the links among polyvinyl chloride exposure, illness, and what is at stake in silencing vital information. She concludes by illustrating the importance of the individual's action in affecting change and by building a web of connection across nation, class, race, and regions.[6]

The use of film as a potential medium for informing and transforming should be noted; with new media technologies, it is becoming less costly to make a film, and now with high-definition video, film is not even a necessity. As this collection is in production, we are witnessing a surge in documentary films that engage with intersections among environmental, social, and political issues: *An Inconvenient Truth*, featuring Al Gore, who provides accessible data and a strong narrative exposé on global warming, and Bernadine Mellis's *The Forest for the Trees*, which documents the posthumous lawsuit brought by Earth First!'s Judi Bari against the FBI, are two recent and highly recommended films that give us environmental activism that is both heroic and practical. There are many films that offer transnational, environmental, and social-justice activism; two that I can highly recommend are *Total Denial*, directed by Milena Kaneva, about fifteen villagers from Burma whose quest for justice leads them to bring a suit against two oil giants, Unocal and Total, for environmental and human rights abuses, and *Darwin's Nightmare*, directed by Hubert Sauper, about the corruption of the multinational fish industry, specifically on Lake Victoria in Africa. The link between documentary and fiction is bridged by Ozeki, who had worked as a documentary filmmaker before turning to novel writing, and her protagonist, Jane Takagi-Little, is directing episodes of *My American Wife*, a weekly television series for Japanese housewives sponsored by the Beef Export and Trade Syndicate. The image of the "all-American" wife and her family in the advent of global capital is conjoined with the taste for meat.[7] In *Meats* and *Vinyl*, the failure to make connections between consuming and desiring is shown to be dangerously naive; there is a direct and insidious relation among the production of meat and polyvinyl chloride and public health issues, which has effects on workers, women, children, and the poor. Both Helfand and Takagi-Little are "DES daughters," suffering from the effects of a "miracle" drug (diethylstilbestrol) of the past given to their mothers to prevent miscarriage. Helfand had made an earlier documentary, *A Healthy Baby Girl*, about her DES experience with cancer, and Takagi-Little has a misshapen uterus and the potential to develop cancer. Thus, gendered health and sexual and political agency evoke the legacies of the many women, especially of color, who have been leaders of the environmental justice movement.[8] When conjoined and compromised, the intersection of these experiences become key sites of resistance. In the readings and discussions, we also raise the issue of how toxins such as Agent Orange and pesticides used on crops would also expose soldiers and agricultural workers to cancers and disease and how and why it is important to form alliances with victims of these various exposures.

Other documentaries and fictional films can offer to educate and illustrate a range of the complexities that environmental justice encompasses, including urban environmentalism as linked to social justice. *Holding Ground: The Rebirth of Dudley Street*, an award-winning documentary, chronicles the struggles and rebirth of Boston's Dudley Street neighborhood in Roxbury, through the efforts of the grassroots-community-based Dudley Street Neighborhood Initiative (DSNI). The film chronicles how the black, Latino, Cape Verdean, and white residents took control of the community, which had been decimated by illegal toxic dumping in vacant lots, years of neglect and abandonment, and arson-induced fires. Beginning in the 1980s with a 'Don't Dump on Us' campaign, DSNI's intergenerational collaboration with residents and agencies became the nation's first neighborhood group to win the right of eminent domain and began to transform their surroundings (Medoff and Sklar 4–5).[9]

The issues in this film allowed our class to make many intersections with literature, including June Jordan's poetry and her "Letter to Buckminster Fuller," in which she links environmental and social-justice issues such as housing, race, space, and design, and Ana Castillo's essay, "The Watsonville Women's Strike." Castillo illustrates the way women workers in communities of color draw on strengths that arise from their cultures, their collaborative resources, and their emphasis on protest, raising consciousness in various ways, mobilizing for survival. Another short documentary film, *Sustainable Atlanta*, explores the intersections of race, class, place, and environmental justice in the city's "empowerment zone," which has more than its share of infrastructure problems, and shows how community-based organizations are attempting to build safer, more sustainable neighborhoods. For my students at the City University of New York, awareness of the work of Peggy Shepard and the organization she founded, West Harlem Environmental Action (WEACT), becomes a key local contact point. The group's collaboration with Columbia University's Center for Children's Environmental Health demonstrates a fruitful partnership between a grassroots organization and the academy to study and document the effects of pests, pesticides, lead poisoning, nutrition, pollution, garbage, and cigarette smoke on local children. The class members read and discusss not only the newsletters and Web sites from WEACT but also reports that document research studies about lead poisoning; they also learn from scholars who are collaborating on related projects.[10] Some electronic sources, newsletters, and alternative media go beyond the mainstream press's coverage of an environmental justice issue to the more complex realities that reflect different cultural traditions and interpretations. One student wrote her research paper on environmental racism in her hometown of Tulsa, Oklahoma. In the local papers, the Environmental Protection Agency's version of how it is cleaning up the Tar Creek Superfund site did not take into account the complexity of the Quapaw tribe's continued health risks and threats to the tribe's cultural traditions; she investigated the Quapaw's viewpoint through Web sites and personal connections to hear the voices of the tribal community and to understand perspectives that were not generally represented.

Environmental Justice in and out of Hollywood

Popular Hollywood films such as *Erin Brockovich*, directed by Steven Soderbergh, or *A Civil Action*, directed by Steven Zaillian, provide fruitful comparisons and contrasts with documentary film, since discussion of how the role of the whistle-blower, when acted by appealing white movie stars such as Julia Roberts and John Travolta, affects the public's perception of the issues, and how race, class, and gender issues are foregrounded or minimized in the discovery of corporate foul play and toxic exposures. A fictional film that uses a documentary style and that is less Hollywood blockbuster than independent inquiry is John Sayles's *Sunshine State*, which chronicles the economic, social, and psychic effects of commercial development and real estate speculation on communities in northeastern Florida. In Sayles's typical style of mixing the personal with the political, his characters display a complex mixture of desire for personal gain and thwarted dreams, raising the question of who is the real endangered species—the assimilated Native American distanced from his history, the small businessman being bought and replaced by chain tourism and gated communities, the members of a historic African American enclave who stand to gain financially by having homes on desirable beachfront property but who lose coherence and independence because they no longer own businesses? Or is it the sandhill crane, its habitat crassly exploited? A character played by the late comedian Alan King represents the omniscient power broker teeing off with his buddies (the golf course representing "nature on a leash"). He sighs that, after all, "nature is overrated"; one of his friends responds, "Yeah but we'll miss it when it's gone."

Environmental Links to Cancer: Memoir, Science Studies, and Film

One of the most powerful units in the course linked film, memoir, scientific studies, and other works that cross genres and fields to demonstrate the environmental causes and treatment of breast cancer and to illustrate how the toxic is physical, social, scientific, psychic, public, and textual. We read sections of Audre Lorde's autopathography *The Cancer Journals* as well as of Sandra Steingraber's scientific memoir *Living Downstream: An Ecologist Looks at Cancer and the Environment* and studied the writing of Rachel Carson to discuss the reasons she would have omitted references to her breast cancer in *Silent Spring*. Then we view the film *Rachel's Daughters: Searching for the Causes of Breast Cancer*, directed by Allie Light and Irving Saraf, which continues Carson's discussion of investigating the environmental causes of cancer and how the complexities of proof place the burden on the victim. The "daughters" of various geographic, racial, and class backgrounds investigate potential environmental links to their breast cancer, from pesticide exposure to genetics, hormone exposure, and electromagnetic fields. Each daughter meets with doctors, scientists, and policy makers in a quest for answers, which, of course, are inconclusive. Blending scientific statistics with personal and cultural histories, these works complement and build on one another and illustrate the investigative, legal, and scientific mode that runs through much literature of environmental justice. Marcy Jane Knopf-Newman's work and class discussions consider the rhetoric of detecting and the burden of becoming a detective to fight for one's life and rights. The powerful final scene of *Rachel's Daughters* shows the results of this mass "slaying," as women on a hillside wear black robes, representing the large numbers of women who have and who are dying from breast cancer. Such symbolism has a powerful impact beyond personal threat: many students noted how the personal accounts of illness stress the high cost of environmental hazards by appealing to our sense of sympathy and how the disturbing facts detailing the local and global repercussions of such abuses make clear that we are all at risk.

Such a course and the body of work it generates ideally go beyond acknowledging risk and instigating fear; rather they create an embodied dialogue through which environmental justice becomes a focal point to create alliances and alternatives and enable us to see the complicated nexus of resistance, compromise, "progress," and identity; although toxins in our lands and cities affect us differently, they affect us all.

Notes

1. Students at University of Colorado and at Colgate had service-learning projects that included volunteering for Habitat for Humanity, working with the Rocky Mountain Justice and Peace Center, assisting attorneys in cases on toxic torts, and raising awareness of environmental justice in the primary schools. They were required to spend three to ten hours a week performing service, to give a presentation to their class, and to write an essay on their project (Figueroa 323).

2. The chapter "What Has Gone Before: Why Race Was Not on the Original Environmental Agenda," from Edwardo Lao Rhodes's book *Environmental Justice in America: A New Paradigm* (30–42) is useful in historicizing the exclusion of urban concerns and minority populations by some United States environmental organizations. David E. Newton's chapter "The Road to Environmental Justice" includes case histories from diverse locations across the United States where environmental inequities have been contested (1–55).

3. Other sources of video for grassroots activism in environmental justice around the world include Big Noise Films (www.bignoisefilms.com), Earth Visions (www.earthvisions.com), and Third World Newsreel (www.twn.org). For a more extensive listing, see Zehle (349n38).

4. Neoliberalism is a mode of free-market economic theory that has become the dominant ideological rationalization for globalization and contemporary state reform. It has become the overarching schema of competitive globalization and programs of state restructuring in a wide range of national and local contexts. See Peck and Ticknell.

5. A fruitful conversation might compare Helfand's documentary persona and style with that of the well-known and controversial Michael Moore and contemplate what the similarities say about the gendering of the muckraking style and the implications for environmental justice activism and representation. For instance, Helfand includes a scene in her film in which she hires a coach to help her pick the appropriate outfit to wear and to practice her approach to confronting William F. Carroll, the head of the Vinyl Institute. For a thorough close reading and analysis of the film, see Plevin.

6. See Helfand and Gold's *Blue Vinyl* homepage (www.Bluevinyl.org); their organizing campaign is My House Is Your House Consumer Organizing Campaign, Working Films and Judith Helfand (www.myhouseisyourhouse.org/report/pdf). A Web site that voices opposition to Helfand's film is supported by the Vinyl Institute and is one of the organizations she takes on in her film; see www.aboutbluevinyl.org.

7. Other texts we read that connected many of the issues raised in *My Year of Meats* regarding the cattle industry, workers' rights, toxic exposure and illness, and the discourse surrounding consumption of meat and gender oppression included Upton Sinclair's novel *The Jungle*; Eric Schlosser's muckraking account of the meat industry, *Fast Food Nation* (also a motion picture); Michael Pollan's essay "An Animal's Place"; Carol J. Adams's *The Sexual Politics of Meat*; and Vandana Shiva's, *Staying Alive*. Works by Temple Grandin such as *Thinking in Pictures* that describe her interest in the "humane" treatment of cattle in slaughterhouses and in connecting her own autism with her relationship to animals make for very provocative and disturbing discussion in the context of the other readings; the film by Morgan Spurlock, *Super Size Me*, would also be appropriate to add to the mix, as would *The Meatrix*, a parody in flash animation that uses the theme of the popular film *The Matrix* to expose the truth about factory farming, located on the Web at www.themeatrix.com/. *The Meatrix* provides a clever and effective way to discuss the use of parody and humor as a form of education and activism, and the Web site provides various links to organizations.

8. In the year 2000 directory *People of Color Environmental Groups*, compiled by Robert D. Bullard, essays by women of color, such as "Environmental and Economic Justice for Immigrant and Women Workers," by Helen Sunhee Kim, and "Environmental Justice Leaders Plead Their Case at the U.N.," by Margie Richard, describe leadership roles played by women of color in the movement. Collections such as *Confronting Environmental Racism: Voices from the Grassroots* and *Unequal Protection: Environmental Justice and Communities of Color*, edited by Bullard, and *Toxic Struggles: The Theory and Practice of Environmental Justice* edited by Richard Hofrichter, include many essays by and about women of color, documenting the activism of particular communities in response to environmental injustices and their relation to gender, race, class, and politics. See also S. Riley.

9. The Dudley Street Neighborhood initiative can help faculty members set up "field trips" for groups of students to see the work firsthand.

10. The collaborative project "the Community Outreach and Education Core (COEP) is comprised of scientific investigators from Columbia University, a lead community partner—West Harlem Environmental Action, Inc. (WEACT)—and a Community Advisory Board (CAB) consisting of eight longstanding community-based health service and environmental advocacy organizations in Washington Heights, Harlem, and the South Bronx" (*Community Education*). J. Sze also addresses this study.

William Slaymaker

Ethnic Ecoethics: Multicultural Environmental Philosophy and Literature

Environmental ethics, ecophilosophy, and surveys of literary nature writing are course topics I frequently teach. In this essay I outline how environmental philosophy and creative nature writing can be taught in classes that are comparative, interdisciplinary, and multicultural. I briefly survey not only North American creative nature writers who represent multicultural perspectives but also the intersections of their environmentalist positions with key ecophilosophical concepts put forth by scholars.

I teach mainly undergraduate courses for a general student audience. Therefore, I rely on readily available environmental-philosophy anthologies and their standardized offerings. I pair anthologized and canonized ecophilosophical selections with the diverse array of nature writers that are commonly found in collections such as *The Norton Book of Nature Writing* (Finch and Elder) or *Literature and the Environment* (Anderson, Slovic, and O'Grady), which has a good selection of multicultural nature writers. I recommend the more specific and circumscribed anthology *The Colors of Nature: Culture, Identity, and the Natural World* (Deming and Savoy) as an ancillary text for those who want a shorter, more focused selection of American multicultural nature writers. College and university instructors have many environmental-philosophy and environmental-ethics texts to choose from. Most follow the same basic formats and offer readings from a standardized repertoire of environmental philosophers and approaches. The textbooks I have preferred are the various editions of Louis Pojman's *Environmental Ethics: Readings in Theory and Application* and J. Baird Callicott's *Earth's Insights: A Multicultural Survey of Ecological Ethics from the Mediterranean Basin to the Australian Outback.* These texts, like the legion of similar anthologies published for academic markets, are organized around the major environmental issues of animal rights, anthropocentrism versus biocentrism and ecocentrism, deep ecology, religion-based ecoethics, ecofeminism, agricultural ethics, and ecojustice—which includes (eco)nomics, or how human consumption and monetary policies impact the health of natural environments. Almost every ecophilosophy reader ends with a chapter on stewardship and sustainability, which are the ethical standards that are most likely to help resolve many of the environmental crises human beings encounter and cause.

Creative nature writers treat environmental topics that fit more or less into these same key ethical categories that philosophers favor, though creative writers tend to wander through labyrinths of ethical domains and combine various environmental concerns in imaginative and nonlinear ways. Multicultural North American nature writing can be used in the philosophy classroom as nondiscursive presentations of analytic arguments, while ecophilosophical readings can provide a disciplined vocabulary and a discriminating heuristic for poems and narratives that rely not on carefully constructed arguments but on metaphoric and affective language that illuminates human-nature interactions. I conclude my brief survey of ethnic ecoethics and its multicultural literary parallels with a more defined and refined example of environmental philosophy as it informs recent Native American narratives by looking at the ecophilosophy of Callicott and the environmentally directed narratives of the Anishinaabe (Ojibwa and Chippewa) writers Louise Erdrich, Winona LaDuke, and Gerald Vizenor. These four can be taught as a unit in an interdisciplinary class that follows environmental and ecological threads through the complex weave of multicultural philosophy and narrative.

There are many nature writers in the American literary canon who view nature from particular ethnic platforms. Native American nature writers make up the largest number who are committed to ecoethnic and ecoethical concerns. Other ethnic groups such as Hispanic, black, and Asian American are represented to varying degrees. Multicultural environmental philosophers and philosophy are a recent academic phenomenon, which means that standardized anthologies suited to the college classroom offer few examples. There is an established and high-profile cadre of black academic philosophers and scholars—Cornel West comes to mind—but few are committed to research and writing on ecoethical topics because of the weight and insistence of racial issues and social justice. Thus when West in *The American Evasion of Philosophy* examines Emerson's famous essay "Nature," he evades environmental issues central to Emerson's work in order to concentrate on the political and racial dimensions of Emersonian ideology. In the sphere of politics, however, West is often linked to the American Green Party and its candidates, and he has taken well-defined stances on animal rights and other environmental concerns. A review of George Yancy's collection of interviews, *African-American Philosophers: Seventeen Conversations,* corroborates the impression that the main interests of black philosophy and philosophers are not dedicated to environmentalism. Black and Green are not mutually or naturally exclusive, but the mix and merger have been and are elusive. This sort of scholarly and academic apartheid is not evident in environmental justice studies, where books like Robert Bullard's *Dumping in Dixie*, Laura Westra and Bill Lawson's *Faces of Environmental Racism*, and Joni Adamson, Mei Mei Evans, and Rachel Stein's *The Environmental Justice Reader* are recognized for their investigation of the impact of pollution on African American and other ethnic communities.

While environmentalism is a main focus of Native American cultural views, it requires some investigative effort to identify academic, anthologized, and canonized philosophers who claim to be doing environmental Native American or Indian philosophy. There are hubs and networks of academic Native and indigenous philosophy to be found: the Native American Philosophy Project at Lakehead University in Thunder Bay, Canada, is a physical (brick-and-mortar) example; the Indigenous Environmental Network is a virtual one; *Ayaangwaamizin: The International Journal of Indigenous Philosophy* is a paper resource of Native American scholarship on environmental ethics and all areas of philosophy. According to Anne Waters in *American Indian Thought*, which is a good introduction to Native American philosophers and philosophy, there were no Native American PhDs in philosophy until 1992 (v). Nonetheless, there has been no lack of sociological, economic, and cultural studies essay collections and monographs that link environmental causes and Native American tribal groups. Vine Deloria, a lawyer, academic activist, and promoter of indigenous studies, was a visible defender of Native American environmental attitudes. Less well known, but important, is the work of the environmental-education scholar Gregory Cajete. The controversial former University of Colorado scholar Ward Churchill has written extensively on Indian land and environmental issues. It is worthwhile to consult his *Struggle for the Land* and to use this work in class for stimulating discussions and debates that wrestle with ecological issues and Native American land tenure and rights and with a variety of turf issues related to positions, poses, and posses that wrangle for power and political attention.

Much Hispanic and Latino philosophy is oriented toward issues and ideas that have percolated up to North America from prominent South and Central American scholars. While Hispanic nature writers are fairly well represented in anthologies such as *Literature and the Environment* (Anderson, Slovic, and O'Grady), which contains essays and stories by Clarissa Pinkola Estés, Simon J. Ortiz, Alberto Ríos, Pat Mora, Benjamin Alire Sáenz, Jimmy Santiago Baca, and Rudolfo Anaya, their work in philosophy is not often encountered in multicultural philosophy anthologies that are available for undergraduate classes. An access point for North American Hispanic philosophy and philosophers is the American Philosophical Association Web site (www.apaonline.org), which publishes the *Newsletter on Hispanic/Latino Issues in Philosophy* as well as newsletters that cover American Indian philosophy and black philosophy. Also, a sweep of the Radical Philosophy Association Web site (http://home.grandecom .net/—jackgm/RPA.html) and its associated links will produce names of multicultural scholars who pursue research on ethnic ecoethics.

Whatever the status and visibility of multicultural environmental philosophy and philosophers, at the very least there are well-known representatives— often but not exclusively white male academics—voicing the key points of ecophilosophical debate and contention. And they and their arguments can be made to function as analogues of multicultural nature writers, who are relatively easy to identify and encounter in environmental readers and anthologies, which are available to college and university instructors.

The best-known animal-rights philosophers are Tom Regan and Peter Singer. Excerpts and essays from their major works are almost always included in environmental-philosophy anthologies. Their arguments for the liberation and better treatment of animals and for preservation of wild and domestic species are widely accessible and generally acceptable to most students, even in the feedlot-rich prairie where I teach. Usually students are not prepared to accept animals as equals, nor are they quite ready for the sophisticated and thought-provoking utilitarian (Singer) and egalitarian

(Regan) arguments to cease concentrating (incarcerating) animals, to stop stuffing market animals with excessive proteins and hormones, and to reduce the human consumption of meat. Students generally remain committed carnivores and only rarely become convinced Regan vegans. The essay "Am I Blue?" by the African American writer Alice Walker (found in Finch and Elder's and many similar anthologies), nonetheless works on students' natural sympathies for animals and has greater impact on their emotional views on or ties to animals than the rigor of philosophical arguments. Literary encounters with rigor mortis and the tragic deaths of animals at human hands are almost always more effective (and affective) than *rigor moralis*, the rigorous and careful analysis of the human abuse of power over animals. "Am I Blue?" describes Walker's deepening concern and compassion for a white horse named Blue, whose career as a stud and a neglected intelligent and sympathetic being depresses her. By the end of this literary essay, Walker has difficulty eating meat because it seems to be an unethical act of hostility against animals, who share many of our same sentiments and thoughts. The realization that human beings and animals share existential spaces and consciousness is the conclusion that Regan, Singer, and Walker lead us to. Walker's brief essay gets students to that shared space with more emotive impact than philosophers could ever hope for.

The philosophical debates over anthropocentrism versus biocentrism and ecocentrism focus on the role of human beings in the natural world. The central question is, who should be the moral arbiters or what should be the criteria determining the preservation or destruction of nature? Anthropocentrism favors human beings and their capacity to make moral and rational judgments that will condemn unnatural and inhumane acts and defend the naturalistic nonhuman. Biocentrism defends the claims of all life to its right to live with minimal human interference. Ecocentrism focuses on the claims and necessities of ecosystems as unified or hierarchically arranged energy-transfer chains that should not be disrupted on pain of major dysfunctions in the system and inevitable loss for the human and natural worlds. A key concept in this triadic debate centers on pain—who and what feels it, and to what degree it is felt. The pain problem is a major philosophical controversy for not just this category of ecoethics, but for all of them. Most ecophilosophers weigh in on the controversies swirling around centers of power and pain. Many conclude that human beings need to do their best to reduce suffering for human and nonhuman life alike, whatever their philosophical conception of moral priorities might be. Creative nature writers, however, naturally slip into a biocentric groove because they are inclined to sympathize or empathize with other-than-human life and because they feel that human beings—especially Euro-American settlers and colonists—have been excessively destructive. In particular, Native American writers who portray indigenous attitudes toward animals desire to show not only human integration into or connection with animal communities but also respect for the animals that are hunted. Luther Standing Bear and Black Elk have become the literary Lakota representatives for this ecophilosophical position. Their depictions and constructions of human-animal harmonies and balances have been contested by anthropological scholars such as Shepard Krech in *The Ecological Indian: Myth and History*. He doubts and resists those writers who romanticize Native-nature relations.

Most multicultural nature writers fit into a category that might be labeled regional naturalism or place-based space. All cultural groups find certain environments friendly and homely and other landscapes inimical and alienating. Philosophers sometimes take up these natural sympathies and artificial antipathies under the rubric "The Aesthetics of Natural Spaces." In the realm of aesthetics, philosophers are allowed to get in touch with their feelings and to write eloquently about beauties as well as beasts. But creative writers express emotional states elicited by natural places much better than philosophers. So it is that an urban (Chicago) Hispanic writer like Sandra Cisneros can remove herself to Texas where she confesses in an interview with Gregg Barrios that she has found a spiritual home and a landscape that liberates and inspires her natural imagination. Other Hispanic writers such as Ray Gonzalez, Alberto Ríos, or Gloria Anzaldúa as well as the Native American writers Leslie Marmon Silko, Simon Ortiz, Paula Gunn Allen, Scott Momaday, and Joy Harjo—all of whom are anthologized in Finch and Elder or in Adamson, Slovic, and O'Grady—can be read for the same feelings of connectedness to Southwestern landscapes.

The Southwest functions as an epicenter for nature and landscape writing by Native Americans who lovingly detail their reservation experiences and feelings of community not only with local human populations but also with regional plants and animals. The anthropological and philosophical work *Wisdom Sits in Places* by Keith Basso inspects the literal and linguistic landscapes of the Arizona Apache and their desert but not deserted homeland, where the Apache continue to dwell in the company of landforms, animals, and plants that have been a part of their collective consciousness for hundreds of years. For all of these Native writers, whatever their ethnic roots, "inhabitation" of a landscape means a special Heideggerian sort of "indwelling," which bespeaks earth and animals and vegetation of a place. Joni Adamson surveys Southwestern Indian authors and their relation to place as well as the environmental justice issues that confront them in *American Indian Literature, Environmental Justice, and Ecocriticism*. Often these literary evocations of home and habitation revive pastoral literary traditions and figure forth the tropes of a golden age in an original and edenic garden landscape. Native American and Hispanic nature writers can be compared with the land-ethics school of ecophilosophy as it has been developed and argued by Callicott and his intellectual mentor Aldo Leopold, whose seminal work, *A Sand County Almanac*, has determined the direction of agricultural ethics and a philosophy of land management. Southwestern multicultural nature writers also may be related to the deep ecology and ecosophy positions taken by the Californians Bill Devall and George Sessions, who plead for land preservation as a part of human spiritual needs.

In the interdisciplinary arenas of nature writing, ecology, philosophy, and religion, theosophy morphs into ecosophy, the special attitude and approach to the study and understanding of the environment that describes and analyzes the spiritual feelings that human beings have for places and spaces. Alice Walker stands out as a California, new age, literary ecosopher who values wilderness; works to preserve it; and writes about it in those novels, essays, and poems she wrote after moving to the West Coast in 1978. Especially accessible as classroom texts are her collections of poems *Her Blue Body Everything We Know* and *Absolute Trust in the Goodness of the Earth*. The "blue body" is Mother Earth or Gaia. Connected to Walker and her ecofeminist rootedness to wilderness and naturalness is the often-anthologized essay by her biographer, Evelyn White, whose "Black Women and the Wilderness" details her conversion from an alienated black woman to whom wild natural tracts of land represented places where slaves and African Americans were hunted when attempting to escape racial oppression to a spiritual promoter of uninhabited and formerly threatening natural spaces. Both Walker and White can be contrasted with Gary Snyder's white male California wilderness aesthetics and ethics, which are fundamentally Buddhist in nature. Sylvia Mayer's *Restoring the Connection to the Natural World: Essays on the African American Environmental Imagination* is a good introduction to the various ways that black writers have written about nature and the environment in harmony with and in opposition to white nature writers such as Snyder.

Not frequently do multicultural nature writers sing hymns of praise for agriculture and write garden pastorals of the sorts that flow naturally from the pens of white male poets like Wendell Berry. But there are some. Jamaica Kincaid is an interesting hybrid transplant from the Caribbean island Antigua who has settled into Vermont and likes it. She praises its gardens and vegetation. She contrasts her Caribbean and New England experiences with rich floral descriptions and herbal interpretations. While gardens and landscapes in the Caribbean are often artificially British, French, Spanish, or Dutch, in New England they seem more genuine to Kincaid, or at least more democratically authentic. Her essay "Alien Soil" is often found in nature-writing anthologies. Langston Hughes, the black poet who is most often associated with the Harlem Renaissance, had positive experiences in the prairie while living in Lawrence, Kansas, during his adolescence. He too can often be encountered in readers and collections.

Asian American writers like David Mas Masumoto and Jeanne Waka-sutki Houston also are horticultural enthusiasts. Masumoto's *Epitaph for a Peach: Four Seasons on My Family Farm* is ripe for selective harvesting of excerpts about agricultural practices; the environment; and cultivation of vineyards, peach orchards, and fields of nitrogen-fixing legumes and wild-flowers. Houston's essay "Rock Garden" is fascinating as an example of a Japanese American interned in a World War II concentration camp who is able to create a sense of belonging to an unnatural prison by cultivating a garden that has cultural connections to the Japanese love of rock gardens. Very much in the spirit of Houston's essay, Joy Kogawa's novel *Obasan* depicts Canadian Japanese persons who have been displaced by the war and reconnects them with an alien landscape (this time the prairie of Alberta). Arthur Sze is not often anthologized but is an excellent nature poet and is very useful for his refracting of American Western landscapes through an Asian lens. Precise philosophical analogues to these pastoral poets and essayists are lacking. Perhaps Paul Taylor, a professional philosopher who defends egalitarian biocentrism, or Holmes Rolston, a proponent of naturalizing values, could be segued into the pastoralist literary perspective, but not easily or seamlessly. Unlike their more creative counterparts, philosophers rarely deal with the anguished alienation coupled with rhapsodic exaltation that characterizes the double-barreled aims of multicultural literary pastoralists. Literary license allows creative writers to positively personify and simultaneously vilify their natural havens and homes, which often are located in the boundaries of love-hate and racialized relationships that are outside the discursive logic of academic philosophy.

The issues and approaches of literary and philosophical ethnic ecoethics funnel into the two categories that most writers and thinkers agree are the solutions to ecological and environmental degradation and depredation: stewardship and sustainability. These are the magic words and formulas that will help restore an injured earth. Some environmental writers and philosophers have adopted codes of earth ethics from religious teachings such as Christianity or Buddhism. Others depend on what the science of ecology teaches about saving and conserving natural resources. An example of the scientific approach is the work on sustainable agricultural and cultural practices among the indigenous groups of the Southwest by the Lebanese American creative essayist and scientist Gary Nabhan, whose work is well known and readily available. Bell hooks is neither theologian nor ecologist; instead she issues lively essayistic apologies to the earth and apologies for sustainability from her perspective as a black feminist writer with rural mid-Southern roots. Both Nabhan and hooks are included in Deming and Savoy's anthology *The Colors of Nature*.

To provide a more specific inspection of the intersections of multicultural ecoethics and nature writing, I propose a transcontinental, geophysical jump from the Southwest to the Old Northwest and to the prominent Native American writers and one philosopher who represent, portray, and defend the naturalistic and environmental attitudes of the indigenous peoples and natural spaces of the upper Midwest. Baird Callicott is an exemplary environmental philosopher whose multicultural aims, themes, methods, and language contain mainly parallels to multicultural creative nature writing and environmental literature. The section "Traditional Native American Attitudes toward Nature" of chapter 6 of his multicultural ecoethics text *Earth's Insights* is a good summary of his environmental-philosophical assessment of the ecological practices of the Lakota and the Ojibwa. In particular, Callicott and Michael Nelson's *American Indian Environmental Ethics: An Ojibwa Case Study* works as a philosophical springboard into the stories and essays by Vizenor, Erdrich, and LaDuke. Much of Callicott's ethnic-environmental philosophy is based on his studies of the Ojibwa, who inhabit the northern plains and Great Lakes regions. Vizenor, Erdrich, and LaDuke voice the cultural histories and experiences of the Ojibwa and Chippewa groups, known collectively as the Anishinaabe. The concluding "Interpretive Essay" from Callicott and Nelson's *American Indian Environmental Ethics* attempts to get to the environmental and philosophical meanings of thirteen Ojibwa nature and hunting stories. From these stories Callicott and Nelson draw some ordinary but also some surprising conclusions that would merit discussion and debate in the classroom. The issues are such that students do not have to be professional philosophers to appreciate the controversies and to want to take sides on the issues. If they become interested enough in the debates, they may want to look at Callicott's essay "Many Indigenous Worlds or *the* Indigenous World," which lays out his philosophical and professional self-defense against attacks from Native American philosophers. One of these retaliatory raids, sardonically titled "Callicott's Last Stand" (Hester, McPherson, Booth, and Cheney), may be found in Wayne Ouderkirk and Jim Hill's *Land, Value, Community*, a collection of philosophical responses to and critiques of Callicott's ecophilosophical positions.

In courses where literary theory or cultural studies is important, Callicott's work and views can be used as springboards to launch into postmodern critical spaces. Callicott defends a postmodern environmental philosophy in chapter 9, "A Postmodern Evolutionary-Ecological Environmental Ethic," in his *Earth's Insights*. His postmodern land ethics is an agglomerative methodology that merges ecological and evolutionary sciences with the land ethics of Aldo Leopold, adding a substantial mixture of alternative traditional tribal narratives about environmental practices in order to produce a legitimate—but never complete—explanatory cause-and-effect model of the ways that human-nature interactions have been conceived, how they have been idealized, and how they ought to be ethically realized in a contemporary globalized multicultural world. In response to critics and changes in ecological paradigms and practices, Callicott has revised his land-ethics approach. His collection of essays *Beyond the Land Ethic* is worth consulting for its renewed perspectives on environmental philosophy.

The postmodern connections of Callicott's environmental philosophy to the narratives and essays of Vizenor, Erdrich, and LaDuke are multiple and worth pursuing. There are the obvious links to the Ojibwa narrative environments and ecoactivism. Just as interesting and fertile are the threads of a postmodern aesthetics that can be followed through Callicott, Vizenor, and Erdrich. While Callicott is not as linguistically playful as his literary counterparts, there is a shared emphasis on multilayered referential systems and antifoundationalist approaches. An effective Vizenor story to examine is "Landfill Meditation" in the collection of related stories with the same title. In this, as in most of his work, the narrator is a trickster figure who is at once a cosmic clown and philosophical shaman. This story introduces Clement Beaulieu, who "conducts seminars on Native

American Indian philosophies, pantribal landfill meditation, environmental fantasies, wild animal languages, transcendental sounds" to rapt groups in California (98). He is aided by Martin Bear Charme, a "crossblood master meditator" from Turtle Mountain Reservation in North Dakota. In addition, there are Oh Shinnah, the celebrator of Mother Earth, and Belladonna Winter Catcher, born at Wounded Knee and the interpreter of tribal naturalism. Magically realistic—characters fly through space and time—and hilariously satirical, "Landfill Meditation" creates ironically humorous Native "earth dreamers" of "holistic waste" and "refuse meditators" on the transcendental creeds from the crossbreeds (105). Vizenor and his literary characters are re-creations of the Ojibwa trickster figure Nanabosho, to whom Callicott devotes considerable attention in *Earth's Insights* (126–27). In Callicott and Nelson's *American Indian Environmental Ethics*, narrative tales 8–12 (79–96) are devoted to this trickster figure, and numerous references to "Nanabushu" (Callicott's spelling) are found in the concluding "Interpretive Essay." Nanabosho is a disobedient trickster spirit who often loses the "blessing" of some animal or natural force but is subsequently chastened and, as a penitent, finally receives the natural reward. Nanabosho becomes the moral of the story that Callicott himself wishes to relate to the Western world and to its past abuses of land and animals. He makes the bold move of integrating Nanabosho's lessons and Ojibwa nature ethics into a Leopoldian land ethic.

For a postmodern satirist like Vizenor, such merging moves and emergent mythmaking are farcical and provide the stage for his comic narrative dramas as well as the gist for his critical mill. "Naanobosho" (Vizenor's spelling) is everywhere: China, Japan, North America, wherever a "trickster of liberty" (the persona of Vizenor himself) has a role to play. Vizenor is literally and literarily all over the map. It is difficult to pick one critical essay or presentation or performance that secures his approach to Nanabosho, the Ojibwa dissimulator who has so many transformations in Vizenor's work. The collection *Shadow Distance: A Gerald Vizenor Reader* can be used as a general overview of Vizenor's major positions and dispositions. As a "postindian" "Crossblood" (Vizenor's terms) his theoretical perspective is not as easy to pin down as Callicott's arguments, which may be difficult but rarely "tricky." Vizenor's postmodernist and playful repositionings lend themselves to French poststructuralist readings and a plentitude of reader responses. Students oriented to film studies can try to find and watch *Harold of Orange*. The script is taken directly from *Shadow Distance*. The work mocks how Euroamericans have constructed the "Native" and how nature has been reconstructed to fit a European cultural image. More brutal and less humorous is the film *Clearcut*. While not scripted by Vizenor nor focused precisely on the Ojibwa, the film nonetheless visualizes destructive logging practices on Native lands in Canada. There is plenty of landscape behind these two cinematic narratives, which filmically supply, as backdrops, the message that the disruption of Native and natural cultures (human and nonhuman) has had tragic consequences.

Like Vizenor, Erdrich has created hyperbolic narrative frames with eccentric Native crossbreeds who are seriously comic and magically real. For example, "Nanabozho" (Erdrich's spelling) plays a role in the chapter "Love Medicine," in the novel with the same title, and appears as Wenabojo in a chapter titled "Almost Soup" in her novel *The Antelope Wife*. Almost Soup is the name of the dog who almost became the meat of the tribal soup and who narrates his own precocious story after having been rescued by an Ojibwa woman. Vizenor's novel *Hotline Healers* offers a similar Ojibwa narrative "hero" with the ironic name, Almost Browne, who, as a mixed blood, is almost brown and whose tragicomic life and thoughts match Erdrich's serious and hilarious narrative temper. Almost Soup is a "windigo dog," a spirit dog that sacrifices itself to save human beings because dogs were created by Wenabojo to be the companions of human beings. Much of what Erdrich has borrowed from Anishinaabe tales and stories can be found in the collection of Ojibwa tales in the central section of Callicott and Nelson's *American Indian Environmental Ethics*. Erdrich, in contrast to Callicott, creatively modernizes the tales, but she maintains a similar ethical intent: human beings learn respect for other human beings and animals and their land through traditional rituals, narratives, and inspiration. Spiritual creatures, like the "manitous," as well as animals like Almost Soup and the Antelope People—the deer and antelope who marry with human beings and watch over them in *The Antelope Wife*—are moral mentors, protectors, and guardian spirits of the environment.

Callicott's ecoethnic ethics directly relate to the environmental activism and writing of Winona LaDuke. In particular, LaDuke's essays "Traditional Ecological Knowledge and Environmental Futures" and "Honor the Earth: Our Native American Legacy," from *The Winona LaDuke Reader*, are pertinent to Callicott's ecoethical interpretation of Ojibwa natural worldviews as well as to Erdrich's and Vizenor's creative narrative attempts to capture Anishinaabe history and culture. LaDuke's fictional historical account of the Ojibwa and White Earth Reservation in Minnesota, *Last*

Standing Woman, provides additional information from a dramatized narrative point of view that reflects LaDuke's own experiences as a resident on the reservation and an active supporter of Ojibwa and Native American environmental causes. She does not affect a playful postmodern stance. Her views are realistically presented and argued. She is accessible to student readers and provides a clear entrance into the complexities of environmental justice and current Native American thinking about the use of land and natural resources.

In conclusion, all four writers—Callicott, Vizenor, Erdrich, and LaDuke— adopt Indian environmental worldviews as models worthy of examination in the classroom. Callicott is an academic skeptic who is concerned with truth claims and rigorous arguments that lead him to embrace natural nativism and pluralistic multiculturalism. Unlike John Neihardt or Richard Nelson and other non-Native nature writers who have spent time with Native American peoples and written sympathetically about their ecoethics, Callicott rarely abandons the hard-edged and hard-nosed approach of a professional philosopher. Nonetheless, the ethnic, ethical, and naturalistic components of literary and popular-culture enactments and vocalizations of environmentalism can often be found in Callicott's richly textured and multilayered ecophilosophy, which he has profusely and intensely argued and defended. Callicott's work is a "natural" choice for classroom analysis and research assignments because of its links to other disciplines and media and because of the richness and variety of environmental topics and topographies. His work does not and cannot put to rest ecoethnic controversies surrounding the authenticities and genuineness of Native and indigenous environmental voices. But his scholarly intent to be inclusive and to balance Western and non-Western philosophical worldviews is admirably well suited to classroom uses that are interdisciplinary and multicultural. His study of Ojibwa environmental attitudes is easily linked to the Anishinaabe narrativists Vizenor, Erdrich, and LaDuke, who creatively reflect, with some distortions and intentional ironies, his postmodern approach to and realistic concern for preservation and restoration of the natural values of the human and nonhuman in the Old Northwest as well as the whole world.

Christopher J. Cobb

Teaching the Literature of Agriculture

If a culture goes for too long without producing poets and others who concern themselves with the problems and proprieties of humanity's practical connection to nature, then the work of all poets may suffer, and so may nature.

— Wendell Berry

Historically, the teaching of environmental literature has attended primarily to nature writing. Although nature writing has been described as including "all texts that describe or study nonhuman environments, including texts that examine the interactions between such environments and humans" (Cooley 1), most attention to nature writing has been given to personal, reflective essays that engage appreciatively with the natural world (Wallace and Armbruster 2), usually in a pastoral mode that associates the entry into the natural world with leisure (Cooley 2–3; Sweet 2–4). The literature of agriculture falls just outside these circles of attention. It is concerned not with "nonhuman environments" but with farms, environments profoundly shaped by human activity. It associates the entry into this environment not with leisure but with the labor of the georgic mode. American agricultural literature, like nature writing, appears in many forms, including poetry, novels, personal essays, history, and technical writings. Writers who stand self-consciously in the American agrarian tradition, which runs from Thomas Jefferson through the Southern agrarians to the new agrarianism (Wirzba 4–10), use descriptions of agricultural labor as a basis for environmental, political, and cultural criticism.

To bring agricultural literature into a course on environmental literature, then, involves broadening students' views of what "nature" might mean and of how people interact with the natural world. This sort of broadening is now taking place in ecocriticism as scholars recognize the insufficiency of a dualistic conception of nature and culture for an accurate understanding of human beings' relationships to their environments. Such dualism is therefore also an insufficient basis for an ethic or aesthetic that can contribute to the health of both people and places (Wallace and Armbruster 3–5; Buell, *Writing* 3–6). This imperative is as pertinent in the classroom as it is in criticism.

Agricultural writing offers opportunities to introduce students to the interaction of nature and culture because agriculture is the practice by which culture in its most basic forms (with the exception of hunter-gatherer culture) is made out of nature. In historical terms, the formation of what most people recognize as culture began with the development of settled farming communities (Heišer 1–13; Critchfield 1–39). In practical terms, modern civilization grows up (as most civilizations have) from an agricultural base. Most students have never given a thought to their complete dependence on agriculture and on the human work with natural environments that makes agriculture possible. Since the literature of agriculture, from its origins in Hesiod and Vergil to the present, is typically concerned to teach its readers how to observe and how to work, reading the literature of agriculture can teach students to perceive the relation of culture to nature and to conceive of their personal relationships to nature more fully.

Wendell Berry's essay "Preserving Wildness" can effectively introduce agricultural writing into a class on environmental literature. Echoing and going beyond Thoreau, Berry's essay shows both the human dependence on wilderness and the present dependence of wilderness on human domestic culture:

> The awareness that we are slowly growing into now is that the earthly wildness that we are so complexly dependent upon is at our mercy. It has become, in a sense, our artifact because it can only survive by a hu-

man understanding and forbearance that we now must make. The only
thing we have to preserve nature with is culture; the only thing we have
to preserve wildness with is domesticity. (143)

Berry explores the ramifications of this awareness by touching on all the
interrelated issues that drive current writings about agriculture: biodiversity
versus monoculture (and by implication genetically modified organisms,
or GMOs), family farming versus corporate agriculture, organic farming
versus industrial agriculture, food security, the value and dignity of human
labor, and local versus global responses to all these issues. The essay, therefore, can serve as a starting point for any approach to the literature of
agriculture that would fit the larger design of the course. Approaches that
may be suitable to many types of environmental literature courses include
a focus on contemporary (possibly local) issues or a focus on agricultural
literature as part of the history of American environmental writing.

A focus on contemporary issues follows easily from Berry's essay since
it raises so many itself. Most of these issues have been intensely debated,
so they offer students an opportunity to study the role of rhetoric and ideology in writers' representations of environmental and agricultural problems. An agrarian perspective takes its distinctive place among ecological,
economic, sociological, and technical writings about agricultural problems
by its perception that work has a role in creating and possibly solving these
problems. For Berry and other agrarians, farmers can learn to work well
only by acting responsively to the nature of the place in which they work.
Working well produces not only sustainable material abundance but also
the qualities of character and the disciplines that enrich human cultures
and relationships. When work is done poorly, land, character, and culture
are all degraded. It is this perception of work that turns the meeting of
nature and culture in agriculture from a clash of opposites into a mutually constitutive union. To show how this perception can issue in practical
solutions to current problems is the challenge agrarian writing faces in its
encounter with other agricultural discourses.

In presenting these encounters to students, I generally use a variety of
short pieces, drawn primarily from several excellent anthologies. Three collections of essays usefully bring together a range of views on these issues. *The
Ethics of Food*, edited by Gregory E. Pence, includes many essays on GMOs
and food-security issues. *Is There a Moral Obligation to Save the Family
Farm?*, edited by Gary Comstock, offers a range of views on what is important about how people farm. Christopher Hamlin and Philip T. Shepard's

Deep Disagreement in U.S. Agriculture studies the conflict between industrial and agrarian views of farm policy and practice. *Deep Disagreements* contains fewer points of view than Pence's and Comstock's collections, but it may be especially valuable to courses focused on rhetoric because it undertakes discourse analysis of the perspectives it studies, instead of simply providing the material for a teach-the-conflicts approach. For views of the diversity in contemporary agrarian thought, two essay collections have much to offer. *The Essential Agrarian Reader*, edited by Norman Wirzba, includes essays on a variety of issues by many prominent agrarians. *Our Sustainable Table*, edited by Robert Clark, gathers a set of more personal, reflective essays. Perspectives compatible with agrarian and environmentalist perspectives but presented in more technical discourses can be found in James E. Horne and Maura McDermott's *The Next Green Revolution: Essential Steps to a Healthy, Sustainable Agriculture*, a readable how-to book; in Dominic Hogg's *Technological Change in Agriculture*, which assesses and defends sustainable agriculture with a thoroughly academic socioeconomic analysis; and in Richard Manning's *Food's Frontier*, which surveys current efforts at agricultural innovation in many parts of the world in the style of science journalism, showing the impact of changing farming practices on local environments and local cultures.

Consideration of contemporary issues in agriculture can also provide opportunities for local environmental and cultural studies. What is happening on farms in your region? How is farming in your region shaped by its environment? What are the environmental, economic, and social impacts of how people eat and how people farm? How are these impacts of agriculture being made visible or invisible locally in advertising and the news media? As public awareness of organic farming and the environmental impact of industrial agriculture continues to grow, so too will opportunities for teaching agricultural writing through current, local writings and activities.

A focus on agricultural literature as part of the history of American environmental writing also follows easily from Berry's essay, and this focus may be useful in environmental literature courses of a more historical bent. Berry places his defense of wildness in the context of the history of American agriculture "from the Indian wars and the opening of agricultural frontiers to the inauguration of genetic engineering" (146–47), so from his essay a course can pick up the history of agricultural writing at any point since the start of colonization. The role of agriculture in the alteration of wilderness is reflected by its prominence in narratives about settlement and success in North America and in the development of the American environmental movement.[1] The inclusion of agricultural writings among narratives of settlement and success requires no defense, and instructors might find Frank Norris's *The Octopus*, Willa Cather's *O Pioneers!* and *My Ántonia*, and Ellen Glasgow's *Barren Ground* to be useful texts.[2] I have myself found that teaching Cather's *O Pioneers!* with Wes Jackson's *Becoming Native to This Place*, which treats the history of human settlement in Kansas and his work at the Land Institute, brings out what Cather's representations of the settlement of Nebraska and of Great Plains agriculture reveal and conceal. For much of the twentieth century, the narratives of settlement have been reversed in narratives of unsettlement: stories of the displacement of rural people and the degradation of farmland. The fullest agrarian view of this unsettlement as an environmental and cultural disaster is Berry's *The Unsettling of America*, his Port William novels (especially *A Place on Earth*), and his poetry, but this view also appears strongly in John Steinbeck's *The Grapes of Wrath* and in the writings of the Southern agrarians, including their manifesto *I'll Take My Stand* and later works on the Tennessee Valley Authority's displacement of Appalachian communities (on the Southern agrarians, see Conkin). The novels of Miguel Ángel Asturias retell the similar, but more brutal, stories of the disruption of Native American communities in Guatemala by the agents of industrial agriculture (see *Strong Wind* and his difficult masterpiece *Men of Maize*).

If the relevance of the literature of agriculture from the nineteenth and early twentieth centuries to narratives of settlement is obvious, its relevance to the development of environmentalist thought may seem surprising, since the use of land for agriculture is contrary to its preservation as wilderness. But the history of conservationist thought does not begin with the dominant environmentalist goal of the twentieth century. Study of the literature of agriculture can provide a way for the instructor of an environmental literature course to address the history of this question: How have people come to an awareness that nature is not a given and that, therefore, care for the environment matters?[3] In American history, this awareness has often come in reaction to environmental disasters, many of which have been agricultural. America's first agricultural disaster—the exhaustion of soils on much of the eastern seaboard's agricultural lands—provoked the agricultural-improvement movement, in which an American environmental consciousness began to form.[4] The writings of this movement (on its history, see Stoll; Sweet 97–121, 164–76) stand with those of the transcendentalists as part of the foundation of American environmental literature. Thoreau's environmental writings especially can gain by being read together with the writings of the agricultural improvers like J. Hector Saint-John de Crèvecoeur, Jefferson, and Charles Brockden Brown in the late eighteenth century and George Perkins Marsh in the nineteenth. Marsh especially merits attention, as his *Man and Nature*, grounded in a georgic perception of life as labor, includes both attention to agricultural practice and a call for a systematic program for wilderness preservation (Sweet 164, 171).

So far I have offered ideas about ways to include agricultural litera-ture in courses that introduce environmental literature, because these are the most widely taught courses in the field. It can also be worthwhile, however, to teach a course wholly devoted to the literature of agriculture. Such a course derives part of its value from its attraction for students who would not necessarily think of themselves as interested in environmental literature. Particularly at schools that draw many students from rural areas, a course on the literature of agriculture can provide students from rural backgrounds with the opportunity to integrate their own experience into an education typically urban and cosmopolitan in its assumptions about what is worth knowing. In my own classes, I have found the dialogue that develops between students from rural backgrounds and students from (typically) suburban backgrounds to be one of the most valuable outcomes of the course.

Starting this dialogue entails overcoming two kinds of resistance to the study of agricultural literature. On the one hand, suburban students who have ended up in the class for no particular reason may arrive with an attitude of contemptuous dismissal toward its subject (agriculture equals boring). Beginning the semester with a dual emphasis on food security and the essential part played by agriculture in the beginnings of civiliza-tion tends to change their view. On the other hand, students with farm-ing backgrounds may get defensive when agrarian writers, as part of their explanation of the dignity and the importance of farming, criticize the environmental and social damage caused by industrial agriculture. Rural students may take the view that farmers are doing the best they can to make a living and to protect their land and that environmentalists should just leave them alone. Addressing their serious resistance is central to the design of the course.

To promote openness to new ideas I present different points of view on the issues in the readings so that the class can freely debate the merits of each position and study the role of the writers' representations in shaping their readers' perceptions. More important, the subjects of each unit in the course regularly shift the distance of the students from the material. The further away the writer's subject is from the students' lives, the more willing students are to accept ethical representations of agricultural work. The nearer the writer's subject, the more likely the students are to prefer representations that focus on pragmatic, economic considerations. Regular changes in distance push students to recognize the ways in which their habits of representing their place in the world to themselves can be confused by self-interest. Agricultural writers, in seeking to comprehend nature and culture together, push their readers to go beyond the shifting representations that promote self-interest: "Happy is he," claims Vergil, "who knows the reasons for things" (74).

A unit on ancient agricultural writings, chiefly drawn from Hesiod's *Works and Days*, Vergil's *Georgics*, and the Bible prompts students to begin analyzing agricultural work as having an ethics that involves care for nature and care for others. Making the connection between work and ethics is a central concern of most ancient representations of farming. A unit on the development of American agriculture, which traces (through the agricultural historian Hurt and the writers Thoreau, Cather, Jackson, and Berry) the cycle of settlement, success, and environmental disaster and social crisis that colonizing and industrializing agriculture has produced, focuses on the transformation of traditional agrarian values when farmers do not have a long-established relation with the land and brings close to home the issues raised at a distance in ancient agricultural writings. A unit on the Green Revolution in India shows the global impact of industrial agriculture and the struggle of writers to represent the momentous changes to nature and culture that have followed from it. Finally, a unit on Jane Smiley's *Moo* brings agricultural literature as close to the students' current home as possible, considering the place of agriculture in a land-grant agricultural university quite similar to their own.

The central subject of the course is how the literature of agriculture helps us see both the places we inhabit and the places and the work from which we derive our lives. That subject is reflected in the course's writing assignments and projects. Two short projects at the start of the semester introduce students to the challenges and the values of writing about agriculture. In the first week of class, I bring a sweet potato (purchased at a farmer's market) to class and pass it around. The students in groups then work on figuring out what they would need to know to write "the sweet-potato story." What would it need to show? Whose story would it be? In the second week of class, I ask the students to write about their personal connection to agriculture. They can write about their family, what they eat, or any way that farming has affected their lives. With students' permission, I share some of their essays with the class, and they also see one another's work in peer workshops on first drafts of the essay. Last year, I had essays about working in a Whole Foods market, about raising a calf for 4-H, about the changes in a small town when many Mexican immigrants settled there to work on the surrounding farms, about how a family fought to save their farm from being annexed for a landfill. These stories show clearly the importance of agriculture for the class, right now.

Once the students have gained some direct experience of writing about agriculture, the class projects turn to analyzing rhetoric and representation. They are assigned two essays in a traditional literary-critical mode. One asks them to analyze the representation of work in Vergil, Cather, or Berry. The other asks them to examine the different ways that the success of agriculture is represented in nonfictional writings about the Green Revolution in the Indian state of Punjab. This second project seeks to show that the effect of representation on meaning is just as important in nonfictional writing as it is in fictional writing: a fact is a rhetorical representation of truth, not an unmediated snapshot of reality. This assignment also follows from the course's largest project: a conference to propose a future course for agriculture in Punjab. The Green Revolution, which is essentially the export of American industrial agriculture to the Third World, has transformed Punjab more fully than any other Third World region, for better and for worse, and its impact on Punjab has been studied extensively.[5] I provide a variety of sources, including Lennard Bickel's biography of Norman Borlaug (the father of the Green Revolution); Richard Critchfield's decades-long journalistic study of a Punjabi village; Vandana Shiva's critique of the Green Revolution (*Violence*); Himmat Singh's economic analysis of its impact; and Web sites hosted by the Indian government, by nongovernmental organizations concerned with Punjab, and by the international organizations and multinational corporations that fund and monitor agricultural-development projects. From these sources and others that they find on their own, students gather the information that they need to represent the positions for four groups who are influencing Punjabi agriculture: residents, government agencies, environmental and consumer-advocacy groups, and international organizations. Each student group must develop a platform for agricultural reform that represents the concerns of their group. These platforms are presented and debated, and the class chooses the platform proposals that seem best. This project moves from literary to cultural study, showing students how representations of a situation can influence policy development and the global network of human interests that shapes human impact on the environment through agriculture. Having put students in the role of people seeking to reshape an environment in this project, I turn the students' attention in the opposite direction in the course's final examination. It asks students to analyze *Moo*'s depiction of the relation of person to place and of institution to place, which the novel's satire shows unsparingly in its depiction of people who see the whole world through the lens of their own narrow academic specialty (a narrowness that agrarian writers have vigorously criticized). The end of the class thus seeks to return students to an awareness of the human experience of being produced by an environment, which must inform the human experience of laboring to produce their own lives within nonhuman nature, if both humans and nature are to thrive.

Notes

The epigraph to this essay is from Berry's *Standing by Words* 154.

1. Recent ecocritical scholarship offers many ideas about how to place agricultural texts in the histories of settlement and of the environmental movement. See especially Sweet; Stoll; Sarver; and Conlogue.

2. On these texts as narratives of success through industrial agriculture, see Conlogue; for a survey of fiction about the American farm, better for the twentieth century than the nineteenth, see Goreham 427–30.

3. One might also open the subject with the counterquestion: How could people not have been aware of this? This question draws attention to the colonial relation to land that displaced or extirpated the Native American relations to land that had preceded the European settlement. Reading of early colonialist texts by such as Richard Hakluyt and John Smith (on both of these as agricultural writings, see Sweet) or reading contemporary agrarian historical analysis of the colonialist attitude to land (as, for example, Berry's *The Unsettling of America*) can reveal the development of blindly exploitative relations to the given, natural world.

4. Two twentieth-century agricultural disasters—the Dust Bowl and the widespread use of DDT—are well known and generally well covered in environmental literature.

5. Since the Green Revolution originated in Mexico, it would be possible to build a similar unit exploring the impact of the Green Revolution there, if one wanted to keep the focus of one's class entirely on North America. On this topic, see Bickel's chapters on Borlaug's work in Mexico; Hogg's chapter on Mexican agricultural policy; and both Cotter's and Simonian's histories of the Green Revolution and the Mexican conservation movement.

Alanna F. Bondar

Ecofeminist Canadian Literature

We approach theorizing ecofeminism in Canadian ecological writing in the classroom with some difficulty, knowing that in Canada ecological writing, ecocriticism, and ecofeminism are still emerging as valid forms of literary criticism. Thus, teaching ecofeminism presents many challenges to the instructor who recognizes that inherited from British literature and its attitude toward nature is a consciousness in English Canada theorized by Northrop Frye and best described by Margaret Atwood as a "violent duality" (Afterword 62); in this much-discussed cultural imagination to which Canadians have subscribed, comforts of the European pastoral and Old World nostalgia are pitted against a vast, terrifying, and disparately alienating Canadian wilderness. This love-hate dynamic leaves the wilderness, according to Gaile McGregor, "not accessible," where "no mediation or reconciliation is possible"; Canadians are "reluctant or unable to get past its immanence, the obtrusive 'thereness' of the thing-in-itself" (27). Many scholars wrongly argue that, to date, there is no such thing as Canadian ecofeminist literature; nonetheless, writers have recently emerged in Canada as if to answer Atwood's poignant question in *Survival* concerning women's reaction to a masculine-encoded notion of the Canadian North as "a sort of icy and savage *femme fatale* who will drive you crazy and claim you for her own" (*Survival* 89).

In the Canadian literary history consumed by a masculinist agenda, Diane M. A. Relke argues that this "story of the garrison" has "obscur[ed] a 'second story' about nature—the one told by the women who find that 'the natural world offers an alternative way of being human through harmony with the land'" (126). Though ecofeminist writing is not gender-specific, Heather Murray argues, Canadian women writers—"within and without culture, within and without discourse" (82)—are "particularly socially placed to examine the problems of nature/culture mediation, which seem to characterize the literature" (81). Furthermore, because women are viewed historically in terms of their identification with the natural world, they are culturally considered less evolved than men, and, as such, their "symbolic ambiguity of the middle ground helps [women] to see how representation of woman is always double" (82).

Since ecological and ecofeminist writing is not clearly defined in Canadian scholarship, teaching Canadian ecofeminism must necessarily include the following stages:

> literary examples that make distinctions between feminism and ecofeminism, between proto-ecological and ecological writings, and between ecological and ecofeminist writings
>
> an exploration not only of the problematic woman-nature dynamic in the myth of the logic of dualisms but also of how the ensuing ecofeminist values of "practical essentialism" (King 23) allow for "revisionist mythmaking" (Murphy, *Literature, Nature* 119)
>
> suggestions for how this innovative literature explores ways of making our relations with nature less alienated and thus has the potential to inspire life-altering changes in individual belief systems and communal practices

All such courses should first satisfy student interest on the topic of hierarchy and of the myth of the logic of dichotomies as they are subverted by the cycle-oriented holistic theoretical code of ecofeminism. Like feminism, ecofeminism recognizes how certain masculine-identified ideologies defend false cultural constructions of the feminine, of women, and of nature in order to continue a secured acceptance of denigration and violence against these cultural participants. Once fundamental theoretical elements of ecofeminism are understood, discussion of Patrick Murphy's revisioning of Gregory Cajete's theory of the "geopsyche"—which replaces the tired paradigm of othering with a revised concept of "anotherness"

(119)—can ensue. This essay identifies early proto-ecofeminist writing by women—that is, writing that precedes ecofeminist theoretical influences and direction for creative ecofeminist responses to self, body, and place in biotic communities—and suggests ecofeminist writers and approaches to their work for consideration when planning a course on Canadian eco-feminist literature.

One can identify early proto-ecofeminist work in Canada as beginning with colonial journals and letters written by authors such as Catherine Parr Traill, Susanna Moodie, and Anna Brownell Jameson and as moving to late modernist writers publishing from the 1940s on. From British high soci-ety to the backwoods of Canada, these women were confronted with the unique opportunity to interpret their experience of the feminine as other through their cultural connection to womanhood and denigration, abuse, loss, life cycles, and extinction. The Canadian reader will recall Jameson's diatribe on how a Canadian settler "hates a tree" (64), "regards it as his natural enemy, as something to be destroyed, eradicated, annihilated by all and any means" (231), after which she makes a correlation between "ringing timber"—the slow death method of tree killing (65)—and how she is "like an uprooted tree, dying at the core" (16). For the next wave of proto-ecofeminist writing in Canadian literature the instructor will want to consider the poets Miriam Waddington, P. K. Page, and Anne Marriott, in particular, since their struggles against the strictures of high modernism, as an elitist measure of civilization and its art, provide interesting insight into essential aspects of the Canadian women's poetry movement in which the human-nature dynamic remains at the forefront. Like the first wave of Canadian proto-ecofeminist writers, these poets explore identification with already established myths, mappings, and metaphors concerning the woman-nature link; however, their process of identification remains not an ecofeminist but a feminist agenda that primarily seeks emancipation from masculine-identified and thus falsely constructed codes of self-identification and, oftentimes ironically, liberation from the woman-nature metaphor, as it is again defined by masculine-encoded strictures. Discussion in the classroom setting of this countertradition in Canadian nature writing as the literature evolves into a more ecofeminist consciousness bridges gaps between early colonial nature writing and the emergence of stricter eco-feminist writings.

From modernist female poets to Canadian women novelists of the late 1960s and 1970s, consciously ecofeminist Canadian literature primarily begins in a third wave of proto-ecofeminist literature through women-on-

spiritual-quest novels. Informed by Frye's convictions that nature as terrifying other was irreconcilably opposed to human consciousness, Marian
Engel's *Bear*, like Atwood's *Surfacing*, Aritha van Herk's *Tent Peg*, and
Ethel Wilson's *Swamp Angel*, seeks a new subgenre of protoecological
prose that, in breaking from colonial inheritance, explores a tropological
wilderness as a necessary underworld running counter to codified masculinist expectations of feminine strength and womanhood. From an ecofeminist perspective, and despite ecological shortcomings, this literature
of "dangerous middles" (Kroetsch qtd. in H. Murray 76), instructors will
note, is both a literature of "safe wilderness trails" where the wilderness—
albeit a pseudo-wilderness—is exploited as a tool for human expression
and expansion without any regard for the wilderness's oppression and
expression and a brave venturing into wilderness space as a place of reju-
venation and renewal—a significant inversion of the traditional Canadian-
nature-as-enemy and human-disaster story.

Discussion that explores differences between feminist and ecofeminist
strategies and interpretations are particularly well suited to novels such
as Atwood's *Surfacing* and Engel's *Bear*, since they reveal a gender distinction between the masculine quest for the pastoral *outside* the self
and the feminine-identified findings of the pastoral *within*. In particular, the ecofeminist reader will interpret how the wilderness is a place of
healing and instruction, regardless of its apparent and non-eco-friendly
tropological "use" by questing female characters; the feminist reader, in
contrast, will interpret the wilderness as a place without patriarchy and,
as such, a place of healing and instruction. Engel's female protagonist in
Bear enters—in ignorance—a wilderness as green world through which
nature as enemy is replaced by nature as lover. By making her body's sexual impulses explicit with an affair with a wilderness bear, Engel's woman
on spiritual quest inscribes both body and desire into what is believed to
be, at least in the masculine-encoded version of Canadian literary history,
a place of extreme danger.

The feminist agenda apparent in *Bear*, as with other pseudowilder-
ness continuums, limits the extent to which women identify the exploitation of self with the exploitation of wilderness. The exception is Atwood's
Surfacing, which hints at an ecofeminist agenda by linking a first-person
narrator's oppression symbolically with otherness, namely animal victims.
Thus the female narrator is metaphorically shot like the loon; useless, since
"proper food was in cans" (129); hung by her feet from a tree like the
pointless killing of the heron (124, 197); and turned into "a new kind of

centrefold" placed in "the hospital or the zoo" (204) through Atwood's links between woman and nature. *Surfacing*, like *Bear*, however, fails to meet the criteria necessary for classification as a postpastoral novel since the focus remains on a symbolic nature to illustrate feminist politics of denigration through animal imagery. For example, her girlfriend's husband, David, degrades women by objectifying their bodies and by equating them with animal status: he jokes about "hook[ing] a beaver" and a "split-beaver," derogatorily aligning woman's genitalia with the "national emblem" (128). The response of Atwood's female narrator is that his comments are no joke; "it was like skinning the cat, I didn't get it" (128).

In an attempt to argue in favor of Canadian pseudo-wilderness continuums or Canadian women on spiritual-quest-novels as ecofeminist or proto-ecofeminist, instructors ought to show that shortcomings celebrating feminism fail to meet important ecofeminist criteria: the wilderness still serves as a tool for self-discovery and not as a means of discovering, defining, and forging healthy new relationships. Both texts celebrate the finding of womanhood through the essentialist notion of woman as creator; the protagonist in *Surfacing* does have intercourse with the bear, or, at least, she actively pursues impregnation (which had earlier in the novel been considered a thing to avoid with her boyfriend) in an outdoor healing-seduction of her ex-lover, who she wishes were a bear: "he needs to grow more fur" (172). Though Atwood and Engel attempt feminist shifts in the human-nature literary paradigm (Engel more radically so), an ecofeminist reading ultimately exposes *Bear* and *Surfacing* as texts that fall short of recognizing the tenets of ecological literature as laid out by Lawrence Buell in *The Environmental Imagination* and by Murphy's call for "revisionist mythmaking." Like feminism, ecofeminism is a dynamic topic of discussion in the classroom since it continues to examine those persistent questions of feminine identity: What is woman? What do women want? What are "natural" instincts and desires for women? What happens when we lose our connection to civilized instincts? Are the reactions that result (e.g., the *Surfacing* protagonist's descent into an underworld madness as a component to self-discovery) considered "unnatural" despite what might very well be a closer link to our "natural" selves?

Instructors will find it exhilarating to move into close analysis of poetry that meets the criterion for ecological poetry and serves in that context as ecofeminist. By applying "practical essentialism" to gender differences in early ecological poetry (after Rachel Carson's publication of *Silent Spring*, in 1962), the instructor of Canadian ecopoetics will find a division between male poets who exhibit ecoguilt and female poets who show rage against patriarchal injustices to women, nature, and the planet; neither tendency, however, reflects the geopsyche. Ultimately, this proto-ecological poetry shifts into anotherness through the collapsing of male-female and self-wilderness-other paradigms to move into shared visions contained in the parameters of ecofeminist theories. Through a speculative male guilt, I surmise that most Canadian ecological poets express confusion, discomfort, dis-ease, hesitancy, self-loathing, historical embarrassment, paralysis, and apology for their continued cultural position as the dominant gender and race through their poetry. Instructors may consider contrasting the poets Tim Lilburn, John O'Neil, and Christopher Dewdney with the ecofeminist poets Don McKay, Kristjana Gunnars, Karen Connelly, Lorna Crozier, and Daphne Marlatt to explore how the mind and psyche become paralyzed by a Canadian colonial past and, thus paralyzed, how the body remains contentious. Through the ecofeminist space, however, defined by geopsychic considerations of the earth body (individual) and the body Earth (planet), a more legitimate ecological poetic practice emerges. This evolution away from a masculine agenda reveals how an ecofeminist poetic voice emerges from a countertradition to assert itself as a dominant articulation in contemporary Canadian poetry.

This emerging ecofeminist practice connects not only the geopsyche to a process of writing through the body as nature but also a return to presymbolic jouissance—desire that runs strong in the ecofeminist post-pastoral: it defines the parameters of both the artist's creative process and the existence of the work itself. The geopsyche, then, at odds with gender and race exclusivity, reveals a postcolonial, and postfeminist ecorevolution found in the poetics of poetic ecoerotica. Often leaning toward experimental poetics in *l'écriture féminine,* isomorphic amalgamations of text and psyche as reflections of the geopsyche reject "phallic monosexuality" (Cixous 41). This quest, as Hélène Cixous argues, is for that "endless body, without 'end,'" which is "not simple . . . but varied entirely, [in] moving and boundless change" (44). Thus, writing through the body makes strategic a defiance of critical attention that attempts to lock, pin, define, or label it. As boundary crossers into territories of both frontier and survival, the ecofeminist poets Anne Szumigalski, Miriam Waddington, Karen Connelly, Erin Mouré, Lorna Crozier, Eva Tihanyi, Daphne Marlatt, and Kristjana Gunnars write revisionist poetry that searches for feminine responses to *le nom de père* as a hegemonic spiritual construction, and they develop feminine-identified spiritual answers that are derived from their explorations of bioregional "belonging"; the result is exemplary, a woman "running green upon the streets / like freshly sprouted grass / in her a woman breathing a greener grace" (Tihanyi 60–61).

What becomes particularly interesting and complex are the ways in which theorists and poets alike disarm feminist fears of women's essentialism by reconnecting women and nature as a point of positive departure for discovering aspects of womanhood and the biosphere (instructors including drama might want to consider Cowan's "A Woman from the Sea" as a segue into ecofeminist poetics). As a kind of micro-macrocosmic link, women's bodies become a space of physical, intellectual, and psychological understanding because, like the planet Earth, they are linked to creation. Oftentimes employing presymbolic language and experimentation beyond linear, logical forms of writing, emerging ecofeminist poets create a kind of origin poetry that resists traditional notions of seeking enlightenment through transcendence and that instead seeks to reinscribe the mind-body-spirit into a harmonious biosphere. In awe of what "[I] never hear / creatures like that, so unmoved / so out-of-reach," ecofeminist poets, such as Kristjana Gunnars, create the necessary continuum for changes in the human-nature connection: when she observes, "where forget- / me-not flowers crowd / and hemlocks stay green" she does not simply admire the beauty of these flowers, as Moodie might have in the early beginnings of Canadian proto-ecofeminist literature, but "wonder[s] how they knew" (67).

A summary of a classroom agenda includes the following:

Link early proto-ecofeminist writing (Jameson, Parr Traill, and Moodie) to Atwood's *Survival* and Frye's theories of garrison in the Canadian cultural imagination.

Read mid-century proto-ecofeminist poets (Waddington, Page, Marriott) and discuss their identification with nature in a practical essentialism.

Consider women-on-spiritual-quest novels of the 1970s as points of departure between feminist and ecofeminist theories.

Discuss Murphy's theory of anotherness and the geopsyche as they are applied to the recent emergence of ecofeminist poets, as well as how the emergence of ecological poetry in Canada is strongly ecofeminist.

Place-Based Approaches

Hal Crimmel

Place-Based Courses and Teaching Literature Outdoors: An Overview

As I plan a creative nonfiction course in the deep river canyons of Dinosaur National Monument, I am reminded how geography determines text, from the landscape the students and I will work in and interpret to essays we will read about desert rivers and the high, arid region they flow through. Though they have existed in one form or another for over a century, such place-based courses and the practice of teaching outdoors are increasingly central to ecocritical practice.[1] As Michael Cohen suggests, ecocriticism's future will depend in part on a "focus on place and region," which will also "include critique of global paradigms—scientific and cultural—as they fit in discussions of local place and future environmental outcomes" (par. 73).[2] In the first half of this essay I'd like to discuss options for incorporating place in our teaching.

Admittedly, *place* is a complex term, familiar yet of indeterminate definition. Is it fluid or fixed? Fixed by what and by whom? Indigenes or immigrants? Cartographers or poets? And when we finally define a particular place, are we content with the results? Not really. "Places are by definition bounded, but human-drawn boundaries usually violate both subjectively felt reality and the biotic givens," says Lawrence Buell (*Environmental Imagination* 268). Despite the hazy, porous, unsatisfactory nature of the term *place*, it is still possible to sketch out possibilities for place-based teaching. In literary studies this traditionally has revolved around geographic space. These divisions, in their broadest disciplinary manifestations, such as British or American, still exist, as do more classically "regional" offerings such as New England literature or Southern women's regional writing. Following from these geographic definitions were specialty courses focused on a particular state, province, or subregion, such as Adirondack literature.

But the literary establishment has typically been quick to dismiss courses or texts focused on specific geographic areas with the perjorative "regional" label. Wallace Stegner once said that the more different a place is from New York "the more likely it is that a novel will be labeled regional. A Brooklyn novel is as regional to me as one laid in Canyonlands would be to a Brooklynite. But his isn't called *regional* and mine is" (qtd. in Stegner and Etulain 137). Regionalism, seen as a career-killing backwater, languished on the sidelines as English departments began to embrace post-structuralist criticism.[3] Those interested in place found themselves on the disciplinary fringes.

But as the environmental movement increased awareness of the fragility, importance, and uniqueness of specific places, regionally focused courses underwent a renaissance. The work of prominent humanistic geographers such as Edward Relph, D. W. Meining, and Yi-Fu Tuan also breathed new life into the work of literary critics searching for relationships between place and text. Place, wrote Tuan, is more than mere geographic space; it is "a center of meaning constructed by experience" ("Place" 152). This shift helped broaden conceptions. Subjective experience of particular place came to be seen as desirable—not merely provincial—and now-canonical authors such as Edward Abbey, Mary Austin, and Willa Cather moved toward the mainstream.

Today, the movement to integrate the humanities with the sciences has influenced the direction of our teaching. E. O. Wilson, David Orr, and Glen Love, among others, have articulated its value in ecocritical contexts, and one of the most important developments is the bioregional movement, which foregrounds an interdisciplinary-based understanding of place. Bioregionalism, famously defined by Gary Snyder as "the entry of place into the dialectic of history" (*Practice* 41), has added a new dimension to our teaching. Distinct places produce distinct forms of literary expression best understood by focusing on aspects such as natural history, Native American history, geology, botany, zoology, physical geography, and others, all of which contribute to a region's identity. Snyder's observation that "we

might say that there are 'classes' which have so far been overlooked—
the animals, rivers, rocks, and grasses—now entering history" (*Practice* 41)
has been taken to heart by those teaching place-based environmental literature courses. Knowing the physical world enhances understanding of
literature; bioregional courses attempt to make students aware of the entry
of place into the dialectic of history, and particularly of their own history.

Wild nature and open spaces are as important to bioregionalism as they
are to ecocriticism. But they are not the sole focus. As Snyder notes, "The
bioregional movement is not just a rural program: it is as much for the restoration of urban neighborhood life and the greening of the cities" (*Practice*
43). This notion has contributed to growth in studies of urban environmental justice and urban nature writing, for example, which expanded the
boundaries of ecocriticism as a critical practice. It likewise stimulated interest in the urban and suburban places where most of the population lives. J.
Scott Bryson's essay in this collection provides a welcome example of how
the idea of urban place—in this case, Los Angeles, helps students make connections with the region they inhabit—freeways, suburbs, and all.

Valuing where we live suggested that place-based education also
"might be characterized as the pedagogy of community, the reintegration
of the individual into her homeground and the restoration of the essential
links between a person and her place"(Lane-Zucker ii).[4] Thus it "is not
simply a means to integrate the curriculum around a study of place, but a
means of inspiring stewardship and an authentic renewal and revitalization
of civic life" (iii). Service learning and stewardship and environmental-
restoration projects can help accomplish that goal. Laird Christensen's
essay "Writing the Watershed" provides an illustration of service learning at work. It details his experience teaching a course focused on the
process of revaluing a badly polluted Michigan watershed. Connecting to
the past helps students imagine "what it would be like to live in a healthy,
vibrant watershed" (134), providing a glimmer of hope for the future of
the abused region in which they live. Valuing wilderness remains crucial.
But when understood as a place "where man is a visitor who does not
remain" (Wilderness Act), wilderness should not be the only site for students to explore how their lives intersect with place, since local landscapes
tend to be diminished and compromised.

But in an era when environmental debates are sharply polarized and
anything connected with the word *environmentalist* engenders immediate opposition in a segment of the population, we should consider audience carefully. "Authentic renewal" often occurs in an artificial way. Few

instructors intend to help students become a part of a community, if that community has a perceived antienvironmental outlook that values unrestricted motorized access to wilderness areas or uncontrolled development. Place-based courses geared toward civic life need to combine existing local definitions with an envisioned ideal. Expecting students to embrace values having more in common with the ivory tower than the local diner can breed profound resentment. Being attuned to local attitudes ensures that such courses reach the broadest possible audience.

Acknowledging the human influence on place, perhaps most evident in the study of built environments, facilitated an instructional shift from those necessarily tied to physical geography to others focused on social place. This might be, as Elizabeth Dodd suggests, "constructed through race" (1095), but it can also include the familiar themes of gender, ethnicity, and class, among others. Courses focus on how a sense of place emerges not just from the landscape, weather, and flora and fauna but also from the social, political, and economic landscapes. They provide a context for integrating aesthetic, scientific, and culturally bound ways of knowing. But they also help us consider place as the province not just of Cather, N. Scott Momaday, or Austin but also of such writers as Sandra Cisneros or Toni Morrison. In doing so we expand our notion of the possibilities for teaching about place.

In the remainder of this essay, I sketch out the six most popular field-based learning models, which describe the possibilities for working with students outdoors across a wide range of instructional settings. Twenty years ago, literature-course field trips leaned toward excursions to museums, authors' homes, and historical sites. The growing interest in environmental literature changed that. Today, field sessions range from hour-long urban forays to multiweek wilderness trips. Students in environmental literature courses are becoming accustomed to researching, sketching, taking notes, idea collecting, writing, and discussing—all while gathered on rock outcrops, sandbars, tree stumps, or city streets.

As we become more skilled in incorporating field-learning experiences into our courses, this practice will continue to evolve and flourish. Environmental literature, now recognized as an important contribution to the humanities, means instructors spend less time justifying topics and approaches. As my 2003 anthology, *Teaching in the Field: Working with Students in the Outdoor Classroom*, illustrates, we now can focus on developing and publicizing field practices.[5] As instructors continue to refine practice, these pedagogies become increasingly sophisticated.

The first model to consider is the short field trip during class time, consisting of near-nature excursions, not only in campus arboretums and woodlots or along a creek or river but also in a cornfield, next to a parking lot, or across from a strip mall. These in-class field sessions are reliable techniques for getting students outdoors because they minimize scheduling conflicts. Fifty-minute outings are easily coordinated and are effective at institutions where students may be unwilling or unable to participate in longer trips because of jobs, finances, or family responsibilities. These trips work well in any course, from lower-division general-education and writing courses to graduate-level seminars. Fifty minutes is adequate time to get students outdoors and engaged in journal writing, sketching, or other activities. This model offers exceptional flexibility. Instructors can take classes outdoors with little notice should it seem helpful to explore a place or an idea encountered in the reading; doing so also avoids weather-related cancellations.

An illustration comes from my ecocriticism course, taught where the Austrian Alps meet the eastern plains. Known as the German Rome, but with a history stretching back to the Celts, the city of Salzburg is an ideal place to explore the intersection of nature and culture. But it is notorious for being exceptionally rainy. As one powerful low after another spun down from the North Sea, it seemed we would never get outside, unless in heavy rain. Finally we seized a ninety-minute class period to complete an urban transect, identifying examples of the picturesque, exploring gardens and the pastoral ideal, discussing urban nature, and identifying how the landscape reflected uniquely Austrian attitudes toward nature. Taking the field trip on short notice helped us accomplish our mission without fighting the weather, and I could tailor the trip's objectives to cap the reading done in the previous month.

A variation of the in-class field trip is the workshop or lab, in which one class period a week—or a certain amount of time each class period—is devoted to outdoor instruction. Instructors who build experiential sessions into the syllabus find that it helps normalize field excursions, making them as integral to the curriculum as reading, writing, or library research. Working outdoors regularly allows students to become comfortable with exploring the connections between their reading and the environment. Different examples come to mind. At Weber State University, where I teach, Russ Burrows and Dave Sumner designed a course called Literary Naturalists, which met one afternoon each week. One hour of most class sessions was devoted to exploring nearby environments relevant to the readings. They visited Antelope Island in the Great Salt Lake, performed community service such as trail work, and spent time with Wildlife Service officials working to reclaim the Weber River from ranching-related damage. Instructors elsewhere have had students "adopt" a particular object or place and then spend time observing, writing, or tending it each week.

A second popular model is the half-day excursion, often consisting of trips to locations integral to understanding a particular text, author, or concept. Easily scheduled for a morning or an afternoon, these trips permit off-campus travel to nearby urban areas, working landscapes, or wild places. John Elder's essay, "The Poetry of Experience," provides a fine example of the symbiosis between field learning and the study of environmental literature on a half-day trip. Working from the idea that we need to "ground criticism and teaching alike in the natural experience from which so much of the world's great literature has emerged" ([Armbruster and Wallace] 314), Elder discusses a workshop on scything that takes place in a hayfield on a fresh Vermont morning. Placing Robert Frost's poem "Mowing" into a historical, geographic, and ecological context lets Elder and his class fully enter into the poem and the labor in nature that inspired it. "Regardless of the length of a class's time outside," writes Elder, "the goal would be the same: to experience personally the images and rhythms we meet again on the page" ([Armbruster and Wallace] 320). His analysis of the poem emerges from experiencing the rhythms and techniques of mowing. In the process we see how such exercises can connect students with nature and text. "The fact is the sweetest dream that labor knows," wrote Frost in "Mowing" (*Early Poems* 24); Elder's class shows us how physicality and imagination likewise become inseparable in the outdoors classroom. Thus half-day excursions enable in-depth exploration of a topic in a way difficult to achieve in the fifty-minute class model. They are logistically uncomplicated and require little time away from campus, making them a good choice for most instructors.

The third field-based model to consider is a two-to-three day, off-campus trip. During the semester these typically need to take place on a weekend to avoid conflict with other courses. In most regions, such trips are best taken early in the fall semester to avoid the short daylight hours and winter conditions found in November and December. In the spring semester, usually the reverse is true: longer days and warmer temperatures make late spring a good time to head out. Note that seeking ideal conditions has pedagogical and theoretical implications—namely, that scheduling trips only when landscapes and weather are perfect reinforces aesthetic expectations that cause us to devalue many places. But the converse is also true—poor weather, light, and location can sabotage any attempt at learning, since students will struggle to meet basic needs. In either case, weekend trips require careful planning. The instructor can ensure participation by building the trip into the syllabus and making it part of the students' grades. Costs can be kept low by basing out of or camping in state or national parks, Bureau of Land Management or Forest Service lands, or national monuments.

Even in states such as Texas, where public lands are relatively few, creative solutions exist.[6] Two-to-three-day trips naturally require advance planning. But they let instructors and students spend blocks of time together, which, in addition to giving students a greater appreciation for a particular place, can also foster group cohesion. One disadvantage is that by the time a group gets into the rhythm of camping, the trip is over. This focus on meeting physical needs can distract from intellectual inquiry. But it also breaks down inhibitions and prejudices, which increases receptivity to new places or new ideas encountered in discussion, reading, or lecture.

An exemplar comes from Don Scheese, a professor at Gustavus Adolphus College and an early advocate of teaching literature outdoors. In his interdisciplinary first-term seminar, The Green American Tradition, Scheese typically takes students off campus early in the semester for a weekend of camping at a Minnesota state park. This acquaints students with an unfamiliar bioregion—the prairie—but it also fosters social bonding that translates into improved group dynamics, which in turn improves classroom performance.

A fourth model, long popular with environmental literature instructors, is the extended excursion, involving several days of camping or overnight stays at cabins, yurts, or mountain huts. Longer trips let students escape from their campus routines long enough to immerse themselves in the topic at hand. Since these trips often are components of semester-length on-campus courses, careful advance planning is needed. To avoid interfering with students' other courses, the field sessions tend to take place before or after the semester. One intriguing example is a course, entitled Storytelling in Native American Literature, that included a one-week hiking trip to the Havasupai Reservation in the bottom of the Grand Canyon. The instructor of this course, Roberta Rosenberg, cites Walker Percy's idea that we need to remove the "educational package" that prevents students from understanding different cultures and perspectives (41). Doing so facilitates the students' understanding of such Native

American concepts as "1) a belief in the people and land as one; 2) story-telling and a sense of the sacred; and 3) the history and impact of discrimination" (43). By staying for a week on Indian land in the canyon, experiencing place, and interacting with villagers, students had a view "of another culture, unclouded by preconception, nostalgia, prejudice or wish projection" (59). In turn, this deepened their understanding of Native American texts and the nature-culture relation found in them.[7] Week-long excursions tend to work best in specialty-topics courses, where the level of interest is generally high enough to get students to commit to a trip.

The fifth field-based model largely, if not exclusively, takes place off campus in a stand-alone program. There are two versions of this model: base camp and nomadic. In the base-camp version, a group typically lives off campus at a camp, in cabins, on a ranch, or at an institute for an extended period of time, ranging from a month to a semester.[8] Significant amounts of time are spent outdoors. An example would be the international field-studies course operated through the Great Basin Institute at the University of Nevada, Reno, which takes place on the central Pacific coast of Mexico (see Keir's essay in this volume). Many others exist that take students far from campus, where their worldviews can be profoundly influenced and learning has a fluid, less institutional feel.[9]

In the nomadic version, students are on the trail or on the road for several weeks or months, a feature that allows for true transformative learning. For years the Sierra Institute at the University of California, Santa Cruz, offered courses along these lines, taught by pioneers of this sort of teaching, including John Tallmadge and Ed Grumbine. An excellent example of this model in action appears in Greg Gordon's book-length narrative, *Landscape of Desire: Identity and Nature in Utah's Canyon Country*. Gordon describes teaching natural history, nature writing, and wilderness education to a group of Sierra Institute students for three weeks as they crossed a remote stretch of the Colorado Plateau's canyon country.[10]

The sixth and final model, independent field-study projects, affords students tremendous flexibility but requires self-discipline and initiative. It is applicable to literature and creative writing courses, as Andrew Wingfield has described in "Road Trip: Self-Directed Field Work as a Learning Journey," and to courses with a service-learning component. Another excellent example comes from Annie Merrill Ingram, whose students consult with members of the local community and work in the field in two areas: "service learning and activist (or action) research" (212). Students have worked on "establishing a community organic garden, at a local land conservancy site, with the Sierra Club's Inner City Outings Program" and have participated in "water quality management and shoreline erosion research" (213–14). Such work is immensely rewarding for those wanting to reach beyond the academy to their communities. It is also "potentially exhausting for faculty and students," as John Harris cautions in "Teaching Place and Community History to Undergraduates" (in this volume). Field-based learning enhances environmental literature courses and is applicable to most courses in most contexts, including natural history, nature writing, wilderness literature, urban nature, bioregionalism, ecocomposition, or place-based fiction. What value does it have? Practitioners tend to identify three areas. First, field learning provides an opportunity for interdisciplinary work, linking the work of science with that of the humanities in ways that expand the work of both. Second, it provides a deeper understanding of the ways self, text, and place intersect in works of environmental literature. Third, it moves the idea of environment from abstract to the real, by actively engaging students with the world outside the classroom.

In short, fieldwork has become an important component of teaching environmental literature. Elder, one of the earliest advocates, states:

> [W]e have arrived at a point . . . where we need to begin integrating this experiential dimension of teaching and scholarship in a more strategic way. The increasing refinement of our critical terminology can be complemented now by an equally deliberate pedagogy. ("Poetry" [Armbruster and Wallace] 313)

It is my hope that the models sketched out above will help instructors choose an appropriate model for their courses and that outdoors pedagogy will continue to evolve in directions fruitful for both students and teachers.

Integrating the sciences with the humanities, valuing urban environments as well as wild places, connecting the ideal with the real and the global with the local—all are important goals for education in our century. Incorporating place and making field-based pedagogies central to teaching environmental literature are two avenues that will help us accomplish these goals.

Notes

1. David Orr reminds us that the "idea that place could be a significant educational tool was proposed by John Dewey in an 1897 essay" (127).

2. Citations to Cohen's "Blues in the Green" are from the version available on the *History Cooperative* Web site (www.historycooperative.org/journals/eh/9.1/Cohen.html), which has 108 paragraphs.

3. Paul Lindholdt comes to a similar conclusion in "Restoring Bioregions through Applied Composition." Yet some feminist critics, including Judy Fetterley and Marjorie Pryce, have dedicated much of their scholarship to redefining regionalism and recovering it from its historically marginalized position, especially in the work of American women writers.

4. David Sobel writes, "Desirable environmental education, or what we're calling place-based education, teaches about both the natural and built environments" (*Place-Based Education* 9).

5. The growth in books "integrating personal narrative and critical analysis . . . insists that field study is integral and essential to understanding literary and aesthetic representations of landscape." This growth also inaugurates "a trend that has generated more sophisticated techniques for teaching field studies courses" (Cohen, "Blues" par. 60). My *Teaching in the Field* contains sections on justifications for field teaching, the pedagogy of teaching outdoors, and practical considerations for taking students into the field. Waage's *Teaching Environmental Literature* also includes one of the earliest discussions of field teaching in the context of environmental literature courses.

6. For more on this topic, see B. Nelson, "Building Community on a Budget in the Big Bend of Texas."

7. Rosenberg cites Joseph Bruchac, who tells us that teachers should "begin any Native American literature course not in the classroom, but in the woods," to get a "sense of the American earth, of the land as people as one" (39).

8. Bergman's "The Literature and Experience of Nature" describes such an approach. In the context of two January trips, Bergman recounts trips to the North Woods of Minnesota, where students lived on-site in cabins; and to the Chiricahua Mountains of Arizona, where students stayed at a ranch.

9. Other programs using the base-camp model include the Summer Environmental Writing Program (SEWP), located in the coal fields of eastern Kentucky, discussed in Randall Roorda's essay in this collection; the Adirondack semester at Saint Lawrence University; and many others.

10. *Reading the Trail: Exploring the Literature and Natural History of the California Crest*, by Corey Lewis, is the latest work to discuss the nomadic model of teaching outdoors.

Cheryll Glotfelty

Finding Home in Nevada?
Teaching the Literature
of Place, on Location

In 1990, I drove a Ryder van from Ithaca, New York, to Reno, Nevada, with a head full of ideas and a heart full of yearning. After a childhood of family relocations and more than a decade of educationally necessitated itinerancy, I longed to sink roots and stay put. Few people imagine Nevada as Shangri-la, but I did. I needed it to be. Reno—The Biggest Little City in the World. My new home. Thank God for a job.

In graduate school, I had periodically strayed from course work to become self-tutored in deep ecology and literary ecology, absorbing works such as Bill Devall and George Session's *Deep Ecology* and Joseph Meeker's *The Comedy of Survival.* The bioregional notion of reinhabitation struck a powerful chord, providing a theory to validate my deepest desires to have a lasting home. To those of us who cannot claim to be native to anywhere but the road, reinhabitation offers the hope that it is possible to become native to a place. The process of reinhabiting a place entails learning the natural history, indigenous lifeways, and cultural traditions of a place and, in turn, actively participating in the continuous making of the place. As the eloquent bioregionalist Gary Snyder suggests, "find your place on the planet, dig in, and take responsibility from there" (*Turtle Island* 101). That's exactly what I aimed to do.

Wanting to learn the stories of my new place, I volunteered to teach a curiously titled, nearly defunct course moldering in the University of Nevada catalog, called Literature of the Far West and Nevada. Despite my green commitment to the Sagebrush State, I had not yet heard of any Nevada literature that would stack up to the best of the West; therefore, my first syllabus included no Nevada texts. Nevertheless, mindful of the "and Nevada" postscript in the course title, I asked students to find a Nevada book and report on it to the class. Their reports changed my life, setting the course of my research for the next decade and beyond. Not only did the books sound good, but the investment that students showed in discussing literature from *their* state revealed that the assignment had tapped a vital nerve and that Nevada readings were not just interesting but important to my students. The next time I offered the course, I taught exclusively Nevada texts, eventually proposing and teaching a new, interdisciplinary, capstone course called Nevada in Literature. The examples herein are drawn from this course, but the reflections on and strategies for teaching a place-based literature course apply to any region.

Although most of the course's required texts are not environmentalist per se, I believe that Nevada in Literature is at least as environmentally influential as my courses in environmental literature. Students who enroll in Environmental Literature tend to be environmentalists already, forcing me into the role of devil's advocate to show these young zealots that every issue is complex. In contrast, Nevada in Literature fills with a diverse mix of students whose viewpoints reflect those of the broader society. Urban students hear the perspective of rural students, and vice versa. Bartenders talk with backpackers, organic gardeners mingle with dirt bikers, and natives meet newcomers. In the process of considering place from so many angles, the place itself becomes intriguing, indeed, becomes visible. Sadly, all too often our professional and personal lives so monopolize our attention that we become oblivious to our surroundings, navigating through life by PDA.

In 1995 *Orion* magazine ran an issue on sense of place, whose editorial introduction well expresses my agenda. The introduction begins by referring to the quiz "Where You At?" by Jim Dodge and others that appeared years earlier. It contains about twenty questions designed to test readers' knowledge of their local bioregion. For example, "Describe the soil around your home" (Dodge et al. 22); "From where you are reading this, point north" (23); "Name five native edible plants in your bioregion and their season(s) of availability"; "Trace the water you drink from precipitation to tap"; "Where does your garbage go?" (22). *Orion's* introduction surmises that most people today would perform poorly on this test. We do not know where we live. *Orion's* editors speculate that because we lack knowledge of and attachment to the specific places where we live, we fail to defend these places when they are threatened. The consequences can be seen across America, in the form of "strip malls, toxic dumps, unlivable housing developments, poisoned farmlands, mountains razed for minerals, towering landfills, clearcuts and monocultured forests, [and] cities stripped of all things green" ("From the Editors"). The editors' introduction offers the hope that if we can relearn to form meaningful attachments to where we live, we will not only enrich and deepen our lives, curing a numbing sense of alienation, but also be more apt to defend these places from environmental degradation.

How then to reestablish a sense of place? How can we grow to love where we live with the fierceness and loyalty of our love for the people with whom we live? *Orion's* answer might surprise the average environmentalist. We can start not by diligently learning the answers to the bioregional quiz—not by acquiring knowledge and memorizing facts about a place—but, as the essay suggests, by understanding that attachments to places are fostered through stories. In the words of Wallace Stegner, "No place is a place until it has had a poet" (qtd. in "From the Editors"). Poets, storytellers, and writers do the important cultural—and environmental—work of transforming space into place, of investing the land with meaning, of encouraging people to form emotional attachments to place.

On the first day of class, I have students fill out a brief survey, telling me where they are from, where in Nevada they have lived, what their major is, and why they are taking the class. They then write a half-page answer to the question, How do you feel about Nevada? The survey rouses them out of that slump-seated, blank-stare lethargy that can deaden the first day of class, and it provides me with valuable information. Good teachers know not only what they teach but *whom* they teach. Thus, I call on my Las Vegas student to comment on representations of that city; I ask my student from the Philippines to share her first impressions of the desert; and I appeal to my geography student to help us interpret a relief map of basin-and-range topography.

The survey initiates a follow-up discussion of the unusual wording of the question itself. *Feel* about Nevada? What kind of a question is that! Are we not drilled in freshman composition to eliminate "feel" from our writing? We learn to revise the sentence "I feel that smoking marijuana should be legal" to the confident declaration, "Smoking marijuana should be legal." Feelings should be kept extracurricular, we intuit. It is this banishing of feelings from the classroom that makes some literature courses seem clinical, becoming, in the pejorative sense, academic. A book that made us cry at home becomes, to quote T. S. Eliot, "a patient etherized on a table" when the professor critically dissects this "text" in class. I invite feelings back to college. One of the highest virtues of good writing, I argue, is precisely that it evokes feelings. "Can literature change one's feelings toward a place?" I ask. We will find out. "You'll answer the same question—How do you feel about Nevada?—at the end of the semester," I tell them, "and then I'll hand back these first-day surveys so you can decide for yourself."

The first few assignments establish commitment and orient students. Homework for the first day asks them to read the brief *Orion* introduction and then to write a page that describes a place they love very much (not necessarily in Nevada) and to explain why they chose this place and what it means to them. Many students write about places associated with their childhood or, as one student observed, "places in time." It is comforting if these places are unchanging, a reliable touchstone for life. On the other hand, if the places have changed—have been burned, developed, or sold—students feel a painful sense of loss. In another common pattern, students have had to move away from the cherished home ground of their youth, and sometimes the sense of homesickness that attends this uprooting never goes away. Surprisingly, given that most of us spend much of our daily lives indoors, typically more than ninety percent of the places described are outdoors. No student has ever written that he or she could not think of a beloved place. The exercise reveals the strong connections between place and identity, awakens students' emotions, and teaches me about my class.

A second homework assignment helps prepare students for the readings to come. I ask them to think of a place in Nevada that they know well; to write one paragraph describing this place positively, in glowing terms rich with detail; and to then write a second paragraph that describes the very same place in heavily negative terms. Students may imagine different characters, from whose perspective the place is viewed. Usually I can tell which view the student holds, but sometimes both paragraphs are so convincing that I cannot discern the student's own standpoint. And, paradoxically, both paragraphs may seem true together, because places are complex and our responses to them may be ambivalent. We talk about how sometimes it takes a guide, a sympathetic interpreter, to help us appreciate places. A geologist can turn us on to roadcuts. A fly fisherman can help us pay attention to the swarm of insects that we were just about to swat away in irritation. A child can rekindle the fun of commonplace things under-foot—rocks; sticks; dandelions; pennies; and, if you are in a Nevada desert, sun-faded shotgun shells. Books, of course, can be our guides.

That beauty is in the eye of the beholder, that love of landscapes is an acquired taste—like a taste for wine or coffee—and that the right guides can help us live well in a place are helpful notions for setting up the first book in the course, which is *Earthtones: A Nevada Album*, a photo-essay collaboration between the essayist Ann Ronald and the photographer Stephen Trimble. Similarly attractive, coffee-table-format books of nature writing and landscape photography are available for most parts of the country. They make a good starting point for a class on place. Nevada's scenery has been so often maligned and regarded as a wasteland, and students generally have so little experience in wild places, that it is very helpful to expose them first to an accessible book that represents local natural areas in a positive light.

Beginning with rhapsody fortifies the class to venture into more hostile literary terrain. In the case of Nevada, most of the acclaimed writing about the state is caustic. Examples are legion. Mark Twain's *Roughing It* describes Nevada as "all one monotonous color" (177). John Muir depicts Nevada's mountains as presenting "a singularly barren aspect, appearing gray and forbidding and shadeless, like heaps of ashes dumped from the blazing sky" (*Steep Trails* 164). Hunter S. Thompson's *Fear and Loathing in Las Vegas* describes Circus-Circus as "what the whole hep world would be doing on Saturday night if the Nazis had won the war" (46). Bill Bryson opens his chapter on Las Vegas with a riddle: "What is the difference between Nevada and a toilet? Answer: You can flush a toilet" (244). He then proceeds to offer up grisly statistics on crime, rape, highway fatalities, gonorrhea, transients, and prostitutes that reinforce Nevada's national image as Sin State.

Such pessimistic accounts would seem to work against my goal of fostering a positive sense of place. One possible strategy would be to omit negative texts from the reading list, kicking the authors out of the canon, as it were, to expose students to the many lesser known but affirmative literary takes. But to value engineer the reading list in this way would fail to expose students to the most famous literary accounts of the state. I feel obligated, in other words, in the name of cultural literacy, to include these classic portrayals. So I do. To my surprise, far from being persuaded by these works that Nevada is a wasteland, my students usually rise up to defend Nevada against such attacks from the outside. They quite rightly resent that some acerbic wordsmiths possessing only a superficial knowledge of this place create the images that poison a whole nation's attitude toward Nevada. Why do outsiders' versions of Nevada sell and enjoy cultural power, whereas works written by Nevadans themselves rarely reach a national audience? We talk about literary economics and politics—who writes for what audience, how works get published and marketed, what effect writing has on actual places. Have so-called literary place bashers perpetuated such a negative stereotype of Nevada that America thinks it is OK to dump the entire nation's nuclear waste in our state? How is one to resist a continuing history of domestic colonialism? One way, as Ronald's *Earthtones* exemplifies, is to deploy alternative images. Fight back! Write back! Get counternarratives into the world! Create an audience! The insight that stories have political consequences provides a rationale for the writing assignments for the course.

Two major papers focus and structure our study. The first, due about a third of the way into the semester, is a creative paper about Nevada. I accept poetry, but class exercises are geared toward prose, either creative nonfiction or fiction. It may seem odd to have a creative paper due in a literature course, and my initial adoption of this assignment was happenstance. A donor established the James MacMillan Writing Contest years before I was hired, giving an annual $500 prize for the best student poetry or prose about the state of Nevada. Having juried this contest in years past, I knew how pitifully few entries are submitted. Aha! I thought, wouldn't it be inspiring to groom my Nevada in Literature students for the contest and later announce that a student in our class won the prize? To prepare students to meet the submission deadline, I assign a creative paper early in the semester. Therefore, I begin the course with contemporary literature—pieces that can serve as models for the students' own writing—instead of adopting the more typical chronological survey approach, that predictable plod from past to present. Luckily, this atypical ordering proves effective pedagogically. Beginning immediately with current writers engages the class swiftly. Once hooked, students start wondering who the earlier writers are, so, as if in answer to their inquiries, in the second half of the semester we explore Nevada's literary roots, reading some Native American and nineteenth-century authors.[1]

Thus the James MacMillan Writing Contest unwittingly shaped my class in two ways that I would now recommend to anyone teaching a literature-of-place course. First, begin with contemporary works. Second, include a creative writing assignment, preferably as the first paper. Writing creatively draws students out of their shells and into the course. Nevada literature gets personal immediately. By sharing these pieces in class, mutual interest in one another develops that creates a climate of respect and boldness when we discuss the later literary works and issues they raise. A creative writing assignment asks students to *be* Nevada writers and convinces them—and me—that they can be. I like to think that the next great Nevada novelist will be one of my former students.

The second major paper for the course is a combination of book review and biography. Students working alone or in pairs pick a Nevada book that is not assigned in the course. They read it and then write a review of it and a biographical profile of the author, including a photo of the author or another illustration. In the early years, I compiled the reports into a class book that I distributed to each student. Collaborating on a book creates a valuable sense of community, and most students produce better work when they know that their peers will read it. Because my own time and skills are so limited, I began delegating the book-making and cover design to students, which produced not only a better product but also a pedagogical benefit, since students took ownership of the project. Recently, I have had my students create the *Nevada Authors* Web site instead of making a book (www.scsr.nevada.edu/~glotfelt/nvauthors.html). Again, I enlist a couple of students to spearhead this project, excusing these webmasters from doing a book report themselves. A Web site saves photocopy money and paper, is available to the general public, and lends a degree of hipness to the assignment. Our class mission, then, expands grandly beyond sharing good books with one another to educating the world about Nevada literature. My current class will build on the Web site created by my first generation of students, choosing new authors and books. As the years go by, this Web site will become truly compendious, an impressive display of the literary riches of the Silver State. Most places have an extensive literary record, and our collective documentation of that record is like archaeology, with hidden bones and shards—stunning surprises—still waiting to be unearthed. The project is a nice way to end the semester since it culminates in student presentations, which not only save the instructor preparation time but also transfer authority in the end to the students, who become the teachers. The reports send us away with good ideas for further reading that will extend beyond the class.

It would be flattering if students took Nevada in Literature because they heard rave reviews of it, but, alas, day-one surveys show that the overwhelming number of students take the course because it fulfills a requirement for a general capstone. Therefore, practical advice for those wishing to develop similar courses is to make sure that your course fulfills a requirement, either for the major or for graduation. Running the course under the capstone rubric has proved ideal. Since all students at the University of Nevada, Reno, need to take a general capstone course in a department outside their major, Nevada in Literature fills with many majors, creating a fruitful mix of disciplinary perspectives. Moreover, the capstone curriculum guidelines mandating interdisciplinarity afford ample rationale for including films and field trips. These mixed-media and experiential approaches further my goals of helping students not just to know but to feel for our place. Another boon of teaching a course on the literature of one's place is that authors may be nearby and available for class visits. In the literature classes that I took in college, we lowly students read "great books" written by "masters," works so famous, so old, and so faraway that they seemed like documents from another world. In my class, though, the gulf between reader and writer, students and texts, is bridged, since students are writers, the texts are about our places, and we meet some of the authors. Presto! Literature is alive in our world.

Because my motivations are bioregional, I have often pondered why I gravitate toward a state-based rather than a bioregional course like, say, Literature of the Great Basin, whose contours would be set by the environment. I think the truest answer is that I want to. It has to do with desire, gut feeling, and personal identification rather than with theoretical consistency. I completely agree with bioregionalists that state boundaries are most often arbitrary, political artifacts, bearing little relation to the properties of the land—straight lines imposed, gridlike, on a rumpled terrain, dividing habitats, watersheds, and the territories of indigenous peoples. I agree that it would make more sense to start thinking and managing natural resources in terms of bioregions. But even as my head nods to these sensible arguments, my heart cleaves to "the great state of Nevada," a phrase one hears in political speeches—speaking of which, one could argue that precisely because state boundaries are political, the political process operates at the state level. Hence, it is beneficial to teach students the issues that affect their jurisdiction and to empower them to participate in local democracy. And while there is value in radically rethinking and dismantling institutions such as the state, one can also work effectively within the system, reinvesting the state with new meaning by taking an existing institution and making it personal. Teach the place that speaks to your heart, and you will find ways to justify the choice.

Given that most of my students had little initial interest in Nevada literature, the strong evaluations they wrote are heartening.[2] One confesses, "I loved this class. I've defended it and suggested it to many who have laughed at the concept of Nevada as having any 'real' literature." Besides noting that they improved their writing and ability to critically analyze literature, students said they developed a "sense of place, pride, and curiosity about Nevada"; that they gained "a better understanding of a state [they] used to loathe, but can now appreciate"; and that they "have learned to love Nevada." Another concluded, "This was an amazing class. I came in really disliking the state; however, I've seen some interesting thought-provoking things. I can honestly say this class has made a difference on my opinion of the state. Thank you." Literature *can* change students' feelings toward a place.

For me, Nevada in Literature is a renewable source of energy. It is the only course that I look forward to teaching over and over again. Offering it regularly allows me to experiment with different texts, feature recently released books, and meet new authors. Perhaps most meaningful, teaching this place-based literature course refreshes my own feelings for the place I now call home.

Notes

1. The course readings and films include, in order of appearance, *Earthtones: A Nevada Album*, by Ann Ronald, with photographs by Stephen Trimble; *Mountain City*, by Gregory Martin; *A Man in the Wheatfield*, by Robert Laxalt; *Desert Wood: An Anthology of Nevada Poets*, edited by Shaun T. Griffin; the films *Las Vegas, Viva Las Vegas*, and *Casino; The Lucky*, by H. Lee Barnes; *Fear and Loathing in Las Vegas: A Savage Journey to the Heart of the American Dream*, by Hunter S. Thompson; the film *The Misfits; Roughing It*, by Mark Twain; and *Life among the Piutes: Their Wrongs and Claims*, by Sarah Winnemucca Hopkins. Interspersed throughout the semester are scholarly essays from *East of Eden, West of Zion: Essays on Nevada*, edited by Wilbur S. Shepperson.

2. Quotations from student writing are used with permission.

John R. Harris

Teaching Place and Community History to Undergraduates

Locations are not fully places until we are able to reconcile and unify their natural and cultural features into a single coherent narrative. In my experience, that narrative expands from observations and sensory impressions to the scrutiny of genealogical records, agricultural census data, journal entries, and historical photographs—and ultimately to recollections of local elders who often serve as repositories of communal wisdom. Ideally, this process of reinhabitation involves relationships that are both incremental and reciprocal, for information gleaned in an archive or a casual conversation will often inform and alter the way one sees and responds to the land.[1]

Originally trained in nineteenth-century British and American literature, I began to explore the themes of place and community history by taking long walks through the woods of New Hampshire more than a decade ago. Motivated by works like Annie Dillard's *Pilgrim at Tinker Creek*, John Hanson Mitchell's *Ceremonial Time*, and John K. Terres's *From Laurel Hill to Siler's Bog*, I set out to learn something about the plants and animals in my own backyard. I followed stone walls up and over the hillside behind our home in Westmoreland, New Hampshire, and retraced old logging roads that disappeared into woods and wetlands. I learned to slow my pace, listened for the voices of the crow and jay, anticipated where the beaver would break the water's surface, and pieced together stories from footprints in soft mud or scat along the trail.

After a year of such sauntering, I assumed that I knew my nearby woods. Then, one afternoon, while returning from a pond that had become my latest object of study, I happened on a neighboring farmer who was a lifelong resident of the town. As we chatted about animals we each had recently seen, I asked him what he knew of the beaver pond a mile away.

"Locals call that place the Lord's Meadow," Linwood Burt replied, and then went on to share the following story: In the spring of 1741, five Massachusetts men set out on a flatbed raft up the Connecticut River, headed north from Deerfield. They followed the river's eastern bank until they reached the Great Meadow, where they came ashore at a site just north of Sheep's Rock. In addition to the implements they needed to settle, these men brought with them a single workhorse. However, sometime that summer, their horse escaped and disappeared into the old-growth forest east of the river. Later that autumn, after leaf fall, one of these men—I've always been told it was my great-great-great-great grandfather Joseph Burt—set out up and over Seventy Acre Hill to find his runaway horse. Several miles east of the river, he wandered from deep woods into an extensive hay meadow, where grasses took the place of trees. And there, along the meadow's edge, he discovered his runaway horse, relaxed and well fed. The man approached slowly, slipped a makeshift halter over the animal's neck, and led his horse back home. Before leaving, however, in acknowledgment of his great good fortune, he named that place the Lord's Meadow.

This remarkable tale, more than any empirical knowledge gained from my previous walks, fired my imagination about the stories of places I assumed I had known. As a result, I set out to investigate what had happened to that hay meadow, how those earliest settlers had fared, and why the stone walls I followed to this site disappeared beneath the water. The more I explored, the more this once-familiar landscape yielded new questions, and, in the end, these attempts to comprehend the Lord's Meadow transformed both the site and its interpreter. I began to understand how each seemingly insignificant artifact is layered with meaning and invested with memories of those who have come before.

In the case of the Lord's Meadow, that narrative begins with the earliest European contact with Native people in the area, an interaction that included the extirpation of the beaver to supply European fashion demands and the consequent subversion of the Abenaki economy before 1700. The story also includes New England's "sheep fever" craze, where subsistence farmers in the 1820s began to rely on imported merino sheep to reshape their relationships with the land. Stone fencing to contain these sheep and a dramatic increase in pasturage transformed the town of Westmoreland and the surrounding Monadnock region. Hay was cut to meet the winter needs of these foraging animals, and hay continued to be harvested from the Lord's Meadow until the 1970s, when, as a neighbor recalled, "the pasture became so wet that a hay wagon sunk to its axles."[2] Shortly thereafter, when the field was abandoned, a pair of beavers reappeared and began the process of flooding the meadow and reclaiming their original homesite.

In my desire to comprehend and articulate the story of this single parcel of land from multiple and at times seemingly contradictory perspectives, I discovered that I needed not only local sources of wisdom but also literary models for synthesizing natural and cultural history. In this regard I found the work of Robert Finch particularly helpful. Finch writes about Cape Cod, unquestionably one of New England's most complicated, storied, and endangered landscapes, and each of his essays brings together the subtleties of observation, the nuances of local ways of knowing, and a delicate balance between restraint and self-discovery:

> Every town needs a certain amount of unfixed history, an outback of the mind, just as it needs a certain amount of undesignated and unmapped hinterland. This is especially true for young people, who have such a strong need to discover things on their own. After all, isn't that what we all value most in our lives: those things about ourselves, our landscape, and our community that we have discovered, or re-discovered, on our own, rather than what we have been shown or presented with in some finished or "authentic" version? History, human and natural, must have room for mystery. (*Death* 131–32)

Self-discovery, humility, and making room for mystery are important lessons for today's technologically savvy undergraduates to learn. As such, relying on the joy I continue to experience while poking around my neighborhood, complemented by the rich archive of print materials and engaging conversations with local inhabitants, I began to envision an American studies offering at Franklin Pierce University. Franklin Pierce, a four-year liberal arts institution serving sixteen hundred undergraduates in rural Rindge, New Hampshire, is situated on twelve hundred acres of woods and wetlands. Four hiking trails offer access to most of these woods, although students tend to remain clumped near classroom buildings and manicured lawns nestled beside Pearly Pond, a kidney-shaped body of water that once functioned as a reservoir for a nearby gristmill. Franklin Pierce, which opened in 1964, is organized around a central quadrangle that features a restored inn and barn as well as modern classroom buildings and a library. The course I designed, Place, Community, and American Culture, relies on a lab-science format where students meet once a week for one hour to discuss ideas and then, in a second class meeting, spend two hours observing and interpreting out of doors. I sought the advice of my colleagues in environmental science to develop a structure for these outdoor excursions that would ensure student learning. Catherine Owen Koning was particularly helpful in this regard, suggesting that I devise a list of questions to help students focus and that I cap the class at fifteen students. In addition, because the emphasis of the course is experiential, and because we need to interpret subtle landscape clues, I proposed this 300-level course as a fall-semester offering.

I have taught the course on four occasions, and I begin each time by focusing students' attention on the oldest building on campus, a late-eighteenth-century farmhouse located near the university entrance. This structure is so familiar to students that it remains unseen, although it is situated only a few short steps from our classroom. I ask class participants to walk around the building silently several times and then to answer a series of questions designed to encourage them to look more closely and imagine the life of those who lived there in the past. What do you notice about the foundation of this building and about its windows, and what do you make of these observations? How do you imagine this structure was used in the past, and what evidence can you find nearby to support your speculations?

Careful observation of a complicated artifact like a building often generates a number of unanticipated questions and intriguing personal reflections. To accommodate this diversity of individual interest, I encourage students to meet in small groups before we come together as a class to share our insights. It is important that each class member has an opportunity to articulate and explain her or his observations and that others listen and process the explanation before challenging or offering alternative ways of seeing. I have found that most undergraduates like this process of learning to see: they are often shocked by how little they have noticed

beforehand, and at the same time they seem appreciative that our emphasis on the senses and direct experience "levels the field" compared with
more traditional academic strategies.

In their attempts to articulate their conclusions about this former
homesite and adjoining yard, students are also quick to recognize that
emotions and feelings are embedded in their observations. I reinforce this
impression, pointing out that a comprehensive understanding of any given
locale must necessarily include one's feelings as well as the observable facts.
Because traditional undergraduate instruction in the humanities and natural sciences often fails to give students sufficient opportunities to examine
their feelings about an object or concept, I nurture these expressions of
emotion early on by asking students to recall and write about places to
which they feel a special affinity. A place one regards as special, whether it
is a childhood memory or a recent site of deep attachment, leaves its mark
on each of us; and, as a result, students have little difficulty intuiting that
their semester-long study must come to terms with feelings as well as facts.
While students practice observing and articulating how they feel about
their observations during the first week, I also assign a series of outside
readings to provide a context for the work ahead.[3]

Following our preliminary investigation of the oldest house, an investigation that several students will likely continue to pursue in the weeks
ahead, we devote the next six classes to a comprehensive study of a single
wooded site on campus that includes cellar holes, stone walls, stumps, and
pasture trees. To make sense of these features, and to instruct students in
environmental history, I rely on *Reading the Forested Landscape*, a remarkable field guide by Tom Wessels, an ecologist at Antioch New England
Graduate School. Organized around different disturbance patterns, such
as cultivation and pasturage, fire, wind, and logging, the text offers specific and detailed clues for reading these events, as well as a concise history
summarizing their significance to central New England. Most class members, even those who have had little exposure to the natural world, enjoy
Wessels's sequential and detective-like analysis of landscape clues. For two
hours on three consecutive weeks we explore this ten-acre parcel of mixed
hardwoods bounded by stone walls and a dry creek bed. Each week I give
students a different set of guiding questions, questions that reinforce the
lessons Wessels has introduced. Students fan out across the site, making
their own decisions about what is important to record in their journals and
referring back to my questions when their own resources flag.[4] They count

whorls of tree limbs, interpret stone walls, check for the presence of barbed wire, and distinguish between hardwood and softwood tree stumps.

After each student has made sense of his or her observations, I distribute some relevant cultural history. In week one we study and discuss a detailed 1858 map of Rindge and a genealogy of the Symonds family, who occupied this site before 1900. We talk about maps, about the kind of information they convey, and about why it is important to construct a visual record of the sites one studies. The next week I distribute copies of the agricultural census records for this farm from 1850 through 1880, and we work together to interpret the data and explain the changes in crop selection and production values.[5] During week 3 a retired professor with more than thirty years of service to Franklin Pierce University stops by to share recollections of the old farmhouse that occupied the cellar hole, as well as memories of the nearby barn and sugarhouse. For a student like Jesse, an environmental-science major who grew up in rural Maine, learning to read a new set of cultural as well as natural-landscape clues dramatically enriched his conception of the New England landscape: "I now interpret stone walls where I used to pass by them, and when I encounter a new site, I ask myself who might have lived there, and what it might have looked like two generations ago."

Over the next three weeks we become familiar with three additional sites on campus. One, a forested parcel that was likely never plowed, requires students to grapple with Wessels's chapter "Pillows and Cradles" in order to read the complicated history of wind events and winter storms in the area. A second site includes one of the oldest cellar holes with adjoining well in the town of Rindge. This focus encourages students to explore the motivations and challenges of the earliest European settlers to populate the region. The final research site, located adjacent to a newly constructed athletic field, requires students to read the history of logging on campus and to reflect on current as well as past land-use practices. From this point forward, I encourage students to follow their inclinations and choose research paths that engage their individual interests and competencies. To illustrate the range of possible approaches for synthesizing landscape features and historical records, I ask students to read several additional selections by Finch.[6]

In addition to researching natural and cultural clues, students who enroll in Place, Community, and American Culture are encouraged to interact with members of the local community. The first community member I introduce to the class is Amy Raymond, the former director of the Rindge Historical Society, a lifelong inhabitant of town, and the last resident to occupy the oldest house on the Franklin Pierce campus. She is an active and generous individual, and students come to rely on her expertise for the remainder of the semester. I have noticed that each undergraduate is remarkably respectful of her age and work schedule, and participants go out of their way to acknowledge their appreciation for her assistance. Although Amy, like so many New Englanders, is unimpressed by ceremony, students are nonetheless deferential to her and to other community members they come to know during the semester. My hypothesis is that young people have few opportunities to engage their elders as resources and that both groups recognize at some level the importance of transmitting wisdom from one generation to the next. As one student noted, "This class was a fantastic way to learn the foundation of the land. Having contact with resources like Amy Raymond is the best way to learn about a community."

Our exploration of place also inculcates and models a number of skills and values that are essential for community participation. Students not only test their individual composition skills by articulating what they have discovered about one of the sites we have studied, they also work in groups of two to four to expand on their individual observations by designing a *PowerPoint* presentation that synthesizes and summarizes the research they have undertaken.[7] For students, learning to work cooperatively in order to research and present on various sites they elect to study is an integral component of the research process, since what one student discovers in the historical archives directly affects how another reads and interprets the land. Thus, the study of place creates a community of learners who recognize the importance of sharing hypotheses and synthesizing data with others to arrive at a broad understanding of a site they together have selected to research. Or as one student puts it, "the presentations on five different sites almost creates a little town of its own, complete with a history of local work and a record of how people supported one another." In their interactions with local residents, students also gain a better understanding of community service and civic commitment and a better appreciation for the reciprocal relation of nurture and need that exists between a small university and its surrounding community.

Once students have presented their research focused on a campus site, we expand our inquiry beyond campus to include parcels scattered throughout the nearby towns. One week we explore Converse Meadow, the site of an important pre-Revolutionary gristmill and sawmill in Rindge. Students read and reflect on the importance of waterpower in shaping community design across the Monadnock region. The following week we walk the railbed in Jaffrey and discuss how trains transformed the manufacturing and recreational components of the region's economy following the Civil War. In week three we visit Cheshire Place, a magnificent and short-lived economic utopia constructed in the 1890s by the eccentric entrepreneur Jones Warren Wilder, the marketing genius behind the Butterick dress-pattern company. The focus of week 4 is Cathedral of the Pines, a nondenominational religious site in Rindge dedicated as a memorial to Sanderson Sloane, a World War II pilot shot down and killed behind enemy lines in Germany. At each of these sites students sketch, take notes, answer questions, and attempt to integrate details of the place with larger social and cultural trends that shaped New England's past.

Near the close of the semester we expand beyond the Monadnock region and turn again to the words of Finch. I ask students to reflect on the personalities and stories they have encountered over the course of the semester and to consider whether any of these individuals or their recollections have begun to "haunt" them in a way that Finch describes: "they frequent my life, they inhabit my imagination and dwell there unbidden, like the melodies of old songs" (*Death* 127). We talk about how and why certain stories resonate in us and what we can do to cultivate this "haunting" in ourselves and others. We revisit the power of place-names like the Lord's Meadow, reconsider the sense of belonging that comes with participation in communal ways of knowing, and reacknowledge how local stories not only "change the way we see a familiar, present landscape, giving it a depth of layering in the mind's eye" but also add to our stores of empathy and preserve a sense of mystery (*Death* 127).

Learning to inhabit one's place, rather than merely residing there, provides an antidote to the forces of homogenization that are continually eroding our individuality and diminishing the distinctive attributes of our communities. Like any set of skills, however, the lessons of place require continual practice and are achieved only through accretion. To maintain our patience, we are obliged to spend time observing and listening; to replenish the well of empathy, we must interact frequently with diverse and unfamiliar points of view. Fortunately, the complement of skills that ground one in a specific locale is portable, and it is capable of being applied and nurtured in any region of the country where one makes the decision to put down roots. Ultimately, I hope that experiential, interdisciplinary courses like Place, Community, and American Culture will foster a change in outlook among young adults, a deepening of values akin to what Kristen, an American studies major from Rhode Island who confided at our first class meeting that she was more comfortable looking things up on the World Wide Web than setting foot outdoors, experienced. "As a result of this course my appreciation for history and my understanding of my role as citizen has changed dramatically. I now recognize that a large part of history is the effort made by individuals to shape or maintain or change their community. Quirky random details sometimes hold the most interesting clues, and stories are the things that make people, places, and towns unique."

Notes

1. Writers who have added significantly to my understanding of place include John Elder, Terry Tempest Williams, David W. Orr, and Scott Russell Sanders.

2. Mary Fredette, who gave me this information, lived in the house closest to the meadow for fifty years. She became an invaluable source of information about the site and town. All quotations from students and community members are used with permission.

3. These readings include "American Geographies," by Barry Lopez; the chapter "Place and Pedagogy," by David W. Orr (125–31); "Settling Down," by Scott Russell Sanders (*Staying Put* 97–121); and "White Mountain Snow Dissolved," by Jane Brox (54–76).

4. A hardcover, spiral-bound journal is essential for recording field observations. I encourage students to purchase a journal that includes both lined and unlined pages for writing and sketching.

5. Detailed agricultural and manufacturing census records were collected for each town in New Hampshire from 1850 through 1880. Students learn to read and interpret records like these as well as property deeds for each site they explore during the semester.

6. Finch essays I have had particular success with as models include "The Tactile Land" in *Outlands*; "God's Acre" and "Punkhorn" in *Primal Place*; and "The Once and Future Cape," "A Town Ghost," and "A Day of Roads" from *Death of a Hornet*.

7. *PowerPoint*, with its ability to display images and text on the same slide, provides an ideal presentation medium. I encourage students to include slides that highlight the primary materials and sources they have used.

J. Scott Bryson

Children of the Asphalt: Teaching the Nature of Los Angeles Literature

If we don't know where we are, we have little chance of knowing who we are. . . . If we confuse the time, *we confuse the* place; *and . . . when we confuse these we endanger our humanity, both physically and morally.*

—Ralph Ellison

What do you do when you are trying to teach students about the world around them and all they know about trees are the palms that line city streets and serve as holders for stapled bills and parking notices? when all they know about air quality is that the layer of smog they see from the 134 freeway cannot be too good for them? when all they know about the city's water supply are the Splash Mountain ride at Disneyland, the waterfall in the outfield of Angel Stadium, and the concreted Los Angeles River where John Travolta races in *Grease*? (Yes, in case you did not know it, *that* is the Los Angeles River, which in the late 1930s was "channelized" to control flooding.) When I arrived in Los Angeles in 2000 as a young academic whose primary research interest was nature poetry and ecocriticism, I immediately came to see that the nature-writing courses I had taught in Kentucky and Texas—to engaged and sometimes even excited undergraduates with camping and hiking backgrounds—were not going to play the same way to my new student population, composed mostly of first-generation college students, many of whom had grown up in the heart of downtown LA. Despite my attempts to help them see the humor and inspiration in the story of a seeker living near Walden Pond or the thrill of discovery experienced by a pilgrim exploring her world around Tinker Creek, it seemed that classic nature writing just did not resonate with my urban-oriented students. So, I came to realize that I needed a different approach as I sought to help them begin to connect with their environment.

At the same time, I wanted to begin to get to know my own new environment, my new place. As a native Texan who originally wanted to live anywhere but Southern California, I needed to introduce myself to a city I had quickly begun to appreciate more than I expected I would. And as a teacher of English who had been trained in literary analysis, books seemed one of the best vehicles to help me better understand my new surroundings. I thus set about reading and teaching what I now call Los Angeles literature. I titled the freshman English course I teach every semester Writing about Los Angeles Literature. We read classics like Raymond Chandler's *The Big Sleep*, Nathanael West's *Day of the Locust*, Chester Himes's *If He Hollers, Make Him Pay*, and John Fante's *Ask the Dust*. We also read more recent LA works like Bret Easton Ellis's *Less than Zero*, Walter Mosley's *Devil in a Blue Dress*, Luis Valdez's *Zoot Suit*, and Carolyn See's *Golden Days*. And thus the LA-literature project began, driven by the dual motivations of finding a way to introduce my students to the idea that they live in a place with which they can connect and of finding a way to connect with that place myself.

I soon began to see that the field of LA literature was only beginning to be examined as a body of work and that, by looking at it as a body, my students and I could actually offer a contribution to an emerging field of literature. Since they were for the most part freshmen and unprepared to share their findings in more sophisticated venues like academic conferences and journals, a Web site seemed the most logical place for us to present the knowledge we were acquiring. I enlisted the help of our Office of Informational Technology staff, who trained me in the basics of creating Web pages, and I was pleased to see that the mechanics of creating the Web site were surprisingly simple. The ultimate goal of the LA-literature project became to produce an exercise that would benefit my students, me, and the reading community. Having completed our first few pilot semesters, I am ready to say that it is doing just that.

The course has three primary goals for the students: to help them read closely with a focus on the role of place in literary texts; to help them improve their writing and rhetorical skills by having them address a particular audience with specific goals in mind; and to help them more fully connect with the history and personality of their own particular place, the city in which they live. To help them reach these goals, I ask students to read four short LA novels, write four essays, and work in groups to produce subsites devoted to the phenomenon of Los Angeles literature.

To understand the details of the course, it is helpful to have an idea about the makeup of the LA-literature Web site (www.msmc.la.edu/pages/1761.asp). Its main page contains introductory materials about LA literature and an explanation of the rationale behind the project. From this site visitors can link to a growing number of subsites—at this point twenty-one—created by groups made up of Mount St. Mary's freshmen and devoted to different Los Angeles texts. For instance, from our home page visitors can follow links to our subsites, which are devoted to all the books mentioned above, as well as to other less-known LA works like Yxta Maya Murray's *Locas*, Luis J. Rodriguez's *The Republic of East L.A.*, and Robert Crais's *L.A. Requiem*.

So that the entire Web site maintains a consistent feel, all twenty-one student subsites contain several of the same general components. One of these is a traditional secondary bibliography containing all the sources that offer analysis of that particular text. I explain to the students that some of them will face the problem of finding too much information, whereas some will meet the opposite obstacle, discovering that not as much has been written about their text. I do not assign a certain number of works that should be included in the bibliography; I require only that it be exhaustive. Then I often define the word *exhaustive*, explaining that I am not (only) describing how tired they should be, but that I am requiring that they provide every book review, journal article, interview, and book chapter that has been published about their book.

Also, student groups compile a list of helpful links to other Web sites about their particular author and text, including biographies of and interviews with the author; interpretations or reviews of the work; historical information that relates to the book; and anything else they can find on the Web. The students' goal for this part of the assignment is again to produce as exhaustive a list as possible, and each link is accompanied by a brief, one-sentence annotation.

The heart of the project is devoted to what we call a geographical reading of each particular text. Here students examine the place awareness on display in a work, keeping in mind that their audience is someone who lives in, say, Houston or Atlanta or Chicago and who is counting on the Web site to help him or her more fully experience the "LA-ness" of the novel. This element of the Web site is introduced by a few paragraphs' discussion of how much effort the author seems to have made at being geographically accurate. Then, students list significant references their book makes to LA landmarks, street names, buildings, neighborhoods, and so forth. Finally, they provide information and images that will prove useful to someone who is studying this book: actual locations of local businesses that are mentioned in the story, maps of routes that characters in the book take, digital and scanned pictures of landmarks around LA, quotes about the city.

In addition to all this, students provide a plot summary of the story and a brief biography of its author. I also ask for any additional materials relating to the text that a prospective student-scholar might find helpful. Past groups have provided, for instance, a glossary containing English translations of Spanish words and phrases used in a book; recommended reading of the author's other works; suggestions for what actors might play the characters were a movie to be made of the story; and frequently asked questions concerning the book, its author, and the LA community in which the story is set. And while I stress that each group will be graded primarily on the content it provides and how clearly it delivers it, students have consistently astounded me with the visual quality of their Web sites. As you might imagine, the act of choosing the artistic design of the individual sites turns out to be one of the favorite parts of the project.

Generally speaking, we spend the first two-thirds of the course discussing and writing about the texts we read and the last third creating the Web site. I am still tinkering with the course organization, but typically we begin the semester by reading two short novels. During that time we work on close reading and literary analysis, and we talk in detail about the concept of place while examining the ways that each author depicts Los Angeles. Then, having read the two texts, the students' first writing assignment is to produce a short (three-to-five-page) essay in which they compare characters from the first two novels we have read, again emphasizing the way characters interact with and respond to their environment. After completing their first paper, students then read and discuss two more novels over the next few weeks. They then write their next paper, this time responding to a literary critic or reviewer who has written about one of the course texts.

These activities occupy us through the first two-thirds of the course, meaning that in the first ten or so weeks, each student has read four LA novels and written two papers about them. While all of this is taking place, students are also preparing the different components of their Web sites. For example, while they read the first two novels of the semester, they are also preparing the list of Web links for their particular author and book. They complete this project with their word-processing software, so they do not have to worry at this point about placing it on the Web. I usually stagger the assignments so that the Web links are due a week or two before the first essay. They then compile the secondary bibliography and the plot summary while reading the second pair of novels. The first two-thirds of the semester is thus also spent compiling the bulk of the material that will be included in their Web sites.

The final third of the class is devoted to teaching the basics of Web writing, placing compiled information and images on the Web, and creating and publishing the geographical reading. Students also have two more essays due at the close of the semester: an introduction to their semester's-end writing portfolio and an in-class final.

There are still obstacles to overcome and goals to achieve. Some of these are minor and, at least as far as I can tell at this point, simply have to be accepted and lived with. For example, since students complete their first assignments for their Web sites early in the semester, some groups begin compiling information about a book they have not yet begun to read. Also, despite my attempt to stress the importance of place in terms of understanding ourselves, some students simply may not be developmentally prepared to grasp this connection in a meaningful way. (And I do not blame them for this; I did not get it as an eighteen-year-old either.) The biggest obstacle to avoid, in my opinion, is the temptation to let the virtual bells and whistles overshadow the basics of writing, rhetoric, and research. In theory, the course is more than capable of helping students in these areas, since it makes it easy to understand the importance of these fundamentals when creating a Web site. Students can see, for instance, why it is critical to write clearly and avoid distracting mechanical errors, to consider their audience, to do their homework and provide accurate and documented information. Still, though, as an instructor, I have to be sure that these fundamentals do not get lost as we discuss the importance of place and work with cool graphics to spice up a Web site.

The reason I continue to work on improving this project semester after semester, despite these potential roadblocks and the extra time and energy the course requires, is that it offers so many benefits to my students. In putting together the Web site, they improve their skills in close reading, writing, literary analysis, audience awareness, research (both traditional and contemporary), and critical thinking. If all goes as planned, they leave the course with a strong general knowledge of themes often explored in fiction about LA, as well as extensive specific knowledge about at least one text in particular. My hope is that this knowledge of texts will not remain strictly "academic" but will enter the personal realm and help students more fully interact with and know the strange and exciting city in which they live.

The site also offers much to its visitors. We are designing the pages with an eye toward an audience of what we are calling students-scholars. Each student page is dedicated to offering in-depth knowledge regarding a work of Los Angeles literature, and we envision the site as a good beginning place for someone researching, for example, a book like Karen Tei Yamashita's *Tropic of Orange* or Oscar Zeta Acosta's *Revolt of the Cockroach People*. However, the pages are also simply an attempt to help readers enjoy these books in ways otherwise unavailable. For instance, visitors to the pages dedicated to Joan Didion's *Play It As It Lays* will find a video-taped LA-freeway excursion that students put together so that viewers of their site could experience secondhand how Maria Wyeth, Didion's main character, spends much of her time in the novel. In the future, we will not only increase the number of LA texts but also branch out into other genres, examining plays, poetry, essays, and films, which will contribute to the understanding of LA literature and the city itself.

And, last, I personally reap a number of benefits. For one thing, I get to stay connected, if only tangentially, to my own nature-writing background, even though I am teaching in the heart of the second largest metropolitan area in the United States. On top of that, I get to spend my working hours reading books about and interacting with the environment I now inhabit, and, in so doing, getting to know it better. And I do all of this with the knowledge that I am challenging myself and my students to think in new ways—both in an academic sense and in a more grounded, place-based sense—about who they are and where they come from. So, in the end, I am hoping that the class can tip its hat to Ralph Ellison and help us all discover more about who we are by determining where we are.

Stacy Alaimo

The Trouble with Texts; or, Green Cultural Studies in Texas

Having spent the last ten years teaching multicultural literatures of the United States, searching for ways to defuse but not defang the political bite of the particularly volatile topics of race, gender, and sexuality, I was surprised by the relative "ease" of teaching environmental literatures. Since I teach in a region where environmental consciousness is as rare as snowfall, I was a little suspicious when students seemed to enjoy, even devour, writers from Henry David Thoreau to Terry Tempest Williams. Was nature a tamer topic, a refuge from the political morass of identity politics? Or could it be that the concept of nature is so firmly articulated to notions of the transcendent, the sublime, the enlightening that it has become, well, natural, to exult rather than to examine? And is the practice of exultation comfortably personal, rather than uncomfortably agonistic and political? A full discussion of these questions is beyond the scope of this essay; however, I would like to address what I see as a couple of key issues in environmental pedagogy by discussing the inclusion of a place-based natural/cultural studies analysis in environmental literature courses. The goal of such an assignment is to connect the literary landscapes with the material-discursive landscapes of cultural politics and everyday life and to encourage students to understand how both nature and culture interact to construct particular places.

Rationale

William Cronon, in his often-cited piece "The Trouble with Wilderness," argues that one problem with the wilderness ideal is that it may lead us to ignore or devalue the places we actually inhabit and encounter, since they do not measure up to the glorious ideal of the wilderness. As he puts it, his "principal objection to wilderness is that it may teach us to be dismissive or even contemptuous of such humble places and experiences" as the "wildness in our own backyards" (86). It is possible to extend Cronon's criticism in a pedagogical direction and to argue that the trouble with texts is that the experience of reading, of approaching what we call nature, solely within a literary, or linguistic, realm is that it becomes contained—an untouched wilderness existing within the confines of the course packet, to be discussed Tuesdays and Thursdays from 12:30 to 2:00. This nature, expressed in sumptuous poetry or delicious prose, effortlessly upstages the many, but probably compromised, natural-cultural landscapes that most of us inhabit. Here in the North Texas metroplex, where no soaring mountains or raging ocean announces its presence, only a disregarded river and miles and miles of highways and suburban sprawl, it is easy to discount the nature of the place. Since many students enter the classroom with the deeply rooted assumption that the safest approach to nature—especially in a course taught by an environmentalist instructor—is to idealize it, a wide gulf may develop between the imagined natures of the course and the actual places that the students inhabit.

Moreover, reading nature writing can take on the sense of a devotional practice, a mystification that obstructs a more open and critical intellectual, philosophical, aesthetic, and political analysis. Indeed, the inspiration that many people expect from nature writing may elevate nature (ironically, of course) into a transcendent, otherworldly, nonmaterial realm. Including the study of film and popular culture can help break a comfortable sense of containment that literary texts may unwittingly elicit. Car advertisements that mix spectacular landscapes with an ideology of machinic domination, monster movies that incite both desire for and aversion to their starring beasts,[1] and children's books and films that teach an embrace of only the most ridiculously anthropomorphic imaginings of nature all offer avenues of approach to the messy, complicated, ethically perplexing landscapes that shape our understanding and experiences of the more-than-human world. What texts, films, and popular-culture representations cannot do, however, is provide an immediate sense of "nature itself."

Although it is not possible to leave behind the discursive landscapes—from *Walden* to *Jaws*—that have shaped us, I would like to make an argument here for complementing the study of texts, films, and other representations with an analysis of an actual, physical place. For even while I think it is crucial to understand the myriad ways that the concept of nature has been culturally constructed and has served, historically and presently, as a potent site for political struggle, I also think it is crucial to understand nonhuman nature as an active, signifying presence rather than as plastic matter that is shaped (entirely) by cultural forces. Recognizing the sovereignty, difference, and agency of nature is crucial for environmental ethics as put forth by Val Plumwood, Donna Haraway, Carolyn Merchant, and Catriona Sandilands. Moreover, valuing the "wild" is at the root of environmental philosophy from Thoreau to Gary Snyder. Examining an actual place carves out a time and space in which students can regard the actions and incommensurate agencies of nonhuman creatures and natural forces. Even in and around places that are predominantly humanly made, such as houses or high-rises, one might consider the activities of birds, cockroaches, and other uninvited guests. Even as we recognize how ideology and expectation shape what we see, paying attention to an actual space may leave room to experience nature "itself." As Brian Massumi puts it, "What is nature 'in itself' if not the world's dynamic reserve of surprise?" (236).

Including a place-based natural/cultural studies analysis in an environmental literature course encourages students to analyze the natural-cultural world around them in such a way that they extend the various concepts, questions, and frameworks they have learned from their readings into an understanding of actual places. This unit hopes to bridge the disconnect between the pastoral ideals or wilderness fantasies of the literary realm and the real, lived spaces that the students encounter. This modest assignment that combines fieldwork with theory, an analysis of nature and an analysis of culture, may actually be asking undergraduates to do something that few scholars in ecocriticism and environmental philosophy have been able to do: to think through, simultaneously, how places, practices, and experiences are constructed by both human and more-than-human forces. The divide between those who would embrace theories of social construction and those who would refuse them seems unnecessary and unproductive at this point, given the theoretical work of Bruno Latour, Haraway, Andrew Pickering, Karen Barad, and others who map ways of understanding the interrelated cocreations of what were once called nature and culture.[2] The complicated arguments in science studies about these matters may well be too difficult for most undergraduates; however, the basic question is not. Yesterday, in fact, during the first day of class, a student raised his hand and asked me, "Are you talking about nature itself or about how humans represent nature?" The only response, it seems to me, is to reiterate a "both/and" position that is troubled by continual epistemological questioning. By analyzing an actual place, students can sort through ways of understanding something as both "nature itself" and as culturally constructed. While this may seem far too ambitious from a theoretical perspective, in actual practice it is rather commonsensical, since nearly any place the students choose to analyze would, in fact, be created by human and more-than-human forces.

Specifics: The Context and the Assignment

I have used this essay assignment in two courses, Nature in Literature, Theory, and Popular Culture and Nature in Film. The first course began with "traditions of American nature writing," which included Ralph Waldo Emerson, Thoreau, Edward Abbey, and Mary Austin and continued with Louise Erdrich's *Tracks* and the poetry of Snyder and Mary Oliver. We then discussed the "political natures" of Meridel Le Sueur, Susan Griffin, Ana Castillo, Evelyn C. White, bell hooks, Abbey, and Julia Butterfly Hill in which the concept of nature is embroiled not only in environmental politics but also in race, class, and gender inequalities. The assignment itself was preceded by a week devoted to "analyzing constructed spaces," which discussed cultural studies analyses of specific places and practices of looking, such as John Berger's "Why Look at Animals," Haraway's "Teddy Bear Patriarchy" (*Primate Visions* 26–58) and Valerie Kuletz's "Science Cities in the Desert."

The essay assignment asks students to experience and then critically analyze one specific place from several different perspectives, asking how the constructed place embodies particular conceptions of nature and how nature itself acts within that place.[3] Parks, arboretums, campgrounds, zoos, and aquariums are obvious choices for the assignment, but students could also study residential areas, a college campus, or a site downtown. One of my students last year, in fact, wrote a brilliant essay about pigeons in a downtown parking garage whose inhabitation and consequent defecation wreaked havoc upon hordes of business people who dashed and ducked in vain. He analyzed this comic scene in terms of the surprising agency and potency of urban natures (reminding me of the trickster-crows in Vizenor's *Bearheart*). This essay, in particular, demonstrated the potential for the assignment to engage students in perceiving the overlooked and undervalued "nature"—whether that be pigeons, insects, or weeds—that is always right here.

Students can also analyze their own reactions, expectations, and experiences and then reflect on how their encounters with a place parallel or diverge from those described by Thoreau, Austin, Abbey, T. Williams, or other authors they have read. A wildly funny model for this sort of examination is Tim Morris's "Grey Water Rafting," which juxtaposes enlightening and uplifting passages from classic nature writing with his own wretched experience of the great outdoors—surrounded by the lawn chairs, televisions, and "turkey deep fryers" of his neighboring Texas campers. One of the best student papers I received was written by an African American student who had never visited a park near her house (nor any other park) because of a profound fear that the park would be a racist territory. Taking Evelyn C. White as her inspiration, she bravely set out for her first walk in a park, writing an illuminating account of her reactions.

Crucially, the assignment asks students to examine how a particular place is constructed by multiple forces that are simultaneously natural and cultural. They may examine whether the place is physically constructed to embody particular definitions of nature or to shape the visitor's experience of nature. Berger's "Why Look at Animals" and Haraway's "Teddy Bear Patriarchy" provide excellent models for analyzing how built environments construct visual encounters. Depending on their site, students may conduct a small-scale ethnographic study, observing how people engage with nature and perhaps conducting interviews. Finally, students could research how the flow of money and power shapes particular places. One could discover, for example, that the reason why the Fort Worth Zoo contains an entire area devoted to praising the ranching and oil industries as the twin saviors of environmentalism is that people who made their fortunes in these enterprises donated large sums of money to the zoo. Analyzing a particular place using two or three of these methods would reveal the complicated interrelationships between "nature" and "culture" that shape the many environments we inhabit. Doing so would also enable students to make vital connections between environmental literature as an academic enterprise and the natural/cultural environments that they themselves inhabit. Experiencing and analyzing an actual place may make it more difficult for students to contain the idea of "nature" in a tidy, manageable, conceptual space.

Despite my rationale for the assignment and the preparatory readings, some of the papers were disappointingly predictable. Some students neglected both the cultural and natural complexities of a particular place and produced papers that followed a nature-essay formula in which merely stepping foot "in nature" results in immediate personal inspiration. The second time around, in the Nature and Film course, I have addressed this problem by including Cronon's anthology *Uncommon Ground* and by beginning the course with his essay, "The Trouble with Wilderness." I am also including more cultural studies analyses of particular places such as Jennifer Price's "Looking for Nature at the Mall," complemented by a unit on "Experiencing the More-Than-Human World," including an excerpt from David Abram's *Spell of the Sensuous*, which demonstrates the patient and deliberate practice of paying attention to nonhuman nature. Even though few of the readings—oddly enough—attend to both natural and cultural forces, students can learn from both models and then create ways of combining them. The readings can also be supplemented with a lecture and slide show on environmental art and architecture—human creations that account for and provide space for the presence and action of the more-than-human world.

Drawbacks and Difficulties

I would like to conclude by discussing some practical as well as theoretical and political difficulties that this unit creates. The most obvious obstacle to making this unit really work in the classroom is that the reading material and, especially, the essay assignment are quite difficult. It may confuse students to think through two paradigms within a single assignment, but that confusion could be rather productive because they could realize the limitations and benefits of different approaches. Also, most undergraduates do not have the political, cultural, historical, or ecological knowledge necessary for some aspects of the analysis. If this assignment were constructed as a research paper, however, the instructor could point students toward relevant sources. Moreover, the students could draw on knowledge and skills that they have acquired from other courses, probably those outside the English department.

Another caveat would be that to emphasize nature or nature/culture as place reaffirms the sense that nature is something out there, somewhere else, rather than always already inextricably here and now. A complement to this assignment would be to discuss the toxic bodies of environmental justice and environmental-health movements, which demonstrate that the flow of toxins, as well as nutrients, interconnect human corporeality and nonhuman nature. Another shortcoming of this approach to place is that it may emphasize nature as resource for recreation rather than nature as a site of work. Students could, of course, visit a logging area, factory, or farm, but few will probably choose these less-than-scenic sites. Instead, complementing the assignment with environmental justice texts (or field trips or service projects) that emphasize human labor as enmeshed in particular environments would help mitigate this shortcoming. John Elder's remarkable account of taking his class scything to better understand Robert Frost's poem "Mowing" illustrates the possibilities for students to experience human labor as inextricably connected with particular landscapes ("Poetry" [Armbruster and Wallace]).

Analyzing a particular place as both a natural and a cultural construction probably does not foster a sense of being inspired by nature. This way of experiencing a place may be disappointing to some students, especially when contrasted with the American tradition of nature writing in which experiencing nature results in (personal) revelation. From the instructor's standpoint, I must wonder whether the assignment is unproductively demystifying, especially when given at a university in a region that is nearly devoid of environmental consciousness. For students who are only just beginning to embrace an environmentalist stance, the cultural studies aspect of this assignment, which insists that even the most "wild" of places is, in part, culturally constructed, may be a bit deflating. The wilderness ideal, as an ideal, remains personally inspiring and politically potent—to deflate it without offering alternatives may abandon students in a quagmire of cynicism. Similarly, students who are only just beginning to develop a philosophical framework for valuing nature may be thrust into a mode of multifaceted critique that may be paralyzing. Furthermore, if the students live in a region that is not exactly environmentally friendly, they may be left with a hopeless sense that, as Bill McKibben would put it, there is no longer anything we could call nature left. However, the other half of the assignment—the analysis of the sometimes surprising agency of nature as well as the possibilities for the wild to arise in the most unlikely places—should complement and complicate the cultural analysis in a way that may well redefine "nature" but that will also reaffirm its significance.

Moreover, I would advocate an open discussion of these questions in class and the inclusion, near the end of the course, of positive actions and built environments, such as the protests of the tree sitters in the Pacific Northwest, the Audubon society's habitat program, and the "Lightning Raptor Roosts" of the artist Lynne Hull.[4] Even while acknowledging the importance of protecting particular areas from human incursion, we can imagine the possibilities for creating urban and suburban places that provide more-than-human, as well as human, habitats. This ethic of inhabiting complements the wilderness ideal and opens out the human into the larger-than-human world.[5] My hope is that the students emerge from the course with an environmental consciousness that is firmly grounded in social and political (as well as natural) realities. Such a foundation may foster an undaunted commitment to the complicated practice of living in an ethical manner in a less than ideal world.

Notes

1. See Alaimo, "Discomforting Creatures: Monstrous Natures in Recent Films," which argues that monster movies could be the single most important genre for ecocriticism and green cultural studies.

2. Dana Phillips has exacerbated this divide with his straw-man critique of social construction that targets something someone else heard Andrew Pickering say. Pickering's actual published work offers complex and nuanced approaches to many of the problems that Phillips identifies.

3. The strangeness of this assignment, from a humanities perspective, or even a cultural studies perspective, is that it asks students to attend to the actions of the nonhuman world. Field biologists are trained to do such things, but most English majors (or humanities faculty members) certainly are not. Michael Whitmore, in "When the Mirror Looks Back: Nature in the Scholarship of the Humanities," challenges us to consider "the consequence of allowing nature a role in the production of knowledge in the humanities." Incisively, he asks, "To what degree do we want to exclude, in advance, any appeals to nature in shaping either the artifacts we study in the humanities or the process by which we come to understand those artifacts?" (95). These sorts of questions—crucial, indeed, for ecocriticism—could be discussed in the classroom, along with the simple observation that the philosophical divide between "nature" and "culture" is instantiated by the disciplinary divide between the sciences and the humanities.

4. See Alaimo, "This Is about Pleasure," for more on Hull and other environmental artists and architects.

5. See Alaimo, "This Is about Pleasure."

Randall Roorda

Living as Equipment for Literature: The Summer Environmental Writing Program

This essay concerns a small program in environmental writing, broadly construed, that some colleagues and I have run for three summers so far, four weeks each summer, on site in the hills of eastern Kentucky. Many readers of this collection will take as granted the virtues of such a program—one that gets students and teachers outside, attending closely to their surroundings, making something of it. I take these virtues for granted myself; my impulses precede explanations. Even so, I'll venture some rationales for what we do: first a complaint about disciplinary formations in English, which approaches of this sort may address or at least circumvent; then an appeal to precedent, a comparison with a long-established, successful program of this type, featured in the earlier version of this collection. I'll proceed to description of particulars of our program, which may redeem these generalities.

Equipment for Literature

Years ago, in *Textual Power*, Robert Scholes analyzed the disciplinary structure of English in a way that, though convincing and influential, hasn't much budged the profession's prevailing ways. According to Scholes, English is structured by a binary divide between production and consumption of texts, with the upper hand granted to consumption. This divide is crossed by other binaries: between texts that are or are not "literature" and between perceived authenticity or its absence in texts produced or consumed. By this logic, English accords privilege to literary criticism—consumption of literature. Production of literature takes second place, with critics determining whether what's produced qualifies as literature and warrants consumption as such. What aspires to that state but falls short—mainly writing by students—comes under the imprimatur of "creative writing," what Scholes calls "pseudo-literature." Production of texts that don't qualify as literature—that is to say, "nonliterature"—rates lower than literary production, of course. Lowest of all is production of nonliterary texts by students in rhetorical situations that render those texts inauthentic: where occasions are stilted, audiences faked, and normal presumptions to inform or entertain ignored or feigned. Scholes deems this the production of "pseudo-non-literature," in English sited under "composition."[1]

What would teaching in English look like if these divides did not prevail? Those concerned with this situation—with ways this disciplinary logic dictates curricular choices and professional rewards through distinctions that are in some ways invidious—seek to undermine this structure by disputing the binaries: scrutinizing the grab bag of habits and rationales through which literature is roped off from other texts, disrupting the curricular divide by which textual consumption is sundered from production, refreshing the rhetorical situations in which student reading and writing take place. Such work has proceeded on a number of fronts for years, among professionals housed in all sectors of English yet dissatisfied with the rigidity and exclusivity of these categories. Yet the dispensation is so entrenched as to shrug off programmatic initiatives for change. After all, the persistence of "English" itself is imperiled if its structuring divides are undermined. If "literature" (as Todorov argues in *Genres in Discourse*) is seen as an inconsistent, insupportable category best supplanted by attention to genres and situations, English loses a key underpinning of its distinction from adjoining fields similarly concerned with production and consumption of texts. If in some sense all studies are textual studies, English persists mainly as the sector of education devoted to extending this sense.

An environmental perspective, loosely speaking, reinforces how "English" is compromised if elements of its constitutive logic lose force. For binary busting of the sort Scholes prescribes would amount to a sort of ecological holism, by which everything concerning texts and contexts is connected to everything else. If, as David Orr avers, "all education is environmental education" (90), education in English is not excepted and so not necessarily distinct. Yet this formula sits uneasily beside a view holding all studies to be textual studies, for an environmental perspective is necessarily extratextual, concerned with a world before, aside, and beyond written texts. Our term *environment* entitles circumstances transcending textuality, the environing or enveloping of self and society in a creation not tantamount to its versions. Yet the transcending itself is a terministic function—a retrieving or contriving of language adequate to the fullness of our experience and situation. This back-and-forthness of text and not-text is *mediation*: a reciprocity, a shuttling between world and language through experience, with (environmental) education the offering, structuring, and dramatizing of occasions for such. "English" in this scheme is just the name given to that end of the shuttle that swings us back toward text. If its end, as Scholes asserts, is to resist manipulation in a pervasively textual world (15–16), environmentally this is equivalent to asserting that its end is *adaptive*: the retrieving or contriving of language adequate to our circumstances, as manipulation, by definition, is not. The term *environment* entitles as well the recognition that our circumstances are troubled in pressing, extratextual ways—ways we *need* to adapt to.

Comprehended thus, the notion of "teaching environmental literature" shifts from the ready sense of classroom approaches to selected genres and texts, toward something more dynamic, concrete, and synoptic. It entails teaching in modes that are environmental (making occasions for mediation in experience), toward consonant (environmentalist) ends, through activities that situate instances of literature within environment as several among many elements of a discursive ecology, addressing tangible extratextual situations. Teaching *environmental* literature means putting literature, and with it English, in its place.

The title of this essay signals such an approach. It reverses a key formulation by Kenneth Burke, his notion of "literature as equipment for living."[2] Burke was an early proponent of what he termed a sociological approach to literature, one stressing its rhetorical functions and essential relations to and continuity with other aspects of textual, social, and biological existence. Reading this formula in reverse, I mean to stress the reciprocity of textual production and consumption in teaching that disputes English's suspect binaries. Living itself triggers and situates acts of reading and writing—mediation by text—from which "literature" in varied senses takes shape. Production and consumption are equally valued, intertwined, deemed symbiotic, so to speak.

Teaching from such precepts rarely fits within disciplinary forms in English or elsewhere. It is tough to record on the transcript. It spills over requirements for the major while mixing up categories of general education. It is not well accommodated through the university's spatial and temporal arrangements: too-large classes in comfortless, klieg-lit rooms, convening in lockstep schedule blocks. And so it takes place best as an exception, even evasion to the university's rule, through moves that literally distance its participants. In this sense, it depends on a form of pastoral—a motivated remove from habitual circumstances, which puts them in relief. This is a recognition forwarded by Walter Clark in both his essays in the first version of *Teaching Environmental Literature*—a precept informing the University of Michigan program he cofounded, the New England Literature Program, known as NELP.

The Precedent of NELP

NELP has been around for more than thirty years now, returning to life in late spring at lakeside summer camps in New Hampshire or Maine, a self-contained learning culture, with established ways, rituals, and stages, emerging from hibernation and reproducing itself annually—a pedagogical Brigadoon or spadefoot toad. I taught at NELP for one season (its nineteenth), in part under the tutelage of Walter Clark, though by 1992, the year I took part, he no longer directed but rather served as a long-term visitor and grey eminence to the group.[3] In my experience of the program and in conversations with Walter, I formed the ambition to start a similar program once circumstances allowed: impulse preceding explanation. Not just Walter's genial yet provocative presence and long-standing example helped generate this impulse; his essay on NELP in Waages's *Teaching Environmental Literature* has been a major underpinning of my thinking, explaining, and planning toward what's become the Summer Environmental Writing Program (SEWP). In several respects discussed in that essay, our program takes after his. All along, we've conceived of SEWP as a pastoral retreat, both idyll and trial, one meant to place the quotidian of campus and metropolis into altered perspective, affecting students' relations thereto. We've engaged in reading writers from the region *in* the region, believing that immersion in landscape affects relations to texts, though we have focused on regional writing less intensively than our predecessor. Though we distance ourselves from campus, we do operate as an offshoot of the university, not escapees from it—in ways perhaps more concentrated than NELP's, since we occupy a university facility, involve faculty members from more varied disciplines, and bear the university's reputation in travels through its home state. We grant credit in both content area and creative pursuit, separating these for convenience, as NELP does.[4] In these and more specific respects—the reliance on student journals, the role of spoken poetry, even the jaunty acronym, to name a few—we are Walter Clark's followers, aspiring to cultivate something like what he's made in largely the same terms.

Yet there are differences, the chief one stemming from what I've just mentioned: that literature of the region plays a less central role to our program than it does to NELP. This is so not just because Appalachia is less storied than New England in literary annals, with Kentucky's eastern coalfields hardly rivaling Amherst and Concord in prestige, influence, and sheer volume of work produced. This differential is a matter of historical and socioeconomic import, of course, a backdrop to regional writing we do explore. Our emphasis differs, further, because our take on "environment" differs from NELP's, is more particular and pronounced; because this is so, we don't have time. We dwell on environment in ways NELP does not. In my experience of NELP, "environment" was so implicit as to be nearly invisible—like air. The conviction, in effect, was that the student is environed in place and texts alike and would learn something telling yet ineffable thereby. Environment is pervasive but not featured. The year I participated, a single session I offered on tree identification (framed, naturally, in terms of poems and essays) was the closest our whole staff came to environmental education in the usual sense, that of imparting knowledge and experience of natural history. To the extent the word came up at all, it figured in casual remarks by Walter as to the fuzziness of its limits, the sense in which *all*, after all, is environment. At SEWP we do sometimes make an issue of the term as Clark did in such remarks as in his lead essay to the predecessor to this collection (Clark, "What"). We've even had Wendell Berry, a friend and visitor to our program, explain point blank why he feels the term is not useful. We do take a broad view of *environment* as inclusive of culture and community; this is crucial to our peregrinations in this much-ravaged region, in ways I'll discuss. But we are not much inclined to dwell on this key term's vagaries, the ways it may imply that the individual or community is surrounded or bounded rather than interpenetrated by natural phenomena. We are concerned rather that our students have opportunities to learn something about what *environment* signifies for those who make it their business, who carry its varied import through fieldwork and writing into the university and world at large: naturalists, ecologists, conservation biologists, activists, communicators. *Environment*, we feel, has a substantial, reasonably dependable valence in the culture at large: we tend to go with that.

Regional literature figures in but does not preoccupy us because *literature* is not our other key term. *Writing* is: we're SEWP, not SELP. Our guests from other disciplines do not make or evaluate literature, but they do write, as most academics do. Our visiting writers (Berry, Bobbie Ann Mason, Gurney Norman, and others) produce literature (so recognized by critics) but are interested in relations of natural and social environments; they don't run workshops but discuss with us how such relations figure in their work and life. In any one aspect or activity, our program is hardly original; yet in emphasizing writing at large against production-consumption divides, we tend to fall between types. We are not a "literature" program (neither is NELP, finally, despite its name), though we read and discuss poems, essays, and stories. We are not an environmental-education program per se: we are intensive but not systematic in our learning, tending to stress the latter word in *ecological literacy*. Though we work on writing, we are not a writing workshop in pastoral guise in the mold of Bread Loaf or a hundred other such ventures, where natural setting figures as bucolic milieu for aspiring writers absorbing glow and blows from their betters in workshop sessions, their writing only incidentally related to the place. We share features of these and other curricular models but are given over to none. If our curriculum bodes always to evanesce into cross-disciplinary ether, it's through writing in environment—the shuttling back toward text—that we cohere.

The Company of Scientists

I've said that we mostly accept the valence of this key term, the vowel in SEWP: environment. That valence, obviously, has much to do with science— the shuttling toward the extratextual—and a fair way to characterize much of what we do at SEWP would be this: we tag along after scientists. On our arrival at the Robinson Forest, we're met by a conservation biologist, John Cox, a frequent resident and researcher at the place and an activist for its protection from the strip-mining that mostly surrounds it and has claimed sections of it already. He leads us up a trail to a fire-lookout tower on a ridge top over the camp, stopping frequently to point out features of the place—birdcalls, ground plants, fungi, especially the profusion of trees, the glory of the mixed mesophytic forest, in succession from moist hollows to xeric heights. From the tower we survey the Cumberland Plateau, the waves of hills weathered out of rock sedimented from Carboniferous swamps and seas. We see the strip mines in the distance, dust rising. In the days following, we move about the forest in like manner, down pristine Clemons Fork with its riffles, plunges, and cobbles of sandstone and coal, up near-vertical slopes to caprocks in treetops where scarlet tanagers nest. We venture out to the mine sites, rising before dawn to watch elk herds ranging through "reclaimed" spaces before they bed down, learning firsthand what a particular travesty this is in ecological and rhetorical terms (of which more later). Our scientist escort is our native guide through our first several days. He is succeeded by others, whom our students have accompanied in copter tracking and netting elk calves, cage trapping and releasing flying squirrels, seining and identifying fish species in branch creeks, snare trapping and studying the bears now reoccupying Kentucky for the first time since the 1830s, and various less charismatic pursuits. Our scientist guides are only modestly compensated for their aid but are enthused to pitch in with a group of this size and type. We take after them, but these scientists take something from us as well, as we've seen when, for instance, we've had them take part in the collaborative circle poems (the *rengas*) we write on the caprocks. These researchers contribute cheerfully. I think there's something about scientists absorbed in environmental fieldwork that predisposes them to appreciate such expression, even if, professionally channeled as they (like we) are, they regard such activities as largely out of their realm. In our mingling, I wonder if we don't all, scientists and humanists alike, at least tacitly retrieve a sense that precedes our occupational choices and exposes them, in retrospect, as contingent: a sense that our methods do not subsume our identities, that any one of us might do any number of things. In our scientists we find the flip side of the remark attributed to a teacher of Henry David Thoreau's: that if Emerson had not got hold of him, he might have made a fine entomologist. Our visiting geologist might have been a poet had the cross beds in sediments not snared him.

Regional Survey

Our exploits with scientists and naturalists figure centrally in the sequence of readings, class sessions, and activities comprising our program curriculum— what we undertake as a group rather than on our own. The curriculum takes the imprimatur of Regional Survey—one of the two course titles under which academic credit is awarded. (The other, Projects in Environmental Writing, involves individual work and is discussed below.) Some readers may recognize the phrase as originating with Lewis Mumford and featured in the essay "Place and Pedagogy" in Orr's *Ecological Literacy*. Regional survey, Orr reports, entails "the intensive study of the local environment by specialists and by every member of the community," toward the end of promoting cross-disciplinary thinking and cooperation, reconciling facts and values, and investigating relations between nature and human society (128). This is a tall order but a fair account of what, in our limited way, we seek to model and pursue with our students.

The region we're surveying can be cast at various levels. First and foremost, it consists of the primary program site: the Robinson Forest, a university-owned forest-study tract in the hills of eastern Kentucky. Expansive enough to be marked and green-shaded on the Kentucky State Highway map, the Robinson Forest is Kentucky's largest remaining intact tract of mixed mesophytic forest: the most diverse forest type in North America, seedbed to the forests of the continent, with some thirty canopy species and scores of understory types. Since being left to the university as a lumberman's bequest in the 1920s, the forest has served primarily as an experimentation and training facility for the School of Agriculture, the site of its summer field programs in forestry and, more recently, natural-resource conservation. Rare for this region, the forest has been logged altogether just once, about eighty years ago—an event that left a measure of its topsoil and its species diversity fairly intact. Its steep wooded ridges drain into streams among the most pristine in the eastern United States. One of these, Clemons Fork, runs next to Camp Robinson, a Works Progress Administration–era compound of dining hall, classrooms, sawmill and workshop, and multibedroomed residence cabins sided in American chestnut, a once prevalent species now all but extirpated by an imported blight. The staff cabin's broad front porch serves as classroom for our compact group. The camp also features the office and home of the forest's manager, and the camp employs members of his family—a family resident in this hollow for well over two centuries, which set of relationships also figures in the character of the place. The life-forms, landforms, history, levels of moisture, shadow patterns, particularities, and impressions of this place constitute the core of our survey, our reason for being here. We have that rare experience, one most people never have and few of us will reprise, of staying put for a while in what is, for most intents and purposes, an intact ecosystem.

Yet the forest exists in relation and contrast to its surroundings, far from intact, which too are subject to our survey. In this region, what surrounds us is coal: King Coal, as geology, landform, history, economic motive, social force, ecological blight. Coal crops up on our first day, as scraped patches, dust plumes, machine noises, and stray explosions witnessed in the distance from the tower above camp. By our third day out, we are venturing to adjacent mine sites, gaining entrance past guards to view herds of elk, then lingering to creep in on the operations. We learn a great deal about forest ecology yet nearly as much about coal's extraction. Not just concrete aspects of the operation occupy us, though these are overwhelming: rubble-strewn plains and blast-spawned faux-Western plateaus; gigantic, literally awful machines, Cat-yellow trucks on ten-foot tires carting eighty tons of spoil, the dragline's shovel scoop dwarfing pickups beside it, itself diminutive in the pit it excavates. Rhetorical aspects are surveyed, too—are forced upon us, in fact. We learn what a fiction and fiasco strip mine "reclamation" is: how rubble gets bulldozed into a crude semblance of previous landforms; how "hollow fills," the heaping of blasted rock over former streambeds, are sanctioned by definition of streams as "periodic"; how "revegetation" consists of a spray mix of invasive exotics, selected for the capacity to take root without soil; how coal operators in cahoots with politicians routinely flout such meager regulations as nominally govern their exploits; how rationales for the devastation, besides that of naked profit, get propounded, including the ostensible need for more flat land in a country of ridges, suitable, for instance, for construction of golf courses and malls. (The secretary of energy, we were told, showed up for a "groundbreaking ceremony" at one—a notion that would be hilarious if it were not so horrific and corrupt.) We learn, naturally, that even strip jobs have ecology: that elk, opportunistic ungulates, find the living easier here than among the trees; that some birds, like the common yellowthroat, inhabit this place as they would not the forest it was. This ecology, though, is not the spurious version portrayed on the park-style interpretation sign mounted at a pond on a Star Fire Mine reclamation site, near step-up telescopes you might find at Niagara Falls—a sign depicting black bear and pink lady's slipper among species "you might find here." We learn, in sum, not just where but how coal lies. Few residents of Kentucky and this nation get to see this firsthand, to learn to what circumstances our appliances apply—what it means to plug anything in.[5]

In the sense that we in the Bluegrass share a geopolitical dispensation, some weather and tree species, and a larger watershed (the Kentucky River and tributaries) with this forest, while consuming electricity generated by the devastation of this place, we can be said to be studying the "local environment," as Orr says regional survey does. Yet *region*, of course, is a flexible term. Especially, relations between pastoral locale and homeplace are at issue: whether *region* encompasses both or construes them as poles, far removed. For NELP, pastoral entails a considerable remove: a student road trip from Ann Arbor to the northeast coast, two days of driving with an overnight at the Flying Dutchman Motel. Our group drives less than three hours from our campus in Lexington, yet we come to a place no less strange to most of us than is Maine to Michiganians. It's a place not unrelated to our own: the locals know the University of Kentucky, cheer its basketball squad, send their accomplished daughters and sons to us, losing many for good in so doing. Still, it's strange as Appalachia can be strange to outsiders, in topography, history, and language: a place that's long tended to insiderness for its inhabitants. The specific isolation of the camp and forest; the prevailing isolation of the ridge-and-hollow landscape, so steep that, until recent decades, creek beds doubled as roads; the impoverished aspect of the built landscape, palpable in what the Appalachian writer Gurney Norman teaches us to see as the "texture" of its makeshiftedness, dilapidation, and abandonment—all this makes a near locale a distant one to us, and our program, as I like to say, a domestic form of study abroad. Our survey takes stock of this in deliberate ways, not just in wanderings with Gurney through back roads and his home town of Hazard but in sessions with visiting faculty members from sociology and communications and through visits to Appalshop in Whitesburg, the media-arts workshop that serves as voice, cultural conservator, and documentary mirror to the region. We ponder the vagaries of being a "stranger with a camera," in the phrase that entitles the acclaimed Appalshop film by Elizabeth Barret, who has showed us around the shop and visited us at the forest: we consider what this means for the stranger with a pen.

Projects and Genres in Environmental Writing

For these elements of our shared curriculum give way to the pen at last, as students are called upon to write projects from their experience—to make literature with the equipment of living. Our program is not divided, exactly, but sketches a trajectory between activities associated with these. Early on, we emphasize direct experience, mediated through the perception of expert guides, inscribed and transmuted through journals—something to write about and with. Though group activities and excursions continue, our emphasis turns increasingly toward individual projects. The informal apogee between these arcs of living and literature is our major outing, a three-day canoe trip on the Big South Fork of the Cumberland River, occurring roughly at the program's midpoint. On our return, we are turning—both inward, in consideration of projects we might devise, and outward, from writing as participation in place toward writing as publication, to be disseminated and read. Working writers rather than scientists tend to appear as guests. We start up workshop groups, allied loosely by genre or emphasis, to respond to drafts. During the last several days, outside visits have ceased, class sessions on readings have been pared to a handful of poems. The computer room is occupied late into the night: coal into electricity into words.

The trials and accomplishments our students experience in creating their projects are concentrated instances of what Kenneth Burke says about literature as barometer or bellwether for situation. What mode or genre of response will precipitate from and suffice for what they've been through, what they wish to impart? How, if at all, will their fresh learning inform their work? How might impressions of all sorts—of caprocks on ridge tops, torso-sized magnolia leaves, the cemetery a strip job blasted around and left aloft on a remnant hill, the turbulence of rapids on a stretch of the Big South Fork, the herbal-musk smell of a bear and texture of its paws—find a place in or impinge on their words? Where are representative anecdotes, expressive forms, commensurate with this welter of experience?

From the start we insist that all fields and genres of writing are welcome in our program; we are adamantly nondirective about what *environmental writing* can mean and what shapes the projects might take. By environmental writing, we mean something like what Lawrence Buell does in preferring the term *environmental literature* to the more circumscribed *nature writing* for texts representing relations with the natural world (*Environmental Imagination* 429)—only with the notion of "literature"

itself set aside, to stress the range of discourses and disciplinary formations by which such relations may be represented. In course readings we
sample many such formations—belletristic, informational, polemical, meditative, hybrid—and we are open to them all in projects as well. We ask only
that students draw on and enact their experience of the place somehow.
Students respond variously to this invitation and charge, refracting their
experience and concerns in different genres and approaches. After three
seasons, student projects have fallen fairly evenly into three types—poem
sequences, essays, and short stories. It's inevitable and desirable that students should work in these genres, ones compact and manageable enough
to be credibly accomplished during our program's brief span (four weeks
at the forest, plus the week after we leave). Still, we await students who
will take us up on the invitation to embark on projects more extensive than
they can finish in this span: ones they can rough out and start composing
for the program grade but that will call them forth into further research
and back to the region for realization.

On our last full day at the forest, our students give presentations on
their projects, each speaking about and reading from their work for twenty
minutes or so. They present not just to our group but to a small audience of returning program visitors—mostly scientists who've helped them
understand and give words to the place now reflected in their texts. To
me, SEWP has been worth cooking up for the novelty alone of witnessing
students of English read poems to foresters—and foresters responding in
appreciative and detailed ways. Where else in academia would you see this?
A representative anecdote indeed.

Idylls and Trials

SEWP is an idyll, to be sure. Four weeks in primeval woods; hiking, wad-
ing, canoeing; class on a porch; kicking back in cabins and at fireside with
fun peers who become friends instantly; time and encouragement to write:
our program exerts these forms of appeal, which go far to account for the
enthusiasm and allegiance it arouses among participants. As with NELP,
whose enrollees become "Nelpers" in a nonce, an identity and panache
for our program starts coalescing right away, as if precipitating from the
mixture of students with place: our students turn quickly to "Sewpers,"
while our acronym crops up finger-scrawled in creek sand and in road dust
on our long blue van. SEWP is like summer camp, with Thoreauvian "fine

baskets" the weaving we pursue. Summer camp, I think, would make a fine model for a university, could one be devised to accommodate twenty thousand students.

That it can't be is a chief difficulty of this approach. Our program is small: *too* small at present, with students outnumbered by visiting teachers, yet *necessarily* small, its potential enrollment circumscribed by facilities at the camp, seats in the vehicles, square feet on our front-porch classroom and the table rock topping the ridge above camp. Enrolling in such a program involves some hardships but is still a sort of luxury; in this respect, too, it's like study abroad. Unless buttressed with outside funding (as ours has been in its formative stage), the program involves additional expense for students, not because it's wasteful (our life in camp is less so than habitual life in town, even factoring in vehicle travel) but because it's an exception. Proceeding by exceptions is essential, by exclusions less so: as grant funds dwindle and our fee goes up, our students, like NELP's, will tend increasingly to be not just white but also well-heeled. In defense, it can be said that an inability to offer opportunities for all is no argument against their being offered at all. It can be noted, too, that besides transforming student participants, programs like ours affect participating teachers as well—with effects from both rippling outward, at least mildly, into larger circles and spheres.

Idyll entails trials of curricular sorts as well. Just as my appeal to experience as recourse to disciplinary ills is romantic and pragmatic in essence, so our curricular precepts and practices are romantic (like environmental literature at large).[6] Attendant on this is a certain tension between experiential abandon and intellectual rigor, intuition and reason, feeling and thought, the instant and its retrospection, surprise and direction. It's a tension we reenact daily, in class sessions on readings, in assignments and prompts, in use and scheduling of time, in course expectations and evaluation. We prefer to stay open, let things happen, give students their heads, acknowledge and credit what doesn't get measured or even inscribed. Yet we get concerned that our methods are not rigorous enough, that student learning is not sufficiently consolidated and secured, that contemplation of relations between reading and experience is sporadic and stray, that the major artifacts of our course—the project, plus journal and cover essay for the survey—will seem meager in comparison with a semester's output on campus. Though our students attest that they find the program intellectually as well as experientially challenging, we are not settled in these respects and continue to look especially for ways to tease out further a dialectic between reading and experience. All the same, we will err toward indirection and autonomy, if err we must.

There are further trials, in group dynamics, student exuberances and excesses, disposition of booked and free time, and the like, worth contemplating but predictable enough. I'll conclude with the trial of conclusion: leaving the forest and program. This is tough: in four weeks we get so acclimated that it's hard to conceive of leaving behind even our difficulties, let alone our friends and the feel of these hills. ("I shall not leave these prisoning hills," begins James Still's fine poem "Heritage" [82]; he never did, yet we must.) One student likened her withdrawal to the bends: the sickness of surfacing after having been immersed in something deep. To fend off the bends, one surfaces in stages: a process NELP is accomplished at, one we in SEWP are still feeling through. A measure we've sometimes adopted is to stop at the tourist attraction Natural Bridge on our trip home. We get the hills, rocks, and prospects with urban accoutrements thrown back in: a parking lot you could land a jet on; novelty-shirted families and scout troops at the summit; big-screen in the chilled lounge by the lodge's gift-shop door. We gape and gasp. Soon we're back at our campus parking lot, packs tossed on the lawn. Cell phones get signals again. We drift off in our several directions. In weeks and months to come, we will all, students and teachers, see what this idyll has come to—what this so-called English has equipped us for.

Notes

I'd like to acknowledge the indispensable contributions of SEWP's codirectors: Erik Reece, my colleague in the English department at the University of Kentucky and my collaborator and coteacher for the program's full duration; and Phil Crowley, professor of biology and former research director for the University of Kentucky's Tracy Farmer Center for the Environment, frequent visitor and participant as well as prime mover in SEWP's origins, whose impetus and encouragement got us off the dime. Our thanks go to these guest teachers, writers, and guides: Wendell Berry, Bobbie Ann Mason, David Orr, Gurney Norman, and James Baker Hall; the conservation biologists Dave Maehr (also a neighbor and friend), John Cox, Mike Orlando, Hanna Harris, and Dave Unger; Jim Krupa, Rob Paratley, and Bill Bryant (naturalists); Michael Handke, geologist; Chike Anyaegbunum (communications researcher and "professional stranger"); the environmental activist, writer, editor, geographer and caver Hilary Lambert; Roger Brucker (writer and caver extraordinaire); Shauna Scott, sociologist; and Greg Howard (administrator) as well as Elizabeth Barret and Robert Salyer (filmmakers) of Appalshop. Profuse thanks to former SEWP student and program assistant Jess Miller, who orchestrated our move to preparing our own meals in ways as local and conscionable as possible; also to grad student and program associate Leah Bayens, who helped with kitchen arrangements, class sessions, a workshop group, and myriad intangibles.

We thank the Department of English at the University of Kentucky for sponsorship of SEWP. We are deeply grateful for grant support from the National Endowment for the Humanities and the Honorable Order of Kentucky Colonels.

1. See Scholes 1-17 for this discussion.

2. Burke's essay by this title sets forth his view of literature as *"strategies* for dealing with *situations"* (296), to be propounded by a "sociological criticism" meant to "codify" those strategies (301).

3. So too did Alan Howes, Clark's colleague in English at Michigan and NELP's cofounder.

4. These features are discussed in Clark's essay "The New England Literature Program."

5. Many more in the region and nation have been instructed in the devastations of mountaintop removal through writings by my SEWP coteacher Erik Reece: his article in *Harper's* and his subsequent book *Lost Mountain* focus on the destruction of a single mountain—Lost Mountain—in proximity to the Robinson Forest. Reece formulated and started work on this undertaking during SEWP's first season. His writings have been key in catalyzing resistance by other Kentucky writers to the depredations of mountaintop removal—efforts orchestrated by Berry in much-publicized visitations to mine sites he's instituted for writers and disseminated in *Missing Mountains,* a collection of writings by participants in these events, edited by Kristin Johannsen, Bobbie Ann Mason, and Mary Ann Taylor-Hall.

6. This coinage and discussion thereof is from Roskelly and Ronald, *Reason to Believe.*

Bob Henderson

Experientially Teaching Canadian Travel Literature on the Trail and in the Classroom

The pleasantest of all diversions is to sit alone under the lamp, a book spread out before you, and to make friends with people of a distant past you have never known.

—The Tsurezuregusa of Kenkô

I am fond of the expression I first heard from Peter Seeger in speaking of his fellow folk songwriter Woody Guthrie; "Any damn fool can get complicated, but it takes genius to attain simplicity" (qtd. in Haslam 722). Thinking of teaching generally, the "simplest" determinants of success are twofold: firstly, you must love people, and secondly, you must love your subject. This is not complicated. For the purposes of this paper, I complicate that just a little bit. Firstly, you must love engaging people experientially in the nature and manner of the inquiry in question, and secondly, you must love your subject—must, in other words, build a relationship such that the subject and students and you are stretched to move beyond the facts and details to the broader inquiry out to where their world is. That still sounds simple enough.

I teach Outdoor Education and Environmental Inquiry to senior students in a Canadian university kinesiology program and in an arts-and-science degree program. All courses involve field experience to complement the direct classroom time and assignments. I will consider here two courses with extended field-trip experience: a summer nine-day canoe-travel course (roughly forty students break up into five groups) and a winter travel course of seven days for one large group of twelve to eighteen. It is hard to teach outdoor education in the classroom and best to teach travel literature on the trail. These points proved to win over a predominantly bioscience faculty that was initially reluctant.

Small-group travel experiences by canoe and snowshoe inevitably involve learning in four basic components: some technical skills (travel mode and camping), social skills, self-awareness, and place-based education. In outdoor education, place-based education is most easily neglected, though I, for one, believe it is equally important. Once the technical, social, and self-awareness aspects settle into place (more or less a given to my mind in a well-run travel experience), one can attend to place-based curricular aspects. Where are we? Who has been here before us? How did they live and travel? How has this place been perceived and understood imaginatively through time in the written word and as oral storytelling? Students begin to open up to literature, folklore, history, anthropology, archaeology, and geography not so much as subjects but as lived experiences. Their world becomes a bigger place in time and space. Sparking their imagination is a healthy part of all this. Mostly we explore travel literature by telling stories on the trail and around campfires.

Our place for travel and inquiry is the North Woods regions of Ontario, Temagami, and Algonquin in the Canadian Shield. This place, the North Woods of the Canadian Shield, encompasses close to three-quarters of the Canadian landscape. This means you can, at times, be specific to Temagami or Algonquin and also address stories of summer canoe travel and winter-snowshoe and dog-team travel for a large part of Canada as a whole. I will always remember the moment on the last day of the trip when a student who had mostly known urban environments in Canada commented from the canoe something like "so this is what it looks like, most of the blue and green on all the maps of Canada look mostly like this. Wow!" Now that is something to learn and a necessary precursor to any study of Canadian literature and of heritage study generally.

What follows are curricular ideas for courses from the trail and classroom that distill an awareness of a self-propelled traveler's place in Canadian travel heritage. For most students a new literary genre is being introduced, travel literature. To this literature, they add their own stories of travels on the trail.

Peppering the Trail with Heritage

> I enjoyed the numerous readings. I felt that they gave a sense of Canadian tradition. The stories were a good reminder of who came before us. Stopping to see the pictographs and the axe markings on trees at portages [blazes] gave us a good visual of the same idea. It was interesting to learn about the places we were visiting instead of just passing through. We didn't pass by just another lake anymore. The places became unique. They became real places with history that others had discovered before us, that they had built up and that they experienced. (Angelina)[1]

On the trail we are living out time-honored traditions. Once over that particularly tough portage with canoes and all our gear we glow in the satisfaction of purposeful work well done as a group. We read from P. G. Downes's *Sleeping Island* as a source of inspiration before we head out on the portage (136–38). If the portage is the trip's longest or farthest or crosses a height of land, extra (really the only) rations of rum (a thimble full) are given out once the portage is finished with an acknowledgment that the crossing is a "watershed" moment. This setting of inspiration using the journals of a previous explorer and the reward at the end (the extra rations of rum draw on the practice of the Canadian voyageur heritage) are part of a long tradition. Why not make the tradition specific? Call it "great Canadian tradition number 268." Help make students feel the extra satisfaction, as if finishing the long portage was not enough, of being connected through time to historical precursors. The rum rations involve a ceremony that refers back to the Downes reading. It is a special moment in time and through time.

Later we will draw warmth from our campfire and read how Peter Browning, in *The Last Wilderness*, felt when experiencing this sensation (26). His words about the primal security of fire may bring articulation to one's thoughts or may expand one's understanding and lead to a reflection on such differences as the warmth of a group by the fire compared with the hearth or the warmth and related dynamic of one's central-air heating back home. Browning's campfire passage may connect to a thousand fires at this spot or throughout the North. I might tell the story of arriving at the end of a remote Labrador portage and wondering if a friend left the neatly stacked firewood about ten years earlier—a fair question in that remote corner of Canada. "It looked like his style," I might say—and, yes, there is a style to enacting this story of travel through time such that past travelers inform the present with the ways (great Canadian traditions) of the North Woods. We, fellow travel guides and I, prepare travel-literature readings for the first campfire, for starting out, for the last portage of the trip, for canoe sailing, for exploring not only body versus mechanical time but also ways of being with time on the trail, for meeting spirits of the land, and for visiting native pictographs (rock art) sites. It is a healthy list.

We pepper the trail with readings and stories. Stories include those about explorers who, not having the benefit of maps, climbed hills from the lake shoreline to see the next day's passage through the maze of bays and islands; those from the Ojibwe about going bushed, or going wendigo, in the winter woods and of becoming a cannibalistic monster; and those about loggers and trappers. One favorite story concerns Peter Freuchen becoming encased in snow after rolling his winter sled as shelter against a storm in the open Arctic barrens. His mistake was leaving his knife outside the sled. His solution, once encased, was to fashion a dagger out of his frozen excrement for digging (by the by, this didn't work). In the end he sacrificed a few fingers (407–11).

We pepper the trail with ceremony and ritual throughout the trail: leaving an offering at a pictograph site, sharing a reading about a pictograph from Louise Erdrich's *Books and Island in Ojibwe Country* (16), taking a break from paddling on the water and having a pipe break (we use licorice pipes), holding story circles around the campfire. The point here is that history is seamlessly woven into the fabric of the travel experience. It is never forced and is mostly shared with the moment of activity: students learn about the First Nations' presence on the land and about exploration history and pioneering trapping, logging, and farming efforts. These are not comprehensive lessons taught on the trail but romantic insights. Detail can follow students to the classroom or into later life.

My hope is that students will follow up on a story (or two) told on the trail, drawing lessons from the story broader than those they initially garnered and making generalizations to life themes. If they can accomplish this, Alfred North Whitehead's rhythms of education are neatly followed (17–21). As educator and travel guide, I may or may not see all these stages of romance, precision, and generalization through to completion. With such experiential learning, the educator cannot be accountable for all that is learned.

Wayne Franklin notes that early American writers

> often turned to writing with an urgency, which suggests that it was a means of self-understanding, an essential way of shaping their lives after the facts. They seem too, to have been painfully aware of the many problems which language proposed for people separated as they were from their own world. (2)

Students are required to keep a trip journal. Staff members keep one too. Reflective, factual—it can take whatever shape they like. This work is not graded for quality or quantity. The act of turning to writing is meant to again connect with "great Canadian tradition number 141" and to allow the writer, in the process, to become aware of the problems that language poses in recording the newness of life experience. Here are two different student journal excerpts:

> So yeah, I am commando in my New Balance navy shorts that did not see the light today (seeing how we're camping in friggin' Antarctica), and my Nike wind pants that are not only navy and light blue, but also carry that "never been washed" (seriously in the last week) permanent dirt from top to bottom . . . now seeing as I have been away from camp now for about, heck, who knows, I'm telling time by the flippin' sun for goodness sakes! . . . (Carly)

> True beauty, true happiness and true comfort for me is feeling like I can live in the moment, breath fresh air, see nature's beautiful gifts of animals, plants, trees, rock waterfalls and feel my body alive as part of something greater. I know I can't stay here forever but I want to take with me this feeling of being alive. Truly knowing that my body is strong and healthy, and is not just something to feed, dress up in a way that others will find attractive and trendy, and to complain about. I feel a connection to myself (my soul?) out here that I have honestly never felt before. . . . Although I have yet to look in a mirror I am wearing a new glow, sparked by this fresh connection with the earth, nature, living things and people that polluted, rushed, obnoxious city living had all but taken over. Knowing now that true beauty is not the renovated face of "The Swan's" winner, but the way a tree stands for hundreds of years and wears its scars with pride. For me true beauty is in the way nature has so many treasures that are so fleeting they compel everyone to stop and stare. (Jess)

For many students, like the David Thompsons of the Canadian Northwest or Henry David Thoreau in his Maine Woods, there is an urgency to their writing, not for grades but for self-expression as a means of heightened self-understanding. But failing this urgency, it is hoped, all students capture that imaginative spark of feeling part of the long tradition of the field of travel writing. My fellow educator Andrew Wingfield captures the imaginative spark poetically: "Through their writing, students jump into a conversation that began in the fifteenth century. They can't simply eavesdrop from the margins" (192).

Back in the Classroom

Back in the classroom, students of the summer travel course read the Canadian novel *Halfway Man* by Wayland Drew. The book is a natural extension to the canoe trip. Set in the Canadian Shield, the plot involves a native community's struggles to preserve its setting from a planned tourist resort. They turn the tides of "progress" and in the end have the development plan revoked by kidnapping the resort plan's leader. Once kidnapped the Native community leader and industrialist are flown north and dropped without maps on a river with the simple plan to paddle back over a few weeks. The gentle environment of the Canadian Shield works its magic as it did for many on our school trip. *Halfway Man* serves to broaden the canoe-trip experience of being on the land with questions such as, what is our relationship of self and culture(s) with the land and is there an innate spiritual impulse for the larger reality of wild places? For many students, some in a science-dominated program, *Halfway Man* is their first read of a novel in over two years.

Another assignment involves a book-club gathering. After the canoe trip, students in their travel groups get together to share the themes and story of some Canadian classic canoe- or conservation-based literature. They each read a different book. Brief individual reports, oral and written, are shared. The written report and minutes of the book-club meetings are handed in. The assignment handout reminds students that school need not be somber and encourages the meeting to be planned for a coffee shop but not a favorite watering hole. Book club encourages a party with literature: getting the tripping group together one more time with learning objectives to sample from a rich heritage of travel and conservation literature. This is a quick and friendly experiential way to introduce all to the likes of Grey Owl (the native impostor of the 1930s who wrote eloquent travel and conservation prose), Sigurd Olson (a contemplative writer of the North Woods), and classics such as Mina Hubbard's *A Woman's Way through Unknown Labrador* and R. M. Patterson's *Dangerous River*. A list to encourage student selections is provided.

The following is one book club group's telling feedback about this posttrip class assignment.

> We were talking about how it was weird that for this book club we all read different books, because in most book clubs everyone reads one and comes prepared for a thorough discussion. . . . at first we were saying how this way might be better, but then thought about it, and realized that it's actually kind of cool that we all read different books because for *Halfway Man* we all read the same book and discussed it, and this switched things up a bit.
>
> Initially almost all of us thought that the assignment was kind of dumb, and just something that was taking up more of our time because we were already so busy with our group and individual projects, let alone other classes . . . but there was a huge turn-around by the end of the meeting because . . . not only did we learn a lot and were motivated to read other books, but we laughed A LOT and had a lot of fun. (The Chickadee Group, 2004)

For a group assignment, in groupings of four to six, students might turn to literature of the Voyageur or to First Nations legends or, more specifically, star-constellation stories and identification. Groups are always encouraged to take on one or more epic Canadian travel stories with the challenge to tell and present this back to the class experientially. Two course highlights include the writing and performing of a one-act play that puts the two surviving members of Leonidas Hubbard's 1903 Labrador expedition on trial for the death by fatigue and starvation of their leader in the bush. The two struggled but return from the aborted mission. Dillon Wallace's (one of the two survivors) book *Lure of Labrador* and the secondary source *Great Heart: The History of a Labrador Adventure* by J. W. Davidson and J. Rugge compose the main literature used to introduce a fictional but very plausible addition to the story. This fictional play manages to involve the class audience as jurors and, more important, tells the story and introduces the literature of the area at the time in a provocative way. (A performance of the play was later given at the Toronto Wilderness Canoe Association Symposium to an audience of eight hundred. Now that's some jury.)

Another epic story, well told in George Whalley's *The Legend of John Hornby*, had students with construction paper re-create a 1920s cabin on the edge of the treeline on the Thelon River in order to report the final days of three northern adventurers in a winter season when the life-giving caribou migration passed them by. It was magic to see the ingenuity with which the presenters re-created the cabin both physically and in terms of mood in a sterile classroom one afternoon. To set the mood, they used excerpts from Edgar Christian's journal. He was the last to die, only 18 years of age, still idealizing his Uncle Jack. His journal was found in the metal firebox that was well preserved from the elements. To be succinct, these particularly ambitious and memorable presentations made northern literature and history come live as a felt experience.

Individual assignments following the trip can involve studying literature experientially. In the past, students have, using our "on the trail" reading kits as a model, compiled their own travel-reading kits with passages and quotations of their own, choosing to pepper the trail with heritage literature. One favorite topic is the student interest in a follow-up trip as the next challenge. Solo travel and fishing trips are most common. Once the technique issues are addressed they must delve into the literature related to this interest. For the solo trip I recommend Robert Perkins's *Against Straight Lines* and Kamil Pecher's *Lonely Voyage*. These are interesting because Perkins advocates solo travel while Pecher does not. For the fisher's interest, they might see *A River Runs Through It* by Norman Maclean, but I strongly recommend *The River Why* by David James Duncan.

A personal favorite over the years was the student who imaginatively took the journal writings and overall personality of the explorer-surveyor David Thompson and placed him on a surveying mission over our class canoe-trip route. This is a compelling way of coming to know this explorer, his literature, and his time of travel. It was a fine short story in keeping with Brian Fawcett's *The Secret Journal of Alexander Mackenzie*. Fawcett's work is historical fiction and tells of the finding of the long lost private and secret journals of this explorer. Once the student had the semblance of her idea, she read Fawcett's *Secret Journal* to help ease her into historical fiction.

Many students are surprised to learn there is a literary genre associated with their specific group or individual project interests. Given the variety of group and individual assignments and of readings on the trail, students can be exposed to a rich array of literature, for the most part completely new to them, that they feel connected to experientially. Also, surprisingly, travel literature, a genre most compelling to students, is generally poorly represented at the university level.

The Winter Northern Storytellers Assignment

> After my story I was like "why did I forget that?" but I soon realized that it didn't matter because it was *my* story and the important thing was not getting all the information in—but capturing the audience in a fun way. Although I did slip out of character—I think because of nervousness—I was able to make the story fun and I hope they never forget it!
>
> Things to work on: staying in character, maintaining the accent, not going too fast, not worrying on getting hung up on parts you've missed. Telling this story will be something that I think [I] will remember forever. It just was so much fun and felt so good. I think it is because the story meant so much to me and I was able to relate it to my heritage. Story telling can be an extremely powerful device!! Cheers to that. (Lydia, reflecting on a telling of the French Canadian legend La Chasse Galerie)

The summer travel course for up to forty students is the prerequisite for the winter travel course. We travel by snowshoes, hand hauling winter sleds. We camp with a variety of cold and warm camping techniques: sleeping in snow shelters (*quinzees*), sleeping in open lean-tos, and sleeping in canvas wall-tents heated by a portable wood stove. There is a course reading kit that explores the themes of place, story, and technology in preparation of the six-day winter camp, which has some time in a rustic cabin and camping. Readings include Robert Service and Jack London.

Students also read the 1930s northern traveler Elliott Merrick's *True North*, a snowshoe traveler's bible for the how-tos and the why and whats of living in a more primal way in the Canadian North with northern peoples. We hope to connect their upcoming winter trip experience to the importance of place, story, and technology in education as well as to Canadian winter's ways of living through the themes of travel-heritage literature. A working premise for this outdoor-education course is that we are a northern people who enact a semi-Nordic way of dwelling largely in denial of our winter season. What would the liberation feel like to learn to embrace our "Nordicity"? A winter, experienced well, is a good time to bring this inquiry centrally to our lives through literature, song, travel, and stories.

On the trail more stories and readings are introduced by staff members but now the students, in the main, take over. Each student is to prepare a "northern story"—usually a winter tale for sharing on the trail. These stories will dominate our evening campfires, and some are told during walking breaks on the trail. Students are not giving presentations. They are "storytellers." They do not use notes or overheads or *Power-Point*. It is often an exposing, raw experience. Many students tell me that this assignment is the most difficult yet rewarding experience in their four years at university. For some it is just too difficult. For some it is a natural way to go. For all, it attracts attention by its difference. The storytelling should be ten or fifteen minutes followed by questions. Examples of stories and books told include the Franklin expeditions in the Arctic; the boreal-forest windigo legend or psychosis; *Elle*, a novel by Douglas Glover; accounts of Marguerite de Roberval's exile on Quebec's lower north shore; *The Beothuk Saga*, concerning this Native group's extinction story from Newfoundland, by Bernard Assiniwi; *Isobel Gunn*, by Audrey Thomas, concerning an Orkney-islander woman posing as a male in the fur trade; the Klondike gold-rush story; and the life story of the early trader and settler George Nelson.

Again, a wide array of northern travel literature and classic northern legends is shared that has over time become part of the well-informed northern winter travelers' psyche connected imaginatively to the season and the land. For the greenhorn, it can be the same, but certainly there is a memorable exposure to a Northern Canadian literature.

Once back from the winter trail, students' practice story notes are organized in a written form so that others, especially classmates who have heard the personal telling, can have a guide for retelling the story another time. The story notes are compiled into a booklet—a collection of our "On the Trail Winter Stories"—for distribution to the class and any course guests. In this way each year we produce our own anthology of northern stories organized in a storytelling-friendly format. We are all proud of our work with winter travel literature. As the teacher and guide, I tell a story too.

The business of self-propelled travel dominates our time in the North Woods of Canada, summer and winter. The trail, however, is peppered with formal and informal readings and with stories told from this literature of travel, legends, and reflections of the North. This pedagogical place-based component to our travels (and classroom time) is "the pleasantest of all diversions," allowing the mind to be active and to wander back in time with the companionship of another traveler. The goal is an imaginative heritage-extended personality we can learn to cultivate. Once students are back in the classroom, assignments and required reading advance this objective connected experientially with the trail. It is a simple, rewarding task for those who love their subject (outdoor education and travel literature) and who love working experientially with people.

Note

1. Student writing is used with permission throughout.

Jerry Keir

"Come to Paradise—
While It Lasts":
Teaching Literary Ecology
on Mexico's Costa Alegre

> *These forms I see at the edge of the ocean*
> *Which breed immediate*
> *Metaphoric association—*
> *Are they Inspiration and its agents,*
> *Or a trick of literary allusion?*
>
> *Estas formas que veo al lado del mar*
> *y engendran de inmediato*
> *asociaciones metafóricas*
> *son instrumentos de la Inspiración*
> *o de falaces citas literarias?*
>
> —José Emilio Pacheco

"The best way to read Mexican literature," says Jorge with a grin, "is with a palm tree overhead and playa sand between your toes." As we slouch in hammocks beneath a thatched-roof *palapa* and gaze out across Tenacatita

403

Bay, I ply Jorge for homegrown insights into his country's literature. Jorge has grown accustomed to my seaside prodding. For the past four years, I have migrated south of the border to join Jorge outside a Pacific coastal town where I teach Mexican literary ecology to American university students. From our beach camp on Jorge's ocean-view lot, we venture out to the surrounding coastal ecosystems to explore mangrove lagoons, tropical deciduous forests, and a fringing coral reef, while connecting these complex biotic systems to regional Mexican nature writing. In this biologically and culturally rich environment, I challenge students to understand how literature reflects place.

This year our field course has joined a larger research project funded by Earthwatch Institute.[1] After years of augmenting the course with the occasional biology guest lecture, I sought to involve students in making a lasting contribution to a region under extreme environmental stress. Collaborating with United States and Mexican wildlife biologists and aquatic ecologists, I wrote a proposal for a five-year project that unites volunteers, students, and the local community in restoration and conservation efforts. With Earthwatch's monetary and volunteer support, students press plants, collect soil samples, count birds, and trap crocodiles, establishing baseline data for the restoration of an imperiled mangrove—a natural resource central to the town's tourism industry. My role in the project is to provide a cultural framework for these scientific investigations by facilitating student involvement in the language and themes of this country's complex histories. Selecting from an assortment of genres and periods, I bring into relief the cultural products that have emerged from this land over the centuries, situating this bioregion in a social, historical, and political context.

In this essay, I explore the pedagogical benefits and challenges of studying another culture's literature while in country. By immersing students in the landscape and culture from which this coastal literature arises, I argue that students achieve a uniquely vital experiential perspective from which to understand and value literary works. I also examine the ethical dimensions intrinsic to international field studies, reviewing the postcolonial implications of our presence in a country whose economic, environmental, and literary histories have been so profoundly influenced by the United States. Finally, I provide examples of how educators might address issues of cultural exploitation by involving students in service-learning projects that benefit both the land and the local community.

Shoreline Poetics

Locating Mexican literature in the coastal landscape begins with a field-observation exercise along the Bay of Tenacatita, an idyllic half-moon stretch of sand where students first orient themselves to the tropical land and sea. The primary goal of this exercise is to establish practical, concrete literary connections to the field research through the close reading of bio-regional writing. To serve as credible, scientific observers of biological conditions, students must quickly attune themselves to this radically different environment, and poetry closely read can effectively alert them in uniquely satisfying ways to the unfamiliar surroundings they find before them. The overarching objective is to reflect on the manner in which well-developed observational skills result not only in sound field science practices but also in recognition of how an ethic of careful attention is essential to the success of place-based literature.

To establish a sense of the observational proficiency required for the fieldwork, students are challenged to read and interpret species-specific poems and then to observe independently these species in their local habitats. After recording observations in a scientific journal, noting information such as species name, habitat, and behavior, students craft their own short poems based on their field notes. Juxtaposing these tasks raises important questions regarding the role of the academic disciplines in defining and solving coastal environmental problems, and a discussion of such concepts as C. P. Snow's "two cultures" and E. O. Wilson's "consilience" clarifies for students the theoretical basis of our interdisciplinary goals.

The coastal themes found in the works of the Mexican poet José Emilio Pacheco are particularly well suited for this exercise. In his 1978 collection of poetry, *Don't Ask Me How the Time Goes By* (*No me preguntes como pasa el tiempo*), we encounter octopus, scorpion, fish, crab, cricket, mosquito, and bat in spare, imagistic poems that introduce students to the often unseen inhabitants along the coast. In "An Address On Crabs" ("Discurso sobre los cangrejos"), Pacheco announces that "On the coast they maintain that crabs are animals bewitched / incapable of turning to see their own claw marks." These "nomads of the mud / or inhabitants of a double exile" occupy the liminal space between shifting earth and surging sea, remaining "foreigners / compared to the populators of the water, compared to the animals of the land." Enlisting anthropomorphic modifiers, Pacheco describes these "nocturnal mountaineers, wandering skeletons" as "sullen and forever furtive" yet skilled in their evolution-ary adaptation and as "avoiding immortality in impossible square-shaped circles" (127). The poet's projection of human traits elicits a discussion of style, and we explore the question of representation and the disciplinary distinctions between literary description and scientific notation. In addition to raising issues regarding empirical, objective diction and qualitative, sub-jective voice, the poet's artistic rendering of the crab's survivalist existence calls our attention to the extreme environmental stress endured by all spe-cies subsisting along the Pacific shoreline.

Reading and interpreting Pacheco's poems in the localized context of the La Manzanilla beach camp heightens student awareness of this ecosytem—the very crabs we read of lie dormant in their sandy burrows just inches below our bare feet. While we swat mosquitoes, we read of Pacheco's "little frail vampires / miniature dragonflies / small picadors / with the devil's own sting," and, while on the beach, we consider the fate of fish stranded by the low tide: "the net / the harpoon / you were made for these / for lures / asphyxia / and frying pans," and the fate of the human collective: "for pure profit we have tainted your seas / Now you exact justice / recontaminating us" (101). These poetic meditations on seaside natural history illustrate the creative reciprocity that emerges between poet and place; they show how the students, too, can begin to access and interpret their research environment on both scientific and artis-tic terms, locating what Gary Paul Nabhan calls "the ecotone between the cultivated skill of careful observation and the wilds of the human imagina-tion" ("Between" 269).

Pacheco's poems span a wide range of tropical species and settings, many of which feature organisms whose nocturnal doings often go unno-ticed. Not only do the poems enhance student understanding of littoral ecology and express what Ronald Friis considers the poet's "uneasy eco-logical consciousness," but they also serve more utilitarian purposes, rais-ing an awareness of the potential for real danger along this wild stretch of coast (104). In "Scorpion," Pacheco's subject is the deadly peculiarity of the species' reproductive process, a macabre biological ritual only a well-seasoned, beachcombing naturalist would discern. "The scorpion attracts its mate," explains Pacheco, "And, pincers locked together / they gaze at one another for one gloomy day / Or night before their curious coupling / And the conclusion of the nuptial encounter: The male succumbs / And is devoured in his turn by the female" (155). Pacheco's portrayal of the scorpion's lethal courtship alerts us to discrete biological phenomena, and we discuss the poem's implicit cautionary message—among the palm leaves and beach grass lie hidden threats we would do well to note. Such poems as this succinctly reinforce our earlier safety lecture on the venomous, potentially deadly possibilities presented by crocodile, viper, and the ubiquitous scorpion, strengthening student awareness of the hazards of tropical research. Moreover, in an environment of such splendor, where the expanse of emerald sea, cobalt sky, and tropical green conspires to eclipse the more subtle biological dramas, Pacheco's poetry returns our gaze to the smaller biotic interactions so vital to our understanding of coastal ecology.

Seeds and Stories

After two days of orientation and training, students have learned the theoretical and methodological basis for their field investigations. One of the more challenging collection tasks is the botanical inventory, where students traverse the thickly populated mangrove forest, measuring species' density and composition while collecting and identifying plant specimens. Beneath the full tree canopy, students trudge through the dank, boggy coastal forest, slapping mosquitoes, juggling global positioning systems, diameter-at-breast-height tapes, and spherical densiometers, while slipping and stumbling through the mangrove's tentacular prop-root system. Tropical research is often depicted as a glamorous, exotic experience, but any lingering romantic notions of such work are dispelled here.

Aside from disabusing students of fieldwork misconceptions, the research also offers an experiential preamble for a discussion of regional land-use history, a richly storied past well documented in the activist tradition of Mexican literary realism. In this context, students explore intersections among literature, history, and the natural sciences. The physically rigorous work can heighten student receptivity to Mexico's literature of the campesino, the rural peasant, granting students important insight—whether it is a campesino harvesting chiles for subsistence farming or a student collecting red mangrove propagules for scientific analysis, the experience of intimate contact with the land is fundamentally similar.

To reflect on the struggles endured by campesinos and the tenacity with which they will fight for their right to farm, sell, or develop their property, we read major writers of the Mexican Revolution and its aftermath, principally Mariano Azuela, Agustín Yáñez, and Juan Rulfo. Their works of social protest—such as Azuela's *The Underdogs* (*Los de abajo*), Yáñez's *The Edge of the Storm* (*Al filo del agua*), and Rulfo's "*The Burning Plain*" *and Other Stories* (*El llano en llamas*)—describe the historical antecedents that have led to persisting land-use conflicts that challenge the protection of the mangrove. Celebrated for their ability to critically portray the plight of the Mexican rural community, these writers describe ethically compelling characters whose struggles continue in the lives of farmers and ranchers populating the Costa Alegre landscape today.

For example, in Rulfo's naturalistic short story "The Burning Plain," we follow four archetypal campesinos on an eleven-hour walk across a barren, hot plain to address an indifferent government official on the quality of ejido land granted to them. The story dramatizes the historical events after the revolution of 1917, when all rural Mexico was guaranteed "land to those who work it," only to find the land mostly unsuitable for cultivation (Riding 45).[2] The failure of the agrarian reform movement is summarized by Rulfo's defeated campesino:

> So they've given us this land. And in this sizzling frying pan they want us to plant some kind of seeds to see if something will take root and come up. But nothing will come up here. . . . You can't do anything when there's nothing to work with. (14)

A single drop of rain signals the narrative's denouement, which is, as Lanin A. Gyurko points out, "symbolic of the desperation of their state and also of the impossibility of redemption" (262). Rulfo's disillusioned farmer continues to speak for those whose lands remain "all washed away and hard" and where "not even a mouthful of water" is available for irrigation (14). The story particularizes for students the chronic problem of poverty and deprivation among campesinos whose land has little agricultural value but now has increasing worth for development. Indeed, the tragedy of the agrarian reform movement continues to be written today, not as short stories but on the *Se Vende* (For Sale) signs that sprout on the fringes of the mangrove.

Problematizing the Postcolonial Pacific

The conservation goals of the Earthwatch project extend beyond the gathering of scientific data. In addition to establishing the biological significance of the mangrove, students work on science-education initiatives to increase the ecological literacy of the rural population. Students and volunteers assist with community meetings, school visits, and sustainable-development workshops, and, while these efforts are mostly met with interest and enthusiasm, there remains a certain reluctance in the community. Although our team includes local biologists and educators, the project is still perceived as the work of privileged outsiders whose transient presence is viewed by some with suspicion.

Such bilateral challenges in uniting the community require students to see themselves not just as visitors but as provisional members of, and active participants in, a multinational community. Indeed, the rapid rise in local foreign investment has foregrounded our paradoxical role as conservation-minded interlopers. To situate the outreach work in a cultural context, students examine the expository prose of Jose Vasoncelos's *La raza cosmica* (*The Cosmic Race*) and Octavio Paz's *The Labyrinth of Solitude* (*El laberinto de la soledad*) from a postcolonial perspective. These classic statements of *mexicanidad* contemplate the ambiguities of Mexico's nationhood and help explain the hesitancy among locals to embrace the findings and recommendations of field science, which may be seen as yet another form of authoritative oppression. Octavio Paz, in his chapter "Mexican Masks," analyzes *lo mexicano* through a poetic characterization of the representative Mexican, a "hermetic being," shaped as much by a complicated history of imperial conquest as by the austerity of his country's provincial landscape (43). "The harshness and hostility of our environment," suggests Paz, "and the hidden, indefinable threat that is always afloat in the air, oblige us to close ourselves in, like those plants that survive by storing up liquid within their spiny exteriors" (30). Summarizing the troubling effects of centuries of political betrayal and failed reforms on Mexico's collective psyche, Paz states plainly the lingering implications: "the colonial world has disappeared, but not the fear, the mistrust, and suspicion" (43). Although such generalizations of a vastly diverse people have come under intense scrutiny in recent years, the writings of Paz and Vasconcelos—with their eloquent thematic expressions of mestizo diaspora, hybridity, and exile—reveal the strengths and virtues of the country's polyvalent cultural underpinnings and highlight for students the profound differences between the United States and Mexico. The fieldwork, if it is to succeed, must also bridge vast cultural divides.

Globalization and the Postmodern Tropical Pastoral

Such a diverse range of activities has attracted students and volunteers from throughout the United States and abroad, and, while most come to La Manzanilla with an authentic desire to make a contribution, the tropical vacation atmosphere can challenge their best intentions. The soporific Pacific sun, the ambient lull of surf, and the lush coastal greenery run counter to an ambitious work schedule. Everything about the beach camp suggests a retreat from, not acceptance of, responsibility.

This holiday sensibility, with its escapist underpinnings, no doubt entices many students to join the program, yet it is also one of the indirect causes of Mexico's environmental crisis. The recruitment message used by Earthwatch Institute, our university course brochures, and the global tourism industry is essentially the same: "Come to Paradise—while it lasts" (D. McLaren 117). As small coastal towns like La Manzanilla are "discovered" and commodified, the marketing strategies for such threatened areas employ a rhetoric of anticipatory nostalgia that smacks of a postmodern tropical pastoral, where one is encouraged to indulge in seaside pleasures in a rarified environment "before it is gone." The attraction of such marketing ploys has its ideological roots in Old World desires, when European explorers set sail with the glory of God and gold to conquer what they deemed a *terra nullius*. Indeed, the narratives of Mexico's conquistadors and the explorers who followed them are echoed in contemporary travel guidebooks in which one encounters the alluring language of idyllic, guiltless consumption. Students can trace the narrative threads of Hernán Cortés, Bernal Díaz del Castillo, and Alexander von Humboldt through the centuries, discerning only slight ideological departures from a dominant motif of exploitation.[3] Mexico's literature of discovery, with its evocative language of pristine, primal landscape, continues in the recent edition of the Lonely Planet guide, which recommends "exploring the desolate beaches of Mexico's undeveloped *Costa Alegre* . . . if you have a taste for adventure" (Palmerlee and Bao 176). The guide's authors even go so far as to suggest that "the beauty of Mexico's Pacific coast is that it can be whatever you want it to be," perpetuating the imperial conceit of an exhaustible locus of desire (9).

It is in the face of such contradictions that international field studies must resist becoming, under the guise of educational innovation, another form of extractive, bourgeois adventure travel. In his recent essay, "Postmodern Pastoral, Advertising, and the Masque of Technology," Scott Hess explicates a conflicted worldview dominated by what he terms a "popular pastoral of consumerism," calling our attention to a Club Med idea of arcadian repose no longer ecologically viable. Instead, Hess imagines a more "sustainable pastoral" that leads to action and participation, not to quiescence and escapism. It must be a pastoral which remembers, even as it imagines an ideal human happiness in harmony with nature, the difference between the imaginary Arcadia and the actual one. (95)

While Hess's call for "action and participation" is essential, he does not explain how we might cultivate a "sustainable pastoral." It is a concept unrealized. The fieldwork in Mexico takes this abstract mandate and grounds it in a localized pedagogy that encourages engagement and experimentation. By approaching the study and teaching of Mexican literature in this way educators negotiate the ethical problems intrinsic to travel programs, offering students opportunities to respond affirmatively to themes of environmental despoliation. Connecting this meaningful work to literary studies offers transformative possibilities, subverting student assumptions of powerlessness and cynicism, addressing the question of hope in a time when most stories from developing nations suggest inexorable crisis. To adopt such methods is to believe that the private, inward experience found in a poem, essay, or story is inextricably linked to the larger public act of living and that literature can inform and inspire our civic engagement and enlarge our sense of global citizenship. Finally, this experience suggests that we, as educators, learners, and scholars, may have something more to give Mexico than a few pesos for beer and tacos.

Notes

The epigraph to this essay is from "Live Experience" ("La experiencea vivida") in *Don't Ask Me How the Time Goes By* (*No me preguntes como pasa el tiempo*).

1. Earthwatch Institute is an international not-for-profit organization that recruits volunteers to serve on environmental field-research projects in over fifty countries from around the world. For more information on the institute, their grants program, and our project Mexico Mangroves and Wildlife, go to www .earthwatch.org.

2. Article 27 of the 1917 constitution granted the peasant's right to a piece of land, establishing the concept of communal ownership, the ejido. However, this agrarian model, which espoused a return to the Indian tradition of communal farming, has been abandoned by "revolutionary" governments who have allowed for the ejidos to rent and sell their properties, betraying the promise of a more sustainable agricultural practice. Riding comments that, "[i]t was the government policy to stimulate industrial development with the result that urban wages were allowed to rise while rural prices were held down. The *Ejidos* came to be viewed merely as 'parking lots' for the peasantry until their cheap labor could be incorporated into the new urban and industrial nation" (184).

3. Mary Louise Pratt notes that while Humboldt detailed in his journal a Mexico untouched and wild, he could only "discover" such remote wilderness through the use of colonial trading infrastructure, for example, roads, towns, haciendas, and colonial labor, to further his remote explorations (127).

Part IV

Resources

Mark C. Long

Resources for Teaching Environmental Literature: A Selective Guide

This guide is designed for nonspecialists, new as well as experienced teachers, and researchers seeking a bibliographic overview of the scholarship that has shaped the study of North American environmental literature. Each topical section provides an overview of the history of the critical conversation as well as a guide to recent work in the field. Additional materials not included here may be found in the list of works cited at the end of the volume. Dissertations, articles, and special issues of journals are not listed, and single-author studies and biographies have been excluded. These works are available in print and electronic resources, such as the *MLA International Bibliography*. Resources relevant to the study of North American environmental literature continue to appear at a rapid rate. Those not included at the time of this compilation in the spring of 2006 may be found by consulting the reviews and books-received sections of the journal *ISLE: Interdisciplinary Studies in the Environment*. The limited Internet sources included here are offered merely to suggest the current and potential uses of electronic sources and digital archives.

The materials in this guide incorporate a more narrowly defined literary concern with nature writing in the United States into a much broader consideration of the ways language and thought mediate human relations with the natural environment. This proliferation of scholarship on environmental writing since the publication of *Teaching Environmental Literature* in 1985 reflects a broader cultural shift in concern during the age of globalism and environmental crisis. Moreover, the scholarship on Mexican, Mexican American, Chicana/o, and Canadian environmental literatures foregrounds the complexities of cultural formation in North America in a field of inquiry that, until quite recently, was organized around a singular national literature (American).[1] Exactly how this recent work will reshape the intellectual and geographic horizon of the field remains an open question. What is certain is that the archive of materials and methods of study available to teachers of North American environmental literature will continue to expand.

Many of the subject areas in this guide also cross departmental and disciplinary lines. Ecocritical readings of nature writing and the study of discourse in ecocomposition continue to produce new scholarship and inspired teaching. But this work is increasingly practiced by scholars and teachers with expertise in complementary fields such as biology, ecology, feminism, geography, anthropology, linguistics, psychology, ethics, and philosophy. New areas of study that combine fields of study—such as religion and nature studies with the theory and practice of social justice—further suggest emerging directions in the field. This interdisciplinary work reflects not only the collaborative enterprise of environmental studies but the willingness (and ability) to work beyond the parochial self-interest of academic disciplines.

The subject areas in this guide are offered to complement the essays in this collection. The authors describe diverse and interesting courses by teachers in a variety of fields, at both the undergraduate and graduate levels, in a number of different kinds of institutions. We are grateful for the intellectual work of these scholars and teachers. Their work has contributed to a growing archive of materials that will guide future work in the field.

General Reference

John Elder's two-volume *American Nature Writers* (1996) compiles seventy biographic and critical overviews of authors writing in the genre and provides an extensive list of primary and secondary readings—including a subject-area essay on nature writing in Canada. *Literature of Nature: An International Sourcebook* (1998), edited by Patrick D. Murphy, Terry Gifford, and Katsunori Yamazato, offers a broader geographic focus to the field, including Canada, Latin America, and the Pacific Rim. Carolyn Merchant has edited two reference works that are especially useful for scholars in the field: *Ecology: Key Concepts in Critical Theory* (2002) and *The Columbia Guide to Environmental History* (2002). Also see Patricia D. Netzley's *Environmental Literature: An Encyclopedia of Works, Authors, and Themes* (1999) and the Dictionary of Literary Biography volumes, *Twentieth-Century American Nature Writers: Prose* (2003) and *Twentieth-Century American Nature Writers: Poetry* (forthcoming). A survey of three decades of environmental journalism is available in *A People's History of Wilderness: A High Country News Reader* (2004), edited by Matt Jenkins.

Ecocriticism

Cheryll Glotfelty and Harold Fromm's *The Ecocriticism Reader: Landmarks in Literary Ecology* (1996) remains a touchstone for students of the emerging field. David Mazel's *American Literary Environmentalism* (2000) and *A Century of Early Ecocriticism* (2001) together provide a survey of the critical practices grouped under the term *ecocriticism*. Among the best examples of ecocriticism focused on the tradition after Henry David Thoreau is Lawrence Buell's *The Ecological Imagination: Thoreau, Nature Writing, and the Formation of American Culture* (1995). *Writing for an Endangered World: Literature, Culture, and Environment in the U.S. and Beyond* (2001) offers Buell's extended argument, which treats a wider range of texts and contexts. More recent books that demonstrate the range of assumptions and practices that fall under the rubric of ecocriticism include the essays by fifteen scholars in William Cronon's *Uncommon Ground: Toward Reinventing Nature* (1995). Also see Richard Kerridge and Neil Sammells's edited collection, *Writing the Environment: Ecocriticism and Literature* (1998); Karla Armbruster and Kathleen R. Wallace's collection, *Beyond Nature Writing: Expanding the Boundaries of Ecocriticism* (2001); and four books that demonstrate the myriad of approaches that fall under the rubric of ecocriticism: John Tallmadge and Henry Harrington's *Reading under the Sign of Nature: New Essays in Ecocriticism* (2000); Patrick D. Murphy's *Farther Afield in the Study of Nature-Oriented Literature* (2000); Steven Rosendale's edited collection, *The Greening of Literary Scholarship*

(2002); and *The ISLE Reader: Ecocriticism, 1993–2003* (2003), edited by Michael P. Branch and Scott Slovic. Michael Bennett and David Teague's *The Nature of Cities: Ecocriticism and Urban Environments* (1999) works with cultural studies and urban experience to question the assumption that built environments are apart from nature. Alan Bleakley deploys an interdisciplinary approach to the significance of animals in *The Animalizing Imagination: Totemism, Textuality, Ecocriticism* (2000), and Barney Nelson examines assumptions about domestication in *The Wild and the Domestic: Animal Representation, Ecocriticism, and Western American Literature* (2000). The most recent assessments of ecocriticism include Dana Phillips, *The Truth of Ecology: Nature, Culture, and Literature in America* (2003); Greg Garrard, *Ecocriticism* (2004); and Buell, *The Future of Environmental Criticism: Environmental Crisis and Literary Imagination* (2005).

Anthologies and Collections

Two reissued collections are *The Wilderness Reader* (1980; rev. ed. 1994), edited by Frank Bergon, and *Words from the Land: Encounters with Natural History Writing* (1988; rev. ed. 1995), edited by Stephen Trimble. Also see *Ecological Crisis: Readings for Survival*, edited by Glen Love and Rhoda Love, and *Eco-Fiction* (1971), edited by John Stadler. Thomas J. Lyon's *This Incomparable Land: A Guide to American Nature Writing* (1989), a seminal text at the time of its publication, has been reissued in a revised edition in 2001. Also see *The Norton Book of Nature Writing*, edited by Robert Finch and John Elder (1990; rev. ed. 2002), and *Finding Home: Writing on Nature and Culture from Orion Magazine* (1992), edited by Peter Sauer. *On Nature: Nature, Landscape, and Natural History* (1986), edited by Daniel Halpern, and *On Nature's Terms: Contemporary Voices* (1992), edited by Thomas J. Lyon and Peter Stine, offer surveys of contemporary nature writing. Also see *Nature's New Voices* (1992), edited by John A. Murray; *Heart of the Land: Essays on the Last Great Places* (1994), edited by Joseph Barbato and Lisa Weinerman; *Place of the Wild* (1994), edited by David Clark Burks; *The World of Wilderness: Essays on the Power and Purpose of Wild Country* (1995), edited by T. H. Watkins and Patricia Byrnes; *Constructing Nature: Readings from the American Experience* (1996), edited by Richard Jenseth and Edward E. Lotto; and *Reading the Landscape: Writing a World* (1996), edited by Peter Valenti. John A. Murray edits an annual collection, *American Nature Writing*, published by Sierra Club Books. A useful anthology of writings before Thoreau is *Reading the Roots: American Nature Writing before* Walden (2003), edited by Michael P. Branch. For nature writing by women, see the collections *Sisters of the Earth: Women's Prose and Poetry about Nature* (1991), edited by Lorraine Anderson; *Celebrating the Land: Women's Nature Writing, 1850–1991* (1992), edited by Karen Knowles, Lorraine Anderson, and Thomas S. Edwards; *At Home on This Earth: Two Centuries of U.S. Women's Nature Writing* (2002), edited by Anderson and Edwards; and *A Sweet, Separate Intimacy: Women Writers on the American Frontier, 1800–1922*, edited by Susan Cummins Miller. A collection that encompasses historical and cultural aspects of the human being–nature relationship is Jill Ker Conway, Kenneth Keniston, and Leo Marx's *Earth, Air, Fire, Water: Humanistic Studies of the Environment* (2000). Anthologies of nature poetry include *News of the Universe*, edited by Robert Bly; *Urban Nature: Poems about Wildlife in the City* (2000), edited by Laure-Anne Bosselaar; Christopher Merrill, *The Forgotten Language: Contemporary Poets and Nature* (1991); and Robert Pack and Jay Parini, *Poems for a Small Planet: Contemporary American Nature Poetry* (1993). More specialized anthologies include *American Sea Writing: A Literary Anthology* (2000), edited by Peter Neill; *Nature's Fading Chorus: Classic and Contemporary Writing on Amphibians* (2000), edited by Gordon L. Miller, Robert Michael Pyle, and Ann Haymond Zwinger; and *An Exhilaration of Wings: The Literature of Birdwatching* (1999), edited by Jen Hill. A call for a more expansive vision of writing about nature is *Naked: Writers Uncover the Way We Live on Earth* (2004), edited by Susan Zakin.

Mexican, Mexican American, and Chicana/o Environmental Literature

Mexican and Mexican American environmental literature is productively set in the contexts of the environmental history of Mexico since the globalization of its economy, the environmental crisis of Mexico City, and the impact of the Zapatista uprising. Useful starting points for the environmental history of Mexico include *Artistas e intelectuales sobre el ecocidio urbano* (1989), edited by Homero Aridjis and Fernando Cesarman; Exequiel Ezcurra and others, *The Basin of Mexico: Critical Environmental*

Issues and Sustainability (1999); Karen L. O'Brian, *Sacrificing the Forest: Environmental and Social Struggles in Chiapas* (1998); Joel Simon, *Endangered Mexico: An Environment on the Edge* (1997); and Lane Simonian, *Defending the Land of the Jaguar: A History of Conservation in Mexico* (1995). For exploration on the uprising in Chiapas and the ecological discourse on the Zapatistas, see Efraín Bartolomé, *Ocosingo: Diario de una guerra y algunas voces* (1995); Carlos Monsiváis, *La marcha del color de la tierra* (2004); Carlos Montemayor, *Chiapas, la rebelión indígena de México* (1998) and *La guerrilla recurrente* (1999). Literature on and from indigenous peoples in contemporary Mexico includes Montemayor, *La literatura actual en las lenguas indígenas de México* (2001) and *Los pueblos indios de México hoy* (2001). Other sources for studying the chronicle come from the chroniclers themselves. See José Joaquín Blanco, *Crónica literaria: Un siglo de escritores mexicanos* (1996); Linda Egan, *Carlos Monsiváis: Culture and Chronicle in Contemporary Mexico* (2001); Carlos Monsiváis, *A ustedes les consta. Antología de la crónica en México* (1980, 2001) and *Salvador Novo: Lo marginal en el centro* (2000). Other resources for the study of environmental themes in Mexican and Mexican American literature include Noreen Groover Lape, *West of the Border: The Multicultural Literature of the Western American Frontier* (2001); Thomas E. Sheridan, *Where the Dove Calls: The Political Ecology of a Peasant Corporate Community in Northwestern Mexico* (1988); and Cynthia Radding, *Wandering Peoples: Colonialism, Ethnic Spaces, and Ecological Frontiers in Northwestern Mexico, 1700–1850* (1997). The relation between Chicana/o writing and environmental issues is addressed by Devon Peña in the collection of essays *Chicano Culture, Ecology, Politics: Subversive Kin* (1998). Also see Peña's *Mexican Americans and the Environment: Tierra y Vida* (2005) and *The Terror of the Machine: Technology, Work, Gender, and Ecology on the U.S.–Mexico Border* (1997), about *maquila* workers and resistance. Laura Pulido's *Environmentalism and Economic Justice: Two Chicano Struggles in the Southwest* (1996) and Robert Bullard's collection *Confronting Environmental Racism: Voices from the Grassroots* (1993) make evident the concept of environmental justice for the study of Chicana/o environmental writing. For additional perspective on environmental issues in Chicana/o literary history see the four-volume collection of essays on Latina/o literary history, *Recovering the U.S. Hispanic Literary Heritage* (1993–2002). Also see Tey Diana Rebolledo, *Women Singing in the Snow: A Cultural Analysis of Chicana Literature*

(1995); Krista Comer, *Landscapes of the New West: Gender and Geography in Contemporary Women's Writing* (1999); Raúl Homero Villa, *Barrio-Logos: Space and Place in Urban Chicano Literature and Culture* (2000); Mary Pat Brady, *Extinct Lands, Temporal Geographies: Chicana Literature and the Urgency of Space* (2002); and Stephen J. Pitti, *The Devil in Silicon Valley: Northern California, Race, and Mexican Americans* (2003).

The Environmental Literature of Canada

The vast territories and diverse cultures of Canada have produced a distinctive literary history. Marcia B. Kline's *Beyond the Land Itself: Views of Nature in Canada and the United States* (1970) and W. H. New's *A History of Canadian Literature* (2nd ed., 2003) offer general overviews. *Canadian Exploration Literature: An Anthology, 1660–1860* (1993), edited by Germaine Warkentin, and *From the Country: Writings about Rural Canada: A Harrowsmith Anthology* (1991) and *Treasures of the Place: Three Centuries of Nature Writing in Canada* (1992), edited by Wayne Grady, focus on the history of environmental writing in Canada. The early critical conversation about the environment in Canadian literature appears in Northrup Frye's *The Bush Garden: Essays on the Canadian Imagination* (1971). Also see Margaret Atwood's argument for the distinctive features of Canadian writing in *Survival: A Thematic Guide to Canadian Literature* (1972); Laurie Ricou's *Vertical Man / Horizontal World: Man and Landscape in Canadian Prairie Fiction* (1973); Gaile McGregor's focus on the northern frontier in *The Wacousta Syndrome: Explorations in Canadian Langscape* (1985); Susan Joan Wood's *The Land in Canadian Prose, 1840–1945* (1988); and Dick Harrison's *Unnamed Country: The Struggle for a Canadian Prairie Fiction* (1977). The essays collected by the range ecologist and writer Don Gayton in *The Wheatgrass Mechanism: Science and Imagination in the Western Canadian Landscape* (1991) and *Landscapes of the Interior: Re-explorations of Nature and the Human Spirit* (1996) offer a contemporary perspective on the Canadian landscape of British Columbia. Also see D. M. R. Bentley's *The Gay Grey Moose: Essays on the Ecologies and Mythologies of Canadian Poetry, 1690–1990* (1992) and the essays on western Canada in Kevin van Tighem's *Coming West: A Natural History of Home* (1997). More recent critical studies include W. H. New's

Land Sliding: Imagining Space, Presence, and Power in Canadian Writing (1997); Susie O'Brien's "Nature's Nation, National Natures? Reading Ecocriticism in a Canadian Context," in *Canadian Poetry* 42 (1998): 17–41; and *This Elusive Land: Women and the Canadian Environment* (2004), edited by Melody Hessing, Rebecca Raglon, and Catriona Sandilands. For a focus on poetry and nature, see Don McKay, *Vis-à-Vis: Field Notes on Poetry and Wilderness* (2001), and Tim Bowling, editor, *Where the Words Come From: Canadian Poets in Conversation* (2002). Also see *Don McKay: Essays on His Works* (2005), edited by Brian Bartlett. Useful anthologies of the environmental literature of Canada include *Native Literature in Canada: From the Oral Tradition to the Present* (1990), edited by Terry Goldie and Daniel David Moses; *Northern Wild: Best Contemporary Canadian Nature Writing* (1996), edited by David R. Boyd; *Fresh Tracks: Writing the Western Landscape*, edited by Pamela Banting (1998); and *Fifteen Canadian Poets X 3* (2001), edited by Gary Geddes.

Backgrounds to United States Environmental Writing

The study of environmental literature in North America has until quite recently focused on a narrow group of writers concerned with the cultural formation of the United States. Norman Foerster's *Nature in American Literature* (1927) represents the early-twentieth-century consensus about New World attitudes toward nature, which would be elaborated in Henry Nash Smith's *Virgin Land: The American West as Symbol and Myth* (1950), Leo Marx's The *Machine in the Garden: Technology and the Pastoral Ideal in America* (1964), and Perry Miller's *Nature's Nation* (1967). Annette Kolodny's *The Lay of the Land: Metaphor as Experience and History in American Life and Letters* (1975) and Cecilia Tichi's *New World, New Earth: Environmental Reform in American Literature from the Puritans through Whitman* (1979) reflect a significant shift in literary assumptions and methodology that would inform subsequent work in English and American studies.

United States Environmental Writing through the Romantic Period

John Bakeless's *The Eyes of Discovery: The Pageant of North America as Seen by the First Explorers* (1950) focuses on writing about nature in North

America during the period of contact. Tony Rice's *Voyages of Discovery: Three Centuries of Natural History Exploration* (1999) and Michael A. Bryson's *Visions of the Land: Science, Literature, and the American Environment from the Era of Exploration to the Age of Ecology* (2002) offer readings of the depictions of the non-European world through the middle part of the eighteenth century. Also see Robert Lawson-Peebles, *Landscape and Written Expression in Revolutionary America: The World Turned Upside Down* (1988). Ernest Earnest's *John and William Bartram, Botanists and Explorers* (1940); Robert Elman's *First in the Field: America's Pioneering Naturalists* (1977); Annette Kolodny's *The Land before Her: Fantasy and Experience of the American Frontiers, 1630–1860* (1984); and Bruce A. Harvey's *American Geographics: U.S. National Narratives and the Representation of the Non-European World, 1830–1865* (2001) extend their focus through the middle decades of the nineteenth century. Supplementing these broad overviews are more regionally concentrated studies, such as Conevery Bolton Valencius's *The Health of the Country: How American Settlers Understood Themselves and Their Land* (2002), an account of nineteenth-century American settlers in Arkansas and Missouri. Also see Russell T. Newman's *The Gentleman in the Garden: The Influential Landscape in the Works of James Fenimore Cooper* (2003). For an argument that examines the nature and culture relationship before Thoreau, see Timothy Sweet, *American Georgics: Economy and the Environment in Early American Literature* (2002).

Natural History Writing

Early studies of natural history writers include Marston Bates, *The Nature of Natural History* (1950); Henry Savage, Jr., *Lost Heritage: Wilderness through the Eyes of Seven Pre-Audubon Naturalists* (1970); and Wayne Hanley, *Natural History in America: From Mark Catesby to Rachel Carson* (1977). Charlotte M. Porter's *The Eagle's Nest: Natural History and American Ideas, 1812–1842* (1986) focuses attention on natural history as cultural history; Marcia Bonta's *Women in the Field: America's Pioneering Naturalists* (1991) expands the canon of natural history writers; and Pamela Regis's *Describing Early America: Bartram, Jefferson, Crèvecoeur, and the Rhetoric of Natural History* (1992) revises earlier assumptions about the relation between natural history and science. Also see Margaret Welch's examination of what she calls a social history of natural history through a range of documentary evidence both rhetorical and iconographic in *The Book of Nature: Natural History in the United States, 1825–1875* (1998). More recent studies of natural history writers include Christoph Irmscher, *The Poetics of Natural History: From John Bartram to William James* (1999); Lester D. Stephens, *Science, Race, and Religion in the American South: John Bachman and the Charleston Circle of Naturalists, 1815–1895* (2000); and John Moring, *Early American Naturalists: Exploring the American West, 1804–1900* (2002).

Nature Writing

Nature writing after Thoreau is defined as a distinctive genre in the literature of the United States in William Beebe's *The Book of Naturalists* (1944), Joseph Wood Krutch's *Great American Nature Writing* (1957), and Frank Bergon's *The Wilderness Reader* (1980). Paul Brooks's *Speaking for Nature: How Literary Naturalists from Henry Thoreau to Rachel Carson Have Shaped America* (1980) discloses a wider range of writing in the genre. The historical introduction, taxonomy of the genre, and bibliography in Thomas J. Lyon's *This Incomparable Lande* (1989; rev. ed. 2001) remains indispensable. More recent collections of note include *On Nature: Nature, Landscape, and Natural History* (1986), edited by Daniel Halpern, and *On Nature's Terms: Contemporary Voices* (1992), edited by Thomas J. Lyon and Peter Stine. Also see *Heart of the Land: Essays on the Last Great Places* (1994), edited by Joseph Barbato and Lisa Weinerman; *Place of the Wild* (1994), edited by David Clark Burks. Critical studies of the genre include *The World of Wilderness: Essays on the Power and Purpose of Wild Country* (1995), edited by T. H. Watkins and Patricia Byrnes. John A. Murray also edits an annual collection, *American Nature Writing*, published by Sierra Club Books. John Cooley and James I. McClintock, editors, *Earthly Words: Essays on Contemporary American Nature and Environmental Writers* (1994); Daniel G. Payne, *Voices in the Wilderness: American Nature Writing and Environmental Politics* (1996), and Peter A. Fritzell, *Nature Writing and America: Essays upon a Cultural Type* (1990) offer a reading that contrasts with the intertextual history of Frank Stewart's *A Natural History of Nature Writing* (1995) or Katrina Schimmoeller Peiffer's focus in *Coyote at Large: Humor in American Nature Writing* (2000). Don Scheese, in *Nature Writing: The Pastoral Impulse in America* (1996), and Thomas Hallock, in *From the Fallen Tree: Frontier Narratives, Environmental Politics, and the Roots of a National Pastoral, 1743–1826* (2003), look at the genre and cultural activity of pastoralism. There are numerous studies of selected nature writers. They include Sherman Paul, *For Love of the World: Essays on Nature Writers* (1992); Scott Slovic, *Seeking Awareness in American Nature Writing: Henry Thoreau, Annie Dillard, Edward Abbey, Wendell Berry, Barry Lopez* (1992); John P. O'Grady, *Pilgrims to the Wild: Everett Ruess, Henry David Thoreau, John Muir, Clarence King, Mary Austin* (1993); James McClintock, *Nature's Kindred Spirits: Aldo Leopold, Joseph Wood Krutch, Edward Abbey, Annie Dillard, and Gary Snyder* (1994); Randall Roorda, *Dramas of Solitude: Narratives of Retreat in American Nature Writing* (1998); Michael Pearson, *Imagined Places: Journeys into Literary America* (2000); Mark Allister, *Refiguring the Map of Sorrow: Nature Writing and Autobiography* (2001); and John R. Knott, *Imagining Wild America* (2002). Robert L. Dorman's *A Word For Nature: Four Pioneering Environmental Advocates, 1845–1913* (1998) and Charles T. Rubin's *Conservation Reconsidered: Nature, Virtue, and American Liberal Democracy* (2000) focus on the emergence of the modern conservation movement in the United States. Daniel J. Philippon's *Conserving Words: How American Nature Writers Shaped the Environmental Movement* (2003) connects particular nature writers, their texts, and their readership to formative events in environmental history. For conversations with contemporary American nature writers, see *Writing Natural History: Dialogues with Authors* (1989), edited by Edward Lueders, and *Listening to the Land: Conversations about Nature, Culture, and Eros* (1995), edited by Derrick Jensen.

Regional and Place-Based Writing

Region and *place* are key terms in the study of North American writing in general and in the study of environmental literature in particular. Leonard Lutwack's *The Role of Place in Literature* (1984) anticipates recent attention to regionalism and the literature of place in Robert M. Nelson, *Place and Vision: The Function of Landscape in North American Fiction* (1993); David M. Jordan, *New World Regionalism: Literature in the Americas* (1994) and *Regionalism Reconsidered: New Approaches to the Field* (1994); *All over the Map: Rethinking American Regions* (1996), by Edward L. Ayers, Patricia Nelson Limerick, Stephen Nissenbaum, and Peter S. Onuf; Judith Fetterley and Marjorie Pryse, *Writing out of Place: Regionalism, Women and American Literary Culture* (2002). See also Tom Lutz's call for a new regionalism in *Cosmopolitan Vistas: American Regionalism and*

Literary Value (2004). The field of cultural geography provides exceptional insight into inhabited and working landscapes. A good starting point is John Brinckerhoff Jackson, *A Sense of Place, a Sense of Time* (1994) and W. J. T. Mitchell, editor, *Landscapes and Power* (1994). Kent C. Ryden's *Mapping the Invisible Landscape: Folklore, Writing, and the Sense of Place* (1993) examines the physical landscape and the stories that determine the significance and meaning of those places. Other studies include Edward S. Casey, *The Fate of Place: A Philosophical History* (1997); Paul Gruchow, *The Necessity of Empty Places* (1999); Lynn Geesaman, *The Poetics of Place* (1999); Anne Whiston Spirn, *The Language of Landscape* (1999); and Mary Gordon, *Seeing through Places: Reflections on Geography and Identity* (2000). Cecelia Tichi examines geographical embodiment in *Embodiment of a Nation: Human Form in American Places* (2001). A more regionally focused study of the overlap of nature and culture is Kent C. Ryden's *Landscapes with Figures: Nature and Culture in New England* (2001). In *Surveying the Interior: Literary Cartographers and the Sense of Place* (2003), Rick van Noy examines four American literary cartographers concerned with what it means to map or survey a place and to write about it. Also see Edmund Ruffin, *Nature's Management: Writings on Landscape and Reform, 1822–1852* (2000); Kate A. Berry and Martha Henderson, editors, *Geographical Identities of Ethnic America: Race, Space, and Place* (2002); and Christopher J. Preston, *Grounding Knowledge: Environmental Philosophy, Epistemology, and Place* (2003). The literature of agriculture includes Stephanie L. Sarver, *Uneven Land: Nature and Agriculture in American Writing* (2000), and William Conlogue, *Working the Garden: American Writers and the Industrialization of Agriculture* (2001). Selections of writings from North American landscapes include David W. Teague, *The Southwest in American Literature and Art: The Rise of a Desert Aesthetic* (1997); John Lane and Gerald Thurmond, editors, *The Woods Stretched for Miles: New Nature Writing from the South* (1999). Numerous collections of regional and place-based American nature writing illustrate the various ways different writers represent the same region (the West, the Southeast, the Great Plains), state (Nevada, Oregon, Texas), or bioregion or natural feature (watersheds, rivers, deserts). A few recent examples of such texts include *The Last Best Place: A Montana Anthology* (1988), edited by William Kittredge and Annick Smith; *A Republic of Rivers: Three Centuries of Nature Writing from Alaska and the Yukon* (1990), edited by John Murray; *The Desert Reader: Descriptions of America's Arid Regions* (1991), edited by Peter Wild, and its companion *Getting Over the Color Green:*

Contemporary Environmental Literature of the Southwest (2001), edited by Scott Slovic. See also *The Height of Our Mountains: Nature Writing from Virginia's Blue Ridge Mountains and Shenandoah Valley* (1998), edited by Michael P. Branch and Daniel J. Philippon. Regional anthologies of writing include Steven Gilbar's *Natural State: A Literary Anthology of California Nature Writing* (1988) and *Pride of Place: A Contemporary Anthology of Texas Nature Writing* (2006), edited by David Taylor.

Bioregional Approaches

Bioregional approaches to environmental literature move from a general concern with landscape and region to a more specific concern with the biological and the ecological contours of place. The work of Gary Snyder in *Earth House Hold: Technical Notes and Queries to Fellow Dharma Revolutionaries* (1969), *The Practice of the Wild* (1990), and *A Place in Space: Ethics, Aesthetics, and Watersheds* (1995) offers the most comprehensive philosophical rationale for bioregionalism. Also see *Reinhabiting a Separate Country* (1978), edited by Peter Berg; Kirkpatrick Sale, *Dwellers in the Land: The Bioregional Vision* (1985); *Home! A Bioregional Reader*, edited by Van Andruss, Christopher Plant, Judith Plant, and Eleanor Wright (1990); and *Lifeplace: Bioregional Thought and Practice* (2003), by Robert L Thayer, Jr.

Environmental Poetry and Ecopoetics

The concern of poetry with the natural world in North America ranges from the pastoral inclinations of nature poetry to more recent explorations of nature and ecology. The anthology of essays *Ecopoetry: A Critical Introduction* (2002), edited by J. Scott Bryson, is a useful starting point for teachers and scholars interested in possibilities for further study. An early introduction to environmental poets and poetics is John Elder's *Imagining the Earth: Poetry and the Vision of* (1985; rev. ed. 1996). Leonard M. Scigaj's *Sustainable Poetry: Four American Poets* (1999) uses the phenomenologist Maurice Merleau-Ponty to offer an ecological alternative to poststructuralist poetics. Bernard Quetchenbach's *Back from the Far Field: Speaking of (and for) Nature in the Work of Three Contemporary American Poets* (2000) and David Gilcrest's *Greening the Lyre: Environmental Poetics and Ethics* (2002) elaborate the condition of nature poetry and poetics in the age of environmentalism. More recent approaches to poets and schools of poetry include Jed Rasula, *This Compost: Ecological Imperatives in American Poetry* (2002); Bonnie Costello, *Shifting Ground: Reinventing Landscape in Modern American Poetry* (2003); M. Jimmie Killingsworth, *Walt Whitman and the Earth: A Study in Ecopoetics* (2004); Angus Fletcher, *A New Theory for American Poetry: Democracy, the Environment, and the Future of Imagination* (2004); and J. Scott Bryson, *The West Side of Any Mountain: Place, Space, and Ecopoetry* (2005).

Native American Literature

Nature, landscape, and *geography* are contested terms in the literature of indigenous peoples and in the historical struggle to define Native American identity. For a collection of 120 stories from eight tribal regions see *Myths of Native America* (2003), edited by Tim McNeese. General historical overviews of the association of American Indian cultures and nature include R. G. Collingwood's *Changes in the Land: Indians, Colonists, and the Ecology of New England* (1983); Winona LaDuke's *All Our Relations: Native Struggles for Land and Life* (1999); Charles E. Kay and Randy T. Simmons's *Wilderness and Political Ecology: Aboriginal Influences and the Original State of Nature* (2002); and Alice Beck Kehoe's *America before the European Invasion* (2003). In *The Ecological Indian: Myth and History* (1999) the anthropologist Shepard Krech questions the historical evidence for Native Americans living in harmony with nature; Krech's controversial argument can be followed in the essays collected by Charles E. Kay and Randy T. Simmons in *Wilderness and Political Ecology: Aboriginal Influences and the Original State of Nature* (2002). Studies concerned with nature in Native American literature include Robert M. Nelson, *Place and Vision: The Function of Landscape in Native American Fiction* (1993); Donelle N. Dreese, *Ecocriticism: Creating Self and Place in Environmental and American Indian Literatures* (2002); Elizabeth Lynn-Cook, *Why I Can't Read Wallace Stegner and Other Essays: A Tribal Voice* (1996); and, more recently, Joni Adamson, *American Indian Literature, Environmental Justice, and Ecocriticism: The Middle Place* (2001).

Environmental Science and Ecology

A useful introduction to the history of environmental science is Donald Worster's *Nature's Economy: A History of Environmental Ideas* (1977; rev.

ed. 1986) and Carolyn Merchant's *Ecological Revolutions: Nature, Gender, and Science in New England* (1989) and *Ecology: Key Concepts in Critical Theory* (2002). These studies can be supplemented with *The Relations of Literature and Science: An Annotated Bibliography of Scholarship, 1880–1980* (1987), edited by Walter Schatzberg, Ronald A. Waite, and Jonathan K. Johnson. More general studies of scientific ecology include Paul R. Ehrlich, *The Machinery of Nature* (1986); Anna Bramwell, *Ecology in the Twentieth Century: A History* (1989); and Daniel Botkin, *Discordant Harmonies: A New Ecology for the Twenty-First Century* (1990). Edward O. Wilson's writings are also useful, most notably *The Diversity of Life* (1992) and *Biophilia* (1984). Also see *The Biophilia Hypothesis* (1993), edited by Stephen R. Kellert and Edward O. Wilson. More recent studies of environmental literature and science include Robert. J. Scholnick, *American Literature and Science* (1992); Karl Kroeber, *Ecological Literary Criticism: Romantic Imagining and the Biology of Mind* (1994); Joseph Carroll, *Evolution and Literary Theory* (1995); Amy R. Meyers, *Art and Science in America: Issues of Representation* (1998); Brett Cooke and Frederick Turner, *Biopoetics: Evolutionary Explorations in the Arts* (1999); *The Philosophy of Ecology: From Science to Synthesis* (2000), edited by David R. Keller and Frank B. Golley; and Ralph H. Lutts, *The Nature Fakers: Wildlife, Science and Sentiment* (2001). Two books that refocus the conversation are Glen E. Love's *Practical Ecocriticism* (2003) and Dana Phillips's *The Truth of Ecology* (2003). Also see Joseph Carroll, *Literary Darwinism: Evolution, Human Nature, and Literature* (2004).

Environmental History

George Perkins Marsh's *Man and Nature; or, Physical Geography as Modified by Human Action* (1864) remains a landmark in changing attitudes concerning the human impact on nature. The most comprehensive survey of the field of environmental history is Carolyn Merchant's *The Columbia Guide to Environmental History* (2002). For a documentary history, see *American Environmentalism: Readings in Conservation History* (1990), edited by Roderick Nash. Also see Donald Worster's *The Wealth of Nature: Environmental History and the Ecological Imagination* (1993) and *Major Problems in American Environmental History: Documents and Essays* (1993), edited by Carolyn Merchant. Major studies of the culture-nature relationship include Hans Huth, *Nature and the American: Three*

Centuries of Changing Attitudes (1957); Clarence Glacken, *Traces on the Rhodian Shore: Nature and Culture in Western Thought from Ancient Times to the End of the Eighteenth Century* (1967); Carolyn Merchant, *The Death of Nature: Women, Ecology, and the Scientific Revolution* (1980); Roderick Nash's classic intellectual history, *Wilderness and the American Mind* (1982); Keith Thomas, *Man and the Natural World: A History of the Modern Sensibility* (1983); Max Oelschlaeger, *The Idea of Wilderness: From Prehistory to the Age of Ecology* (1991); and Neil Evernden, *The Social Creation of Nature* (1992). See also *The Wilderness Condition: Essays on Environment and Civilization* (1992), edited by Max Oelschlaeger; and *Reinventing Nature? Responses to Postmodern Deconstruction* (1995), edited by Michael Soulé and Gary Lease. Two histories of the modern environmental movement are Philip Shabecoff, *A Fierce Green Fire: The American Environmental Movement* (1993), and Kirkpatrick Sale, *The Green Revolution: The American Environmental Movement, 1962–1992* (1993).

Environmental Ethics and Ecology

Mary Anglemeyer's bibliography, *The Natural Environment: An Annotated Bibliography on Attitudes and Values* (1984), provides a listing of books and articles on deep ecology, ecophilosophy, and environmental ethics. Nash outlines the development of environmental ethics in *The Rights of Nature: A History of Environmental Ethics* (1989), and Warwick Fox offers a review of ethical positions in *Toward a Transpersonal Ecology: Developing New Foundations for Environmentalism* (1990). Further explorations of ethics and the environment can be found in *Planet in Peril: Essays in Environmental Ethics* (1994), edited by Dale Westphal and Fred Westphal; *Environmental Philosophy: From Animal Rights to Radical Ecology* (1993), edited by Michael E. Zimmerman, J. Baird Callicott, George Sessions, Karen J. Warren, and John Clark; *Postmodern Environmental Ethics* (1995), edited by Max Oelschlaeger; *The Great New Wilderness Debate* (1998), edited by J. Baird Callicott and Michael P. Nelson; and *Philosophy and Geography III: Philosophies of Place* (1999), edited by Andrew Light and Jonathan M. Smith. The conversation continues in *Beyond the Land Ethic: More Essays in Environmental Philosophy* (1999), edited by J. Baird Callicott; *Ethnoecology: Knowledge, Resources, and Rights* (1999), edited by Ted L. Gragson and Ben G. Blount. Also see Pablo A. Iannone, *Philosophical Ecologies: Essays in Philosophy, Ecology, and Human Life* (1999); Peter H. Kahn, Jr., *The Human Relationship with Nature: Development and Culture* (1999); Lee Keekok, *The Natural and the Artefactual: The Implications of Deep Science and Deep Technology for Environmental Philosophy* (1999); Angelika Krebs, *Ethics of Nature* (1999). The effort to transform environmental ethics is at the heart of the deep-ecology movement and the various movements of radical environmentalism. See *Beneath the Surface: Critical Essays in the Philosophy of Deep Ecology* (2000), edited by Eric Katz, Andrew Light, and David Rothenberg, and Carolyn Merchant's overview of radical environmentalism in *Radical Ecology: The Search for a Livable World* (1992). Also see Jack Turner, *The Abstract Wild* (1996). For a critique of radical environmentalism see Martin W. Lewis, *Green Delusions: An Environmentalist Critique of Radical Environmentalism* (1992). Robert Paehlke attempts to establish a *via media* in *Environmentalism and the Future of Progressive Politics* (1989).

Religion and Nature

The study of religion and nature is inseparable from the history of environmental discourse and the concerns of contemporary environmental literature. General studies include Catherine Albanese, *Nature Religion in America: From the Algonkian Indians to the New Age* (1990); *Religion and Environmental Crisis* (1986), edited by Eugene Hargrove; *Spirit and Nature: Why the Environmental Crises Is a Religious Issue* (1992), edited by Steven C. Rockefeller and John C. Elder; *This Sacred Earth: Religion, Nature, Environment* (1996), edited by Roger S. Gottlieb; *The Greening of Faith: God, the Environment, and the Good Life* (1997), edited by John E. Carroll, Paul Brockelman, and Mary Westfall; *The Sacred Place: Witnessing the Holy in the Physical World* (1996), edited by W. Scott Olsen and Scott Cairns; and Beldon C. Lane, *Landscapes of the Sacred: Geography and Narrative in American Spirituality* (2001).

Ecofeminism

The theoretical and philosophical issues raised by ecofeminism have transformed the study of environmental literature. Annette Kolodny's work is foundational to the argument that women writers deepen our understanding of human relations to nature in Marcia Bonta, *Women in the Field: America's Pioneering Naturalists* (1991); Vera Norwood, *Made from This Earth: American Women and Nature* (1993); Louise Westling, *The Green Breast of the New World: Landscape, Gender, and American Fiction* (1996); and Krista Comer, *Landscapes of the New West: Gender and Geography in Contemporary Women's Writing* (1999). Additional scholarship on women and nature includes Donna J. Haraway, *Simians, Cyborgs, and Women: The Reinvention of Nature* (1991); Val Plumwood, *Feminism and the Mastery of Nature* (1993); and Noël Sturgeon, *Ecofeminist Natures: Race, Gender, Feminist Theory, and the Political Action* (1997). Surveys of ecofeminism include *Reweaving the World: The Emergence of Ecofeminism* (1991), edited by Irene Diamond and Gloria Feman Orenstein; *Healing the Wounds: The Promise of Ecofeminism* (1989), edited by Judith Plant; *Ecofeminism: Women, Animals, Nature* (1993), edited by Greta Gaard; and *Ecological Feminist Philosophies* (1996), edited by Karen J. Warren. Other works on gender and nature include Greta Gaard, *Ecological Politics: Ecofeminists and the Greens* (1998), and Catriona Sandilands, *The Good-Natured Feminist: Ecofeminism and the Quest for Democracy* (1999). Also see Stacy Alaimo, *Undomesticated Ground: Recasting Nature as Feminist Space* (2000), and Elizabeth Englehardt, *The Tangled Roots of Feminism, Environmentalism, and Appalachian Literature* (2003). Thomas S. Edwards and Elizabeth A. DeWolfe's anthology, *Such News of the Land: U.S. Women Nature Writers* (2001), and *Ecofeminist Literary Criticism: Theory, Interpretation, Pedagogy* (1998), edited by Greta Gaard and Patrick D. Murphy, suggest new directions in the field of ecofeminism and environmental literature.

Environmental Justice

Joni Adamson, Mei Mei Evans, and Rachel Stein's collection of essays, *The Environmental Justice Reader: Politics, Poetics, and Pedagogy* (2002), is the most comprehensive introduction to the field of environmental justice. Also see David E. Newton, *Environmental Justice: A Reference Handbook* (1996). The literature of environmental justice includes *Toxic Struggles: The Theory and Practice of Environmental Justice*, edited by Richard Hofrichter (1993); Robert Bullard's *Confronting Environmental Racism: Voices from the Grassroots* (1993), *Unequal Protection: Environmental Justice and Communities of Color* (1994), and *Dumping in Dixie: Race, Class, and Environmental Quality* (2000); Andrew Szasz, *Ecopopulism: Toxic Waste and the Movement for Environmental Justice* (1994). Other studies include Benjamin Goldman, *Not Just Prosperity: Achieving Sustainability with Environmental Justice* (1993); Kathlyn Gay, *Pollution and Powerless: The Environmental Justice Movement* (1995); Fen Osler Hampson and Judith Rippey, *Environmental Change and Social Justice* (1996); Laura Pulido, *Environmentalism and Economic Justice: Two Chicano Struggles in the Southwest* (1996); Jace Weaver, *Defending Mother Earth: Native American Perspectives on Environmental Justice* (1996); Jim Schwab, *Deeper Shades of Green: The Rise of Blue-Collar and Minority Environmentalism in America* (1996); Tom Athanasiou, *Divided Planet: The Ecology of Rich and Poor* (1996); Sandra Steingraber, *Living Downstream: An Ecologist Looks at Cancer and the Environment* (1997); Michael R. Edelstein, *Seeking Environmental Justice in a Contaminated World* (1998); Dorothee E. Kocks, *Dream a Little: Land and Social Justice in Modern America* (2000); and *The Colors of Nature: Culture Identity and the Natural World* (2002), edited by Alison H. Deming and Lauret E. Savoy.

Ecocomposition and Environmental Rhetoric

Ecocomposition: Theoretical and Practical Approaches (2001) and *Natural Discourse: Toward Ecocomposition* (2002), both edited by Sidney I. Dobrin and Christian R. Weisser, outline the current debates in the field. The study of environmental rhetoric is the subject of M. Jimmie Killingsworth and Jacqueline S. Palmer's *Ecospeak: Rhetoric and Environmental Politics in America* (1992). How people argue for environmental issues in nature writing and nonliterary discourse is the subject of Carl G. Herndl and Stuart C. Brown, editors, *Green Culture: Environmental Rhetoric in Contemporary America* (1996). The role of discourse and communication in environmentally oriented praxis is the subject of the essays in *The Symbolic Earth: Discourse and Our Creation of the Environment*, edited by James G. Cantrill and Christine L. Oravec (1996). Practical tools and advice from a practiced environmental journalist is found in Michael Frome's *Green Ink: An Introduction to Environmental Journalism* (1999). Also see Akira Mizuta Lippit, *Electric Animal: Toward a Rhetoric of Wildlife* (2000). Available readers and rhetorics for the composition classroom include *The Green Reader: Essays toward a Sustainable Society* (1991), edited by Andrew Dobson; *The Endangered Earth: Readings for Writers* (1992), edited by Sarah Morgan and Dennis Okerstrom; *Being in the World: An Environmental Reader for Writers* (1994), edited by Scott Slovic and Terrell Dixon; *Reading the Environment* (1994), edited by Melissa Walker; *Green Perspectives: Thinking and Writing about Nature and the Environment* (1994), edited by Walter Levy and Christopher Hallowell; *The Environmental Predicament: Four Issues in Critical Analysis* (1995), edited by Carol J. Verburg; *Writing Nature: An Ecological Reader for Writers* (1995), edited by Carolyn Ross; *Literature and the Environment: A Reader on Nature and Culture* (1999), edited by Lorraine Anderson, Scott Slovic, and John P. O'Grady; and *A Forest of Voices: Conversations in Ecology* (2000), edited by Chris Anderson and Lex Runciman.

Pedagogy

David Orr's argument for the need to redefine literacy in terms of environmental responsibility is elaborated in *Ecological Literacy: Education and the Transition to a Postmodern World* (1992). C. A. Bowers's *Critical Essays on Education, Modernity, and the Ecological Imperative* (1993) and Orr's *Earth in Mind: On Education, Environment, and the Human Prospect* (1994) provide useful analysis, as does Jonathan Collett and Stephen Karakashian's *Greening the College Curriculum: A Guide to Environmental Teaching in the Liberal Arts* (1996). A practical teacher's guide to environmental education that focuses on identity and citizenship is Mitchell Thomashow's *Ecological Identity: Becoming a Reflective Environmentalist* (1995); Thomashow's more recent argument for a place-based perceptual ecology is *Bringing the Biosphere Home: Learning to Perceive Global Environmental Change* (2002). For practical tips and useful overview materials geared to teaching literature and environment, see the first incarnation of this volume, *Teaching Environmental Literature: Materials, Methods, Resources* (1985), edited by Frederick Waage. Clare Walker Leslie, John Tallmadge, and Tom Wessels's *Into the Field: A Guide to Locally Focused Teaching* (1999) and William Morrish and Catherine R. Brown's *Planning to Stay: Learning to See the Physical Features of Your Neighborhood* (2000) are extremely useful for place-based pedagogies as well. An example of narrative scholarship and memoir is John Tallmadge's *Meeting the Tree of Life: A Teacher's Path* (1997). The most comprehensive compilation of essays on field-based practices is Hal Crimmel's *Teaching in the Field: Working with Students in the Outdoor Classroom* (2003). Corey Lewis, *Reading the Trail: Exploring the Literature and Natural History of the California Crest* (2005) elaborates a nomadic model for teaching outdoors.

Studies of Film

Jhan Hochman's *Green Cultural Studies: Nature in Film, Novel, and Theory* (1998) uses a comparative approach to the relation between nature and culture. Books on films about place and nature include *Mass Media and Environmental Conflict: America's Green Crusades* (1996), edited by Mark Neuzil and William Novarik; Gregg Mitman's *Reel Nature: America's Romance with Wildlife on Film* (1999); David Ingram's *Green Screen: Environmentalism and Hollywood Cinema* (2000); and Kim Newman's *Apocalypse Movies: End of the World Cinema* (2000). Also see Scott MacDonald's study of independent experimental and narrative films, *The Garden in the Machine: A Field Guide to Independent Films about Place* (2001).

Journals and Magazines

Amicus Journal
ASLE News
Audubon
Canadian Journal of Environmental Education
Earth
Earth First! The Radical Environmental Journal
Ecologist
Environment
Environmental Ethics
Environmental History
Environmental Values
High Country News
ISLE: Interdisciplinary Studies in Literature and the Environment
Orion: People and Nature
Science
Science News
Sierra
Terra Nova
Western American Literature
World Watch

Electronic Resources

The available materials on the World Wide Web are beyond the scope of this anthology. The Association for the Study of Literature and the Environment Web site (www.asle.umn.edu) includes current resources for teachers and scholars, such as electronic bibliographies, syllabi collections, and back-issue indexes for the association's journals and newsletters. The comprehensive environmental- and sustainability-studies resource page, *George* (named for George Perkins Marsh, author of *Man and Nature* [1864]), currently maintained by Ralph Lutts of Goddard College, is among the most useful portals to resources available on the World Wide Web (http://web.goddard.edu/ESresources/).

Note

1. In addition to the contributors to this volume, a list of people too long to mention here made helpful suggestions about the contents of this guide. For the materials on Canada I would like to especially acknowledge Pamela Banting, and for the materials on Mexican, Mexican American, and Chicana/o environmental literature I am grateful to Jorge Marcone and Priscilla Ybarra.

Notes on Contributors

Joni Adamson is associate professor of literature, writing, and film at Arizona State University, Polytechnic. She is the author of *American Indian Literature, Environmental Justice, and Ecocriticism: The Middle Place* and coeditor, with Mei Mei Evans and Rachel Stein, of *The Environmental Justice Reader: Politics, Poetics, and Pedagogy*. Her essays have appeared in *Globalization on the Line: Culture, Capital, and Citizenship at the U.S. Borders; Reading the Earth: New Directions in the Study of Literature and the Environment;* and *Studies in American Indian Literatures.*

Stacy Alaimo is associate professor of English at the University of Texas, Arlington, where she teaches multicultural American literatures, critical theory, and green cultural studies. She has published *Undomesticated Ground: Recasting Nature as Feminist Space*, as well as articles on feminism and environmentalism, American literature, film, and cultural studies. She has edited a collection with Susan J. Hekman, entitled *Material Feminisms*, and is finishing a manuscript entitled "Bodily Natures: Science, Environment and the Human Self."

Karla Armbruster teaches American literature, interdisciplinary humanities, and professional writing at Webster University, where she is associate professor in the English department. Her research interests include women's writing about nature, environmental activism in literary and cultural texts, bioregional and community studies, and representations of animals. With Kathleen R. Wallace, she is editor of *Beyond Nature Writing: Expanding the Boundaries of Ecocriticism*. Her current project is a book of narrative criticism about dogs and the significance of how we position them on the border between nature and culture.

Pamela Banting is associate professor in the English department, University of Calgary. She is the author of *Body Inc.: A Theory of Translation Poetics* and editor of the anthology *Fresh Tracks: Writing the Western Landscape*. She has published articles on such topics as geography as intertext, ethnicity and signature effects, the archive as literary genre, the postcolonial body, the body and landscape, and representations of grizzly bears. She is currently researching the question of the animal and working on a book of creative nonfiction essays about the Swan River Valley.

David Landis Barnhill is director of environmental studies and professor of English at the University of Wisconsin, Oshkosh. He has edited or coedited two ecologically oriented anthologies, *Deep Ecology and World Religions: New Essays on Sacred Ground* and *At Home on the Earth: Becoming Native* *to Our Place.* His book "Engaging the Earth: Radical Politics in American Nature Writing" is forthcoming. His interests include Asian influence on American nature writing, radical politics and spirituality in American nature writing, and Japanese nature writing.

Alanna F. Bondar is assistant professor of English and creative writing at Algoma University in Canada. She has published articles in *Canadian Poetry, Studies in Canadian Literature,* and *Theatre Research in Canada.* Her current poetry manuscript, "There are Many Ways to Die While Travelling in Peru," critically explores links between the Andean region and the quirky "wilds" of northern Ontario. Her scholarly work explores, through the lens of ecocriticism, how Canadian literature revisions our connections within biotic communities.

J. Scott Bryson teaches at Mount Saint Mary's College. He has edited one of the most important collections on ecocriticism, *Eco-poetry: A Critical Introduction* and is the author of *The West Side of Any Mountain: Place, Space, and Ecopoetry.* He has coedited volumes in the *Dictionary of Literary Biography.* Scott's current scholarship focuses on urban theory and culture, primarily as it relates to Los Angeles literature.

SueEllen Campbell is professor of English at Colorado State University. She has published ecocritical essays in various journals and books and is an editor for the University of Virginia's Under the Sign of Nature ecocriticism series. Her books of creative nonfiction are *Even Mountains Vanish: Searching for Solace in an Age of Extinction* and *Bringing the Mountain Home.* Currently she is working on a natural-history and cultural guide to landscapes.

Katherine R. Chandler teaches in the English department of Saint Mary's College of Maryland and is an originating member of the college's environmental studies program. She is coeditor of *Surveying the Literary Landscapes of Terry Tempest Williams: New Critical Essays.* Her articles have focused on Williams, Linda Hogan, and the teaching of environmental literature. Currently she is researching how Beatrix Potter's study of natural history and mycology influenced the creation of her children's stories.

Laird Christensen is associate professor of English and environmental studies at Green Mountain College, where he directs the graduate program in environmental studies. His articles on literature and bioregional pedagogy have appeared in a number of anthologies and journals, including *Northwest Review* and *Renascence;* his poems and creative nonfiction have appeared in such magazines as *Utne Reader, Wild Earth,* and *Whole Terrain.*

Christopher J. Cobb is assistant professor of English at Saint Mary's College in Notre Dame, Indiana, where he teaches Renaissance literature, modern drama, fantasy literature, and environmental literature. He is the author of *The Staging Romance in Late Shakespeare: Text and Theatrical Technique* and coeditor of *Renaissance Papers*. His interest in the literature of agriculture developed while he was teaching at North Carolina State University.

Hal Crimmel teaches writing and literature at Weber State University. He is the author of *Dinosaur: Four Seasons on the Green and Yampa Rivers* and editor of *Teaching in the Field: Working with Students in the Outdoor Classroom*. His essays on wilderness and outdoor-related topics have appeared in *Pacific Northwest Quarterly*, *South Dakota Review*, and *ISLE*. He is a former Fulbright Scholar to Austria.

Cheryl J. Fish is associate professor of English at City University of New York, Borough of Manhattan Community College, and was a Fulbright lecturer in Finland. She is the author of *Black and White Women's Travel Narratives: Antebellum Explorations* and coeditor of *A Stranger in the Village: Two Centuries of African American Travel Writing*. She is currently working on essays that examine environmental and social-justice narratives and films that draw on humor, memory, and grassroots activism.

Cheryll Glotfelty became the world's first professor of literature and environment, at the University of Nevada, Reno, where she and her colleagues founded the Association for the Study of Literature and Environment. With Harold Fromm, she edited the foundational text, *The Ecocriticism Reader: Landmarks in Literary Ecology*. She has published articles on environmentally oriented writers and is currently compiling an anthology of Nevada literature.

John R. Harris is executive director of the Monadnock Institute of Nature, Place, and Culture at Franklin Pierce University and the author of four stories in *Where the Mountain Stands Alone: Stories of Place in the Monadnock Region*. His teaching interests include American studies, New England's natural and cultural history, and the evolution of environmental thought. His research interests include the study of place and the collection of local stories about the inhabitants of the Monadnock region of New Hampshire.

Ursula K. Heise is associate professor of English at Stanford University, specializing in contemporary American and European literatures and literary theory. She published a book on the postmodern novel, *Chronoschisms: Time, Narrative, and Postmodernism* and coedited the *Longman Anthology of World Literature*. Her most recent book, "Sense of Place and Sense of Planet: The Environmental Imagination of the Global," is forthcoming. She is currently working on a book project entitled "The Avantgarde and the Forms of Nature."

Bob Henderson teaches outdoor education at McMaster University and writes a heritage-travel column for *Kanawa* magazine. His book, *Every Trail Has a Story: Heritage Travel in Canada*, explores heritage stories and pedagogical themes.

Annie Merrill Ingram is associate professor of English at Davidson College. She has published articles on environmental-justice literature, ecocomposition, and nineteenth-century American women writers. She is currently working on a project investigating the culture of flowers in nineteenth-century America.

Stephen R. Johnson is a freelance ecologist. His research interests include diversity in prairie remnants in Iowa.

Jerry Keir is the cofounder and director of the Great Basin Institute, an interdisciplinary environmental field-studies program at the University of Nevada, Reno. His essays have appeared in *Whole Terrain, Interdisciplinary Literary Studies*, and the United Nations' *Natural Resource Forum*.

Mark C. Long is associate professor of English and American studies and chair of the Department of English at Keene State College. He is cofounder and cofacilitator of the Calderwood Institute on the Teaching of Writing at Keene State College. He has published essays on teaching and the profession, theories of reading, environmental literature, and American poetry.

Glen A. Love is professor of English, emeritus, at the University of Oregon. He is the author of *Practical Ecocriticism: Literature, Biology and the Environment*. With Rhoda Love, he edited the first reader on modern environmental issues, *Ecological Crisis*. Other books include *Babbitt: An American Life* and *New Americans: The Westerner and the Modern Experience in the American Novel*. He was twice a visiting Fulbright senior lecturer in Germany.

Jorge Marcone is associate professor of Spanish and comparative literature at Rutgers University, New Brunswick. He has taught and researched on literacy and orality; nature, modernization, and writing in Latin America; representations of Amazonia; romances of the jungle; and "ecology" and the interconnectedness of the human and nonhuman in literature and the humanities since the end of the cold war. He was a visiting professor at the Center for Environmental Studies, Williams College.

David Mazel is professor of English at Adams State College, where he teaches courses in American literature, biotechnology and literature, and literary theory. He is the author of *American Literary Environmentalism* and *A Century of Ecocriticism*. He has written articles on ecocritical subjects and written or coauthored books on hiking and climbing.

Catriona Mortimer-Sandilands is Canada Research Chair in Sustainability and Culture at York University (Toronto). She is the author of *The Good-Natured Feminist: Ecofeminism and the Quest for Democracy*, editor (with Melody Hessing and Rebecca Raglon) of *This Elusive Land: Women and the Canadian Environment*; and author of articles on ecological feminisms, literatures, politics, and cultures. Currently she is working on a book entitled "Pastoral Traditions, Sexual Subversions: Lesbians Write Nature."

Patrick D. Murphy is professor of English at the University of Central Florida. He was founding editor of *ISLE: Interdisciplinary Studies in Literature and Environment*. He is the editor of *The Literature of Nature: An International Sourcebook* and author of *Farther Afield in the Study of Nature-Oriented Literature,* as well as periodical articles. He is currently writing a study of nature in the contemporary American novel.

Jeffrey Myers is assistant professor of English at Manhattan College, where he teaches nineteenth-century and multicultural American literature and environmental literature. He is the author of *Converging Stories: Race, Ecology, and Environmental Justice in American Literature,* as well as essays in journals including *African American Review* and *Interdisciplinary Studies in Literature and Environment*. His scholarship focuses on the intersection of race and the environment as they are represented in literature and culture, with particular attention to the implications for environmental justice.

Barbara Barney Nelson is associate professor at Sul Ross State University. She researches and teaches topics and authors related to environmental subjects that have an agricultural connection: West Texas, the Southwest, rural women, Mary Austin, and Edward Abbey. She is the author of *The Wild and the Domestic: Animal Representation, Ecocriticism, and Western American Literature* and is currently working on a memoir of her thirty years as a livestock journalist.

Daniel J. Philippon is associate professor of English at the University of Minnesota, Twin Cities, where he teaches courses in environmental rhetoric, history, and ethics. He is the author of *Conserving Words: How American Nature Writers Shaped the Environmental Movement,* editor of *The Friendship of Nature,* and coeditor of *The Height of Our Mountains* and *Coming into Contact.*

Bernard Quetchenbach teaches literature and writing at Montana State University, Billings. He is the author of *Back from the Far Field: American Nature Poetry in the Late Twentieth Century* and coeditor of *Lake Hollingsworth: Reflections and Studies on a Florida Landmark*. He has published poems, essays, and articles in journals and collections. *Everything as It Happens,* a book of poems, was published in 2007.

Anne Raine is assistant professor of English at the University of Ottawa, where she teaches courses in American literature and literature and environment. She has published articles on female modernist writers, nature writers, and earth art. Her book in progress explores how female modernist writers and nature writers negotiated the gendered divide between the professionalizing sciences and the feminized field of "nature work."

Randall Roorda is associate professor of English at the University of Kentucky, where he directs the writing program. He is author of *Dramas of Solitude: Narratives of Retreat in American Nature Writing* as well as essays in nature writing, ecocriticism, and teaching. He is past president of the Association for the Study of Literature and Environment (ASLE) and founder of ASLE-CCCC, a special-interest group of the Conference of College Composition and Communications promoting ecological approaches to composition. His interests center on genres of participation and valences of ecology in English studies.

William Slaymaker teaches environmental ethics, nature literature, and comparative literature and philosophy classes at Wayne State College. He has published essays on philosophical aesthetics and ecocriticism and, in *PMLA*, on African literature and ecocriticism. His most recent work focuses on environmental writing and literature in the Black Atlantic since 1950.

Scott Slovic is professor of literature and environment at the University of Nevada, Reno. He is the author of articles on ecocriticism and environmental literature and author, editor, or coeditor of seventeen books, including *Seeking Awareness in American Nature Writing* and *Wild Nevada*. The founding president of the Association for the Study of Literature and Environment from 1992 to 1995, he has served since 1995 as the editor of *ISLE*.

Cheryl C. Smith is assistant professor of English and the Writing across the Curriculum / Writing in the Disciplines faculty coordinator at Baruch College, City University of New York. She has published articles on Anne Hutchinson, Mina Shaughnessy, Henry David Thoreau, the role of English departments in general education, and the relation between writing programs and writing-across-the-curriculum initiatives. Her current research looks at building communities of practice for faculty development and using new technologies, such as Weblogs, in the writing classroom.

Mary Stark is chair of the English department at Central College. She has published articles and presented papers on environmental literature, environmental history, and Native American literature. She is active in promoting interdisciplinary science and literature teaching.

John Tallmadge is an independent scholar, writer, and educator based in Cincinnati. He has taught at Carleton College and the Union Institute and served as a director of the Orion Society and president of the Association for the Study of Literature and Environment. His writings on nature and culture include *Meeting the Tree of Life: A Teacher's Path* (1997) and *The Cincinnati Arch: Learning from Nature in the City* (2004), in addition to essays for *Audubon*, *Orion*, and *ISLE*.

Fred Waage is the editor of *Teaching Environmental Literature: Materials, Methods, Resources*. He has published poetry, fiction, and creative nonfiction as well as articles on Renaissance literature, Shakespeare, popular culture, and environmental literature. He was the founding editor of the Appalachian periodical *Now and Then*. As a teacher, he is interested in Renaissance drama, creative writing, Irish literature, and literature of the environment. He is the author of *The Crucial Role of the Environment in the Writings of George Stewart: A Life of America's Literary Ecologist*.

Priscilla Solis Ybarra is assistant professor of Latina and Latino literature in the Department of English at Texas Tech University. Her current book project will be the first study to engage a long-range environmental literary history of Chicana/o writing. She is the author of an article on Cherríe Moraga published in *New Perspectives on Environmental Justice: Gender, Sexuality, and Activism*. She has taught at Rice University; the University of California, Los Angeles; and Yale University.

Works Cited

Abbey, Edward. *Desert Solitaire: A Season in the Wilderness.* New York: Touchstone, 1968.

———. *Desert Solitaire: A Season in the Wilderness.* 1968. New York: Ballantine, 1971.

———. *The Monkey-Wrench Gang.* New York: HarperTrade, 2000.

———. "The Serpents of Paradise." Finch and Elder 614–20.

Abram, David. *The Spell of the Sensuous.* New York: Vintage, 1996.

Abrams, Kathleen S. "Literature and Science: An Interdisciplinary Approach to Environmental Studies." *Curriculum Review* 18.4 (1979): 302–04.

Adams, Carol F. *The Sexual Politics of Meat: A Feminist-Vegetarian Critical Theory.* New York: Continuum, 1995.

Adams, Douglas, and Mark Carwardine. *Last Chance to See.* New York: Ballantine, 1990.

Adamson, Joni. *American Indian Literature, Environmental Justice, and Ecocriticism: The Middle Place.* Tucson: U of Arizona P, 2001.

———. "'Throwing Rocks at the Sun': An Interview with Teresa Leal." Adamson, Evans, and Stein 44–57.

Adamson, Joni, Mei Mei Evans, and Rachel Stein, eds. *The Environmental Justice Reader: Politics, Poetics, and Pedagogy.* Tucson: U of Arizona P, 2002.

———. "Introduction: Environmental Justice Politics, Poetics, and Pedagogy." Adamson, Evans, and Stein, *Reader* 3–14.

Adams-Williams, Lydia. "Conservation: Woman's Work." *Forestry and Irrigation* 14 (1908): 350–51.

"Agnew Unleashed." *Time* 31 Oct. 1969. 22 Aug. 2007 <http://www.time.com>.

Alaimo, Stacy. "Discomforting Creatures: Monstrous Natures in Recent Films." *Beyond Nature Writing: Expanding the Boundaries of Ecocriticism.* Armbruster and Wallace 279–96.

———. "This Is about Pleasure: Human Habitats, Animal Memories, and Corporeal Ethics." *Architecture, Ethics, and the Personhood of Place.* Ed. Gregory Caicco. Hanover: UP of New England, 2007.

———. *Undomesticated Ground: Recasting Nature as Feminist Space.* Ithaca: Cornell UP, 2000.

Allen, Grant. Introduction. *The Natural History of Selborne.* By Gilbert White. 1789. Ed. Allen. Ware, Eng.: Wordsworth Eds., 1996. ix–xx.

Altman, John, and Aimée Larrabee. *Last Stand of the Tallgrass Prairie.* Videocassette. Inland Sea Productions, 2001.

America's Lost Landscapes. Dir. David O'Shields. New Light Media, 2004.

Ammons, A. R. *Corson's Inlet.* Ithaca: Cornell UP, 1965.

———. *Garbage.* New York: Norton, 1993.

Anaya, Rudolfo A., and Francisco A. Lomelí, eds. *Aztlán: Essays on the Chicano Homeland.* Albuquerque: Academia-El Norte, 1989.

Anderson, Lorraine, and Thomas S. Edwards, eds. *At Home on This Earth: Two Centuries of U.S. Women's Nature Writing.* Hanover: UP of New England, 2002.

Anderson, Lorraine, Scott Slovic, and John O'Grady, eds. *Literature and the Environment: A Reader on Nature and Culture.* New York: Longman, 1999.

And Justice For All. Louisville: Media Services Presbyterian Church, n.d.

Andrews, William L., ed. *Classic American Autobiographies.* New York: Mentor, 1992.

Anglemyer, Mary, and Eleanor R. Seagraves, comps. *The Natural Environment: An Annotated Bibliography on Attitudes and Values.* 2nd ed. Washington: Smithsonian Inst. P, 1984.

The Animal—Part I. Spec. issue of *Mosaic: A Journal for the Interdisciplinary Study of Literature* 39.4 (2006): 1–218.

The Animal—Part II. Spec. issue of *Mosaic: A Journal for the Interdisciplinary Study of Literature* 40.1 (2007): 1–213.

Annals of the Cakchiquels. Ed. and trans. Daniel G. Brinton. Vol. 6 of *Library of Aboriginal American Literature 1882–1899.* Philadelphia: n. p., 1885. 8 vols.

Anzaldúa, Gloria. *Borderlands / La Frontera: The New Mestiza.* San Francisco: Spinsters–Aunt Lute, 1987.

Aranda, José F., Jr. "Contradictory Impulses: María Amparo Ruiz de Burton, Resistance Theory, and the Politics of Chicano/a Studies." *American Literature* 70 (1998): 551–97.

———. *When We Arrive: A New Literary History of Mexican America.* Tucson: U of Arizona P, 2003.

Arendt, Hannah. *The Human Condition.* Chicago: U of Chicago P, 1958.

Arguedas, Jose Maria. *Deep Rivers.* 1958. Trans. Frances Horning Barraclough. Prospect Heights: Waveland, 2002.

Aridjis, Homero. *¿En quién piensas cuando haces el amor?* Mexico City: Alfaguara, 1996.

———. *Eyes to See Otherwise / Ojos, de otro mirar: Selected Poems.* Ed. Betty Aridjis and George McWhirter. New York: New Directions, 2001.

———. *Imágenes para el fin del milenio and Nueva Expulsión del Paraíso.* Mexico City: Mortiz, 1990.

———. *La leyenda de los soles.* Mexico City: Fondo de Cultura Económica, 1993.

———. *La montaña de las mariposas.* Mexico City: Alfaguara, 2000.

———. *Ojos de otro mirar.* Mexico City: El Tucán de Virginia, 1998.

———. *Tiempo de ángeles.* Mexico City: Fondo de Cultura Económica, 1997.

Armbruster, Karla. "Buffalo Gals, Won't You Come Out Tonight: A Call for Boundary-Crossing in Ecofeminist Literary Criticism." Gaard and Murphy 97–122.

Armbruster, Karla, and Kathleen R. Wallace, eds. *Beyond Nature Writing: Expanding the Boundaries of Ecocriticism.* Charlottesville: UP of Virginia, 2001.

Assiniwi, Bernard. *The Beothuk Saga.* Toronto: McClelland, 2000.

Asturias, Miguel Ángel. *Men of Maize.* Trans. Gerald Martin. Pittsburgh: U of Pittsburgh P, 1993.

———. *Strong Wind.* Trans. Gregory Rabassa. New York: Delacorde, 1987.

Atwood, Margaret. Afterword. *The Journals of Susanna Moodie*. Toronto: Oxford UP, 1970. 62–64.

———. *Surfacing*. Toronto: McClelland, 1972.

———. *Survival: A Thematic Guide to Canadian Literature*. Toronto: Anansi, 1972.

Auerbach, Erich. *Mimesis: Dargestellte Wirklichkeit in den Abendlandischen Literatur*. 2nd ed. Bern: Francke, 1959.

Austin, Mary. "Bitterness of Women." 1909. *Western Trails: A Collection of Short Stories by Mary Austin*. Ed. Melody Graulich. Reno: U of Nevada P, 1987. 76–82.

———. *The Ford*. 1917. Berkeley: U of California P, 1997.

———. *The Land of Little Rain*. 1903. New York: Modern Lib., 2003.

———. "Speaking of Bears." *One Smoke Stories*. New York: Houghton, 1934. 110–30.

———. "The Wolf Pack: A Review of *The Last Stand of the Pack*." *Saturday Review* 21 Dec. 1929: 587.

Azuela, Mariano. *The Underdogs*. Trans. Enrique Munguía. New York: Brentano, 1929. Trans. of *Los de abajo*. 1915.

Babstock, Ken. "The Appropriate Gesture; or, Regular Dumb-Ass Guy Looks at Bird." *Where the Words Come From: Canadian Poets in Conversation*. Ed. Tim Bowling. Roberts Creek: Nightwood, 2002.

Baca, Jimmy Santiago. *Black Mesa Poems*. New York: New Directions, 1989.

———. "Carrying the Magic of His People's Heart: An Interview with Jimmy Santiago Baca." By Gabriel Meléndez. *Americas Review* 19.3-4 (1991): 64–86.

———. *Healing Earthquakes*. New York: Grove, 2001.

———. *Martin and Meditations on the South Valley*. New York: New Directions, 1987.

Bailey, Liberty Hyde. "Excerpts from *Holy Earth*." *This Incomparable Lande: A Book of American Nature Writing*. Ed. Thomas J. Lyon. Boston: Houghton, 1989. 247–57.

Bakeless, John. *America as Seen by Its First Explorers: The Eyes of Discovery*. New York: Dover, 1961.

Baker, Houston A., Jr. *Modernism and the Harlem Renaissance*. Chicago: U of Chicago P, 1987.

Baker, Steve. *Picturing the Beast: Animals, Identity, and Representation*. 1993. Champaign: U of Illinois P, 2001.

———. *The Postmodern Animal*. London: Reaktion, 2000.

Balbuena, Bernardo de. *Grandeza mexicana*. 1604. Mexico City: Porrúa, 1985.

Banfield, A. W. F. Rev. of *Never Cry Wolf*, by Farley Mowat. *Canadian Field Naturalist* 78 (1964): 52–54.

Bangs, Ed. Lecture. "Dancing with Wolves: Reality and Imagination." Western Lit. Assn. Conf. Big Sky. 1 Oct. 2004.

Banting, Pamela, ed. *Fresh Tracks: Writing the Western Landscape*. Victoria: Polestar, 1998.

———. "The Land Writes Back: Notes on Four Western Canadian Writers." Murphy, *Literature of Nature* 140–46.

Barlow, Joel. *The Columbiad*. 1807. *Project Gutenberg*. 5 Aug. 2007 <http://gutenberg.org/etext/8683.html>.

———. *The Vision of Columbus: A Poem in Nine Books*. 1787. Ann Arbor: UMI, n.d.

Barnes, H. Lee. *The Lucky*. Reno: U of Nevada P, 2003.

Barnhill, David Landis, trans. *Bashō's Haiku: Selected Poems of Matsuo Bashō*. Albany: State U of New York P, 2004.

———, trans. *Bashō's Journey: The Literary Prose of Matsuo Bashō*. Albany: State U of New York P, 2005.

———."Indra's Net as Food Chain: Gary Snyder's Ecological Vision." *Ten Directions* 11.2 (1990): 20–28.

———. "An Interwoven World: Gary Snyder's Cultural Ecosystem." *Worldviews: Environment, Culture, Religion* 6.2 (2002): 111–44.

———. "Relational Holism: Huayan Buddhism and Deep Ecology." *Deep Ecology and World Religions*. Ed. Barnhill and Roger S. Gottlieb. Albany: State U of New York P, 2001. 77–106.

———. "Through an Eastern Window: East Asian Culture and the Writings of Scott Russell Sanders." Biennial Meeting of the Assn. for the Study of Lit. and the Environment. Flagstaff. 22 June 2001.

Baron, David. *The Beast in the Garden: A Modern Parable of Man and Nature*. New York: Norton, 2004.

Barr, Nevada. *Blood Lure*. New York: Berkley, 2002.

Barry Lopez. Dir. Dan Griggs. Santa Fe: Lannon Foundation, 1992.

Barthes, Roland. "L'effet de reel." *Le bruissement de la langue: Essais critiques IV*. 1968. Paris: Seuil, 1984. 179–80.

Bartholomae, David. "Inventing the University." *When A Writer Can't Write: Studies in Writer's Block and Other Composing Process Problems*. Ed. Mike Rose. New York: Guilford, 1985. 134–65.

Bartolomé, Efraín. *Ciudad bajo el relámpago*. Mexico City: Katún, 1983.

———. *Cuandernos contra el ángel*. Querétaro, Mex.: Universidad Autonoma de Querétaro, 1987.

———. *Oficio: Arder. Obra poética 1982–1997*. Mexico City: UNAM, 1998.

———. *Ojos de jaguar*. 1982. Mexico City: Punto de Partida-UNAM, 1990.

Bartram, William. *Travels*. 1791. New York: Viking, 1988.

Baruch College Faculty Handbook. Academic Integrity Taskforce, Baruch Coll. 25 May 2004. 16 Feb. 2007 <http://www.Baruch.cuny.edu/facultyhandbook/taskforce.htm>.

Bary, William Theodore de. " 'Think Globally, Act Locally,' and the Contested Ground Between." Tucker and Berthrong 23–34.

Basso, Keith. *Wisdom Sits in Places: Landscape and Language among the Western Apache*. Albuquerque: U of New Mexico P, 1987.

Baym, Nina. *American Women of Letters and the Nineteenth-Century Sciences: Styles of Affiliation*. New Brunswick: Rutgers UP, 2002.

———, ed. *Norton Anthology of American Literature*. New York: Norton, 1998.

Begley, Sharon. "Can Pesticide Tests on Humans Ever Meet Standards for Ethics?" *Wall Street Journal* 17 Jan. 2003: B1.

Bennett, Michael. "Anti-pastoralism, Frederick Douglass, and the Nature of Slavery." Armbruster and Wallace 195–210.

———. "Manufacturing the Ghetto: Anti-urbanism and the Spatialization of Race." Bennett and Teague 169–88.

Bennett, Michael, and David W. Teague, eds. *The Nature of Cities: Ecocriticism and Urban Environments.* Tucson: U of Arizona P, 1999.

Bentham, Jeremy. *An Introduction to the Principles of Morals and Legislation.* Ed. J. H. Burns and H. L. A. Hart. Oxford: Clarendon, 1996.

Beongcheon Yu. *The Great Circle: American Writers and the Orient.* Detroit: Wayne State UP, 1983.

Berger, John. "Why Look at Animals?" *About Looking.* New York: Pantheon, 1980. 1–26.

Bergman, Charles. "Academic Animals." *ISLE* 9.1 (2002): 141–47.

———. "The Literature and Experience of Nature." Waage, *Teaching* 122–29.

Bergon, Frank, ed. *The Journals of Lewis and Clark.* New York: Penguin, 1995.

Berman, Morris. *The Twilight of American Culture.* New York: Norton, 2001.

Berry, Wendell. "A Citizen's Response to the National Security Strategy of the United States." *Citizens Dissent: Security, Morality, and Leadership in an Age of Terror.* Ed. Wendell Berry and David James Duncan. Great Barrington: Orion, 2003.

———. *Home Economics.* New York: North Point, 1987.

———. *In the Presence of Fear: Three Essays for a Changed World.* Great Barrington: Orion, 2005.

———. "The Peace of Wild Things." Bly 177.

———. *A Place on Earth.* Rev. ed. San Francisco: North Point, 1983.

———. "The Prejudice against Country People." *Progressive* 66.4 (2002). 31 Oct. 2004 <http://www.progressive.org/April%2022002/berry0402.html>.

———. "Preserving Wildness." Berry, *Home Economics* 137–51.

———. *Sayings and Doings and an Eastward Look.* 1974. Frankfort: Gnomon, 1990.

———. *The Selected Poems of Wendell Berry.* Washington: Counterpoint, 1998.

———. *Standing by Words.* San Francisco: North Point. 1983.

———. *The Unsettling of America: Culture and Agriculture.* 3rd ed. San Francisco: Sierra Club, 1997.

Berthoff, Ann E. *The Making of Meaning.* Montclair: Boynton-Cook, 1981.

Beston, Henry. *The Outermost House: A Year of Life on the Great Beach of Cape Cod.* 1928. New York: Holt, 2003.

Bibb, Henry. *The Life and Adventures of Henry Bibb, an American Slave.* 1849. Madison: U of Wisconsin P, 2001.

Bickel, Lennard. *Facing Starvation: Norman Borlaug and the Fight against Hunger.* Pleasantville: Reader's Digest, 1974.

Bierhorst, John, ed. and trans. *Cantares Mexicanos: Songs of the Aztecs.* Stanford: Stanford UP, 1985.

Binns, Niall. *¿Callejón sin salida? Las crisis ecológica en la poesía hispano-americana.* Zaragoza, Spain: Prensas Universitarias de Zaragoza, 2004.

———."Landscapes of Hope and Destruction: Ecological Poetry in Spanish America." *ISLE* 9.1 (2002): 105–19.

———. "Landscapes of Hope and Destruction: Ecological Poetry in Spanish America." *The ISLE Reader: Ecocriticism, 1993–2003.* Ed. Michael P. Branch and Scott Slovic. Athens: U of Georgia P, 2003. 124–39.

Bishop, Elizabeth. *The Complete Poems, 1927–1979.* New York: Farrar, 1980.

Blake, William. "The Tiger." *Oxford Book of English Verse: 1250–1900.* Ed. Arthur Quiller-Couch. Oxford: Clarendon, 1919. 489. <http:www.bartleby.com/101/ 489.html>.

Blanco, Alberto. *El corazón del instante.* Mexico City: Fondo de Cultura Económica, 1998.

———. *Dawn of the Senses: Selected Poems of Alberto Blanco.* Ed. Juvenal Acosta. Introd. José Emilio Pacheco. Bilingual ed. San Francisco: City Lights, 1995. Trans. of *Amanecer de los sentidos.* 1993.

———. *The Desert Mermaid / La sirena de desierto.* Trans. Barbara Paschke. San Francisco: Children's Book, 1992.

———. *El origen ya la huella / The Origin and the Trace.* Trans. Julian Palley. San Diego: Circa, 2000.

———. *También los insectos son perfectos.* Mexico City: Centro de Información y Desarrollo de la Comunicación y la Literatura Infantiles-Consejo Nacional para la Cultura y las Artes, 1993.

Blanco, José Joaquín. *Un chavo bien helado. Crónicas de los años '80.* Mexico City: Era, 1990.

———. *Cuando todas las chamacas se pusieron medias de nylon.* Mexico City: Enjambre, 1989.

———. *Función de medianoche.* Mexico City: Era, 1997.

Blau, Sheridan, and John von B. Rodenbeck, eds. *The House We Live In: An Environmental Reader.* New York: Macmillan, 1971.

———. Introduction. Blau and Rodenbeck, *House* 1–6.

Bleakley, Alan. *The Animalizing Imagination: Totemism, Textuality, and Ecocriticism.* New York: St. Martin's, 2000.

Blend, Benay. "Intersections of Nature and the Self in Chicana Writing." *Bucknell Review: New Essays in Ecofeminist Literary Criticism.* Ed. Glynis Carr. Lewisburg: Bucknell UP, 2000. 56–70.

Blue Vinyl. Dir. Judith Helfand and Daniel B. Gold. Toxic Comedy, 2002.

Bly, Robert, ed. *News of the Universe: Poems of Two-Fold Consciousness.* San Francisco: Sierra Club, 1980.

The Book of Chilam Balam of Chumayel. Trans. Ralph L. Roys. 1933. Norman: U of Oklahoma P, 1967.

Borges, Jorge Luis. With Esther Zemborain de Torres. *An Introduction to American Literature.* Ed. and trans. L. Clark Keating and Robert O. Evans. Lexington: UP of Kentucky, 1971.

Bost, Suzanne. "West Meets East: Nineteenth-Century Southern Dialogues on Mixture, Race, Gender, and Nation." *Mississippi Quarterly* 56 (2003): 647–56.

Botkin, Daniel. *Discordant Harmonies: A New Ecology for the Twenty-First Century.* New York: Oxford UP, 1990.

———. *Our Natural History: The Lessons of Lewis and Clark.* New York: Oxford, 2004.

Botstein, Leon. "Beyond Great-Books Programs and Fads in the Curriculum." *Chronicle of Higher Education* 1 Dec. 1982.

———. *Jefferson's Children: Education and the Promise of American Culture.* New York: Doubleday, 1997.

Bowerbank, Sylvia. *Speaking for Nature: Women and Ecologies of Early Modern England.* Baltimore: Johns Hopkins UP, 2004.

Bowers, C. A. *Educating for an Ecologically Sustainable Culture.* Albany: State U of New York P, 1995.

Boyle, T. Coraghessan. *A Friend of the Earth.* New York: Penguin, 2001.

———. *The Tortilla Curtain.* New York: Viking, 1995.

Bradford, William. *Of Plymouth Plantation: 1620–1647.* Ed. Samuel Eliot Morison. New York: Modern Lib., 1967.

Branch, Michael P., ed. *Reading the Roots: American Nature Writing before Walden.* Athens: U of Georgia P, 2004.

———. "Saving All the Places: The Place of Textual Editing in Ecocriticism." Rosendale 3–25.

Brand, Dionne. *Land to Light On.* Toronto: McClelland, 1997.

Brinkley, Alan. *The Unfinished Nation.* 4th ed. Boston: McGraw, 2004.

Brotherston, Gordon. *Image of the New World: The American Continent Portrayed in Native Texts.* London: Thames, 1979.

Brown, Charles Brockden. *Edgar Huntly; or, Memoirs of a Sleep-Walker.* 1799. Ed. Norman S. Grabo. New York: Penguin, 1988.

Brown, Donald E. *Human Universals.* Philadelphia: Temple UP, 1991.

———. "Human Universals and Their Implications." *Being Humans: Anthropological Universals and Particularity in Transdisciplinary Perspectives.* Ed. Neil Roughley. New York: Gruyter, 2000. 157–74.

Browning, Peter. *The Last Wilderness: Eight Hundred Miles by Canoe and Portage in the Northwest Territories.* Lafayette: Great West, 1989.

Brox, Jane. *Five Thousand Days like This One: An American Family History.* Boston: Beacon, 1999.

Bruchac, Joseph. "The Connections: An Introduction." *Come to Power.* Ed. Dick Lourie. Trumansburg: Crossing, 1974. 5–8.

Bryant, William Cullen. "The Prairies." Baym, *Norton Anthology* 1042–44.

Bryson, Bill. *The Lost Continent: Travels in Small-Town America.* 1989. New York: Harper, 1990.

Bryson, J. Scott. Introduction. *Ecopoetry.* Ed. Bryson. Salt Lake City: U of Utah P, 2002. 1–13.

———. *The West Side of Any Mountain: Place, Space, and Ecopoetry.* Iowa City: U of Iowa P, 2005.

Buell, Lawrence. "The Ecological Insurgency." *New Literary History* 30 (1999): 699–712.

———. *The Environmental Imagination: Thoreau, Nature Writing, and the Formation of American Culture.* Cambridge: Harvard UP, 1995.

———. *The Future of Environmental Criticism: Environmental Crisis and Literary Imagination.* Oxford: Blackwell, 2005.

———. "Toxic Discourse." *Critical Inquiry* 24 (1998): 639–65.

————. *Writing for an Endangered World: Literature, Culture, and Environment in the U.S. and Beyond.* Cambridge: Harvard UP, 2001.

Bullard, Robert D., ed. *Confronting Environmental Racism: Voices from the Grass-roots.* Boston: South End, 1993.

————. *Dumping in Dixie: Race, Class, and Environmental Quality.* 1990. Boulder: Westview, 1999.

————, ed. *Unequal Protection: Environmental Justice and Communities of Color.* San Francisco: Sierra Club, 1997.

Burke, Edmund. *A Philosophical Enquiry into the Origins of Our Ideas of the Sublime and Beautiful.* London: n.p., 1757.

Burke, Kenneth. "Literature as Equipment for Living." *The Philosophy of Literary Form.* 2nd ed. Baton Rouge: Louisiana State UP, 1967.

Burroughs, John. *Burch Browsings: A John Burroughs Reader.* Ed. Bill McKibben. New York: Penguin, 1992.

Busch, Robert, ed. *Wolf Songs: The Classic Collection of Writing about Wolves.* San Francisco: Sierra Club, 1994.

Bustillo Oro, Juan. *San Miguel del las Espinas: Trilogía dramática de un pedazo de tierra mexicana.* 1933. *Teatro mexicano del Siglo XX.* Vol. 2. Mexico City: Fondo de Cultura Económica, 1981. 25–148.

Butler, Judith. *Bodies That Matter: On the Discursive Limits of "Sex."* New York: Routledge, 1993.

Cajete, Gregory. *Look to the Mountain: An Ecology of Indigenous Education.* Durango: Kivaki, 1994.

Calarco, Matthew, and Peter Atterton, eds. *Animal Philosophy: Essential Readings in Continental Thought.* New York: Continuum, 2004.

Callicott, J. Baird. *Beyond the Land Ethic: More Essays in Environmental Philosophy.* Albany: State U of New York P, 1999.

————. *Earth's Insights: A Multicultural Survey of Ecological Insights from the Mediterranean Basin to the Australian Outback.* Berkeley: U of California P, 1994.

————. "Many Indigenous Worlds or *the* Indigenous World? A Reply to My 'Indigenous' Critics." *Environmental Ethics* 22 (2000): 291–310.

Callicott, J. Baird, and Michael Nelson. *American Indian Environmental Ethics: An Ojibwa Case Study.* Upper Saddle River: Prentice, 2004.

Camarillo, María Enriqueta. *Álbum sentimental.* Ed. Ángel Dotor. Madrid: Espasa-Calpe, 1926.

————. *El secreto.* Madrid: Editorial América, 1922.

Cameron, Elspeth, ed. *Canadian Culture: An Introductory Reader.* Toronto: Canadian Scholars', 1997.

Carby, Hazel V. *Reconstructing Womanhood: The Emergence of the Afro-American Woman Novelist.* New York: Oxford UP, 1987.

Carhart, Arthur H., and Stanley P. Young. *The Last Stand of the Pack.* New York: Sears, 1929.

Carpentier, Alejo. *The Lost Steps.* 1956. Trans. Harriet de Onis. Minneapolis: U of Minnesota P, 2001.

Carr, Glynnis, ed. *New Essays in Ecofeminist Literary Criticism.* Lewisburg: Bucknell UP, 2000.

Carroll, Joseph. *Evolution and Literary Theory.* Columbia: U of Missouri P, 1994.

———. *Literary Darwinism: Evolution, Human Nature, and Literature.* New York: Routledge, 2004.

———. "Organism, Environment, and Literary Representation." *ISLE* 9.2 (2002): 27–45.

Carson, Rachel. *Silent Spring.* Boston: Houghton, 1962.

———. *Silent Spring.* Boston: Mariner, 2002.

Carter, Angela. *The Bloody Chamber.* New York: Harper, 1979.

Casino. Dir. Martin Scorsese. Universal, 1995.

Castellanos, Rosario. *The Book of Lamentations.* Trans. Esther Allen. New York: Marsilio, 1996. Trans. of *Oficio de tinieblas.* 1962.

———. *The Nine Guardians.* Trans. Irene Nicholson. New York: Vanguard, 1960. Trans. of *Balún-Canán.* 1957.

Castillo, Ana. *So Far from God: A Novel.* New York: Plume, 1994.

———. "The Watsonville Women's Strike, 1986. A Case of Mexican Activism." *Massacre of the Dreamers: Essays in Xicanisma.* New York: Plume, 1994. 43–62.

Castro Leal, Antonio, ed. *Las cien mejores poesías mexicanas modernas.* Mexico City: Porrúa, 1958.

Cather, Willa. *My Ántonia.* 1918. Boston: Houghton, 1954.

———. *O Pioneers!* 1913. Ed. Marilee Lindemann. Oxford: Oxford UP, 1999.

———. *The Professor's House.* 1925. Lincoln: U of Nebraska P, 2002.

———. *The Song of the Lark.* 1915. Boston: Houghton, 1988.

Catlin, George. *Letters and Notes on the Manners, Customs, and Conditions of North American Indians.* 1841. Vol. 1. New York: Dover, 1973.

Catton, William R., and Riley E. Dunlap. "A New Ecological Paradigm for Post-exuberant Sociology." *American Behavioral Scientist* 24.1 (1980): 15–47.

Cervantes, Lorna Dee. *Enplumada.* Pittsburgh: U of Pittsburgh P, 1981.

Chenette, Jon. *Broken Ground.* 6 Aug. 2004. 16 Feb. 2007 <http://web.grinnell .edu/individuals/Chenet/bg_guide.html>.

Childs, Craig. *The Secret Knowledge of Water.* Boston: Little, 2000.

Christensen, Laird. "Trends in Teaching Literature and Environment: From Overview to Application." Pacific Ancient and Modern Lang. Assn. Conf. Portland State U. Apr. 1999.

———. "Writing the Watershed." Crimmel 124–36.

Christensen, Laird, and Peter Blakemore, eds. *The ASLE Collection of Syllabi in Literature and Environment.* 16 Feb. 2007 <http://www.asle.umn.edu/pubs/ collect/surveys/Buell.PDF>.

Christian, Edgar. *Death in the Barren Ground.* Ed. George Whalley. Ottawa: Oberon, 1980.

Churchill, Ward. *Struggle for the Land: Indigenous Resistance to Genocide, Ecocide, and Expropriation in Contemporary North America.* Monroe: Common Courage, 1993.

Cisneros, Sandra. Interview with Gregg Barrios. *Nature Conservancy* Fall 2003: 12.

Cixous, Hélène. "The Newly Born Woman." *The Cixous Reader.* Ed. Susan Sellers. New York: Routledge, 1994. 35–46.

Clark, Robert, ed. *Our Sustainable Table*. San Francisco: North Point, 1990.

Clark, Walter H., Jr. "The New England Literature Program." Waage, *Teaching* 158–64.

———. "What Teaching Environmental Literature Might Be." Waage, *Teaching* 4–8.

Clarke, Bruce. "Science, Theory, and Systems: A Response to Glen A. Love." *ISLE* 8.1 (2001): 149–65.

Clavijero, Francisco Javier. *Historia Antigua de México*. 1780–81. 4 vols. Mexico City: Porrúa, 1958.

Clearcut. Dir. Riszard Bugajski. Cinezus, 1991.

Cohen, Michael P. "Blues in the Green: Ecocriticism under Critique." *Environmental History* 9.1 (2004): 9–36.

———. *The Pathless Way: John Muir and the American Wilderness*. Madison: U of Wisconsin P, 1984.

Colborn, Theo, Dianne Dumanoski, and John Peterson Myers. *Our Stolen Future*. New York: Plume, 1997.

Coleman, James William. *The New Buddhism: The Western Transformation of an Ancient Tradition*. Oxford: Oxford UP, 2001.

Comer, Krista. *Landscapes of the New West: Gender and Geography in Contemporary Women's Writing*. Chapel Hill: U of North Carolina P, 1999.

Commoner, Barry. *The Closing Circle: Nature, Man, Technology*. New York: Knopf, 1971.

Community Education and Outreach. Mailman School of Public Health, Columbia U. 5 June 2007 <http://www.ccceh.org/research/community-education .html>.

Comstock, Anna Botsford. "A Little Nomad." Anderson and Edwards 107–09.

Comstock, Gary, ed. *Is There a Moral Obligation to Save the Family Farm?* Ames: Iowa State UP, 1987.

Conkin, Paul K. *The Southern Agrarians*. Knoxville: U of Tennessee P, 1988.

Conlogue, William. *Working the Garden: American Writers and the Industrialization of Agriculture*. Chapel Hill: U of North Carolina P, 2001.

Connelly, Karen. *This Brighter Prison: A Book of Journeys*. London: Brick, 1993.

———. *The Small Words in My Body*. Toronto: Gutter, 1990.

Conrad, Dan, and Diane Hedin. "National Assessment of Experiential Education: Summary and Implications." Kraft and Kielsmeier 382–403.

Connolly, Kevin. "Poethead: Concrete Poetry Mixer." 31 Oct. 2004. 16 Feb. 2007 <http://www.eyeweekly.com/eye/issue/issue_02.12.98/plus/books.php>.

Cooke, Brett. "Edward O. Wilson on Art." *Biopoetics: Explorations in the Arts*. Ed. Cooke and Frederick Turner. Lexington: ICUS, 1999. 97–118.

Cooley, John. "Introduction: American Nature Writing and the Pastoral Tradition." *Earthly Works: Essays on Contemporary American Nature and Environmental Writers*. Ed. Cooley. Ann Arbor: U of Michigan P, 1994. 1–15.

Cooper, James Fenimore. *The Pioneers; or, The Sources of the Susquehanna: A Descriptive Tale*. 1823. Introd. James Franklin Beard. Albany: State U of New York P, 1980.

Cooper, Susan Fenimore. *Rural Hours*. 1850. Ed. Rochelle Johnson and Daniel Patterson. Athens: U of Georgia P, 1998.

Corbett, Jim. *The Temple Tiger and More Man-Eaters of Kumaon*. New Delhi: Oxford UP, 1954.

Cornyn, J. H. *The Song of Quetzalcoatl*. Yellow Springs: Antioch, 1930.

Cortés, Hernán. *Cartas de relación*. 1519–26. Mexico City: Porrúa, 1963.

Cotter, Joseph. *Troubled Harvest: Agronomy and Revolution in Mexico, 1880–1920*. Westport: Praeger, 2003.

Coupe, Laurence, ed. *The Green Studies Reader: From Romanticism to Ecocriticism*. London: Routledge, 2000.

Cousins, Norman. "The Third Culture." *Saturday Review* 7 May 1966: 42–43.

Cowan, Cindy. "A Woman from the Sea." *The CTR Anthology*. Ed. Alan Filewood. Toronto: U of Toronto P, 1993. 342–88.

Cowper, William. "Epitaph on a Hare." *The Norton Anthology of Poetry*. 3rd ed. Ed. Alexander W. Allison et al. New York: Norton, 1983. 481–82.

Crichton, Michael. *Prey*. New York: Harper, 2002.

Crimmel, Hal. Introduction. Crimmel, *Teaching* 1–11.

———, ed. *Teaching in the Field: Working with Students in the Outdoor Classroom*. Salt Lake City: U of Utah P, 2003.

Critchfield, Richard. *The Villagers: Changed Values, Altered Lives: The Closing of the Urban-Rural Gap*. New York: Anchor, 1994.

Cronon, William. Introduction. Cronon, *Uncommon Ground* 23–68.

———. *Nature's Metropolis: Chicago and the Great West*. New York: Norton, 1991.

———. "The Trouble with Wilderness; or, Getting Back to the Wrong Kind of Nature." Cronon, *Uncommon Ground* 69–90.

———, ed. *Uncommon Ground: Rethinking the Human Place in Nature*. New York: Norton, 1996.

Crozier, Lorna. *Apocrypha of Light*. Toronto: McClelland, 2002.

———. *The Garden Going on without Us*. Toronto: McClelland, 1985.

———. *Inventing the Hawk*. Toronto: McClelland, 1992.

Cushman, John H., Jr. "After *Silent Spring*, Industry Put a Spin on All It Brewed." *New York Times* 26 Mar. 2001: A14.

Cussler, Clive. *Sahara*. 1992. New York: Pocket, 1993.

Cuthbertson, Brent, et al. "Engaging Nature: A Canadian Case Study of Learning in the Outdoors." Crimmel, *Teaching* 77–98.

Da Jandra, Leonardo. *Arousiada*. Mexico City: Joaquín Mortiz, 1995.

———. *Los caprichos de la piel*. Mexico City: Seix Barral, 1996.

———. *Entrecruzamientos*. 3 vols. Mexico City: Joaquín Mortiz, 1986–90.

———. *Huatulqueños*. Mexico City: Joaquín Mortiz, 1991.

———. *Samahua*. Mexico City: Seix Barral, 1997.

Darwin's Nightmare. Dir. Hubert Sauper. Celluloid Dreams, 2004.

Davidson, J. W., and J. Rugge. *Great Heart: The History of a Labrador Adventure*. New York: Viking, 1988.

Davidson, Robyn. *Tracks*. 1980. New York: Vintage, 1995.

Davis, Jack. *Black Life: Poems*. Brisbane: U of Queensland P, 1992.

Davis, Wade. *One River: Explorations and Discoveries in the Amazon Rain Forest.* New York: Simon, 1997.

Deleuze, Gilles, and Félix Guattari. *Kafka: Toward a Minor Literature.* Trans. Dana Polan. Minneapolis: U of Minnesota P, 1986.

———. *A Thousand Plateaus: Capitalism and Schizophrenia.* Trans. Brian Massumi. Minneapolis: U of Minnesota P, 1987.

Delgado, Rafael. *Angelina.* 1893. Mexico City: Porrúa, 1947.

———. *Los parientes ricos.* 1902. Coleccíon de Escritores Mexicanos 6. Mexico City: Porrúa, 1944.

DeLoughrey, Elizabeth M., Renée K. Gosson, and George B. Handley, eds. *Caribbean Literature and the Environment: Between Nature and Culture.* Charlottesville: UP of Virginia, 2005.

Deming, Alison H., and Laurent E. Savoy, eds. *The Colors of Nature: Culture, Identity, and the Natural World.* Minneapolis: Milkweed, 2002.

———. "Introduction as Conversation." Deming and Savoy, *Colors* 3–15.

Derrida, Jacques. "And Say the Animal Responded?" Trans. David Willis. Wolfe, *Zoontologies* 121–46.

———. *L'animal autobiographique.* Ed. Marie-Louis Mallet. Paris: Galilee, 1998.

———. "The Animal That Therefore I Am (More to Follow)." Trans. David Willis. *Critical Inquiry* 28 (2002): 369–418.

———. "'Eating Well'; or, The Calculation of the Subject: An Interview with Jacques Derrida." *Who Comes after the Subject?* Ed. Eduardo Cadava, Peter Connor, and Jean-Luc Nancy. New York: Routledge, 1991. 96–119.

———. With Elisabeth Roudinesco. "Violence against Animals." *For What Tomorrow: A Dialogue.* Trans. Jeff Fort. Stanford: Stanford UP, 2004. 62–76.

Devall, Bill. *Simple in Means, Rich in Ends: Practicing Deep Ecology.* Salt Lake City: Smith, 1988.

Devall, Bill, and George Sessions. *Deep Ecology: Living as if Nature Mattered.* Salt Lake City: Smith, 1985.

Dewdney, Christopher. *Signal Fires.* Toronto: McClelland, 2000.

Di Chiro, Giovanna. "Sustaining the 'Urban Forest' and Creating Landscapes of Hope: An Interview of Cinder Hypki and Bryant 'Spoon' Smith." Adamson, Evans, and Stein 284–307.

Dickey, James. "The Heaven of Animals." *Contemporary American Poetry.* 4th ed. Ed. A. Poulin, Jr. Boston: Houghton, 1985. 99–100.

Dillard, Annie. "Living like Weasels." Finch and Elder 876–79.

———. *Pilgrim at Tinker Creek.* New York: Harper, 1974.

Disch, Robert, ed. *The Ecological Conscience: Values for Survival.* Englewood Cliffs: Prentice, 1970.

Dissanayake, Ellen. *Homo Aestheticus: Where Art Comes from and Why.* Seattle: U of Washington P, 1995.

Dixon, Melvin. *Ride Out the Wilderness: Geography and Identity in Afro-American Literature.* Urbana: U of Illinois P, 1987.

Dixon, Terrell, ed. *City Wilds: Essays and Stories about Urban Nature.* Athens: U of Georgia P, 2002.

Dixon, Terrell, and L. Smith. "Service Learning and Environmental Writing." *MLA Newsletter* 30.2 (1998): A3–4.

Dodd, Elizabeth. Letter. *PMLA* 114 (1999): 1094–95.

Dodge, Jim, et al. "Where You At?" *Coevolution Quarterly* 32 (1981): 1. Rpt. in Devall and Sessions 22–23.

Donovan, Josephine. "Ecofeminist Literary Criticism: Reading the Orange." Gaard and Murphy 74–96.

Doubiago, Sharon. *Hard Country.* 1982. Albuquerque: West End, 1999.

Douglas, Marjory Stoneman. *The Everglades: River of Grass.* 1947. Sarasota: Pineapple, 1997.

Douglass, Frederick. *Narrative of the Life of Frederick Douglass.* 1845. Andrews 229–327.

Dowling, Lee H. "The Colonial Period." Foster 31–81.

Downes, P. G. *Sleeping Island: The Story of One Man's Travels in the Great Barren Lands of the Canadian North.* New York: McCann, 1943.

Dragland, Stan. *Floating Voice: Duncan Campbell Scott and the Literature of Treaty 9.* Toronto: Anansi, 1994.

Drew, Wayland. *Halfway Man.* Ottawa: Oberon, 1989.

Duncan, David James. *The River Why.* New York: Bantam, 1983.

Duncan, Robert. *The Opening of the Field.* 1969. New York: New Directions, 1973.

Dunlap, Riley E. "Paradigmatic Change in Social Science." *Ecology and the Social Sciences.* Spec. issue of *American Behavioral Scientist* 24.1 (1980): 5–14.

Durán, Diego. *The Aztecs: The History of the Indies of New Spain.* 1589. Trans. Doris Heyden. Abr. ed. New York: Orion, 1964.

———. *Book of the Gods and Rites and the Ancient Calendar.* 1589. Trans. Fernando Horcistas and Doris Heyden. Norman: U of Oklahoma P, 1971.

Eagleton, Terry. *The Idea of Culture.* Oxford: Blackwell, 2000.

Earle, Scott, and James Reveal, eds. *Lewis and Clark's Green World: The Expedition and Its Plants.* Helena: Far Country, 2003.

Edelman, Murray. "Symbols and Political Quiescence." *American Political Science Review* 54 (1960): 695–704.

Edwards, Jonathan. "Beauty of the World." *Scientific and Philosophical Writings.* Ed. Wallace E. Anderson. New Haven: Yale UP, 1980. 305–06.

Edwards, Thomas S., and Elizabeth A. De Wolfe, eds. *Such News of the Land: U.S. Women Nature Writers.* Hanover: UP of New England, 2001.

Ehrlich, Gretel. *Islands, the Universe, Home.* New York: Penguin, 1991.

———. *The Solace of Open Spaces.* New York: Penguin, 1985.

Ehrlich, Paul R. *The Population Bomb.* 1968. Cutchogue: Buccaneer, 1971.

Eisner, Thomas, and Mary Woodsen. "The Science of Wonder: Natural History in the Balance." *Plant Talk* 37 (2004): 3.

Elbow, Peter. *What Is English?* New York: MLA, 1990.

Elder, John. *Imagining the Earth.* Urbana: U of Illinois P, 1985.

———. Introduction. *American Nature Writers.* Ed. Elder. Vol. 1. New York: Scribner's, 1996. 2 vols. xiii–xix.

———. "The Poetry of Experience." Armbruster and Wallace 312–24.

———. "The Poetry of Experience." *New Literary History* 30 (1999): 649–60.

————. *Stories in the Land.* Great Barrington: Orion Soc., 1998.

————. "The Voice of Experience: An Interview with John Elder." By Laird Christensen. *ISLE* 10.1 (2003): 195–213.

Elder, John, and Robert Finch. Introduction. Finch and Elder, *Norton* 19–28.

Elder, John, and Hertha D. Wong, eds. *Family of Earth and Sky: Indigenous Stories of Nature from around the World.* Boston: Beacon, 1994.

Eliot, T. S. The Waste Land: *Authoritative Text, Contexts, Criticism.* Ed. Michael North. New York: Norton, 2001.

Ellwood, Robert S., ed. *Zen in American Life and Letters.* Malibu: Undena, 1987.

Emerson, Ralph Waldo. "The American Scholar." 1837. Emerson, *Essays and Lectures* 51–71.

————. *Essays and Lectures.* Ed. Joel Porte. New York: Lib of Amer., 1983.

————. *Nature.* 1836. Emerson, *Essays and Lectures* 5–49.

————. "Nature." 1844. Emerson, *Essays and Lectures* 541–55.

Engel, Marian. *Bear.* Toronto: McClelland, 1976.

Engelhardt, Elizabeth S. D. *The Tangled Roots of Feminism, Environmentalism, and Appalachian Literature.* Athens: Ohio State UP, 2003.

"Environmental Studies Programs at Other Institutions." 7 Nov. 2007 <http://envstudies.brown.edu/oldsite/Web/academics/gradprogramsotherinstitutions.htm>.

Erb, Audrey. "A Survey of ASLE Members' Current Teaching Practices: Implications and Questions." 2003. 5 Jan. 2004 <http://jan.ucc.nau.edu/~writcnt/audrey/asle%20survey.html>.

Erdrich, Louise. *The Antelope Wife.* New York: Harper, 1998.

————. *Books and Islands in Ojibwe Country.* Washington: Natl. Geographic Soc., 2003.

Evans, Mei Mei. " 'Nature' and Environmental Justice." Adamson, Evans, and Stein 181–93.

Evans, Nicholas. *The Loop.* New York: Random, 1998.

Farrell, James J. "Shopping: The Moral Ecology of Consumption." *American Studies* 39.3 (1998): 153–73.

Faulkner, William. *Go Down, Moses.* 1942. New York: Vintage, 1990.

Fawcett, Brian. *The Secret Journals of Alexander Mackenzie.* Vancouver: Talon, 1985.

Fernández de Oviedo, Gonzalo. *Historia general y natural de las Indias.* 1535. Madrid: Biblioteca de Autores Españoles, 1959.

Figueroa, Robert. "Teaching for Transformation: Lessons from Environmental Justice." Adamson, Evans, and Stein 311–30.

Finch, Robert. *Death of a Hornet.* Washington: Counterpoint, 2000.

————. *Outlands: Journey to the Outer Edges of Cape Cod.* Boston: Godine, 1986.

————. *The Primal Place.* New York: Norton, 1983.

Finch, Robert, and John Elder, eds. *The Norton Book of Nature Writing.* New York: Norton, 1990.

Finkel, Donald. *What Manner of Beast: Poems.* New York: Atheneum, 1981.

Fletcher, Angus. *A New Theory for American Poetry: Democracy, the Environment, and the Future of Imagination.* Cambridge: Harvard UP, 2004.

Flys-Junquera, Carmen. "Nature's Voice: Ecological Consciousness in Rudolfo Anaya's *Albuquerque Quartet.*" *Aztlán* 27.2 (2002): 119–38.

Folsom, Ed. "Walt Whitman's Prairie Paradise." Sayre, *Recovering* 47–60.

The Forest for the Trees. Dir. Bernadine Mellis. Bullfrog, 2006.

Forns-Broggi, Roberto. "¿Cuales son los dones que la Naturaleza Regala a la Poesia Latinoamericana?" *Hispanic Journal* 19.2 (1998): 209–38.

"Forum on Literatures of the Environment." *PMLA* 114 (1999): 1089–104.

Foster, David William, ed. *Mexican Literature: A History.* Austin: U of Texas P, 1994.

Frankenberg, Ruth. *White Women, Race Matters: The Social Construction of Whiteness.* Minneapolis: U of Minnesota P, 1993.

Franklin, Benjamin. *The Autobiography of Benjamin Franklin.* Andrews 70–228.

Franklin, Wayne. *Discoverers, Explorers, Settlers: The Diligent Writers of Early America.* Chicago: U of Chicago P, 1979.

Frazier, Jane. *From Origin to Ecology: Nature and the Poetry of W. S. Merwin.* Madison: Austin Peay UP, 1999.

Freebairn, A. L. *Sixty Years in Cow Town.* Pincher Creek: Freebairn, 2001.

Freeman, Martha, ed. *Always, Rachel: The Letters of Rachel Carson and Dorothy Freeman, 1952–1964.* Boston: Beacon, 1995.

Freuchen, Peter. *The Arctic Adventurer.* New York: Farrar, 1955.

Friis, Ronald J. *Jose Emilio Pacheco and the Poets of the Shadows.* Lewisburg: Bucknell UP, 2001.

Fromm, Harold. "From Transcendence to Obsolescence: A Route Map." Glotfelty and Fromm 30–39.

"From the Editors." *The Place Where You Live.* Ed. Jennifer Sahn. Spec. issue of *Orion* Spring 1995: 2.

Frost, Robert. *Early Poems.* New York: Penguin, 1998.

———. "The Most of It." Bly 85.

———. "Two Look at Two." Bly, 87–88.

Frye, Northrop. *Reflections on the Canadian Literary Imagination.* Ed. Branko Gorjup. Rome: Bulzoni, 1991.

Fudge, Erica. *Animal.* London: Reaktion, 2002.

———. *Perceiving Animals: Humans and Beasts in Early Modern English Culture.* Urbana: U of Illinois P, 2002.

Fuentes, Carlos. *Christopher Unborn.* 1987. New York: Farrar, 1989. Trans. of *Cristóbal nonato.* 1987.

———. *The Death of Artemio Cruz.* Trans. Sam Hileman. New York: Farrar, 1964. Trans. of *La muerte de Artemio Cruz.* 1962.

———. *Where the Air Is Clear.* Trans. Sam Hileman. New York: Farrar, 1960. Trans. of *La región más transparente.* 1958.

Gaard, Greta, ed. *Ecofeminism: Women, Animals, Nature.* Philadelphia: Temple UP, 1993.

———. "Hiking without a Map: Reflections on Teaching Ecofeminist Literary Theory Criticism." Gaard and Murphy 224–27.

Gaard, Greta, and Patrick D. Murphy, eds. *Ecofeminist Literary Criticism: Theory, Interpretation, Pedagogy.* Urbana: U of Illinois P, 1998.

García, Adriana. "Twentieth-Century Poetry." Foster 171–212.

Garrard, Greg. *Ecocriticism*. London: Routledge, 2004.

Garro, Elena. *Los recuerdos del porvenir*. Mexico City: Joaquín Mortiz, 1963.

George, Jean Craighead. *Julie of the Wolves*. New York: Harper, 1972.

Gerbi, Antonello. *La natura delle Indie Nove: Da Cristoforo Colombo a Gonzalo Fernández de Oviedo*. Milano: Ricciardi, 1975.

Gifford, Terry. *Green Voices: Understanding Contemporary Nature Poetry*. Manchester: Manchester UP, 1995.

———. *Pastoral*. New York: Routledge, 1999.

Gilcrest, David. *Greening the Lyre*. Reno: U of Nevada P, 2002.

Ginsberg, Allen. "By Air: Albany-Baltimore." Disch viii–ix.

Gipson, Philip S., Warren B. Ballard, and Ronald M. Nowak. "Famous North American Wolves and the Credibility of Early Wildlife Literature." *Wildlife Society Bulletin* 26.4 (1998): 808–16.

Girardot, N. J., James Miller, and Liu Xiaogan eds. *Daoism and Ecology: Ways within a Cosmic Landscape*. Cambridge: Harvard UP, 2001.

Gladwell, Malcolm. "The Mosquito Killer." *New Yorker* 2 July 2001: 42–51.

Glasgow, Ellen. *Barren Ground*. San Diego: Harcourt, 1985.

Glotfelty, Cheryll. "Introduction: Literary Studies in an Age of Environmental Crisis." Glotfelty and Fromm, *Ecocriticism* xv–xxxvii.

Glotfelty, Cheryll, and Harold Fromm, eds. *The Ecocriticism Reader: Landmarks in Literary Ecology*. Athens: U of Georgia P, 1996.

Glover, Douglas. *Elle: A Novel*. Fredericton, NB: Goose Lane, 2003.

Goddard, John. "A Real Whopper." *Saturday Night* May 1997: 47+.

Goldie, Terry, and Daniel David Moses, eds. *Native Literature in Canada: From the Oral Tradition to the Present*. Toronto: Oxford UP, 2005.

Gonzales, Ray. *Memory Fever: A Journey beyond El Paso del Norte*. Seattle: Broken Moon, 1993.

Gonzales, Rodolfo. *I Am Joaquin / Yo soy Joaquin*. Denver: Crusade for Justice, 1967.

González, Jovita. *Dew on the Thorn*. Ed. José E. Limón. Houston: Arte Público, 1997.

González, Jovita. *Caballero: A Historical Novel*. Ed. José E. Limón and María Cotera. College Station: Texas A&M UP, 1996.

Gordon, Greg. *Landscape of Desire: Identity and Nature in Utah's Canyon Country*. Logan: Utah State UP, 2003.

Gore, Al. Introduction. *Silent Spring*. By Rachel Carson. Boston: Houghton, 1994. xv–xxvi.

Goreham, Gary A. *Encyclopedia of Rural America: The Land and People*. 2 vols. Santa Barbara: ABC-CLIO, 1997.

Gould, Stephen J. "Deconstructing the 'Science Wars' by Reconstructing an Old Mold." *Science* 287 (2000): 253–61.

Gowdy, Barbara. *The White Bone*. New York: Picador, 2000.

Graff, Gerald. *Clueless in Academe: How Schooling Obscures the Life of the Mind*. New Haven: Yale UP, 2003.

Grey Owl. *The Men of the Last Frontier*. 1931. Toronto: Macmillan, 1976.

Griffin, Shaun T., ed. *Desert Wood: An Anthology of Nevada Poets*. Reno: U of Nevada P, 1991.

Griffin, Susan. *Woman and Nature: The Roaring Inside Her*. New York: Harper, 1980.

Gross, Paul R., and Norman Levitt. *Higher Superstition: The Academic Left and Its Quarrels with Science*. Baltimore: Johns Hopkins UP, 1994.

Grossinger, Richard. Editorial. *Io* 7 (1970): n. pag.

Grover, Jan Zita. *North Enough: AIDS and Other Clear-Cuts*. Saint Paul: Graywolf, 1997.

Gunnars, Kristjana. *Exiles among You*. Regina: Coteau, 1996.

Gyurko, Lanin A. "Twentieth-Century Fiction." Foster 243–304.

Hall, Sands. "Backnotes to Fair Use." *Artmatters, a Quarterly Journal of the Nevada County Arts Council* Spring 2001: 3.

Ham, Jennifer, and Matthew Senior. *Animal Acts: Configuring the Human in Western History*. New York: Routledge, 1997.

Hamlin, Christopher, and Philip T. Shepard. *Deep Disagreement in U.S. Agriculture: Making Sense of Policy Conflict*. Boulder: Westview, 1993.

Haraway, Donna. "The Birth of the Kennel: Cyborgs, Dogs and Companion Species." 22 Sept. 2006. 20 Feb. 2007 <http://www.egs.edu/faculty/haraway/haraway-birth-of-the-kennel-2000.html>.

———. "A Cyborg Manifesto: Science, Technology, and Socialist-Feminism in the Late Twentieth Century." Haraway, *Simians* 149–82.

———. *Primate Visions: Gender, Race, and Nature in the World of Modern Science*. New York: Routledge, 1989.

———. "The Promises of Monsters: A Regenerative Politics for Inappropriate/d Others." *Cultural Studies*. Ed. Lawrence Grossberg et. al. New York: Routledge, 1992. 295–337.

———. *Simians, Cyborgs, and Women: The Reinvention of Nature*. New York: Routledge, 1991.

Harding, Sandra. "After the Neutrality Ideal: Science, Politics, and 'Strong Objectivity.'" *Social Research* 59.3 (1992): 568–87.

Hariot, Thomas. *A Briefe and True Report of the New Found Land of Virginia*. 1588. New York: Da Capo, 1971. N. pag.

Harjo, Joy. "Ancestral Voices." Interview with Bill Moyers. *The Power of the Word*. PBS. WNET. New York. 1989.

———. "Deer Dancer." *In Mad Love and War*. By Harjo. Middletown: Wesleyan UP, 1990. 5–6.

———. *How We Became Human: New and Selected Poems, 1975–2001*. New York: Norton, 2002.

———. "Joy Harjo." Interview with Greg Sarris. Lannan Literary Videos. Videocassette. Lanham Foundation, 1996.

———. *Joy Harjo: Poet, Writer, Musician*. 13 Feb. 2008. 6 Mar. 2008 <http://www.joyharjo.com>.

———. With Stephen Strom. *Secrets from the Center of the Earth*. Tempe: Arizona State UP, 1989.

Harjo, Joy, and Gloria Bird. *Reinventing the Enemy's Language*. New York: Norton, 1997.

Harold of Orange. Dir. Richard Weise. Films in the Cities, 1984.

Harrington, Henry, and John Tallmadge. Introduction. Tallmadge and Harrington ix–xv.

Harris, Joseph. "Negotiating the Contact Zone." *Journal of Basic Writing* 41.1 (1995): 27–41.

Harrison, Dallas. "Where Is (the) Horizon? Placing *As for Me and My House*." *Essays on Canadian Writing* 61 (1997): 141–69.

Haslam, Gerald. "American Oral Literature: Our Forgotten Heritage." *English Journal* 60.6 (1971): 709–23.

———. "Who Speaks for the Earth?" *English Journal* 62.1 (1973): 42–48.

Hatley, James. "The Uncanny Goodness of Being Edible to Bears." *Rethinking Nature: Essays in Environmental Philosophy*. Ed. Bruce V. Foltz and Robert Frodeman. Bloomington: Indiana UP, 2004. 13–31.

Hawken, Paul. *The Ecology of Commerce*. New York: Harper, 1993.

Hawthorne, Susan. *The Falling Woman*. Melbourne: Spinifex, 1992.

Hayles, N. Katherine. "Constrained Constructivism: Locating Scientific Inquiry in the Theater of Representation." *Realism and Representation: Essays on the Problem of Realism in Relation to Science, Literature, and Culture*. Ed. George Levine. Madison: U of Wisconsin P, 1993. 27–43.

A Healthy Baby Girl. Dir. Judith Helfand. Women Make Movies, 1996.

Hegland, Jean. *Into the Forest*. New York: Bantam, 1998.

Heise, Ursula K. "Science, Technology and Postmodernism." *The Cambridge Companion to Postmodernism*. Ed. Steven Connor. Cambridge: Cambridge UP, 2004. 136–67.

Heiser, Charles B. *Seed to Civilization: The Story of Food*. New ed. Cambridge: Harvard UP, 1990.

Hempel, Amy, and Jim Shepard. *Unleashed: Poems by Writers' Dogs*. New York: Three Rivers, 1995.

Henighan, Stephen. *When Words Deny the World: The Reshaping of Canadian Writing*. Erin, Ont.: Porcupine's Quill, 2002.

Hepburn, Allan. "Urban Kink: Canadian Fiction Shakes Off Its Rural Roots." *Quill and Quire* 66.4 (2000): 30.

Herk, Aritha van. *The Tent Peg*. Toronto: McClelland, 1981.

Herrera-Sobek, María. "The Nature of Chicana Literature: Feminist Ecological Literary Criticism and Chicana Writers." *Revista canaria de estudios ingleses* 37 (1998): 89–100.

Hesiod. Works and Days: *A Translation and Commentary for the Social Sciences*. Trans. David W. Tandy and Walter C. Neale. Berkeley: U of California P, 1996.

Hess, Scott. "Postmodern Pastoral, Advertising, and the Masque of Technology." *ISLE* 11.1 (2004): 71–100.

Hessing, Melody, Rebecca Raglon, and Catriona Sandilands, eds. *This Elusive Land: Women and the Canadian Environment*. Vancouver: U of British Columbia P, 2005.

Hester, Lee, Dennis McPherson, Annie Booth, and Jim Cheney. "Callicott's Last Stand." Ouderkirk and Hill 253–78.

Heyen, William. *Pterodactyl Rose: Poems of Ecology.* Saint Louis: Time Being, 1991.

Hinojosa, Tish. "There Must Be Something in the Rain." *Culture Swing.* Rounder Records, 1992.

Hirsch, Edward. "Movement 3, Middle. Edward Hirsch, 'Iowa Flora' (1994)." Jonathan Chenette. Home page. 6 Aug. 2004. 21 Sept. 2007 <http://web .grinnell.edu/individuals/chenet/bg_poems_music.html#3>.

Hochman, Jhan. *Green Cultural Studies: Nature in Film, Novel, and Theory.* Moscow: U of Idaho P, 1998.

Hofrichter, Richard, ed. *Toxic Struggles: The Theory and Practice of Environmental Justice.* Philadelphia: New Soc., 1993.

Hogan, Linda. *Solar Storms.* New York: Simon, 1997.

Hogan, Patrick Colm. "Literary Universals." *Poetics Today* 18 (1997): 223–49.

Hogg, Dominic. *Technological Change in Agriculture: Locking in to Genetic Uniformity.* New York: St. Martin's, 2000.

Holding Ground: The Rebirth of Dudley Street. Hohokus: New Day Films, n.d.

Holthaus, Gary. *Circling Back.* Salt Lake City: Gibbs, 1984.

hooks, bell. "Earthbound: On Solid Ground." Deming and Savoy 67–71.

———. "Touching the Earth." T. Dixon 28–33.

Hopkins, Sarah Winnemucca. *Life among the Piutes: Their Wrongs and Claims.* 1883. Reno: U of Nevada P, 1994.

Horne, James E., and Maura McDermott. *The Next Green Revolution: Essential Steps to a Healthy, Sustainable Agriculture.* New York: Food Products, 2001.

Houston, Jean Wakasutki. "Rock Garden." Anderson, Slovic, and O'Grady 278–82.

Hubbard, Mina. *A Woman's Way through Unknown Labrador.* Saint John's: Breakwater, 1981.

Hubbell, Sue. *A Country Year: Living the Questions.* New York: Random, 1986.

Huerta, Efraín. *Los hombres del alba.* Mexico City: Géminis, 1944.

———. *Poesía completa.* Ed. Martí Soler. Mexico City: Fondo de Cultura Económica, 1988.

———. *El Tajín.* Mexico City: Pájaro Cascabel, 1963.

Hunter, Dan. "Movement 5, Beginning. Dan Hunter, 'Only the Wind' (1995)." Jonathan Chenette. Homepage. 25 July 1996. 28 May 2007 <http://web .grinnell.edu/individuals/chenet/bg_poems_music.html#5>.

Hurd, Barbara. *Stirring the Mud: On Swamps, Bogs, and Human Imagination.* Boston: Beacon, 2001.

Hurt, R. Douglas. *American Agriculture: A Brief History.* Rev. ed. West Lafayette: Purdue UP, 2002.

I'll Take My Stand: The South and the Agrarian Tradition, by Twelve Southerners. 1935. New York: Harper, 1962.

An Inconvenient Truth. Dir. David Guggenheim. Paramount, 2006.

Ingram, Anne Merrill. "Service Learning and Ecocomposition: Developing Sustainable Practices through Inter- and Extradisciplinarity." Weisser and Dobrin 209–33.

Irving, Washington. "A Tour of the Prairies." Baym, *Norton Anthology* 969–80.

Jackson, Wes. *Becoming Native to This Place*. Washington: Counterpoint, 1994.

Jameson, Anna Brownell. *Winter Studies and Summer Rambles in Canada*. 1938. Toronto: McClelland, 1990.

Jeffers, Robinson. "The Eye." *Selected Poems*. New York: Vintage, 1965.

———. "Hurt Hawks." *Cawdor and Other Poems*. New York: Liveright, 1928. 153–54.

Jefferson, Thomas. *Notes on the State of Virginia*. 1785. Ed. William Peden. Chapel Hill: U of North Carolina P, 1995.

———. *Notes on the State of Virginia*. 1785. Ed. Frank Shuffleton. New York: Penguin, 1999.

Jenseth, Richard, and Edward E. Lotto. Preface. *Constructing Nature: Readings from the American Experience*. Ed. Jenseth and Lotto. Upper Saddle River: Prentice, 1996. v–viii.

Jhala, Yadvendradev V., and Dinesh Kumar Sharma. "Child-Lifting by Wolves in Eastern Uttar Pradesh, India." *Journal of Wildlife Research* 2.2. (1997): 94–101.

Joern, Anthony, and Kathleen Keeler. *The Changing Prairie: North American Grasslands*. New York: Oxford UP, 1995.

Johannsen, Kristin, Bobbie Ann Mason, and Mary Ann Taylor-Hall. *Missing Mountains*. Nicholasville: Wind, 2003.

Johnsgard, Paul. *Lewis and Clark on the Great Plains*. Lincoln: U of Nebraska P, 2003.

Jordan, June. "Letter to Buckminster Fuller." *Civil Wars*. New York: Touchstone, 1981. 23–28.

Jordan, Teresa. *Riding the White Horse Home: A Western Family Album*. 1993. New York: Vintage, 1994.

Kahn, Peter H., Jr. *The Human Relationship with Nature: Development and Culture*. Cambridge: MIT P, 1999.

Kahn, Peter H., Jr., and Stephen R. Kellert, eds. *Children and Nature: Psychological, Sociocultural, and Evolutionary Investigations*. Cambridge: MIT P, 2002.

Kahn, Richard. "Is That *Ivory* in That Tower? Representing the Field of Animal Studies." Online posting. Feb. 2005 H-Nilas 4 Aug. 2006 <http://www.h-net.org>.

Kalaidjian, Walter, ed. *The Cambridge Companion to American Modernism*. Cambridge: Cambridge UP, 2005.

Kamo no Chōmei. "An Account of My Hermitage." Trans. Helen Craig McCullough. *Classical Japanese Prose: An Anthology*. Stanford: Stanford UP, 1990. 379–92.

Kanellos, Nicolás. *Herencia: The Anthology of Hispanic Literature of the United States*. Oxford: Oxford UP, 2002.

Keegan, Bridget, and James C. McKusick. *Literature and Nature: Four Centuries of Nature Writing*. Upper Saddle River: Prentice, 2001.

Keith, W. J., ed. *A Voice in the Land: Essays by and about Rudy Wiebe*. Edmonton: NeWest, 1981.

Kellert, Stephen R. *Kinship to Mastery: Biophilia in Human Evolution and Development*. Washington: Island, 1997.

Kellert, Stephen R., and Edward O. Wilson. *The Biophilia Hypothesis*. Washington: Island, 1993.

Kenner, Hugh. *A Homemade World: The American Modernist Writers*. Baltimore: Johns Hopkins UP, 1975.

Kern, Robert. *Orientalism, Modernism, and the American Poem*. Cambridge: Cambridge UP, 1996.

Killingsworth, M. Jimmie. *Walt Whitman and the Earth: A Study in Ecopoetics*. Iowa City: U of Iowa P, 2004.

Kim, Helen Sunhee. "Environmental and Economic Justice for Immigrant and Women Workers." *People of Color Environmental Groups*. Comp. Robert D. Bullard. Flint: CSMOH Foundation, 2000. 46–48.

Kincaid, Jamaica. *A Small Place*. New York: Farrar, 2000.

King, Ynestra. "The Ecology of Feminism and the Feminism of Ecology." *Healing the Wounds: The Promise of Ecofeminism*. Ed. Judith Plant. Santa Cruz: New Soc., 1989. 18–28.

Kingsolver, Barbara. *Small Wonder*. New York: Harper, 2002.

Kinnell, Galway. "The Bear." *Contemporary American Poetry*. 4th ed. Ed. A. Poulin, Jr. Boston: Houghton, 1985. 256–59.

Kissam, Edward, and Michael Schmidt, eds. *Power and Song: Poems of the Aztec Peoples*. Ypsilanti: Bilingual, 1983.

Klinghammer, Erich. "Woman Killed by Captive Wolf Pack." *Wolf!* 13.4-14.1 (1995-1996): 3.

Knapp, Alan, et al. *Grassland Dynamics: Long-Term Ecological Research in Tallgrass Prairie*. New York: Oxford UP, 1998.

Knopf-Newman, Marcy Jane. "Public Eyes: Investigating the Causes of Breast Cancer." R. Stein, *New Perspectives* 161–76.

Kodama, Sanehide. *American Poetry and Japanese Culture*. Hamden: Archon, 1984.

Komunyakaa, Yusef. "Dark Waters." Deming and Savoy 98–112.

Kogawa, Joy. *Obasan*. New York: Knopf, 1993.

Kraft, Richard J. "Closed Classrooms, High Mountains, and Strange Lands: An Inquiry into Culture and Caring." Kraft and Kielsmeier 152–62.

Kraft, Richard J., and James Kielsmeier, eds. *Experiential Learning in Schools and Higher Education*. Dubuque: Kendall, 1995.

Krech, Shepard. *The Ecological Indian: Myth and History*. New York: Norton, 1999.

Kroetsch, Robert. *The Lovely Treachery of Words*. Toronto: Oxford UP, 1989.

Krutch, Joseph Wood. *The Voice of the Desert: A Naturalist's Interpretation*. 1954. New York: Sloane, 1955.

Kuletz, Valerie. "Science Cities in the Desert." *The Tainted Desert: Environmental Ruin in the American West*. By Kuletz. New York: Routledge, 1998. 38–81.

LaDuke, Winona. *All Our Relations: Native Struggles for Land and Life*. Cambridge: South End, 1999.

———. *Last Standing Woman*. Stillwater: Voyageur, 1997.

———. *The Winona LaDuke Reader: A Collection of Essential Writings*. Stillwater: Voyageur, 2002.

LaFleur, William R. "Japan." *Death and Eastern Thought: Understanding Death in Eastern Religions and Philosophies.* Ed. Frederick H. Holk. Nashville: Abingdon, 1974. 226–56.

———. *The Karma of Words: Buddhism and the Literary Arts in Medieval Japan.* Berkeley: U of California P, 1983.

Lancaster, Lewis. "Buddhism and Ecology: Collective Cultural Perceptions." Tucker and Williams 3–20.

Lane-Zucker, Laurie. Foreword. Sobel i–iv.

Larson, Gerald. "'Conceptual Resources' in South Asia for 'Environmental Ethics.'" *Nature in Asian Traditions of Thought: Essays in Environmental Philosophy.* Ed. J. Baird Callicott and Roger T. Ames. Albany: State U of New York P, 1989. 267–77.

Las Vegas. Written and prod. by Andy Thomas. A&E, 1994.

Latour, Bruno. *We Have Never Been Modern.* 1991. Trans. Catherine Porter. Cambridge: Harvard UP, 1993.

Lawrence, D. H. "Snake." Bly 223–25.

Laxalt, Robert. *A Man in the Wheatfield.* 1964. Reno: U of Nevada P, 2002.

Leahy, David. Rev. *Canadian Culture: An Introductory Reader*, ed. Elspeth Cameron, and *New Contexts of Canadian Criticism,* ed. Ajay Heble, Donna Pennee, and J. R. Struthers. 24 May 2004. <http://www.canlit.ca/reviews/index.html>.

LeDuff, Charlie. "At a Slaughterhouse, Some Things Never Die." Wolfe, *Animal Rights* 183–97.

Le Guin, Ursula K. *Always Coming Home.* New York: Bantam, 1987.

———. "Cheek by Jowl: Animals in Children's Literature." *Journal of the Association for Library Service to Children* 2.2 (2004): 20–30.

———. *City of Illusions.* New York: Ace, 1967.

———. *Dancing at the Edge of the World: Thoughts on Words, Women, Places.* New York: Grove, 1989.

———. *The Dispossessed: An Ambiguous Utopia.* New York: Harper, 1974.

———, trans. *Lao Tzu: Tao Te Ching: A Book about the Way and the Power of the Way.* Boston: Shambhala, 1998.

———. *Left Hand of Darkness.* New York: Penguin, 2000.

———. "The Wife's Story." 1979. *Buffalo Gals and Other Animal Presences.* By Le Guin. New York: Penguin, 1987. 67–71.

———. *The Wind's Twelve Quarters: Short Stories.* 1975. New York: Bantam, 1976.

———. *The Word for World Is Forest.* 1972. *Five Complete Novels.* New York: Avenel, 1985.

Leñero, Vicente. *La gota de agua.* Mexico City: Plaza, 1984.

León-Portilla, Miguel. *Literaturas de Mesoamérica.* Mexico City: Secretaría de Educación Pública, 1984.

———. *Pre-Columbian Literatures of Mexico.* 1964. Trans. Grace Lobanov and León-Portilla. Norman: U of Oklahoma P, 1969. Trans. of *Literaturas precolombinas de México.* 1964.

Leopold, Aldo. *A Sand County Almanac.* 1949. New York: Oxford, 1987.

Levertov, Denise. "Come into Animal Presence." Bly 150.

———. Introduction. Baca, *Martin* xiii–xviii.

———. *The Life around Us.* New York: New Directions, 1997.

Levin, Jonathan. "Between Science and Anti-science: A Response to Glen A. Love." *ISLE* 7.1 (2000): 1–8.

———. "Beyond Nature? Recent Work in Ecocriticism." *Contemporary Literature* 43 (2002): 171–86.

Levi-Strauss, Claude. *Totemism.* Boston: Beacon, 1963.

Lewis, Bart. "Modernism." Foster 139–70.

Lewis, Corey. *Reading the Trail: Exploring the Literature and Natural History of the California Crest.* Reno: U of Nevada P, 2005.

Lewontin, Richard C. *Biology as Ideology: The Doctrine of DNA.* New York: Harper, 1992.

Lilburn, Tim. "How to Be Here?" *Poetry and Knowing.* Ed. Lilburn. Kingston: Quarry, 1995. 161–76.

———. *Moosewood Sandhills.* Toronto: McClelland, 1994.

———. *To the River.* Toronto: McClelland, 1999.

Lillard, Richard G. "The Nature Book in Action." Waage, *Teaching* 35–44.

Lincoln, Kenneth. *Native American Renaissance.* Berkeley: U of California P, 1983.

Lindholdt, Paul. "Restoring Bioregions through Applied Composition." Weisser and Dobrin 235–52.

Lingua Franca Editors, eds. *The Sokal Hoax: The Sham that Shook the Academy.* Lincoln: U of Nebraska P, 2000.

Lippit, Akira Mizuta. *Electric Animal: Toward a Rhetoric of Wildlife.* Minneapolis: U of Minnesota P, 2000.

La lira mexicana: Antología de las mejores poesías de los mejores poetas. Mexico City: Editorial Pax-México, 1967.

Living with Animals. Spec. issue of *Papers in Language and Literature* 38.4 (2002): 339–446.

"Location and Habitats." *Konza Prairie Biological Station.* Kansas State Univ. 21 Sept. 2007 <http://www.k-state.edu/konza/location.htm>.

Lockwood, Randall. "Anthropomorphism Is Not a Four-Letter Word." *Perceptions of Animals in American Culture.* Ed. R. J. Hoage. Washington: Smithsonian Inst. P, 1989. 41–55.

London, Jack. "To Build a Fire." The Call of the Wild *and Selected Stories.* New York: New Amer. Lib., 1905. 142–57.

———. *The Call of the Wild.* 1903. New York: Dover, 1990.

———. "The Other Animals." *Collier's* 5 Sept. 1908: 10+.

Lopez, Barry. "The American Geographies." *Openings: Original Essays by Contemporary Soviet and American Writers.* Ed. Robert Atwan and Valeri Vinikurov. Seattle: U of Washington P, 1990. 55–69.

———. *Apologia.* Athens: U of Georgia P, 1998.

———. *Of Wolves and Men.* New York: Scribner's, 1978.

———. *The Rediscovery of North America.* 1990. New York: Vintage, 1992.

———. "Renegotiating the Contracts." Lyon, *Book* 381–88.

———. *Winter Count.* New York: Vintage, 1989.

López Portillo y Rojas, José. *La parcela.* 1898. Mexico City: Porrúa, 1978.

López y Fuentes, Gregorio. *El Indio.* 1935. Trans. Anita Brenner. Indianapolis: Bobbs-Merrill, 1937.

———. *Tierra.* Mexico City: Talleres de El Universal, 1932.

Lorde, Audre. *The Cancer Journals.* San Francisco: Aunt Lute, 1980.

Lousley, Cheryl. "Field Work: Old Patterns and New Directions in Ecocriticism." Northeast Mod. Lang. Assn. Convention. Toronto. Apr. 2002.

Love, Glen. *Practical Ecocriticism: Literature, Biology, and the Environment.* Charlottesville: U of Virginia P, 2003.

———. "Science, Anti-science, and Ecocriticism." *ISLE* 6.1 (1999): 65–81.

Love, Glen, and Rhoda Love, eds. *Ecological Crisis: Readings for Survival.* New York: Harcourt, 1970.

Lovelock, James E. *Gaia: A New Look at Life on Earth.* Rev. ed. Oxford: Oxford UP, 1995.

Luke, Timothy W. *Ecocritique: Contesting the Politics of Nature, Economy, and Culture.* Minneapolis: U of Minnesota P, 1997.

Lutts, Ralph. *The Nature Fakers: Wildlife, Science, and Sentiment.* Golden: Fulcrum, 1990.

———. *The Nature Fakers: Wildlife, Science, and Sentiment.* 1990. Charlottesville: UP of Virginia, 2001.

———, ed. *The Wild Animal Story.* Philadelphia: Temple UP, 1998.

Lynch, Thomas P. "Toward a Symbiosis of Ecology and Justice: Water and Land Conflicts of Frank Waters, John Nichols, and Jimmy Santiago Baca." Adamson, Evans, and Stein 405–28.

Lyon, Thomas J. "A Taxonomy of Nature Writing." *This Incomperable Lande: A Book of American Nature Writing.* Ed. Lyon. New York: Penguin, 1989. 3–7.

———. *This Incomparable Land: A Guide to American Nature Writing.* San Francisco: Milkweed, 2001.

MacDonald, John D. *A Flash of Green.* 1962. New York: Fawcett, 1963.

MacIntyre, Angus A. "The Politics of Nonincremental Domestic Change: Major Reform in Federal Pesticide and Predator Control Policy." Diss. U of California, Davis, 1982.

Mack, Arien, ed. *Humans and Other Animals.* Columbus: Ohio State UP, 1999.

———, ed. *In the Company of Animals.* Spec. issue of *Social Research* 62.3 (1995): 415–838.

Maclean, Norman. *A River Runs through It.* Chicago: U of Chicago P, 1992.

Magoc, Chris J. *So Glorious a Landscape: Nature and the Environmental in American History and Culture.* Wilmington: Scholarly Resources, 2002.

Malamud, Randy. *Poetic Animals and Animal Souls.* New York: Palgrave, 2003.

Manes, Christopher. "Nature and Silence." Glotfelty and Fromm 15–29.

Mannes, Marya. "Hymn of Thanksgiving." *Earth Day: The Beginning.* Ed. Environmental Action. New York: Arno, 1978. 248.

Manning, Richard. *Food's Frontier: The Next Green Revolution.* New York: North Point, 2000.

Mao, Douglas. *Solid Objects: Modernism and the Test of Production.* Princeton: Princeton UP, 1998.

Maracle, Lee. "The 'Post-colonial' Imagination." *Fuse* 15.1 (1992): 12–15.

Marco, Gino J., Robert M. Hollingworth, and William Durham, eds. Silent Spring *Revisited.* Washington: Amer. Chemical Soc., 1987.

Marlatt, Daphne. *This Tremor Love Is.* Vancouver: Talonbooks, 2001.

Marriott, Anne. *The Circular Coast: Poems New and Selected.* Oakville, ON: Mosaic, 1981.

Marsh, George Perkins. *Man and Nature.* 1864. Ed. David Lowenthal. Seattle: U of Washington P, 2003.

Marshall, James Vance. *Walkabout.* 1959. Littleton: Sundance, 1995.

Martin, Calvin. "The American Indian as Miscast Ecologist." *Ecological Consciousness.* Ed. Robert C. Schultz and J. Donald Hughes. Washington: UP of Amer., 1981.

Martin, Gregory. *Mountain City.* New York: North Point, 2000.

Martín-Flores, Mario. "Nineteenth Century Prose Fiction." *Mexican Literature: A History.* Ed. David William Foster. Austin: U of Texas P, 1994. 113–37.

Marx, Leo. *The Machine in the Garden: Technology and the Pastoral Ideal in America.* New York: Oxford UP, 1964.

Massumi, Brian. *Parables for the Virtual: Movement, Affect, Sensation.* Durham: Duke UP, 2002.

Masters, Dexter. *The Accident.* 1955. New York: Penguin, 1983.

Masumoto, David Mas. *Epitaph for a Peach: Four Seasons on My Family Farm.* San Francisco: Harper, 1996.

Matro, Thomas. "Poetry and the Effort of Perception." *Landscape* 22.2 (1978): 14–18.

Matthiessen, Peter. *The Snow Leopard.* New York: Penguin, 1987.

———. "The Wolves of Aguila." 1958. *"On the River Styx" and Other Stories.* New York: Random, 1986. 71–91.

Mayer, Sylvia, ed. *Restoring the Connection to the Natural World: Essays on the African American Environmental Imagination.* New Brunswick: Transaction, 2003.

Mazel, David. *American Literary Environmentalism.* Athens: U of Georgia P, 2000.

———, ed. *A Century of Early Ecocriticism.* Athens: U of Georgia P, 2001.

McBride, Roy. *The Mexican Wolf (Canis lupus baileyi).* United States Department of the Interior Fish and Wildlife Endangered Species Report 8, 1980.

———. *Status of the Gray Wolf (Canis lupus baileyi) in Mexico.* United States Department of the Interior Fish and Wildlife Service Report, 1978.

McBride, R. T., et al. "Do Mountain Lions Exist in Arkansas?" *Proceedings of the Forty-Seventh Annual Conference, Southeastern Association of Fish and Wildlife Agencies.* 9–13 Oct. 1993, Atlanta. N. p.: n. p. 394–402.

McCarthy, Cormac. *The Crossing.* New York: Vintage, 1994.

———. "The Crossing." Read by Brad Pitt. *Cormac McCarthy Value Collection.* Audiocassette. New York: Random, 2000.

McFadden, Margaret. "The 'I' in Nature." Waage, *Teaching* 102–07.

McGregor, Gaile. *The Wacousta Syndrome: Explorations in the Canadian Langscape* [sic.]. Toronto: U of Toronto P, 1985.

McKain, David W. Preface. *The Whole Earth: Essays in Appreciation, Anger, and Hope*. Ed. McKain. New York: St. Martin's, 1972. ix–xii.

McKay, Don. *Another Gravity*. Toronto: McClelland, 2000.

———. *Apparatus*. Toronto: McClelland, 1997.

———. *Night Field*. Toronto: McClelland, 1991.

McKibben, Bill. *The End of Nature*. New York: Random, 2006.

McLaren, Deborah. *Rethinking Tourism and Ecotravel*. West Hartford: Kumarian, 1998.

McLaren, Leah. "A Country Mouse Trapped in a City-Girl Body." *Globe and Mail* [Toronto] 1 May 2004: L3.

McNay, Mark E. "Wolf-Human Interactions in Alaska and Canada: A Review of the Case History." *Wildlife Society Bulletin* 30 (2002): 831–43.

Mech, L. David. *The Way of the Wolf*. Stillwater: Voyageur, 1991.

———. *The Wolf: The Ecology and Behavior of an Endangered Species*. Garden City: Natural History, 1970.

Medoff, Peter, and Holly Sklar. *Streets of Hope: The Fall and Rise of an Urban Neighborhood*. Boston: South End, 1994.

Meeker, Joseph W. *The Comedy of Survival: Studies in Literary Ecology*. New York: Scribner's, 1974.

Meine, Curt. *Aldo Leopold: His Life and Work*. Madison: U of Wisconsin P, 1988.

———. "Reimagining the Prairie: Aldo Leopold and the Origins of Prairie Restoration." Sayre, *Recovering* 144–60.

Méndez de Cuenca, Laura. *Mariposas fugitivas*. Ed. Servín Méndez and Rodolfo García. Toluca, Mex.: Talleres Gráficos de la Escuela de Artes y Oficios, 1953.

———. *Simplezas*. Paris: Ollendorf, n. d.

Merchant, Carolyn. *The Death of Nature: Women, Ecology, and the Scientific Revolution*. San Francisco: Harper, 1980.

———, ed. *Major Problems in American Environmental History: Documents and Essays*. Lexington: Heath, 1993.

Merrick, Elliott. *True North*. 1933. Lincoln: U of Nebraska P, 1989.

Merwin, W. S. *The Folding Cliffs: A Narrative*. New York: Knopf, 1998.

Meyer, C., S. Schuman, and N. Angello. "NWEA White Paper on Aggregating Portfolio Data." Lake Oswego: Northwest Evaluation Assn., 1990.

Micheaux, Oscar. *The Conquest*. 1913. Lincoln: U of Nebraska P, 1994.

———. *The Homesteader: A Novel*. 1917. Lincoln: U of Nebraska P, 1994.

Microcosmos: Le peuple de l'herbe. Dir. Claude Nuridsany and Marie Pérennou. Miramax, 1996.

Mies, Maria, and Vandana Shiva. *Ecofeminism*. London: Zed, 1993.

Miller, James. *"Democracy Is in the Streets": From Port Huron to the Siege of Chicago*. New York: Simon, 1987.

Miller, Perry. *Nature's Nation*. Cambridge: Harvard UP, 1967.

Miner, Earl. *The Japanese Tradition in British and American Literature*. 2nd ed. Princeton: Princeton UP, 1966.

The Misfits. Dir. John Huston. United, 1961.

Mitchell, John Hanson. *Ceremonial Time: Fifteen Thousand Years on One Square Mile*. Boston: Houghton, 1991.

Monsiváis, Carlos. *Amor perdido*. 1977. Mexico City: Era, 1990.

———. *Días de guardar*. 1970. Mexico City: Era, 1998.

———. *Entrada libre; crónicas de una sociedad que se organiza*. 1987. Mexico City: Era, 1998.

———. *Escenas de pudor y liviandad*. Mexico City: Grijalbo, 1988.

———. *Mexican Postcards*. Ed. and trans. John Kraniauskas. London: Verso, 1997.

———. *Los rituales del caos*. Mexico City: Era, 1995.

Montemayor, Carlos. *Abril y otras estaciones (1977–1989)*. Mexico City: Fondo de Cultura Económica, 1989.

———. *Blood Relations*. Trans. Dale Carter and Alfonso González. Kaneohi: Plover, 1995. Trans. of *Mal de piedra*. 1981.

———. *Gambusino*. Trans. John Copeland. Kaneohi: Plover, 1997. Trans. of *Minas del retorno*. 1983.

Montes, Amelia María de la Luz, and Anne Elizabeth Goldman, eds. *María Amparo Ruiz de Burton: Critical and Pedagogical Perspectives*. Lincoln: U of Nebraska P, 2004.

Moodie, Susanna. *Voyages: Short Narrative of Susanna Moodie*. Ed. John Thurston. Ottawa: U of Ottawa P, 1991.

Moore, Marianne. *Becoming Marianne Moore: The Early Poems, 1907–1924*. Ed. Robin G. Schulze. Berkeley: U of California P, 2002.

———. *Complete Poems*. New York: Penguin, 1982.

———. *The Poems of Marianne Moore*. Ed. Grace Schulman. New York: Viking, 2003.

Moraga, Cherríe. *Heroes and Saints and Other Plays*. Albuquerque: West End, 1994.

———. *The Last Generation: Prose and Poetry*. Boston: South End, 1993.

Morris, Tim. "Grey Water Rafting." *Here* 5 (2001): 6–11.

Mouré, Erin. *Furious*. Concord, ON: Anansi, 1988.

———. *The Green World: Selected Poems, 1973–1992*. Toronto: Oxford UP, 1994.

———. *WSW (West South West)*. Montreal: Vehicle, 1989.

Mowat, Farley. *Never Cry Wolf*. Boston: Little, 1963.

Muir, John. *The Mountains of California*. 1894. New York: Penguin, 1989.

———. *My First Summer in the Sierra*. Boston: Houghton, 1911.

———. *My First Summer in the Sierra*. *Nature Writing*. Ed. William Cronon. New York: Lib. of Amer., 1997. 147–309.

———. *Steep Trails: California, Utah, Nevada, Washington, Oregon, the Grand Canyon*. Ed. William Frederic Badé. Boston: Houghton, 1918.

———. "Stickeen: The Story of a Dog." *Sierra Club John Muir Exhibit*. 4 Aug. 2006. <http://www.sierraclub.org/john_Muir_exhibit/writings/stickeen/>. Path: Stickeen: The Story of a Dog.

———. "The Water-Ouzel." *Nature Writing: The Tradition in English*. Ed. Robert Finch and John Elder. New York: Norton, 2002. 258–68.

Muñoz, Boris. "Ciudad, violencia y globaizacion." Diss. Rutgers U, 2003.

Murie, Adolph. "The East Fork Wolves." Busch 29–46.

Murphy, Patrick D. "Anotherness and Inhabitation in Recent Multicultural American Literature." *Writing the Environment: Ecocriticism and Literature*. Ed. Richard Kerridge and Neil Sammels. London: Zed, 1998. 40–52.

———. *Farther Afield in the Study of Nature-Oriented Literature*. Charlottesville: U of Virginia P, 2000.

———. *Literature, Nature, and Other: Ecofeminist Critiques*. Albany: State U of New York P, 1995.

———, ed. *Literature of Nature: An International Sourcebook*. Chicago: Fitzroy, 1998.

Murray, Heather. "Women in the Wilderness." *A Mazing Space Writing Canadian Women Writing*. Ed. Shirley Neuman and Smaro Kamboureli. Toronto: Longspoon, 1986. 74–83.

Murray, John A. Preface. *Nature's New Voices*. Ed. Murray. Golden: Fulcrum, 1992. ix–xiii.

Murray, Les. *Translations from the Natural World*. New York: Farrar, 1992.

Myers, Jeffrey. *Converging Stories: Race, Ecology, and Environmental Justice in American Literature*. Athens: U of Georgia P, 2005.

Nabhan, Gary Paul. "Between Imagination and Observation." *The Essential Aldo Leopold: Quotations and Commentary*. Ed. Curt Meine and Richard Knight. Madison: U of Wisconsin P, 1999. 269–70.

———. *Coming Home to Eat: The Pleasures and Politics of Local Foods*. 2001. New York: Norton, 2002.

———. *Cultures of Habitat: On Nature, Culture, and Story*. Washington: Counterpoint, 1997.

Nafisi, Azar. *Reading* Lolita *in Tehran: A Memoir in Books*. New York: Random, 2003.

Naipaul, V. S. *Miguel Street*. 1959. New York: Knopf, 2002.

Nash, Roderick F. *Wilderness and the American Mind*. 4th ed. New Haven: Yale UP, 2001.

Neely, Barbara. *Blanche Cleans Up*. 1998. New York: Penguin, 1999.

Nelson, Barney. "Building Community on a Budget in the Big Bend of Texas." Crimmel 265–76.

———. "Crossing Borders: A West Texas Wolf Trapper's True Stories Cross over into Cormac McCarthy's Fiction." Western Literature Assn. Tucson. 1 Nov. 2003.

———. "Trap, Trapper, Trapped: Exploiting Scientists and Government Documents as Material for Wild Books." Western Literature Assn. Tucson. Oct. 2002.

———. *The Wild and the Domestic: Animal Representation, Ecocriticism, and Western American Literature*. Reno: U of Nevada P, 2000.

Nelson, George. *My First Years in the Fur Trade: The Journals of 1802–1804*. Ed. Laura Peers and Theresa Schenck. Montreal: McGill-Queen's UP, 2002.

Nelson, Richard. "The Gifts." Finch and Elder 797–810.

Nelson, Richard, Barry Lopez, and Terry Tempest Williams. *Patriotism and the American Land*. Great Barrington: Orion Soc., 2002.

Neruda, Pablo. *Extravagaria*. 1958. Trans. Alistair Reid. New York: Farrar, 1975.

Nevada Authors. 22 Feb. 2007 <http://www.scsr.nevada.edu/~glotfelt/nvauthors.html>.

New, W. H. *A History of Canadian Literature*. 2nd ed. Montreal: McGill-Queens UP, 2003.

———. *Land Sliding: Imagining Space, Presence, and Power in Canadian Writing*. Toronto: U of Toronto P, 1997.

Newton, David E. *Environmental Justice: A Reference Handbook*. N.p.: ABC-Clio, 1996.

Nigro, Kirsten F. "Twentieth-Century Theater." Foster 213–42.

Norris, Frank. *The Octopus*. 1901. New York: New Amer. Lib., 1981.

Norris, Margot. *Beasts of the Modern Imagination: Darwin, Kafka, Nietzsche, Ernst, and Lawrence*. Baltimore: Johns Hopkins UP, 1985.

Norwood, Vera. *Made from This Earth: American Women and Nature*. Chapel Hill: U of North Carolina P, 1993.

Nussbaum, Martha. *Cultivating Humanity: A Classical Defense of Reform in Liberal Education*. Cambridge: Harvard UP, 1997.

O'Brien, Dan. *Buffalo for the Broken Heart*. New York: Random, 2001.

O'Brien, Susie. "Nature's Nation, National Natures? Reading Ecocriticism in a Canadian Context." *Canadian Poetry* 42 (1998): 17–41. 31 Oct. 2004 <http://www.uwo.ca/english/canadianpoetry/cpjrn/vol42/nature.htm>.

O'Connell, Joanna. "Pre-Columbian Literatures." Foster 1–29.

O'Connor, Mark. *The Olive Tree: Collected Poems*. Alexandria, Austral.: Hale, 2000.

Odum, Eugene P. *Ecology: A Bridge between Science and Society*. Sunderland: Sinauer, 1997.

———. "The Emergence of Ecology as a New Integrative Discipline." *Science* 195 (1977): 1289–93.

Oliver, Mary. *New and Selected Poems: Volume One*. Boston: Beacon, 1992.

Olson, Charles. "Projective Verse." *Selected Writings of Charles Olson*. Ed. Robert Creeley. New York: New Directions, 1966. 15–26.

Olson, Sigurd. *The Singing Wilderness*. New York: Knopf, 1987.

Olwig, Kenneth Robert. *Landscape, Nature, and the Body Politic: From Britain's Renaissance to America's New World*. Fwd. Yi-Fu Tuan. Madison: U of Wisconsin P, 2002.

O'Neill, John. *Animal Walk*. Winnipeg: Turnstone, 1988.

———. *Love in Alaska*. Lantzville, BC: Oohichan, 1994.

Opie, John. *Nature's Nation: An Environmental History of the United States*. Fort Worth: Harcourt, 1998.

Orr, David W. *Ecological Literacy: Education and the Transition to a Postmodern World*. Albany: State U of New York P, 1992.

Ortiz, Simon. *Fight Back: For the Sake of the People, for the Sake of the Land*. Ortiz, *Woven Stone* 285–365.

———. "Meanwhile: Soon the Millennia: Burning Forests: Indians Killed: October 6, 1997." Ortiz, *Out There* 139–41.

———. *Out There Somewhere*. Tucson: U of Arizona P, 2002.

———. *Woven Stone.* Tucson: U of Arizona P, 1992.

Osborn, Ron, and Roger Spofford. "Interdisciplinary Involvement in Environmental Field Trips." *Environmental Education: A Sourcebook.* Ed. Cornelius J. Troost and Harold Altman. New York: Wiley, 1972. 359–63.

Ouderkirk, Wayne, and Jim Hill, eds. *Land, Value, Community: Callicott and Environmental Philosophy.* Albany: State U of New York P, 2002.

Owens, Derek. *Composition and Sustainability: Teaching for a Threatened Generation.* Urbana: Natl. Council of Teachers of English, 2001.

Owens, Louis. *Wolfsong.* Norman: U of Oklahoma P, 1995.

Owings, Loren. *Environmental Values, 1860–1972: A Guide to Information Sources.* Detroit: Gale, 1976.

Ozeki, Ruth L. *My Year of Meats.* New York: Penguin, 1998.

Pacheco, José Emilio. *Album de zoología.* Ed. Jorge Esquinca. 2nd ed. Guadalajara: Xalli-U de Guadalajara, 1991.

———. *City of Memory and Other Poems by José Emilio Pacheco.* Trans. Cyntha Steele and David Lauer. San Francisco: City Lights, 1997.

———. *Don't Ask Me How the Time Goes By.* New York: Columbia UP, 1978.

———. *El silencio de la luna (Poemas 1985–1993).* Mexico City: Era-Casa de Poesía Silva, 1996.

———. *Tarde o temprano.* 2nd ed. Mexico City: Fondo de Cultura Económica, 1986.

———. *Los trabajos del mar.* Mexico City: Era, 1983.

Page, P. K. *The Glass Air: Selected Poems.* Toronto: Oxford UP, 1985.

———. *Planet Earth: Poems Selected and New.* Erin, ON: Porcupine's Quill, 2002.

———. *Poems: Selected and New.* Toronto: Anansi, 1974.

Palmerlee, Danny, and Sandra Bao. *Mexico's Pacific Coast.* Melbourne: Lonely Planet, 2003.

Paredes, Américo. *The Shadow.* Houston: Arte Público, 1998.

———. *With His Pistol in His Hand: A Border Ballad and Its Hero.* Austin: U of Texas P, 1958.

Patterson, R. M. *The Dangerous River.* 1966. Sidney, BC: Gray's, 1980.

Paz, Octavio. *The Labyrinth of Solitude.* 1950. Berkeley: U of California P, 1964.

———. *The Other Voice: Essays on Modern Poetry.* 1990. Trans. Helen Lane. New York: Harcourt, 1991. Trans. of *La otra voz. Poesía y fin de siglo.*

———. *A Tree Within.* 1987. Trans. Eliot Weinberger. New York: New Directions, 1988. Trans. of *Árbol adentro.* 1987.

Pecher, Kamil. *Lonely Voyage by Kayak to Adventure and Discovery.* Saskatoon, SK: Western Producer Prairie, 1978.

Peck, Jamie, and Adam Ticknell. "Neoliberalizing Space." *Spaces of Neoliberalism: Urban Restructuring in Western Europe and North America.* Ed. Neil Brenner and Nik Theodore. Spec. issue of *Antipode* 34.3 (2002): 380–403.

Pellicer, Carlos. *Material poético: 1918-1961.* Mexico City: U Nacional Autonoma de México, 1962.

Pence, Gregory E, ed. *The Ethics of Food: A Reader for the Twenty-First Century.* Lanham: Rowan, 2002.

Pepper, David. *Modern Environmentalism: An Introduction.* London: Routledge, 1996.

Perkins, Robert. *Against Straight Lines: Alone in Labrador.* Boston: Little, 1983.

"Pesticides: The Price for Progress." *Time* 28 Sept. 1962: 45–48.

Petrone, Penny. *Native Literature in Canada: From the Oral Tradition to the Present.* Toronto: Oxford UP, 1990.

Philippon, Daniel J. *Conserving Words: How American Nature Writers Shaped the Environmental Movement.* Athens: U of Georgia P, 2004.

Phillips, Dana. *The Truth of Ecology: Nature, Culture, and Literature in America.* New York: Oxford UP, 2003.

Phillips, Rod. "Notes for 'Let Us Throw Out the Word Man': Michael McClure's Mammalian Poetics." *Light and Dust Mobile Poetry Anthology.* 1999. 22 Feb. 2007 <http://www.thing.net/~grist/l&d/mcclure/mc-philn.htm>.

Piasecki, Bruce. "American Literary Environmentalism before Darwin." Waage, *Teaching* 9–18.

Pilkington, Doris. *Rabbit-Proof Fence.* 1996. New York: Miramax, 2002.

Pimlott, D. H. Rev. *Never Cry Wolf,* by Farley Mowat. *Journal of Wildlife Management* 39 (1966): 236.

Pinker, Steven. *The Blank Slate: The Modern Denial of Human Nature.* New York: Viking, 2002.

Platt, Kamala. "Ecocritical Chicana Literature: Ana Castillo's 'Virtual Realism.' " *ISLE* 3.1 (1996): 67–96.

Plevin, Arlene. "Home Everywhere and the Injured Body of the World: The Subversive Humor of *Blue Vinyl.*" R. Stein, *New Perspectives* 225–39.

Plumwood, Val. "Human Vulnerability and the Experience of Being Prey." *Quadrant* 3 (1995): 29–34.

Pojman, Louis, and Paul Pojman, eds. *Environmental Ethics: Readings in Theory and Application.* 5th ed. Belmont: Thomson, 2008.

Pollan, Michael. "An Animal's Place." *New York Times Magazine* 10 Nov. 2002. 23 Oct. 2007 <http://www.nytimes.com>.

Poniatowska, Elena. *Fuerte es el silencio.* Mexico City: Era, 1980.

———. *Massacre in Mexico.* Trans. Helen R. Lane. New York: Viking, 1975. Trans. of *La noche de Tlatelolco.* 1972.

———. *Nada, nadie. Las voces del temblor.* 1988. Mexico City: Era, 1999.

Pound, Ezra, Trans. *Confucius: The Unwobbling Pivot and the Great Digest.* Norfolk: Pharos, 1947.

Pratt, Mary Louise. *Imperial Eyes: Travel Writing and Transculturation.* New York: Routledge, 1992.

Prebish, Charles S. *Luminous Passage: The Practice and Study of Buddhism in America.* Berkeley: U of California P, 1999.

Prebish, Charles S., and Martin Baumann, eds. *Westward Dharma: Buddhism Beyond Asia.* Berkeley: U of California P, 2002.

Prebish, Charles S., and Kenneth K. Tanaka, eds. *The Faces of Buddhism in America.* Berkeley: U of California P, 1998.

Price, Jennifer. "Looking for Nature at the Mall." Cronon, *Uncommon Ground* 186–203.

Pringle, Lawrence. *Wolfman*. New York: Scribner's, 1983.

Quammen, David. "The Face of a Spider." Ross 235–41.

Quinby, Lee. "Ecofeminism and the Politics of Resistance." *Reweaving the World: The Emergence of Ecofeminism*. Ed. Irene Diamond and Gloria Feman Orenstein. San Francisco: Sierra Club, 1990. 122–27.

Rabbit-Proof Fence. Dir. Phillip Noyce. Miramax, 2002.

Rabinowitz, Alan. *Jaguar: One Man's Struggle to Establish the World's First Jaguar Preserve*. Washington: Shearwater, 2000.

Rachel's Daughters: Searching for the Causes of Breast Cancer. Dir. Allie Light and Irving Saraf. Women Make Movies, 1997.

Rajpurohit, Kishan Singh. "Child Lifting: Wolves in Hazaribagh, India." *Ambio* 28.2 (1999): 162–66.

Rasula, Jed. *This Compost*. Athens: U of Georgia P, 2002.

Ray, Janisse. *Ecology of a Cracker Childhood*. Minneapolis: Milkweed, 1999.

Reece, Erik. "Death of a Mountain: Radical Strip Mining and the Leveling of Appalachia." *Harper's* Apr. 2005: 41–60.

———. *Lost Mountain: A Year in the Vanishing Wilderness: Radical Strip Mining and the Devastation of Appalachia*. New York: Riverside-Penguin, 2006.

Reed, T. V. "Toward an Environmental Justice Ecocriticism." Adamson, Evans, and Stein 145–62.

Regan, Tom. "The Radical Egalitarian Case for Human Rights." Pojman and Pojman 82–89.

Relke, Diana M. A. *Greenwor[l]ds: Ecocritical Readings of Canadian Women's Poetry*. Calgary: U of Calgary P, 1999.

Rexroth, Kenneth. *Beyond the Mountains*. New York: New Directions, 1951.

———. *The Collected Longer Poems*. New York: New Directions, 1968.

———. *Communalism: From Its Origins to the Twentieth Century*. New York: Seabury, 1974.

———. *The Complete Poems of Kenneth Rexroth*. Ed. Sam Hamill and Bradford Morrow. Port Townsend: Copper Canyon, 2003.

Reyes, Alfonso. "Discurso par Virgilio." Reyes, *Obras* 11: 157–77.

———. *Obras completas de Alfonso Reyes*. 19 vols. Mexico City: Fondo de Cultura Económica, 1955–68.

———. "Visión de Anáhuac." Reyes, *Obras* 2: 9–34.

Rhodes, Edwardo Lao. *Environment Justice in America: A New Paradigm*. Bloomington: Indiana UP, 2003.

Richard, Margie. "Environment Justice Leaders Plead Their Case at the U.N." *People of Color Environment Groups*. Comp. Robert D. Bullard. Flint: CSMOH Foundation, 2000. 52–54.

Ricou, Laurie. *The Arbutus/Madrone Files: Reading the Pacific Northwest*. Carovallis: Oregon State UP, 2002.

———. *Vertical Man / Horizontal World: Man and Landscape in Canadian Prairie Fiction*. Vancouver: U of British Columbia P, 1973.

Riding, Alan. *Distant Neighbors: A Portrait of the Mexicans*. New York: Vintage, 1989.

Riley, Robert. "Reflections on the Landscape of Memory." *Landscape* 23.2 (1979): 11–15.

Riley, Shamara Shantu. "Ecology is a Sistah's Issue Too: The Politics of Emergent Afro-Centric Ecowomanism." *Worldviews, Religion, and the Environment: A Global Anthology.* Ed. Richard C. Foltz. Belmont: Wadsworth, 2003. 472–80.

Rivera, Tomás. *Y no se lo trago la tierra / And the Earth Did Not Devour Him.* 1971. Houston: Arte Público, 1992.

Robisch, Sean Kipling. "Big Holy Dog: The Wolf in North American Literature." Diss. Purdue U, 1998.

Roethke, Theodore. *Collected Poems of Theodore Roethke.* Garden City: Anchor, 1975.

Rogers, Pattiann. *Song of the World Becoming: New and Collected Poems, 1981–2001.* Minneapolis: Milkweed, 2001.

Rolston, Holmes. "Naturalizing Values: Organism and Species." Pojman and Pojman 107–19.

Ronald, Ann. *Earthtones: A Nevada Album.* Photographs by Stephen Trimble. Reno: U of Nevada P, 1995.

Rosenberg, Roberta. "Being There: The Importance of a Field Experience in Teaching Native American Literature." *Studies in American Indian Literatures: The Journal of the Association for the Study of American Indian Literatures* 21.2 (2000): 38–60.

Rosendale, Steven, ed. *The Greening of Literary Scholarship: Literature, Theory, and the Environment.* Iowa City: U of Iowa P, 2002.

Roskelly, Hephzibah, and Kate Ronald. *Reason to Believe: Romanticism, Pragmatism, and the Teaching of Writing.* Albany: State U of New York P, 1998.

Ross, Andrew. *The Chicago Gangster Theory of Life: Nature's Debt to Society.* London: Verso, 1994.

———. *Strange Weather: Culture, Science and Technology in the Age of Limits.* London: Verso, 1991.

Ross, Carolyn, ed. *Writing Nature: An Ecological Reader for Writers.* New York: St. Martin's, 1995.

Rothfels, Nigel, ed. *Representing Animals.* Bloomington: Indiana UP, 2002.

Roy, Arundhati. *Power Politics.* Cambridge: South End, 2001.

Rue, Loyal. *Everybody's Story: Wising Up to the Epic of Evolution.* Albany: State U of New York P, 2000.

Ruiz de Burton, María Amparo. *Conflicts of Interest: The Letters of María Amparo Ruiz de Burton.* Ed. Rosaura Sánchez and Beatrice Pita. Houston: Arte Público, 2001.

———. *The Squatter and the Don.* 1885. Ed. Rosaura Sánchez and Beatrice Pita. Houston: Arte Público, 2001.

———. *Who Would Have Thought It?* 1872. Ed. Rosaura Sánchez and Beatrice Pita. Houston: Arte Público, 1995.

Rukeyser, Muriel. "The Book of the Dead." 1938. *Anthology of Modern American Poetry.* Ed. Cary Nelson. New York: Oxford UP, 2000. 655–87.

———. *The Collected Poems of Muriel Rukeyser*. Ed. Janet E. Kaufman and Anne F. Herzog. Pittsburgh: U of Pittsburgh P, 2005.

Rulfo, Juan. *"The Burning Plain" and Other Stories*. Austin: U of Texas P, 1967. Trans. of *El ilano en llanas*. 1953.

———. *Pedro Páramo*. 1955. Trans. Lysander Kemp. New York: Grove, 1959.

Sahagún, Bernardino de. *General History of the Things of New Spain: Florentine Codex*. 1569. Ed. and trans. Arthur J. O. Anderson and Charles E. Dibble. Salt Lake City: School of Amer. Research–U of Utah, 1950–82.

Saint-John de Crévecoeur, J. Hector. Letters from an American Farmer *and* Sketches of Eighteenth-Century America. Ed. Albert E. Stone. New York: Penguin, 1986.

Saitoti, Tepilit Ole. *The Worlds of a Maasai Warrior: An Autobiography*. Berkeley: U of California P, 1986.

Salter, Christopher, and William Lloyd. *Landscape in Literature*. Washington: Assn. of Amer. Geographers, 1977.

Samson, Fred, and Fritz Knopf. *Prairie Conservation: Preserving North America's Most Endangered Ecosystem*. Washington: Island, 1996.

Sanders, Scott Russell. *Hunting for Hope: A Father's Journeys*. Boston: Beacon, 1998.

———. *Staying Put: Making a Home in a Restless World*. Boston: Beacon, 1994.

Sandilands, Catriona Mortimer. "The Importance of Reading Queerly: Jewett's *Deephaven* as Feminist Ecology." *ISLE* 11.2 (2004): 57–77.

Sandman, Peter. "Mass Environmental Education: Can the Media Do the Job?" *Environmental Education: Strategies toward a More Livable Future*. Ed. James A. Swan and William Stapp. New York: Wiley, 1974. 207–47.

Santander, Felipe. *El extensionista*. 1979. Havana: Casa de las Américas, 1980.

Sarver, Elizabeth. *Uneven Land: Nature and Agriculture in American Writing*. Lincoln: U of Nebraska P, 1999.

Sayre, Gordon. "Le Page du Pratz's Fabulous Journey of Discovery: Learning about Nature Writing from a Colonial Promotional Narrative." Rosendale 26–41.

Sayre, Robert. Introduction. Sayre, *Recovering* 3–13.

———, ed. *Recovering the Prairie*. Madison: U of Wisconsin P, 1999.

Scharff, Virginia, ed. *Seeing Nature through Gender*. Lawrence: U of Kansas P, 2003.

Schlosberg, David. *Environmental Justice and the New Pluralism: The Challenge of Difference for Environmentalism*. New York: Oxford UP, 1999.

Schmitt, Peter J. *Back to Nature: The Arcadian Myth in Urban America*. New York: Oxford UP, 1969.

Scholes, Robert. *Textual Power: Literary Theory and the Teaching of English*. New Haven: Yale UP, 1985.

Scholtmeijer, Marian. *Animal Victims in Modern Fiction: From Sanctity to Sacrifice*. Toronto: U of Toronto P, 1993.

Schueler, Donald G. *A Handmade Wilderness*. Boston: Houghton, 1996.

———. "McBride's Collar." *Incident at Eagle Ranch: Man and Predator in the American West*. San Francisco: Sierra Club, 1980. 170–86.

Schultz, Charles. *Peanuts*. 1963. Rpt. in *The House of Life: Rachel Carson at Work*. By Paul Brooks. Boston: Houghton, 1972.

Schultz, Elizabeth. "Melville's Environmental Vision in *Moby Dick*." *ISLE* 7.1 (2000): 97–113.

Schumacher, Michael. *Dharma Lion*. New York: St. Martin's, 1992.

Schwartz, Leonard. "A Flicker at the Edge of Things: Some Thoughts on Lyric Poetry." *Telling It Slant: Avant-Garde Poets of the 1990s*. Ed. Mark Wallace and Steven Marks. Tuscaloosa: U of Alabama P, 2002. 95–114.

Scigaj, Leonard. *Sustainable Poetry: Four American Ecopoets*. Lexington: UP of Kentucky, 1999.

Scott, Peter A., Catharine V. Bentley, and Jeffrey J. Warren. "Aggressive Behavior by Wolves toward Humans." *Journal of Mammology* 66 (1985): 807–09.

Seager, Richard Hugh. *Buddhism in America*. New York: Columbia UP, 1999.

Seago, Karen, and Karla Armbruster, eds. *Literary Beasts: The Representation of Animals in Contemporary Literature*. Spec. issue of *Comparative Critical Studies* 2.3 (2005): 303–425.

Sealander, J. A. and P. S. Gipson. "Status of the Mountain Lion in Arkansas." *Proceedings of the Arkansas Academy of Science* 27 (1973): 38–41.

Selfe, Richard J., and Cyntha L. Selfe. "The Politics of the Interface: Power and Its Exercise in Electronic Contact Zones." *College Composition and Communication* 45 (1994): 480–504.

Seton, Ernest Thompson. "Lobo: King of the Carrumpaw." *Wild Animals I Have Known*. 1898. Toronto: n. p., 1991. 19–44.

Shepherd, Reginald. Introduction. *The Iowa Anthology of New American Poetries*. Ed. Shepherd. Iowa City: U of Iowa P, 2005. xiii–xvii.

Shepperson, Wilbur S, ed. *East of Eden, West of Zion: Essays on Nevada*. Reno: U of Nevada P, 1989.

Shiva, Vandana. *Staying Alive*. London: Zed, 1989.

———. *The Violence of the Green Revolution: Third World Agriculture, Ecology, and Politics*. Atlantic Highlands: Zed, 1991.

Siehl, George. "Literature Subsequent to the Environmental Nova." *Library Journal* 96.13 (1971): 2266–70.

Silko, Leslie Marmon. *Almanac of the Dead*. New York: Simon, 1991.

———. *Ceremony*. 1977. New York: Penguin, 1988.

———. *Yellow Woman and a Beauty of the Spirit: Essays on Native American Life Today*. New York: Simon, 1996.

Simms, William Gilmore. *The Cassique of Kiawah: A Colonial Romance*. 1859. Ed. Kevin Collins. Fayetteville: U of Arkansas P, 2003.

———. *The Yemassee: A Romance of Carolina*. 1835. Ed. John Caldwell Guilds. Fayetteville: U of Arkansas P, 1993.

Simonian, Lane. *Defending the Land of the Jaguar: A History of Conservation in Mexico*. Austin: U of Texas P, 1995.

Simons, John. *Animal Rights and the Politics of Literary Representation*. New York: Palgrave, 2002.

Simpson, Louis. "Rolling Up." *American Poetry in 1976*. Ed. William Heyen. Indianapolis: Bobbs-Merrill, 1976. 330–40.

Sinclair, Upton. *The Jungle*. 1906. New York: Barnes, 2003.

Singer, Peter. "A Utilitarian Defense of Animal Liberation." Pojman and Pojman 73–81.

Singh, Himmat. *Green Revolution Reconsidered: The Rural World of Contemporary Punjab.* Oxford: Oxford UP, 2001.

Skinner, Jonathan. "Notes from the Tanaja." *Ecopoetics* 2 (2002): 5–6.

Slicer, Deborah. "Toward an Ecofeminist Standpoint Theory: Bodies as Grounds." Gaard and Murphy 49–73.

Slovic, Scott. "Editor's Note." *ISLE* 11.2 (2004): v–viii.

———, ed. *Getting over the Color Green: Contemporary Environmental Literature of the Southwest.* Tucson: U of Arizona P, 2001.

———. "Love is Never Abstract: Bioregionalism, Narrative Discourse and the Value of Nature." *Watershed: Environment and Culture* 2.1 (2005): 17–23.

———. *Seeking Awareness in American Nature Writing.* Salt Lake City: U of Utah P, 1992.

Slovic, Scott, and Terrell F. Dixon, eds. *Being in the World: An Environmental Reader for Writers.* New York: Macmillan, 1993.

Smiley, Jane. *Moo.* New York: Knopf, 1995.

Smith, Cheryl C. "Writing like a Transcendentalist." *Academic Exchange Quarterly* 7.4 (1993): 67–71.

Smith, John. *The Complete Works of Captain John Smith.* Ed. Philip L. Barbour. Vol. 2. Chapel Hill: U of North Carolina P, 1986.

Smith, Paula V. "Movement 3. Beginning and End. Paula V. Smith, 'Rhizomes' (1994)." Jonathan Chenette. Home page. 6 Aug. 2004. 21 Sept. 2007 <http://web.grinnell.edu/individuals/Chenet/bg_poems_music.html#3>.

Smith, Russell. "Hot Town, Summer in the City." *Globe and Mail* [Toronto] 2 Aug. 2003: T1.

Snyder, Gary. "As for Poets." Snyder, *Turtle Island* 88.

———. "Buddhism and the Possibilities of Planetary Culture." Snyder, *Gary Snyder Reader* 41–43.

———. *Danger on Peaks.* Washington: Shoemaker, 2004.

———. "The Etiquette of Freedom." 1990. Snyder, *Gary Snyder Reader* 167–82.

———. *The Gary Snyder Reader: Prose, Poetry, and Translations, 1952–1998.* Washington: Counterpoint, 1999.

———. "Introductory Note." Snyder, *Turtle Island* n. pag.

———. *Mountains and Rivers without End.* Washington: Counterpoint, 1996.

———. "Nets of Beads, Webs of Cells." Snyder, *Place* 65–73.

———. *No Nature: New and Selected Poems.* New York: Pantheon, 1992.

———. "Piute Creek." Snyder, *No Nature* 6.

———. *A Place in Space: Ethics, Aesthetics, and Watersheds.* Washington: Counterpoint, 1995.

———. "Poetry and the Primitive: Notes on Poetry as an Ecological Survival Technique." Disch 194–204.

———. *The Practice of the Wild.* San Francisco: North Point, 1990.

———. *The Real Work: Interviews and Talks, 1964–1979.* New York: New Directions, 1980.

———. "Reinhabitation." Snyder, *Place* 183-91.

————. *Riprap and Cold Mountain Poems*. San Francisco: Four Seasons, 1965.

————. *Turtle Island*. New York: New Directions, 1974.

————. "The Woman Who Married a Bear." Snyder, *Practice* 155–74.

Sobel, David. *Children's Special Places: Exploring the Role of Forts, Dens, and Bush Houses in Middle Childhood*. Tucson: Zephyr, 1993.

————. *Place-Based Education: Connecting Classrooms and Communities*. Great Barrington: Orion Soc., 2004.

Sokal, Alan D. "Transgressing the Boundaries: Toward a Transformative Hermeneutics of Quantum Gravity." *Social Text* 46-47 (1996): 217–52.

Sommers, Nancy, and Laura Saltz. "The Novice as Expert: Writing the Freshman Year." *College Composition and Communication* 56 (2004): 124–49.

Soper, Kate. "Nature/'nature.'" *Future Natural*. Ed. George Robertson, Melinda Mash, Lisa Tickner, et al. New York: Routledge, 1996. 22–34.

————. *What Is Nature? Culture, Politics, and the Non-human*. Oxford: Blackwell, 1995.

Soule, Michael, and Gary Lease, eds. *Reinventing Nature? Responses to Postmodern Deconstruction*. Washington: Island, 1995.

Sproxton, Birk, ed. *Trace: Prairie Writers on Writing*. Winnipeg: Turnstone, 1986.

Stabb, Martin S. "The Essay." Foster 305–39.

Stadler, John, ed. *Eco-Fiction*. New York: Washington Square, 1971.

Stafford, William. *Stories That Could Be True: New and Collected Poems*. New York: Harper, 1977.

Stedman, Barbara. "Summary of *Our Land, Our Literature*." E-mail to Fred Waage. 6 Dec. 2004.

Steeves, H. Peter. *Animal Others: On Ethics, Ontology, and Animal Life*. Albany: State U of New York P, 1999.

Stegner, Wallace. *Angle of Repose*. New York: Penguin, 1992.

————. "The Wolfer." *Collected Stories of Wallace Stegner*. New York: Wings, 1994. 453–69.

Stegner, Wallace, and Richard W. Etulain. *Conversations with Wallace Stegner on Western History and Literature*. Salt Lake City: U of Utah P, 1983.

Stein, Gertrude. *Last Operas and Plays*. Ed. Carl van Vechten. 1949. Baltimore: Johns Hopkins UP, 1995.

————. *Lucy Church Amiably*. 1930. Normal: Dalkey, 2000.

Stein, Rachel. "Activism as Affirmation: Gender and Environmental Justice in Linda Hogan's *Solar Storms* and Barbara Neely's *Blanche Cleans Up*." Adamson, Evans, and Stein 194–212.

————, ed. *New Perspectives on Environmental Justice: Gender, Sexuality, Activism*. New Brunswick: Rutgers UP, 2004.

————. *Shifting the Ground: American Women Writers' Revisions of Nature, Gender, and Race*. Charlottesville: UP of Virginia, 1997.

Steinbeck, John. *The Grapes of Wrath*. 1939. Ed. Peter Lisca. New York: Viking, 1972.

Steingraber, Sandra. *Living Downstream: An Ecologist Looks at Cancer and the Environment*. Reading: Addison, 1997.

Stephenson, Neal. *Zodiac: An Eco-thriller*. 1988. New York: Bantam, 2003.

Sternberg, Robert J. "What Is Wisdom and How Can We Develop It?" *Annals of the American Academy of Political and Social Science* 591 (2004): 161–74. <http:ann.sagepub.com/cgi/reprint/591/1/164.pdf>.

Stevens, Wallace. *Collected Poetry and Prose.* New York: Lib. of Amer., 1997.

Stewart, George R. *Earth Abides.* 1949. New York: Fawcett Crest, 1971.

Still, James. *The Wolfpen Poems.* Berea: Berea College P, 1986.

Stillwell, Hallie. *I'll Gather My Geese.* College Station: Texas A&M UP, 1991.

Stoll, Steven. *Larding the Lean Earth: Soil and Society in Nineteenth-Century America.* New York: Hill, 2002.

Strachey, William. *The Historie of Travell into Virginia Britania.* 1612. Ed. Louis B. Wright and Virginia Freund. London: Hakluyt Soc., 1953.

Straley, John. *The Curious Eat Themselves.* New York: Soho, 1993.

Stranger with a Camera. Prod. and dir. Elizabeth Barret. Exec. Prod. Dee Davis. Coprod. Judi Jennings. Appalshop, 2000.

Stratton-Porter, Gene. *Homing with the Birds.* Garden City: Doubleday, 1919.

———. *The Song of the Cardinal.* 1903. Whitefish: Kessinger, 2004.

Sturgeon, Noel. *Ecofeminist Natures: Race, Gender, Feminist Theory, and Political Action.* New York: Routledge, 1997.

Sumner, David T. "Don't Forget to Argue: Problems, Possibilities, and Ecocomposition." Weisser and Dobrin 265–80.

Sunshine State. Dir. John Sayles. Sony, 2002.

Sustainable Atlanta. Environmental Justice Research Center and CAU-TV, n.d.

Suvin, Darko. "On the Poetics of the Science Fiction Genre." *College English* 34 (1972): 372–83.

Swanson, Carl. "The Relationship of the Natural Sciences, Social Sciences, and Humanities to Environmental Education." AAAS Symposium. San Francisco. 25 Feb. 1974.

Sweet, Timothy. *American Georgics: Economy and Environment in Early American Literature.* Philadelphia: U of Pennsylvania P, 2002.

Sze, Arthur. *The Redshifting Web: New and Selected Poems.* Port Townsend: Copper Canyon, 1998.

Sze, Julie. "Gender, Asthma Politics, and Urban Environmental Justice Activism." R. Stein, *New Perspectives* 177–90.

Szumigalski, Anne. *Rapture of the Deep.* Regina: Coteau, 1991.

———. *The Word, the Voice, the Text.* Saskatoon: Fifth House, 1990.

Tallmadge, John. Letter to Fred Waage. 25 Mar. 1982.

Tallmadge, John, and Henry Harrington, eds. *Reading under the Sign of Nature: New Essays in Ecocriticism.* Salt Lake City: U of Utah P, 2000.

Tassoni, John Paul. "Deep Response: An Ecofeminist, Dialogical Approach to Introductory Literature Classrooms." Gaard and Murphy 204–23.

Tayebi, Kandi. "Editorial: Teaching Environmental Literature." *Academic Exchange Quarterly* 7 (2003): 5–6.

Taylor, Dorceta E. "Women of Color, Environmental Justice and Ecofeminism." *Ecofeminism: Women Culture Nature.* Ed. Karen J. Warren. Bloomington: Indiana UP, 1997. 38–81.

Tedlock, Dennis, trans. Popul Vuh: *The Definitive Edition of the Mayan Book of the Dawn of Life and the Glories of the Gods and Kings*. New York: Simon, 1985.

Terres, John K. *From Laurel Ridge to Siler's Bog*. New York: Knopf, 1966.

Terry, Mark. *Teaching for Survival*. New York: Ballantine, 1971.

Thomas, Audrey. *Isobel Gunn: A Novel*. New York: Viking, 1999.

Thomas, J. W., and D. H. Pletscher. "The 'Lynx Affair'—Professional Credibility on the Line." *Wildlife Society Bulletin* 30.4 (2002): 1281–86.

Thomashow, Mitchell. *Bringing the Biosphere Home: Learning to Perceive Global Environmental Change*. Cambridge: MIT P, 2002.

———. *Ecological Identity: Becoming a Reflective Environmentalist*. Cambridge: MIT P, 1995.

Thompson, Hunter S. *Fear and Loathing in Las Vegas: A Savage Journey to the Heart of the American Dream*. 1971. New York: Vintage, 1989.

Thoreau, Henry David. *Maine Woods*. 1864. Ed. Joseph J. Moldenhauer. Princeton: Princeton UP, 1972.

———. *Walden and* Resistance to Civil Government. Ed. William Rossi. New York: Norton, 1992.

———. *Walden*. 1854. Introd. Joyce Carol Oates. Princeton: Princeton UP, 1989.

———. Walden [1854] *and* Civil Disobedience [1849]. New York: Penguin, 1983.

———. "Walking." *The Major Essays of Henry David Thoreau*. Ed. Richard Dillman. Albany: Whitston, 2001. 161–89.

Tichi, Cecilia. *Shifting Gears: Technology, Literature, Culture in Modernist America*. Chapel Hill: U of North Carolina P, 1987.

"The Tiger's Whisker." *World Folktales: An Anthology of Multicultural Folk Literature*. Ed. Anita Stern. Lincolnwood: NTC, 1994. 84–89.

Tihanyi, Eva. *Prophecies Near the Speed of Light*. Saskatoon: Thistledown, 1984.

Todorov, Tzvetan. *Genres in Discourse*. Cambridge: Cambridge UP, 1990.

Total Denial. Dir. Milena Kaneva. MK, 2006.

Tuan, Yi-Fu. "Place: An Experiential Perspective." *Geographical Review* 65 (1975): 151–65.

Tucker, Mary Evelyn, and John Berthrong, eds. *Confucianism and Ecology: The Interrelation of Heaven, Earth, and Humans*. Cambridge: Harvard UP, 1998.

Tucker, Mary Evelyn, and Duncan Ryūken Williams, eds. *Buddhism and Ecology: The Interconnection of Dharma and Deeds*. Cambridge: Harvard UP, 1997.

Twain, Mark. *Roughing It*. 1872. Ed. Hamlin Hill. New York: Penguin, 1981.

Tweed, Thomas A. *The American Encounter with Buddhism, 1844–1912: Victorian Culture and the Limits of Dissent*. Bloomington: Indiana UP, 1992.

———. "Night-stand Buddhists and Other Creatures: Sympathizers, Adherents, and the Study of Religion." Williams and Queen 71–90.

Twitchell, Chase. *The Ghost of Eden: Poems*. Princeton: Ontario Rev., 1995.

Ulman, H. Lewis. "Seeing, Believing, and Acting: Ethics and Self-Representation in Ecocriticism and Nature Writing." *Reading the Earth: New Directions in the Study of Literature and Environment*. Ed. Michael P. Branch, Rochelle Johnson, Daniel Patterson, and Scott Slovic. Moscow: U of Idaho P, 1998. 225–33.

United States, Cong. Committee on Govt. Operations. *Hearing before the Environment, Energy, and Natural Resources Subcommittee.* 102nd Cong., 2nd sess. Washington: GPO, 1993.

Valenti, Peter. Preface. *Reading the Landscape; Writing a World.* Ed. Valenti. Fort Worth: Harcourt, 1996. v–vi.

Vargas Llosa, Mario. *The Storyteller.* 1989. Trans. Helen Lane. New York: Picador, 2001.

Vergil. *Georgics.* Introd. and trans. Kristina Chew. Indianapolis: Hackett, 2002.

Vidrine, Malcolm, et al. "The Cajun Prairie Restoration Project." *Proceedings of the Seventeenth North American Prairie Conference: Seeds for the Future, Roots of the Past: Held 16–20, July 2000, North Iowa Area Community College, Mason City, Iowa.* Ed. Neil P. Bernstein and Laura J. Ostrander. Mason City: North Iowa Area Community Coll., 2001. 151–54.

Villoro, Juan. *Los once de la tribu.* 1995. Mexico City: Aguilar, 1998.

Viramontes, Helena María. *Under the Feet of Jesus.* New York: Plume, 1995.

Viva Las Vegas. Dir. George Sidney. Metro-Goldwyn Mayer, 1963.

Vizenor, Gerald. *Landfill Meditation: Crossblood Stories.* Hanover: Wesleyan UP, 1991.

———. *Shadow Distance: A Gerald Vizenor Reader.* Hanover: Wesleyan UP, 1994.

Vogel, Steven. "Marx and Alienation from Nature." *Social Theory and Practice* 14 (1988): 367–87.

Waage, Frederick O. "In the Non-Euclidean Mountains of Robert Morgan's Poetry." *Pembroke Magazine* 35 (2003): 47–54.

———. Introduction [to the volume]. Waage, *Teaching* viii–xvi.

———. Introduction [Part 4]. Waage, *Teaching* 111–13.

———, ed. *Teaching Environmental Literature: Materials, Methods, Resources.* New York: MLA, 1985.

Waddington, Miriam. *Collected Poems.* Toronto: Oxford UP, 1986.

———. *The Last Landscape.* Toronto: Oxford UP, 1992.

Walcott, Derek. *Omeros.* New York: Farrar, 1992.

Walkabout. Dir. Nicolas Roeg. Criterion, 1971.

Walker, Alice. *Absolute Trust in the Goodness of the Earth: New Poems.* New York: Random, 2003.

———. "Am I Blue?" Finch and Elder 863–67.

———. *Her Blue Body Everything We Know: Earthling Poems, 1965–1990.* San Diego: Harcourt, 1991.

———. *Living by the Word: Selected Writings, 1973–1987.* San Diego: Harcourt, 1988.

Walker, Melissa, ed. *Reading the Environment.* New York: Norton, 1994.

Wallace, Dillon. *The Lure of the Labrador Wild.* St. John's: Breakwater, 1983.

Wallace, Kathleen R., and Karla Armbruster. "Introduction: Why Go Beyond Nature Writing and Where To?" Armbruster and Wallace 1–25.

———. "The Novels of Toni Morrison: 'Wild Wilderness Where There Was None.'" Armbruster and Wallace 211–30.

Warkentin, Germaine, ed. *Canadian Exploration Literature: An Anthology.* 1993. Toronto: Dundurn, 2006.

Warren, Karen J. "The Power and the Promise of Ecological Feminism." *Ecological Feminist Philosophies*. Ed. Warren. Bloomington: Indiana UP, 1996. 19–41.

Waters, Anne, ed. Introduction. *American Indian Thought: Philosophical Essays*. Oxford: Blackwell, 2004. xv–xxxviii.

We Act. West Harlem Environmental Action 24 July 2007 <http://www.weact.org>.

Weaver, J. E. *North American Prairie*. Lincoln: Johnsen, 1954.

Weber, David J., ed. *Foreigners in Their Native Land: Historical Roots of the Mexican Americans*. 1973. Albuquerque: U of New Mexico P, 2003.

Weisser, Christian R., and Sidney I. Dobrin, eds. *Ecocomposition: Theoretical and Practical Approaches*. Albany: State U of New York P, 2001.

Wessels, Tom. *Reading the Forested Landscape: A Natural History of New England*. Woodstock: Countryman, 1997.

West, Cornel. *The American Evasion of Philosophy: A Genealogy of Pragmatism*. Madison: U of Wisconsin P, 1989.

Westling, Louise H. *The Green Breast of the New World: Landscape, Gender, and American Fiction*. Athens: U of Ohio P, 1996.

Westra, Laura, and Bill Lawson. *Faces of Environmental Racism: Confronting Issues of Global Justice*. Lanham: Rowman, 2001.

Whalley, George. *The Legend of John Hornby*. Toronto: Macmillan, 1977.

"Where Have All the Flowers Gone?": A Reference Guide and Sourcebook to Ecological Literature. Englewood: Arrow, 1970.

White, Evelyn C. "Black Women and the Wilderness." *Names We Call Home: Autobiography on Racial Identity*. Ed. Becky Thompson and Sangeeta Tyagi. New York: Routledge, 1996. 283–88.

White, Richard. "The Nationalization of Nature." *Journal of American History* 86.3 (1999): 976–86.

Whitehead, Alfred North. 1929. *The Aims of Education*. New York: Free, 1962.

Whitman, Walt. "From 'Song of Myself.'" Bly 75.

———. *Leaves of Grass*. Ed. Sculley Bradley and Harold Blodgett. New York: Norton, 1973.

———. "Song of Myself." Whitman, *Leaves* 28–89.

Whitmore, Michael. "When the Mirror Looks Back: Nature in the Scholarship of the Humanities." *Feminist Science Studies: A New Generation*. Ed. Maralee Mayberry, Banu Subramaniam, and Lisa H. Weasel. New York: Routledge, 2001. 92–96.

Wild, Peter. "John C. Van Dyke." *American Nature Writers*. Ed. John Elder. Vol. 2. New York: Scribner's, 1996. 951–62. 2 vols.

Wilderness Act. Pub. L. 88-577. 3 Sept. 1964. Stat. 78.

"The Wilderness Act of 1964: Public Law 88-57, 88th Congress, S. 4. September 3, 1964." *The Great Wilderness Debate*. Ed. J. Baird Callicott and Michael P. Nelson. Athens: U of Georgia P, 1998. 120–30.

Williams, Duncan Ryūken, and Christopher S. Queen, eds. *American Buddhism: Methods and Findings in Recent Scholarship*. Surrey: Curzon, 1999.

Williams, Joy. "The Inhumanity of the Animal People: Do Animals Have the Same Rights as We Do?" *Harpers* Aug. 1997: 60–67.

Williams, O. W. "The Lobo." *Historic Review of Animal Life in Pecos County*. Fort Stockton: Fort Stockton Pioneer, 1908. 47–51.

Williams, Raymond. *The Country and the City*. New York: Oxford UP, 1973.

———. *Problems in Materialism and Culture*. London: Verso, 1980.

Williams, Terry Tempest. "Lion Eyes." *Nature's New Voices*. Ed. John A. Murray. Golden: Fulcrum, 1992. 215–17.

———. *Red: Passion and Patience in the Desert*. 2001. New York: Vintage, 2002.

———. *Refuge: An Unnatural History of Family and Place*. New York: Vintage, 1992.

———. "Undressing the Bear." *The Soul of Nature: Celebrating the Spirit of the Earth*. Ed. Michael Tobias and Georgianne Cowan. New York: Plume, 1996. 109–13.

Williams, William Carlos. *Selected Essays*. New York: New Directions, 1969.

———. *Spring and All*. Paris: Contact, 1923. Rpt. as *Imaginations*. New York: New Directions, 1971. 83–151.

Wilson, Edward O. *Biophilia*. Cambridge: Harvard UP, 1984.

Wilson, Ethel. *The Swamp Angel*. Toronto: New Canadian Lib., 1954.

Wingfield, Andrew. "Road Trip: Self-Directed Field Work as a Learning Journey." Crimmel 182–202.

Winkler, Karen. "Scholars Embark on Study of Literature about the Environment." *Chronicle of Higher Education* 9 Aug. 1996: A8–9.

Winthrop, John. "A Model of Christian Charity." 1630. *Collections of the Massachusetts Historical Society*. 3rd ser. Vol. 7. Boston, 1838. 31–48.

Winton, Tim. *Dirt Music*. 2001. New York: Scribner's, 2002.

Wirzba, Norman, ed. "Introduction: Why Agrarianism Matters—Even to Urbanites." *The Essential Agrarian Reader: The Future of Culture, Community, and the Land*. Lexington: UP of Kentucky, 2003. 1–20.

Wolfe, Cary. *Animal Rites: American Culture, the Discourse of Species, and Posthumanist Theory*. Chicago: U of Chicago P, 2003.

———, ed. *Zoontologies: The Question of the Animal*. Minneapolis: U of Minnesota P, 2003.

Woodlief, Ann. "American Nature Writing: A Computer and Writing Intensive Course." *ISLE* 2.1 (1994): 141–49.

Worster, Donald. *Nature's Economy: A History of Ecological Ideas*. 2nd ed. Cambridge: Cambridge UP, 1994.

Wright, Harold Bell. *The Shepherd of the Hills*. 1907. Gretna: Pelican 2002.

Wyile, Herb, and Christopher Armstrong. "Firing the Regional Can(n)on: Liberal Pluralism, Social Agency, and David Adams Richards's Miramachi Trilogy." *Studies in Canadian Literature* 22.1 (1997): 1–18.

Yamashita, Karen Tei. *Tropic of Orange*. Minneapolis: Coffee House, 1997.

Yancey, Kathleen Blake. *Portfolios in the Writing Classroom: An Introduction*. Urbana: Natl. Council of Teachers of English, 1992.

Yancy, George, ed. *African-American Philosophers: Seventeen Conversations*. New York: Routledge, 1998.

Yáñez, Agustín. *The Edge of the Storm*. Trans. Ethel Brinton. Austin: U of Texas P, 1963. Trans. of *Al filo del agua*. 1947.

Ybarra, Priscilla Solis. " 'Lo que Quero es Tierra': Longing and Belonging in Cherríe Moraga's Ecological Vision." R. Stein, *New Perspectives* 240–48.

Zaid, Gabriel. *El progreso improductivo*. 1978. Mexico City: Siglo XXI, 1979.

Zakin, Susan. Introduction. *Naked: Writers Uncover the Way We Live on Earth*. Ed. Zakin. New York: Four Walls Eight Windows, 2004. ix–xv.

Zehle, Soenke. "Notes on Cross-Border Environmental Justice Education." Adamson, Evans, and Stein 331–49.

Zepeda, Ofelia. *Ocean Power: Poems from the Desert*. Tucson: U of Arizona P, 1995.

Zubbizarreta, John. *The Learning Portfolio: Reflective Practice for Improving Student Learning*. Boston: Anker, 2004.

Zurita, Raúl. *Anteparadise*. Trans. Jack Schmitt. Berkeley: U of California P, 1986.

Index of Names

Modern Language Association of America
Options for Teaching

Teaching Early Modern English Prose. Ed. Susannah Brietz Monta and Margaret W. Ferguson. 2010.

Teaching Italian American Literature, Film, and Popular Culture. Ed. Edvige Giunta and Kathleen Zamboni McCormick. 2010.

Teaching the Graphic Novel. Ed. Stephen E. Tabachnick. 2009.

Teaching Literature and Language Online. Ed. Ian Lancashire. 2009.

Teaching the African Novel. Ed. Gaurav Desai. 2009.

Teaching World Literature. Ed. David Damrosch. 2009.

Teaching North American Environmental Literature. Ed. Laird Christensen, Mark C. Long, and Fred Waage. 2008.

Teaching Life Writing Texts. Ed. Miriam Fuchs and Craig Howes. 2007.

Teaching Nineteenth-Century American Poetry. Ed. Paula Bernat Bennett, Karen L. Kilcup, and Philipp Schweighauser. 2007.

Teaching Representations of the Spanish Civil War. Ed. Noël Valis. 2006.

Teaching the Representation of the Holocaust. Ed. Marianne Hirsch and Irene Kacandes. 2004.

Teaching Tudor and Stuart Women Writers. Ed. Susanne Woods and Margaret P. Hannay. 2000.

Teaching Literature and Medicine. Ed. Anne Hunsaker Hawkins and Marilyn Chandler McEntyre. 1999.

Teaching the Literatures of Early America. Ed. Carla Mulford. 1999.

Teaching Shakespeare through Performance. Ed. Milla C. Riggio. 1999.

Teaching Oral Traditions. Ed. John Miles Foley. 1998.

Teaching Contemporary Theory to Undergraduates. Ed. Dianne F. Sadoff and William E. Cain. 1994.

Teaching Children's Literature: Issues, Pedagogy, Resources. Ed. Glenn Edward Sadler. 1992.

Teaching Literature and Other Arts. Ed. Jean-Pierre Barricelli, Joseph Gibaldi, and Estella Lauter. 1990.

New Methods in College Writing Programs: Theories in Practice. Ed. Paul Connolly and Teresa Vilardi. 1986.

School-College Collaborative Programs in English. Ed. Ron Fortune. 1986.

Teaching Environmental Literature: Materials, Methods, Resources. Ed. Frederick O. Waage. 1985.

Part-Time Academic Employment in the Humanities: A Sourcebook for Just Policy. Ed. Elizabeth M. Wallace. 1984.

Film Study in the Undergraduate Curriculum. Ed. Barry K. Grant. 1983.

The Teaching Apprentice Program in Language and Literature. Ed. Joseph Gibaldi and James V. Mirollo. 1981.

Options for Undergraduate Foreign Language Programs: Four-Year and Two-Year Colleges. Ed. Renate A. Schulz. 1979.

Options for the Teaching of English: Freshman Composition. Ed. Jasper P. Neel. 1978.

Options for the Teaching of English: The Undergraduate Curriculum. Ed. Elizabeth Wooten Cowan. 1975.